Churchill & Roosevelt
The Complete Correspondence

17. Alliance declining: Roosevelt and Churchill aboard the USS *Quincy*,
Malta, February 2, 1945

Churchill & Roosevelt

The Complete Correspondence

III. Alliance Declining

FEBRUARY 1944 – APRIL 1945

EDITED WITH
COMMENTARY BY

Warren F. Kimball

Princeton University Press, Princeton, New Jersey

Of the great men at the top, Roosevelt was the only one who knew what he was doing: he made the United States the greatest power in the world at virtually no cost.

A.J.P. Taylor, in *English History, 1914–1945*

Contents

VOLUME III

List of Maps   ix

List of Photographs (Volume III)   x

Correspondence: February 29, 1944 – April 13, 1945   3

Editorial Commentary:
The Big Three Powers in Iran   139
De Gaulle versus the Allies   169
The Pacific Theater   191
Disputes over Strategy in Europe   197
De Gaulle's Visit to Washington   237
The Warsaw Uprising   259
British Policy in the Balkans   274
The Second Quebec Conference (OCTAGON)   315
Organizing the United Nations   330
The Moscow Conference (TOLSTOY)   348
Anglo-American Disagreements   436
Trouble in Greece   449
Confusion of Policy toward Poland   461
Roosevelt and Eastern Europe   481
Competition for Iranian Oil   511
The Malta and Yalta Conferences (CRICKET and ARGONAUT)   521
A British Reversal on Eastern Europe   545

Glossary of Codenames, Acronyms, and Common Abbreviations   639

List of Sources Cited   647

Index   655

List of Maps

VOLUME I

The North Atlantic   55

The Western Desert (North Africa) (*Campaign Summaries*, USMA)   271

Initial Japanese Attacks 7–8 December 1941 and Limit of
Advance (*Campaign Summaries*, USMA)   288

The ABDACOM Area, January–February 1942 (*United States
Army in World War II* series; hereafter U.S. Army history)   311

The Pacific Areas, 1 August 1942 (U.S. Army history)   410

Persian Corridor Supply Routes (U.S. Army history)   573

Convoy Routes to Northern Russia   601

The Battle of El Alamein, 23 October – 4 November 1942
(*Campaign Summaries*, USMA)   658

Landings in North Africa 8–11 November 1942, and Advance
into Tunisia November–December 1942 (*Campaign Summaries*,
USMA)   668

VOLUME II

Russian Winter Offensive 1942–43 (*Campaign Summaries*,
USMA)   16

Lines of Communication in China-India-Burma Theater,
December 1942 (U.S. Army history)   111

Campaign in Italy, 1943–45   453

Polish Boundary Proposals   685

India-Burma Theater, 1944–1945 (U.S. Army history)   758

VOLUME III

Campaign in Northern France   184

Situation in the Pacific, 12 March 1944 (U.S. Army history)   192

Campaign in Southern France, 15 August – 15 September 1944
(U.S. Army history)   277

Situation in Europe, 15 January 1945 (U.S. Army history)   525

List of Photographs

VOLUME III

17. (*frontispiece*) Roosevelt and Churchill, aboard the USS *Quincy*, Malta, February 2, 1945 (U.S. Army, SC 199765)   ii

18. Anthony Eden, Churchill, and Harold Macmillan, Algeria, May 6, 1943 (U.S. Army, SC 175202)   4

19. Churchill and Roosevelt, Quebec, September 11, 1944 (Franklin D. Roosevelt Library)   320

20. John Gilbert Winant, Roosevelt, Edward Stettinius, and Harry Hopkins aboard the USS *Quincy*, Alexandria, Egypt, February 15, 1945 (U.S. Army, SC 262654)   522

21. Churchill, Livadia Palace, Yalta, February 8, 1945 (U.S. Army, SC 200222)   529

22. Roosevelt and Stalin, Yalta, February 1945 (U.S. Army, SC 260479)   529

See individual volumes for other photographs

III. Alliance Declining

This letter and its enclosure typify the changes that had begun to develop in the Anglo-American relationship as postwar politics began to rival wartime strategy as the most pressing issue.

Major General Patrick Hurley, whose high military rank had come primarily during service in the reserves, was a favorite of the President. Although Hurley was a Republican, his internationalism put him in the same category as Secretary of War Henry Stimson, who was an old friend, and Navy Secretary Frank Knox, both of whom Roosevelt could count on to support his foreign policy, at least during wartime. After brief service as Ambassador to New Zealand, a far too quiet post to suit him, Hurley went on a number of "fact-finding" missions for the President, including stops in Iran. On the basis of what he learned during those visits, Hurley became a supporter of the State Department's recommendations embodied in the so-called Declaration on Iran (*FRUS*, 1943, IV, 331–36, 355–59). In that paper, the State Department called for postwar American support for the Shah to prevent Britain and the Soviet Union from expanding their influence in Iran. Hurley's letter, written a year later, directly attacked British and Russian imperialism in the Middle East, and it is a measure of Roosevelt's opposition to European colonialism that he would send so strongly worded a letter to the Prime Minister. What neither Roosevelt nor Hurley mentioned was Hurley's close association with the Sinclair Oil Company, then trying to obtain an oil concession from the Iranian government. (See also the headnote to C–678/1.)

James M. Landis (mentioned in Part III of the enclosure) was the American director of economic operations in the Middle East and held the rank of Minister.

R–483/2, letter

Hyde Park, N.Y.
February 29, 1944

Private
Dear Winston:—

The enclosed memorandum was sent to me by Major General Patrick Hurley (former Secretary of War) whom you saw at Teheran.

This is for your eyes only. I rather like his general approach to the care and education of what used to be called "backward countries". From your and my personal observation I think we could add something about cleanliness as well.

The point of all this is that I do not want the United States to acquire a "zone of influence"—or any other nation for that matter. Iran certainly needs Trustees. It will take thirty or forty years to eliminate the graft and the feudal system. Until that time comes, Iran may be a headache to you, to Russia and to ourselves.

You will remember that I suggested to Stalin that a free port could be set up at the head of the Persian Gulf, the management of the railroad internationalized, providing a through route for Russia and for the developing areas of Iran herself.

Would you let me have this copy back, as I have no other?

With my warm regards, As ever yours,

[PSF:Safe:GB]

ENCLOSURE TO R–483/2

Teheran, Iran
21 December 1943

Dear Mr. President:

On your departure from Teheran you outlined to me, during our conversation at the airport, a tentative basis for American policy in Iran which might be used as a pattern for our relations with all less favored associate nations. In response to your suggestion and the directive which I received from the Secretary of State, I wish to submit the following for your consideration.

18. The colonial masters: Anthony Eden, Churchill, and Harold Macmillan

Part I

It is the purpose of the United States to sustain Iran as a free, independent nation and to afford the Iranian people an opportunity to enjoy the rights of man as set forth in the Constitution of the United States and to participate in the fulfillment of the principles of the Atlantic Charter.

The policy of the United States toward Iran, therefore, is to assist in the creation in Iran of a government based upon the consent of the governed and of a system of free enterprise which will enable that nation to develop its resources primarily for the benefit of its own people. Iranian resources are adequate to sustain a program to help Iran to help herself. By this program of self-government and well directed self-help Iran can achieve for herself the fulfillment of the principles of justice, freedom of conscience, freedom of the press, freedom of speech, freedom from want, equality of opportunity, and to a degree freedom from fear.

To accomplish the above, the United States will furnish, upon invitation of the Iranian Government, expert advisors in any or all of the fields of government. All experts and advisors furnished to Iran by the United States will be paid by the Iranian Government and implemented in their operations by authority of Iranian law, and will not be a financial responsibility of the American taxpayer. The United States will not ask or receive any special privileges for these services.

American advisors will be fully indoctrinated in the policy of our government toward Iran and shall make regular progress reports to our State Department. This indoctrination and requirement of reporting will provide a vital element of coordination which is essential to direction of our policy and protection of our interests.

Modern history of this country shows it to have been dominated by a powerful and greedy minority. The people have also been subjected to foreign exploitation and monopoly. In extending American assistance to the building of an improved society in Iran there must be imposed a sufficient degree of supervision and control over free enterprise and personal aggression to protect the unorganized and inarticulate majority from foreign and domestic monopoly and oppression.

Inauguration in Iran of the American pattern of self-government and free enterprise will be an assurance that proceeds from development of Iranian resources will be directed substantially to the building of schools, hospitals, sanitary systems, transportation and communication systems, irrigation systems and improvement of all facilities contributing to the health, happiness and general welfare of the Iranian people.

This plan of nation building may be improved through our experience in Iran and may become the criterion for the relations of the United States toward all the nations which are now suffering from the evils of greedy minorities, monopolies, aggression and imperialism.

The American people, single-mindedly devoted to independence and liberty, are fighting today not to save the imperialisms of other nations nor to create an imperialism of our own but rather to bestow upon the world the benevolent principles of the Atlantic Charter and the Four Freedoms.

Part II

The foregoing is a rather simple plan designed to promote the building of free nations. The job that confronts us is not an easy one. The success of the recent conferences in Moscow, Cairo and Teheran indicates that the major powers can cooperate in the prosecution of the war. The reaffirmation of the Atlantic Charter indicates that there is a basis for postwar cooperation. Notwithstanding these evidences of good will I think that now is the time for us to attempt to analyse the opposition that the building of free nations will be likely to encounter.

Without any opposition from other nations and with the cooperation and support of the intelligent and patriotic leaders of Iran it will take generations to achieve in Iran free enterprise and a government based on the consent of the governed. The population of Iran is approximately 90% illiterate and it is composed, to a large extent, of disorganized and separated tribes. The intelligence and vigilance which will support liberty of the masses must be created. The education of the tribesmen and the establishment of a unity of purpose will require time, patience, diligence, efficiency, and a crusading spirit on the part of our advisors. Above all, the advisors must have the continuous support of the American people which in itself may be difficult to assure.

In addition to the obstacles within Iran, the principles of the above formula are in conflict with the principles of imperialism. Free enterprise may also come in conflict with any forced expansion of communism. Advocates of both of these doctrines may resist the proposed spreading of democracy.

In all the nations I have visited, I have been told, usually by British and Americans, that the principles of imperialism already have succumbed to the principles of democracy. From my own observations, however, I must say that if imperialism is dead, it seems very reluctant to lie down.

The imperialism of Germany, Japan, Italy, France, Belgium, Portugal, and The Netherlands will, we hope, end or be radically revised by this war. British imperialism seems to have acquired a new life. This appearance, however, is illusory. What appears to be a new life of British imperialism is the result of the infusion, into its emaciated form, of the blood of productivity and liberty from a free nation through lend lease. British imperialism is also being defended today by the blood of the soldiers of the most democratic nation on earth.

The names of the imperialistic nations are sufficient to indicate that a large part of the world's population is still committed to the principles of imperialism. These names also indicate the opposition that will be encountered by any effort that has for its purpose the establishment of democracy in nations that are now subjected to the rule of imperialistic nations. We are approaching the irrepressible conflict between world-wide imperialism and world-wide democracy. It is depressing to note how many of our real friends in the world seem to be irrevocably committed to the old order of imperialism.

Woodrow Wilson's policy for America in the first world war was designed "To make the world safe for democracy" and to sustain Britain as a first class world power. Sustaining Britain as a first class power has for many years been the cornerstone of America's foreign policy. Personally I have supported that policy. I have long believed and have many times stated publicly that the ultimate destiny of the English speaking peoples is a single destiny.

We did sustain Britain in the first world war as a first class power but we did not succeed in making the world "safe for democracy". Instead, when we backed away from the League of Nations and failed to make the peace terms an instrument of democracy, we made the world safe for imperialism. In the quarter of a century which has intervened the processes of both eastern and western imperialism set the stage for this new world war.

An effort to establish true freedom among the less favored nations, so many of which are under the present shadow of imperialism, will almost inevitably run counter to the policy of sustaining Britain as a first class world power. This leads us to the conclusion that Britain today is confronted by the same condition that confronted our nation when Lincoln at Gettsburg said "That this nation, under God, shall have a new birth of freedom". Britain can be sustained as a first class power but to warrant this support from the American people she must accept the principles of liberty and democracy and discard the principles of oppressive imperialism.

Soviet Russia has earned for herself an assured place as a first class world power. Friendship and cooperation between the United States and the U.S.S.R. are essential to peace and harmony in the post-war world. There must, therefore, be a mutual understanding and acceptance of the post-war patterns for freedom which the great powers among the United Nations are to offer to their less powerful associates. Without such agreement there would be jealousy, suspicion and conflict.

Part III

In considering the present status of relations between Iran and the United States it must be remembered that although American troops have been here more than a year their presence has not yet been officially recognized by the Iranian Government. Many Iranian officials believe that American troops are in Iran on the invitation and for the purpose of serving as an instrumentality of Britain. For a year or more we have had under negotiation with Iran a treaty wherein Iran would recognize the presence of American troops as an American operation. The ineffective presentation of the treaty has not been helpful to American prestige with the Iranians.

It is the responsibility of the State Department to effect the consummation of the treaty. The necessity for promptness in the negotiation of this agreement was pointed out by me in my report to you of May 13, 1943. I have not personally participated in any of the treaty conferences with the Iranians.

I think it important that we understand that since our troops entered Iran on the invitation of the British, without advance notice to the Government of Iran, it was natural for the Iranians to look upon us as a British instrumentality. In addition to this The United Kingdom Commercial Corporation which was first engaged in preclusive purchasing in Iran has since been selling American lend lease supplies to civilians and to the Government of Iran. Largely through our lend lease supplies, paid for by the American taxpayer, the United Kingdom Commercial Corporation has been attempting and, to a considerable degree, succeeding in establishing a complete trade monopoly in Iran. The United Kingdom Commercial Corporation achieved this position by virtue of being on the scene when American lend lease supplies began entering Iran. United States representatives in Iran engaged the British Corporation, government owned but profit making, to serve as handling agent and middleman for the American goods. This arrangement, which evidently had the approval of the Lend Lease Administration and the State Department, has been profitable to the British Corporation.

There has been a United States Commercial Corporation, government owned, with offices in Teheran. When I was here a year ago, Mr. Philip Kidd was in charge of the corporation. Later Mr. Erik Erikson was in charge. If we were going to enter the commercial field with lend lease goods, I do not know why we did not use our own corporation instead of the British Corporation. I refer again to my report to you on Iran dated at Cairo, May 13, 1943 and my report on Lend Lease in the Middle East dated at Delhi, November 7, 1943. Your Minister, Mr. Landis, has made great improvement in the administration of lend lease in the Middle East. Notwithstanding this I am still of the opinion that the present debate between the Americans and British on lend lease will be ended only when America has taken complete control of the distribution of our own lend lease supplies in this area.

The Iranians believe that the post-war monopoly plans of the United Kingdom Commercial Corporation now have the support of the United States Government.

In addition to all this there have been conflicts between the British and American Ministries that have been evident to the Iranians. This situation has been damaging to both American and British prestige. To offset this impression the Iranians have witnessed the efficiency of the American operations of railroad and road transportation in passing war supplies to Russia. Finally they have been deeply impressed by your masterful handling of the three-power conference and especially by your skill in procuring from the conference the declaration of policy of the United Nations toward Iran.

Meanwhile, Soviet prestige has benefited from their own well ordered conduct and by their direct and positive relations with the Iranians.

Part IV

In a conversation with his Majesty, the Shah and certain of his ministers a few days ago, I was informed that from one source or another the tribesmen in the outlying provinces of Iran have acquired at least 50,000 rifles and ammunition. This the Shah thought made it imperative that our advisors to the Iranian Army and to the Iranian Police Force hasten the organization of the forces for security against internal disorder. He stated that certain foreign influences are being brought to bear on the tribesmen to cause internal disorder in Iran. While on this subject I informed His Majesty that I had heard that Russia had agreed to furnish the Iranian Army with a number of tanks, rifles and airplanes. The Shah admitted that there was such an offer but how much equipment Russia would give he was unable to say. I remarked that we were furnishing Russia equipment under lend lease because Russia did not have enough equipment for her own war necessities. His Majesty said that he understood that fact but that Russia had offered to give his government this much needed equipment. He said he had hoped to acquire the equipment from the United States but had been unable to obtain satisfactory action. In my opinion Iran is able to pay for the equipment which she needs for both her Army and her Police force.

It is a fact, however, that Britain is furnishing lend lease material to other nations at a time when she is being sustained in her war effort by American lend lease. Now Russia seems to be about to embark on a similar program. Britain has been giving and now Russia is about to give our lend lease supplies, or supplies that have been replaced or released by our lend lease supplies, to other nations in return for concessions or to strengthen their own ideologies in the countries to which the supplies are given. The least we should demand is that we be permitted to do our own giving.

Part V

Iranian officials have expressed a desire to establish a closer commercial relationship with the United States.

Under conditions now prevailing there will no doubt be a great rush on the part of American businessmen to get oil, mineral and other concessions in Iran. I suggest that the State Department, with the assistance of the other agencies of our government should be prepared to advise the Government of Iran definitely concerning the character and other qualifications of every applicant for a concession.

Part VI

In proposing to commit you to a world wide plan of building associated free nations, I am not unmindful of the problems that confront you on the home front.

We should, of course, consider the effect of the present and future high taxes and of the expenditure of great amounts of our economic reserve. Our greatest danger, however, lies in the creation of a stupendous bonded indebtedness. If the war and our post-war reconstruction and rehabilitation commitments continue for a long period this indebtedness may become so overwhelming that it will create hopelessness, lethargy and despondency on the part of the world's freest and most resourceful people. We may again have people shouting that "We can't eat the Constitution". They may even add to the non-edibles the Atlantic Charter and the Four Freedoms. This might lead to panic, bankruptcy and revolution. It is needless to add that if anything of this nature occurred at home, all our plans for the future of the world would be futile. Tyranny and oppressive imperialism would again be dominant.

I think the broader aspects of your world diplomacy are now in excellent form. But we can damage that position if we fail to be realistic in whipping the details into conformity with your general plan.

Respectfully yours, s/ Patrick Hurley   Brigadier General, U.S.A.

[PSF:Safe:GB. *FRUS*, 1943, IV, 363–70.]

The precise date and accuracy of this Churchill-Roosevelt telephone conversation is uncertain, for the only record currently available is a summary printed in the memoirs of a German intelligence officer, Walter Schellenberg. For a discussion of German intercepts of this and similar telephone calls, see the headnote to C–R/tel.–4.

C–R / telephone–5

[Feb. 1944?]

"Early in 1944 we hit a bull's eye by tapping a telephone conversation between Roosevelt and Churchill which was overheard and deciphered by the giant German listening post in Holland. Though the conversation was scrambled, we unscrambled it by means of a highly complicated apparatus. It lasted almost five minutes, and disclosed a crescendo of military activity in Britain, thereby corroborating the many reports of impending invasion. Had the two statesmen known the enemy was listening to their conversation, Roosevelt would hardly have been likely to say good-bye to Churchill with the words, 'Well, we will do our best—now I will go fishing.' "

[The only record of this call is printed in Walter Schellenberg, *The Labyrinth: The Memoirs of Walter Schellenberg*, trans. Louis Hagen (New York: Harper and Brothers, 1956), pp. 366–67]

The statistics provided by Churchill illustrate that the Allies had won the Battle of the Atlantic.

C–597

London [via U.S. Army]
Mar. 2, 1944, 1026 Z / TOR 1220 Z

Prime Minister to President Roosevelt. Personal and Most Secret.
Here is a suggested item for your draft of our monthly anti U-boat war statement. Provided later information about sinkings in February 1944 does not considerably increase the figure shown below:

February 1944 was the best month since the United States entered the war. The total sinkings of all Allied shipping in February by enemy action only were less than one fifth of the sinkings in February 1943, and less than one ninth of the sinkings in February 1942.
The figures in British notation are:
February 1944, 70,000 tons;
February 1943, 378,400;
February 1942, 659,500.
We have a very good haul of U-boats, too.

[MR*. WSC, V, 696.]

The changes proposed by Roosevelt and implemented by Churchill improved the efficiency of the supply operation in Calcutta and Assam, and by April 20 the U.S. Army Services of Supply area commander could report that the Calcutta docks were clear and there was no indication that the port had reached the saturation point.

C–598

London [via U.S. Army]
Mar. 2, 1944, 1118 Z / TOR 1220 Z

Prime Minister to President Roosevelt. Personal and Most Secret.
    Your 454.
    I have now received a report by air mail from the Viceroy on the working of the Port of Calcutta and the Bengal-Assam lines of communication. The Chiefs of Staff have reported to me as follows:

> 1. As regards the Port of Calcutta, a man of unquestioned standing and ability will shortly be appointed as Port Director to control the whole working of the Port and all the Agencies therein. He will have working under him two deputies, one of whom will be American.
> 2. Operational control of the metre gauge section of the Bengal-Assam Railway is being taken over by the U.S. Army Railway Units. Machinery, which will be linked with that set up under the Port Director at Calcutta, is being established for the allocation of priorities and the control of movement over all sections of the lines of communication. The allocation of priorities will be determined after consultation with representatives of all interests concerned, including those of the U.S. Forces. The allotment of traffic and the energetic implementation of this allocation will be the responsibility of picked executives.
> 3. These measures have been worked out with the personal collaboration of the Viceroy and have been agreed with the United States Authorities in India. No effort will be spared to gain the maximum efficiency on the Bengal-Assam lines of communication which is fully recognized to be vital to our joint operations in Burma and the U.S. Army Air Forces operating in China.

    I trust this will be satisfactory to you.

[MR*]

The Navy Department officials who drafted this message chose not to argue with Churchill's proposed message on anti-submarine warfare in the Atlantic but instead substituted their own draft. In general, American naval officers preferred to give less information in these press releases since the submarine was the U.S. Navy's most effective weapon against Japan.

R-484

Washington [via U.S. Navy]
Mar. 2, 1944, 5:20 P.M.

From the President for the Former Naval Person.

Your Number 597. In view agreement for alternate origination and your origination last month, I propose the following statement for release March 10th:

> QUOTE. Despite the increasing traffic of United Nations shipping in the Atlantic, February 1944 was the lowest month as to tonnage of Allied merchant ship losses to enemy U-boat action since the United States entered the war; and February was the second lowest month of the entire war.
>
> Again there were more U-Boats destroyed than merchant vessels sunk, so the exchange rate remains favorable to the United Nations. In actual numbers a few more U-Boats were sunk in February than in January.
>
> The lack of aggressiveness on the part of the U-Boat continues. UNQUOTE.

Roosevelt [Navy Dept.]

[MR. *R&C.*]

Roosevelt was technically correct when he promised that the United States would not attempt to take over British oil concessions in Iran and Iraq, but American representatives had already begun discussions with Iranian officials about new concessions. The President may have been enthralled with the idea of helping to modernize such nations, but his policies also pleased those Americans who were more concerned with oil resources than with the problems of underdevelopment. (See, for example, Leahy, *I Was There*, p. 226.) The underlined sentence was added by Roosevelt.

Stalin's response to Churchill's message about Soviet-Polish relations had been clear and curt. The Soviet leader asserted that the time was not ripe for a compromise and cited as an example the Polish insistence that Lvov and Vilna remain part of Poland. (See *Stalin/WSC*, doc. 249, and *Stalin/FDR*, doc. 171. Stalin's message about the deficiencies in the destroyers sent to Russia is in *Stalin/FDR*, doc. 169.)

R–485

Washington [via U.S. Navy]
Mar. 3, 1944, 11:50 A.M.

Personal and Secret. From the President for the Former Naval Person.
  Your 591, 592 and 595 received.
  Referring to 591, I am having the oil question studied by the Department of State and my oil experts, but please do accept my assurances that we are not making sheep's eyes at your oil fields in Iraq or Iran. I cannot hold off the conversations much longer.
  Referring to 592, we also are concerned about the apparent concentration of enemy forces at Singapore and uncertain as to enemy intentions in that area.
  We are sending our best carrier with a destroyer escort to join your naval force in the Indian Ocean.
  Referring to 595, Uncle Joe's attitude toward your suggested compromise on the Polish problem is very disappointing.
  I have Stalin's message of February 26th addressed to both of us in regard to the loan of eight destroyers and requesting that at least half of them be of a modern type. It would seem that the destroyers you agreed to deliver would be very useful to the Soviet Navy. I find them highly efficient for escort duty.
  Can you suggest anything that would assist in making a reply to U.J.'s message regarding the destroyers? Roosevelt [WDL]

[MR*]

Roosevelt's cable to Churchill explaining his statements to the press did not indicate how far the President had really gone. In fact, he had stated that talks with the Soviet Union concerning the transfer of one-third of the Italian fleet or its equivalent were "about half completed," a commitment far beyond what the British were willing to make. The President was not one to let reporters bulldoze him into revealing disagreements among the Allies, and the fact that he sent a copy of this cable to Stalin suggests that he was primarily concerned with the Soviet reaction to the entire episode.

R–486

Washington [via U.S. Navy]
Mar. 3, 1944, 12:04 P.M.

Personal and Secret, from the President for the Former Naval Person.
  In reply to insistent questioning at a press conference today I stated that Italian merchant ships and war ships are now being used in our war

effort by the Allied Mediterranean command and that some of the Italian ships or substitutes therefor from the British and American tonnage will be allocated to the Soviet Navy to assist in their requirements for their war effort. Roosevelt [WDL]

[MR*. *FRUS, Teheran Conf.*, p. 876. *R&C.*]

Negotiations with the Bulgarians dragged on until September 6, 1944, when the Soviet Army invaded and occupied the country.

R–487

Washington [via U.S. Navy]
Mar. 3, 1944, 12:05 P.M.

Secret and Personal, for the Former Naval Person from the President.

Referring your 596. In agreement with your suggestion we have instructed Jadwin Mission to inform Minister of Bulgaria that representatives of the three Allies are prepared to confer in Cairo with a fully qualified Bulgarian Mission. Jadwin also directed to telegraph immediately to Washington any reply that he may receive.

In view of the inclusion of the Balkans in General Wilson's area it seems to me that he is the correct official to control any mission to discuss surrender terms of Bulgaria. Roosevelt [WDL]

[MR*. *R&C.*]

Roosevelt's warning that he had made a statement concerning the transfer of Italian ships to the Soviet Union (R–486) had crossed the following query in transit. Churchill chose to send only the first two sentences of this draft, but his anger and concern are apparent in the portion he deleted.

C–599

London [via U.S. Army]
Mar. 3, 1944, 1805 Z / [TOR] 1926 Z

Prime Minister to President Roosevelt. Personal and Most Secret.

Reuter announces the message in my immediately following. Can this be true? ~~If so it surprises me very much as it is a complete departure from all our arrangements and agreements. I should be most grateful if you would let me know what has happened, as I shall have to make a statement of my own both to the public and to the Russians. Considering Great Britain has suffered at least twenty times the naval losses of your~~

~~Fleet in the Mediterranean and has been fighting the Italians since June~~
~~1940, we had hoped to be consulted or at least informed beforehand.~~

[PREM 3/240/5/438. MR. *FRUS, Teheran Conf.*, p. 875.]

C–600

London [via U.S. Army]
Mar. 3, 1944, 1805 Z / TOR 1926 Z

Prime Minister to President Roosevelt. Personal and Most Secret.

Reference my immediately preceding telegram. Washington Friday from Reuter. Time of receipt 1720 3rd March. Msg begins:

> President Roosevelt today announced that Italian warships are ready to be sent to the Russian Navy. Discussions for transferring roughly ⅓ of the Italian Fleet to Russia, the President said, were about half completed.
>
> President Roosevelt said that the U.S. and Britain are already using some Italian tonnage. Efforts are now being made to determine how many of these ships or their equivalent can be turned over to the Russian Navy. Marshal Stalin had raised the question through his Ambassador in Washington.
>
> President Roosevelt stressed that so long as the war lasted the Allies will use everything afloat against the enemy. After the war something more permanent would have to be decided. Asked whether the ships would be manned by Italians, the President replied that some may and some may not. Italian ships which had escaped to the Ballearic [Balearic] Islands, he said, were a Spanish problem.
>
> President Roosevelt explained that since Italy surrendered to the U.S., Britain and Russia, it was thought advisable to distribute the Italian Fleet roughly on the basis of ⅓ each. He would not say how much tonnage was involved.

[MR*. *FRUS, Teheran Conf.*, pp. 875–76.]

Roosevelt's assurances not withstanding, the British remained wary of the President's oil policy because of his insistence that the conference on postwar petroleum matters meet in Washington in the immediate future. Churchill's emphatic warning that Britain would not submit to the loss of oil concessions in the Middle East was phrased in language similar to that used in his defense of the British keeping possession of Hong Kong.

The German attack against the Anzio beachhead in Italy had finally failed on March 3, but the Allied attack against Cassino did not begin until March 15, even then achieving only partial success. Not until mid-May did the Allies launch a massive and eventually successful offensive against Rome.

Churchill's cryptic closing sentence seems to be a reference to the thorny postwar problems that had begun to crop up.

C–601

London [via U.S. Army]
Mar. 4, 1944, 1925 Z / TOR 2235 Z

Prime Minister to President Roosevelt Personal and Most Secret.

Your number 485. Thank you very much for your assurances about no sheeps eyes at our oilfields at Iran and Iraq. Let me reciprocate by giving you the fullest assurance that we have no thought of trying to horn in upon your interests or property in Saudi Arabia. My position on this, as in all matters, is that Great Britain seeks no advantage, territorial or otherwise, as the result of the war. On the other hand she will not be deprived of anything which rightly belongs to her after having given her best services to the good cause—at least not so long as your humble servant is entrusted with the conduct of her affairs. I will bring the matter before the Cabinet on Monday and hope to telegraph you immediately there-after.

About the India Ocean situation [R–485]. I hope the enemy fleet will stay at Singapore, as this should give you fine opportunities in the main Pacific theatre. Thank you very much for the carrier. I shall be sending you a signal shortly on the wider aspects of our joint action against Japan.

About U.J. and the Poles. I am waiting to receive the official answer of the Soviet Government before attempting to make up my mind whether there is anything else we can do.

About the Italian ships et cetera. I was much startled by the press accounts of your talk with them. The Russians have never asked for one-third of the Italian ships. But only for the specific vessels mentioned at Moscow and agreed to by us at Teheran. See list which follows. We have never agreed, as you know, to anything beyond this. We shall now see what the Italian reaction will be and whether the Combined Chiefs of the Staff were right in their apprehensions set forth in J.S.M. 1372 dated 28th-12-43 [see R–437]. From your 483 I infer that we are to go on with the policy of loaning U.J. some British and American ships till we can get the Italians'. I therefore suggest the following joint message to U.J. from you and me: Begins.

Although the Prime Minister instructed Ambassador Clark Kerr to tell you that the destroyers we are lending you were old, this was only for the sake of absolute frankness. In fact they are good, serv-iceable ships, quite efficient for escort duty. There are only 7 fleet destroyers in the whole Italian Navy, the rest being older destroyers and torpedo boats. Moreover these Italian destroyers, when we do get them, are absolutely unfitted for work in the North without very lengthy refit. Therefore we thought the 8 which the British Government have found would be an earlier and more convenient form of help to you. The Prime Minister regrets that he cannot spare any new destroyers at the present time. He lost 2 last week, one in the Russian convoy; and for the landing at OVERLORD alone he has to deploy, for close inshore work against the batteries, no fewer than 42 destroyers, a large proportion of which may be sunk. Every single vessel that he has of this class is being used to the utmost pressure in the common cause. The movement of the Japanese fleet to Singapore creates a new situation for us both in the Indian Ocean. The fighting in the Anzio bridgehead and generally throughout the Mediterranean is at its height. The vast troop convoys are crossing the Atlantic with the United States Army of Liberation. The Russian convoys are being run up to the last minute before OVERLORD with very heavy destroyer escorts. Finally there is OVERLORD itself. The President's position is similarly strained, but in this case mainly because of the great scale and activity of the operations in the Pacific. Our joint intentions to deliver to you the Italian ships agreed upon at Moscow and Teheran remain unaltered, and we shall put the position formally to the Italian Government at the time when it is broadened and the new ministers take over their responsibilities. There is no question of our right to dispose of the Italian Navy, but only of exercising that right with the least harm to our common interests. Meanwhile, all our specified ships are being prepared for delivery to you on loan as already agreed. Signed: Roosevelt. Churchill. Message to Stalin ends.

I must send you my warmest congratulations on the grand fighting of your troops, particularly the United States Third Division in the Anzio bridgehead. I am always deeply moved to think of our men fighting side by side in so many fierce battles and of the inspiring additions to our history which these famous episodes will make. Of course I have been very anxious about the bridgehead where we have so little ground to give. The stakes are very high on both sides now and the suspense is long-drawn. I feel sure we shall win both here and at Cassino.

We certainly do have plenty to worry us now that our respective democracies feel so sure the whole war is as good as won.

[MR*. p*FRUS, Teheran Conf.*, pp. 876–77. p*FRUS*, 1944, III, 103. p*R&C*.]

C–602

London [via U.S. Army]
Mar. 4, 1944, 1925 Z / TOR 2235 Z

Prime Minister to President Roosevelt. Personal and Most Secret.
  Number 601.
  My immediately preceding telegram. The Admiralty state that one third
of the Italian ships in our possession would amount to:

1.7   battleships
2   6 inch cruisers
0.7   5.3 inch cruisers
3.3   destroyers
7.7   torpedo boats
6.7   corvettes
7.3   submarines

Whereas what the Russians ask for and what the British agreed to was:

1   battleship
1   cruiser
8   destroyers
4   submarines

40,000 tons of merchant shipping.

[MR*. *FRUS, Teheran Conf.*, 877.]

Operation PIGSTICK had called for an amphibious invasion on the southern
end of the Mayu Peninsula, about thirty-five miles south of the Burma-India
border. Although that project had been canceled, the British had still planned
an overland attack down the peninsula with the objective being the port of
Akyab, located on an island about fifteen miles south of the tip of the Mayu
Peninsula (Foul Point). General Wingate's operations in northern Burma were
part of the overall Allied move to protect the construction route for the Ledo
Road. The Japanese offensive referred to by the SEAC (South East Asia
Command) commander, Admiral Lord Mountbatten, was the attack in the
Arakan province of Burma, an area which also included Akyab and the Mayu
Peninsula. Although beaten back, the Japanese aimed another offensive at
the supply center of Imphal in east central Assam, India, which guaranteed
that the British attack against Akyab would be postponed. (See maps, Vol.
II, pp. 111, 758.)

C–603

London [via U.S. Army]
Mar. 4, 1944, 2245 Z / TOR 0130 Z, Mar. 5

Prime Minister to President. Personal and Most Secret.

I have just received the following from Mountbatten which I forward to you knowing the interest you take in these parts.

"At one time, I had every hope even after the cancellation of 'PIGSTICK' that advance in Arakan would be pressed to the south of Mayu Peninsular in time to give a sporting chance of taking Akyab. Japanese counter offensive has imposed a vital three weeks delay which I fear will prevent us from reaching the south of Mayu Peninsular in time to cover the passage of landing craft round Foul Point into river before swell conditions which become rapidly worse from now on prevent it. Wingate's operations are proceeding to plan as follows:

"A. 16 Brigade has crossed the Upper Chindwin about 30 miles southwest of Taro and will operate against communications of 18 and 31 Divisions.

"B. 77 Brigade due to be flown into Okkyi Valley between March 6 and March 9 to operate against communication of 18 Division.

"C. 111 Brigade due to be flown into same airstrip as 77 Brigade between March 10 and March 13 to operate in area Wuntho Katha against communications of 15 Division."

[MR*]

Stalin had already informed the U.S. Ambassador in Moscow, W. Averell Harriman, that he would not deal with the Poles until they reconstructed their government. The Soviet leader warned that if those changes did not take place a new Polish government would make its appearance. He dismissed Churchill's message and accused the Poles of "fooling" the British Prime Minister (Woodward, *British Foreign Policy*, III, 178). Churchill had earlier suggested the postponement of Polish Prime Minister Stanislaw Mikolajczyk's visit to the United States (C–523).

C–604

London [via U.S. Army]
Mar. 4, 1944, 2310 Z / TOR 0130 Z, Mar. 5

Prime Minister to President Roosevelt. Personal and Most Secret.

1. I have now received Stalin's reply about Poland which I send in my

immediately following. I find it most discouraging. I will send you a copy of my answer as soon as it has been approved by the Cabinet.

2. There is now no reason in my opinion why the Polish Prime Minister should not visit the United States as you invited him to do. It may at any rate make the Russians more careful if they see that Poland is not entirely without friends.

[MR*]

C–605

London [via U.S. Army]
Mar. 4, 1944, 2310 Z / TOR 0130 Z, Mar. 5

Prime Minister to President Roosevelt. Personal and Most Secret.
[Stalin to Churchill]

"I received both your messages of the 20th February on the Polish question from Sir A. Clark Kerr on the 27th February.

"I have studied the detailed account of your conversations with the members of the Emigre Polish Government and have come more and more to the conclusion that such people are not capable of establishing normal relations with the USSR. Suffice it to point to the fact that not only do they not wish to recognize the Curzon Line but they still lay claim to Lwow as well as Vilna. As regards designs to place under foreign control the administration of certain Soviet territories, we cannot accept for discussion such aspirations since we consider even the very raising of a question of such a kind insulting for the Soviet Union.

"I have already written to the President that the solution of the question of Soviet-Polish relations has not yet matured.

"It is necessary once more to affirm the justness of this conclusion. 3d March, 1944."

[MR. *R&C.*]

Roosevelt's letter of February 29 (R–483/1) raised questions that Churchill decided to avoid rather than confront. Twice answers to the President were drafted, but each time the Prime Minister decided not to send them. (See memo to the Prime Minister dated June 4, 1944, PREM 3/197/3/61–62.)

C–605/1, not sent

London
Mar. 4, 1944

Prime Minister to President. Personal and Most Secret.

Your letter of February 29. I look at it the same way you do, but it is a long way to Tipperary. All my thoughts are centred in the battle.

[PREM 3/197/3/163]

C–605/2, not sent

London
Mar. 1944

[Churchill to Roosevelt]

I look forward to reading your revised paper about the administration of France. You can be sure that I will do my best to bring our views together. You will remember that we are committed to consultation with Uncle Joe at some stage.

I quite see your point about the desirability of "short" terms. But the whole question is now under active examination in the European Advisory Commission and I am sure that we ought to let the Commission do its work and try to produce an agreed draft. We shall certainly do our best to secure this. Here again it is essential to get the Russians into line if we can.

[PREM 3/194/2/64]

C–606

London [via U S. Army]
Mar. 5, 1944, 1822 Z / TOR 1900 Z

Prime Minister to President Roosevelt. Personal.

Your number 484. We agree. We should prefer to leave out the last sentence but we do not press the point.

[MR*]

Once again, Churchill gently but firmly rejected Roosevelt's suggestion that diplomatic negotiations be left to military leaders. Even though an Englishman, General Sir H. M. Wilson, commanded the Mediterranean theater, the Prime Minister insisted that the British Minister Resident with Allied forces in the Mediterranean, Harold Macmillan, represent the British government in talks with Bulgaria.

C–607

London [via U.S. Army]
Mar. 5, 1944, 2040 Z / TOR 2240 Z

Prime Minister to President Roosevelt. Most Secret and Personal.

Your number 487.

We agree about this being in General Wilson's sphere. But I think that the mission should in the first place be received by representatives of the three Allies and a military representative of General Wilson and the first contacts established through diplomatic channels. General Wilson would, of course, be kept informed and would be responsible to the Combined Chiefs of Staff if and when it came to dictating armistice terms. No doubt you will instruct your representative to keep in touch with Mr. Macmillan who will act for us. I think it most important, however, that you and I should watch this from day to day and settle on the highest level, of course in conjunction with U.J.

[MR*]

Roosevelt accepted Churchill's amendment to the February anti-submarine warfare statement.

R–488

Washington [via U.S. Navy]
Mar. 6, 1944, 6:30 P.M

Personal and Secret. From the President for the Former Naval Person.

Thank you for your message Number 606. We will issue the statement without repeat without the last sentence. Roosevelt [WEB]

[MR*]

Churchill continued to worry about Roosevelt's remark that one-third of the Italian fleet would go to the Soviet Union. Both the French and Greek governments had protested, after Roosevelt's press conference, that they should also share in the spoils, and the British believed that their own losses justified keeping a larger portion of Italian warships. The Italian government protested Roosevelt's formula, but most officers and men in the Italian fleet remained quiet, although the American Naval Attaché in Madrid reported mutinous activity aboard five Italian warships interned in Spanish ports (ALUSNA Madrid to OPNAV, Mar. 6, 1944, MR, "Transfer of Italian Ships" folder).

The battleship *Vanguard* (par. 3), the largest ship ever built in Britain, was not completed until 1946. Ten years later she was deactivated without ever having fired her guns in anger.

C–608

London [via U.S. Army]
Mar. 7, 1944, 1236 Z / TOR 1610 Z

Prime Minister to President Roosevelt Personal and Most Secret.

About the Italian ships.

1. I have never agreed nor have you ever asked me to agree to a division of the Italian Fleet into 3 shares. If this claim were to be based on the fact that we 3 Powers signed the Italian Armistice together, what about all the other Powers that fought Italy? Greece for instance would have an irrefutable claim. It was not until after the Cairo conference that I heard you had mentioned about the ⅓ for Russia. Averell [Harriman] was however able to assure you that nothing of the sort had been said to the Russians. See your number 437. You are therefore quite uncommitted so far as they are concerned.

2. His Majesty's Government would not be able to agree to a division of the Italian Fleet by ⅓ or a pro rata division among signatories to the Armistice. We hold very strongly that losses entailed in the Italian war must be considered. We bore the whole weight of that war from 1940 onwards until British and American troops entered Tunisia as the result of "TORCH". Our Naval losses alone have been very heavy indeed. For instance, from Italy's declaration of war until her unconditional surrender, the Royal Navy lost in the Mediterranean the following major warships:

  1 Battleship
  2 Aircraft Carriers
  1 Monitor
14 Cruisers
48 Destroyers
13 Escorts
  3 Fast Minelayers
  2 Depot Ships
40 Submarines

and the following merchant shipping: 129 vessels of 780,000 gross tonnage. We certainly feel that we are entitled to have our claims for replacements duly considered by our closest Ally.

3. Here I must mention that excepting only *Vanguard* we have suspended our whole battleship programme including the four 16-inch battleships authorized by Parliament even before the war began in order to concentrate upon short-term war necessities freely expended in the common cause. We have borne the whole burden of warship losses in the Russian convoys, to wit:

2 Cruisers
5 Destroyers
3 Minesweepers
1 Fleet Oiler.

4. Up to the present I have been content to leave these matters for adjustment at the end of the war when His Majesty's Government would certainly have represented that they were justly entitled to the 2 surviving Littorios on account of their heavy battleship losses. I do not wish to prejudge this question at the present time. We must however bear in mind that about 100 Italian Warships have been and up to the present moment are still doing useful and important work for both our countries. I therefore suggest that all further discussion of a division of the Italian Fleet apart from what we agreed with Stalin at Teheran, stand over till the end of the war, when no doubt the Japanese Fleet will also come into consideration.

5. At the Moscow conference the Russians asked for certain specified types of Italian ships, namely

1 Battleship
1 Cruiser
8 Destroyers
4 Submarines

and 40,000 tons of merchant shipping. At Teheran we assented to this. The Combined Chiefs of Staff subsequently became alarmed lest the announcement that we meant to turn over Italian ships to the Soviets should impair cooperation by the Italian Naval Forces and possibly lead to scuttling. You and I then agreed to propose to Russia that we lend her the same quantity of ships until the matter could be adjusted with the Italians after the present critical stage of the war in Italy and in the Mediterranean was over. This was accepted by the Russians. I am sure you will recognize that the British Admiralty made a generous contribution to the plan by providing in fact 13 warships out of 14 and half the merchant tonnage. This plan is in actual process of being carried out.

6. Our relations with the Italian Government in this matter must also

be considered. They surrendered their fleet and there is no doubt of the ultimate right of the Allies to dispose of it as they may decide. However Admiral Andrew Cunningham, with General Eisenhower's full assent, made an agreement at Taranto in consequence of which the Italian Fleet, which had bravely escaped from the clutches of the Germans not without heavy loss, thenceforward became actively employed in the Allied interest. A relationship has been established between the Italian Fleet and the British and American Fleets alongside of whom they are operating which certainly implies that we should treat them properly and with due consideration. A prisoner of war is one thing but once you accept a man's services and he fights at your side against the common enemy, a different status and relationship are established. I hope this may be patiently looked into because at present the British Admiralty feel uncomfortable about the position into which we have got.

7. I shall no doubt have to make a statement to Parliament in the near future and would propose, subject to your agreement, something as follows:

> As President Roosevelt has said the question of the future employment and disposal of the Italian Fleet has been the subject of some discussion. In particular consideration has been given to the immediate reinforcement of the Soviet Navy either from Anglo-American or Italian resources. On these discussions I have no statement to make other than to say that at present no change is contemplated in the arrangements with the Italian Naval Authorities under which Italian ships and their crews take part in the common struggle against the enemy in the theatres where they now operate. It may well be found that the general question of enemy or ex-enemy fleet disposal should best be left over till the end of the war against both Germany and Japan, when the entire position can be surveyed by the victorious Allies and what is right and just can be done.

[MR*. R&C.]

The British government reluctantly acceded to the President's demand for talks in Washington on postwar oil policy. British suspicions that the upcoming presidential election was the reason for such a hasty convening of talks were probably accurate, although there is no question that American officials wanted to seize every opportunity to open Middle Eastern nations to American petroleum interests. These talks, which took place in Washington from mid-April through early May, proved amicable, but they produced no concrete results. This message from Churchill was forwarded to the President by Ambassador John Winant, who prefaced and followed it with a few remarks about the arrangements for the oil conference. (See FRUS, 1944, III, 104–5. Winant's message was dated March 6.)

C-608/1

London [via U.S. Embassy]
Mar. 7, 1944

Prime Minister to President Roosevelt. Personal and Most Secret.

The War Cabinet welcome your assurance that there is no desire on the part of the United States Government to propose the transfer of our property and interests in Iraq and Iran which we presume includes our properties elsewhere. In consequence of this, we waive our objection to talks not being in London and will send a delegation to the United States. We still feel, however, that this delegation should be official and expert, and once the ground is clear and facts established, that higher authorities should then intervene.

As the fact that we are sending a delegation will now become public property, I suggest that a communique on the following lines be issued:—

"The Governments of the United States and the United Kingdom are undertaking preliminary and exploratory discussions on petroleum questions. These discussions will be, in the first instance, at the official and expert level, and will take place in Washington."

As I am likely to be questioned in Parliament on the subject, I must reserve the right to make it clear that no question arises of any transfer of existing rights or properties in oil.

[PREM 3/472/519. *FRUS*, 1944, III, 104–5.]

Roosevelt did not press the issue of transferring one-third of the Italian fleet to the Soviet Union, but neither did he back away from his statement to the press. Rather, it was as if he had never made such a commitment. The final sentence of this message was added to the draft in Roosevelt's handwriting.

Churchill's message to Eleanor Roosevelt expressed pleasure over her projected visit to some of the British West Indies (Churchill to Eleanor Roosevelt, March 4, 1944, MR 14).

R-489

Washington [via U.S. Navy]
Mar. 7, 1944, 1:15 P.M.

Personal and Secret. From the President for the Former Naval Person.

Receipt is acknowledged of your messages 598 to 607 inclusive. Thank you for your very kind message to Mrs. Roosevelt.

Reference your 601, I agree with your proposed joint message to U.J. about destroyers to be sent.

I am sending you by the following message (490) my recommendation about the Italian Government.

In order to try to put at rest the concern of the Italian Navy about their ships what do you think of sending the following to General Wilson and to the Naval Commanders in the Mediterranean for confidential information of Italian officials:

> QUOTE. At Teheran it was agreed that ships of the Italian Navy should be used where they could be employed most effectively against the common enemy. It was also agreed in principle that Russia is entitled to her share in the increase of Allied Naval strength resulting from the surrender of the Italian Fleet. Russia is now in urgent need of additional Naval strength. For the present Great Britain and the United States will lend some of their ships to Russia to compensate for the help they are receiving from the Italian Navy. It is not intended to transfer any Italian ships to Russia at present. UNQUOTE.

Your 608 has just come after what appears above had been prepared. I do not think there is any essential conflict. I will wire you again in a short time. Roosevelt [WDL, WEB]

[MR*]

It appears that continued pessimistic reports from the British Commander in Chief in the Mediterranean, General Wilson, concerning the political tension in liberated Italy stimulated this message. The State Department had commented on Wilson's messages and, on March 4, the President instructed the department to draft a message to Churchill on the subject. After discussing it with Admiral Leahy and Presidential Aide Rear Admiral Wilson Brown, Roosevelt deleted the sentence indicated below and approved the message. Benedetto Croce was an old and respected academic and a leader of an anti-Fascist faction in Italy.

R–490

Washington [via U.S. Navy]
Mar. 7, 1944, 1:15 P.M.

Personal and Secret. From the President for the Former Naval Person.

Our advices from Italy indicate that the political situation there is rapidly deteriorating to our disadvantage and that an immediate decision in breaking the impasse between the present Government and the six opposition parties is essential.

General Wilson has had to forbid a strike called by three of the anti-

Fascist parties in the Naples area. I fear we are moving into a situation in which the Allied authorities will have to use force against the anti-Fascist leaders and groups. I feel strongly that our policy should be so designed that it would never be necessary to suppress these elements by using force against them.

One of General Wilson's telegrams of February 29 (NAF 634) reports that the Government and the opposition are waiting for an indication of Allied policy with regard to their respective plans. I would like to give General Wilson an immediate reply. As you know, we prefer the program put forward by the six opposition parties which involves the abdication of Victor Emmanuel and the delegation of the powers of his successor to a "Lieutenant" of the realm, acceptable to the six political parties. Croce has been mentioned as their probable choice. General Wilson and his advisers have recommended the acceptance of this proposal and are awaiting our approval. My feeling is that we should assure at the earliest opportunity the active cooperation of the liberal political groups by bringing them into the Italian Government.

If you will send instructions to your Chiefs of Staff here, we can sent an agreed directive to General Wilson in the early part of the week. Roosevelt [State Dept.]

[MR*. *FRUS*, 1944, III, 1053 (draft). *R&C*.]

Churchill's message to Stalin about the Soviet-Polish controversy conceded to the Soviets all the border questions but, aside from generally supporting the London Polish government, left open the question of its exact composition.

C–609

London [via U.S. Army]
Mar. 7, 1944, 1730 Z

Prime Minister to President Roosevelt. Personal and Most Secret.

Following is text of reply which I have sent, at the desire of the War Cabinet, to UJ in reply to his message of March 3rd repeated to you in my No. 605.

    1. I thank you for your message of March 3rd about the Polish question.

    2. I made it clear to the Poles that they would not get either Lwow or Vilna and the references to these places, as my message shows, merely suggested a way in those areas in which the Poles thought they could help the common cause. They were certainly not intended to be insulting either by the Poles or by me. However since you find

them an obstacle pray consider them withdrawn and expunged from the message.

3. The proposals I submitted to you make the occupation by Russia of the Curzon Line a *de facto* reality in agreement with the Poles from the moment your armies reach it, and I have told you that, provided the settlement you and we have outlined in our talks and correspondence was brought into being, His Britannic Majesty's Government would support it at the armistice or peace conferences. I have no doubt it would be equally supported by the United States. Therefore you would have the Curzon Line *de facto* with the assent of the Poles as soon as you get there, and with the blessing of your Western Allies at the general settlement.

4. Force can achieve much but force supported by the goodwill of the world can achieve more. I earnestly hope that you will not close the door finally to a working arrangement with the Poles which will help the common cause during the war and give you all you require at the peace. If nothing can be arranged and you are unable to have any relations with the Polish Government, which we shall continue to recognize as the Government of the Ally for whom we declared war upon Hitler, I should be very sorry indeed. The War Cabinet asks me to say that they would share this regret. Our only comfort will be that we have tried our very best.

5. You spoke to Ambassador Clark Kerr of the danger of the Polish question making a rift between you and me. I shall try earnestly to prevent this. All my hopes for the future of the world are based upon the friendship and cooperation of the western democracies and Soviet Russia.

[MR*. *R&C.*]

Churchill pulled out all the stops in replying to the President's suggestion that they arrange the formation of a new government in Italy. Not only did the British Prime Minister raise the bogeyman of de Gaulle and refer to the British support for Roosevelt's decision to work with Admiral Darlan in liberated North Africa, but he mocked the ability and questioned the honesty of the Italian anti-Fascists.

Harold Macmillan, the British Minister Resident at Allied Headquarters in the Mediterranean, had been in England for health reasons, but returned to Algiers on March 9. Andrei Vyshinsky represented the Soviet government on the Allied Control Council for Italy. Sforza's letter to Adolf Berle, of the U.S. State Department, is discussed in the headnote to C–422, and reprinted following C–845. Foreign Secretary Eden's message to Ambassador Halifax (no. 1783) is printed in *FRUS*, 1944, III, 1037–38. In it, Eden asked Halifax to propose postponing any political changes in Italy and to propose a warning to the Italian opposition parties that political agitation would not be tolerated.

C–610

London [via U.S. Army]
Mar. 8, 1944, 1244 Z / TOR 1423 Z

Prime Minister to President Roosevelt. Personal.

1. Your number 490 causes me concern. It is a departure from your agreement with me of February 11 (your 464) which you kindly reaffirmed in your number 483 describing the matter as "finished business". On the strength of the first assurances I made my statement to Parliament.

2. My advices do not lead me to believe that any new facts of importance have arisen or that the Allied forces are not capable of maintaining order in the regions they have occupied as the result of the "unconditional surrender" of Italy. It would in my opinion be a very serious mistake to give way to agitation especially when accompanied by threats on the part of groups of office seeking politicians. We should then be liable to set up in Italy an administration which might not command the allegiance of the armed forces, but which would endeavour to make its position with the Italian people by standing up to the Allies. In fact we should have another but more intractable version of the De Gaullist Committee. Meanwhile in the midst of a heart-shaking battle we are to get rid of the tame and helpful government of the King and Badoglio, which is doing its utmost to work its passage and aid us in every way.

3. I readily admit that the course you recommend would be the more popular and would have at least a transitory success. But I am sure that for the victorious conquerers to have their hands forced in this way by sections of the defeated population would be unfortunate. So also would be the obvious open division between you and me and between our two governments. I gave you and the State Department loyal and vigorous support over the Darlan affair. Unity of action between our two governments was never more necessary than at the present time considering the great battles in which we are engaged and which lie ahead.

4. I am quite ready to take up with you now the proposals put forward by General Wilson set out in his number 634, whereby the Crown Prince becomes lieutenant of realm. I have no confidence in either Croce or Sforza for this job. MacMillan tells me Croce is a dwarf professor about 75 years old who wrote good books about aesthetics and philosophy. Vyshinsky who has tried to read the books says they are even duller than Karl Marx. Sforza has definitely broken his undertakings given in his letter to Mr. Berle of September 23. I hope therefore we may open

discussions with you on the basis of the Foreign Secretary's telegram number 1783 to Halifax. I repeat I am most anxious to see a broadly based government assume power in Italy, but this ought not to be done under duress by the Allies and can certainly be done with far better advantage when the battle has been gained or, best of all, when Rome is taken. MacMillan is returning at once.

[MR*. *FRUS*, 1944, III, 1054. p*WSC*, V, 502. *R&C*.]

Roosevelt readily agreed to Churchill's insistence that the discussions with representatives of the Bulgarian government be handled by political, not military, officials. Lincoln MacVeagh was the U.S. Ambassador to the Greek government in exile, located in Cairo.

R–491

Washington [via U.S. Navy]
Mar. 8, 1944, 12:05 P.M.

From the President for the Former Naval Person, Secret and Personal.
    Your 607.
    Mr. MacVeagh will act for us, his instructions at this stage being only to listen to what the Bulgarians have to say. He is being informed that Mr. MacMillan will be the British representative, and directed to keep in touch with him.
    We agree that General Wilson, who will be responsible to the Combined Chiefs in matters pertaining to the activities of the Bulgarian Mission, should be kept fully informed of developments, and that he be directed to have a military representative present. Roosevelt [WDL]

[MR*]

Barring a protest from Stalin, Roosevelt seemed willing to accept Churchill's lead on the final disposition of the Italian fleet.

R–492

Washington [via U.S. Navy]
Mar. 8, 1944, 12:10 P.M.

Personal and Secret from the President to the Former Naval Person.
    Referring to your 608, I can find no fault in your proposed statement to Parliament contained in the last paragraph thereof.

Please give me your reaction to the message proposed in my 489 to be sent to General Wilson and to our naval commanders in the Mediterranean for confidential information of Italian officials. Roosevelt [WDL]

[MR*]

With the presidential election coming in the fall, Roosevelt became increasingly solicitous of the various ethnic groups that made up part of the Democratic Party's coalition. Polish-Americans frequently made unrealistic demands for American assistance to the Polish government in exile in London, and Roosevelt did not want to lose their support, which could prove crucial.

R–493

Washington [via U.S. Navy]
Mar. 8, 1944, 12:15 P.M.

Secret and Personal, from the President to the Former Naval Person.
Your 609. The reply to U.J. contained therein seems to be a very clear and concise statement of the British attitude in the Polish controversy.
It will be of assistance to me in handling our Polish complications here. Roosevelt [WDL]

[MR*. R&C.]

General Wilson had recommended that the Allies accept the program advanced by the Junta of six opposition parties in Italy, which called for the abdication of King Victor Emmanuel and the appointment of a Lieutenant of the Realm as the temporary head of the Italian government. Churchill was willing to consider the appointment of Crown Prince Umberto as Lieutenant of the Realm, but adamantly opposed giving that post to the two most likely candidates, Croce and Sforza. The additions and deletions were apparently made by Roosevelt.

R–494

Washington [via U.S. Navy]
Mar. 8, 1944, 12:17 P.M.

From the President for the Former Naval Person. Secret and Personal.
Your 610. My Number 490 was sent with the purpose of attempting to meet the difficult situation reported by General Wilson ~~and his recommendation in regard thereupon~~ in his NAF 634.

~~I will be very pleased to receive from you~~ I wish very much you would send me suggestions as to a method that will be acceptable to your Government of correcting the serious situation reported by General Wilson.

It is my strongest wish that you and I should continue to work in complete harmony in this matter as in all others. <u>We may differ on timing but things like that can be worked out, and on the big objectives like self-determination we are as one.</u> Roosevelt [WDL, WEB]

[MR*. *FRUS*, 1944, III, 1055.]

C–611

London [via U.S. Army]
Mar. 9, 1944, 0100 Z / TOR 0210 Z

Prime Minister to President. Personal and Secret.

I am most grateful to you for all your four telegrams just received.

[MR]

C–612

London [via U.S. Army]
Mar. 9, 1944, 1620 Z / TOR 1700 Z

Prime Minister to President. Personal.

Your 489 for confidential information of Italian officers. We entirely agree and have signalled Wilson accordingly as from Combined Chiefs of Staff for use at his discretion.

[MR*]

Most Americans, including the President, tended to suspect that British complaints about bearing an excessive share of the financial burdens of war only masked a plan to improve Britain's competitive position with the United States in the postwar world. The pressure for limiting British dollar balances came primarily from anti-administration members of the U.S. House Foreign Affairs Committee. With lend-lease up for renewal and the presidential election around the corner, Roosevelt had become ever more cautious about such matters. (See the headnote to R–474.) Churchill's memo to Harry Hopkins, printed in *FRUS, Teheran Conf.*, pp. 822–28, consisted of three papers written by Lord Cherwell (an adviser to Churchill), Chancellor of the Exchequer Sir John Anderson, and possibly the economist Lord John Maynard Keynes. Each argued strenuously against any American restrictions on the size of British dollar and gold balances (uncommitted gold and dollar assets) by a reduction of lend-lease aid, which would force Britain to spend those assets.

C–613

London [via U.S. Army]
Mar. 9, 1944, 2000 Z / TOR 2245 Z

Prime Minister to President Roosevelt. Personal and Secret.

Your 474.

1. You will remember that we discussed the dollar balances in Cairo on December 8th and that I gave a memorandum to Harry. I certainly understood that you felt we ought not to be treated worse than France or Russia in these matters. France has at least two billions and no overseas liabilities against them. So has Russia. These dollar balances are not, as your telegram might suggest, a particular part of our assets which is available in the United States, but our total reserves. Against these reserves we have incurred for the common cause liabilities of at least ten billions on the other side of the account.

2. Since our talk, Lord Halifax met Mr. Hull and Mr. Morgenthau as recently as January 8th, when the matters mentioned in the first paragraph of your telegram under reply were discussed. Lord Halifax reported to us that Mr. Morgenthau stated to him that it was not at present intended to reduce our dollar balances in any other way, and in reliance on this personal assurance to Lord Halifax, we agreed to the exclusion of the politically difficult item[s] from Lend-Lease.

3. Will you allow me to say that the suggestion of reducing our dollar balances, which constitute our sole liquid reserve, to one billion dollars would really not be consistent either with equal treatment of Allies or with any conception of equal sacrifice or pooling of resources. We have not shirked our duty or indulged in an easy way of living. We have already spent practically all our convertible foreign investments in the struggle. We alone of the Allies will emerge from the war with great overseas war debts. I do not know what would happen if we were now asked to disperse our last liquid reserves required to meet pressing needs, or how I could put my case to Parliament without it affecting public sentiment in the most painful manner and that at a time when British and American blood will be flowing in broad and equal streams and when the shortening of the war even by a month would far exceed the sums under consideration.

4. I venture to put these arguments before you in order that you may be fully armed with our case, for my confidence in your sense of justice and, I may add, in that of the American people is unshakable.

5. But see also my immediately following.

[MR*. *WSC*, V, 697–98. *FRUS*, 1944, III, 45–46. p*FRUS, Teheran Conf.*, pp. 878–79.]

Churchill was correct in surmising that public and congressional scrutiny stimulated the President's decision to raise the dollar-balance question at that time, although one official British historian later described the root cause: "The Americans, being the paymasters, naturally felt themselves entitled to impose conditions which, according to their understanding, appeared reasonable enough" (Sayers, *Financial Policy*, pp. 434–35).

Leo Crowley, who headed the Foreign Economic Administration, had joined Secretary of the Treasury Morgenthau in warning Roosevelt of the dangerous political consequences should Congress learn about the rising British dollar balances (over $1.5 billion by mid-1944), particularly in view of continued lend-lease shipments of consumer goods to England. Undersecretary of State Edward R. Stettinius, who faithfully reflected Secretary Hull's beliefs about international economics, had previously directed the Office of Lend-Lease Administration and was sympathetic to the British argument. He left Washington on March 30 on a four-week visit to England for talks with various British officials. As Churchill had promised, he and other British officials brought up the question of Britain's dollar balances during those conversations, but Churchill only reiterated his previous statements made to Roosevelt. (See Stettinius, *The Diaries*, ed. Campbell and Herring, pp. 44–46.)

C–614

London [via U.S. Army]
Mar. 9, 1944, 2000 Z / TOR 2245 Z

Prime Minister to President Roosevelt. Personal and Most Secret.

1. Further to my number 613. I have laid before you our case about dollar balances in its full strength, but from the informal way in which you refer to it in your number 474, I have wondered whether you might be meaning only that we should search for some arrangement to enable us to put a portion of our balance less conspicuously in the limelight. If this is so, and if you desire it, we will go into this very carefully with Stettinius when he visits us.

2. Since we received your telegram, we now learn that Mr. Crowley on March 8th promised to give Congress the amount of our dollar balances now and at the outbreak of war. This raises serious dangers. I am confident in the justice of our case if it could be stated as a whole, and of course if the matter becomes public property, we shall have to justify ourselves in public. The disclosure of the vast debit balance which is growing up against us outside the United States would certainly have most injurious effects upon our Sterling position, and consequently upon the whole strength of the Allies at this period. We therefore ask that there shall be no disclosure. If this is not possible, that the disclosure shall be in strict confidence, and also that the substance of our case should be stated to the body to whom the disclosure is made.

[MR*. *FRUS*, 1944, III, 46–47. *WSC*, V, 698–99.]

With the sinking of the German battle cruiser *Scharnhorst* and with the *Tirpitz* still undergoing repairs following damage from British midget submarines (see C–425), the British had renewed their convoys to northern Russia. The convoy Churchill referred to (RA 57) consisted of thirty-one merchant ships plus escort vessels. Only one merchant ship was sunk, and three German submarines were destroyed.

C–615

London [via U.S. Army]
Mar. 9, 1944, 2155 Z / TOR 2250 Z

Prime Minister to President Roosevelt. Personal and Most Secret.

You will be glad to hear that the latest Russian convoy has now got safe home, and that four U-boats out of the pack that attacked it were certainly sunk on the voyage by the escort.

[MR*. *R&C.*]

R–495

Washington [via U.S. Navy]
Mar. 9, 1944, 7:00 P.M.

Personal and Secret. From the President for the Former Naval Person.

Your 615. Congratulations, well done. Roosevelt [FDR]

[MR*]

C–616

London [via U.S. Army]
Mar. 10, 1944, 0906 Z / TOR 1010 Z

Prime Minister to President. Personal and Secret.

I am sending you to-day by courier an inscription I have had drawn up for Harry [Hopkins] about his boy who was killed. It would be very kind of you to have it sent to him whenever he is recuperating. How does the operation stand now?

[MR*. *WSC*, V, 699.]

An intense debate over British strategy in the Pacific and the South East Asia theater had been taking place in London following the arrival of the "Axiom" Mission, headed by General Wedemeyer, sent from SEAC Headquarters by Admiral "Dickie" Mountbatten. The British Chiefs of Staff, aware that the main and most glamorous campaign against Japan would take place in the

Pacific, proposed sending British naval and air detachments to the southern flank of the American advance against the Philippine Islands, Formosa, and eventually Japan. Churchill, although finally convinced that CULVERIN (an attack against Sumatra) was not immediately feasible, supported Mountbatten's proposal for concentrating military operations in the Burma/Bay of Bengal area instead of the Pacific. Foreign Office concern for the retention of British colonies and influence in Southeast Asia made Mountbatten's plan even more attractive.

C–617

London [via U.S. Army]
Mar. 10, 1944, 1706 Z / TOR 2050 Z

Prime Minister to President Roosevelt Personal.

1. In the final report of the Cairo conference, the Combined Chiefs of Staff reported that they had "Approved in principle as a basis for further investigation and preparation" an overall plan for the defeat of Japan. This plan contemplated the despatch to the Pacific of a detachment of the British Fleet which was provisionally scheduled to become operational in the Pacific in June 1944. Although you and I both initialled the final report, neither of us had had the opportunity of going into these matters personally as we were concerned with affairs of more immediate urgency. Since then the War Cabinet and Chiefs of Staff have been "investigating" and we have not so far reached united conclusions. Meanwhile the Japanese Fleet has arrived at Singapore which constitutes in my mind a new major fact.

2. After the surrender of the Italian Fleet in September 1943 I was very keen on sending a detachment of our fleet as quickly as possible to the Pacific, but when I opened this to Admiral King he explained to me how very strong the United States Navy was already in those waters compared to the Japanese, and I formed the impression that he did not need us very much. I have also seen several telegrams from our Naval representatives in Washington which tend to confirm the above impression. On the other hand, I am told that Admiral King has informed the First Sea Lord that he would like to have our detachment, provided it did not arrive until August or September, when its logistic requirements could more easily be met. I am, in the upshot, left in doubt about whether we are really needed this year.

3. Accordingly I should be very grateful if you could let me know whether there is any specific American operation in the Pacific

(A) Before the end of 1944 or

(B) Before the summer of 1945

which would be hindered or prevented by the absence of a British Fleet Detachment.

4. On the other hand the movement of the Japanese Fleet to Singapore, which coincided inter alia with their knowledge of the movement of our battleship squadron into the Indian Ocean, seems to show their sensitiveness about the Andamans, Nicobars and Sumatra. It would surely be an advantage to you if, by keeping up the threat in the Bay of Bengal, we could detain the Japanese Fleet or a large portion of it at Singapore and thus secure you a clear field in the Pacific to enable your by-passing process and advance to develop at full speed.

5. General Wedemeyer is able to unfold all Dickie's plans in the Indian Theatre and the Bay of Bengal. They certainly seem to fit in with the kind of requests which Chiang Kai-shek was making which you favoured but which we were unable to make good before the monsoon on account of the Mediterranean and OVERLORD operations. I am personally still of opinion that amphibious action across the Bay of Bengal will enable all our forces and establishments in India to play their highest part in the next 18 months in the war against Japan. We are examining now the logistics in detail and prima facie it seems that we could attack with two or three times the strength the islands across the Bay of Bengal and thereafter the Malay Peninsula than we could by prolonging our communications about 9000 miles round the south of Australia and operating from the Pacific side and on your southern flank. There is also the objection of dividing our fleet and our effort between the Pacific and Indian Oceans and throwing out of gear so many of our existing establishments from Calcutta to Ceylon and way back in the Suez Canal zone.

6. Before however reaching any final conclusions in my mind about this matter, I should like to know what answer you would give to the question I posed in paragraph three, namely, would your Pacific operations be hindered if, for the present at any rate and while the Japanese Fleet is at Singapore, we kept our centre of gravity in the Indian Ocean and the Bay of Bengal and planned amphibious operations there as resources come to hand.

[MR*. *WSC*, V, 576–78.]

Harry Hopkins never regained sufficient vigor to function as the unofficial Chief of Staff to the President, though he did return to government service.

R–496

Washington [via U.S. Navy]
Mar. 11, 1944, 7:20 P.M.

Personal and Secret. From the President for the Former Naval Person.
Your 616. Harry has gone to the Mayo Clinic at Rochester, Minnesota.

He stood the trip well, feels reasonably well but has not gained weight. He is to be fattened up for the next three or four weeks and then they will decide whether an operation is necessary.

As soon as I get your inscription I will sent it out to him. I know it will do him much good. Roosevelt [FDR]

[MR*]

Roosevelt and the Joint Chiefs of Staff saw no need for British naval forces to assist American operations in the Pacific during 1944 and the first half of 1945, but that did not mean the Americans would support Churchill's plans. On March 21, the Joint Chiefs expressed their opposition to any extensive amphibious operations against the Netherlands East Indies or even in the Bay of Bengal, since the expected advance of U.S. forces in the Pacific would reduce the strategic value to Japan of those areas. (See Ehrman, *Grand Strategy*, V, 452.) The final sentence was added in Roosevelt's handwriting.

R–497

Washington [via U.S. Navy]
Mar. 13, 1944, 12:15 P.M.

Personal and Secret. From the President for the Former Naval Person.

Your 617, in specific reply to paragraph 3 thereof:

(a) There will be no specific operation in the Pacific during 1944 that would be adversely affected by the absence of a British Fleet Detachment.

(b) It is not at the present time possible to anticipate with sufficient accuracy future developments in the Pacific to be certain that a British Fleet Detachment will not be needed there during the year 1945, but it does not now appear that such a reinforcement will be needed before the Summer of 1945.

In consideration of recent enemy dispositions it is my personal opinion that unless we have unexpected bad luck in the Pacific your naval force will be of more value to our common effort by remaining in the Indian Ocean.

All of the above estimates are of course based on current conditions and are therefore subject to change if the circumstances change. Roosevelt [WDL]

[MR*. *WSC*, V, 578–79.]

The final paragraph of this message may offer a clue to Roosevelt's reasons for deciding not to let the Italian political situation remain as it was until the occupation of Rome. As the 1944 election approached, public opinion became more and more important.

R–498

Washington [via U.S. Navy]
Mar. 13, 1944, 1:00 P.M.

Personal and Secret, from the President for the Former Naval Person.

With further reference to your No. 610, I am sorry if my earlier messages were not clear. I did not at any time intend to convey to you my agreement that we postpone all political decisions until after Rome had been taken. The political situation in Italy has developed rapidly since our earlier messages; the military situation has not kept pace. The capture of Rome is still remote and major political decisions must be taken.

I do not like having to use stern measures against our friends in Italy, except for good reason. In the present situation the Commander-in-Chief and his political advisers, both British and American, have recommended that we give immediate support to the program of the six opposition parties. Thus we have, happily for once, our political and military considerations entirely in harmony.

We do not need to intervene beyond informing the Executive Junta of our support of their program, as described in NAF 622, 624 and 628, and confirm this to the King if necessary. The Italians can present the solution to the King and work out the program among themselves.

I cannot for the life of me understand why we should hesitate any longer in supporting a policy so admirably suited to our common military and political aims. American public opinion would never understand our continued tolerance and apparent support of Victor Emmanuel. Roosevelt [State Dept.]

[MR*. *FRUS*, 1944, III, 1055. *WSC*, V, 503–4. *R&C*.]

Churchill had instructed General Wilson to consult the British government before making additional recommendations for political changes in Italy, but the damage was already done. As Roosevelt's preceding cable (which Churchill had not received when he drafted this one) indicated, the agreement of British and American officials on the scene seemed to demand that the King and Badoglio be removed. In spite of warnings from Halifax that the State Department wanted immediate changes in the Italian government, Churchill continued to insist that no changes take place until the liberation of Rome, possibly in the hope that a triumphal entry by the King into that city might stimulate support for the monarchy. (Foreign Secretary Anthony Eden's cable number 1783 to British Ambassador Lord Halifax in Washington is in PREM 3/243/8/415–16, 3 pp., and the Ambassador's oral presentation of that cable is summarized in *FRUS*, 1944, III, 1037–38.) (See also C–610.)

C–618

London [via U.S. Army]
Mar. 13, 1944, 2118 Z / TOR 2255 Z

Prime Minister to President. Personal and Secret.

Your number 494.

1. I should be most grateful if you would read Eden's number 1783 to Halifax, which shows the kind of policy we should like to embark upon. I am entirely at one with you in the big objective of self-determination. All I plead for is "timing". I do not believe the ambitious wind-bags, now agitating behind our front that they may themselves become the government of Italy, have any representative footing. I fear that if we drive out the King and Badoglio at this stage, we shall only have complicated the task of the armies.

2. I see that this is also the Soviet view. They are certainly realistic but of course their aim may be a Communist Italy, and it may suit them to use the King and Badoglio till everything is ready for an extreme solution. I can assure you that this danger is also in my mind. My idea remains that we should try to construct a broadly-based government, taking into account the opinion of the democratic North of Italy and seeking representatives from there. Of course, if we cannot get Rome for several months, we shall have to act earlier, but without the favourable conditions which will be open to us once we are in possession of the capital. We shall then have much better chances of finding a really representative footing.

[MR. p*WSC*, V, 503. *FRUS*, 1944, III, 1043–44 (paraphrase). PREM 3/243.]

The Soviet decision to send an Ambassador to the Badoglio government caused some concern within the British and American governments. Although Churchill was pleased because such a move would tend to support the King and Badoglio, the Foreign Office was disturbed by the Russian failure to consult their allies beforehand. American officials shared the sentiments of the Foreign Office, and some even inferred that the Soviets hoped to gain favor with the conservative Italians so as to support Tito across the Adriatic in Yugoslavia. (The entire matter is discussed in *FRUS*, 1944, III, 1038ff.) Whatever Stalin's intentions, his instructions to the Italian Communist Party to cooperate with the Badoglio government forced the other parties of the left to do likewise, and Churchill surmised that, "as a result of the Russian 'lack of decorum,' we could secure almost everything for which we had asked, and that all might be well if we could 'keep that old trickster Sforza out or in a minor position' " (Woodward, *British Foreign Policy*, II, 535).

C–619

London [via U.S. Army]
Mar. 14, 1944, 1148 Z / TOR 1300 Z

Prime Minister to President Roosevelt. Personal.

Your 498 has crossed my 618. Meanwhile the Russians have announced that they have sent a fully-accredited ambassador to the present Italian Government with whom we are still technically at war. I do not think it would be wise, without further consideration, to accept the programme of the so-called six parties and demand forthwith the abdication of the King and the installation of Signor Croce as Lieutenant of the Realm. I will however consult the War Cabinet upon what you justly call a "major political decision". Our war with Italy has lasted since June 1940 and we have suffered 232,000 casualties in men, as well as the losses in ships which I mentioned in my number 608. I feel sure that in this matter our view will receive consideration from you. We ought to make every effort to act together. Pray remember that on the strength of your number 464 I committed myself in public and that any divergence will certainly become known.

[MR*. *FRUS*, 1944, III, 1059 (paraphrase). p*WSC*, V, 504.]

As much as both men enjoyed war stories, Churchill probably passed on this tale in order to convince Roosevelt that the British were exerting every effort in northern Burma. Major General Orde Wingate's long-range penetration forces—about 9,000 men—met with initial success, but eventually failed to achieve their objective, which was to cut off large segments of Japanese forces; those enemy troops would then be attacked by the main Allied armies moving more slowly behind Wingate's troops. Once the Japanese recovered from their surprise, they stripped Wingate of much of his air support and successfully held their positions at Indaw in northeastern Burma. With the death of Wingate in a plane crash on March 24, the long-range penetration concept lost its moving force as well as a leader who had commanded Churchill's support.

C–620

London [via U.S. Army]
Mar. 14, 1944, 1622 Z / TOR 1745 Z

Prime Minister to President Roosevelt. Personal.

I feel you will be interested to hear about the operation just completed to fly two of Wingates Long Range Penetration Brigades into enemy territory in North Burma. Landing strips in two areas were selected, one 60 miles north of Katha and one 20 miles south of it, from which the Brigades could advance westwards primarily to interrupt the Japanese lines of communication and so assist the American/Chinese operations taking place further north. The strips were 100 miles inside enemy territory and 260 miles from the transport base.

First landings were made by gliders whose occupants then prepared the strips to receive transport aircraft. Between March 6th and March 11th, 7500 men with all their gear and with mules were successfully landed. The only losses were a number of gliders, and some of these should be repairable. The Brigades have now started their advance but a small holding party has been left at one of the strips to receive a flight of Spitfires and a squadron of Hurricane fighter/bombers which were to fly in to protect the base and provide air support.

Only serious mishap occurred on the first night. One of the strips in the northern area was found to have been obstructed by the Japanese, and surface of remaining strip was much worse than expected, causing crashes which blocked the strip and prevented further landings that night. A few of the gliders had to be turned back in the air and failed to reach our territory. Another strip was immediately prepared in this area and was ready for landings two days later. The total of killed, wounded and missing is at most 145.

The operation appears to have been a complete surprise for Japanese. There has been no enemy air action against the strips in the northern area, and the one in the south was only bombed on 10th March after our men had left it. As it happened, the enemy were concentrating aircraft at airfields in the Mandalay area as part of their own plans. In consequence, the strong air forces we had collected to protect the landings had a very good bag, and in 2 days destroyed 61 enemy aircraft for the loss of only 3 of our own.

We are all very pleased that Wingate's venture has started so well, and the success of this flying-in operation augurs well for the future. Your men have played an important part both in the transport squadrons and in the supporting air operations.

[MR*. *WSC*, V, 565–66. *R&C*.]

Churchill managed to persuade the British Cabinet to support his policy of opposing changes in the Italian government. North Italy, still under German control, contained the nation's major industrial cities, which provided the Italian Communist Party with the bulk of its membership. Even with Stalin's support for the Badoglio government, British diplomats remained worried that a weak government in Rome could be subverted by Communist pressure.

C–621

London [via U.S. Army]
Mar. 15, 1944, 1507 Z / TOR 1645 Z

Prime Minister to President Roosevelt. Personal.

1. I consulted the War Cabinet this morning on the proposal that the British and American Governments should accept the six party programme without further delay. The War Cabinet asked me to assure you that they agree fully with your wish to establish a more broadly based government in Italy and that the future form of government of the Italian people can only be settled by self determination. They also agree with you that the point to consider is the timing. On this they have no doubt that it would be far better to wait till we are masters of Rome before parting company with the King and Badoglio, because from Rome a more representative and solidly based administration can be constructed than is possible now. They feel that nothing could be worse for our joint interests and for the future of Italy, than to set up a weak democratic government which flopped. Even a settlement reached at Rome could not be final because it would be necessary to review it when the northern provinces and great industrial centres favourable to us and essential to a democratic solution, like Milan and Turin have been liberated. They do not consider that the six parties are representative in any true sense of the Italian democracy or Italian nation or that they could at the present time replace the existing Italian government which has loyally and effectively worked in our interests.

2. In reaching these conclusions the War Cabinet have of course had before them the telegrams sent by the Allied Commander in Chief whose views on this subject they do not share. Meanwhile we should be quite ready to discuss the suggestions put to the State Department in Paragraph 3 of the Foreign Secretary's number 1783. It is also of course recognised that should the capture of Rome be unduly protracted, say for 2 or 3 months, the question of timing would have to be reviewed.

3. Finally they ask me to emphasize the great importance of not exposing to the world any divergencies of view which may exist between our two governments, especially in face of the independent action taken by Russia in entering into direct relations with the Badoglio government

without consultation with other Allies. It would be a great pity if our respective viewpoints had to be argued out in Parliament and the press when waiting a few months may make it possible for all three governments to take united action.

[MR*. *FRUS*, 1944, III, 1060–61 (paraphrase). *WSC*, V, 504–5. *R&C*.]

Wingate's use of mules to carry supplies, particularly mortars and ammunition, says a great deal about the kind of terrain where the fighting took place.

R–499

Washington [via U.S. Navy]
Mar. 15, 1944, 12:55 P.M.

Secret and Personal, from the President for the Former Naval Person.

Your 620. I am thrilled by the news of our success under Wingate. If you wire him please give him my hearty good wishes. May the good work go on. This marks an epic achievement for air-borne troops, not forgetting the mules. Roosevelt [FDR]

[MR*. *WSC*, V, 566. *R&C*.]

Taken from the last scene of *Macbeth*, the promised inscription (C–616) Churchill sent to Harry Hopkins was hand lettered on parchment (OF 4117):

Stephen Peter Hopkins
Age 18

"Your son, my lord, has paid a soldier's debt:
He only liv'd but till he was a man;
The which no sooner had his prowess confirm'd
In the unshrinking station where he fought,
But like a man he died."

Shakespeare.

To Harry Hopkins from Winston S. Churchill
13 February, 1944.

R–500

Washington [via U.S. Navy]
Mar. 15, 1944, 1:10 P.M.

Personal and Secret, for the Former Naval Person from the President.
  Inscription for Harry received and forwarded to Rochester. Roosevelt
[FDR]

[MR*]

Pressure from Congress, particularly strong in an election year, prompted
the State Department to propose some sort of relief program for German-
occupied nations in western Europe. The U.S. Joint Chiefs of Staff were
dubious and the British, convinced that the blockade was seriously hampering
the German war effort, were firmly opposed.

R–501

Washington [via U.S. Navy]
Mar. 15, 1944, 3:55 P.M.

Personal and Secret. From the President for the Former Naval Person.
  We have lately been giving further thought to the matter of limited
feeding programs for children and nursing and expectant mothers in the
German-occupied countries of Europe. Ambassador Winant will shortly
take up with your Government a proposal under which such programs
might be put into effect initially in Belgium, France, the Netherlands,
and Norway.
  I bespeak your most earnest consideration of this proposal. I am convinced that the time has arrived when the continued withholding of food
from these categories of the populations of the occupied countries is likely
to hurt our friends more than our enemies and consequently to be injurious to the United Nations cause. Roosevelt [State Dept.]

[MR*. *FRUS*, 1944, II, 257n. *R&C*.]

Although a copy of this unsent draft is in the Hopkins papers, it was probably
drafted by Leahy and the President since Hopkins was still recuperating at
the Mayo Clinic in Minnesota. It was not sent, possibly because of the receipt
on March 18 of Churchill's number 625.

R–501/1, not sent

Washington
Mar. 16, 1944

To Former Naval Person from the President.

In regard to the general Polish situation, I am inclined to think that the final determination of matters like boundaries can well be laid aside for awhile by the Russians, by the Polish Government and by your Government.

In other words, I think that on these particular matters we can well let nature take its course.

The main current problem is to assure the cooperation of the Polish guerrillas and population with the Russians as they advance into Poland. Most certainly we do not want any Polish opposition to the Russian armies.

In the meantime we will learn much more about Polish sentiment and the advisability of continuing or not continuing to let the Polish Government in London speak for the Poles. It is entirely possible that as the Russians advance they may recognize some other organization as more representative of the people of Poland.

The advancing Russian army will doubtless find many local Poles who will aid them as they proceed westward. This is essentially a military occupation. I still think the future government and matters like boundaries can be put on ice until we know more about it. This, in line with my general thought that we ought not to cross bridges till we come to them.

If you think it would be helpful for me to wire Uncle Joe along the lines of the above, I will do so.

[HLH: Sherwood Col.]

The Allies had permitted Turkish trade with Germany, including shipments of chrome ore, because they could not provide certain goods which Turkey needed and could obtain from Germany. But Lawrence Steinhardt, the American Ambassador in Turkey, acting with his British counterpart, had protested that recent Turkish shipments of chrome ore to Germany had been substantially larger than shipments of the ore to Britain.

R–501/2

Washington
Mar. 16, 1944

President Roosevelt to Prime Minister. Most Secret.

As I am impressed by the importance to Germany of Turkish chrome,

I have today forwarded by air a personal letter to President Inonu on the subject of chrome for delivery in Ankara by Ambassador Steinhardt. I feel sure that you will concur, but if this action runs counter to any steps you are now taking or contemplating, please let me know so that I can stop delivery of the letter. The following is a paraphrase of the text of my letter:

"There are many matters about which I would like to talk to you almost every day in the week, and I wish that you and I were not several thousand miles apart.

I want to write you about the subject of chrome at this time.

By the capture of Nikopol the Russians, as you are aware, have succeeded in denying to the Germans an important source of manganese. Turkish chrome ore for many purposes can be substituted for manganese, and the denial to the Germans of manganese from Nikopol therefore multiplies the importance to the German war key.

It is obvious that it has now become a matter of grave concern to the United Nations that large supplies of chrome ore continues to move from Turkey to Germany.

How the Germans can be denied further access to Turkish chrome ore can best be decided by you. I know of your inventive genius and I hope you will find some method of accomplishing this.

It is my firm belief that you will recognize this opportunity for a unique contribution to what really is the welfare of the world to be made by Turkey.

There is no need to tell you how very happy I was in our talks in Cairo, and I feel that now you and I can talk to each other as old friends.

Please accept all my good wishes. I am counting on our meeting again in the near future."

A similar telegram is being sent by me to Marshal Stalin.

[PREM 3/472/474–75]

Once the British realized that the Japanese were about to launch their long-anticipated offensive against Imphal and Kohima, British military centers in western Assam, India, they began a planned withdrawal toward those towns. British strategy was to hold Kohima and Imphal, relying heavily on airlifted supplies, until the Japanese ran short of food and ammunition—probably in about three weeks. That required the temporary use of aircraft assigned to the Air Transport Command, where they were used to fly supplies over the Hump (the Himalaya Mountains) from India to China (see map, Vol. II, p. 111). Taking good advantage of their almost complete control of the air, the

British held; and by May they had launched a counter-offensive. (See the headnote to C–603 for a discussion of the Arakan offensive.) C-47 (Dakota) and C-46 (Commando) aircraft were cargo planes.

C–622

London [via U.S. Army]
Mar. 17, 1944, 0100 Z / TOR 0404 Z

Prime Minister to President. Most Secret and Personal.

We have had a Most Immediate telegram from Mountbatten operative part of which I am sending you in my immediately following.

2. Upshot is that Japanese are staging an offensive with the apparent object of capturing Imphal plain. Mountbatten thinks he has a good chance of inflicting a sharp defeat on the enemy greater than that achieved in recent Arakan operations.

3. Everything depends on flying up from Arakan the operational portion of 5 Division, ordering the troops to stand fast in places where they cannot be supplied by ordinary means and supplying them by air, and seizing any opportunity offered to use Wingate's two remaining brigades to harass the enemy in the rear. These brigades also would have to be supplied by air.

To do this Mountbatten needs 30 C.47s or the equivalent in load carrying capacity of C.46s to be diverted from the Hump for about a month starting 18th March. He is going ahead unless contrary instructions are issued. The stakes are pretty high in this battle and victory would have far reaching consequences.

5. British Chiefs of Staff have telegraphed their entire agreement with Mountbatten's proposals to Washington. We trust that U.S. Chiefs of Staff will agree.

[PREM 3/472/481. MR (garbled). *R&C* (MR version).]

The U.S. Joint Chiefs of Staff continued to support operations aimed at supplying Chinese and American forces in China, and Mountbatten's argument that the Japanese offensive threatened the Assam line of communication (L of C) and therefore the supply effort into China guaranteed JCS approval of his request for transport planes. Ever suspicious that the British hoped to shift the emphasis away from supplying China and toward greater support for their own operations in SEAC, the Joint Chiefs rejected Mountbatten's assumption that he could divert Air Transport Command (ATC) assets without first referring the request to American military authorities. (See Arnold to Stilwell, AC/AS Plans AFALP OPD no. 5043 and 4755 of Mar. 16, 1944, in MR.) Brigadier General J. S. "Tubby" Lethbridge later became Chief of Staff to the British commander in Burma, General W. J. Slim.

C-623

London [via U.S. Army]
Mar. 17, 1944, 0122 Z / TOR 0404 Z

Prime Minister to President. Most Secret and Personal.

Following is extract referred to in Para 1 of my immediately preceding telegram. Begins.

"Transport aircraft.

"1. Japanese offensive intentions on the IV Corps front have been previously reported in my SEACOS 93 and 96. Enemy has concentrated three divisions with presumed intention capturing Imphal Plain. First phase of offensive has already begun with encircling movement to east and west of 17 Division threatening to cut Tiddim Road and there are now indications that main offensive may start about 20 March. Capture of Imphal Plain would give enemy abundant food and two all weather landing grounds and would:

"A. Constitute direct threat to traffic on air ferry route and Assam L of C and

"B. Jeopardise whole air position in northern Burma.

"2. The Japanese plan appears to be similar to his plan for Arakan in that he is exploiting ability of Japanese troops to advance carrying own supplies for several days and gambling on defeating our forces and reaching food supplies in Imphal Plain quickly. There is thus an opportunity which I welcome of inflicting on him a defeat similar to that he has sustained in the Arakan but on a much larger scale. Enemy does not yet appear to have appreciated the size of Wingate forces behind him which should prove additional factor in achieving his defeat.

"3. Our success in Arakan was due to our ability to order troops to stand fast because we could supply them by air even when encircled. Lethbridge mission emphasised supply by air as essential factor in MacArthur's successes against Japanese and successes of Stilwell's advance from the Ledo area support this view. It is relevant to note that during February Ledo combat troops had over 10,000,000 pounds dropped while total for Arakan and Kaladan together was some 6,500,000 pounds.

"4. Best answer to present Japanese move to Tiddim area would be to order 17 Division to stand fast and to supply them by air. I cannot, however, afford to do this, as I have insufficient reserves within striking distance of Tiddim to enable me to make the necessary counter attacks, nor have I sufficient transport aircraft both to supply troops holding Tiddim area and fly reserves up. 17 Division have therefore been ordered to withdraw northwards about half way towards Imphal. Much as I dislike this, I do not consider it essential to protection of ferry route to hold so far forward as Tiddim and do not therefore consider that I should be justified in asking for diversion of aircraft from the ferry route for this purpose alone.

"5. I do, however, regard it as vital to the ferry route and to the Assam L of C by which it is nourished, and indeed to our whole position in Assam to hold the Imphal Plain. Immediate requirement is to fly up from Arakan ASP reinforcements essential operational portion of 5 Division. This fly in should be started 18 March. It may also be necessary to order troops to stand fast in places where they cannot be supplied by ordinary means and to supply them by US air. At the same time, an opportunity may offer of using Wingate's two remaining brigades of his second wave behind Japanese formations. These too must of course [be supplied by air.]

"6. The dangers of Japanese successes and the magnitude of the defeat which we may inflict upon them are both greater than in the case of Arakan. Troop carrier command are already committed to support of Kaladan Division three LRP brigades and Ledo force and cannot carry out the requirements indicated in my Para 5 without the addition of up to 30 C47's or the equivalent in load carrying capacity of C46's with combat and maintenance crews from 18 March for about a month. All the aircraft borrowed from ATC for Arakan emergency were returned with least possible delay but since the emergency is even greater than in the case of the Arakan and since it is clear that Imphal attack and Arakan are both part of one Japanese plan I think it is justifiable to regard the period of emergency as continuing. I should be glad to receive your confirmation that my interpretation is correct. Unless I receive instructions to the contrary from you, aircraft will have moved by March 18."

[MR*]

This was the last message exchanged by Churchill and Roosevelt on the matter of the Italian government before King Victor Emmanuel appointed his son (Crown Prince Umberto) Lieutenant of the Realm, shortly after the Allies had entered Rome on June 4. The President's position was set forth, however, in an *aide-mémoire* of March 25, 1944, which was sent to the British Embassy. In that paper the State Department reiterated American support for political changes which would bring the six opposition parties into the Italian government. In spite of such opinions, the Badoglio government remained in power until the Allies entered Rome—just as Churchill had hoped. (See C–699.)

R-502

London [via U.S. Navy]
Mar. 17, 1944, 5:00 P.M.

Personal and Secret for the Prime Minister from the President.

Thank you for your Number 621, March 15, reporting the decisions of the War Cabinet with respect to the Italian political situation. I am in full agreement with you and them that we should not permit our divergent views to become known publicly particularly at this time.

However, I still feel that if the pressure of the Six Opposition Parties comes to a point where it will have an adverse effect on the situation, we should support their program. I think that we should watch political developments carefully in Italy for the present with that in mind and keep the matter continually before the Advisory Council. Roosevelt [State Dept.]

[MR*. *FRUS*, 1944, III, 1078. *R&C.*]

Roosevelt's proposed letter to President Ismet Inönü (R–501/2) had expressed a desire that the two men meet. Easter fell on April 9 that year.

The telegram to General Marshall mentioned by the Prime Minister is probably quoted in a letter from Field Marshal Sir John Dill to Marshall cited in Matloff, *Strategic Planning, 1943–1944*, p. 427. In that letter Dill included this from Churchill: "I am hardening very much on this operation [OVERLORD] as the time approaches in the sense of wishing to strike if humanly possible even if the limiting conditions we laid down at Moscow are not exactly fulfilled." According to many other sources, the Prime Minister had overcome his doubts about the OVERLORD invasion and was now enthusiastic.

C-624

London [via U.S. Army]
Mar. 18, 1944, 1715 Z / TOR 2010 Z

Prime Minister to President Roosevelt Most Secret and Personal.

1. Winant gave me your letter this morning. As you are so keen for the company of Inonu, I wonder whether you would care to spend Easter with me at Bermuda. I can arrive there on the 5th and we could separate on the 11th or earlier if you are pressed. I would not suggest bringing the great staffs but only the principals on the scale with which we went to Teheran. It is not so much that there are new departures in policy to be taken but there is a need after more than 90 days of separation for checking up and shaking together.

2. I am hardening for OVERLORD as the time gets nearer. Perhaps Marshall will show you a telegram I sent him.

[MR*. *FRUS, Quebec Conf.*, 1944, p. 3.]

Stalin's complaint concerned revelations in the London *Observer* of his most recent message regarding Soviet-Polish questions (C–609). Churchill's proposed statement to Parliament is outlined in C–630.

C–625

London [via U.S. Army]
Mar. 18, 1944, 1714 Z / TOR 2010 Z

Prime Minister to President Roosevelt Personal.

Following is latest from UJ about Poland. No leakage has occurred for which we are responsible. We did not tell the Poles anything. On the other hand the "Observer" newspaper was unduly well informed about Stalin's attitude. This we think could only have come from the Russian Embassy. The matter is of relative unimportance. What matters is that our talks with him on this subject are at an end. He has definitely avoided seeing Ambassador Clark Kerr. Presently I shall have to make some statement in Parliament which I do not expect he will like very much. Meanwhile I do not propose to send any answer. Telegram from UJ begins

I received from Sir A Clark Kerr on March 12th your message of March 7th on the Polish question.

Thank you for the explanations which you made in this message.

In spite of the fact that our correspondence is considered secret and personal the contents of my letter to you have for some time begun to appear in the English press, and, moreover, with many distortions which I have no possibility of refuting.

I consider this to be a breach of secrecy. This fact makes it difficult for me to express my opinion freely. I hope that you have understood me.

Telegram from UJ ends.

[MR*. p*Stalin*/WSC, doc. 254. *R&C*.]

SEACOS 117 from Admiral "Dickie" Mountbatten presented an optimistic summary of Allied activities in northern Burma along the Ledo Road route. After talks with General Stilwell, the SEAC commander believed that Chinese and American forces would be able to make a substantial advance southward, so much so that they would need to be reinforced by a Chinese division. In addition, Mountbatten reported great success by Wingate's forces because of their effective use of an airfield (named BROADWAY) constructed behind enemy lines. (See SACSEA to Chiefs of Staff, repeated to Joint Staff Mission, Washington, SEACOS 117, dated Mar. 17, 1944, in MR.) The Joint Staff Mission provided administrative support for British representatives on the Combined Chiefs of Staff Committee in Washington.

C–626

London [via U.S. Army]
Mar. 19, 1944, 1130 Z / TOR 1245 Z

Prime Minister to President. Personal and Most Secret.

SEACOS 117 from Dickie repeated to Joint Staff Mission will show you all the possibilities that are open in this theatre and the enormous power of air transportation applied to actual fighting.

[MR*]

Churchill had supported harsh sanctions against Turkey, but the British no longer considered Turkish entry into the war important. The Foreign Office was more concerned with promoting good postwar relations and feared that the letter Roosevelt proposed sending (R–501/2) might work against that goal. The President never sent the letter to Inönü, and quiet British diplomacy including a suspension of military aid, plus the changing fortunes of war, prompted the Turks to suspend chrome shipments to Germany on April 21, 1944.

C–627

London [via U.S. Army]
Mar. 19, 1944, 1719 Z / TOR 1850 Z

Prime Minister to President Roosevelt. Personal.

I have consulted Eden on your proposed message to President Inonu. He says: Begins:

We are already studying how best to induce Turks to limit the supply of chrome to Germany. Question is very complicated one owing to existing Turco-German agreements and I doubt whether personal appeal to Turkish President would help at present stage. As you know Turks are at present in a very selfish and obstinate mood and an appeal to their better feelings might have the opposite effect to what we desire. It is all a question of timing and I would suggest that the President's message should be kept in reserve until we have decided what we actually want the Turks to do and have found out how far they are likely to go. Above all there is danger that they will regard so friendly a message at this juncture as a sign of weakening on our part. Ends.

Perhaps you will consider this point of view.

[MR*]

Ultimately, twenty Commando (C-46) aircraft—the equivalent of thirty Douglas (C-47) planes—were sent to assist in the defense of Imphal.

R–503

Washington [via U.S. Navy]
Mar. 19, 1944, 12:45 P.M.

Personal and Secret. From the President for the Former Naval Person.

Receipt is acknowledged of your 622 and 623. The American Chiefs of Staff have issued instructions authorizing the diversion of 30 C-47's or the equivalent C-46 aircraft from the hump program to meet Mountbatten's immediate necessity with instructions to the American Commander of the Air Forces, India-Burma Sector, that these planes should be returned to the Air Transport Command at the earliest possible time.

The American Chiefs of Staff have advised the Commanding General, American Army Air Forces and the Commanding General, American Army Forces in that area that Mountbatten should request the British Chiefs of Staff to provide the additional transport aircraft which he needs to support his operations during the remainder of this dry season. Roosevelt [WDL]

[MR*. R&C.]

The cruiser USS *Milwaukee*, along with a number of British ships, was being transferred to the Soviet Union in lieu of a portion of the Italian fleet. The Soviet government had requested that the American vessel be delivered directly to a Russian port instead of a British port. A similar request was made of the British government, but the Admiralty insisted that it could not spare the British crews needed to sail the ships to the Soviet Union, and the Russians reluctantly agreed to pick up the warships in Great Britain. Admiral Harold Stark, the former Chief of Naval Operations, headed the U.S. Naval Mission in London.

R–504

Washington [via U.S. Navy]
Mar. 19, 1944, 12:55 P.M.

Personal and Secret. From the President for the Former Naval Person.

For your information I have today sent the following message to Harriman:

> QUOTE. Your 142215. The *Milwaukee* can be delivered at a North Russian Port. Please inform Admiral Stark port at which delivery is desired and inform us by telegram what arrangements can be made for an early return of *Milwaukee*'s personnel. UNQUOTE.

Roosevelt [WDL]

[MR*]

Roosevelt had long been annoyed at the refusal of Irish Prime Minister Eamon de Valera to cooperate in the anti-submarine war by providing bases on the west coast of Ireland. A number of other incidents, particularly an OSS report that the Germans were obtaining a good deal of useful intelligence in Ireland, finally prompted the President to request that Ireland break diplomatic relations with Germany and Japan. Aware that domestic pressures made it difficult for Roosevelt to push the issue, particularly in an election year, de Valera flatly refused. Churchill believed the Irish should be punished for failing to support the Allies, but the security of OVERLORD, especially of U.S. Army units stationed in Northern Ireland, was probably his paramount reason for deciding to cut off contacts between Ireland and other nations. Ambassador Winant's cable (*FRUS*, 1944, III, 236–37) summarized the recommendations of the U.S. Minister in Ireland, David Gray, that the United States should retain the option to force Ireland to cooperate. (The OSS report mentioned above is cited in Brown, *Bodyguard of Lies*, pp. 543–44.)

C–628

London [via U.S. Army]
Mar. 19, 1944, 1830 Z

Prime Minister to President Roosevelt. Personal.

See State Department's message through Winant dated March 14.

1. We have followed Gray's lead in Ireland and it is early days to start reassuring De Valera. There is not much sense in a doctor telling a patient that the medicine he has just prescribed for his nerve troubles is only colored water. I think it would be much better to keep them guessing for a while.

2. I do not propose to stop the necessary trade between Britain and Ireland or to prevent anything going into Ireland. I do propose to stop ships going from Ireland to Spain and Portugal and other foreign ports until OVERLORD is launched. One must remember that a ship may start out in one direction and turn off in another. There is no difficulty in stopping ships. The above also applies to outward bound airplanes which we shall try to stop by every means in our power. The object of these measures is not spite against the Irish but preservation of British and American soldiers' lives and against our plans being betrayed by emissaries sent by sea or air from the German Minister in Dublin. Since the beginning of 1943 only 19 Irish ships have left Irish ports, some several times, so the evil is not very great. We are also cutting off telephones and restricting communications to the utmost and also stopping the Anglo-Irish Air Line from running. I repeat, all our actions will be taken from motives of self preservation and none from those of spite.

3. If however the Irish retaliate by doing something which in no way helps them but merely annoys us, such as stopping the Foynes Airport facilities, I should feel free to retaliate on their cross channel trade. They would have opened a new chapter and economic measures of retaliation would be considered. I would tell you about these before we took them.

4. It seems to me that so far from allaying alarm in De Valera's circles we should let fear work its healthy process. Thereby we shall get behind the scenes a continued stiffening up of the Irish measures which even now are not so bad to prevent a leakage.

5. I gather that the State Department will probably not disagree with the above, for Mr Hull says in the message above quoted: Begins.

I am inclined to believe however that for the time being at least we should not make any statement to the press or commit ourselves to the Irish Government that we have no intention of instituting economic sanctions. Ends.

And I hope this may also be your view.

[MR*. *WSC*, V, 700–701. *FRUS*, 1944, III, 243–44 (paraphrase).]

SEACOS 118 suggested that Chiang Kai-shek would be more likely to provide the Chinese division needed in northern Burma if he were approached by Churchill and Roosevelt. (See SACSEA to British Chiefs of Staff, SEACOS 118, dated Mar. 17, 1944, in MR.) The Chinese eventually sent the forces requested, but only when threatened with a cutoff of American lend-lease supplies (Kirby, *War Against Japan*, III, 231).

R–505

Washington [via U.S. Navy]
Mar. 20, 1944, 12:40 P.M.

Secret and Personal, for the Former Naval Person from the President.

Replying to your No. 626, I have read SEACOS 117 and 118 with much interest. On 17 March I telegraphed to the Generalissimo an urgent request that he utilize his Yunnan troops to assist the effort reported in SEACOS 117 and 118. I have as yet received no reply. Roosevelt [WDL]

[MR*]

Roosevelt's attack of influenza shortly after the Teheran Conference had left him weak, listless, and bothered by frequent headaches. As various message-routing slips indicate, he had spent a good deal of time in the office of his personal physician, Admiral Ross T. McIntire. A week after this cable was sent, Lieutenant Commander Howard Bruenn, a doctor stationed at Bethesda Naval Hospital, examined the President and found that he suffered from hypertension and congestive heart failure. Roosevelt was put on digitalis and a weight-loss program, but attempts to get him on a more restful routine were only partly successful. (For additional discussion of Roosevelt's health see Burns, *Soldier of Freedom*, pp. 448–50.) Changes in the message were made in Roosevelt's handwriting. An earlier draft of this message, later changed by Admiral Leahy, suggested a Churchill-Roosevelt meeting in Bermuda beginning on April 25.

R–506

Washington [via U.S. Navy]
Mar. 20, 1944, 6:30 P.M.

Personal and Secret. From the President for the Former Naval Person.

~~Replying to your 624 and in reference to your suggestion that we have a staff meeting on the Teheran scale in Bermuda about the fifth of April, it is not now possible for me to meet that date.~~

~~Not having had any opportunity for relaxation since my recent attack of grippe which has not been completely eliminated leaves me from time to time with a temperature.~~

~~My doctor considers it~~ I am very angry with myself. The old attack of grippe having hung on and on, leaving me with an intermittent temperature, Ross decided about a week ago that it is necessary for me to take a complete rest of about two or three weeks in a suitable climate which

I am definitely planning to do beginning at the end of this month. <u>I see no way out and I am furious.</u>

It will therefore be impossible for me to get to a staff meeting in early April. I believe that such a meeting on the Teheran scale in early April would be most useful and if you agree I will send my Chiefs of Staff to Bermuda for that purpose at any time that suits your convenience.

<u>I am glad you feel hardened about OVERLORD. Its accomplishment may synchronize with a real Russian break-through.</u> Roosevelt [WDL]

[MR*. *FRUS, Quebec Conf.*, 1944, pp. 3–4.]

The "great event" was OVERLORD, the cross-channel invasion.

C–629

London [via U.S. Army]
Mar. 21, 1944, 1516 Z / TOR 1655 Z

Prime Minister to President Roosevelt. Most Secret and Personal.
   Your 506.
   1. I am indeed grieved and trust rest will do you good.
   2. I do not think the staff meeting worthwhile without our being there.
   3. I hope you are still planning your visit here for the great event after you are fully recovered.

[MR*. *FRUS, Quebec Conf.*, 1944, p. 4.]

The tone of exchanges between Churchill and Stalin concerning the Polish question had become markedly strained, and the Prime Minister's threat publicly to oppose any Soviet-Polish boundary arrived at unilaterally by the conquering Red Army was bound to exacerbate the situation. Churchill tried to lessen the harshness of his message by thanking Stalin for being gentle with the Finns. Soviet forces had broken the German siege of Leningrad and, in the process, isolated Finland. In mid-February the Finnish government had opened talks with the Russians. (Britain and the United States had not declared war on Finland even though the Finns had allied with Germany; the Soviets had reacted similarly to Bulgaria's alliance with Germany.) Soviet negotiators had been surprisingly moderate, demanding only a return to the political relationship and boundaries of 1940, but the Finns distrusted the Russians and requested additional safeguards. The talks broke off in March when the Finnish government claimed it was not capable of disarming the German forces in northern Finland and would not permit Soviet troops to enter the country for that purpose. It was not until September 1944 that the Finns bowed to the inevitable and accepted the Russian demands. The "leak" about which Stalin had complained is discussed in C–625. Feodor T. Gusev (Gousev) had replaced Ivan Maisky late in 1943 as Soviet Ambassador to Britain. Maisky had been recalled, along with Maxime Litvinov, the Soviet Ambassador in Washington, in July 1943 as part of Stalin's protest against the TRIDENT decision to delay the second front.

C–630

London [via U.S. Army]
Mar. 21, 1944, 1052 Z / TOR 0015 Z, Mar. 22

Prime Minister to President Roosevelt. Personal and Most Secret.
  Reference my telegram number 625.
  I have today sent following reply to Uncle J. So what!

  Prime Minister to Marshal Stalin. "Personal and most secret.
  Your telegram of March 16th.
  1. First of all I must congratulate you again on all the wonderful victories your Armies are winning and also on the extremely temperate way in which you have dealt with the Finns. I suppose they are worried about interning the nine German Divisions in Finland for fear that the nine German Divisions should intern them. We are much obliged to you for keeping us in touch with all your action in this Theatre.
  2. With regard to the Poles, I am not to blame in any way about revealing your secret correspondence. The information was given both to the American *Herald Tribune* correspondent and to the London *Times* correspondent by the Soviet Embassy in London. In the latter case it was given personally by Ambassador Gusev.
  3. I shall have very soon to make a statement to the House of Commons about the Polish position. This will involve my saying that the attempts to make an arrangement between the Soviet and Polish Governments have broken down; that we continue to recognize the Polish Government, with whom we have been in continuous relations since the invasion of Poland in 1939; that we now consider all questions of territorial change must await the armistice or peace conferences of the victorious powers; and that in the meantime we can recognize no forcible transferences of territory.
  4. I am repeating this telegram to the President of the United States. I only wish I had better news to give him for the sake of all.
  5. Finally, let me express the earnest hope that the breakdown which has occurred between us about Poland will not have any adverse effect upon our cooperation in other spheres where the maintenance of our common action is of the greatest consequence."

[MR*. p*Stalin/WSC*, doc. 256. *R&C*.]

Roosevelt continued to look for an alternative to de Gaulle's leadership in liberated France. The President often referred to the French General's lack of popular support in France, although deeper motives seem to have determined American policy. De Gaulle had annoyed Roosevelt personally, but the President also seemed to oppose any strong leader in France who did not accept Anglo-American leadership. The decision to give the Supreme Commander, General Eisenhower, such broad authority was aimed at preventing de Gaulle from assuming power. The British Foreign Office, convinced that de Gaulle would establish control anyway, vigorously opposed this "French Directive," but Churchill refused to confront the President on the matter. (See C–643, R–538, and ff.)

R–506/1, letter

Washington
March 21, 1944

Dear Winston,

As I told you in my letter of February 29th, I have been putting the finishing touches on a directive to Eisenhower which would make him solely responsible for OVERLORD and for the administration of good order and reasonable justice when we get ashore.

The paper is now being cleared through the usual channels of the Combined Chiefs of Staff for presentation to Eisenhower, and I am sending you a copy herewith.

I hope you will agree that my efforts to keep it simple and to provide primarily for the first few months of occupation are on a sound basis and have not been in vain.

With warm regards, As ever,

ENCLOSURE TO R–506/1

Mar. 15, 1944

Dear Mr. Secretary:— (Secretary of War)

After much thought, and many revisions, and with the approval of yourself and the Secretary of State, I request that the following order be sent to General Eisenhower. I think it covers the practical objective of giving the final command in the forthcoming occupation to General Eisenhower and, at the same time, leaving him free to consult any and all French organizations as circumstances may be determined by him.

General Eisenhower:

This memorandum is directed to you as Supreme Allied Commander in the event of the occupation of French territory:

I.

The three paramount aims which are to be the landmarks of your policy are the following:

A. The prompt and complete defeat of Germany.

B. The earliest possible liberation of France from her oppressors.

C. The fostering of democratic methods and conditions under which a French government may ultimately be established according to the free choice of the French people as the government under which they wish to live.

II.

The following powers and instructions are given you for your guidance in the achievement of the foregoing aims:

1. The Supreme Allied Commander will have supreme authority in order that the war against Germany may be prosecuted relentlessly with the full cooperation of the French people. As such Allied Commander you will have the ultimate determination as to where, when, and how the civil administration in France shall be exercised by French citizens, remembering always that the military situation must govern.

2. When and where you determine that there shall be set up a civil administration in any part of France, so far as possible there shall not be retained or employed in any office any person who has wilfully collaborated with the enemy or who has acted in any manner inimical to the cause of the United States.

3. In order to secure the setting up of any such civilian administration locally in any part of France, you may consult with the French Committee of National Liberation and may authorize them in your discretion to select and install the personnel necessary for such administration. You are, however, not limited to dealing exclusively with said Committee for such purpose in case at any time in your best judgment you determine that some other course or conferee is preferable.

4. Nothing that you do under the powers conferred in the preceding paragraph 3 in connection with the French Committee of National Liberation or with any other group or organization shall constitute a recognition of said Committee or group as the government of France even on a provisional basis.

5. In making your decision as to entering into such relations with the French Committee of National Liberation or other committees or persons for that purpose, you should as far as possible obtain from it the following restrictions upon its purposes:

a. It has no intention of exercising indefinitely in France any powers of government, provisional or otherwise, except to assist in the establishment by the democratic methods above mentioned a government of France according to the free choice of the French people, and that when such government is established it will turn over thereto all such powers as it may have.

b. It favors the reestablishment of all the historic French liberties and the destruction of any arbitrary regime or rule of personal government.

c. It will take no action designed to entrench itself or any particular political group in power pending the selection of a constitutional government by the free choice of the French people.

6. In any area of liberated France, whether or not there has been set up local control of civil affairs as aforesaid, you will retain the right at any time to make such changes in whole or in part which in your discretion may seem necessary (a) for the effective prosecution of the war against Germany; (b) for the maintenance of law and order; and (c) for the maintenance of civil liberties.

7. As Supreme Commander you will seek such uniformity in the administration of civil affairs as seems advisable, issue policy directives applicable to British, French, and American commands, and review all plans.

8. You may at your discretion incorporate in your Civil Affairs Section members of the French Military Mission and other French officials.

9. You will have no talks or relations with the Vichy regime except for the purpose of terminating its administration in toto.

10. Instructions on economic, fiscal, and relief matters will be furnished you later by the Prime Minister, by the President, or by the Combined Chiefs of Staff. Franklin D. Roosevelt Commander-in-Chief

[MR. *R&C* (w/o enclosure).]

R–507

Washington [via U.S. Navy]
Mar. 22, 1944, 12:25 P.M.

Personal and Secret. From the President for the Former Naval Person.
Your 629 received and my Chiefs of Staff have been told.
I join you in hoping that we may arrange to have a meeting before the great event is launched. Roosevelt [WDL]

[MR*. *FRUS, Quebec Conf.*, 1944, p. 4.]

R–508

Washington [via U.S. Navy]
Mar. 22, 1944, 12:10 P.M.

Personal and Secret, for the Former Naval Person from the President.

Your 630, thank you for the information as to the present status of the Anglo-Soviet disagreement about Poland. I hope your strategy will accomplish the best possible advantage to both of us. Roosevelt [WDL]

[MR*. R&C.]

With the attention of Republicans in Congress (Karl Mundt, R–S.Dak., was the concerned member of the Foreign Affairs Committee mentioned below) directed to growing British dollar-balances and possible non war-related use of lend-lease, Roosevelt could not promise Churchill that the dollar-balance question would not come up in the future. Nevertheless, at Morgenthau's urging, everyone agreed to let the matter drop, at least until after the Normandy invasion. On lend-lease, however, Congress had become increasingly adamant. As one proposed amendment to the lend-lease arrangement with Britain put it, ". . . nothing in this paragraph shall be construed to authorize the President in any final settlement to assume or incur any obligations on the part of the United States with respect to post war economic or post war military policy except in accordance with established constitutional procedure." In other words, lend-lease was not to be used for postwar reconstruction. (Oscar Cox Diary, FDRL, Mar. 23, 1944.)

R–509

Washington [via U.S. Navy]
Mar. 24, 1944, 3:15 P.M.

Secret and Personal, from the President for the Former Naval Person.

1. Thank you for your reply contained in your cables 613 and 614 of March 9. The points you raised have already been brought to my attention several times by Secretary Morgenthau and Secretary Hull.

I am sorry if my message caused you anxiety. There is no dispute as to the understanding on the handling of questionable items under Lend-Lease which was reached between Mr. Crowley, Secretary Hull, Secretary Morgenthau and Lord Halifax, and to which I had given my prior approval. As Secretary Morgenthau stated at the meeting, this understanding did not deal with the dollar position question and did not preclude the possibility of our reopening that question in the future should the situation seem to call for it.

I raised this dollar position question since it is a troublesome one of continuing concern with us here and doubtless with you. I hope that we may be able together to find some reasonable solution to this problem before it becomes more troublesome.

2. In any further discussion of these matters the Treasury would be the normal center of such conversations. The agenda which Stettinius has of topics to be discussed in London does not include the question of British dollar balances.

3. The question to which you refer in paragraph two of 614 may be withdrawn, although the Congressman concerned and the entire Foreign Affairs Committee are now alerted to the issue. We will let you know as soon as a definite decision is reached, and will consult fully before any information is proffered. Roosevelt [CH, HM, L. Crowley]

[MR*. *FRUS*, 1944, III, 47–48.]

The British remained eager to obtain a compromise agreement with the Spanish on limiting wolfram exports to Germany, particularly since a break-down of good relations between the two nations could jeopardize British imports of iron ore and potash from Spain. Although the two Allied Ambassadors in Madrid, Sir Samuel Hoare for Britain and Carlton J. H. Hayes for the United States, supported a compromise, the State Department had insisted that Spain completely cut off wolfram shipments to Germany. The previous messages referred to by Churchill are C–577, R–467, C–586, R–478, and C–590.

C–631

London [via U.S. Army]
Mar. 30, 1944, 2325 Z / TOR 0300 Z, Mar. 31

Prime Minister to President Roosevelt. Most Secret and Personal.

1. In the messages we exchanged last month about Spain, ending with your Nr. 478 of February 23rd, you indicated your agreement with my view that we should reach a rapid settlement with the Spanish Government on a basis which would obtain for us the political and military requirements to which we have always attached great importance, and at the same time secure in effect a cessation of Spanish wolfram exports to Germany for the first half of this year.

2. In the subsequent negotiation conducted by our two ambassadors at Madrid, in which Sir S. Hoare has given the strongest support to your representations, it has become clear that, while we can still obtain full satisfaction of our other requirements, we cannot within the next few months obtain a complete embargo on Spanish wolfram exports for the

whole of this year, which is what I understand you are now expecting of the Spanish Government. There has, however, been a temporary embargo since early January.

3. We have, therefore, reached a situation in which we must either accept some slight compromise over wolfram or prolong the present deadlock. This would mean running certain serious risks, quite apart from postponing our enjoyment of such valuable benefits as the closing of the German consulate at Tangier and the cleaning up of the German espionage system throughout Spanish territory.

4. I have no doubt that by increasing our economic pressure we can eventually bring Spain to heel. In fact, with reasonable people the mere threat should be enough. The Spaniards are not, however, reasonable and they have a capacity for tightening their belts in resistance to foreign pressure. This would, I am convinced, postpone any settlement for several months. Meanwhile, we should run the following serious risks:—

(1) Between 700 and 1000 tons of wolfram representing Spanish stocks now on the Pyrenees, might be handed over to the Germans in exchange for important supplies, including gasoline, which the Germans are now offering to Spain. This would be a far greater help to the German war effort than the 100 or 200 tons on which our present discussions are centered;

(2) The Spaniards will clearly apply economic counter measures. This would mean that we should lose the Spanish iron ore which at present provides 42% of British requirements at a great economy in shipping and fuel. We should also lose Spanish potash, which is essential for the maintenance of British agriculture. Finally, our purchases in Spain are only made possible by Spanish financial facilities, without which we should run out of funds in a few weeks. Although these considerations have been put to your government I am not aware of any satisfactory method by which these essential needs could be replaced from other sources.

5. I understand that the State Department have suggested that the Spaniards might be brought to accept a total wolfram embargo now by the offer of a long term economic agreement. Our view which is, I understand, shared by all our experts in Madrid, is that such a prospect is illusory. Such a settlement would mean replacing the very important supplies which Spain now gets from German-controlled Europe, including in particular machinery and arms. It would, in any case, take several months to negotiate during which we should run all the risks I have mentioned above. Nor do I think we should be well advised to enter into any long term commitments with the present Spanish Regime. Surely what we should aim at is a short term arrangement which will secure important tangible benefits now at a very small cost in wolfram exports to Germany. When we have, as we hope, established the second front

successfully, the whole picture will change. The supply of even 50 tons of wolfram a month to Germany meanwhile, which is what is now in question, can be of little real assistance to the German war effort and can certainly not be balanced against the much greater advantages Germany would probably obtain if we fail to break the deadlock now.

6. I hope, therefore, you will agree that, having tried unsuccessfully to obtain a total wolfram embargo but having nevertheless made more satisfactory progress than might originally have been expected, we should now authorize our ambassadors to secure immediately the most favourable wolfram settlement they can obtain. This should be on the basis of not more than 50 tons of wolfram a month being allowed through to Germany during the next few vital months.

7. In making this proposal I would venture to remind you that we have gone along with you in Argentina and that we feel entitled to ask you to take our views seriously into account in the Iberian Peninsula, where our strategic and economic interests are more directly affected than are those of the United States.

8. It seems to me that we should make a fatal mistake if we risk throwing these 750 to 1000 tons of wolfram into German hands as well as losing all the other advantages which are now open. I earnestly hope that you will give your consideration to our appeal without which we shall be in very serious difficulties. Among other things Ambassador Hoare who has held most of our offices of state and is a member of Parliament now evidently wishes to resign. I could not support in public the policy which is now being enforced upon us. Do please consider the arguments of this telegram.

[MR*]

Churchill's threat of a public statement criticizing the Soviet government for its intransigence toward Poland (C–630) brought an angry reply from Stalin. The British believed Stalin had grossly misinterpreted Churchill's message, but they also realized that the Soviet leader was correct when he noted that the Big Three had agreed on the Curzon line during the Teheran talks. The War Cabinet decided the best thing would be to downplay the dispute; hence the British sent a formal response to Stalin through their Ambassador, Clark Kerr.

C–632

London [via U.S. Army]
Apr. 1, 1944, 1100 Z / TOR 1345 Z

Prime Minister to President Roosevelt. Personal and Most Secret.

1. I send you in my immediately following the recent telegrams I have

received from UJ. The War Cabinet did not think there was much use in going on with the personal correspondence on this subject at this time as evidently he is determined to find fault and pick a quarrel on every point. We are therefore instructing Ambassador Clark Kerr as in my next following telegram.

2. I have a feeling that the bark may be worse than its bite and that they have a great desire not to separate themselves from their British and American allies. Their conduct about Finland has been temperate and their attitude towards Rumania and Bulgaria seems to be helpful. It may be that, while unwilling to say anything of a reassuring nature to us about Poland, they will in fact watch their step very carefully. This may be of great benefit to the Poles in Poland. It would, I believe, help the situation if you invited Monsieur Mikolajczyk to pay his visit to the United States on your return from your holiday, and thus show the Russians the interest which the United States takes in the fate and future of Poland.

[MR*. R&C.]

C–633

London [via U.S. Army]
Apr. 1, 1944, 1139 Z / TOR 1700 Z

Prime Minister to President Roosevelt. Personal and Most Secret.

My immediately preceding telegram. Following are recent telegrams I have received from UJ. Begins.

"1. Premier J. V. Stalin to Mr. Prime Minister W. Churchill 23.3.44 recd 25.3.44.

"I have recently received from you two messages on the Polish question and have studied the statement which Sir A. Clark Kerr made to V. M. Molotov on your instructions on the same question. I was unable to reply at the time as matters at the front often take me away from non-military questions.

"I now reply on these questions.

"It is patent that your messages, and especially the statement of Sir A. Clark Kerr, are full of threats concerning the Soviet Union. I should like to draw your attention to this fact, as the method of threats is not only incorrect in the mutual relations of allies but is also harmful and can lead to contrary results.

"In one of your messages, you qualified the efforts on the Soviet Union in the matter of the maintenance and realization of the Curzon Line as a policy of force. This means that you now seek to qualify the Curzon Line as inequitable and the struggle for it as unjust. I can, on no account, agree with such an attitude. I cannot but remind you that at Teheran you, the President, and I agreed as to the justice of the Curzon Line. You considered then the attitude of the Soviet Union regarding this question as perfectly just, and you said that the representatives of the Emigre Polish Government would be mad to refuse the Curzon Line. Now you maintain something which is directly the contrary. Does this not mean that you no longer acknowledge what we agreed upon at Teheran, and that by this very fact you are breaking the Teheran agreement? I have no doubt that if you had continued to stand firmly, as before, by the attitude you adopted at Teheran, the dispute with the Polish Emigre Government would already have been settled. As for myself and the Soviet Government, we continue to stand by the attitude we adopted at Teheran and have no intention of departing from it, since we consider that the realization of the Curzon Line is not a manifestation of a policy of force but a manifestation of the policy of the restoration of the legal rights of the Soviet Union to those territories which even Curzon and the Supreme Council of the Allied Powers recognised in 1919 as being non-Polish.

"You state in your message of the 7th March that the question of the Soviet-Polish frontier will have to be deferred until the summoning of the armistice conference. I think we have here some misunderstanding. The Soviet Union is not waging war and has no intention of waging war against Poland. The Soviet Union has no dispute with the Polish people and considers itself the ally of Poland and the Polish people. For this very reason, the Soviet Union is shedding blood for the sake of the liberation of Poland from German oppression. For this reason, it would be strange to speak of an armistice between the USSR and Poland. But the Soviet Government has a dispute with the Emigre Polish Government, which does not reflect the interests of the Polish people and does not express its hopes. It would be even more strange to identify with Poland the Emigre Polish Government in London separated (literally "torn away") from Poland. I find it difficult even to point to the difference between the Emigre Government of Poland and the similar Emigre Government of Yugoslavia, or between certain Generals of the Polish Emigre Government and the Serbian General Mikhailovich.

"In your message of the 21st March you state that you intend to make a statement in the House of Commons to the effect that all questions of territorial changes must be deferred until the armistice or the peace conference of the victorious powers, and that, until then, you cannot recognise any transferences of territories *carried out by force*. I understand this to mean that you represent the Soviet Union as a power hostile to Poland, and that the essence of the matter is that you deny the emancipatory character of the war of the Soviet Union against German aggression. This is equivalent to attempting to ascribe to the Soviet Union what is not in fact the case and to discrediting it thereby. I have no doubt that such a statement of yours will be taken by the peoples of the Soviet Union and world public opinion as an undeserved insult directed at the Soviet Union.

"Of course, you are free to make whatever statement you please in the House of Commons—that is your affair. But if you do make such a statement, I shall consider that you have committed an unjust and unfriendly act towards the Soviet Union.

"In your message you express the hope that failure over the Polish question will not influence our collaboration in other spheres. As for myself, I stood for, and continue to stand for collaboration. But I fear that the method of threats and discrediting, if it continues in the future, will not conduce to our collaboration." Stalin.

"2. Premier Stalin to Prime Minister 25.3.44.

"I have carried out a thorough enquiry into your statement that the disclosure of the correspondence between us occurred between the fault of the Soviet Embassy in London and of Ambassador F. T. Gousev personally.

"This enquiry has shown that neither the Embassy nor F. T. Gousev personally were at all guilty in this matter and that they did not even have in their possession certain of the documents the contents of which were published in the English newspapers. Thus the leakage occurred not on the Soviet but on the English side.

"Gousev is willing to undertake any investigation of this matter in order to prove that he and the members of his staff are in no way implicated in the matter of the disclosure of the contents of our correspondence. It seems to me that you have been led astray with regard to Gousev and the Soviet Embassy." Stalin.

[MR*. *Stalin/WSC*, docs. 257, 258. *R&C*.]

C–634

London [via U.S. Army]
Apr. 1, 1944, 1225 Z / TOR 1700 Z

Prime Minister to President Roosevelt. Personal and Most Secret.

My telegram number 632. Following is text of telegram which we propose sending to Ambassador Clark Kerr. Begins.

"1. Please inform Monsieur Molotov that the Prime Minister thought it necessary to refer Marshal Stalin's message of March 23 about

Poland to the War Cabinet whose considered views are set out below for communication to the Soviet Government.

"2. Marshal Stalin's references to power politics and threats are not understood here. The Prime Minister had only thought it necessary to say what he would have to do to make the position of His Majesty's Government quite clear to the British Parliament and public if no settlement of the Polish problem could be agreed now. He felt that his personal relations with Marshal Stalin and Anglo-Soviet relations in general demanded that degree of frankness. It is regretted that Marshal Stalin should characterise this as a threat.

"3. To avoid any possible misunderstanding the Soviet Government should be informed that the Prime Minister has not departed in any way from what he regarded as just and reasonable at Teheran. His attitude has the approval of the War Cabinet. The Prime Minister has never suggested that the Poles should refuse to accept the Curzon Line. On the contrary, he has most strongly urged them to do so. His exchange of messages with Marshal Stalin related however to what he had been able to do in mediating between the Soviet Government and the Polish Government in London. In his message of February 21st, he explained in particular why it was difficult for a government and especially a government in exile to agree publicly to the Curzon Line in isolation from other important issues concerning the future of Poland, which cannot be finally settled now. He had, therefore, proposed a de facto working arrangement to get around this difficulty. This was as far as he had been able to bring the Poles and he had hoped that it might have been considered acceptable to the Soviet Government.

"4. His Majesty's Government felt very strongly that it was of the utmost importance, more particularly in order that means might be found to ensure the full cooperation of the Polish underground movement, controlled by the Polish Government in London, in the common struggle against the Germans, to find some working arrangement for the purposes and for the duration of the war. They still considered that coordination of the Polish underground movement with the advancing Soviet forces would be of immediate value to the war effort and a real advantage to future relations between Poland and the USSR.

"5. The Prime Minister and the War Cabinet therefore deeply regret Marshal Stalin's inability to accept the proposals of February 21st.

"6. His Majesty's Government welcome Marshal Stalin's statement that the Soviet Union considers itself the ally of Poland and the Polish people and they trust that means can still be found providing for the

active cooperation of the Soviet forces and the Polish population in
the liberation of Poland from German oppression. It had never, of
course, been the Prime Minister's intention to suggest that any war
was being waged between the Soviet Union and Poland or that there
was any need for a peace between the two countries. He had only
referred to the practical difficulties which are likely to arise in the
absence of a working arrangement on the lines suggested in his message of February 21st. His reference to the peace conference was, of
course, based upon the fact that all the future territorial arrangements in Europe, and not only the frontiers between enemy states,
will eventuallly require the formal ratification and sanction of the
victorious powers. His Majesty's Government would have preferred
to reach some de facto understanding on the question now, but, in
view of the Soviet Government's inability to accept a working arrangement now, the formal settlement, so far as His Majesty's Gov-
erment are concerned, must clearly await ratification and agreement
at the peace conference. Meanwhile, His Majesty's Government can
only maintain the attitude they have hitherto consistently adopted
and publicly stated in regard to the non-recognition of territorial
changes effected since the war other than by agreement between the
parties concerned.

"7. In the present circumstances, His Majesty's Govenment must
continue to regard the Polish Government in London as the legitimate government of Poland, with whom their relations have never
been interrupted since the Germans attacked Poland in 1939 and so
brought this country into the war. Quite apart from this consideration, the Polish Government controls important armed forces now
actively engaged with us in the struggle against our common enemy.
These are, in themselves, sufficient reasons for our continued recognition of and co-operation with the Polish Government. Furthermore, our information goes to show that it is they who control the
general resistance in Poland to the German oppressor and more
particularly that of the organized underground movement.

"8. If, as His Majesty's Government now understand, the Soviet
Government see no prospect of further discussion between them
leading to a settlement, His Majesty's Government can only retire
from the ungrateful role of mediator and announce their failure. In
any statement the Prime Minister will make it plain that he has not
departed from the views he has hitherto held regarding the proper
settlement of this question. His Majesty's Government have, however,
never disguised from the Soviet Government the important factor in
all this of public opinion, more particularly here and in America.
Public opinion, which would have welcomed a working arrangement

on the lines proposed in the Prime Minister's message of February 21st, will be sadly disappointed that the Soviet Government have not been able to accept these proposals. The Prime Minister must, therefore, make the position of the British Government perfectly plain, although he does not think anything which he will say will be of a character to arouse adverse reactions in the Soviet Union. As he has already told M. Stalin in an earlier message, nothing is further from the intention of His Majesty's Government than to insult or discredit our Soviet ally.

[MR*]

The standard prescription for Roosevelt's heart condition was complete rest— an impossibility for the President. Nevertheless the doctors persuaded him to spend a month at "Hobcaw Barony," Bernard Baruch's plantation in South Carolina. Churchill apparently learned of Roosevelt's plans through Ambassador Halifax.

The "little trouble" referred to by Churchill was a dispute over an education-bill amendment calling for equal pay for men and women teachers. Churchill had insisted on treating the issue as a major one and called for a Vote of Confidence. (See further the headnote to R–511.)

C–635

London [via U.S. Army]
Apr. 1, 1944, 2147 Z / TOR 2315 Z

Prime Minister to President Roosevelt Personal and Most Secret.

1. As I expect you will now be going off to a "Suitable climate" may I express the earnest hope that you will be accessible to my personal telegrams and that full arrangements will be made for their speedy transmission to you. I shall be sending a lot of stuff unless you tell me not to, which would be disastrous. I am so relieved to hear through Louise that Harry has borne the operation well and that they are pleased with the progress he has made so far.

2. I have had some little trouble here which has been coming to a head for some time and at length forced me to fall back upon the House of Commons which as usual showed itself steadfast in the cause and put all malignants in their proper places. It is an immense comfort to me to feel this mighty body behind me when troubles like Singapore, Tobruk or untimely yearnings for reconstruction come along. I wonder whether this solidity in our Legislature will be helpful on your side.

3. I have seen a lot of your splendid troops over here lately. As you know I harden for it the nearer I get to it. Eisenhower is a very large man.

4. Every good wish to you on your journey, and please keep the wires open to me.

[MR*]

Stalin claimed that the Soviet Union could not participate in the International Labor Organization so long as that group continued to claim to be an organ of the League of Nations. He promised, however, that Soviet representatives would join if the ILO affiliated with the proposed United Nations organization (*Stalin/FDR*, docs. 181, 182, 185, 186). Ernest Bevin was Minister of Labour in the British War Cabinet.

R–510

Washington [via U.S. Navy]
Apr. 3, 1944, 11:30 A.M.

Secret and Personal, from the President for the Former Naval Person.

I have been informed that the U.S.S.R. will not take part in the ILO Conference in Philadelphia. It is generally believed here that the absence of Russia will have bad effect upon prestige of ILO both here and among labor in occupied areas.

In order to offset possible loss of prestige by the conference and to strengthen such agreements as may be arrived at, I am convinced that it is essential that Bevin come to the conference as a British Government delegate. His presence will be evidence of the importance placed upon the conference by the British Government.

I trust that it will be possible for him to come even though it may not be possible for him to stay throughout the entire period of conference, and personally I should much like to meet him even if he could come to Washington for only a day. I hope to get back from my trip about April 24th. Roosevelt [Isador Lubin]

[MR*]

The Department of State drafted another message to Irish Prime Minister de Valera, but on the recommendation of the British government and the U.S. Ambassador in Ireland, David Gray, it was not sent. Gray and the British concluded that de Valera might publicize the note in an attempt to marshal public opinion against the British and Americans (see *FRUS*, 1944, III, 246–49, 254–56).

R-510/1

Washington [via Winant]
Apr. 3, 1944, midnight

Please deliver the following message to Prime Minister Churchill from the President:

I have discussed with Secretary Hull your message of March 19 [C-628] on the further steps which you contemplate in relation to Ireland. We believe that you are pursuing the right line in taking the security measures mentioned without, however, adopting measures of coercion designed only to harm Ireland.

We wonder, however, if measures forbidding Irish ships to go to all foreign ports from Ireland might not be interpreted as economic sanctions. Would not your purpose be accomplished by limiting the prohibition to Irish shipping going to any part of the continent? I realize that, as you say, a ship can start in one direction and turn in another, but any ship violating the prohibition could be dealt with in an appropriate manner. This would leave Ireland free to send its ships to North America to carry wheat and other essential supplies. The fact that no ban was made on Irish shipping to Canada and the United States would in itself constitute proof that the measures against shipping were not in the nature of economic sanctions.

For our part we are considering a further message to Mr. de Valera once more making plain that the continued presence of Axis representatives in Ireland constitutes a danger to our forces and their operations for which the Irish Government cannot escape responsibility. We shall let you see it in advance.

[MR. *FRUS*, 1944, III, 245–46.]

Churchill continued to hope that British forces could retake Singapore and Malaya, and pressed the United States for a larger allocation of landing craft.

C-636

London [via U.S. Army]
Apr. 4, 1944 / TOR 1055 Z

Prime Minister to President Roosevelt. Top Secret and Personal.

Our Chiefs of Staff are telegraphing to yours on the subject of LST. A review of our requirements for amphibious operations against Japan clearly shows that LST will be the limiting factor. We are trying every expedient to increase our own output, but it appears inevitable that for operations in the spring of 1945 we shall have a shortage between 80 and 100 of these ships.

I understand that on your present programme you will reach an output of 55 per month by June, and that thereafter your monthly rate drops to about 40. If you could see your way to maintain the monthly rate at 55, then by the 1st December the greater part of the shortage would be met.

It is my earnest wish to operate against the Japanese as soon as our amphibious resources are released from the European theatre and I very much hope you will find it possible to meet this request.

[MR*]

The President's ignorance about the reasons why he might have needed additional medical tests was of his own choosing. According to all the evidence, he never asked questions of his doctors, and his personal physician, Dr. Ross McIntire, did not tell him the details. The President finally left for his vacation in South Carolina on April 8.

The vote in the House of Commons, mentioned by Roosevelt, concerned an amendment to an education bill. Proposed by Conservative M.P. Thelma Cazalet, the amendment called for equal pay for male and female teachers. Government leaders were caught off guard and the proposal passed by a single vote. Churchill argued that such important principles should not be established in a minor amendment but required full debate, and he insisted upon making the matter a Vote of Confidence. Faced with the threat of the government's resignation, the House voted confidence by 425 to 23, and Cazalet withdrew her amendment. Roosevelt obviously liked the idea of being able to coerce legislators by forcing the vote of confidence on what was a relatively minor issue. But one of Churchill's staunchest supporters, Harold Nicolson, complained that the Prime Minister had treated the Commons like "naughty schoolboys" instead of ignoring the whole matter. (See Nicolson, *The War Years*, pp. 357–58.)

The Prime Ministers of Australia and New Zealand, John Curtin and Peter Fraser, visited Washington late in April enroute to London for a meeting of British Commonwealth Prime Ministers. Roosevelt did not return to Washington until May, so the two Prime Ministers instead met with Secretary of State Hull.

R–511

Washington [via U.S. Navy]
Apr. 4, 1944, 7:15 P.M.

Personal and Secret from the President for the Former Naval Person.

My trip has again been postponed and still other researches and studies are being made. I do not approve of this for the principal reason that I do not understand it all. I hope to get off in four or five days and will let you know. The place I am going has full equipment for our lines of communication, and messages ought not to take more than ten minutes longer than in the White House itself.

Congratulations on your splendid vote in the House. Results here would be almost as good if we operated under your system.

Curtin will get here about April twenty-sixth and Fraser approximately the same time. Let me know if there is anything you want me to stress. Roosevelt [FDR]

[MR*]

With the presidential election coming in the fall, Roosevelt and the State Department had become sensitive to criticism that the United States had been too easy on the neutrals, particularly the pro-German regimes in Spain and Portugal. The President sent this message without changing the State Department draft, and it lacked the usual candor of Roosevelt-Churchill exchanges. The State Department had no intention of compromising on the basic issue of stopping all Spanish wolfram exports to Germany, but Churchill misinterpreted the cable to mean that the United States would negotiate.

R–512

Washington [via U.S. Navy]
Apr. 4, 1944, 7:15 P.M.

Personal and Secret from the President for the Former Naval Person.

I have studied with considerable care your message Number 631 of March 30 with regard to our negotiations with Spain concerning wolfram. I am most reluctant to accept any compromise on this matter with the Spanish Government. It can hardly be helpful in the present wolfram negotiations with the Portuguese. At the same time I appreciate that in the absence of full agreement between us on the measures to be adopted we cannot anticipate an early successful conclusion of these negotiations. I am therefore asking the Department of State to work out with your Embassy a mutually agreeable line to take with the Spanish. Roosevelt [CH]

[MR*. R&C.]

Germany's sinking fortunes were reflected in the March anti-submarine warfare statement.

C–637

London [via U.S. Army]
Apr. 5, 1944, 1308 Z / TOR 1430 Z

Prime Minister to President Roosevelt Personal and Most Secret.

I propose the following joint statement regarding U-Boat warfare in March for issue on April 10. I am also telegraphing the text to Mackenzie King. Begins.

> March was an active month in the war against the U-Boats which operated in widely dispersed areas from the Barents Sea to the Indian Ocean.
>
> The enemy has persevered vainly in strenuous endeavours to disrupt our flow of supplies to Russia by the northern route.
>
> Our merchant shipping losses were mainly incurred in far distant seas: Though a little higher than in February they were still low and the rate of sinking U-Boats was fully maintained.
>
> The Allied merchant fleet continues to improve both in quantity and quality but the strength of the U-Boat force remains considerable and calls for powerful efforts by surface and air forces.

[MR*]

Roosevelt preferred to stay out of the Soviet-Polish dispute and, in keeping with that policy, emphasized the immediate problem of military coordination between the Red Army and the Polish Underground. Nevertheless, the approaching presidential election made it impossible for the President to ignore Polish-American demands for a public expression of United States support for the Polish government in London; hence the concern over the visit of Polish Prime Minister Stanislaw Mikolajczyk.

R–513

Washington [via U.S. Navy]
Apr. 5, 1944, 11:30 A.M.

Personal and Top Secret from the President for the Former Naval Person.

Referring to your 634 of April first, it seems to me the essential consideration in the Polish-Russian controversy at the present time is to get the Polish military power, including the underground, into effective action against the Nazis.

It would therefore appear that your proposed reply to Uncle Joe's explosion of 23 March is correct in its purpose and considerate beyond reasonable expectation. I do not see how he can find any fault therewith.

I am considering the advisability of having a visit from Mikolajczyk after my return from vacation. Roosevelt

[MR*]

Churchill wanted what seemed to be mutually exclusive things in Yugoslavia— effective military resistance to the Germans, and the restoration of the monarchy under King Peter. The forces of General Draža Mihailović were loyal to the King, but they had been compromised by collaboration with the Germans and by their attacks on political opponents. Tito's Partisans had also engaged in civil war but had simultaneously inflicted heavy damage on the Germans, and Churchill appreciated results. Early in 1944 the British decided to shift all support to the Partisans, trying at the same time to get Tito to support King Peter. The King, recognizing better than Churchill that Tito would never permit the restoration of a monarchy, refused to eliminate Mihailović from the Yugoslav government.

C–638

London [via U.S. Army]
Apr. 6, 1944, 1010 Z / TOR 1120 Z

Prime Minister to President Roosevelt. Personal.

It is said that OSS have received instructions, which have been approved by you, to arrange for a small Intelligence Mission to be infiltrated to General Mihailovic's Headquarters, and we have been asked to organize the necessary arrangements.

We are now in process of withdrawing all our missions from Mihailovic and are pressing King Peter to clear himself of this millstone, which is dragging him down in his own country and works only to the assistance of the enemy. If, at this very time, an American Mission arrives at Mihailovic's Headquarters, it will show throughout the Balkans a complete contrariety of action between Britain and the United States. The Russians will certainly throw all their weight on Tito's side, which we are backing to the full. Thus we shall get altogether out of step. I hope and trust this may be avoided.

[MR. R&C.]

Churchill mistakenly interpreted Roosevelt's cable 512 as an expression of willingness to accept the British compromise with Spain concerning wolfram exports.

C–639

London [via U.S. Army]
Apr. 6, 1944, 1705 Z / TOR 1810 Z

Prime Minister to President Roosevelt Personal and Secret.
  Your number 512.
  Thank you so much. I am entirely in agreement with you on the principle: But, I think we can get more out of it by the method you now approve.

[MR*]

Churchill understood the President's desire to avoid antagonizing Irish-American groups unnecessarily.

C–640

London [via U.S. Army]
Apr. 7, 1944, 0900 Z / TOR 1000 Z

Prime Minister to President Roosevelt Personal and Top Secret.
  I thank you for your message dated April 5th about Ireland [R–510/1].
  We considered the question of stopping Irish shipping and came to the conclusion which you yourself have reached that there was no need to interfere with the transatlantic sailings to North America. Only their direct services from Southern Ireland to the Iberian Peninsula will, therefore, be suspended. They have accepted this and there is no question of their regarding this as the imposition of economic sanctions.
  I note that you are considering the despatch of a further message to Mr. De Valera. It is very good of you to say that you would let us see it in advance, if you decided to send it.

[MR*]

R–514

Washington [via U.S. Navy]
Apr. 7, 1944, 7:15 P.M.

Personal and Secret. From the President for the Former Naval Person.
  Your 637. I agree on the submarine statement as proposed by you for releases on 10 April. Roosevelt

[MR*]

The United States chose to stay out of the Yugoslav imbroglio.

R–515

Washington [via U.S. Navy]
Apr. 8, 1944, 12:30 P.M.

Personal and Secret. From the President for the Former Naval Person.

Your 638 my thought in authorizing an O.S.S. Mission to the Mihailovic Area was to obtain intelligence and the mission was to have no political functions whatever.

In view however of your expressed opinion that there might be misunderstanding by our Allies and others, I have directed that the contemplated mission be not repeat not sent. Roosevelt [WDL]

[MR. R&C.]

The need to keep additional landing craft in the Italian theater made it obvious that ANVIL, the invasion of southern France, would be delayed, though how long was still a question. (See headnote to R–481.) Led by General Marshall, who believed that ANVIL was an essential part of the OVERLORD strategy, the Americans threatened not to transfer promised equipment from the Pacific unless a major invasion of southern France were planned. As ever, Roosevelt was concerned lest Stalin interpret changes in strategy as a failure to live up to commitments.

R–516

Washington [via U.S. Navy]
Apr. 8, 1944, 12:32 P.M.

Personal and Secret, for the Former Naval Person from the President.

In view of prospective change in plans for ANVIL I believe that U.J. should be fully informed at once when we reach decision in regard to ANVIL on recommendation of the Combined Chiefs of Staff. Roosevelt [WDL]

[MR*. R&C.]

The Canadian government, wishing for more direct control over its own forces, hoped to establish channels which would bypass the British Imperial General Staff in London as well as the Anglo-American Combined Chiefs of Staff. The Canadian contribution to the war effort was sizeable and the suggestion seemed reasonable, but it would have destroyed the unity of Allied command, for every national contingent would have demanded direct control over its own forces. The American Joint Chiefs did not object to Canadian nationalism being assuaged by a political gesture, but nothing would be permitted to jeopardize the unified command structure.

R–517

Washington [via U.S. Navy]
Apr. 8, 1944, 1:30 P.M.

The President to the Former Naval Person, Secret and Personal.

For your information I have today sent the following quoted letter in reply to the Canadian Prime Minister's letter of March 10 regarding participation of Canadian forces in Allied operations. He sent you an identical message.

QUOTE. Upon receipt of your communication dated March 13, 1944, and transmitting a letter from the Prime Minister of Canada in regard to the command of Canadian troops with the Allied forces overseas, I referred the questions therein contained to the Joint Chiefs of Staff.

The Joint Chiefs of Staff this date have given me the following report with which I am in agreement:

'We have examined the message addressed to you on 10 March 1944 by the Canadian Prime Minister, in which he informed you of his government's consideration of the establishment of a Canadian Joint Staff Mission in London. In the same message he proposed that appropriate formal announcements be made to clarify the command authority exercised by Generals Eisenhower and Wilson over the participating forces of the United Nations.

'Although the establishment of a Canadian Joint Staff Mission in London is a question for decision by the governments of the United Kingdom and Canada, military implications involved make it necessary that, should such a Mission be established, the appropriate channel of communications between the Canadian Chiefs of Staff and the Supreme Commands must be through the Combined Chiefs of Staff and not directly through the Mission, to the Supreme Commands, as proposed by the Canadian Prime Minister.

'We feel that there is no need from the military standpoint, to make any announcement clarifying command authority since the chain of military command is well established. There is no objection, however, to such an announcement if other than military considerations warrant it. An announcement should make clear that the Supreme Commanders derive their authority from the Governments concerned through the Combined Chiefs of Staff and not directly from the governments, as suggested in the letter from the Canadian Prime

Minister. We recommend that if any announcement is made, it be general in scope and cover all participating nations.' UNQUOTE.

Roosevelt [WDL]

[MR*]

On April 4, the American representative to the French Committee of National Liberation at Algiers reported receiving a note from the committee requesting that agreements with the committee be made by the Allied governments, not the Combined Chiefs of Staff. In addition to other demands for treatment as a legitimate government and equal partner in the war, the French Committee also asked for the right to communicate directly and secretly with its military and political commands free of Allied censorship. Angered by what he considered the arrogance of the demands (see *FRUS*, III, 668–69), Roosevelt dictated a curt condemnation of the French action. The British, however, had been trying to arrange a de Gaulle–Roosevelt meeting in the hope of getting American support for the French National Committee.

R–518

Washington [via U.S. Navy]
Apr. 8, 1944, 5:00 P.M.

Personal and Secret. From the President for the Former Naval Person.

I am a good deal concerned by the French National Committee's demands in regard to military matters. The tone of these communications verges on the dictatorial, especially when we consider the simple facts.

Personally I do not think that we can give military information to a source which has a bad record in secrecy. The implied threat to stay out of operations in France would, if carried out, do the Committee and its leader irreparable harm.

If De Gaulle wants to come over here to visit me I shall be very glad to see him and will adopt a paternal tone, but I think it would be a mistake for me to invite him without an intimation from him that he wants to come. Roosevelt [FDR]

[MR. PREM 3/121/2. *R&C.*]

With the cross-channel invasion imminent, the British government had no desire to become involved in protracted relief operations within occupied Europe. As the report to Winant later stated, "The occupied countries are however looking forward to liberation rather than relief" (*FRUS*, 1944, II, 260). The President commented in a marginal notation that "I don't know

but what Prime is right on that." Winfield Riefler of the Foreign Economic
Administration was a Special Assistant to the U.S. Ambassador in London.

C–641

London [via U.S. Army]
Apr. 8, 1944, 1940 Z / TOR 2230 Z

Prime Minister to President Roosevelt Personal and Top Secret.
Your telegram No. 501.

1. The proposals of your government for a limited relief scheme were
put forward by Mr. Riefler on March 29th and have been most earnestly
considered by my colleagues and by myself. I share your desire to do
everything possible to ameliorate the lot of the peoples of the occupied
countries in so far as this is possible without detriment to the war effort.
I find it however difficult to accept the view that the maintenance of our
blockade policy is likely to hurt our friends more than our enemies.

2. The whole question seems to me to be governed by the impending
military operations for the invasion of Europe. Our experience of the
working of the Greek relief scheme has conclusively shown that it causes
considerable difficulties for, and imposes restrictions on, our naval and
air forces, and these difficulties will increase as new operations are begun.
The opening of further channels of importation into Europe at the present moment would, in our view, be wholly incompatible with the naval
and military situation which is developing. It would involve not only the
granting of safe-conducts for ships to sail to designated ports within the
operational zones, but also the preservation of routes of inland transport
from those ports to the countries in which the food is to be distributed.
It would clearly be impossible to undertake to keep any ports or routes
to them open, or to keep intact any railways between now and the end
of this year: and if it were possible to give such an undertaking we should
thereby give the Germans valuable information as to our military intentions. Any relief action now undertaken would therefore inevitably hamper impending military operations.

3. Even if military considerations were not decisive there are also grave
objections from the blockade point of view. These are being explained
in detail to Mr. Winant and I do not think I need trouble you with them,
if we are agreed that nothing can be allowed to hamper or interfere with
forthcoming operations.

[MR*. *FRUS*, 1944, II, 257–58. *R&C*.]

R-519

Washington [via U.S. Navy]
Apr. 8, 1944, 9:15 P.M.

Secret and Personal for the Prime Minister from the President.

Your 641. While I remain of the opinion that it would be humane and wise to provide such relief as is practicable to the under-nourished women and children of friendly people in Nazi occupied Europe, I am in complete agreement with you that nothing should be done that will interfere with or hamper forthcoming operations. Roosevelt [WDL]

[MR*. R&C.]

Churchill appreciated Roosevelt's decision not to send an OSS mission to Mihailović's headquarters in Yugoslavia.

C-642

London [via U.S. Army]
Apr. 9, 1944, 0910 Z / TOR 1210 Z

Prime Minister to President Roosevelt. Personal.

I am most deeply grateful to you for your number 515.

[MR*]

During a radio broadcast on April 9, Secretary of State Hull gave credit to the French Committee of National Liberation as a valuable symbol of resistance, and he said that the United States would permit the committee to exercize civil authority in liberated France so long as it operated under the supervision of the Supreme Allied Commander. Even though Hull denied that the committee constituted a legitimate French government, the statement was a major departure from previous American refusals to work with the French Committee (FCNL). The British were pleased, for they had patiently urged the United States to recognize the French Committee, while trying to reduce de Gaulle's influence. Churchill's personal annoyance with the FCNL was evident, however, in his brusque denial of French claims to any of the captured Italian warships since the French in similar straits had failed to bring their fleet over to the Allied side. Nevertheless, the Prime Minister tried to seize upon Hull's speech as a lever with which to shift American policy toward accepting the French Committee. But Roosevelt would have none of it and continued to hold de Gaulle and the FCNL at arm's length. (See R–521.)

De Gaulle had requested that the French Second Armored Division, commanded by General Jacques Philippe Leclerc, be transferred from North

Africa in time to take part in the cross-channel invasion. De Gaulle was thinking of more than just French pride; he also wanted his own forces to be in a position to take control of liberated France ahead of the Resistance or any other political factions.

British Field Marshal Sir Bernard Montgomery was scheduled to command the Allied assault forces during the Normandy invasion. Assistant Secretary of War John J. McCloy and the Army's Deputy Chief of Staff, Lieutenant General Joseph T. McNarney, were on an inspection trip in the European Theater of Operations (ETO). Duff Cooper was the British Representative to the FCNL.

C–643

London [via U.S. Army]
Apr. 12, 1944

Prime Minister to President Roosevelt Private Personal and Most Secret. Your number 518.

1. I was very glad to read Hull's references to the French Committee of National Liberation in which I observed your guiding hand. His Majesty's Government will take an early opportunity of making clear that we are in full accord with this declaration. I take it that it modifies in some respects, though not in principle, the form of the enclosure to your letter of March 21st [R–506/1] which presented some difficulties here. These might be talked over between the Foreign Office and State Department before issue.

2. In the first phase of OVERLORD there will be no opportunity for the French Civil Government to function, as the ground captured by our troops will be the battlefield, and it may be some time before we have advanced far enough to be clear of what was called in the last war by the French "The Zone of the Armies" and often extended some 50 miles from the front. I agree cordially with you that nothing must hamper the freedom of action of the Supreme Commander and that no disturbing political agitation should be allowed until we have got well inland.

3. I am becoming very hard set upon OVERLORD. On Good Friday [April 7] I gave a talk to all the Generals, British and American, who were gathered at General Montgomery's Headquarters, expressing my strong confidence in the result of this extraordinary but magnificent operation. I understand that you will have received some account of this from General Eisenhower, Mr. McCloy and General McNarney who were present. I do not agree with the loose talk which has been going on on both sides of the Atlantic about the undue heavy casualties which we shall sustain. In my view it is the Germans who will suffer very heavy casualties when our band of brothers gets among them.

4. I agree that the FCNL should not be made a party in any way to the

details of OVERLORD. I have tried to further their earnest wish to have the Leclerc armoured division included in the forthcoming battle. But the presence of this single division will not give them any right to be informed of our secrets, and they should be told so without delay. A different situation might arise if ANVIL were to materialize at the new date. In this operation I believe 6 or 7 French divisions were to be employed, in fact they would be more than half of the Allied Army. There I think they should be made full partners. The 74,000 men they have already in Italy have fought very well and have a very small proportion of missing to killed. These facts give them claims to be taken into our confidence in that theatre with of course proper restrictions and safeguards such as we ourselves impose at home. I suggest an answer on these lines. Shall I draft for your agreement or vice versa?

5. You will also have received the demand of the FCNL about our giving them a portion of the Italian fleet. If they had brought their own fleet over, as Badoglio did, they would not be short of ships. I am inclined to think it would be best to leave their unwarrantable demand unanswered, at any rate for some weeks to come.

6. Your number 516 last sentence. I think it would be a very good thing if De Gaulle came over to see you but obviously you must know where you are with a man like this before you send an invitation. I have asked Ambassador Duff Cooper to put the point to him in the following way: "Mr. Churchill is worried about the danger of bad relations growing between you (De Gaulle) and the United States Government. He (Mr. Churchill) thinks that after Mr. Hull's important speech which has been welcomed by the FCNL it would be a very good and important thing for you to pay a short visit to the President and make a personal contact there. This would be helpful also to our British relations with the FCNL for you (De Gaulle) will readily understand that it is the foundation of our British policy to keep in step with the United States with whom we are sharing such great war schemes. If you felt like making this visit and would let me (Duff Cooper) know, Mr. Churchill would suggest to the President that he send you a formal invitation".

[MR. PREM 3/121/2.]

The U.S. Joint Chiefs had no intention of diverting American landing ships from the successful central Pacific campaign or from the politically important invasion of the Philippines in order to help the British reconquer their empire.

During the time that the President stayed in South Carolina (April 9–May 7), the log sheets frequently do not indicate the drafter of Roosevelt-to-Churchill cables. It is, however, prudent to assume that Admiral Leahy, who was with Roosevelt, continued to be the President's primary adviser and probably drafted most of the messages sent to the Prime Minister.

R–520

Waccamaw, S.C. [via U.S. Navy]
Apr. 13, 1944, 4:05 P.M. (Washington)

Personal and Secret. From the President for the Former Naval Person.

Your Number 636, I have today received a report from the U.S. Chiefs of Staff on the possibility of increased American production of LST in order to provide for anticipated British operations in the Pacific in 1945.

Our program has recently been increased, as you know, to take care of the large needs for OVERLORD and the impetus thus acquired will continue for some time after June so that the drop you mention does not occur so soon. It is not possible further to accelerate or increase our program without interference with other programs which have already been reduced to the limit to permit going ahead with the present landing craft program.

In view of the gains made in accelerating our building schedule for OVERLORD, in view of the larger number of U.S. survivors now expected on the basis of experience in European operations, and in view of a better knowledge as to U.S. requirements in the Pacific, the United States Chiefs of Staff believe that the combined needs for prosecuting the war against Japan can be met under present programs and that allocations should not be made until operations have been definitely decided upon. Roosevelt

[MR*]

Roosevelt remained unwilling to make any conciliatory gesture to de Gaulle. Even though American officials agreed that General Giraud had failed to provide effective leadership for the French military and should be replaced, Roosevelt resented the French Committee's failure to consult the United States. (See R–275/1 for background information.)

R–521

Waccamaw, S.C. [via U.S. Navy]
Apr. 13, 1944, 4:10 P.M.
(Washington)

Top Secret and Personal, from the President for the Former
Naval Person.

Your 643. The questions therein presented necessitate consultation with the State Department and my Chiefs of Staff when I return to Washington, but at this distance all seems well.

I have no objection to a visit from De Gaulle but I should like to have your opinion of the action of the Committee in dismissing General Giraud.

Some time ago I was asked if I would receive De Gaulle in Washington if he came over and I replied in the affirmative. I think it should remain in this situation. I would be glad to see him if he asks to see me but I will extend no formal or informal invitation.

In addition to a probability of compromising the security of our plans for operations which might have disastrous effects, it does not appear to me that any military advantage could result from divulging confidential information to the Committee.

I agree with you that no reply should be made to the unwarranted demand for Italian ships. Roosevelt

[MR. PREM 3/121/2.]

Churchill was eager to emphasize to the Russians the vast scale of the Allied offensive and to obtain a firm commitment from Stalin for the promised Soviet offensive to coincide with the cross-channel attack.

C–644

London [via U.S. Army]
Apr. 14, 1944, 0957 Z / TOR 1200 Z (Washington)

Prime Minister to President Roosevelt Personal and Top Secret.

Would it not be well for you and me to send a notice to Uncle J. about the date of OVERLORD? I do not see why this particular communication should not go from us both unitedly. I suggest for your consideration, the following message. Message begins:

1. Pursuant to our talks at Teheran, the general crossing of the sea will take place around the date mentioned in my immediately following, with 3 days margin on either side for weather. We shall be acting at our fullest strength.

2. Our action in the Mediterranean Theatre will be designed to hold the maximum number of German divisions away from the Russian front and from OVERLORD. The exact method by which this will be achieved will depend on the outcome of the heavy offensive which we shall launch in Italy with all our strength about mid-May.

3. Since Teheran your armies have gained and are gaining a magnificent series of unforeseen victories for the common cause. Even in months when you thought they would not be active they have gained these great victories. We ask you to let us know, in order to make our own calculations, what scale your effort will take in the 3 months following the date mentioned, when we shall certainly strike.

We send you our very best wishes and hope we may all fall on the common foe together. Message ends.

Please let me have your amendments to this and I will send it off signed Roosevelt-Churchill.

[MR*. R&C.]

There was no mistaking Churchill's bitterness over the American refusal to allot more landing craft to British forces in the South East Asia Command. Ever inclined to avoid arguments, Roosevelt instructed his staff not to acknowledge or reply to Churchill's cable.

C–645

London [via U.S. Army]
Apr. 14, 1944, 0900 Z / TOR 0005 Z, Apr. 15

Prime Minister to President Roosevelt Most Secret and Personal.
  Your No. 520.
  1. I am sorry you cannot help in this way. Our only wish is to help you as much as possible in the war against Japan in accordance with our pledge. There is no possibility of increasing our LST programme here and this may well be a limiting factor. I hope you will bear this in mind if there are any complaints hereafter. Considering we are freely engaging five sixths of the naval forces to be used at OVERLORD much of which may be destroyed by the mines and short shore batteries, and that our merchant ship building is down to a bare million a year, I hope you will reconsider keeping your mass production of LST going on a little longer at the high levels it is about to attain. You will certainly want them even if you do not give any to us.
  2. We are working very hard to prepare plans for amphibious operations destined to support your left flank against Japan, and I hope soon to have definite proposals to make to your Chiefs of Staff. Perhaps you will allow me to recur to the above topic then.
  3. Your number 521. I regret the Committee's action in dismissing General Giraud, and have done all I could to prevent it. I have acceded to Giraud's request to grant him and his daughter of seventeen asylum over here. I am very conscious of the dangers of an unfriendly France on the morrow of its deliverance by the English-speakers.
  4. I hope you are benefitting from your rest. I am very glad to hear frequent and good accounts of Harry's progress.

[MR*]

At the insistence of Eisenhower and Montgomery, the British government instituted a wide range of measures aimed at providing security for the Normandy invasion. The most controversial of these was the imposition of censorship on all diplomatic communications in and out of the United Kingdom. Only the Soviet Union and the United States were excluded, although outraged protests from the French Committee finally brought a partial relaxation of the censorship for that group.

C–646

London
Apr. 15, 1944, 1735 Z / TOR 1920 Z

Prime Minister to President Roosevelt. Personal and Top Secret.

To safeguard the security of OVERLORD, we have decided to prohibit foreign representatives in this country from sending or receiving uncensored communications, whether cypher telegrams or diplomatic bags. We shall also forbid couriers or other members of diplomatic staffs from leaving the country. The ban will come into force from midnight Monday, April 17, and continue until after the launching of the operation. It will not, of course, apply to your representatives or to the Soviet representative; but it will cover both neutral representatives and representatives of other Allied Governments, including representatives of the French Committee of Liberation and exiled governments in this country.

We are imposing this ban because of our desire to leave nothing undone which might promote the success of OVERLORD, and we have been much influenced by the view of General Eisenhower, who pressed strongly for it.

We shall explain to the foreign governments that the ban is being imposed for compelling military reasons and that many other restrictions are being imposed on our own people in the interests of security.

We hope that no foreign government will be tempted to retaliate by forbidding our diplomatic representatives to send uncensored communications. If, however, any were to do so, may we count on the help of your representative in the country concerned to enable us to continue to send and receive uncensored communications?

So much information about military plans is constantly passing between here and Washington that valuable information might well reach the enemy through cypher telegrams sent by representatives of foreign governments in the United States.

I have no doubt that you will be ready to consider whether some corresponding action should be taken to prevent leakages through diplomatic representatives in the United States.

[MR*. *R&C*.]

Churchill continued to avoid any commitment to postwar Anglo-American economic collaboration, preferring instead to speak of "preliminary" and "initial" discussions. Stettinius had been in England since April 6, sent there to discuss economic issues.

C–647

London
Apr. 15, 1944, 1920 Z

Prime Minister to President Roosevelt. Personal and Top Secret.

Your messages numbers 476 and 477 (of the 24th February). I agree that we should clear our minds on the question of which economic matters might profitably be discussed internationally before the end of the war. Mr. Stettinius' visit to London should provide an opportunity for discussing, anyhow in a preliminary way, the procedure best calculated to ensure that all these economic questions are dealt with at the right time and in the right order.

On the subject of combined boards, and their future status, (your 477) I entirely agree with you that the boards have done very good work and that the part which they could and should play in our future arrangements should be further studied between us. I think that the initial discussions on this had better take place in Washington between our representatives there and the appropriate United States agencies; and I propose to send instructions to our representatives in Washington accordingly.

[MR*. *FRUS*, 1944, II, 36.]

General Marshall, who drafted this cable, assumed that Churchill did not know that the Combined Chiefs of Staff had already informed Stalin that OVERLORD would take place on or about May 31. Marshall also disliked paragraph 2 of Churchill's proposed message (C–644) because it seemed to imply that ANVIL had been canceled. The President agreed and sent the General's message without changes.

R–522

Waccamaw, S.C. [via U.S. Navy]
Apr. 16, 1944, 5:15 P.M. (Washington)

Personal and Top Secret. From the President for the Former
Naval Person.

Replying to your 644, as the Combined Chiefs of Staff dispatched a message on April 6th to General Burrows, head of your mission in Moscow, and General Deane, who heads our Mission, with instructions to inform the Soviet General Staff that in accordance with the agreement reached at Teheran, it is our firm intention to launch OVERLORD on the agreed date (which date was furnished in a succeeding message) I do not believe we should repeat to U.J. information which has already been given to the Russian Military authorities. In this same message, Deane and Burrows were instructed to pay a handsome tribute to the magnificent progress of the Soviet Armies and to ask the Soviet General Staff to confirm, that they, for their part, would fulfill the undertaking given at Teheran by Marshal Stalin to organize a large scale offensive at the appropriate time to assist OVERLORD by containing the maximum number of German divisions in the East.

With reference to paragraph two of your proposed message, it would be better to wait until our Chiefs of Staff have come to a firm agreement on the scope and timing of operations in the Mediterranean.

As to the question regarding the scale of the Soviet effort raised in paragraph three of your proposed message, U.J. made a definite commitment at Teheran, and I believe he meant it. The C.C.S. message to Deane and Burrows directed them to ask for confirmation of the Soviet Teheran undertaking.

The British Chiefs of Staff did not consider it advisable to ask directly for Soviet plans for scale of effort because the Soviet decisions must depend on the development of their operation between now and the middle of May. The U.S. Chiefs of Staff took the same view. I am inclined to agree that U.J. should not be asked this specific question unless you have strong reasons to the contrary.

If you feel it timely to dispatch a message, I suggest the following redraft to which you may attach my signature if you concur:

1. Pursuant to our talks at Teheran, the general crossing of the sea will take place around a date which Generals Deane and Burrows have recently been directed to give the Soviet General Staff. We shall be acting at our fullest strength.

2. We are launching an offensive on the Italian mainland at maximum strength about mid May.

3. Since Teheran your Armies have been gaining a magnificent series of victories for the common cause. Even in the months when you thought they would not be active, they have gained these great victories. We send you our very best wishes and trust that your Armies and ours, operating in unison in accordance with our Teheran agreement, will soon crush the Hitlerites.

Roosevelt

[MR*. R&C.]

This cable signaled the beginning of what became a harsh dispute between Britain and the United States, although the President initially lent firm support to Churchill's policy. The problem in Greece was longstanding: an unpopular monarchy and an oligarchic, dictatorial government, both in exile in Cairo, were challenged by anti-monarchial nationalists within Greece who had gained popularity by effectively resisting the German occupation. The bulk of the Greek partisans were led by the National Liberation Front (EAM), an organization dominated by the small but well-organized Greek Communist Party. Churchill invariably assumed that the EAM and all opposition to the monarchy was Communist-sponsored with support from both the Soviet Union and Yugoslavia, although it is likely he would have opposed any movement to depose the King and displace British influence. Churchill had originally expected Greece to be liberated by British forces which would also re-instate the monarchy, but Anglo-American decisions not to mount an offensive in the eastern Mediterranean had changed that picture.

By 1944, morale among Greek forces stationed in Egypt had become a serious problem. There was little for either the Army or the Navy to do, and the government of Prime Minister Emmanouel Tsouderos had become a target of political dissidents among the officer corps. After the Greek government rejected a demand that Tsouderos resign, mutiny broke out among troops stationed in Alexandria. Churchill instructed the British Ambassador to the Greek government, Reginald Leeper, to authorize the use of force if necessary to restore order. Sophocles Venizelos (Venezelos) had been the Minister of Marine in the Tsouderos government.

C–648

London
Apr. 16, 1944, 1603 Z

Prime Minister to President Roosevelt. Personal and Top Secret.

1. You will be aware of the disturbances which have broken out among the Greek Armed Forces in the Middle East and of the difficulties which have arisen with the Greek Government in Cairo.

2. The outbreak in the Greek Army and Navy followed closely on the establishment in the mountains of Greece of the political committee sponsored by E.A.M. and there is little doubt that the extremist elements who have long been working to subvert the allegiance of the Greek forces to their legitimate King and Government seized on this as a heaven-sent opportunity for open and violent action. The dissident elements are undoubtedly opposed to the King and in favour of a republic but, through the disturbances, there have been almost no direct attacks on the King's personal position and the only specific demand put forward is that the Greek Government should take immediate and effective steps to recognize and associate with themselves the political committee in Greece.

3. This crisis came at a particularly unfortunate moment since Monsieur Tsouderos had already sent an invitation to a number of moderate politicians in Athens, urging them to come to Cairo to join the government. He had also invited representatives of E.A.M., the Communist-controlled organization which has created and now dominates the political committee. Tsouderos was thus doing everything in his power to create a truly representative Greek Government.

4. In this programme, he had the support of his colleagues and they appear to have had no hand in provoking the disturbances in the Greek forces. But they were extremely jealous of Tsourderos' position and used the trouble in the Greek Army, which was at first on a small scale, to get rid of him. Feeling that he had lost control of the situation, Tsouderos resigned and proposed Venezelos for the Premiership. The trouble in the Greek Army rapidly spread to the Navy and assumed proportions of a full scale mutiny in both forces. The politicians in Cairo realized that the matter had gone beyond one of personal rivalries or ambitions and their only thought was to find some candidate for the Premiership sufficiently notorious for his left-wing views to be acceptable to the mutinous elements in the forces.

5. The King of Greece was reluctant to accept a new government whose composition was in effect dictated by the mutineers. He considered that order in the Greek Armed Forces must be restored before any lawful reconstruction of the government could be undertaken. I entirely agreed with him and instructed our ambassador to the Greek Government to do his utmost to induce the Greek Ministers to remain at their posts until the King could get back to Cairo and take stock of the situation. This, I am glad to say, they agreed to do. I also gave instructions to the military authorities in the Middle East to deal firmly with indiscipline in the Greek Forces under their command. Order in the Greek Army and Navy has not been completely reestablished but the dissident elements are being isolated and once the ring leaders are under arrest the mutiny should rapidly subside.

6. The King of Greece has now reached Cairo and, after studying the position for himself, has formed a government under Monsieur Venizelos. For the future, I have informed our ambassador to the Greek Government that he should be guided by the following considerations:—

"Our relations are definitely established with the lawfully-constituted Greek Government headed by the King, who is the ally of Britain and cannot be discarded to suit a momentary surge of appetite among ambitious emigres nonenties. Neither can Greece find constitutional expression in particular sets of Guerillas, in many cases indistinguishable from banditti, who are masquerading as the saviours of their country while living on the local villagers. If necessary, I shall denounce these elements and tendencies publicly in order to emphasize the love Great Britain has for Greece whose suffering she shared in a small measure being, alas, not then armed as we are now. Our only desire and interest is to see Greece a glorious, free nation in the Eastern Mediterranean, the honoured friend and ally of the victorious powers. Let all, therefore, work for this objective and make it quite clear that any failure in good conduct will not be overlooked.

"I had been working very hard to arrange the movement of the Greek Brigade in Italy. Here they might still take part in the entry into Rome which is to be expected during the summer. This brigade, the First Greek Brigade, representatives of the army which had beaten back the Italian invader and were only felled by the treacherous and brutal intervention of the German hoardes, had and still has the chance of raising the name of Greece high in the world. It is a lamentable fact that they should have signalised this opportunity by an undignified, even squalid, exhibition of indiscipline which many will attribute to an unworthy fear of being sent to the front.

"In the same way the Greek Navy, which is full of daring seamen and is playing a worthy part upholding its country's good name, should not suddenly have tried to meddle with politics and presume to dictate a constitution to the Greek people. I believe that both of these two forces can be brought back to a high sense of national honour and duty if courageous leadership is forthcoming backed by overwhelming force in reserve.

"All the time I have been planning to place Greece back high in the counsels of the victorious nations. Witness how we have included them in the Italian Advisory Council and tried to send a brigade to take part in the impending victories in Italy. Greeks who are in safety in Egypt under our protection equipped with our vessels or armed with our weapons or otherwise in security under the military authority of the British Commander in Chief, Middle East, will place themselves in an abject and shameful position before all history if they allow their domestic fueds to mar their performance of the solemn duties to their country of which they have become the heirs. They may easily, by selfish excitable behaviour reduce Greece to a country without expression either at home or abroad and their names will be stained as long as history is written.

"The King is the servant of his people. He makes no claim to rule them. He submits himself freely to the judgment of the people as soon as normal conditions are restored. He places himself and his royal house entirely at the disposition of the Greek Nation. Once the German invader has been driven out, Greece can be a republic or a monarchy, entirely as the people wish. Why then cannot the Greeks keep their hatreds for the common enemy who has wrought them such cruel injuries and would obliterate them as a free people, were it not for the resolute exertions of the great Allies?"

7. In sending these instructions, I have asked Ambassador Leeper to make use of all these arguments freely in my name, if necessary, both to the troops and to the sailors as well, of course, as to the politicians, who have been clattering around him. In making it clear to them that this is the policy of His Majesty's Government, I have asked him to emphasize that we seek no advantage for ourselves and have no interests but in the upholding of Greek independence, freedom and honour.

[MR*. *FRUS*, 1944, V, 96–98. p*WSC*, V, 547–48.]

Roosevelt's initial reaction to the Greek mutiny was to emphasize the need for unity against Germany.

His family's contributions to Greek independence are obscure, but the comment in this message to Churchill may have been a reference to the Howlands. Rebecca Howland Roosevelt was the first wife of James Roosevelt, Franklin's father. She died in 1876, six years before Franklin Roosevelt's birth, but the President's definition of family was very extended, particularly when he found something to brag about. In the early 1820s, the firm of G. G. & S. Howland, presumably connected to Rebecca Howland, helped finance the construction of two frigates "intended to secure the independence of Greece." Since the pamphlet which describes this venture was in the President's personal library he probably knew the story. (See Alexander Contostavlos, *A Narrative of the Material Facts in Relation to the Building of the Two Greek Frigates*, New York: n.pub., 1826. The quotation is from p. 3.)

The underlined portion was added to the draft in Roosevelt's handwriting.

R–523

Waccamaw, S.C. [via U.S. Navy]
Apr. 17, 1944; 2:00 A.M., Apr. 18

From the President for the Former Naval Person. Top Secret and Personal.

Your 648, thank you for the information regarding recent difficulties encountered in Greek participation in our Allied effort.

I join with you in a hope that your line of action toward the problem may succeed in bringing the Greeks back into the Allied camp and to a participation against the barbarians that will be worthy of traditions established by the heroes of Greek history. Frankly, as one whose family and who personally have contributed by personal help to Greek inde-

pendence for over a century, I am unhappy over the present situation
and hope that Greeks everywhere will set aside pettiness and regain their
sense of proportion. Let every Greek think of their glorious past and
show a personal unselfishness which is so necessary now. You can quote
me if you want to in the above sense. Roosevelt

[MR*. *FRUS*, 1944, V, 98–99 (paraphrase). *WSC*, V, 548.]

As Roosevelt had indicated before (R–512), the American government was
reluctant to accept anything less than a complete cessation of Spanish wolfram
sales to Germany. General Francisco Jordana Gómez was the Spanish Minister
for Foreign Affairs. The Duke of Alba was the Spanish Ambassador to Great
Britain.

C–649

London [via U.S. Army]
Apr. 17, 1944

Prime Minister to President Roosevelt Most Secret and Personal.
  Subject: Spanish Wolfram.
  1. The only difference outstanding between our 2 countries and the
Spaniards is that we should like to accept Jordana's final offer of 60 tons
between now and the end of June in rising monthly installments of 15,
20, and 25 tons, the remaining 240 tons to be sent in monthly installments
of 40 tons between July and December.
  2. When considering what turned out to be an unauthorized proposal
from the Duke of Alba, you have agreed that 51 tons might go to Germany
in monthly installments of 17 tons between now and the end of June.
This is the most important period and the difference between us is 9 tons
on the 3 months.
  3. For the sake of this trifle we ought not surely to run the risk of the
Spaniards sending in to Germany nearly a thousand tons which is waiting
at the frontier, as well as lose all the other points which are of a very
great interest to us both. I do hope you will be able to give the point your
personal consideration.

[MR*. *FRUS*, 1944, IV, 386 (paraphrase).]

Roosevelt referred most questions of postwar economic cooperation to his
Secretaries of State and the Treasury.

R–524

Waccamaw, S.C. [via U.S. Navy]
Apr. 18, 1944, 2:00 A.M.

Personal and Top Secret. From the President to the Former Naval Person.
    Your number 647 received and delivered to Hull and Morgenthau for their information. Roosevelt

[MR*]

Churchill readily accepted the American revisions to his message to Stalin about the timing of the Normandy invasion. A few days after receiving this cable, Stalin renewed his Teheran promise to launch a major offensive at the same time as OVERLORD. (See *Stalin/FDR*, doc. 188.)

C–650

London
Apr. 18, 1944, 0940 Z

Prime Minister to President Roosevelt. Personal and Most Secret.
    Your number 522.
    I certainly think that it would be a good thing to send the message as redrafted by you beginning at "1. Pursuant to our talks" and ending "will crush the Hitlerites". This engages Stalin's direct personal attention and is more worthy of the tremendous event to which we are committed heart and soul than a Staff notification. It may even be followed by a friendly response. I have ventured to omit the word "soon" as it seems safer, and have sent it off over our joint signatures.

[MR*. *R&C.*]

R–525

Waccamaw, S.C. [via U.S. Navy]
Apr. 18, 1944, 11:00 P.M. (Washington)

Personal and Secret from the President to the Former Naval Person.
    Your 650 received and your message to Uncle J. reported therein has my approval. Roosevelt

[MR*]

State Department officials saw no need to antagonize other governments, particularly those in Latin America, by imposing an unnecessary censorship on diplomatic messages. The U.S. military agreed. (See below, R–533/1.)

R–525/1

Waccamaw, S.C. [via U.S. ambassador]
Apr. 18, 1944, midnight (Washington)

Personal and Secret for the Ambassador.

Please transmit to the Prime Minister the following message from the President in reply to his No. 646 of April 15:

> "The situation here is so different from that in the United Kingdom that restrictions here would have to be handled differently. We are nevertheless considering what can be done to tighten up, and are consulting our military people on the point." [CH]

[MR*]

Churchill eagerly seized the opportunity to associate the United States with British policy toward Greece.

C–651

London [via U.S. Army]
Apr. 18, 1944, 1504 Z

Prime Minister to President Roosevelt Personal and Top Secret.

Your number 523.

Thank you so much. I have told our people to make use of your message to the King and his new Ministers, and to read it to the mutinous brigade and recalcitrant ships. It may have a most salutary effect. I am not publishing anything here.

[MR*. *FRUS*, 1944, V, 99. *R&C*.]

Ernest Bevin was most certainly busy with his duties as Churchill's Minister of Labour, but the decision to send George Tomlinson to the International Labour Organization meeting may have reflected the usual British inclination to play down the prestige of such organizations. The reference to R–514 should read 510.

C–652

London [via U.S. Army]
Apr. 19, 1944, 0856 Z / TOR 1350 Z (Washington)

Prime Minister to President Roosevelt Most Secret and Personal.

1. I have talked to Mr. Bevin upon this. Personally he would like to come and greatly appreciates the kindness of your invitation and references to him. He very much regrets that he finds it impossible. What with the demands of OVERLORD and its follow-up and with the very delicate situation here with labour unrest, he feels he would not be doing his duty in quitting his post. I must say that he is so much in the centre of our affairs here at this time that I should find it very difficult to spare him.

2. On the other hand the labour M.P., George Tomlinson, a minister of the Crown, is going with a pretty strong team and we hope that they will make a good contribution towards solving our international problems. Great pains have been taken here by Mr. Bevin and other labour leaders to make sure that our people have a constructive case to present.

[MR*]

Churchill continued to encourage de Gaulle to meet Roosevelt more than halfway, although the Prime Minister made it clear to his subordinates that they should not push the matter with the President—Anglo-American relations were far more important than French politics. (British communicators dropped their usual classification, "most secret," for the American term, "top secret," after security officials in the United States expressed fears that "most" might be interpreted as "almost." Montagu, *Beyond Top Secret ULTRA*, p. 32n.)

C–653

London [via U.S. Army]
Apr. 19, 1944, 2350 Z / TOR 0055 Z, Apr. 20 (Washington)

Prime Minister to President Roosevelt Personal and Top Secret.

General De Gaulle would like to inquire, through his representative in Washington, whether a visit from him to you would be agreeable when you return from your holiday. I hope in these circumstances you will tell me I may encourage him to take this course. You might do him a great deal of good by paternal treatment and indeed I think it would be a help from every point of view.

[MR*]

To Churchill's annoyance, Canadian Prime Minister Mackenzie King tried throughout the war to enhance his own prestige and that of the Canadian Government. (See the headnote to R–517.)

C–654

London [via U.S. Army]
Apr. 20, 1944, 1253 Z

Prime Minister to President Roosevelt. Top Secret and Personal.
   Many thanks for your 517.
   Following is text of telegram I have sent to Mackenzie King.

"Many thanks for your telegrams numbers 34 and 35 of the 10th March. I have now examined these with the Chiefs of Staff and I have seen a copy of the reply which President Roosevelt has sent you. We welcome the proposal for the establishment of a Canadian Joint Staff Mission in London to act as a link with the British Chiefs of Staff and with the Supreme Allied Commanders. Our Chiefs of Staff will work out detailed arrangements for the necessary liaison between themselves and the Canadian Joint Staff Mission as soon as we hear that it has been appointed.

"President Roosevelt has explained that the appropriate channels of communication between the Canadian Chiefs of Staff and the Supreme Commands must be through the Combined Chiefs of Staff and not directly through your Joint Staff Mission. You will I think understand that it is essential not to disturb the well-established chain of command whereby the Supreme Commanders receive their instructions on all subjects from the Combined Chiefs of Staff. There will of course be no objection to your Joint Staff Mission having contact on day to day liaison matters with the Supreme Commands, but all matters of high policy can only be dealt with through the Combined Chiefs of Staff.

"In your telegram number 34 you expressed the opinion that it would be desirable that appropriate announcements should be made to make clear that General Wilson and General Eisenhower are Commanders in Chief of the participating forces of the United Nations. I agree with President Roosevelt that on military grounds there is no call for such an announcement. I am inclined to doubt its desirability on other grounds. The Supreme Command in the Mediterranean has been in existence for 18 months and has been directing the forces of many nations, which have been placed at its disposal, under arrangements satisfactory to all. Any general announcement at the present time might give rise to misunderstandings and cause difficulties with the many participants in the European campaigns. I suggest therefore that if you desire to announce the authority of General Eisenhower over the Canadian Forces under his command, that you should do so on behalf of the Canadian Government alone, rather than that we should seek to get agreement from all concerned for a general announcement."

[MR*]

R–526

Waccamaw, S.C. [via U.S. Navy]
Apr. 20, 1944, 11:30 P.M. (Washington)

Personal and Top Secret from the President for the Former Naval Person.

Replying to your number 652, I am sorry that Bevin finds it impossible to attend International Labor Conference in Philadelphia but the need for his services at home is understood and I am sure that Mr. Tomlinson with his assistants will prove to be welcome.

[MR*]

Roosevelt and his advisers saw no reason to enhance de Gaulle's prestige or to be distracted from more important things by a visit from the French General.

R–527

Waccamaw, S.C. [via U.S. Navy]
Apr. 20, 1944, 11:30 P.M. (Washington)

Personal and Top Secret from the President for the Former Naval Person.

Your 653. Owing to accumulation of work here I think it would be much better not to have the inquiry of a visit made at present. It would be much better timing from my standpoint to have the question raised about a month from now by the French Representative in Washington. Roosevelt

[MR*]

Basic English had been conceived in the 1920s by C. K. Ogden of Cambridge University. Consisting of 850 basic words plus a few additional words for each specialized field of science, the system was designed to be an efficient yet easily learned language. During the QUADRANT Conference, held in

August 1943 in Quebec, Churchill and Roosevelt had discussed the possibility of using Basic English as an international language.

L. S. Amery's primary appointment was as Secretary of State for Burma. He had previously been Secretary of State for India and had long been a staunch defender of the British Empire.

C–654/1, letter

London
April 20, 1944

My dear Mr. President,

When I was with you in the United States last August you expressed to me your interest in Basic English. The Cabinet Committee which I appointed here to consider the possibilities of Basic and means of promoting its wider use have reported and we have adopted the recommendations they have made. I thought it might be of interest to you to see the Report and am sending you copies.

Amery, who presided over the Committee, is also sending a copy personally to Hull.

If the United States authorities feel able to give their powerful support to the promotion of Basic English as a means of international intercourse, I feel sure that that would ensure its successful development. My conviction is that Basic English will then prove to be a great boon to mankind in the future and a powerful support to the influence of the Anglo-Saxon peoples in world affairs.

Yours ever, [signed] Winston S. Churchill

[PSF:GB:WSC]

R–528

Waccamaw, S.C. [via U.S. Navy]
Apr. 21, 1944, 6:30 P.M. (Washington)

Personal and Secret. From the President for the Former Naval Person.

Your 654 is received and I am in full agreement with your telegram to Mackenzie King quoted therein. Roosevelt

[MR*]

In urging that the President send the following message, drafted in the State Department, holding to a hard line on the question of Spanish wolfram shipments to Germany, Cordell Hull offered two reasons which Roosevelt found hard to differ with. First, the Secretary mentioned the need to do everything possible to cut off essential war materials from the enemy until the invasion of Europe made shipments impossible. Second, he referred to "the unanimous attitude of the American people" in support of restricting neutral trade with the enemy. Such language usually meant that any other policy would bring strong congressional criticism, something Roosevelt wanted to avoid in an election year (Hull to Roosevelt, Apr. 20, 1944, MR.)

R–529

Waccamaw, S.C. [via U.S. Navy]
Apr. 21, 1944, 6:30 p.m. (Washington)

Personal and Secret. From the President for the Former Naval Person.

Your 649. As you say, the only point which divides us on Spanish policy is whether to resume oil shipments concurrently with the resumption of wolfram shipments from Spain to Germany to the extent of 60 tons over the three months of April, May and June, or whether to do all in our power by a united effort to continue the suspension of wolfram shipments until July 1 in the hope and belief that thereafter shipments in the second half of the year in the amounts agreed to will not be practicable. It seems to us that to agree to the resumption of wolfram shipments prior to July 1st would frustrate the efforts which we are jointly making in Sweden and Turkey and would impair our position in dealing with Switzerland and Portugal. To these negotiations we attach great importance, as I know you do also.

Furthermore, our public attaches the greatest importance to Spanish shipments of wolfram and is most critical of oil supplies going to that country while these shipments continue. They are most insistent upon a policy of firmness in this matter and a contrary course on the eve of military operations would, I believe, have the most serious consequences.

The Duke of Alba's repudiated proposal to which you refer required shipments of only half the wolfram now proposed for the rest of 1944 and even in that case we said that only as a last resort would we consent to shipments before July 1st.

We have gone a very long way to meet your difficulties as you describe them in your long cable to me [C–631]. Will you not, therefore, reconsider an instruction to our two Ambassadors to join in a determined effort to settle the matter upon the basis of a suspension of shipments during the first half year. I do not believe that we have yet done all that is possible along this line. Roosevelt [CH]

[MR*. *FRUS*, 1944, IV, 396–97. *R&C*.]

While awaiting Roosevelt's response to this appeal for a compromise with Spain, Churchill proposed telling the President that the British would "retire from the business," leaving it in the hands of the Americans (Woodward, *British Foreign Policy*, IV, 27). Roosevelt's message of April 25 (R–531), accepting the British proposal, finally brought the matter to a close.

C–655

London [via U.S. Army]
Apr. 22, 1944, 1543 Z / TOR 1725 Z

Prime Minister to President Roosevelt Personal and Top Secret.
Your number 529 (of April 22nd: Spanish Wolfram).

1. Since I sent you my number 649, Lord Halifax has been discussing this question with Mr Cordell Hull who, after drawing attention to your difficulties with your public opinion, proposed that we should ourselves sponsor Spanish oil shipments on the basis of our special strategic interests and supply needs in Spain. The United States Government would not be directly concerned with this arrangement but Mr Hull intimated that we would be able to make a much better case for it than for the same action taken by you. He concluded that this was the best way we could help you.

2. As I have already explained to you, I am convinced that the present Spanish offer is a good one, which I shall be glad to sponsor as a practical and prestige victory over our enemies. I am also sure that it is the best we can get. Our latest information indicates that if we do not close on it within a day or two the Spanish Minister for foreign affairs will resign and there will be a temporary swing away from us in Spain. This will automatically bring about all the disadvantages which I have set out in my earlier messages, including an immediate increase in Spanish Wolfram exports to Germany. I have no doubt that Sir Samuel Hoare has already done all that is possible to prevent the 60 tons, to which you attack some importance, going to Germany before the end of June. The course you now suggest would only mean future delay which might prove very dangerous.

3. As regards your references to the other neutrals, I cannot believe that they will be deterred from meeting our wishes by the fact that a negligible quantity of wolfram (a few lorry loads) goes to Germany from Spain before the end of June. On the contrary, a settlement with Spain which will be a clear victory for us could, in my view, only have a good effect on the other neutrals, more particularly as Spain has hitherto been the most pro-German among them. In fact, I regard an immediate settlement with Spain on the lines now proposed as offering the best prospects for bringing about a reduction in Portuguese Wolfram exports. Some here fear that your recent decision to raise your legation at Lisbon

to an embassy may give Salazar the impression that we do not mean business. We [are] already dealing with Turkey separately and I am not aware of any demands that we are now making upon Switzerland. If Switzerland did not exist it would have to be invented.

4. I understand difficulties about public opinion. It is for that reason that I have already instructed Lord Halifax to inform Mr Hull that I am ready to fall in with his wishes, and take upon myself the whole responsibility for this settlement. I have already instructed Sir S. Hoare to make a communication accordingly to the Spanish Government as soon as I receive confirmation that the United States Government would acquiesce in the above arrangement as suggested by Mr Hull. It is important that Sir S. Hoare should act early next week and I therefore hope that either you or Mr Hull will confirm United States acquiescence in the above procedure before then.

[MR*]

Churchill continued to try to get de Gaulle and Roosevelt together.

C–656

London [via U.S. Army]
Apr. 22, 1944, 1730 Z

Prime Minister to President Roosevelt. Personal and Top Secret.
    Your 527.

From our previous correspondence, especially number 518 on which I took action, I had hoped you would go a little further with this. After all this man, whom I trust as little as you do, commands considerable forces including Naval Forces and the *Richelieu*, which are placed most freely at our disposal and are in action or eager for action. He presides over a vast empire, all the strategic points in which are at our disposal. May I send the following:

> "Prime Minister to General De Gaulle. The President tells me that he will be very much pressed with work immediately after his return to Washington. But if the French Representative in Washington raises the question after the middle of May, your visit would be agreeable to him, subject of course to the unforeseeable events of war."

I hope you can go as far as this.

[MR*]

Roosevelt's response was quick and curt. The *Richelieu* was a French battleship which had become available to the Allies after the capture of Dakar in 1943. The Great Duke is apparently a reference to the Duke of Marlborough, an accomplished diplomat and courtier, although like so many others Roosevelt may have meant the 1800s when he wrote "18th Century," and thus may have been referring to the Duke of Wellington.

R–530

Waccamaw, S.C. [via U.S. Navy]
April 23, 1944, 7:15 P.M. (Washington)

To the Former Naval Person from the President, Personal and Top Secret.

Your number 656, I do not have any information that leads me to believe that De Gaulle and his Committee of National Liberation have as yet given any helpful assistance to our Allied war effort. It seems to me that the "forces including naval forces and the *Richelieu*" were placed at our disposal before De Gaulle.

While it is impossible for me to make at this time a definite commitment to a visitation from him at a later date, I have no objection to his being informed that a request from him made about the end of May will receive such favorable consideration as is permitted by the conditions then existing.

Circumstances are so often misconstrued later that I will not ever have it said by the French or by American or British commentators that I invited him to visit me in Washington. If he asks whether I will receive him if he comes, I will incline my head with complete suavity and with all that is required by the etiquette of the 18th Century. This is farther than the Great Duke would have gone, don't you think so. Roosevelt

[MR. PREM 3/121/2.]

Churchill's seriatim cables require explanation in kind. The first paragraph refers to the proposed invitation for de Gaulle to visit the United States. Roosevelt had promised to visit the British Isles around the time of the Normandy invasion and Churchill did not want de Gaulle to interfere with that commitment.

Undersecretary of State Edward Stettinius was in London to discuss a wide variety of issues, particularly those concerning postwar Anglo-American relations. Assistant Secretary of State Adolf A. Berle had gone to England to work on the preliminary arrangements for an international conference on postwar civil aviation agreements. Assistant Secretary of War John J. McCloy was on a pre-OVERLORD inspection trip, but also discussed Mediterranean strategy with the British Chiefs of Staff and political/military relations regarding France and de Gaulle with Churchill.

Georgios Papandreou, leader of the Greek Social Democratic Party, opposed the monarchy but believed such questions should await the liberation of Greece. When Tsouderos resigned as Prime Minister, Papandreou formed a temporary government.

Political problems in Egypt (Egyptians were derisively labeled "Wogs" on the log sheet accompanying this cable) stemmed from a combination of poverty, a corrupt government under King Farouk, and the rise of anti-British nationalism. In an attempt to prevent a more radical solution and a possible challenge to British predominance, Churchill's government had arranged the appointment of Nahas Pasha, a moderate opposition leader, as Prime Minister. Farouk's candidate, Ahmad Muhammad Hasanain (Hassanein), had been associated with the Egyptian court since 1925. The WAFD Party was strongly nationalistic, and aimed at eliminating the monarchy and the British from Egypt.

In Italy, King Victor Emmanuel had, on April 12, abdicated in favor of his son as Lieutenant of the Realm, effective once Rome was liberated. At the same time, Badoglio had reformed the government, bringing in Croce, Sforza, and Palmiro Togliatti, the leading Italian Communist, as Ministers without portfolio. As Churchill had hoped, Badoglio reserved the Ministry of Foreign Affairs for himself, while continuing as Prime Minister. The military campaign, however, had bogged down despite Churchill's prodding as OVERLORD and ANVIL continued to monopolize resources which might otherwise have gone to General Alexander in Italy.

Churchill had acted as Foreign Secretary and leader of the House of Commons for three weeks in April while Anthony Eden, exhausted by his duties, took a rest; that was Churchill's "busman's holiday."

C–657

London [via U.S. Army]
Apr. 24, 1944, 1557 Z / TOR 1835 Z (Washington)

Prime Minister to President Roosevelt Personal Private and Top Secret.
Your number 530.

1. You started me off on this by your number 518. However I press it no more, especially as the date you mention is one round about which I am hoping you will remember you have a prior engagement.

2. I have had very good talks with Berle, McCloy and above all Stettinius. I am most relieved by what I have heard about Harry [Hopkins].

3. I am glad we sent our joint telegram to UJ because it is a great thing to have on record that he accepts what we are going to do as fulfillment of the Teheran undertakings and in addition that he himself will move accordingly.

4. Thank you very much for your message about the Greeks [R–523].

I have made use of it in all quarters concerned. The Greek naval mutineers have now surrendered unconditionally to a boarding attack by loyal Greek sailors. I think the mutinous brigade will be brought to its bearings to-morrow. At any rate if it is not, we shall have to use artillery against its batteries, which are pointing at us. There are two small heights to be taken during the night. With the dawn comes a heavy shower of leaflets. Smoke is then dropped so as to leave a quarter of an hour when all will be in darkness and when it is hoped a large number of these gentry will make their way out from the abodes of the guilty. By these means we hope to establish order without bloodshed. King George has shown great steadfastness and has got hold of a Greek named Papandreou, said to be a man of high and firm character and of public distinction, who has lived in Greece all the time and consequently is one up on the earlier emigres. I expect he will make Papandreou Premier. Generally the position seems to be clearing up.

5. It will be well to get these Greek matters out of the way, as His Majesty King Farouk is on his high horse. He wishes to dismiss the Nahas government, which has a large majority in the chamber, the chamber having 3 years to run. Nahas as you know represents the WAFD [Wafdist] party of the democracy and the peasants, and is viewed with much distaste by the palace circles and the wealthy Pashas and it is believed by the Egyptian army. We are quite ready to have an election and so is Nahas, provided it can take place at once. This the King thinks is a horrible idea: he wishes to put his palace minister Hassanein in as Prime Minister with a court clique around him to rig the election in the next 3 or 4 months. We cannot allow this, as it would make great enemies of the working class and peasant parties who stood so firm and steady when the enemy was but 60 miles from Cairo and when Farouk might have slipped off any day to join the Italians or Germans. Here again we are proceeding with great caution but also with force behind. To be quite fair I must admit that Nahas and company fall below the standards which idealists have always hoped for in Oriental democracy. He and his party are corrupt, incompetent but fully capable, I blush to say, influencing elections otherwise than by oratory.

6. I am very glad at what has happened in Italy. It seems to me that we have both succeeded in gaining what we sought. The only thing now lacking is a victory. I had long talks with Alexander when he was here for a few days consultation. He defended his actions or inactions with much force, pointing out the small plurality of his army, its mixed character, there being no fewer than 7 separate nationalities against the homogeneous Germans, the vileness of the weather and the extremely awkward nature of the ground. At latest by the date in my immediately following he will attack and push everything in as hard as possible. If this

battle were successful or even going at full blast it would fit in very well with other plan.

7. I hope that you have benefitted by your rest and that a sea voyage may be prescribed in due course to consolidate the effects of your holiday. I have had a busman's holiday myself having been acting Foreign Secretary and leader of the house as well as my other odd jobs.

Every good wish to you and yours.

[MR*. p*WSC*, V, 514–15.]

C–658

London [via U.S. Army]
Apr. 24, 1944 / TOR 2030 Z (Washington)

From Prime Minister to President Roosevelt Personal and Top Secret.
My immediately preceding telegram, para 6. May 14th is date.

[MR*]

The U.S. Tenth Fleet had been established in May 1943 to coordinate anti-submarine warfare in the Atlantic. Admiral Ernest King, the U.S. Chief of Naval Operations, officially commanded the shipless fleet, but its day-to-day operations were run by its Chief of Staff, Rear Admiral Francis Low. Back on September 28, 1943, during a radio interview, Low had claimed that the Allied campaign against German U-boats in the Atlantic had been so successful that the German Navy was on the verge of the kind of demoralization it had experienced in 1917, just prior to the outbreak of mutiny. Apparently, that was the statement to which Churchill referred.

C–659

London [via U.S. Army]
Apr. 24, 1944 / TOR 2030 Z (Washington)

From Prime Minister to President Roosevelt Personal and Top Secret.
Have just read Rear Admiral Francis Low Chief of Staff of US 10th Fleet about anti submarine warfare. All this matter might have come in very well in our monthly statement as agreed. You instituted, with my agreement, the monthly statements which seem to have worked pretty well on the conventions agreed. Would you consider whether this pronouncement is not rather outside the scope of our arrangement. Tell me if anyone here has offended.

[MR*]

General Sir Bernard Paget was the British Commander in Chief, Middle East.

C-660

London [via U.S. Army]
Apr. 24, 1944, 2030 Z / TOR 2130 Z (Washington)

Prime Minister to President Roosevelt Personal and Top Secret.

Further to my number 657 I have just heard from General Paget that the British troops occupied key positions on the ridge overlooking the Greek camp last night and encountered slight opposition. There were no Greek casualties but one British Officer was killed. The Greek brigade surrendered this morning and laid down its arms. The brigade is now being evacuated to the prisoner of war cage where the ring leaders will be arrested.

The mutinous Navy surrendered unconditionally 24 hours earlier.

[MR*]

Roosevelt also received a copy of Stalin's promise to launch an offensive at the same time as the Normandy invasion.

C-661

London [via U.S. Army]
Apr. 25, 1944, 1032 Z / TOR 1217 Z (Washington)

Prime Minister to President Roosevelt Personal and Most Secret.

My telegram number 650.

I have received following telegram dated April 22 from Premier Stalin in reply to our joint message. Begins:

> I have received your message of the 18th April. The Soviet Government is satisfied with your statement that in accordance with the Teheran agreement, the crossing of the sea will take place on the date planned regarding which Generals Deane and Burrows had already informed our General Staff and that you will be acting at your fullest strength. I express my confidence in the success of the planned operations.
>
> I, also, hope for the success of the operation to be undertaken by you in Italy.
>
> As we agreed at Teheran, the Red Army will undertake at the same time its new offensive order to give the maximum support to the Anglo-American operations.

I beg you to accept my thanks for the wishes which you express regarding the success of the Red Army. I subscribe to your declaration that your armies and ours supporting one another will crush the Hitlerites and fulfil their historic missions. Ends.

I am not inclined to press them for details of their operations as we are such a great distance apart and they certainly have played up with grand vigour.

[MR*. p*Stalin/FDR*, doc. 188.]

When the Spanish offered to restrict wolfram shipments to Germany to twenty tons a month for May and June and forty tons a month thereafter, Hull recommended that the United States accept the compromise. He was particularly worried that a split with the British on this issue would weaken the joint Anglo-American leverage against other neutrals.

R–531

Waccamaw, S.C. [via U.S. Navy]
Apr. 25, 1944, 2:00 P.M. (Washington)

Personal and Top Secret, from the President for the Former
Naval Person.

Referring to your 655, I have today authorized Hull to accept Halifax's proposal to restrict shipments of wolfram from Spain. Roosevelt

[MR*. *R&C*.]

A quick victory in Italy was essential if ANVIL was to be carried out since there were not enough landing craft to support both campaigns. Once again comments on the Egyptian scene came under the label "Wogs" on the log sheet.

R–532

Waccamaw, S.C. [via U.S. Navy]
Apr. 25, 1944, 11:00 P.M. (Washington)

Secret and Personal from the President for the Former Naval Person.

Your 657, 658 and 660. I am very pleased indeed by your success in handling the Greek naval and military mutiny.

I will hope for a similar success in your efforts with the Egyptian political problem.

Our prospects of assisting OVERLORD by vigorous action in Italy do look much better with a fixed date upon which we may expect all-out pressure against the enemy. In view of our postponement of ANVIL a real success in Italy now seems essential.

Referring to your 659, I will upon my return look into the matter of Rear Admiral Low's talk about submarine warfare and will endeavor to prevent in the future any publicity regarding submarines that might properly be included in our monthly statement.

Everything goes well here in my vacation residence. The doctor agrees with me that I am better.

Your 661, I have received from Uncle Joe an identical message. Roosevelt

[MR*. p*WSC*, V, 550–51.]

Churchill was happy to have another minor irritant—the wolfram matter—out of the way.

C–662

London [via U.S. Army]
Apr. 26, 1944, 0727 Z / TOR 0825 Z (Washington)

Prime Minister to President Roosevelt Personal and Most Secret.
   Your number 531.
   We are all here greatly obliged for your consideration.

[MR*]

The split in Yugoslavia between monarchists and republicans/communists roughly corresponded to the ethnic division between the Serbs (monarchists) and other minorities, particularly the Croatians. Shortly before the outbreak of World War II, King Peter of Yugoslavia tried to defuse the ethnic tension by creating an autonomous state of Croatia. The Ban (Viceroy) of Croatia was Dr. Ivan Subasić. At the time of the Italo-German occupation of Yugoslavia, Subasić fled to the United States, where he worked to unify the various Yugoslavian organizations which functioned there. Supported by the British, King Peter hoped to reorganize the Yugoslavian government in exile, although the King was still unwilling to abandon General Mihailović, in spite of Churchill's warning that the General might fight against Soviet forces in the event that they entered Yugoslavia and lent support to Tito and the Partisans. Roosevelt instructed Hull to find Subasić.

C–663

London
Apr. 26, 1944 / TOR 1240 Z (Washington)

Prime Minister to President Roosevelt Personal and Top Secret.

King Peter is very anxious to have the Ban of Croatia over here as soon as possible. I am most anxious he should form a government which will not tie him to Mihailovitch, a weight which cannot well be borne. The Ban is essential to his plans for forming a broad-based administration not obnoxious to the Partisans. Could you find the gentleman and put him on an aeroplane as early as possible? He may need a little encouragement. Halifax will do this if the Ban is directed to the British Embassy.

[MR*. R&C.]

King Farouk of Egypt had little choice but to go along whenever the British insisted.

C–664

London [via U.S. Army]
Apr. 26, 1944, 1149 Z / TOR 1240 Z (Washington)

Prime Minister to President Roosevelt Personal and Top Secret.
Your 532.

The Egyptian political crisis is at an end as the King has agreed not to make any changes at present. An attempt is being made to patch up things between him and the government.

Thank you so much for all your kindness. I am greatly delighted that your health has improved.

[MR*]

Famine had long plagued India, and war only heightened the problem. A poor rice crop in 1943, followed by an equally small wheat harvest early in 1944, put an enormous strain on British grain and shipping resources, and when the explosion of two ammunition ships at the Bombay docks destroyed over 36,000 tons of grain, the British reluctantly turned to the United States for aid. Field Marshal Sir Archibald Wavell, the Viceroy of India, and Admiral Louis Mountbatten, the SEAC commander, feared that the shortages could precipitate food riots and serious political unrest.

C–665

London [via U.S. Army]
Apr. 29, 1944 / TOR 1525 Z (Washington)

Prime Minister to President Roosevelt Personal and Top Secret.

1. I am seriously concerned about the food situation in India and its possible reactions on our joint operations. Last year we had a grievous famine in Bengal through which at least 700,000 people died. This year there is a good crop of rice, but we are faced with an acute shortage of wheat, aggravated by unprecedented storms which have inflicted serious damage on the Indian spring corps. India's shortage cannot be overcome by any possible surplus of rice even if such a surplus could be extracted from the peasants. Our recent losses in the Bombay explosion have accentuated the problem.

2. Wavell is exceedingly anxious about our position and has given me the gravest warnings. His present estimate is that he will require imports of about one million tons this year if he is to hold the situation, and so meet the needs of the United States and British and Indian troops and of the civil population especially in the great cities. I have just heard from Mountbatten that he considers the situation so serious that, unless arrangements are made promptly to import wheat requirements, he will be compelled to release military cargo space of SEAC in favour of wheat and formally to advise Stilwell that it will also be necessary for him to arrange to curtail American military demands for this purpose.

3. By cutting down military shipments and other means, I have been able to arrange for 350,000 tons of wheat to be shipped to India from Australia during the first nine months of 1944. This is the shortest haul. I cannot see how to do more.

4. I have had much hesitation in asking you to add to the great assistance you are giving us with shipping but a satisfactory situation in India is of such vital importance to the success of our joint plans against the Japanese that I am impelled to ask you to consider a special allocation of ships to carry wheat to India from Australia without reducing the assistance you are now providing for us, who are at a positive minimum if war efficiency is to be maintained. We have the wheat (in Australia) but we lack the ships. I have resisted for some time the Viceroy's request that I should ask you for your help, but I believe that, with this recent misfortune to the wheat harvest and in the light of Mountbatten's representations, I am no longer justified in not asking for your help. Wavell is doing all he can by special measures in India. If however he should find it possible to revise his estimate of his needs, I would let you know immediately.

[MR*. Ehrman, *Grand Strategy*, V, 578–79. *FRUS*, 1944, V, 271–72 (paraphrase).]

Secretary of the Navy Frank Knox unexpectedly died of a heart attack on April 28.

C–666

London [via U.S. Army]
Apr. 29, 1944 / TOR 1900 Z (Washington)

From Prime Minister to President Roosevelt.

I have learned with great sorrow of the sudden death of Colonel Knox. If you will allow me to say so, His Majesty's Government and especially the Admiralty feel his loss acutely, for no-one could have been more forthcoming and helpful in all our difficult times than was this distinguished American Statesman and War Administrator.

The War Cabinet have desired me to express their sympathy with you in losing so invaluable a colleague, to which I add my own expressions of sincere sorrow.

[MR*]

C–667

London
Apr. 29, 1944

Prime Minister to President Roosevelt. Personal and Top Secret.

My immediately preceding telegram. We propose that this message should be published, unless you have any objection.

[PREM 3/472/388]

R–533

Waccamaw, S.C. [via U.S. Navy]
Apr. 29, 1944, 11:59 P.M. (Washington)

Secret and Personal from the President for the Former Naval Person.

Your 666. Thank you very much for your sympathetic message of condolences on the loss of Secretary of the Navy Knox.

I think it would be an added kindness if you should release your message for publication. Roosevelt

[MR]

Discussions about ANVIL, the invasion of southern France, had broadened into a consideration of an assault against other portions of southern France or even against western France from the Bay of Biscay. During a meeting of the Combined Chiefs in Washington, Admiral King had promised that the landing craft allocated from the Pacific for ANVIL would also be available for other attacks on France which would support the OVERLORD assault.

DIADEM was the codeword for the Allied offensive against the Germans in Italy planned for mid-May. The Allies still held the beachhead at Anzio, and part of the offensive was designed to link that beachhead with the main Anglo-American forces. SHINGLE was the codename for the Anzio assault.

General Sir H. M. Wilson, the Allied Commander in Chief in the Mediterranean, had been called to London to participate in the debate over strategy in Italy and southern France.

C–668

London [via U.S. Army]
Apr. 29, 1944, 1640 Z / TOR 2015 Z (Washington)

Prime Minister to President Roosevelt Personal and Most Secret.

1. We are deeply grateful for a statement made by Admiral King reported to us in our JSM 23, holding out the hope that the L.S.T's which have been considered in relation to some form of ANVIL may even yet be made available to us for the greatest amphibious operation we can stage after the big battle in Italy is decided. This has followed our COS (W) 16 of April 27th and gives me hope that the difficulties are clearing away. Admiral King is being informed that as soon as the conference between Wilson, who is coming home, Eisenhower and the British Chiefs of Staff has reached a definite point, we will submit our proposals.

2. Let me repeat that I do not consider that the objective of the forthcoming battle in India called DIADEM is the taking of Rome good though that would be or even the joining of the bridgehead which is indispensable. Its prime purpose is the destruction of the armed forces of the enemy, and if by mid-May we find the enemy before us in present strength I have every hope we shall be so closely engaged and entangled with them, we being the superior force, that much of the life may be struck out of this German army. Meanwhile everything not wanted for this battle is being prepared for the biggest amphibious operation we can mount on which decisions will be taken and laid before you as soon as Wilson arrives on Monday.

3. Like the United States C.O.S. I too fear a sudden and swift withdrawal through the tunnels of the Alps, but I do not consider on the whole that it is very likely. Hitler obstinate by habit vide Stalingrad, the Crimea, Tunis etc and also he would be very much afraid of his position in the Balkans. If he let us get swiftly up to the north of Italy he would not be able to tell which way we would go. Moreover he must now be very expectant of an OVERLORD move in the favourable moon and tide

period at the beginning of May as indeed was originally aimed at by us. Notwithstanding this, he has made no move to withdraw the eight extra divisions sucked down to the south of Rome by the SHINGLE operation and our joint fighting there.

[MR*]

Even though matters of state took precedence, exchanges such as this letter demonstrate the close relationship that existed between Churchill and Roosevelt. The portrait of Churchill is at the Roosevelt Library.

C–668/1, letter

London
May 1, 1944

My dear Franklin,

You kindly sent me recently a portrait of yourself which I like very much and have hung in my bedroom. Here is a tit for your tat. I hope you will accept it, flattering though it be to me, and like it as much as I do yours.

Yours ever, [signed] Winston S. C.

[PPF 7683]

After the Joint Chiefs of Staff and the State Department agreed that stopping diplomatic communications to and from embassies in the United States would not "do any good" for OVERLORD security, Roosevelt approved the following draft cable to Churchill. But without explanation the President decided not to send the message, and he instructed Admiral Leahy to take the necessary security measures at the appropriate time.

R–533/1, not sent

Washington
May 4, 1944

To Prime Minister Churchill from President Roosevelt.

The factors set forth in your 646 have been carefully considered, and much thought has been devoted to the probable results of the imposition of similar restrictive measures on the privileged communication channels of diplomatic officials accredited to this country. The special circumstances that necessitated such action in the case of Great Britain are fully appreciated, but in view of the geographical location of this country it seems clear that the military justification for such restrictive measures is not nearly so strong in our case. In England there is vital information to be observed at first hand, the lines of communication which have been closed are short and direct, and the measures in question can be made effective; with us, on the other hand, vital information concerning the invasion would not be obtainable by observation, lines of mail communication are long and slow, and the restrictions in question would not be fully effective in preventing information from crossing the border.

Our observation of the reaction in other countries to your recently imposed measures indicates the likelihood that if we take similar action retaliatory measures will be imposed against us and we will lose our privileged channels of communication. Not only are these channels proving highly valuable but their retention will enable us to afford our facilities to your representatives wherever this may be helpful or desirable. There seems little doubt that the imposition of such measures by us would cause such resentment in this Hemisphere that it would negative to a substantial degree whatever contribution the various countries therein are making to the war effort.

For the reasons given, I have come to the conclusion that there is more to be lost than gained by a change in our present procedures. We will, of course, continue to lend our full support to the measures that you have so wisely placed in effect.

[MR]

As usual, the American draft of the monthly anti-submarine warfare statement was succinct and uninformative.

R–534

Waccamaw, S.C. [via U.S. Navy]
May 5, 1944, 4:30 P.M. (Washington)

Personal and Secret. From the President for the Former Naval Person.

I propose the following joint statement regarding U-boat warfare in April for release on May 10:

QUOTE. The following Joint Anglo-American statement on submarine and anti-submarine operations is issued under the authority of the President and the Prime Minister.

In April 1944, the United Nations anti-submarine activity continued at a highly satisfactory level. Again for another month the extraordinary fact continues that the number of enemy submarines sunk exceeds the number of Allied merchant ships sunk by submarines. UNQUOTE.

Roosevelt [Navy Dept.]

[MR*]

How best to use Allied air power preparatory to the OVERLORD attack prompted a major argument. General Eisenhower, supported by his Chief of Staff, Lieutenant General W. Bedell Smith, and two British Air Chief Marshals, Sir Arthur Tedder, who was Eisenhower's Deputy Commander, and Sir Charles Portal, who was Chief of the British Air Staff, favored tactical air strikes against railways in France which could be used to supply German forces near the Normandy beaches. Some U.S. and British air officers opposed the plan for fear it would divert aircraft from the strategic bombing of Germany, but the strongest objections came from Churchill and his War Cabinet. They believed that excessive civilian casualties would cause a backlash among the French population and leave serious wartime and postwar problems for Britain.

C–669

London [via U.S. Army]
May 7, 1944, 1720 Z / TOR 2120 Z (Washington)

Prime Minister to President Roosevelt. Personal and Top Secret.

1. The War Cabinet have been much concerned during the last three weeks about the number of Frenchmen killed in the raids on the railway centres in France. We have had numerous Staff meetings with our own officers and I have discussed the matter with Generals Eisenhower and Bedell Smith. There were and are great differences of opinion in the two Air Forces not between them but criss cross about the efficacy of the "Railway Plan" as a short term project. In the end Eisenhower, Tedder, Bedell Smith and Portal all declare themselves converted. I am personally by no means convinced that this is the best way to use our Air Forces in the preliminary period, and still think that the G.A.F. [German Air Force] should be the main target. The matter has been discussed in very great detail on the technical side, and it would not be wise to dismiss lightly the arguments for or against.

2. When this project was first put forward a loss of 80,000 French civilian casualties including injured, say 20,000 killed was mentioned. The War Cabinet could not view this figure without grave dismay on account of the apparently ruthless use of the Air Forces, particularly of the Royal Air Force on whom the brunt of this kind of work necessarily falls, and the reproaches that would be made upon the inaccuracy of night bombing.

The results of the first, say, three-sevenths of the bombing have however shown that the casualties to French civil life are very much less than was expected by the commanders, in fact Air Chief Marshal Tedder has now expressed the opinion that about 10,000 killed, apart from injured, will probably cover the job.

3. I am satisfied that all possible care will be taken to minimize this slaughter of friendly civilian life. Nevertheless the War Cabinet share my apprehensions of the bad effect which will be produced upon the French civilian population by these slaughters, all taking place so long before OVERLORD D Day. They may easily bring about a great revulsion in French feeling towards their approaching United States and British liberators. They may leave a legacy of hate behind them. I have just now received the telegram contained in my immediately following from our Ambassador at Algiers, which I am pretty sure represents a serious wave of opinion in France. It may well be that the French losses will grow heavier on and after D Day, but in the heat of battle, when British and United States troops will probably be losing at a much higher rate, a new proportion establishes itself in men's minds. It is the intervening period that causes me most anxiety. We are of course doing everything in our power by leaflets etc to warn the French people to keep clear of dangerous spots, and this may prove beneficial in the remaining interval. However both on technical and political grounds, which latter are very gravely involved, the War Cabinet feel very great distress and anxiety.

4. Accordingly they ask me to invite you to consider the matter from the highest political standpoint and to give us your opinion as a matter between governments. It must be remembered on the one hand that this slaughter is among a friendly people who have committed no crimes against us, and not among the German foe with all their record of cruelty and ruthlessness. On the other hand we naturally feel the hazardous nature of operation OVERLORD and are in deadly earnest about making it a success. I have been careful in stating this case to you to use only the most moderate terms, but I ought to let you know that the War Cabinet is unanimous in its anxiety about these French slaughters, even reduced as they have been, and also in its doubts as to whether almost as good military results could not be produced by other methods. Whatever is settled between us, we are quite willing to share responsibilities with you.

[MR*. pWSC, V, 529–30. R&C.]

The protest by René Massigli, French Commissioner for Foreign Affairs, was not echoed by the French military. Major General Pierre Joseph Koenig, commander of French forces in the United Kingdom, remarked that "this is

War, and it must be expected that people will be killed. We would take twice the anticipated loss to be rid of the Germans" (as quoted in *Eisenhower Papers*, III, 1810n).

C–670

London [via U.S. Army]
May 7, 1944, 1730 Z / TOR 2120 Z (Washington)

Prime Minister to President Roosevelt. Personal and Top Secret.

The text of the telegram referred to in my number 669 follows:

"Massigli handed me this morning a memorandum concerning Allied bombardments of French targets, expressing the serious psychological effect they are having on the French population and French resistance groups when the loss of human life involved does not seem to correspond with the results obtained, notably in the case of stations and factories in populated districts. It is suggestd that sabotage operations would achieve a better result without risk of life.

2. Massigli told me that he had had a letter from a friend of his in France in whom he has complete confidence, speaking of reactions amongst the French population particularly with regard to Rouen and Paris.

3. The memorandum ends with a request that the French and Allied high commands should collaborate in the choice of targets on French territory.

4. I do not know whether a French expert from their mission in London is consulted by target committee. If this is not the case, I think it would have a good psychological effect here if a French transport expert several of whom are now in London, could be coopted on target committee for consultation when targets in France are being examined. He might have useful information to communicate."

5. Text of note goes to you by bag.

[MR*]

Sir Walter Citrine was General Secretary of the British Trades Union Congress and a leader of the Labour Party. Though he and Churchill were political opponents, Citrine was a moderate who opposed the radical wing of the Labour Party and who condemned the communists—just the kind of Labour leader Churchill could work with.

C–671

London [via U.S. Army]
May 8, 1944 / TOR 1345 Z

Prime Minister to President Roosevelt. Personal and Secret.

I hope you will be able to find time to have a talk with Sir W. Citrine. As a Privy Councillor and leader of the British Trades Union Congress he is a person of consequence with us.

[MR]

Roosevelt scheduled a fifteen-minute meeting with Citrine on May 11, 1944.

R–535

Washington [via U.S. Navy]
May 8, 1944, 7:00 P.M.

Personal and Secret, from the President for the Former Naval Person.

Your 671. I will be very glad to see Sir W. Citrine and I am planning to do so.

[MR*]

Ever sensitive to British morale as well as to the efforts of his beloved Navy, Churchill drafted this vigorous reply to the American proposal for the April U-boat statement.

C–672, draft A, not sent

London
May 7, 1944

Prime Minister to President. Personal and Secret.

I am quite content with your declaration, but I should prefer to insert instead of the words quote the United Nations unquote, the words quote the British and United States Anti-submarine activity unquote. We are always ready to go fifty fifty with you in anything; but I do not consider that it is either the United States or United Nations, and by this procedure completely omit any reference to the contribution made by the British Navy. The facts are United States 7, British 7, Norwegian 1. I should be quite satisfied with quote United States-British unquote, or quote Anglo-American unquote or, if you will, quote British, United States and other

United Nations unquote. When it is our turn to draft the communique, we will always put the U.S.A. first, being sure you would return the compliment. But considering that all the 33 United Nations, apart from you and we, have only sunk one submarine during the month in question, I think we run the risk of deceiving our publics.

[PREM 3/413/5/166]

When the British Admiralty made no protest to Roosevelt's use of the phrase United Nations, Churchill chose to accept the American draft.

C–672

London [via U.S. Army]
May 8, 1944 / TOR 1925 Z

Prime Minister to President Roosevelt Personal and Secret.
   Thank you for the joint U-boat warfare statement for April [R–534]. I have no alterations to suggest and Mackenzie King, to whom I showed it, agrees with its terms. We will accordingly release it on May 10th.

[MR*]

As ever, the President was concerned that Stalin would misinterpret changes in Allied strategy to mean that the second front would be less than an all-out effort. For that reason Roosevelt changed the wording in the third sentence of this proposed message to Stalin.

R–536

Washington [via U.S. Navy]
May 10, 1944, 12:05 P.M.

Personal and Top Secret, from the President for the Former Naval Person.
   I believe we should inform Marshal Stalin that ANVIL will not be launched in conjunction with the OVERLORD assault. If you agree to the following message, will you send it as being from both of us.

   "In order to give maximum strength to the attack across the sea against northern France, we have transferred part of our landing craft from the Mediterranean to England. This, together with the need for using our Mediterranean land forces in the present Italian battle, makes it impracticable to attack the Mediterranean coast of

France in conjunction with the OVERLORD assault. We are ~~consid-ering~~ expecting to make such an attack ~~at a~~ later ~~date~~. In order to keep the greatest number of German forces away from northern France and the eastern front, we are attacking the Germans in Italy at once on a maximum scale and, at the same time, are maintaining a threat against the Mediterranean coast of France."

Roosevelt [WDL/JCS]

[MR*. R&C.]

Roosevelt continued to support American military planners closest to the action, who believed that the tactical bombing of railroads in the Normandy area was worth the unfortunate losses of civilian lives and property. Military analysts are unanimous in agreeing that the bombings were effective.

R–537

Washington [via U.S. Navy]
May 11, 1944, 12:00 A.M. (noon)

Top Secret and Personal, from the President for the Former
Naval Person.

Replying to your 669 and 670, I share fully with you your distress at the loss of life among the French population incident to our air preparations for OVERLORD.

I share also with you a satisfaction that every possible care is being and will be taken to minimize civilian casualties. No possibility of alleviating adverse French opinion should be overlooked, always provided that there is no reduction of our effectiveness against the enemy at this crucial time. The message from your Ambassador at Algiers [C–670] referred to the good psychological effect to be obtained if a French transport expert were consulted by the target committee. This matter should be referred to the responsible military commanders for their decision.

However regrettable the attendant loss of civilian lives is, I am not prepared to impose from this distance any restriction on military action by the responsible commanders that in their opinion might militate against the success of OVERLORD or cause additional loss of life to our Allied Forces of invasion. Roosevelt [WDL]

[MR*. pWSC, V, 530. R&C.]

Churchill suggested changes in the cable to Stalin designed to imply an even firmer commitment to the invasion of southern France.

C–673

London [via U.S. Army]
May 11, 1944

Prime Minister to President Personal and Secret.

Your No. 536. The Chiefs of Staff suggest the amendments contained in the following text. They seem to strengthen our statement.

"From President Roosevelt and Prime Minister Churchill to Marshal Stalin.

In order to give maximum strength to the attack across the sea against northern France, we have transferred part of our landing craft from the Mediterranean to England. This, together with the need for using our Mediterranean land forces in the present Italian battle makes it impracticable to attack the Mediterranean coast of France simultaneously with the OVERLORD assault. We are planning to make such an attack later, for which purpose additional landing craft are being sent to the Mediterranean from the United States. In order to keep the greatest number of German forces away from northern France and the eastern front, we are attacking the Germans in Italy at once on a maximum scale and, at the same time, are maintaining a threat against the Mediterranean coast of France. Signed Roosevelt Churchill."

[MR. *FRUS*, 1944, III, 682.]

Although Foreign Secretary Eden and most of the Foreign Office believed that General de Gaulle commanded the respect and loyalty of the overwhelming majority of the French Resistance fighters as well as the French public at large, Churchill and Roosevelt remained reluctant to work with the General. Churchill not only distrusted de Gaulle, but was unwilling to break with Roosevelt in order to placate the French leader. Roosevelt may not have accepted the advice given by Admiral Leahy that Marshal Henri Pétain, the old Vichy leader, was the most reliable Frenchman to whom the Allies could turn (Eden, *The Reckoning*, p. 519), but the President definitely wanted someone other than de Gaulle. Nevertheless, Eisenhower's plea for a resolution of the impasse so the Allies could work effectively with the Resistance during OVERLORD prompted Churchill to recommend some sort of agreement with de Gaulle.

C-674

London [via U.S. Army]
May 12, 1944, 1116 Z

To President Roosevelt from Prime Minister Personal and Top Secret.

As the hour approaches we feel it indispensable to have some kind of understanding with the French National Committee. Owing to the restrictions we have found it necessary to put on cypher communications and on comings and goings from this island, which gained your approval, we find it impossible to allow any French who have come or may be permitted to come to this island in order to join in the Eisenhower-Koenig conversations, to leave it again before the event. De Gaulle and his committee refuse to accept these conditions and state that no reasonable discussion is possible.

2. In these circumstances we must presently be faced with a public complaint that no kind of arrangement has been made with the French National Committee for the employment of French forces outside or inside France. We could quite well dispense with French aid from outside in the operation, because the LeClerc [French] Division does not reach the scene until D plus 90, and as the FNCL will have no troops till then the military aspect would not be involved. However General Eisenhower says that he attaches great importance to the action to be taken by the French resistance groups on and after D Day, and undoubtedly we must take care that our joint troops do not suffer heavier losses owing to the fact that no agreement has been made for the employment of the French resistance groups. The French Committee state that the resistance army numbers 175,000 men and they intend to incorporate them officially in the French Army under the name of French Forces of the Interior.

3. I therefore propose to you that General De Gaulle, together with one or two of his committee, should be invited to come here on say May 18th in the utmost secrecy: That you should either entrust your case to General Eisenhower or send over someone specially to meet them: That we should discuss outstanding matters affecting military and political collaborations together face to face, showing all our substantial reasons against any extreme demands but endeavouring to reach a working arrangement. The Foreign Secretary or I would conduct the discussion with De Gaulle and any of your representatives you may choose. We will make the best proposals we can to you without agreeing to anything until we have heard from you. It may be that no agreement will be reached because they are unreasonable, in which case we have done our best, and he will have put himself hopelessly in the wrong. In any case we shall have done

our duty by the soldiers and you will have the fullest opportunity of seeing the best lay-out we can get for you to consider.

[MR*]

Roosevelt continued to insist that de Gaulle be held at arm's length. At the same time General Marshall endeavored to keep Eisenhower out of the political dispute so he could concentrate on the military task at hand.

R–538

Shangri-la, Md. [via U.S. Navy]
May 12, 1944, 9:00 P.M.

Personal and Top Secret from the President for the Former Naval Person.

Your 673 meets with my approval. Please send it as being from both of us.

Your 674. I have no objection whatever to your inviting De Gaulle and others of the French Committee to discuss your association in military or political matters; however, you must consider in the interest of security keeping De Gaulle in the United Kingdom until the OVERLORD landing has been made.

It is my understanding that General Eisenhower now has full authority to discuss with the Committee all matters on a military level. I do not desire that Eisenhower shall become involved with the Committee on a political level and I am unable at this time to recognize any government of France until the French people have an opportunity for a free choice of government. Roosevelt [WDL, GCM]

[MR*. *FRUS*, 1944, III, 683.]

The pun was added in Roosevelt's handwriting.

R–539

Shangri-la, Md. [via U.S. Navy]
May 13, 1944, 1:20 P.M.

Personal and Top Secret, from the President for the Former
Naval Person.

Replying to your Number 663, I am informed that the Ban of Croatia is now in England. I am generally opposed to any kind of ban but have no objection to this variety. Roosevelt

[MR*]

The message as received by Stalin is in *Stalin/FDR*, doc. 192.

C–675

London [via U.S. Army]
May 13, 1944, 1534 Z

Prime Minister to President Roosevelt Personal and Most Secret.
   Your 538. Joint message to Uncle Joe has been despatched.

[MR*]

Though the humor would have been lost on the Yugoslavs, the punning continued.

C–676

London [via U.S. Army]
May 14, 1944, 1442 Z / TOR 1645 Z

Prime Minister to President Personal and Secret.
   Ban duly lifted and safely received.

[MR*]

Yielding to British pressure, King Peter agreed to remove Mihailović as Minister of War and form a new, non-political government with the Ban of Croatia, Ivan Subasić, replacing Bozidar Purić as Prime Minister. Although the Serbian politicians in London refused to join such a government, Subasić did become Prime Minister on June 1. (See C–706.) The words deleted in paragraph 2 of the telegram to Tito were removed at the suggestion of the Foreign Office. Brigadier Fitzroy Maclean, head of the British Liaison Mission to Marshal Tito, strongly favored British support for the Partisans.

C–677

London [via U.S. Army]
May 18, 1944, 1506 Z / TOR 1615 Z

Prime Minister to President Roosevelt Personal and Top Secret.
   I send you herewith a message which I have sent to Marshal Tito, which I hope you will like. The King hopes to announce his new government on Monday. He has just left me, and seems in very good form. Telegram runs as follows:

This morning, as the result of British advice, King Peter II dismissed Monsieur Purić's administration, which included General Mihailović as Minister of War. He is now about to form a small government under the Ban of Croatia. This course has the strong approval of his Britannic Majesty's Government.

We do not know what will happen in the Serbian part of Yugoslavia. Mihailović certainly holds a powerful position locally as Commander in Chief, and it does not follow that his ceasing to be Minister of War will rob him of his influence. We cannot predict what he will do. There is also a very large body, amounting perhaps to 200,000, of Serbian peasant proprietary who are anti-German but strongly Serbian and who naturally hold the views of a peasants' ownership community, contrary to the Karl Marx theory. My object is that these forces may be made to work with you for a united, independent Yugoslavia which will expel from the soil of Yugoslavia the filthy Hitlerite murderers and invaders till not one remains.

It is of importance to the common cause and to our relations with you that these changes should be given a fair chance to develop in a favourable way to the main object. I should greatly regret it if you were at all in a hurry to denounce them in public. Crucial events impend in Europe. The battle in Italy goes in our favour. General Wilson assures me of his resolve to aid you to the very utmost. I feel therefore that I have a right to ask you to forbear any utterance adverse to this new event, at least for a few weeks till we can have exchanged telegrams upon it.

Brigadier MacLean, who is with me now, will be with you in less than 3 weeks with all the views he has gathered here, and I hope that at the very least you will await his return.

Meanwhile, I congratulate you once more upon the number of enemy divisions which you are holding gripped on your various fronts. You will realize, Marshal Tito, that the war will soon come to a very high pitch of intensity and that British, American and Russian forces will all hurl themselves on the common foe. You must be at your strongest during this climax. While I cannot guarantee a speedy breakdown of the enemy's power, there is certainly a chance of it.

[MR*. R&C.]

King Peter II of Yugoslavia had been in the United States from June 22 through July 29, 1942. He visited the President at the White House on July 24, which is probably when the talk mentioned in paragraph 2 of this cable took place. In an exchange of letters with the King (see *FRUS*, 1944, IV, 1359–61, 1366–68), Roosevelt had responded to a plea for support by advising

Peter to dismiss Mihailović and accept the British proposal for a non-political government under the leadership of Ivan Subasić. The President put off the King's argument that Yugoslavia was "the test case for all of Central Europe" in the fight to escape communism. He resorted to vague truisms accompanied by a reference to America's "less direct interest in Southeastern Europe." As Roosevelt recognized, part of the monarchy's weakness lay in the identification of Peter with Serbian nationalism. Pouritch is apparently an Anglicization of Purić, the recently replaced Yugoslavian Prime Minister.

R–540

Washington [via U.S. Navy]
May 18, 1944, 8:00 P.M.

Personal and Secret. From the President to the Former Naval Person.

I am delighted with your telegram to Marshal Tito and I wish you would tell King Peter that I am heartily in accord. I sent him yesterday a letter in reply to a very nice letter I had from him.

Incidentally, do you remember my telling you over a year ago of my talk with Peter in which I discussed the possibility of three nations in place of the one, he to be the head of a reconstituted Serbia. This created no excitement on his part or that of Pouritch.

The King, with real fire in his eyes, remarked that he was a Serb. I think that you and I should bear some such possibility in mind in case the new government does not work out. Personally I would rather have a Yugoslavia, but three separate states with separate governments in a Balkan confederation might solve many problems. Roosevelt

[MR*. *FDR LTRS*, p. 1509. *R&C*.]

The stimulus for this proposed appeal to the German people came when Stalin, during the Teheran Conference, had suggested issuing precise surrender terms for Germany since the vague demand for "unconditional" surrender tended to support Nazi propaganda that the Allies sought to destroy the entire German nation, thus stiffening German resistance. Discussions on the question began in earnest in American government circles after Eisenhower said that he favored a revision of the unconditional-surrender formula in favor of more specific terms. But the President remained firm in his insistence upon unconditional surrender. Convinced that the German character had to be totally reformed, Roosevelt told the Joint Chiefs of Staff that "the change in German philosophy must be evolutionary and may take two generations. . . . Please note that I am not willing at this time to say that we do not intend to destroy the German nation. As long as the word 'Reich' exists in Germany as expressing a nationhood, it will forever be associated with the present form of nationhood. If we admit that, we must seek to eliminate the very word 'Reich' and all that it stands for today" (*FRUS*, 1944, I, 502). The President's proposed public statement was designed to wean the German people from the Nazis without compromising the complete freedom for the victors implied by unconditional surrender.

R–541

Hyde Park, N.Y. [via U.S. Navy]
May 18, 1944; 3:50 P.M., May 19

Personal and Secret. From the President for the Former Naval Person.

Instead of a tripartite statement to be issued by the U.S., U.K. and Soviet Governments, and in place of a Message to the Congress, what would you think of a statement by me alone along these lines, to be issued after D DAY?

QUOTE. It has been suggested that the Allied Governments join in a general statement to the German people and their sympathizers emphasizing the landings recently made on the Continent of Europe. I have not been in agreement with this because it might over-emphasize the importance of these landings. What I want to impress on the people of Germany and their sympathizers is the inevitability of their defeat. What I want to emphasize to them is their continuation of the war from now on is unintelligent on their part. They must know in their hearts that under their present leadership and under their present objectives it is inevitable that they will be totally defeated.

Every German life that is lost from now on is an unnecessary loss. From a cold-blooded point of view it is true that the Allies will suffer losses as well, but the Allies so greatly outnumber the Germans in population and in resources that on a relative basis the Germans will be far harder hit—down to every family—than the Allies. And in the long run mere stubbornness will never help Germany. The Allies have made it abundantly clear that they do not seek the total destruction of the German people. They do seek total destruction of the philosophy of those Germans who have announced that they could subjugate the world.

The Allies are seeking the long range goal of human freedom—a greater true liberty—political, religious and intellectual; and a greater justice, social and economic.

Our times are teaching us that no group of men can ever be strong enough to dominate the whole world.

The Government and people of the United States—with nearly twice the population of Germany—send word to the people of Germany that this is the time to abandon the teachings of evil.

By far the greater part of the world's population of nearly two billion people feel the same way. Only Germany and Japan stand out against all the rest of humanity.

Every German knows this in his heart. Germany and Japan have made a terrible and disastrous mistake. Germany and Japan must atone reasonably for the wanton destruction of lives and property which they have committed; and they must give up an imposed philosophy the falsity of which by now must be very clear to them.

The more quickly the end of the fighting and the slaughter the more quickly shall we come to a more decent civilization in the whole world.

The attacks which are now being made in the European theatre by the Americans, by the British, by the Russian armies and their associates will, we hope, continue with success, but the German people can well realize that they are only a part of a series of attacks which will increase in number and volume until the inevitable victory is completed. UNQUOTE.

Roosevelt

[MR*. *FRUS*, 1944, I, 513–14.]

Fearing that de Gaulle would refuse to come to England if he were not permitted to leave or send enciphered messages until after D-day (the date of the assault on the Normandy beaches—OVERLORD), Churchill proposed to avoid the problem by not inviting him at all. The Foreign Office advised telling de Gaulle the date for OVERLORD and inviting him to Britain at least two days before the invasion, but the Prime Minister was not willing to do that, particularly since the British Chiefs of Staff suspected that underground organizations in France had been infiltrated by the Germans.

The French Committee for National Liberation had proclaimed itself the provisional government of France, but did not formally adopt that designation until June 2. Pierre Viénot and General Pierre Joseph Koenig represented the French Committee in political and military dealings with the British government and in discussions with General Eisenhower.

A meeting in Lebanon between May 17 and 21, between representatives of the Greek government in exile (Cairo) and delegates from the EAM (National Liberation Front), resulted in an agreement to pursue the fight against Germany under the leadership of the EAM but in the name of the Greek government in Cairo, temporarily headed by the moderate anti-monarchist Georgios Papandreou. But Churchill's optimism was premature, for the EAM leadership in Greece rejected the compromise.

The Allied offensive in Italy began on May 11, and a week later a Polish corps took the German stronghold at Monte Cassino. By May 23 the Germans had begun to fall back in most sectors along the front, though Allied troops did not enter Rome until June 4.

C–678

London [via U.S. Army]
May 19, 1944, 1242 Z

Prime Minister to President Roosevelt Personal and Top Secret.

In your No. 538 you assented to my idea of asking De Gaulle over here. On further reflection I think the following course would be better: Namely, once D-day has started, I will send him a cordial invitation to come and talk things over. There will then be no chance of his making difficulties about going back with any entourage he has brought with him, or sending back individual members, or demanding, as head of a considerable Empire, Free French cypher communication with them. Our ban will be off and anybody can cable or come and go as they please.

In the meantime, I recommend that we allow Koenig or Vienot to send a few messages in their own cypher, subject to their giving us the substance of these messages and giving their word that they do not refer to military affairs other than those specifically affecting French troops. Neither will be informed of D-day or anything military.

There will be plenty of time after De Gaulle arrives here (if he deigns to come) when the show has started, to settle up the French collaboration in their own country. It seems probable to me that for a week, or perhaps a fortnight, it will be a shot-torn, bomb-crumbled battlefield, and I cannot see any question of a civil government arising there. If you agree with me I will hold to this decision. At the same time if you agree, I will telegraph to General Wilson to take the French more into their confidence about the battle in Italy. Considering the fine performance of the two French Corps they deserve to be consulted. There would, I think, be feeling here that we were treating them roughly if we do not act in comradeship with them in this Italian battle.

I do not think we are called upon to notice at all the Algiers declaration that they are the provisional Government of France unless or until the Committee inform us officially. We will of course consult you then. Meanwhile, our action remains regulated by the terms of recognition we, in unison, have already given them. It may be that the Russians will recognize them as what they now call themselves. In this case it is important that we should be together. Personally I do not think the Russians will dare to draw such dangerous lines of demarcation, but I may well be wrong.

Further about the Russians. I have found it practically impossible to continue correspondence with them, but I note that after each very rude message they send to me, they have done pretty well what was asked. For instance, I do not think they have done any great harm to the Poles, and the tide seems to have turned in favor of the Polish Government here making themselves less disagreeable to the Soviets. Again, although Molotov was most insulting about Rumania, they have today told us they accept the broad principle that they take the lead in the Rumanian business and give us the lead in Greece. I am quite content with this. A portent of the Soviet policy is to be found in the gushing message which I have received from the Representatives of EAM gathered, with all other Greek parties, in the Lebanon. I do not think it at all impossible that we may get a united Greece which we can support in accordance with what I know are your heart-felt wishes. Your message, backing up my message, and a little firmness in putting down the mutiny, may prove to have had a salutary effect.

The battle in Italy has been very good and may be still better. We are most grateful to your Chief's of Staff for sending the LST's as desired. This battle is being fought, not so much to join with the bridgehead army or even to take Rome—valuable though that may be—but rather to destroy the German Armies which have been sent by Hitler away from OVER-LORD.

The moment the Italian battle is over and we can see clear on the chess board, every effort will be made to mount the largest and strongest amphibian we can conceive and to direct it upon the point which will best help OVERLORD.

All goes well here, and everything will be hurled in at the appointed hour. Kindest regards.

[MR*]

Roosevelt disliked and distrusted French policies long before Charles de Gaulle became the *soi-disant* leader of the FCNL, though the French General's self-righteous and unyielding attitude intensified that dislike. Any proposal to postpone recognition of a French provisional government—a recognition de Gaulle would push for during any meeting with the President—met with Roosevelt's enthusiastic approval. He was willing to use the FCNL for whatever military benefits might accrue, but only if the committee remained under Eisenhower's jurisdiction. The additions and deletions were made by the President.

R–542

Hyde Park, N.Y. [via U.S. Navy]
May 19, 1944, 6:15 P.M.

Top Secret and Personal. From the President for the Former
Naval Person.

Replying to your 678 it seems to me that your proposed course in handling the De Gaulle visitation after D-day is the most promising solution.

Whether or not Koenig or Vienot should be permitted to send code messages from U.K. to Algiers can be safely left to your discretion.

I have no objection to the Committee's sending agents to France after D-day as Eisenhower now has authority to utilize their services at his discretion for the advantage of our military effort. I also have no objection to the Supreme Commander Mediterranean consulting with the Committee about the battle of Italy.

I have no official information in regard to the self constituted provisional government of France alleged in press reports to have been announced in Algiers. We will have to take a joint interest in that when and if it officially comes to our attention. I hope we and the Soviet can come to a common agreement before action is taken by any one of us. You are familiar with my repeated announcements that in America's opinion the French people in France should have a free choice of their own government and I really cannot go back on my oft repeated statement that ~~this has been their aim for months~~ the Committee and De Gaulle have aimed to be recognized as the provisional government of France without any expression or choice by the people themselves and that I could not recognize it.

Our battle in Italy seems to be progressing favorably and I am hopeful of a major military success in the near future. Best of luck. Roosevelt [WDL]

[MR*]

After thanking Churchill for sending a portrait of himself (see C–668/1), Roosevelt discussed his own health without even hinting at the heart problem diagnosed by doctors. The President stuck faithfully to his regimen and maintained the lower weight, giving him a gaunt look for the rest of his life. The "boat" Roosevelt missed was the Normandy invasion. He had promised Churchill he would come to England around the time of D-day, although firm plans had never been made for that trip. Lord Moran was Churchill's personal physician and Roosevelt had cautioned the Prime Minister to follow the doctor's orders back in December 1943, when Churchill contracted pneumonia. (See R–420.) Now the President changed that warning into an order, for, as he pointed out, in terms of protocol Roosevelt held a higher position since he was both head of state and head of the government, whereas Churchill was head of the government while King George VI was head of state. (In addition to being Prime Minister, Churchill was also Minister of Defence.)

The offensive in Italy, under the command of General Sir Harold ("Alec") Alexander, had developed slowly but successfully, and reports from the front were optimistic.

R–542/1, letter

Hyde Park, N.Y.
May 20, 1944

Dear Winston:—

That picture of you I particularly like. So much so that it too becomes an inhabitant of my bedroom wall. I am awfully glad to have it.

I am safely back in Washington trying to catch up and I am really practically all right again though I am still having some tests made on my plumbing and am keeping regular hours with much allocation to sleep. The old bronchial pneumonia has completely disappeared. The real triumph is that I have lost nearly ten pounds in the last couple of months and now I have begun the struggle to maintain the loss.

I do not believe I can get away for over a month. Of course, I am greatly disappointed that I could not be in England just at this moment, but perhaps having missed the boat it will be best not to make the trip until the events of the near future are more clear.

I got awfully good reports of you from Averell and Winant. Remember what I told old Moran to make you do—obey his orders. Thus the Commander-in-Chief in one country orders around a mere Minister of Defense in another country.

At this writing the news from Italy looks good. I hope old Alec keeps up the good work.

With my affectionate regards, As ever yours,

[PSF:WSC. p*FRUS, Quebec Conf.*, 1944, p. 7n.]

THE BIG THREE POWERS IN IRAN

Iran (which Churchill insisted on calling Persia to distinguish it from Iraq) was one of the few places where the United States found itself in competition with both Soviet and British designs. As Churchill readily admitted in the following letter, Iran's "strategic supplies of oil" were a prize worthy of a struggle. The British had made inroads before World War II, but both the United States and the Soviet Union were trying to use their military presence in Iran, recently expanded to develop the supply route from the Persian Gulf to Russia, as a springboard for increased economic and political influence. Although Roosevelt enthused to Hull about the opportunity Iran presented for demonstrating what unselfish American policy could do, the British and the Iranians believed the primary American concern was oil. American influence in Iran had been enhanced when, at the end of 1942, the government asked the United States to send a special financial mission to assist Iran in managing its economy. Hoping to escape the British and avoid the Russians, the Iranians soon found that the Americans were equally dangerous. By 1944, the head of the mission, Dr. Arthur C. Millspaugh, had become a major force in Iranian politics, in spite of vigorous opposition from nationalist leaders. At the time Churchill wrote the following letter, those nationalists were trying to cut back Millspaugh's plenary economic authority to financial matters only. Through diplomatic channels as well as in talks with Undersecretary of State Stettinius and his party, then in England to discuss a wide range of Anglo-American questions, the British expressed support for the Millspaugh Mission since an economic collapse in Iran would help no one. (See Woodward, *British Foreign Policy*, IV, 417n.) Another step toward greater economic leverage, the President's suggestion for a free port and international control of railroads in Iran, made during the Teheran Conference, came to naught, although the Soviets did sound out the Iranian government on the matter. (See *FRUS*, 1944, V, 455, 483.)

Meanwhile the British also sought to buttress their position in Iran. General Patrick Hurley, after visiting the Middle east on a "fact-finding" mission for the President, had accused the United Kingdom Commercial Corporation (U.K.C.C.) of selling lend-lease goods in Iran as a means of establishing a British trade monopoly—in flagrant violation of Anglo-American agreements. (See R–483/2.)

C–678/1, letter

London
May 21, 1944

My dear Mr. President,

Many thanks for letting me see General Hurley's memorandum on Persia, which I am returning to you herewith as requested. I am sorry to have delayed answering it, but several Departments of State had to be consulted on the points which it raised. The General seems to have some ideas about British imperialism which I confess make me rub my eyes. He makes out, for example, that there is an irrepressible conflict between imperialism and democracy. I make bold, however, to suggest that British imperialism has spread and is spreading democracy more widely than any other system of government since the beginning of time.

As regards Persia, however, I do not think that "British imperialism" enters into the picture. It is true that we, like the United States, are inevitably concerned about our strategic supplies of oil, the more so because, unlike the United States, we have no metropolitan sources. From the same security point of view, we have responsibilities which we cannot at present abandon for the western frontier of India and the eastern frontier of Iraq. Apart from this, we have the same wartime interest as the United States in the safety of the trans-Persian supply route to Russia. For all these reasons we want a strong and friendly Government in Persia, and have no wish to see the establishment of foreign "zones of influence". In short, we are certainly no less interested than the United States in encouraging Persian independence, political efficiency and national reform.

I agree with what you say about Persia's need for outside assistance. Whether she would welcome the principle of international trusteeship seems open to doubt. It sounds rather like the mandatory system. I think that our best way of helping the Persians is through the American advisers. Dr. Millspaugh and his colleagues have undertaken a very necessary but a long, arduous and thankless task. We are giving them, and intend to continue giving them, all the help in our power, as we have since made clear in our discussions with the Stettinius Mission.

I assume that you have had no reply from Stalin to your suggestion for a free port at the head of the Persian Gulf, and for international management of the Persian Railway. On this point we might await Russian reactions. I am by no means certain that after the war, when the Black Sea ports are again open, the trans-Persian route will continue to be necessary for Russian trade, or indeed could be operated under such conditions as would enable it to compete commercially with the Black Sea route.

I quite recognize that the position of the U.K.C.C. and the use of Lend-Lease supplies in Persia, to which Hurley drew your attention, required some looking into. I am glad to be able to say that since the date of your letter to me, the matter has been discussed with your people and a mutually satisfactory arrangement reached. I think they also appreciate that we have no intention whatever of trying to establish a British monopoly through the U.K.C.C. which is under instructions not to interfere with private trade unless absolutely necessary for the purposes of the war.

I return General Hurley's memorandum, of which I have kept a copy.

Yours sincerely, [signed] Winston S. Churchill

[MR]

As Churchill indicated in this and the following cable to the President, the British feared that the Germans might interpret the statement proposed by Roosevelt as a retreat from unconditional surrender—precisely what the President did not mean.

C–679

London
May 22, 1944

Prime Minister to President Roosevelt Personal and Top Secret.

Your number 541. I will bring this matter before the Cabinet today Monday. Personally I think it would be best you should speak for all three of us. I can easily do a follow-up on some of the points later on. But the main principle of the note we should strike towards Germany seems to require considerable thought. Also the time of any such statement should have relation to the success or otherwise of our operation.

[MR*. *FRUS*, 1944, I, 515.]

Prime Ministers John Curtin of Australia and Jan Smuts of South Africa were in England for a Commonwealth meeting, and so they also passed judgment on Roosevelt's appeal to the German people. Churchill was correct in recalling that Roosevelt and Stalin had, at Teheran, held out for harsh treatment of Germany. As Churchill suspected, Stalin also opposed publication of Roosevelt's statement. (See *Stalin/FDR*, doc. 196.) Churchill made corrections to the final paragraph of this message in his cable C–683.

The German reinforcements mentioned by Churchill were almost cut off from retreat when Allied forces broke out from the Anzio beachhead. However, much to the distress of the British, the American commander of the U.S. Fifth Army, General Mark Clark, insisted on heading toward Rome instead of moving to capture the German forces.

C–680

London [via U.S. Army]
May 25, 1944 / TOR 2440 Z [?]

Prime Minister to President Roosevelt Top Secret and Personal.

I brought your No. 541 before the Cabinet yesterday, Curtin and Smuts also being present. Considerable concern was expressed at the tone of friendship shown to the Germans at this moment when the troops are about to engage. There was a feeling that the message, if sent before the battle is won, might be distorted by the enemy into a sort of peace appeal. If there were nothing between us except that the Germans have an evil philosophy, there would be little ground for the war going on. I think myself that the message might conceivably be taken as a peace feeler, and that the Germans might reply that they accepted your note as a basis for further discussion.

In truth there is much more between them and us than a philosophy. Nearly all Europe cries for vengeance against brutal tyranny. At Teheran my suggestion for the isolation of Prussia was considered far too modest by you and U.J. Everybody expects complete forcible disarmament of Germany, possibly extending to civil aviation, to be made and maintained. There are other very grave questions open. For instance, how are the Poles going to be compensated if they do not get East Prussia and certain territories up to the line of the Oder in return for the Curzon Line which the Russians will certainly demand?

I do not know what U.J. will say about your declaration, but we here earnestly hope you will not make it in its present form and, above all, at this present time. There was also a feeling that a document so grave addressed to the enemy, should emanate from the three principal Allies. I may add that nothing of this document would get down to the German pillboxes and front line in time to affect the fighting troops.

The battle is going well in Italy and Alexander has high hopes. Up to the present, so far from trying to bolt to the northwards, Hitler has been bringing down at least three more divisions, one from Istria and two from the north of Rome. Even the Hermann Goering Division which is in Hitler's Special General Reserve may be drawn in. All our Allied troops are fighting magnificently and everywhere the enemy has been pressed back. I think myself tomorrow and the day after may be very important days.

I go every weekend to see the armies preparing here and I have visited some of your finest divisions. Even more striking are all the extraordinary structures and mass of craft already prepared. The weather is a great gamble but otherwise I am full of hope.

All this brings me to my great hope, which is that you will yourself be able to come over. It could not now I suppose be till after D Day as your movement would be taken as heralding it. But if you could start as soon as the signal has been given, the very greatest advantages might be derived from our close talks about all matters including any address to the ~~Commons~~ Germans by you. This _meeting_ is also becoming a practical necessity in respect of the Chiefs of Staff. We have the whole Far Eastern Campaign to discuss and our execution of our promise to help in it to the very utmost of our strength. We need you here so much as the great battle will be of a profound and heart-shaking character, not by any means only in its opening phase. The King will of course send you a formal invitation at any moment that you let me know. There is a very good place in London which would give you perfect safety and comfort. I greatly desire to see you again. It is six months since we met.

[MR*. pFRUS, 1944, I, 517–18. pFRUS, *Quebec Conf.*, 1944, p. 5.]

Treasury Secretary Morgenthau shared the distrust of many New Dealers for bankers and financiers. He opposed the appointment of Robert Brand to represent the British Treasury in the United States because Brand had connections with the British financial community.

C–681

London [via U.S. Army]
May 26, 1944, 0930 Z / TOR 1157 Z

Prime Minister to President Roosevelt Personal and Top Secret.

I am letting you know that we have decided to appoint Robert Brand, who has been head of our Food Mission in Washington and the British Representative on the Combined Food Board, to the post of Treasury Representative in succession to the late Sir Frederick Phillips.

Halifax has explained to Morgenthau our reasons for choosing Brand for this very important appointment, even at the cost of loosing him from his work on the Food Board and Food Mission.

Brand is known to you personally and I think you will agree that we have chosen the right man for a difficult post. Brand got on very well with the Administration on his work for our Ministry of Food and I have no doubt that he will soon be on equally good terms in his new work. I vouch for him.

[MR]

If Roosevelt did read the statements made in the House of Commons by members of the British Cabinet, he must have been wary if not confused. On May 24, Churchill acknowledged the French contributions to the alliance against Hitler, particularly two divisions fighting in Italy, but explained that the Allies had not recognized the French Committee of National Liberation because they were not convinced that the committee represented the "whole body of their people." He went on to promise that the British government would never work with anyone connected with the Vichy French government (Churchill, *Speeches*, VII, 6941). The next day Foreign Secretary Anthony Eden told the House that "Allied armies would deal with the Committee as 'the French authority which will exercize leadership in France as the liberation progresses'" (Woodward, *British Foreign Policy*, III, 47n).

C-682

London
May 26, 1944, 1615 Z / TOR 1725 Z

Prime Minister to President. Personal and Top Secret.

1. You will have seen what has passed about De Gaulle coming here and what I said in Parliament on the subject. There is a very strong feeling here after their recent fighting in Italy in favour of the French. We are going to liberate France at the cost of much British and American blood. The feeling is that she should be with us in this. But who is "She"? When this works out in the person of De Gaulle, all those difficulties which you and I know so well, emerge.

2. I feel, however, that we should be in a difficulty if it were thought that more British and American blood was being spilt because we had not got the French national spirit working with us. There is a strong French movement here and of course they do not know, nor can we tell them, all the faults and follies of De Gaulle. This is only another reason why you and I should consult together in the near future. Of course I shall keep you informed every day about any talks that may occur with De Gaulle. He has lately shown some signs of wishing to work with us and after all it is very difficult to cut the French out of the liberation of France. I should be grateful for a full expression of your views and any other points.

[MR*]

It is not clear whether poor health, American politics (visiting England in an election year could cost votes), or a desire to postpone further arguments about ANVIL and overall strategy lay behind Roosevelt's refusal to have full-fledged staff meetings with the British. Probably a combination of all three is the answer. The President added the final sentence.

R-543

Washington [via U.S. Navy]
May 27, 1944, 1:00 P.M.

Personal and Top Secret. From the President for the Former
Naval Person.

Your 680. In view of your comments on my 541 and the attitude of your Cabinet, I am in agreement with you that a statement along the lines suggested by me is not necessary and I shall therefore not make any statement at that time to the German people.

I am informing U.J. of this decision.

Conditions here will not permit of my visiting the U.K. shortly after D-day, and after consultation with my Joint Chiefs of Staff I do not believe that a full staff meeting at that time is necessary.

Small staff conversations can and will be conducted immediately after the attack is launched.

At a later date after our forces are established on the Continent it does appear necessary to have a full Staff meeting to decide upon our future moves, and I hope and expect that it will then be possible for me to be present.

I join you in a hope that the present magnificent performance of our Forces in Italy will continue and inflict a major disaster upon the enemy. Things look well at this moment. Roosevelt [WDL]

[MR*. p*FRUS, Quebec Conf.*, 1944, pp. 5–6.]

Once again the President emphasized that Allied cooperation with de Gaulle and the FCNL should be limited strictly to military matters. Recognition of the committee was out of the question. Roosevelt made the addition to the final paragraph.

R–544

Washington [via U.S. Navy]
May 27, 1944, 1:30 P.M.

Top Secret and Personal. From the President for the Former Naval Person.

Your 682 received. I am in complete agreement with you that the French National Spirit should be working with us in OVERLORD to prevent unnecessary loss of American and British lives.

You are fully informed in regard to my belief that Allied military power should not be used to impose any particular group as the Government of the French people.

At the present time I am unable to see how an Allied establishment of the Committee as a Government of France would save the lives of any of our men.

Any assistance that the Committee or any other Frenchmen can give to our Army of liberation is of course highly desirable from our point of view as well as to the interest of France.

I am hopeful that your conversations with General De Gaulle will result in inducing him to actually assist in the liberation of France without being

imposed by us on the French people as their Government. <u>Self deter-</u>
<u>mination really means absence of coercion.</u> Roosevelt [WDL]

[MR*. *FRUS*, 1944, III, 692. *R&C*.]

Roosevelt continued to insist that the United States would occupy northwestern Germany after the war. The argument made by British and American
military planners, that a switch of U.S. forces from the southern flank where
they would fight to the northwestern part of Germany would cause enormous
logistical problems, made little impression on the President. As he wrote
Edward Stettinius, then Acting Secretary of State: "Various points have been
raised about the difficulties of transferring our troops, etc., from a French
front to a northern German front—what is called a 'leap-frog'. These objections are specious because no matter where British and American troops are
on the day of Germany's surrender, it is physically easy for them to go anywhere—north, east or south." Roosevelt closed with the warning "that political
considerations in the United States makes [*sic*] my decision conclusive" (memo
from Roosevelt to Stettinius, Feb. 21, 1944, DS 740.00119 Control (Germany/
-2-2144), printed in Kimball, *Swords or Ploughshares?*, pp. 80–81).

The directive quoted in the following message to Churchill was drafted by
General Marshall. The President approved and gave instructions for it to be
sent to General Eisenhower, but, at Marshall's suggestion, the statement was
first cabled to London for the Prime Minister's approval.

R–545

Washington [via U.S. Navy]
May 27, 1944, 1:00 P.M.

Top Secret and Personal. From the President for the Former
Naval Person.

I propose that the Combined Chiefs of Staff be directed by both of us
to send the following message to Eisenhower:

> QUOTE. You are hereby directed to make such plans as are prac-
> ticable to send American troops to the Netherlands and northwest
> Germany as forces of occupation when hostilities with Germany cease.
> For planning purposes, the area in Germany to be occupied by U.S.
> Forces will comprise the states of Schleswig, Hanover, Brunswick,
> Westphalia, Hesse-Nassau and the Rhine Province.
>
> It will be assumed in this plan that France, Austria, and the Balkans
> will not be included in an American zone of responsibility and that
> Berlin will be occupied jointly by the U.S., British and Soviet Forces.
> UNQUOTE.

Roosevelt [GCM]

[MR. *FRUS*, 1944, I, 223. *R&C*.]

C–683

London [via U.S. Army]
May 27, 1944, 1315 Z / TOR 1445 Z

Prime Minister to President Roosevelt. Top Secret and Personal.

I have noticed a bad mistake in paragraph 6 of my telegram number 680. For "address to the commons by you" read "address to the Germans by you". Also insert "meeting" before "is also becoming" in the next sentence.

I am so sorry about this mistake.

[MR*]

Churchill was reluctant to invite de Gaulle to England before the launching of OVERLORD because the Frenchman would insist upon passing the time of D-day to French Resistance forces, and British intelligence believed the Germans had penetrated the Resistance. Yet, if de Gaulle were not given adequate notice he might refuse to broadcast an appeal to the French people to support the invasion. At the same time, Churchill and Roosevelt wanted to avoid doing anything which would enhance de Gaulle's prestige or seem to indicate recognition of him as the legitimate political leader of France. Shortly after Churchill sent this message, press reports reaching London claimed that de Gaulle would refuse to go to England unless the United States sent representatives to discuss, at an official level, Allied plans for postwar France. Although de Gaulle claimed he had expressed only a wish, not a demand, the news stories exacerbated the bad feeling between the Prime Minister and the French leader.

In a radio broadcast on April 9, Secretary of State Hull had stated that the United States was willing to have the FCNL "exercize the leadership to establish law and order" in liberated France, but he went on to indicate that such authority came under the supervision of the Supreme Commander, General Eisenhower. Later in the speech Hull emphasized that the United States would not recognize the French Committee as the government of France. (See Woodward, *British Foreign Policy*, III, 29.)

Churchill had hoped that the bulk of German forces in Italy would be cut off as Allied forces struck out from the Anzio beachhead and joined the main Anglo-American drive from the south. (See the headnote to C–680.)

C–684

London [via U.S. Army]
May 27, 1944, 2043 Z

Prime Minister to President Roosevelt. Top Secret and Personal.

1. I do not propose to invite De Gaulle who is bringing three members

of his Cabinet with him till D day at dawn. I would earnestly ask you to send over someone of the rank of Stettinius to express your point of view. I see the growth of opinion very powerful here and the feeling that France should be with us when we liberate France. Naturally, there is a great wave of sentiment for France on account of the bravery and success of French troops mainly African but well led by French officers, in our Italian battle. There is also the sense that they should share in the work we have in hand. No one will understand their being cold-shouldered. I feel I ought to let you know how things are moving. The word "leadership" in Hull's speech has been very helpful here.

2. The Anzio bridgehead looks like paying a dividend six months later than I hoped, but none the less welcome. Besides we have enticed about ten divisions down into the south of Italy and not all of them will see their homes in Germany again unmauled.

[MR*]

Churchill continued to press for a major conference between Anglo-American leaders, possibly because he wanted to cancel ANVIL and concentrate on liberating all of Italy. Likewise Churchill again repeated his urging that Roosevelt consider the strong political pressures building in England, and the urging of the Foreign Office, to recognize de Gaulle and the FCNL. The left-handed hook Churchill hoped for in Italy was frustrated by the swing of the American Fifth Army toward Rome instead of across the path of the German retreat.

C-685

London
May 28, 1944, 1723 Z

Prime Minister to President Roosevelt Top Secret and Personal.

1. Cabinet and I are most grateful to you for your number 543 about my 680.

2. I still think that a short visit is, above all things, desirable for the Staffs and above all for you, but any time after D + 14 might be convenient to you, and would be received with rejoicing by us. I am delighted at what you say and that you are keeping this in view. Doctor Churchill informs you that a sea voyage in one of your great new battleships would do you no end of good.

3. Your number 544 and the fact that you will not be here at the time, make it all the more necessary that you should send someone who will express your views. I do not think it is impossible that De Gaulle will subscribe to the last two sentences of 544, but of course there ought to

be a responsible United States representative at all the discussions. I will help all I can to act in harmony with our long association on this subject, but the situation and my sentiment are somewhat changed by the substantial fighting of the French troops in these Italian battles.

4. Finally I am hoping that Alexander will turn his battle into left-handed hook so as to get as many as possible.

[MR*. p*FRUS, Quebec Conf.*, 1944, p. 6.]

Roosevelt had reiterated his refusal to become involved in postwar French problems after the Prime Minister protested the proposal that the United States occupy northwestern Germany. (See R–483/1 and R–506/1.)

C–686

London [via U.S. Army]
May 31, 1944, 0708 Z / TOR 0850 Z

Prime Minister to President Roosevelt Personal and Top Secret.

Reference your number 545. As you had not reverted to the question of the zones of occupation by our respective forces since I sent you my number 589 of 23rd February, I had the impression that all this was settled.

It has however occurred to me that in sending your number 545 you might possibly have overlooked the arguments in my number 589 which, in our view, are just as cogent now as they were in February last.

I hope that if there has been a misunderstanding we can clear it up, as a change of policy such as you now propose would have grave consequences.

[MR*. *FRUS*, 1944, I, 224. R&C.]

According to the log sheet, Admiral Leahy wrote the initial draft of this message (presumably the draft printed below) and then the President rewrote the message. If that is true, then Roosevelt took a far more demanding position regarding de Gaulle than did Leahy, even though the latter had long distrusted de Gaulle. Admiral Raymond Fénard, who relayed Roosevelt's comments to de Gaulle, was the Washington representative of the FCNL for naval matters. According to British reports, de Gaulle was surprised by Fénard's visit as well as the message from the President, particularly when the Admiral claimed that Roosevelt sent assurances that he did not dislike de Gaulle personally.

General Marshall, along with Admiral King and General Arnold, planned to arrive in England on June 7, " 'to be on hand in case major decisions by the Combined Chiefs of Staff were necessary.' " Marshall feared that one of two contingencies might arise: first, " 'a very insecure hold on a beachhead' " requiring a decision on whether or not to withdraw; second, a major German counter-attack about a week after D-day (quoted in Brown, *Bodyguard of Lies*, p. 624).

R–546, draft A, not sent

Washington
May 19, 1944

President to Prime:

Your 684 and 685 received.

I will instruct General Marshall who will arrive U.K. about June 8 to express my views at your meeting with De Gaulle in regard to the utilization by General Eisenhower of all services that can be provided by the French Committee.

I am in full agreement with the feeling expressed by you that France should be with us in its liberation. I have no doubt whatever that France will be with us and I hope that General De Gaulle and his Committee will do whatever is within their capacity to expell the invaders from France. We should expect General De Gaulle to be enthusiastic in this effort of ours to aid his countrymen in their distress.

I should like very much to accept Dr. Churchill's advice to make a sea voyage in your direction and I hope to do so at a later date. Conditions here will not permit it shortly after D plus fourteen as suggested by you.

Developments of the OVERLORD campaign should point with some accuracy to the time when a meeting of the Combined Staff is necessary. I prefer to await developments of OVERLORD before making a decision as to the next full staff meeting.

[MR]

R–546

Washington [via U.S. Navy]
May 31, 1944, 7:20 P.M.

Personal and Top Secret from the President for the Former Naval Person.

Your 684 and 685 received.

I do want to make this De Gaulle matter clear from my point of view beyond peradventure of a doubt.

Less than a week ago, on May twenty-fifth, Admiral Fénard said goodbye on his way to see De Gaulle in Algiers. We had a very satisfactory talk and I think he is a first class man in every way, besides being Senior Officer of the French Navy.

He asked me if I had any message for De Gaulle. I told him that I had been hoping for a message from De Gaulle to me asking if I would see him if he came over here and that he could tell De Gaulle that if I received such a message my answer would be an immediate and cordial affirmative.

I explained to him, as I thought I had made the whole matter clear to many people before, that as the head of the Government and the head of the State I could not well invite De Gaulle to come, as the latter is only the head of a Committee and is not the head of the French Government or the French State. Fénard was in complete accord, and that message ought to have been delivered to De Gaulle by now.

I feel very strongly that in his position he, in person and through nobody else, should ask if he will be received. This is simple, straightforward, and the reply would be expressed in cordial terms.

Now as to your 682, in further reply, of course you and I must do everything possible to encourage the French national spirit and to get it working with us at top speed in the immediate future.

We do not know definitely what the state of that French spirit is and we will not know until we get to France, but we hope for the best.

Marshall will be with you about D plus 4. We cannot give him plenary powers to negotiate with De Gaulle singly or with you and De Gaulle jointly, because this is wholly a matter in the political and not in the military field. Marshall can, of course, talk about all military matters.

My suggestion is that after you talk with De Gaulle that he should ask me whether I would see him if he came here direct from London. Meanwhile you could send me a summary of your talks with him and we can be in complete accord by the time he reaches here.

As a matter of practical fact, the French military strength could not be used on OVERLORD until then anyway. All plans are for later than D-DAY.

I think I can only repeat the simple fact that I cannot send anyone to represent me at the De Gaulle conversations with you.

I should like very much to accept Dr. Churchill's advice to make a sea voyage in your direction and I hope to do so at a later date. Conditions here will not permit it shortly after D plus fourteen as suggested by you.

Developments of the OVERLORD campaign should point with some accuracy to the time when a meeting of the Combined Staff is necessary. I think we had best await developments of OVERLORD before making a decision as to the next full Staff meeting. Roosevelt

[MR. *FRUS*, 1944, III, 693–94. p*FRUS, Quebec Conf.*, 1944, pp. 6–7.]

Churchill's real concern about political affairs in the Balkans was masked by disingenuous protestations that he had no intention of carving up the area into spheres of influence. Early in May, the Prime Minister had asked Eden to examine the question of resisting the communization of the Balkans and Italy, and later that month the British had indicated that they expected Soviet support in Greece in return for British acquiescence to Soviet dominance in Roumania. The Soviet Ambassador responded by asking if the United States had been consulted about such an arrangement. Churchill's immediate concern was increased by Russian interest in the conflict in Greece beween the communist EAM and the British-sponsored government in exile.

Roosevelt referred this cable to the State Department for a draft reply, knowing that Secretary Hull was an ardent believer in the Wilsonian creed that spheres of influence were the causes of war, beliefs which Hull soon passed on to Ambassador Halifax when the British representative raised the issue.

C–687

London [via U.S. Army]
May 31, 1944, 1050 Z / TOR 1310 Z

Prime Minister to President Roosevelt Personal and Most Secret.

There have recently been disquietening signs of a possible divergence of policy between ourselves and the Russians in regard to the Balkan countries and in particular towards Greece. We therefore suggested to the Soviet Ambassador here that we should agree between ourselves as a practical matter that the Soviet Government would take the lead in Roumanian affairs, while we would take the lead in Greek affairs, each government giving the other help in the respective countries. Such an arrangement would be a natural development of the existing military situation since Roumania falls within the sphere of the Russian armies and Greece within the Allied command under General Wilson in the Mediterranean.

The Soviet Ambassador here told Eden on May 18th that the Soviet Government agreed with this suggestion but before giving any final assurance in the matter they would like to know whether we had consulted the United States Government and whether the latter had also agreed to this arrangement.

I hope you may feel able to give this proposal your blessing. We do not of course wish to carve up the Balkans into spheres of influence and in agreeing to the arrangement we should make it clear that it applied only to war conditions and did not affect the rights and responsibilities which each of the three great powers will have to exercise at the peace settlement and afterwards in regard to the whole of Europe. The arrangement would of course involve no change in the present collaboration between you and us in the formulation and execution of Allied policy towards these countries. We feel, however, that the arrangement now proposed would be a useful device for preventing any divergence of policy between ourselves and them in the Balkans.

Meanwhile Halifax has been asked to raise this matter with the State Department on the above lines.

[MR*. *FRUS*, 1944, V, 114–15. *WSC*, VI, 73–74. *R&C*.]

After receiving Churchill's letter about Basic English (C–654/1), Roosevelt referred it to Hull. A month later, the Secretary sent a memo to the President which enclosed a draft reply to Churchill as well as the comment that "before we go very far we should take steps to ascertain the views of competent Government specialists and private linguistic experts" (Hull to Roosevelt, May 31, 1944, PSF:WSC). Roosevelt responded that waiting for the views of " 'competent Government specialists' " would "sound the death knell of Basic English." He went on to emphasize that he did not want to "pour ice water" on the scheme and asked Hull to find a "sympathetic" congressional committee which could discuss the question with the British (Roosevelt to Hull, June 5, 1944, ibid.).

R–546/1

Washington
June [?], 1944

My dear Mr. Prime Minister:

Thank you for your letter of April 20, 1944, concerning Basic English. It is a matter in which I am most interested and I have discussed it with Mr. Hull. I have asked him to sound out opinion in the Congress and to take appropriate steps with a view to looking carefully into both the scientific and the practical aspects of the matter.

Incidentally, I wonder what the course of history would have been if in May 1940 you had been able to offer the British people only "blood, work, eye water and face water", which I understand is the best that Basic English can do with five famous words.

Seriously, however, we are interested and will look into the matter thoroughly.

Very sincerely yours,

[PSF:WSC]

R–547

Washington [via U.S. Navy]
June 1, 1944, 12:15 P.M.

Personal and Top Secret. From the President for the Former
Naval Person.

Your 681. I am delighted to know of your appointment of Robert Brand
to the post of Treasury Representative. As you know he is an old friend
of mine. Roosevelt [WDL]

[MR]

American officials estimated that serious deficits of cargo ships would continue
in the Pacific area throughout the summer and fall of 1944, making it impossible to transfer shipping assets for use in supplying wheat to India.

R–548

Washington [via U.S. Navy]
June 1, 1944, 6:45 P.M.

Personal and Top Secret. From the President for the Former
Naval Person.

I refer to your telegram number 665 of April 29, 1944 in which you
set forth the urgent need for additional shipping in order that greater
quantities of wheat than now contemplated may be imported within the
year into India from Australia.

Upon receipt of your telegram I immediately directed that the matter
be taken under urgent consideration by the appropriate authorities of
this Government. The appeal has my utmost sympathy and you may be
sure that there is full realization of the military, political and humanitarian
factors involved. The American Joint Chiefs of Staff have reported, however, that they are unable on military grounds to consent to the diversion
of shipping necessary to meet the request because of the adverse effect
such a diversion would have upon military operations already undertaken
or in prospect.

Needless to say, I regret exceedingly the necessity of giving you this
unfavorable reply. Roosevelt [CH]

[MR. *FRUS*, V, 273.]

The "camouflage" series of radio broadcasts (apparently codenamed TOP-FLITE) was designed to confuse the Germans as to the location of the main Allied attack against German-controlled western Europe. In addition to King Haakon of Norway and Queen Wilhelmina of the Netherlands, Hubert Pierlot, the Belgian Prime Minister, and General de Gaulle were scheduled to make prerecorded broadcasts ostensibly directed at their countrymen but actually aimed at the Germans.

De Gaulle, who arrived in London on June 4, refused to deliver the speech prepared for him by the Psychological Warfare Division of SHAEF (Supreme Headquarters Allied Expeditionary Force—General Eisenhower's command) and eventually made a broadcast which called for the French to obey the instructions of their government (the Allies would not permit him specifically to name the French Committee of National Liberation), hardly mentioning the supervisory authority of SHAEF. Even then, de Gaulle had infuriated Churchill and Roosevelt by procrastinating and arguing just before the launching of the most critical Anglo-American operation of the war.

C–688

London [via U.S. Army]
June 1, 1944, 2045 Z / TOR 2315 Z

Prime Minister to President Roosevelt. Personal and Top Secret.
Your 546.
1. The War Cabinet feel that De Gaulle and some of the principal representatives of the FCNL should be told about OVERLORD before it happens. Otherwise it may become a very great insult to France. The only safe place to inform them is here. The following programme will, I think, meet all security obligations. I have invited him to come as soon as he will. I have not yet had an answer from him, but I have offered to send my own York airplane to fetch him. This would reach him on D minus 3 and he could be here by D minus 1. He will then be taken to Eisenhower's Headquarters and told what is necessary and brought into the show. Eisenhower agrees with this plan.
2. Eisenhower thinks it important that De Gaulle should broadcast to France in the camouflage series. Eisenhower's proclamation would be followed by King Haakon then Queen Wilhelmina and now De Gaulle. To leave a broadcast from France out of the series would be to destroy the confusing effect we wish to establish by leaving one gap. I have very little doubt De Gaulle can be persuaded to say the right thing. Thereafter on D plus 3 or 4 we will have discussions with him and his people in London, and I must explain to him that there will be no French territory

worth speaking of for a good many days, only the bombed and shell-torn beaches. I will do the best I can with him during the week D 2 to 8 or 9. I will tell him what you say, namely, that if he sent you a message asking if you would see him, you would answer an immediate and cordial affirmative. Meanwhile, I shall have explored the ground as far as possible with him beforehand. If he comes, he comes. If he won't, he won't, and that is the moment when we may be able to take a further decision.

3. I am delighted to hear that Marshall will be with us about D plus 4 and I will certainly bring him in to discussions with De Gaulle with me on the military field alone or, as you say, he can have them singly on the military field alone. I will report to you the upshot.

4. Besides the Eisenhower-Wilhelmina series of broadcasts to the Continent on D day, the King proposes to broadcast to his people at 9:00 P.M. that day and I presume you will be doing the same to yours. It seems to me that this can all be fitted in to a programme on D day. Would you let me have your wishes.

5. I am indeed sorry to hear the long time that must elapse before we meet on your programme. When the immediate situation in OVERLORD clarifies I would make an effort to meet you at Quebec or Bermuda. The former seems easier if this were agreeable to you. It would probably be better for me not to come in to the United States as you approach the election crisis or our enemies might try to make mischief.

[MR*. p*FRUS, Quebec Conf.*, 1944, p. 7.]

Churchill appreciated Roosevelt's willingness to accept Robert Brand as the representative of the British Treasury despite Morgenthau's opposition.

C–689

London [via U.S. Army]
June 1, 1944, 2350 Z / TOR 0120 Z, June 2

Prime Minister to President Roosevelt. Personal and Secret.
Your 547. Thank you so much. I vouch for him.

[MR*]

King George VI delivered this speech, with only minor changes, over the radio at nine o'clock on the evening of D-day.

C–690

London [via U.S. Army]
June 2, 1944, 0806 Z

Prime Minister to President Roosevelt Personal and Top Secret.

Reference my telegram No. 688, Paragraph 4. It may be convenient to you to know what the King proposes to say. Following for your most private information is text of his draft speech. Begin:

"At this time four years ago our nation and empire stood alone against an overwhelming and implacable enemy, with our backs to the wall. Tested as never before in our history, in God's providence we survived the test; the spirit of the people, resolute, dedicated, burned like a bright flame, lit surely from those unseen fires which nothing can quench.

Now once more a supreme test has to be faced. This time the challenge is not to fight to survive but to win the final victory for the good cause. Once again what is required from us all is something more than courage and endurance; we need a revival of spirit, a new unconquerable resolve. After nearly five years of toil and suffering, we must renew that crusading impulse on which we entered the war and met its darkest hour. We and our Allies are sure that our fight is against evil and for a world in which goodness and honour may be increasingly the foundation of the life of men in every land.

That we may be worthily matched with this new summons of destiny, I desire solemnly to call my people to prayer and dedication. We are not unmindful of our own shortcomings, past and present. We shall ask not that God may do our will, but that we may be enabled to do the will of God; and we dare to believe that God has used our nation and empire as an instrument for filfilling His high purpose.

I hope that throughout the present crisis of the liberation of Europe there may be offered up earnest, continuous and widespread prayer. We who remain in this land can most effectively enter into the sufferings of subjugated Europe by prayer, whereby we can fortify the determination of our sailors, soldiers, and airmen who go forth to set the captives free.

The Queen joins with me in sending you this message. She well understands the anxieties and cares of our womenfolk at this time, and she knows that many of them will find, as she does herself, fresh strength and solace in such waiting upon God. She feels that many women will be glad in this way to keep vigil with their menfolk as they man the ships, storm the beaches, and fill the skies.

At this historic moment none surely are too busy, none too young, none too old to play their part in a nation-wide, perchance a world-wide, vigil of prayer as the great crusade sets forth. If from every place of worship, from home and factory, from men and women of all ages and many races and occupations, our intercessions rise, then, please God, both now and a future not remote the predictions of an ancient psalm may be fulfilled: "The Lord will give strength unto His people: The Lord will give His people the blessing of Peace."

[MR*]

Convoys to northern Russia had been suspended because OVERLORD required all available shipping, but now Churchill sought to renew the shipments, particularly since the Soviet offensive was so important to the success of OVERLORD. Oliver Lyttelton and Lord Frederick Leathers held the posts of Minister of Production and Minister of War Transport respectively.

C–691

London [via U.S. Army]
June 2, 1944; 0830 Z, June 3 / TOR 1015 Z, June 3

Prime Minister to President Roosevelt Personal and Top Secret.

I am anxious to reopen the northern convoys to Russia after OVERLORD is well launched. We think we shall be able to find the escorts and so I have told Lyttelton and Leathers to get into touch with your people and see what can be done. We have sent pretty nearly all that we have to send but it would be very important to keep the Russian armies well supplied during the increasing severity of this year's campaign. I cannot make a fixed arrangement as to date until after the battle has revealed our casualties but I am hoping that it might be possible to do something at the end of July.

Will you let me know if this commands your sympathy and support.

[MR*]

This restatement of the President's earlier refusal to accept the southern occupation zone in Germany was, according to the log sheet, written by Roosevelt himself. Even though his advisers were willing to accept the southern zone, the President apparently believed that an American presence there would involve the United States in the postwar political affairs of Austria, the

Balkans, and possibly even Italy. Worst of all, it would place the Americans adjacent to France—a nation in which, Roosevelt was convinced, political chaos would follow the war. Although the President referred to the domestic American opposition to any long-term involvement in Europe, associates such as Secretary of War Stimson and General Marshall understood that Roosevelt's main objection to the southern zone was the fear that it would force the United States to "police" France. Although Churchill chose not to answer this cable, the question of occupation zones was discussed frequently during the meetings of the European Advisory Commission being held in London. It was finally settled during the Quebec Conference in September 1944, discussed below. (See *FRUS*, 1944, I, 233–341 for the European Advisory Committee discussions.)

The political problems to which the President referred included a congressional override of his veto of a tax bill (Roosevelt labeled the legislation "a tax relief bill providing relief not for the needy but for the greedy") and a fight with Congress on the question of making it easier for military personnel to cast absentee ballots.

R–549

Washington [via U.S. Navy]
June 2, 1944, 6:20 P.M.

Top Secret and Personal. From the President for the Former
Naval Person.

Referring back to your message of February twenty-third, No. 589, and in reply to your 686, my telegram No. 457 of February seventh on this subject contained the following statements: "I am absolutely unwilling to police France and possibly Italy and the Balkans as well".

I am worried lest you also did not receive my letter to you of February twenty-ninth [R–483/1] and I was really waiting to hear from you in response to that letter of mine.

I am worried because I fear you did not get it and that that was the reason for your silence until the other day.

A good part of the letter does not refer to the subject but I am now quoting it to you in full lest it did not reach you [not printed: see R–483/1].

As a result of this exchange back in February and March, I believed until recently that at least tentative plans would be made for occupation of northwestern Germany by American forces.

I am just as strongly for this point of view as I was before, and your special problems can be perfectly easily handled on the naval side even if American forces are in northwest Germany.

In view of my clearly stated inability to police the south and southwestern areas now occupied by the Germans, I really think it is necessary that General Eisenhower shall even now make such plans as are practical to use American forces of occupation in northwestern Europe during the occupation period. Such plans as it is practicable for Eisenhower to prepare in advance would help to meet the contingency of your not being able to provide forces of occupation in all of the surrendered and liberated areas not occupied by the Soviets and of my inability to police the southern areas—France, Italy, etc.

There is ample time for this unless Germany suddenly collapses because, as you and I know, the present timetable proves this point.

Under my plan all of your needs can and will be taken care of in the northwest area, but I hope you will realize that I am in such a position that I cannot go along with the British General Staff plan. The reasons are political, as you well know, though, as a result, they enter necessarily into the military.

Over here new political situations crop up every day but so far, by constant attention, I am keeping my head above water. Roosevelt

[MR. *FRUS*, 1944, I, 232. p*R&C*.]

Tidal conditions would not permit a landing on the Normandy beaches from June 7 through mid-June, a delay which would be hard on the morale of troops already primed for the attack. Moreover, it would give the Germans time to launch the pilotless aircraft the Allies knew were being readied and might compromise various cover-and-deception plans designed to confuse the Germans as to the actual point of the main invasion. Understandably then, Eisenhower was very concerned about the bad weather flowing over southern England and across the channel. High winds and bad visibility forced the Supreme Commander to postpone the invasion scheduled for the morning of June 5, but meteorologists predicted the skies would clear and the winds abate on the morning of June 6 and thereafter for about thirty-six hours; so Eisenhower gave the go-ahead signal from his headquarters just outside Plymouth, England.

On May 24, Churchill made a conciliatory speech in the House of Commons regarding Spanish foreign policy during the war. He argued that Spain had "made amends" for its earlier support of Germany and went on to criticize those who constantly attacked and ridiculed Generalissimo Franco and the Spanish government (Churchill, *Speeches*, VII, 6935).

Harry Hopkins' health had improved enough for him to move from the Mayo Clinic in Rochester, Minnesota, to Ashford General Hospital, run by the U.S. Army, in White Sulphur Springs, West Virgina. On July 4, 1944, Hopkins returned to Washington and slowly reinvolved himself in government work. His health remained frail, and that, combined with his long absence during the crucial period since December 1943, prevented Hopkins from ever regaining his position as Roosevelt's closest adviser. By the summer of 1944, his role had been assumed by a number of other advisers, such as Admiral Leahy, rather than a single person as before.

"Alex" referred to the Allied commander in Italy, Sir Harold Alexander. The outcome of de Gaulle's trip to London is discussed in the headnote to C–688.

C–692

London [via U.S. Army]
June 4, 1944, 0830 Z / TOR 1150 Z

Prime Minister to President Roosevelt Personal and Top Secret.

I was so glad to get your charming letter of May 20th [R–542/1]. Our friendship is my greatest stand-by amid the ever-increasing complications of this exacting war. Averell [Harriman] brought me a good account of your physical health, and I have sustained from many quarters impressions that your political health is also greatly improved.

2. I am here near Ike's Headquarters in my train. His main pre-occupation is the weather. There are wonderful sights to see with all these thousands of vessels.

3. De Gaulle's Committee by a large majority decided that he should accept my invitation to come here. He hemmed and hawed, but Massigli and several others threatened to resign if he did not do so. We expect him on D minus one. If he arrives, Eisenhower will see him for half an hour and explain to him the position exclusively in its military aspect. I shall return to London during the night of D day.

4. We will then take on De Gaulle. I do not expect that very much can be done, but I still hope the word "Leadership", which I am told you approved in Hull's speech, may prove serviceable. I do not expect we shall get more than a certain number of miles from the beaches, and probably what we get will be a depopulated area wearing the aspect of a battlefield. This I can explain to De Gaulle safely here when he arrives. I will also deliver him your friendly message to come over to see you. I shall keep you constantly informed.

5. I see some of your newspapers are upset at my references in the House of Commons to Spain. This is very unfair, as all I have done is to repeat my declaration of October 1940. I only mention Franco's name to show how silly it was to identify Spain with him or him with Spain by means of caricatures. I do not care about Franco but I do not wish to have the Iberian Peninsula hostile to the British after the war. I do not know how I can depend on a De Gaullist France. Germany will have to be held down by main force, and we have a 20 years alliance with Russia. You must remember that we are very near to all this present outlook.

6. We should not be able to agree here in attacking countries which have not molested us because we dislike their totalitarian form of government. I do not know whether there is more freedom in Stalin's Russia

than in Franco's Spain. I have no intention to seek a quarrel with either.

7. After D day, ought not you and I to send a short message to Stalin, which can be published? Perhaps it would be well to wait till we are definitely established over the other side.

8. We have the all-time high record for the U-boat war—only 4 ships of all the United Nations, amounting to about 20,000 tons, sunk. In addition we have 4 U boats sunk for every ship and a tremendous plurality of enemy ships sunk by our own Combined Fleets.

9. I am so glad Alex has not belied your support and impressions of him. How magnificently your troops have fought. I hear that relations are admirable between our armies in every rank there, and here certainly it is an absolute brotherhood. I am looking forward to seeing your Chiefs of Staff.

10. I have been delighted to receive increasingly good news about Harry. I earnestly hope that this will be maintained. I am deeply grieved that you cannot come before that very distant date. Let me know if I can help matters by a journey.

[MR*. *WSC*, V, 626–28. p*FRUS, Quebec Conf.*, 1944, p. 7.]

Believing that the bulk of German first-line forces in Italy might be cut off by advancing Allied armies, Churchill thought it appropriate to consider immediately moves which would support the OVERLORD invasion scheduled for either June 5 or 6. Churchill was extraordinarily tense on the eve of the Normandy landings, and his concern reflected itself in this hasty proposal. The British Chiefs of Staff preferred an attack in southern France to Churchill's old idea of an attack against the ports of western France (Operation CALIPH). They also suggested holding off on such a cable until the Allied commander in Italy, General Alexander, proposed a strategy following the capture of Rome. Presaging what would later become a serious disagreement between Churchill and Roosevelt, the British military emphasized "the *threat* of ANVIL" as sufficient to force the Germans to maintain forces in the south of France. Churchill readily agreed with their arguments and decided not to send this cable. (Memo by CoS, 7 June 1944, PREM 3/271/8/697–98.)

C–692/1, not sent

London
June 5, 1944

Prime Minister to President.

1. Tonight our joint Forces have entered Rome. If it should prove that the bulk of the German Army south of Rome is mauled, cut-off, stripped of its heavy weapons, it may well be that we can afford in a few weeks to

begin to move troops from Italy either to prepare to deliver some form of ANVIL or far better to come round and strike at the Biscay Ports. The reason why it is better to strike between Bordeaux and St. Nazaire rather than on the Riviera is that the first course will be in intimate relation with the main battle and that it is possible not only to gain new Ports for direct Transatlantic debarkation; but to join hands with Eisenhower when he has landed and deployed. The distances are so much less. In fact it may be said that an action 500 miles distant will not influence the main battle till that main battle is decided.

2. I advise therefore that if we have good success in Rome and in the round-up of the German armies south of it, which is quite possible, we should consider immediately planning the descent upon a Biscay Port or ports of the largest Forces we can get together. This was foreshadowed in my telegram about Operation CALIPH [C–668]. There might easily be 4 or 5 French Divisions, 2 or 3 Divisions from across the Atlantic for which no berthing accommodation can be found in the British Isles, and 5 or six Divisions from Italy—possible total about 12 or 14 Divisions. This army coming in at the end of July or in August will make a decisive effect on Eisenhower's operation, provided the delivery of Divisions from the United States as already planned will be in no wise diminished. Once Eisenhower has got well established ashore, air refueling bases can be arranged which will give us the power to use shore-based aircraft to cover the new landings southward in the Biscay region. Besides this, we have seaborne Air quite sufficient to encounter the German Air which will have survived the prolonged battle in the OVERLORD area. If successful, we gain great new Ports for Transatlantic deliveries and our troops advance into a country ardent for our cause and suitable in terrain for our large superiority in armour.

3. Should the operations in Italy turn out as we hope and those in OVERLORD be successfully launched and maintained, I am of opinion that this shaping of our policy demands earnest and urgent consideration.

[PREM 3/271/8/699–701]

D-day became a proper noun in the English language with the Allied invasion of France on June 6, 1944. At dawn, six Allied divisions—three American, two British, and one Canadian—landed on the north side of the Normandy peninsula, due south across the English Channel from Plymouth and well below the Strait of Dover (Pas de Calais), where the Germans expected them. Plans called for 200,000 men to go ashore within the first forty-eight hours, with another 440,000 to land within eleven days. It was history's most massive amphibious invasion; carried by over 5,000 vessels of every conceivable type, preceded by British and American airborne forces landed inland a few hours earlier, and supported by a naval bombardment and by 11,000 aircraft sorties that dropped 12,000 tons of bombs. The invasion spelled the end of German domination of western Europe and the return of Anglo-American power and influence to the Continent.

Air and naval superiority, effective planning, and a successful cover and deception plan (JAEL) spelled victory for the Allies, although a combination of poor intelligence (a German division had moved undetected into the area), unfavorable terrain, and tricky wind and current conditions resulted in near disaster at one American landing area, OMAHA beach. Within twenty-four hours the beachheads were safely established. The Germans, their attention firmly focused on the Pas de Calais, never launched the all-out counterattack that Eisenhower feared might split Allied forces and drive them back into the sea.

Yet, Churchill and Roosevelt, seized by both fear and exhilaration at this crucial moment, exchanged no important comments, no unforgettable rhetoric, no cheers of joy. Perhaps each was reluctant to celebrate prematurely lest the invasion turn out to be a flop. Probably they had little or no idea of what was happening at Normandy—certainly Eisenhower at Allied headquarters in England was in the dark. Or perhaps they sensed that June 6, 1944, was a day that belonged to the soldiers, sailors, and airmen—but especially the soldiers—who were there on the beaches. Whatever the reason, the long-awaited cross-channel attack, the major Anglo-American operation of the war, passed almost unremarked in the Churchill-Roosevelt correspondence.

EVEN while the massive invasion of Normandy was underway, the routine business of the war—such as drafting the monthly anti-submarine warfare statement—continued.

C–693

London [via U.S. Army]
June 6, 1944, 1215 Z / TOR 1430 Z

Prime Minister to President. Personal and Top Secret.

Following is text of proposed anti U-boat statement for May. I am also sending it to Mr. MacKenzie King. Begins:

During May our shipping losses have been by far the lowest for any month of the war, and they have in fact been a fraction of the losses inflicted on enemy shipping by our warships and aircraft, although their merchant shipping is petty compared to that of the Allies.

There has been a lull in the operations of the U-boats which perhaps indicates preparations for a renewed offensive. The change which has come over the scene is illustrated by the fact that in spite

of the few U-boats at sea, several are now sent to the bottom for each
merchant ship sunk whereas formerly each U-boat accounted for a
considerable number of merchant ships before being destroyed.

This is to be ascribed to the vigilance and to the relentless attacks
of our Anglo-American-Canadian and other anti-U-boat forces, including the scientists who support them in a brilliant manner.

[MR*]

R–550

Washington [via U.S. Navy]
June 6, 1944, 11:15 A.M.

Top Secret and Personal. From the President for the Former
Naval Person.

Your 691. I am in full agreement with you as to the high desirability
of reopening the northern convoys to Russia at the earliest practicable
date after the results of OVERLORD are known to us.

We should give to the Soviet attack on Germany all the support and
assistance that we can provide. Roosevelt [WDL]

[MR. *R&C.*]

Admiral Fénard, the FCNL's naval representative to the United States, returned to Washington from Algiers with a message that de Gaulle would like
to visit the President. The first draft of cable R–551, prepared by the Map
Room staff, contained the following sentence: "I feel it unnecessary for you
to come to this side now, but that is a decision which can be quickly and
readily made if circumstances require." Although the President did not include that phrase when he redrafted the cable, it presumably reflected his
feelings as expressed orally to his aides.

R–551

Washington [via U.S. Navy]
June 6, 1944, 4:00 P.M.

Top Secret and Personal. From the President for the Former
Naval Person.

Thank you very much for your 688, 690, and 692.

In view of today's stupendous events the subjects already seem like
ancient history. I have sent word to De Gaulle that in view of his expression
of hope that I will see him over here, I shall be very glad to do so if he
will come to Washington between June 22 and 30 or else between July 6

and 14. Fénard has gone to London this morning with the above.

I agree that you and I should send a joint message to Stalin in the near future—preferably when his plans and ours are in full swing. How I wish I could be with you to see our war machine in operation! Roosevelt [FDR]

[MR]

Roosevelt spent the weekend before the Normandy invasion (June 3–4) at the Charlottesville, Virgina, home of his military aide, General Edwin "Pa" Watson. This message was written there on June 4 but not sent until two days later. The generals mentioned in the first paragraph were Sir Harold Alexander, the Allied commander in Italy; Mark Clark, commander of the U.S. Fifth Army which had occupied Rome; Sir Oliver Leese, commander of the British Eighth Army; and Field Marshal Sir H. M. "Jumbo" Wilson, the Supreme Commander of Allied forces in the Mediterranean.

Admiral Fénard's missions are discussed in the headnotes to R–546 A and R–551.

The Randolph mentioned in the final paragraph was Major Randolph Churchill, who had been in Yugoslavia as the personal representative of his father to the Partisan leader, Tito. On May 25, Tito narrowly missed being killed or captured when the Germans made a parachute attack on his headquarters at Drvar. Tito and his staff escaped and were evacuated, first by a British seaplane and then by a British destroyer, to the island of Vis on the Adriatic coast of Yugoslavia. Randolph Churchill stayed behind assisting arrangements for further evacuation flights and left for Bari, Italy, on one of the last of those flights.

R–552

Charlottesville, Va. [via U.S. Navy]
June 4, 1944; 5:10 P.M., June 6

From the President for the Former Naval Person.

1. I have your No. 692 at Charlottesville where I am spending the weekend with General Watson. We have just heard of the fall of Rome and I am about to drink a mint julep to your very good health. I have sent telegrams to Alex and Clark and Leese and Jumbo. The whole operation was a magnificent example of perfect teamwork.

2. Marshall and the others will be able to talk with you in regard to next moves. I will see them on Tuesday.

3. All good luck in your talks with prima donna. Admiral Fénard is just back in Washington from De Gaulle with a very important message to me. I will see the Admiral on my return to Washington Monday afternoon. I will let you know at once.

4. In your paragraph 4, please for the love of Heaven do not tell De Gaulle that I am sending him a "friendly message to come over to see me." The whole point of it is that I decline absolutely as head of the state to invite him to come over here. My message via Admiral Fénard was that if he asked me if I would see him if he came over I told Fénard that I would reply in the affirmative most cordially. The distinction is a very important one.

5. Don't worry about chit-chat over here in regard to Franco. It is an old controversy and soon I hope that he will not be able to worry us much one way or the other.

6. Harry is really better and I think will be back in Washington within the next two weeks and he will be able to resume a part of his work.

7. It is great news that Randolph got out of the cave safely. I note that he is now a major and that makes me very happy.

[MR. PREM 3/121/2.]

R–553

Washington [via U.S. Navy]
June 6, 1944, 6:35 P.M.

From the President for the Former Naval Person.

We think your submarine statement excellent and plan to release it exactly as received.

It was indeed a grand month. Roosevelt

[MR]

After returning from a visit with British military officials in England, General Joseph T. McNarney had written to thank the Prime Minister for his hospitality. Churchill indicated that he would like two typewriters which had the typeface used in McNarney's letter (a modified "square serif") and after General Marshall so informed the President, Roosevelt sent this letter along with two new typewriters. Fortunately, the "strong bond between the people of America and Great Britain" was symbolized by more than just two typewriters.

R–553/1, letter

Washington [via courier]
June 6, 1944

My dear Winston:

I am informed that you liked the type script of a letter recently sent you by General McNarney, U.S. Army Deputy Chief of Staff. Two electric typewriters that produce this type script are being shipped without delay which I hope you will accept as a gift from me and as a symbol of the strong bond between the people of America and Great Britain.

With warm regards and best wishes, Very sincerely yours,

[OF 7683]

Sir William Brown, Permanent Secretary of the Ministry of Home Security and previously with various British agencies which dealt with the petroleum industry, headed the British delegation at the preliminary oil conference in Washington in late April–early May 1944. With a presidential election coming up in the fall, Churchill did not want to let American politics force Britain into more formal conversations, but the Foreign Office argued that delaying tactics would arouse resentment, particularly since two major American government figures—Secretary of State Hull and Secretary of the Interior Ickes—were pushing for a conference.

R–554

Washington [via U.S. Navy]
June 7, 1944, 4:40 P.M.

From the President for the Former Naval Person.

I am sorry to learn that Sir William Brown and staff departure has been delayed. I personally hope much that they can come as quickly as possible, as the situation is becoming embarrassing. Roosevelt [FDR]

[MR. *FRUS*, 1944, III, 117.]

DE GAULLE VERSUS THE ALLIES

De Gaulle suspected that the Allies, particularly the Americans, planned a military occupation of France along the lines of what had developed in Italy. Accordingly, he demanded formal recognition of the French Committee of National Liberation, which had proclaimed itself the provisional government of France. Although most of the British War Cabinet and General Eisenhower were willing to accept the FCNL, Roosevelt and his closest advisers, supported by Churchill, adamantly refused. Before coming to England, de Gaulle had insisted that an accredited representative of the United States government be present to discuss civil affairs in liberated France, but the President refused, insisting that only military matters were relevant and that Eisenhower was in full command of such affairs. Churchill, only slightly more willing to deal with the FCNL, had asked de Gaulle to bring with him the French Commissioner for Foreign Affairs, René Massigli; the Commissioner to the Liberated Territory, André Le Troquer; and the Commissioner of the Interior, Emmanuel R. d'Astier; but de Gaulle refused. (Pierre Viénot was the diplomatic representative of the FCNL to the British government.)

Churchill was correct in pointing out that no French military forces participated in the assault on Normandy, but de Gaulle had previously established the French Forces of the Interior, which included all Resistance troops, and the work of the Resistance was an integral part of SHAEF's OVERLORD plan. And a French division commanded by General Jacques Philippe Leclerc came ashore at Normandy in late July as part of General George Patton's Third Army.

De Gaulle finally gave his speech to the French people on the evening of June 6. Although he failed to heed the Allied request to emphasize SHAEF authority, he did express gratitude to the British for their efforts on behalf of the liberation of France. Upon hearing that, Churchill, who was sitting with a group of British officials listening to the speech, began to cry and, noticing General "Pug" Ismay staring at him, snorted, "You great tub of lard! Have you no sentiment?" (This anecdote is repeated by the courtesy of Forrest Pogue, historian of SHAEF and biographer of George C. Marshall. General Ismay told Dr. Pogue this story, among many others, in an interview in London in November 1946.)

The currency question, mentioned in paragraph 4 of Churchill's cable, was again a problem of Allied versus French provisional government (FCNL) authority. The Allies asked de Gaulle to endorse the occupation francs to be issued by SHAEF, but the French General refused, insisting that only his government had monetary powers.

Churchill continued to hope that the other members of the FCNL would prove more cooperative than de Gaulle. Eisenhower, on the other hand, was more realistic about the hold de Gaulle had over his associates. In a letter written a month and a half earlier to General Marshall, he commented that only two groups remained in France: "one is the Vichy gang, and the other [is] characterized by unreasoning admiration for De Gaulle." In the original draft Eisenhower had put it even more strongly, asserting that the second group "seems almost idolatrous in its worship of De Gaulle" (*Eisenhower Papers*, III, 1867–68).

Churchill's expression of faith in an Anglo-American rather than an Anglo-French entente was made in far more colorful language than the Prime Minister used in this cable. Even de Gaulle recalled the phrases, though he surmised that Churchill's passion was aimed primarily at the ears of his British associates: "each time we must choose between Europe and the open sea, we shall always choose the open sea. Each time I must choose between you and Roosevelt, I shall always choose Roosevelt" (de Gaulle, *Unity*, p. 153).

Someone on the American side underlined the final three words of Churchill's message: "all the luck." Even if the line was not drawn by the President, that phrase was the sort of sarcasm which appealed to his sense of humor and fit his annoyance with de Gaulle.

C-694

London [via U.S. Army]
June 7, 1944, 2354 Z / TOR 0210 Z, June 8

Prime Minister to President. Personal and Top Secret.

1. You will have seen from Eisenhower's No. SH. 2511 [apparently the cable from Eisenhower to the CCS, June 4, 1944, *Eisenhower Papers*, III, 1906–7] part of General De Gaulle's activities over here. He has arrived without the three commissioners, Massigli, Le Troquer, and d'Astier, whom we understood he was going to bring. This is to make clear his position that he will not discuss the civil administration of France only with us, and that an American representative fully charged must be present.

2. You have probably been informed of his attitude in refusing to allow the French liaison officers to go with our forces into France until the civil administration question has been settled. Under severe pressure from the Foreign Secretary he consented at last to broadcast, though not in Eisenhower's series. You will no doubt read the broadcast for yourself. It is remarkable, as he has not a single soldier in the great battle now developing. Further, he has also modified his attitude about the liaison officers and will allow some of them to go. It is probable that all would go in any case, whatever he said if called upon by General Eisenhower and their British and American comrades.

3. I can assure you that every courtesy and personal attention was lavished upon General De Gaulle. After a full discussion with his two generals and Monsieur Viénot, his representative here, we have had luncheon in my train, and the Foreign Secretary and I then took him personally to see General Eisenhower at his headquarters in a woodland camp. Generals Eisenhower and Bedell Smith went to the utmost limit in their endeavour to conciliate him, making it clear that in practice events would probably mean that the Committee would be the natural authority with whom the Supreme Commander would deal. It was after this that he proceeded to London and acted in the sense of my Paras 1 and 2.

4. We are still persevering. We have told De Gaulle that if he sends for three or four of his commissioners, we will then begin conversations designed to clarify and smooth the difficulties about the civil administration in France. Meanwhile, I have assured General Eisenhower that we will certainly support him in making the necessary proclamation about currency.

5. It is not impossible that the commissioners will differ from De Gaulle and may show themselves disposed to make friendly arrangements with the American and British Governments. There might even be a sort of isolation of De Gaulle.

6. If he refuses to send for the commissioners, we shall suggest he had better go back to Algiers. If he accepts, I hope you will consider whether Winant might not sit in in order to give you an American slant on the talks. After this we will let you know what our view is. I have repeatedly told De Gaulle and he acknowledged it without irritation that failing an agreement, I stand with you.

7. Supposing all this fails, we shall express the hope that he will return to Algiers and then later proceed to Washington as the result of your message sent through Admiral Fenard or if he cares he can stay here and proceed by the dates named. I think it would be a great pity if you and he did not meet. I do not see why I have all the luck.

[MR*. R&C.]

Churchill had reported to Stalin that OVERLORD "has started well." Stalin's reply, quoted below by the British Prime Minister, was also sent to Roosevelt with the introductory statement that "I feel it necessary to let you know that, on June 6, in reply to a message from Mr. Churchill I sent the following personal message about the plan for a Soviet summer offensive" (*Stalin/WSC*, doc. 273; *Stalin/FDR*, doc. 201).

C–695

London [via U.S. Army]
June 9, 1944, 0946 Z / TOR 1100 Z

Prime Minister to President Roosevelt Personal and Top Secret.
I have received the following from Uncle J. It looks good.

"I have received your communication about the success of the beginning of the OVERLORD operations. It gives joy to us all and hope of further successes.

The summer offensive of the Soviet Forces, organized in accordance with the agreement at the Tehran Conference, will begin towards the middle of June on one of the important sectors of the front. The general offensive of the Soviet Forces will develop by stages by means of the successive bringing of armies into offensive operations. At the end of June and during July offensive operations will become a general offensive of the Soviet Forces.

I shall not fail to inform you in due course of the progress of the offensive operations."

[MR*]

Given the long delay before the second front in Western Europe, Roosevelt's complaint that the promised Soviet offensive would be held off a few weeks has a certain irony. The final phrase, added in the President's writing, may only be vague optimism—or it may betray his concern that Soviet armies would have a chance to occupy more of Europe than he thought was safe. America had entered two world wars, at least in part, to prevent Europe from being dominated by a single nation. The Normandy invasion, important as it was, may not have been the single most important military effort of the war, but its political significance was vast; it signaled the return of British and American power to the Continent.

R–555

Washington [via U.S. Navy]
June 9, 1944, 12 noon

Top Secret and Personal. From the President for the Former
Naval Person.

Your 695 received. The plans of U.J. promise well even if the beginning is a little later than we hoped for, <u>but it may be for the best in the long run.</u> Roosevelt [WDL]

[MR]

Both Churchill and Roosevelt resented what they viewed as de Gaulle's irresponsibility for trying to resolve political questions on the eve of the Normandy invasion.

R–556

Washington [via U.S. Navy]
June 9, 1944, 12 noon

Personal and Top Secret. From the President for the Former
Naval Person.

Your 694 received. It appears that de Gaulle is performing in accordance with his previous record of lack of cooperation in our effort to liberate France.

He may visit Washington at the end of this month or about mid July but there is no indication yet that he will be helpful in our efforts in the interest of his country. I will do my best to attract his interest to the Allied war effort. Roosevelt [WDL]

[MR. *R&C.*]

In order to avoid a devaluation of the French franc (already overvalued in relation to the British pound and the American dollar), British and American officials planned to issue a special occupation franc. Working with the Commissioner for Finance for the FCNL, Pierre Mendès-France, Secretary of the Treasury Morgenthau had worked out the details designed to prevent inflation and economic chaos in liberated France. Roosevelt, however, refused to permit any mention of the newly proclaimed provisional government of France (de Gaulle's FCNL) either on the currency or in public statements about the currency, and de Gaulle responded by refusing to endorse the money.

C–696

London [via U.S. Army]
June 9, 1944, 2127 Z / TOR 2306 Z

Prime Minister to President Roosevelt. Personal and Top Secret.

1. I want to know your wishes about the notes issued for the troops in France. Eisenhower has urgent need to make a proclamation announcing it. De Gaulle is quite ready to make a supporting proclamation but there is reason to expect he will press for his proclamation to contain the words "Provisional Government of France" or "of the French Republic" and publish it in the "Official Journal of the French Republic" which he produces at Algiers. We shall naturally endeavor to persuade him to stick to the French Committee of National Liberation but he fights at every point. The Treasury fear that if he does not endorse the issue, the notes will have no backing behind them and alternatively I feel that Eisenhower's proclamation will commit our two governments jointly or separately to redeem them. How does this stand in your mind?

2. Others even say that he might denounce the notes as false money. I do not myself think that he will dare. I should myself think, if I were a French shopkeeper, that a note printed in the United States tendered to me by a British or American soldier and declared legal by General Eisenhower was well worth having whether De Gaulle endorsed it or not.

3. Would you please let me know what is your view? Shall we get De Gaulle to take responsibility for these notes as President of the Provisional Government of France in which case the French nation will ultimately face the problem of redeeming them? Or shall we say the United States and Great Britain assume responsibility for these notes and will fix the ultimate responsibility at the peace settlement? I should be grateful for an early answer.

[MR*. R&C.]

C-697

London [via U.S. Army]
June 9, 1944, 2358 Z / TOR 0144 Z, June 10

Prime Minister to President Roosevelt. Personal and Top Secret.

1. Further to my No. 696. I have now seen the specimens of the notes in question. They do not strike us as very reassuring. They look very easy to forge. Nothing is said on whose responsibility they are issued and who is responsible for redeeming them. Surely there must be some authority behind them.

2. These views expressed after seeing the notes affect Paragraph 2 of my No. 696 and make it all the more necessary that someone should take responsibility for meeting them when they are presented. Please, my dear friend, look at them for yourself and say what we ought to do. Should we let De Gaulle obtain new status as his price for backing these notes or should we take the burden on ourselves for the time being and improve the issue later on and settle up at the peace table where there will be many accounts to be presented?

[MR*. R&C.]

The attack along the Leningrad front, mentioned by Stalin, was directed against the Finns and was not the major offensive the Allies awaited. That latter attack began on June 23, in the area north of the Pripet Marshes in White Russia.

C-698

London [via U.S. Army]
June 10, 1944, 1124 Z

Prime Minister to President Roosevelt. Personal and Top Secret.

I have received the following from U.J.

"I have received your message of the 7th June with the information of the successful development of the operation OVERLORD. We all greet you and the valiant British and American armies and warmly wish you further successes.

"The preparation of the summer offensive of the Soviet armies is concluding. Tomorrow, the 10th June, the first stage will open in our summer offensive on the Leningrad front."

[MR. Stalin/WSC, doc. 274. R&C.]

As a British official historian, Sir Llewellyn Woodward, has pointed out, it had become increasingly difficult "to reconcile the legal and practical anomolies of her [Italy's] position as a co-belligerent and also as a defeated enemy" (Woodward, *British Foreign Policy*, II, 540). British inclinations to be harsh on the Italians, particularly once it became clear that Italy would make no significant military contribution to the Allied cause, were offset by fears that such a policy could drive Italy toward communism.

When Allied armies occupied Rome, King Victor Emmanuel abdicated, as previously arranged, and appointed the Crown Prince, Umberto, as Lieutenant of the Realm. When the Crown Prince asked Marshal Badoglio to form a new government, various opposition politicians—with tacit American approval—demanded that Badoglio step aside and permit Ivanoe Bonomi, a seventy-year-old conservative socialist, to form a government. Bonomi did so and appointed Count Carlo Sforza, a favorite of the Americans, to the post of Foreign Minister. When a British representative in Italy stated that the Allied governments would not approve of Sforza's appointment, the State Department protested that British representatives could not speak for the United States government. The British believed that General Wilson, the Supreme Allied Commander in the Mediterranean, and his authorized subordinates could speak for the Allies regarding an area still under military control, but the Americans were looking at postwar politics just as much as the British.

Though Churchill did not specifically make the comparison, his complaint that the new Italian government had taken over "without the slightest pretence of a popular mandate" was reminiscent of the President's arguments against recognizing the provisional government of de Gaulle.

C–699

London [via U.S. Army]
June 10, 1944, 1943 Z

Prime Minister to President Roosevelt. Personal and Top Secret.

I think it is a great disaster that Badoglio should be replaced by this group of aged and hungry politicians. He has been a useful instrument to us from the time when he delivered the fleet, in spite of the enemy, safely into our hands. I thought it was understood that he was to go on, at any rate till we could bring the democratic north in and have a thoroughly sound Italian government. Instead we are confronted with this absolutely unrepresentative collection. As far as I can make out, the Italian Advisory Committee have not been consulted. I have had no opportunity of bringing the matter before the Cabinet, nor I suppose have you had much time to consider it. I was not aware, at this present time, that we had conceded to the Italians who have cost us so dear in life and material the power to form any government they chose without reference to the victorious powers, and without the slightest pretence of a popular mandate. I take a most serious view of the situation, and I hope before you take a final decision you will let me know your views and give me an opportunity of replying.

[MR*. *FRUS*, 1944, III, 1129 (paraphrase). *R&C*.]

Historians may argue about Roosevelt's motives in protesting what was clearly a division of the Balkans into British and Soviet "spheres of influence." Whether the President desired to maintain an "open door" for American contacts and commerce, sincerely hoped to promote long-term cooperation with the Soviet Union, or vaguely believed that such spheres were unstable and would frustrate any permanent peace—there was no mistaking his firm opposition to the Anglo-Soviet agreement. In this case, the President and the State Department were on the same wavelength, for Roosevelt made no changes in the draft sent him by Acting Secretary of State Stettinius.

R–557

Washington [via U.S. Navy]
June 10, 1944, 11:30 P.M.

Personal and Secret from the President to the Former Naval Person.

The proposed agreement between your Government and Russia concerning Rumania and Greece, outlined in your telegram no. 687 of May 31, was discussed by Lord Halifax with Mr. Hull on May 30. The State Department has communicated to Lord Halifax the reasons why this Government is unwilling to approve the proposed arrangement. Briefly, we acknowledge that the militarily responsible Government in any given territory will inevitably make decisions required by military developments but are convinced that the natural tendency for such decisions to extend to other than military fields would be strengthened by an agreement of the type suggested. In our opinion, this would certainly result in the persistence of differences between you and the Soviets and in the division of the Balkan region into spheres of influence despite the declared intention to limit the arrangement to military matters.

We believe efforts should preferably be made to establish consultative machinery to dispel misunderstandings and restrain the tendency toward the development of exclusive spheres. Roosevelt [State Dept.]

[MR. *FRUS*, 1944, V, 117–18. p*WSC*, VI, 75.]

This "interim" message about the Italian political situation was sent while the State Department prepared a formal reply to Churchill's protest.

R–558

Washington [via U.S. Navy]
June 11, 1944, 11:55 A.M.

Personal and Top Secret from the President for the Former Naval Person.

Your 699. Before forming an opinion on this question I should like to have a recommendation from the Italian Advisory Committee and General Wilson. Roosevelt

[MR. R&C.]

Some officials in the State Department had interpreted the Anglo-Soviet arrangement in Roumania and Greece and Churchill's subsequent request for Roosevelt's approval as an attempt to get the United States to accept British leadership in Greece. As one memo put it: "The British are giving us informal notice that the U.K. expects to follow a strong policy in regard to the Eastern Mediterranean even if it means standing up and making deals with the Soviet Union. This is part and parcel of the British policy of regarding the Mediterranean as a British sea . . ." (John Hickerson, Div. of British Commonwealth Affairs, May 30, 1944, DS 870.00/46, as quoted in Davis, *Cold War Begins*, pp. 145–46). Churchill's emotional plea lends credence to that interpretation.

The Egyptian situation is discussed in C–648, C–657, and C–660. Lord Killearn (Sir Miles Lampson) was the British Ambassador in Cairo.

C–700

London [via U.S. Army]
June 11, 1944

Prime Minister to President. Secret, Personal and Private.

1. I am much concerned to receive your number 557. Action is paralysed if everybody is to consult everybody else about everything before it is taken. The events will always outstrip the changing situations in these Balkan regions. Somebody must have the power to plan and act. A consultative committee would be a mere obstruction, always overriden in any case of emergency by direct interchanges between you and me, or either of us and Stalin.

2. See, now, what happened at Easter when I had charge not only of the Foreign Office but of the British armed forces. We were able to cope with this mutiny of the Greek forces entirely in accordance with your own views. This was because I was able to give constant orders to the military

commanders, who at the beginning advocated conciliation, and above all, no use or even threat of force. Very little life was lost. The Greek situation has been immensely improved and, if firmness is maintained, will be rescued from confusion and disaster. The Russians are ready to let us take the lead in the Greek business, which means that EAM and all its malice can be controlled by the national forces of Greece. Otherwise, civil war and ruin to the land you care about so much. I always reported to you and I always will report to you. You shall see every telegram I send. I think you might trust me in this.

3. Similarly, troubles arose in Egypt, where King Farouk wished to sack Nahas and put in his court minister to rig the elections. This might easily have led to wide-spread riots and disorder throughout Egypt. Here again the military advise that no action should be taken which involved the use of force. I was in a position to give the necessary orders to the military without having to consult anybody, and none is more pleased than they are at the result. Here again I kept you informed, and Lord Killearn kept your ambassador at Cairo informed. All passed off happily without the slightest struggle.

4. If, in either of these two difficulties, we had had to consult other powers and a set of triangular or quadrangular telegrams got started, the only result would have been chaos or impotence.

5. It seems to me, considering the Russians are about to invade Rumania in great force and are going to help Rumania recapture part of Transylvania from Hungary, provided the Rumanians play which they may, considering all that, it would be a good thing to follow the same leadership considering that neither you nor we have any troops there at all and that they will probably do what they like anyhow. Moreover I thought their terms, apart from indemnity, very sensible and even generous. The Rumanian Army has inflicted many injuries upon the Soviet troops and went into the war against Russia with glee. I see no difficulty whatever in our addressing the Russians at any time on any subject, but please let them go ahead upon the lines agreed as they are doing all the work.

6. Similarly with us in Greece. We are an old ally of Greece. We had 40,000 casualties in trying to defend Greece against Hitler, not counting Crete. The Greek King and the Greek Government have placed themselves under our protection. They are at present domiciled in Egypt. They may very likely move to the Lebanon which would be a better atmosphere than Cairo. Not only did we lose the 40,000 men above mentioned in helping Greece, but a vast mass of shipping and warships, and by denuding Cyrenaica to help Greece, we also lost the whole of Wavell's conquests in Cyrenaica. These were heavy blows to us in those days [April 1941]. Your telegrams to me in the recent crisis worked wonders. We were entirely agreed, and the result is entirely satisfactory. Why

is all this effective direction to be broken up into a committee of mediocre officials such as we are littering about the world? Why can you and I not keep this in our own hands considering how we see eye to eye about so much of it?

7. To sum up, I propose that we agree that the arrangements I set forth in my Number 687 may have a trial of three months, after which it must be reviewed by the three powers.

[MR. pFRUS, 1944, V, 118–19. WSC, VI, 75–77.]

Churchill agreed to seek additional information and advice about the situation in Italy, possibly because the British political representative in Italy, Harold Macmillan, reported that there was no sense in trying to undo what had taken place.

C–701

London [via U.S. Army]
June 11, 1944, 2207 Z / TOR 2335 Z

Prime Minister to President Roosevelt Top Secret and Personal.
    Your number 558.
    I entirely agree.

[MR*]

Roosevelt added only a final sentence to the message, prepared by the Treasury Department, about occupation currency in France. As things turned out, the Americans were correct in guessing that the currency situation was less critical than Churchill feared. Early reports from the Normandy invasion area indicated that the invasion currency was being accepted by the French even without an endorsement from de Gaulle (Pogue, *Supreme Command*, p. 233). Jean Monnet, the representative of the FCNL in Washington, and Pierre Mèndes-France, the FCNL's Finance Commissioner, had discussed and approved the occupation francs as well as the economic concepts which underlay their use. But politics, not economics, was de Gaulle's concern.

R–559

Washington [via U.S. Navy]
June 12, 1944, 5:20 P.M.

Personal and Top Secret. From the President for the Former Naval Person.
    I share your view [C–696] that this currency issue is being exploited

to stampede us into according full recognition to the Comité. Personally I do not think the currency situation referred to in your cable is as critical as it might first appear, nor do I feel that it is essential from the point of view of the acceptability of the supplemental currency that De Gaulle make any statement of support with respect to such currency. I propose that De Gaulle should be informed as follows:

1. We intend to continue to use the supplementary franc currency in exactly the same manner as we have planned and as we have agreed with the British Treasury and as has been fully understood by Messrs. Monnet and Mèndes-France of the French Comité.

2. If for any reason the supplementary currency is not acceptable to the French public, General Eisenhower has full authority to use yellow seal dollars and British Military Authority notes. Accordingly, if De Gaulle incites the French people into refusing to accept supplementary francs then the Comité will have to bear the full responsibility for any bad effects resulting from the use of yellow seal notes and BMA notes in France. One of the certain consequences will be the depreciation of the French franc in terms of dollars and sterling in a black market which will accentuate and reveal the weaknesses of the French monetary system. This is one of the important reasons why we accepted the request of the French Comité that we not use yellow seal dollars and BMA notes as a spearhead currency. There would be other adverse effects which would be apparent to De Gaulle and his advisers.

I would certainly not importune De Gaulle to make any supporting statement whatever regarding the currency. Provided it is clear that he acts entirely on his own responsibility and without our concurrence he can sign any statement on currency in whatever capacity he likes, even that of the King of Siam.

As far as the appearance of the notes is concerned, I have seen them before but I have looked at them again and think them adequate. I am informed by the Bureau of Engraving and Printing counterfeiting experts that they will be extremely difficult to counterfeit by virtue of the intricate color combination. I am also informed that the British Treasury officials approved the note and that the French representatives here not only approved the note but were satisfied with the designs and the color.

It seems clear that prima donnas do not change their spots. Roosevelt [HM]

[MR. p*FRUS*, 1944, III, 707–8. *R&C.*]

Roosevelt agreed to a three-month trial period for the Anglo-Soviet arrangement in Roumania and Greece, though he reiterated his opposition to continuing the division after the war. The President drafted this cable and failed to send a copy to the State Department, which caused a good deal of confusion since Hull and Stettinius assumed that the arrangement had been rejected.

R–560

Washington [via U.S. Navy]
June 12, 1944, 6:40 P.M.

Top Secret and Personal. From the President for the Former Naval Person.

Your 700. I am in agreement with your proposal in paragraph seven of subject message.

We must be careful to make it clear that we are not establishing any post war spheres of influence. Roosevelt [FDR]

[MR. *FRUS*, 1944, V, 121. *R&C*.]

Churchill still harbored the hope that Badoglio could be persuaded to return and form a new government with Allied support, and Stalin's apparent willingness to see the Allies reject the Bonomi government only strengthened the Prime Minister's resolve. (See C–699.)

In addition to a message to Stalin about political developments in Italy, Churchill had also reported on Allied military successes in Normandy and in the Italian campaign (*Stalin/WSC*, docs. 277, 278).

C–702

London [via U.S. Army]
June 12, 1944, 2143 Z / TOR 2250 Z

Prime Minister to President Roosevelt Personal.

I have just received the following from Premier Stalin.

1. I have received your message about the departure of Badoglio. To me, too, the departure of Badoglio was unexpected. It seemed to me that without the consent of the Allies, the British and the Americans, the removal of Badoglio and the appointment of Bonomi could not take place. From your message, however, it is evident that this took place regardless of the will of the Allies. One must assume that certain Italian circles purpose to make an attempt to change to their advantage the armistice conditions. In any case, if for you and the Americans circumstances suggest that it is necessary to have another government in Italy and not the Bonomi Government, then you can count on their being no objections to this from the Soviet side.

2. I have also received your message of the 10th June. I thank you for the information. As is evident, the landing, conceived on a grandiose scale, has succeeded completely. My colleagues and I cannot but admit that the history of warfare knows no other like undertaking from the point of view of its scale, its vast conception and its masterly execution. As is well known, Napoleon in his time failed ignominiously in his plan to force the channel. The hysterical Hitler, who boasted for two years that he would effect a forcing of the channel, was unable to make up his mind even to hint at attempting to carry out his threat. Only our Allies have succeeded in realising with honour the grandiose plan of the forcing of the channel. History will record this deed as an achievement of the highest order.

[MR*. *Stalin/WSC*, doc. 279. *R&C*.]

In thanking the President for his approval of a three-month trial for the Anglo-Soviet arrangement in the Balkans, Churchill carefully left the door open for the establishment of a more permanent deal.

Despite advice from the War Cabinet and representatives in Italy recommending that Britain work with the new Bonomi government, Churchill continued to favor the re-installation of Badoglio as Premier.

Soon after Churchill sent this cable, de Gaulle visited the British sector in Normandy where General Sir Bernard Montgomery commanded all ground forces involved in OVERLORD as well as the British Twenty-first Army Group. In a memo to Eden, Churchill complained that de Gaulle "only wishes to pose as the saviour of France" and should not be permitted to hold any public demonstrations while visiting Normandy. But, as de Gaulle recalled, "the inhabitants stood in kind of a daze, then burst into bravos or else into tears. Rushing out of their houses, they followed after me, all in the grip of an extraordinary emotion." A British liaison officer on the beachhead reported that the average Frenchman believed de Gaulle "the natural and inevitable leader of Free France," and the General himself, in writing about his enthusiastic reception in Bayeux and Isigny, concluded that "the proof was given. . . . The French people had shown to whom they entrusted the duty of leading them" (Woodward, *British Foreign Policy*, III, 62; Pogue, *Supreme Command*, pp. 233–34; de Gaulle, *Unity*, pp. 260, 261).

During a press conference on June 13, Roosevelt had promised to accept any currency issued by whatever legitimate French authority was finally recognized by the Allies, but that was not a move toward de Gaulle. On the contrary, the President commented that he would not permit that "jackenape" to take over (Blum, *Years of War*, p. 174). Churchill's proposal for Anglo-American guarantees to redeem the occupation currency were opposed by the U.S. Treasury Department. (See R–572.)

One can only speculate on Churchill's disappointment and the relief of his escorts, particularly the ship's captain, when the Germans failed to return the

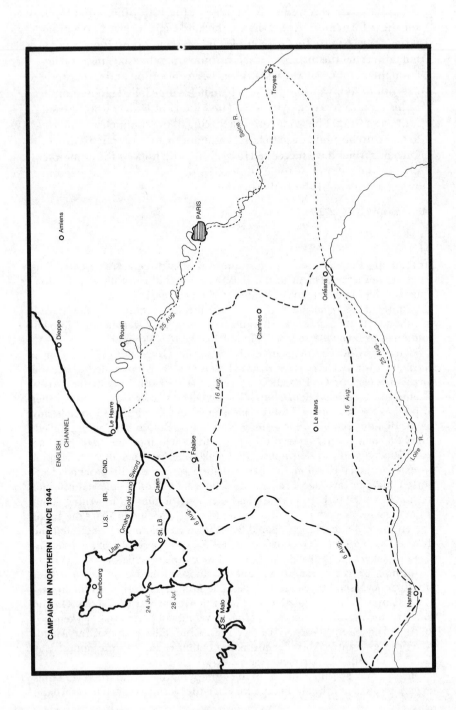

CAMPAIGN IN NORTHERN FRANCE 1944

ENGLISH CHANNEL

Cherbourg

Utah · Omaha · Gold · Juno · Sword

U.S. | BR. | CND.

St. Lô

Caen

St. Malo

Le Havre

Rouen

Dieppe

Amiens

PARIS

Seine R.

Troyes

Falaise

24 Jul.

28 Jul.

6 Aug.

9 Aug.

16 Aug.

25 Aug.

Chartres

Le Mans

Orléans

16 Aug.

25 Aug.

Loire R.

Nantes

9 Aug.

gunfire from the British destroyer carrying the Prime Minister on a tour of the Normandy beaches. The artificial harbors ("Mulberries") mentioned by Churchill were constructed of metal and concrete in sections which were towed from England and assembled at the beachheads. The British completed one at Arromanches, but the American one at OMAHA beach was broken up during a mild storm which began on June 19. (See Weigley, *Eisenhower's Lieutenants*, p. 103.) The landing craft and operations about which General Marshall cabled to Admiral "Dickie" Mountbatten had been developed, to some degree, by Mountbatten's Combined Operations Staff earlier in the war. (The cable is reprinted in *WSC*, VI, 13–14.) The "problems as between the Mediterranean and OVERLORD" soon erupted in a serious dispute over the decision to launch an attack on southern France (ANVIL) in spite of delays.

C–703

London [via U.S. Army]
June 14, 1944, 1129 Z / TOR 1135 Z

Prime Minister to President Personal and Top Secret.

1. Your number 560: I am deeply grateful to you for your reply to my number 700. I have asked the Foreign Secretary to convey the information to Monsieur Molotov and to make it clear that the reason for the three months limit is in order that we should not prejudge the question of establishing postwar spheres of influence.

2. Your number 558: Please note the remarks I had had on this question from Marshal Stalin. I share your opinion that the matter should be examined by the Joint Advisory Committee and that they should report to the three governments, who will consult together and give a united answer. Meanwhile Badoglio remains nominally in charge, and the delay in bringing the new government into office is to be explained by the needs of consulting the victorious powers. This is what Badoglio and Bonomi have, I believed, settled amicably at Salerno, whither they have both repaired. It appears that they are quite friendly and I see great difficulties in persuading Badoglio to resume the thankless task he has quitted, at his great age. I consider that if we cannot do this it will be detrimental to the interests of the Allies.

3. When De Gaulle arrived here at my invitation, in my first efforts to make him friendly I held out the hopes that he would plant his foot upon the soil of France. After making as much trouble for us as was in his power, he has now expressed a great desire that these should be made good. I have therefore consented that he should visit the British Sector in France today, 14th, where he will be received by General Montgomery at his headquarters and may possibly be allowed to go to Bayeux. No demonstrations will be permitted on military grounds, as crowds might attract bombardment. He will give no addresses there, but a statement,

which we shall have the power to censor, may be made on his return. I did not want to give him the grievance that we had refused him his desire to set foot on his native soil, and also I was a bit compromised myself by our first conversation. I imparted the above decision of mine, that he should go to our sector, to Eisenhower and Bedell Smith, and the responsibility for it is mine. I hope you will not think I was wrong.

4. I understand that you issued a statement last night about the currency. You may be sure I shall try to support you in every way. I am quite sure that if an old woman in Bayeux sells a cow to an American Quartermaster and is paid in these notes, when she presents them at Morgenthau's office in Washington he will have to see that she is no loser on the transaction. My information from France last night was that the French people are taking the notes.

5. I had a jolly day on Monday on the beaches and inland. There is a great mass of shipping extending more than fifty miles along the coast. It is being increasingly protected against weather by the artificial harbours, nearly every element of which has been a success, and will soon have effective shelter against bad weather. The power of our air and of our anti U-boat forces seems to ensure it a very great measure of protection. After doing much laborious duty, we went and had a plug at the Hun from our destroyer, but although the range was 6,000 yards he did not honour us with a reply.

6. Marshall and King came back in my train. They were greatly reassured by all they saw on the American side, and Marshall wrote out a charming telegram to Dickie, saying how many of these new craft had been produced under his organization and what a help they had been. You used the word "stupendous" in one of your early telegrams to me [R–551]. I must admit that what I saw could only be described by that word, and I think your officers would agree as well. The marvelous efficiency of the transportation exceed anything that has ever been known in war. A great deal more has to be done, and I think more troops are needed. We are working up to a battle which may well be a million a side. The Chiefs of Staff are searching about for the best solution of problems as between the Mediterranean and OVERLORD.

How I wish you were here.

[MR. p*FRUS*, 1944, V, 123. p*WSC*, VI, 15. *R&C*.]

The additions to this cable were made in the President's handwriting.

R–561

Washington [via U.S. Navy]
June 14, 1944, 11:55 A.M.

Personal and Top Secret, from the President to the Former Naval Person.

Your 703. I can see no objection to your action in permitting de Gaulle to visit France and feel that his visit may have the good effect of stimulating that part of the French underground over which he has authority or which he can influence to work against the common enemy.

In my opinion we should make full use of any organization or influence he may have in so far as is practicable without imposing him by force of our arms upon the French people as their government <u>or giving recognition to his outfit as the Provisional Government of France. After all, the Germans control over 99% of the area of France.</u>

His unreasonable attitude toward our supplementary French currency does not disturb me. My reaction to his action in the matter of currency is fully covered in my number 559 of 12 June.

I join with you in a hope that the Italian situation will clear up to the advantage of our military effort in Italy and elsewhere, and I regret exceedingly that it was not possible for me to be with you on your visit with our splendid soldiers who have made the first breach in Hitler's "citadel of Europe." <u>But don't do it again without my going with you.</u>
Roosevelt [WDL]

[MR. *FRUS*, 1944, III, 713. *R&C*.]

Churchill still wanted to delay any major conference about oil interests until after the American elections in November, but the Foreign Office soon persuaded him that such a move would only alienate those Americans who had guaranteed that the United States would not seek to gain control of British oil concessions in the Middle East.

Sir William Brown headed the British delegation sent to Washington to discuss "a basic understanding between the two Governments regarding Middle Eastern oil" (R–474/1). The talks, which took place between April 18 and May 3, were broadened to include worldwide oil supplies. The British delegation returned to London believing that a working agreement had been reached. Despite support for such an agreement from both the British and American governments, American oil companies and a number of Senators opposed what they considered government interference in private business, and in January 1945 Roosevelt dropped the idea (Woodward, *British Foreign Policy*, pp. 398–402, and C–608/1).

C–704

London [via U.S. Army]
June 14, 1944, 1801 Z / TOR 1900 Z

Prime Minister to President Roosevelt. Personal and Secret.

Many thanks for your telegram of 7th June, No. 554. Points of principle have arisen in connection with Brown's report which it has been necessary to take in Cabinet and, oil being so vital to us for security and other reasons, we have referred them to a ministerial committee. But I hope this will not mean any great delay and that I shall be able to let you know how matters stand in the very near future.

[MR*. *FRUS*, 1944, III, 117–18.]

Roosevelt had referred Churchill's cable about the change of government in Italy to the State Department for a draft reply. Predictably, given the department's longstanding support for Count Sforza and other anti-monarchists, the suggested reply advised that the Allies work with the new Italian Cabinet. The President agreed, but made a few changes to the State Department draft.

R–562

Washington [via U.S. Navy]
June 15, 1944, 4:45 P.M.

Personal and Top Secret. From the President for the Former
Naval Person.

With further reference to your telegram No. 699 and my reply No. 558, I have consulted with my advisers here and in the field and, despite some surprise here that the Deputy President of the Control Commission apparently acted without consulting the other Allied Governments, I have reached the conclusion that it would be a grave mistake for us not to permit the Bonomi cabinet to be promptly installed.

Though regretting Badoglio's withdrawal, I nevertheless feel that this may be of distinct advantage to us. Aside from allaying criticism at home and abroad of our Italian policy and pointing to the implementation of our proclaimed policy, it would seem well that the surrender terms— hitherto in the public mind associated with Badoglio's person—should become the obligation of the most representative men today available in Italy, forming a cabinet regarded as one hundred percent anti-fascist. I understand that the new cabinet have pledged themselves to assume all the commitments the Badoglio government contracted with the Allies, including both the long terms of surrender and the postponement of the institutional question until the hostilities are ended.

The broadening of the Government when Rome was reached had long been foreseen. Negotiations following Rome's fall were held with the approval of the Allied Control Commission and in constant consultation with its Deputy President and his British and American political advisers. While the parties were divided in willingness to serve under Badoglio, Bonomi was the unanimous choice of all the parties represented in that Rome Committee of National Liberation which seems to be the best available channel existing in Italy today for the expression of popular will.

Interference on our part at this late moment in the establishment of what appears to be a representative government would have, I fear, serious repercussions both at home and in Italy, to the detriment of the military situation and the profit of mischievous elements there, <u>and would not this be in direct violation of our announced policy to let the people choose their own government.</u>

~~I hope, therefore, that you will agree that we should permit the new cabinet to take oath without delay and I have instructed the United States member of the Advisory Council to support this view in the Council.~~ Roosevelt [State Dept.]

[MR. *FRUS*, 1944, III, 1133–34 (paraphrase). pR&Cn.]

Churchill's thank-you note was typed on one of the typewriters sent to him by the President. (See R–553/1.)

C–704/1, letter

London
June 16, 1944

My dear Franklin,

I am indeed grateful for your kind thought in sending me two electric typewriters. I was greatly struck by the typescript of the letter which General McNarney sent me from Washington, and am delighted to have these typewriters for use in my own office.

Yours always, [initialed] W.

[PSF:WSC]

Churchill finally gave in to the arguments of the Foreign Office and British officials in Italy, though he wanted the Bonomi government formally to accept the conditions imposed on Badoglio by the Allies. Churchill had previously

opposed Soviet participation in the supervision of liberated Italy, but with
Stalin supporting the Prime Minister's opposition to easing the Italian surrender terms, prior consultation with the Soviet Premier became useful.

C–705

London [via U.S. Army]
June 17, 1944, 1334 Z / TOR 1505 Z

Prime Minister to President Roosevelt Personal and Top Secret.
    Your No. 562.
    I have reluctantly come to the conclusion that it will not be possible to
press the return of Badoglio, and I am so informing U.J. We ought I
think to wait for his answer before taking final action. Also matters should
be regularized through the Advisory Council.
    The important thing now is to make sure that all these ministers who
have elected themselves to office shall be cognizant of all the engagements
into which Badoglio entered. We also think the time has come to publish
the long terms of surrender.

[MR* R&C.]

Roosevelt and the American Joint Chiefs had steadfastly opposed the long
surrender terms because, in spelling out the details of Italy's responsibilities,
the local Allied military commander lost the flexibility he might need in order
to deal with military questions. Moreover, they feared the long terms might
cause a drop in morale within the Italian armed forces and make them less
willing to fight the Germans—although they had not been much help to the
Allies in any case.

R–563

Hyde Park, N.Y. [via U.S. Navy]
June 17, 1944, 12:45 P.M.

Personal and Secret, from the President for the Prime Minister.
    I am in agreement with your 705, but believe we should obtain advice
General Wilson and the Combined Chiefs of Staff before publishing the
long terms of surrender. Roosevelt [WDL]

[MR]

With the elimination of Mihailović from the Yugoslav Cabinet, Tito agreed
to meet with the new Yugoslav Prime Minister, Dr. Ivan Subasić, on the island
of Vis, where Tito had fled after a German attack on his headquarters in

Croatia. Caught between cross-purposes, the British, who occupied Vis, did not want to force Tito into the arms of the Soviets by cutting off military aid, yet they realized that continuing their support for the Partisan leader would put him in a position to prevent the establishment of a monarchy or any other pro-British government after the war. Forced to hedge, the British tried to get Tito and the Royal Yugoslav Government to suspend politics for the duration of the war. With OVERLORD's success still uncertain, Churchill would do nothing to jeopardize the military situation, and Tito's forces held down a significant portion of German troops.

Roosevelt instructed the State Department to give the widest possible publicity to the joint communiqué quoted in this cable.

C–706

London [via U.S. Army]
June 18, 1944, 2143 Z / TOR 2100 Z

Prime Minister to President. Personal and Top Secret.

The following looks good.

Dr. Subasic and Tito agreed today the following joint communique which will be issued by Tanjug [Yugoslav News Agency] afternoon of June 18th. I should be grateful if wide publicity and warm welcome could be given it in local press.

> "The 'New Yugoslav' News Agency has been authorised to issue the statement: 'From June 14th to June 17th discussions have been going on in liberated territory of Yugoslavia between the President of the National Liberation Committee of Yugoslavia, Marshal Josip Broz-Tito, and Prime Minister of the Royal Yugoslav Government, Dr. Subasic. Several members of the National Liberation Committee of Yugoslavia and of the Presidium of Anti-Fascist Council of National Liberation Yugoslavia took part in these discussions. These negotiations have been led from both sides in spirit of mutual effort towards strengthening the liberation fight of the nations of Yugoslavia and with the aim of achieving broadest unity of the national forces. Agreement and mutual accord was reached regarding many questions. This will undoubtedly help to strengthen still further our relations with the Allies and help the peoples of Yugoslavia to liberate their country as speedily as possible' ".

[MR*. R&C.]

THE PACIFIC THEATER

With rumors circulating about his poor health and lack of energy, Roosevelt decided an inspection trip to the Pacific Coast, Hawaii, and Alaska made good

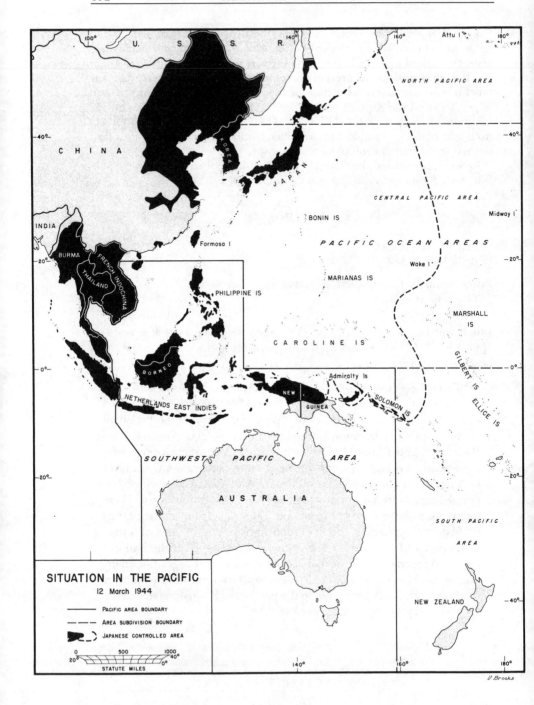

SITUATION IN THE PACIFIC
12 March 1944

——————— PACIFIC AREA BOUNDARY
– – – – – AREA SUBDIVISION BOUNDARY
◥◣ ⊃ JAPANESE CONTROLLED AREA

0   500   1000
STATUTE MILES

U Brooks

political sense. Moreover, it permitted him to deal directly with the argument between the Navy, which favored a strike against Formosa from the central Pacific, and the Army, particularly General Douglas MacArthur, which argued that the Philippine Islands should be secured first in order to prevent a flanking movement against any invasion of Formosa. Whether or not MacArthur actually told the President that a failure to carry out the American promise to liberate the Philippines would arouse the American people to "register most complete resentment against you at the polls this fall," Roosevelt decided against bypassing the islands (Burns, *Soldier of Freedom*, p. 489).

The war against Japan in the Pacific had come up infrequently in the Churchill-Roosevelt exchanges largely because the Americans saw no need to consult the British about what was almost exclusively an American theater of operations, but the situation had altered there in recent months as radically as it had in Europe. Navy and Marine Corps forces in the central and northern Pacific, under the overall command of Admiral Chester Nimitz, had followed up the victory at Midway in June 1942 with a series of amphibious invasions. Tarawa in the Gilbert Islands fell in November 1943, followed by Kwajalein and Eniwetok in the Marshall Islands in February 1944. Then, on June 15, 1944, only nine days after the launching of OVERLORD, American Marines landed on Saipan in the Mariana Islands, located 1,600 miles from Tokyo— within striking distance for the new B-29 "Superfortress" bombers. Even though 20,000 Marines were ashore by nightfall, the defenders (who numbered a little over 30,000) fought tenaciously and controlled the heights overlooking the beachhead, slowing the American advance.

More important than the assault on Saipan was the naval and naval-air battle which took place in the Philippine Sea west of the island. A combination of good intelligence, judicious positioning, effective use of radar, and more experienced pilots brought on what the Americans later called the Marianas "Turkey Shoot." Within two days, the Japanese had lost about 480 aircraft, three irreplaceable aircraft carriers, and suffered extensive losses and damage to other fleet units. Saipan did not come under American control until July 7, but the Battle of the Philippine Sea had already eliminated the Japanese ability to resist amphibious invasions of their island territories.

EVEN though de Gaulle had referred to himself as President of the provisional government of France during his visit to Normandy, Roosevelt remained willing to have the Frenchman visit Washington.

Since the President drafted this message, the use of the French word *Quai* (for quay) was probably intentional and not a mistake in transmission.

R–564

Hyde Park, N.Y. [via U.S. Navy]
June 19, 1944, 12:30 P.M.

Top Secret and Personal. From the President for the Former
Naval Person.

1. I am glad the visit of De Gaulle to France passed off peacefully and
without any apparent harm.

2. I have a third person message, via French Mission here, saying the
General hopes to come here during one of the two specified times I said
I could see him. It was polite but vague.

3. I am thinking of a trip to the Pacific Coast about the middle of July
and this seems important from a good many angles.

4. Our operations at Saipan are progressing slowly, for there are between twenty and thirty thousand Japanese troops on that Island. If it
goes through it will be of the highest importance to future offensives
against Japan.

I do wish I could have seen all you did. The efficiency must have
delighted your soul. I hope that when I get over I will be able to land
along side the Quai at Cherbourg. Roosevelt [FDR]

[MR]

Churchill occasionally gave Roosevelt a gentle shove—as in this cable—toward
an accommodation with de Gaulle, but the British Foreign Office believed
that Anglo-American differences over policy toward the FCNL demonstrated
that Britain "could not have a free foreign policy in Europe as long as there
was an American Supreme Commander responsible to the Combined Chiefs
of Staff in Washington" (Woodward, *British Foreign Policy*, III, 65).

Churchill had talked with the U.S. Chief of Naval Operations, Admiral
Ernest King, during a visit by the American Joint Chiefs to the Normandy
beachhead and to London for a meeting of the Combined Chiefs of Staff.

German forces in Cherbourg, on the seaward end of the Normandy peninsula, were cut off from retreat first by Hitler's order against withdrawals and
then by advancing American armies, but did not surrender until June 27, a
week later than Allied planners had predicted.

C–707

London [via U.S. Army]
June 20, 1944, 1514 Z

Prime Minister to President Roosevelt Personal and Top Secret.
Your 564.

1. I hope DeGaulle will come to you because it would be a good thing

all round if some sort of arrangement could be fixed. This need not involve recognizing the French National Committee as the provisional government of France. In practice, however, I think it would be found that DeGaulle and the French National Committee represent most of the elements who want to help us. Vichy is a foe and there is a large middle body who only wish to be left alone and eat good meals from day to day. The energizing factor of DeGaulle must not be forgotten in our treatment of the French problem.

2. Your operations in the Pacific assume every day a more vehement and compulsive course. Admiral King gave me a full account in the several good talks I had with him. Everything went well at the meeting of the Chiefs of Staff.

3. However, it is most desirable we have a meeting before October. How about August 20 at the Citadel Quebec? A week in those surroundings and cool air would do you no end of good.

4. Your troops are fighting magnificently and I should not think that Cherbourg would hold out long. Anyhow, the synthetic harbours, which are a miracle of rapid construction, would each of them handle more traffic than Cherbourg, and I hope you will honour one of them with your arrival.

[MR*. p*FRUS, Quebec Conf.*, 1944, p. 8. *R&C.*]

Although Lord Beaverbrook was no longer a member of the British War Cabinet, he had remained a member of the government as Lord Privy Seal. More important, Churchill liked and trusted him and knew he would defend the British Empire against the Americans during the approaching Petroleum Conference. More than most Britons, Churchill was sensitive to the effect of the upcoming presidential elections on Roosevelt, and hence his reference to "political or party difficulties."

On the night of June 12/13, four flying bombs (V-1s) fell on southern England. Thereafter the Germans increased the number (200 were launched on June 15/16) in an attack which Hitler claimed would force the British to negotiate.

Lieutenant General Carl Spaatz commanded U.S. Strategic Air Forces in Europe. A firm proponent of the strategic bombing campaign, he had opposed diverting bombers from attacks on Germany in order to provide tactical air support for OVERLORD. As Churchill promised, the Royal Air Force mounted a massive attack on Berlin on June 21.

C–708

London [via U.S. Army]
June 20, 1944, 2350 Z

Prime Minister to President Roosevelt. Personal and Private.

1. The man I think best capable of stating the British case in the oil conference is without question Beaverbrook. While naturally we must choose our own representative to put our own point of view, I should be grateful if you would let me know in personal privacy whether you would foresee any American political or party difficulties in this choice by me. I should greatly regret if he were not acceptable as I believe he is far and away the best man to work towards a solution by cordial agreement.

2. At this moment a flying bomb is approaching this dwelling. We think we are getting the best of them. We have received the greatest consideration from Eisenhower and Spaatz, and I have given it out that nothing is to impede the battle. This perpetual bombardment is a new feature, but I do not think it will seriously affect production in London. Up to date there are 7,000 casualties of which half are light. The Guards Chapel where 300 occurred was a sad episode. General Bedell Smith was invited by Colonel Ivan Cobbold who was killed to attend the service but did not go.

I consider the battle on land is progressing favourably but the weather has not been kind for June. Bomb has fallen some way off, but others are reported. We have exploded more than half our visitors today by fighter aircraft harmlessly. As you know, tomorrow is a great effort on Berlin. This will give them something else to rejoice about. Every good wish.

[MR. *R&C.*]

Churchill's opening remark presumably refers to his statement of June 14 in the House of Commons on the question of General de Gaulle and Anglo-French relations. In an obvious attempt to avoid giving the Germans the small comfort of knowing that the Allies were quarreling, the Prime Minister tried to convince the House that "leniency and forbearance" should prevail lest the government be forced into premature decisions. Churchill did comment that any currency issued in France should be redeemed, at least in the "first instance," by the government which issued the notes—a position opposed to the U.S. Treasury's insistence that occupation francs should be redeemed by the postwar French government. Roosevelt and Morgenthau considered that the "moral responsibility" of the Allies, which Churchill mentioned in this cable, would be discharged by the liberation of France. (See Churchill, *Speeches*, VII, 6948–50.)

C-709

London [via U.S. Army]
June 21, 1944, 1139 Z

Prime Minister to President Roosevelt Personal and Top Secret.

Your No. 559.

You will see that my statement in Parliament was designed to give no comfort to the enemy. For the moment, you may be right in thinking that the situation about the note is not critical. But, it is not a comfortable situation, and is bound to get worse as we go forward. I think we should explore whether there is a basis for an agreement with the French Committee provided it gives nothing away which you and we do not want to give away.

The notes give no indication of the authority by whom they are issued. Unless we reach an understanding with the French Committee, we shall be morally responsible for seeing that they are honoured. Under the mutual aid arrangements which we are making with the other European allies, they will bear the cost of civil administration and of supplies and services to our troops in their countries. But, if we should become responsible for the whole of the military notes issued in France, the French would contribute no mutual aid to the American and British armies of liberation.

We shall, therefore, see whether a basis of agreement exists by discussion between our officials and the French officials and I will let you know the result.

In this whole matter I am not thinking of the French Committee's position.

[MR*]

DISPUTES OVER STRATEGY IN EUROPE

The U.S. Chief of Naval Operations, Admiral King, had instructed the commander of U.S. naval forces in Europe, Admiral Harold "Betty" Stark, to begin a transfer of naval vessels in preparation for the attack on southern France (ANVIL), an invasion which the Americans believed had been agreed upon. But the British were having second thoughts. The success of the recent offensive in Italy, Operation DIADEM, had not only liberated Rome but offered an opportunity to break through the retreating Germans before they could regroup and establish a new defense line in northern Italy (see map, Vol. II, p. 453. When the Allied commander in Italy, General Alexander, submitted a plan for a post-DIADEM offensive, the Supreme Commander in the Mediterranean, General Wilson, was inclined to support it. Alexander argued that a quick follow-up to DIADEM, using the forces which had already been victorious against the Germans, would provide effective support for OVERLORD faster than ANVIL or an invasion near Bordeaux. A massive attack in Italy would force the Germans to send reinforcements since a break-through, Alexander pointed out, would threaten Hitler's southern flank. It was that threat—an attack across the Po River, through northeastern Italy past Venice and Trieste, through Ljubljana in Yugoslavia and then north into Austria and Vienna—which captured Churchill's imagination, and not only for its military possibilities. The British Prime Minister had become increas-ingly worried about the political situation in the southern Balkans, particularly in Greece. Even though his advisers warned that the Soviet Union would probably redirect its offensive more toward the Balkans if the Allies began major operations there, Churchill remained fascinated by the opportunity to put British armies in Yugoslavia and Greece. He had already tacitly agreed to a division of British and Russian influence in the Balkans, but the presence of British forces would be a far stronger bargaining chip than diplomatic agreements. That was especially true in Yugoslavia, where short-term military requirements had convinced the British to support Tito, a dubious postwar ally. Besides the promise of political gain, an attack through the so-called Ljubljana gap dovetailed with Churchill's long-held strategic views. From the outset of the war he had advocated defeating Germany with a series of attacks around the periphery of Europe, as opposed to a massive OVER-LORD-style assault. Not only were peripheral attacks better suited to the naval strength of a small island-nation, but they would cut down the chances of a World War I–type stalemate in northern France, with trench warfare and massive losses. Adding to the attractiveness of General Alexander's plan was the fact that it would be a British-led operation. The growing prepon-derance of U.S. military and logistical strength in the European theater had guaranteed that SCAEF (Supreme Commander, Allied Expeditionary Force) would be an American, and Churchill realized that the critical British con-tribution—particularly during the first four years of the war—was already overshadowed by the American buildup. Thus convinced that tactical, stra-tegic, and political considerations all favored a major offensive in Italy, the Prime Minister dug in his heels and began his own major offensive to get American agreement for General Alexander's proposal.

Roosevelt may have been reluctant to send Allied armies into the Balkans lest Stalin interpret that as a challenge, and the President eventually warned that any such change in strategy would have to be cleared with the Soviet leader. Yet the immediate military situation in June 1944 played the key role in frustrating Churchill's strategy. Violent gales from June 19 through 24 in the English Channel had seriously disrupted the delivery of supplies and reinforcements to the Normandy beachhead and had also hampered Allied air operations. As a result, OVERLORD fell behind schedule. As Eisenhower put it on June 20, in a cable to General Marshall, "achievement of a successful beachhead in France does not repeat not of itself imply success in Operation OVERLORD as a whole." The Supreme Commander insisted that concen-tration of forces was the key to success and that "wandering off overland via Trieste to Ljubljana repeat Ljubljana is to indulge in conjecture to an un-

warranted degree at the present time. . . . Wilson should be directed to undertake Operation ANVIL at the earliest possible date" (*Eisenhower Papers*,
III, 1938–39). Since ANVIL required the use of troops, equipment, and
supplies which would be necessary for any breakthrough in Italy, the two
operations could not be mounted simultaneously, and Eisenhower was convinced that an attack on southern France would provide the fastest and most
effective assistance to OVERLORD.

Churchill's specific request for a delay in implementing Admiral King's
order to shift three battleships, two cruisers, twenty-six destroyers, and various
landing and support vessels did receive Eisenhower's support—though for
reasons different from those of the Prime Minister. Eisenhower decided not
to release the naval units until after the capture of Cherbourg and its port
facilities, but he continued to insist upon the ANVIL operation (*Eisenhower
Papers*, III, 1941–42).

C–710

London [via U.S. Army]
June 21, 1944, 1840 Z

Prime Minister to President Roosevelt Personal and Top Secret.

We are much concerned at the consequences of the directions which
have been given by Admiral King to Admiral Stark about transferring
the great mass of American ships from the OVERLORD battle to the
Mediterranean. This is surely not the time to withdraw such a great
American naval component without consultation with the Admiralty and
the Supreme Commanders concerned, or the specific approval of the
Combined Chiefs of Staff.

2. Very important strategic decisions have to be taken by the Combined
Chiefs of Staff and by you and me about the form of diversion from the
forces against OVERLORD to be effected from the Mediterranean. These
grave matters are now under close and urgent consideration by General
Wilson and General Eisenhower, following the lead given to them by the
Combined Chiefs of Staff, and arising from the discussions which they
had so recently here in London together. No decisions can be taken until
we have had the considered view of the two supreme commanders concerned.

3. I understand that Eisenhower has telegraphed to you also on this
subject.

[MR*. R&C.]

The Advisory Council for Italy, on June 16, 1944, had passed a resolution
calling on the Bonomi government to reaffirm, in writing, all the commitments
made to the Allies by the Badoglio government and to do nothing toward

resolving the question of the type of government postwar Italy should have until the Italian people could be consulted, after the war.

The summer offensive promised by Stalin began on June 23, with an attack north of the Pripet Marshes against German positions in White Russia. In the first week Soviet forces pushed the Germans back 150 miles, and on July 3 they captured Minsk, about 250 miles from where the offensive started.

C–711

London [via U.S. Army]
June 21, 1944, 2240 Z / TOR 0045 Z, June 22

Prime Minister to President Roosevelt Personal and Top Secret.

Please see following from U J which is important and good:

> Thank you for your communication [see C–691] about your and the Presidents intentions to resume the northern convoys to the Soviet Union about August 10th. This will be of very considerable help to us.
>
> As regards Italian affairs, you know of course already about the resolution of the consultative council in connection with the new Italian Government. On the part of the Soviet Government there is no objection to this resolution.
>
> We are all greatly pleased by the successful progress of the operations conducted in Normandy by British and American Troops which have already acquired such serious scope and strength. From my heart I wish your troops further successes.
>
> In not more than a week will begin the second round of the summer offensive of the Soviet Armies. 130 Divisions will take part in this offensive, including armoured tank divisions. I and my colleagues reckon on considerable (literally—serious) success. I hope that our offensive will render essential support to the operations of the Allied Armies in France and Italy.

[MR*. p*Stalin*/WSC, doc. 283.]

Secretary of State Hull and State Department officials were highly suspicious of the Anglo-Soviet arrangement in the Balkans, and Ambassador Halifax's discussions with Hull had not reassured them. On June 8, Churchill denied any intention of establishing spheres of influence but reiterated his arguments for British predominance in Greece and Yugoslavia and Soviet predominance in Roumania and Bulgaria. In a reference which Hull interpreted as a British insinuation that the United States had a sphere of influence in Latin America, Churchill mentioned that Britain had followed the American lead in South America. Nor did the Secretary of State accept the Foreign Office's lame explanation that the Anglo-Soviet agreement had arisen out of a chance remark which the Soviets turned into a formal proposal before the British could consult the Americans. (See Hull to Roosevelt, June 17, 1944, *FRUS*, 1944, V, 124–25, and attachments to R–565, MR.) For both political and personal reasons, Roosevelt accepted Hull's draft of an answer to Churchill without making significant changes. Anglophobia, particularly opposition to imperialism, was stock in trade for the Republican Party, and any acquiescence by Roosevelt to a spheres-of-influence deal would surely leak out of the State Department before the November election. In addition, even though the President never clearly differentiated between his concept of having "four policemen" and the traditional concept of spheres of influence, he was enough of an heir to the Wilsonian legacy to shrink away from the latter phrase.

R–565

Washington [via U.S. Navy]
June 22, 1944, 2:00 P.M.

Personal and Top Secret. From the President for the Prime Minister.

With reference to your 687 and my 560 regarding matters in the Balkans, I am a bit worried and so is the State Department. I think I should tell you frankly that we were disturbed that your people took this matter up with us only after it had been put up to the Russians and they had inquired whether we were agreeable. Your Foreign Office apparently sensed this and has now explained that the proposal "arose out of a chance remark" which was converted by the Soviet Government into a formal proposal. However, I hope matters of this importance can be prevented from developing in such a manner in the future. Roosevelt [CH]

[MR. *FRUS*, 1944, V, 125. *R&C*.]

Roosevelt saw no contradiction between his agreeing to a three-month trial period for the Anglo-Soviet arrangement in the Balkans and his opposing postwar spheres of influence, although Secretary of State Hull, who did not know that the President had accepted Churchill's suggestion of a temporary division of power in the Balkans (R–560), opposed even the limited deal. The American protest against the temporary arrangement (R–565) was apparently seen by Roosevelt as pertaining to the postwar situation, and by the State Department, which drafted the cable, as relating to both the wartime and the postwar world. Churchill, who had no knowledge of the confusion within the U.S. government, could only protest what seemed to be a shift in the American position.

The fourth paragraph of Churchill's message refers to a statement made on June 20, 1944, by Oliver Lyttelton before a meeting in London of the U.S. Chamber of Commerce. While surveying the development of the Anglo-

American alliance, Lyttelton commented that "the Japanese were forced to attack the Americans at Pearl Harbor." Although he later insisted that he meant only that the Japanese chose to take American aid to Germany as a provocation, news reports in the United States about the speech embarrassed the Roosevelt administration, particularly since some questions about Tyler Kent's claims of prewar conspiracy between Churchill and Roosevelt had been raised recently. (See R–5x and Kimball and Bartlett, "Prewar Commitments," pp. 293–94.)

C–712

London [via U.S. Army]
June 23, 1944, 1437 Z / TOR 1625 Z

Prime Minister to President Roosevelt Personal and Top Secret.
  Your number 565.
  1. The Russians are the only power that can do anything in Roumania and I thought it was agreed between you and me that on the basis of their reasonable armistice terms, excepting indemnities, they should try to give coherent direction to what happened there. In point of fact, we have all three cooperated closely in handling in Cairo the recent Roumanian peace feelers. On the other hand, the Greek burden rests almost entirely upon us and has done so since we lost 40,000 men in a vain endeavour to help them in 1941. Similarly, you have let us play the hand in Turkey, but we have always consulted you on policy and I think we have been agreed on the line to be followed. It would be quite easy for me, on the general principle of slithering to the left, which is so popular in foreign policy, to let things rip when the King of Greece would probably be forced to abdicate and EAM would work a reign of terror in Greece, forcing the villagers and many other classes to form security battalions under German auspices to prevent utter anarchy. The only way I can prevent this is by persuading the Russians to quit boosting EAM and ramming it forward with all their force. Therefore I proposed to the Russians a temporary working arrangement for the better conduct of the war. This was only a proposal and had to be referred to you for your agreement.
  2. I cannot admit that I have done anything wrong in this matter. It would not be possible for three people in different parts of the world to work together effectively if no one of them may make any suggestion to either of the others without simultaneously keeping the third informed. A recent example of this is the message you have sent quite properly to UJ about your conversations with the Poles of which, as yet, I have heard nothing from you [see R–571]. I am not complaining at all of this because I know we are working for the general theme and purposes and I hope you will feel that has been so in my conduct of the Greek affair.

3. I have, also, taken action to try to bring together a union of the Tito forces with those in Serbia and with all adhering to the Royal Yugoslav Government, which we have both recognized. You have been informed at every stage of how we are bearing this heavy burden which at present rests mainly on us. Here again, nothing would be easier than to throw the King and the Royal Yugoslav Government to the wolves and let a civil war break out in Yugoslavia to the joy of the Germans. I am struggling to bring order out of chaos in both cases and concentrate all efforts against the common foe. I am keeping you constantly informed: and I hope to have your confidence and help within the spheres of action in which initiative is assigned to us.

4. On the other hand, I send you my sincere apologies for Oliver Lyttelton's foolish remark which I fear may cause you trouble. If there is anything I can say usefully, pray let me know.

5. Let me congratulate you most wholeheartedly upon the brilliant fighting of the American troops in the Cherbourg Peninsula as well as in Italy. We have immense tasks before us. Indeed, I cannot think of any moment when the burden of the war has laid more heavily upon me or when I have felt so unequal to its ever-more entangled problems. I greatly admire the strength and courage with which you face your difficulties, especially in a year when you have, what I may venture to call, other preoccupations.

[MR*. pFRUS, 1944, V, 126–27. pWSC, VI, 77–79. R&C.]

A key factor in the American insistence on ANVIL was the need to obtain a major port through which forty to fifty divisions of troops waiting in the United States could be brought into action. The destruction of one of the "Mulberry" harbors during the channel gale of June 19–24 and the damage to the port of Cherbourg during the battle for that city, finally occupied by the Allies on June 27, only strengthened the American resolve to push for ANVIL.

R–566

Washington [via U.S. Navy]
June 23, 1944, 11:50 A.M.

Personal and Top Secret, from the President for the Prime Minister.

Replying to your Number 710, Admiral King advises as follows: In their meeting in London on June 13 the Combined Chiefs of Staff approved a telegram to be addressed to General Wilson and General Eisenhower concerning future amphibious operations using forces in the Mediterranean. This despatch was to be sent after the receipt of your approval, which was reported by your secretariat to have been obtained.

The approved despatch expressed the view that an amphibious operation involving a three-divisional lift should be undertaken, the operation to be launched by July 25.

Admiral King's memorandum to Admiral Stark provided for the prospective movement of combat forces and certain amphibious forces to the Mediterranean in time to provide for these operations that had met with the approval of the Combined Chiefs of Staff. The combat forces involved were essentially those originally set up for the support of a two-divisional ANVIL and were later moved, after the postponement of ANVIL, to OVERLORD for the specific purpose of augmenting the support forces to be used in the firm establishment of the beachhead. The amphibious forces to be moved southward were derived after consultation with Eisenhower's staff and were discussed in the Combined Chiefs of Staff meeting. Emphasis on the need for an early date for amphibious operations in the Mediterranean in support of OVERLORD (an earlier date than the August 15 proposed by General Wilson) was particularly stressed by Eisenhower. However, Admiral King's memorandum to Admiral Stark stated that the directive to execute the planned movement could be expected to follow immediately upon *final* Combined Chiefs of Staff decision (which has not yet been made.)

Obviously it is not King's intention to take any steps that would jeopardize OVERLORD. Further the planned steps for the prospective movement of forces were taken after consultation with the British Chiefs of Staff and with General Eisenhower.

It appears that there is a misunderstanding in regard to the directions given by King to Stark. Roosevelt [WDL]

[MR]

When the British announced they were beginning discussions with the French Committee of National Liberation about the civil affairs of liberated France, Secretary of State Hull concluded that those negotiations approximated government-to-government relations. If agreement were reached between the British and the FCNL, Hull warned, it would violate the American policy of maintaining military control in France and would constitute a *fait accompli* that the United States would have "to go along with, or be placed in the position alone of having to object to the terms of the agreement" (Hull to Roosevelt, June 20, 1944, MR).

R–567

Washington [via U.S. Navy]
June 23, 1944, 12:00 A.M., noon

Personal and Top Secret. From the President for the Former
Naval Person.

Your 707. I join with you in a hope that a visit by De Gaulle in Washington will have a corrective effect on what is now a very unsatisfactory situation.

We are informed by your Embassy that your Government plans discussions with the Committee prior to De Gaulle's visit with the thought of "being helpful to the Washington conversations."

I hope you will not make any agreements with the Committee prior to giving me an opportunity to comment thereon.

I should not like to be faced with a fait accompli when De Gaulle arrives in Washington. Roosevelt [WDL]

[MR. *R&C*.]

Although Churchill assured Roosevelt that the talks between the British and the FCNL diplomatic representative in London, Pierre Viénot, were unofficial, the British Cabinet assumed that the reality of the situation would force the Americans to accept FCNL administrative control in liberated France. (The Map Room version of this document substituted "official" for "unofficial" in the opening sentence.)

C–713

London [via U.S. Army]
June 24, 1944, 2100 Z / TOR 2220 Z

Prime Minister to President Roosevelt Personal and Top Secret.

Your number 567.

The conversations now proceeding with Monsieur Vienot the De Gaullist Ambassador in London are on an unofficial level only, De Gaulle having declared himself unwilling to send any of his Committee members unless the United States were represented also.

The object of the conversations is to discover a basis that we might accept for the operation of civil affairs in liberated areas of France in regard to which both the United States Government and we ourselves have agreed that the French Committee of National Liberation should take the leadership. Our people have no power to conclude any agreement. Their work will be submitted to the Foreign Secretary and to me and at that time, before any agreement is made with the French Committee and before His Majesty's Government have pronounced on the result of their work or intimated to the French Committee their decision, we shall consult with you and impart to you our views.

There is of course no question of the recognition of a provisional government being raised at this Committee. You will certainly not be faced by His Majesty's Government with any fait accompli. I hope these assurances, in which Eden concurs will be fully satisfactory to you.

[PREM 3/472. MR.]

Anglo-American conversations on petroleum began on July 25, 1944, with the British delegation headed by Lord Beaverbrook and the American by Cordell Hull.

The counter-measures mentioned by Roosevelt were aimed against the German V-1 "flying bombs" then falling on southern England. British fighter aircraft accounted for most of the flying bombs destroyed in the air, although anti-aircraft shells using proximity fuses later proved effective. Bombing raids on launch sites in France did little damage until later in July, after intelligence from the French Resistance pinpointed the main storage areas for the flying bombs. False information fed to the Germans by British Intelligence caused the bulk of the flying bombs to fall short of the center of London, mostly in the Dulwich area, which cut down the number of casualties. (See Jones, *Wizard War*, pp. 418–28, and Montagu, *Beyond Top Secret ULTRA*, pp. 158–61.)

R–568

Washington [via U.S. Navy]
June 24, 1944, 11:30 A.M.

Personal and Secret, for the Prime Minister from the President.

Your 708. Beaverbrook is as you know an old friend of mine and I shall be very happy to see him.

May the good fortune of you and yours in the bombing continue until the Hun is crushed and we hope your counter measures already producing good results will rapidly increase in their effectiveness. Roosevelt [WDL]

[MR]

R–569

Washington [via U.S. Navy]
June 24, 1944, 11:35 A.M.

Secret and Personal, from the President for the Prime Minister.

Thank you for the message from U.J. contained in your 711.

The immediately prospective new offensive should be of real assistance to our Italian and French efforts which are already moving forward at a rate of progress that is exceeding my expectations. Roosevelt [WDL]

[MR]

CCS 603 expressed the opinion of the U.S. Joint Chiefs that Italy would not be a decisive theater of operations and emphasized that the delay in agreeing on ANVIL seemed to go against the policy of directing all resources toward the speediest possible end of the war.

C–714

London [via U.S. Army]
June 25, 1944, 1330 Z

Prime Minister to President Roosevelt Personal and Top Secret.

I have just read memorandum CCS 603 from the United States Chiefs of Staff and also the immediately following containing the proposed draft orders. These very grave questions will immediately be examined by the British Chiefs of Staff and by the War Cabinet. I earnestly hope you will consent to hear both sides. Our answer will be given within 48 hours.

[MR*. R&C.]

Again without telling the State Department, the President agreed to the three-month trial period for the Anglo-Soviet arrangement in the Balkans.

R–570

Washington [via U.S. Navy]
June 26, 1944, 1:10 P.M.

Personal and Top Secret, from the President to the Prime Minister.

Your Number 712.

It appears that both of us have inadvertently taken unilateral action in a direction that we both now agree to have been expedient for the time being.

It is essential that we should always be in agreement in matters bearing on our Allied war effort.

My next following message quotes the one I sent to U.J. about the Polish Prime Minister's visit.

Oliver Lyttelton's remark reminds me of the well known old prayer that we be spared from our friends—I think that is now a dead issue that should not be resurrected.

Local problems are no doubt occupying much of the time of both of us, but I am sure we do not admit preoccupation with anything but the war. Roosevelt [WDL]

[MR. p*FRUS*, 1944, V, 127. p*WSC*, VI, 78. p*R&C*.]

The President responded quickly to Churchill's chiding (C–712) by sending the Prime Minister a copy of the Roosevelt-to-Stalin cable regarding the visit of Polish Prime Minister Stanislaw Mikolajczyk to Washington. Roosevelt had previously discouraged such a visit lest it stimulate Polish-American groups to insist that he support the Poles against the Soviets in disputes over borders and the political makeup of the Polish government. By June, however, the President had decided that a continued refusal to see Mikolajczyk would be even more damaging to his hopes of maintaining Polish-American support in the election—only five months away. Roosevelt told his aides that the seven million Polish-Americans were the one ethnic group which could be counted on to vote as a bloc, and those votes could swing the election in such key states as Illinois and Ohio.

The talks between Mikolajczyk and American officials began on June 5 and lasted until June 14. As part of the arrangements, the Polish leader had promised not to make any public speeches or to contact any of the Polish-American groups, although a certain amount of public fanfare accompanied the visit. Mikolajczyk tried to obtain firm commitments from Roosevelt, but the President would promise only "moral support." Roosevelt may have preferred a freely elected government in Catholic Poland, assuming that such a regime would not be communist, but wartime and postwar cooperation with the Soviet Union were even more important, particularly since Poland lay in eastern Europe, far from American power and influence. In a statement which Mikolajczyk should have realized meant that Roosevelt would have sided with the Soviets were it not for the forthcoming presidential election, the President repeatedly explained that he could not actively participate in the Soviet-Polish dispute during the "American political year of 1944" (Stettinius, *The Diaries*, p. 79).

Foreshadowing Soviet recognition of the pro-communist Polish government in Lublin, Stalin met with representatives of the Soviet-controlled Polish National Council while Mikolajczyk was meeting with the Americans.

R–571

Washington [via U.S. Navy]
June 26, 1944, 12:30 P.M.

Top Secret and Personal. From the President for the Former
Naval Person.

The following is an accurate paraphrase of the message sent to Stalin
on 17 June 1944:

> QUOTE. The Polish Prime Minister, Mr. Mikolajczyk, as you know,
> has just completed a short visit here. I deemed his visit at this time
> as desirable and necessary for reasons which Ambassador Harriman
> has already explained to you.
>
> Therefore, you know that his visit was not connected with any
> attempt on my part to insert myself into the merits of the differences
> which exist between the Soviet Government and the Polish Govern-
> ment-in-exile. I can assure you that no specific plan or proposal in
> any way affecting Polish-Soviet relations was drawn up, although we
> had a frank and beneficial exchange of views on a wide variety of
> subjects affecting Poland. However, I think you would be interested
> in his attitude towards the problems confronting his country and in
> my personal impression of him.
>
> He impressed me as a very reasonable and sincere person whose
> only aim is to do what is best for his country. Being fully aware that
> the entire future of Poland depends upon the establishment of really
> good relations with the Soviet Union, he will, in my opinion, exert
> every effort to achieve that goal.
>
> His first immediate concern is the vital necessity for setting up the
> fullest kind of collaboration between the forces of the Polish Un-
> derground and the Red Army in the common struggle against our
> enemy. It is his belief that cooperation between the organized Polish
> Underground and your Armies is a military factor of the greatest
> importance not only to your Armies in the East but also to the main
> task of finishing off by our combined efforts the Nazi beast in his
> lair.
>
> The Prime Minister gave me the impression that he will not let any
> minor considerations stand in the way of his attempts to reach a
> solution with you and that he is thinking only of Poland and the
> Polish people. If he felt that you would welcome such a step on his
> part, it is my firm belief that he would not hesitate to go to Moscow
> in order to discuss with you frankly and personally the problems
> involving your two countries, in particular the urgency of immediate
> military collaboration. You will understand, I know, that I am in no

way trying to press my personal views upon you in a matter which is of special concern to you and your country, when I make this observation. However, I felt that a frank account of the impressions I received in talking with the Polish Prime Minister were due you. UNQUOTE.

Roosevelt [WDL]

[MR. p*FRUS*, 1944, II, 1284. p*Stalin/FDR*, doc. 203. *R&C*.]

At Morgenthau's insistence, the United States stood by its refusal formally to back the occupation francs being issued by Anglo-American officials in liberated France. (The last sentence in the second paragraph was deleted from the Treasury Department draft by the President.)

R–572

Washington [via U.S. Navy]
June 26, 1944, 4:55 P.M.

Personal and Top Secret. From the President for the Former Naval Person.

Refer your 709 of June 21.

I do not feel that we should proceed upon the assumption that our governments are responsible for the redemption of the supplemental franc currency merely because no understanding has been reached with the French Committee.

The supplemental franc currency has been issued by the Supreme Allied Commander because at present he is the only authority with the power to issue currency for France. The Supreme Commander has the responsibility during the military period to see that the Frenchmen who accept and hold this currency will not be cheated and that full value will be given for it in France. Ultimately the supplemental currency will be redeemed like any other good currency by the government of the country in which it is issued. In due course, when a government is established in France the United States and British Governments can reach a full settlement with the French Government for Allied expenditures in France. In such a settlement, even in the absence of prior agreement with the French Committee, allowance could be made for assumption by the French of all costs of civil government and of those local expenditures of our armed forces which in the case of other Western European countries will be regarded as mutual aid. ~~If we wanted to drive a hard bargain, a strong case could be made that neither of our governments has any obligation~~

~~to bear the burden for any of our local currency expenditures in France or in other liberated areas.~~

Despite these considerations I have recently proposed financial agreements with Belgium, the Netherlands and Norway under which this Government will pay currently in dollars for the amounts of their currencies used for our troop pay. On the other hand, we expect these governments to pay us in dollars for supplies for the civil population. If dollars accruing to them from troop pay are insufficient to cover their purchases of civilian supplies, we shall expect them to draw on their dollar or gold resources. I understand you have similar arrangements with these countries.

I am willing that we should study the possibility of reaching an understanding with the French Committee consistent with existing political considerations embodying the payment principles of the financial arrangements with Belgium, the Netherlands and Norway. I am giving instructions to the appropriate departments of this government to proceed with the study of this problem in consultation with the French Committee, and I feel it advisable that your studies and consultations be coordinated with ours. Roosevelt [HM]

[MR]

Churchill's claim that "the very best of relations prevail" soon proved incorrect as the dispute over ANVIL became more heated. Admiral Sir Andrew B. Cunningham had become First Sea Lord in October 1943.

C–715

London [via U.S. Army]
June 26, 1944, 2344 Z / TOR 0115 Z, June 27

Prime Minister to President Personal and Top Secret.
Your No 566.

Thank you very much. I have had a talk with Stark and Andrew Cunningham here today. Everything is quite understood and the very best of relations prevail. The matter need not be thought of again. I am greatly obliged for your courtesy and that of Admiral King.

[MR*]

Churchill's "trial" was probably the V-1 attack on southern England, whereas the President was becoming more deeply involved in the fall elections.

C–716

London [via U.S. Army]
June 27, 1944, 2151 Z / TOR 2320 Z

Prime Minister to President Roosevelt Personal and Top Secret.

Your No. 570 let me withdraw at once the word "preoccupation" in Para 5 of my 712 and substitute the word "trials." Thank you very much for what you say. You may be very sure I shall always be looking to our agreement in all matters before, during and after.

I have read your message to Stalin about Mikolajczyk [R–571]. I think it will be most helpful. Every good wish.

[MR*. R&C.]

The dispute over the scheduled invasion of southern France, Operation AN-VIL (discussed in C–710), could no longer be settled by the Combined Chiefs of Staff, and Churchill went over their heads with a direct appeal to Roosevelt. During the Teheran Conference, the President had briefly mentioned the chance of an attack toward the Danube from the head of the Adriatic Sea (Istria), but that suggestion had long since been overtaken by events. (See *FRUS, Teheran Conf.*, p. 493.)

C–717

London [via U.S. Army]
June 28, 1944, 1620 Z / TOR 1745 Z

Prime Minister to President Roosevelt Strictly Private, Personal and Top Secret.

1. The deadlock between our Chiefs of Staff raises most serious issues. Our first wish is to help General Eisenhower in the most speedy and effective manner. But, we do not think this necessarily involves the complete ruin of all our great affairs in the Mediterranean, and we take it hard that this should be demanded of us.

2. I am sending you, in a few hours, a very full argument on the whole matter which I have prepared with my own hands, and which is endorsed by the Chiefs of Staff. I shall consult the War Cabinet on the subject tomorrow, 29th, and I have already circulated the paper to them. Those who have seen it completely endorse it, including those members who belong to the Defense Committee. I have very little doubt of unanimous support upon this issue.

3. I most earnestly beg you to examine this matter in detail for yourself. I think the tone of the United States Chiefs of Staff is arbitrary and,

certainly, I see no prospect of agreement on the present lines. What is to happen then? It was such a pity that they all separated before this issue arose, just like we separated before the Italian climax after QUADRANT.

4. Please remember how you spoke to me at Teheran about Istria, and how I introduced it at the full conference. This has sunk very deeply into my mind, although it is not, by any means, the immediate issue we have to decide.

5. I am shocked to think of the length of the message that I shall be sending you tonight. It is a purely personal communication between you and me in our capacity as heads of the two western democracies.

[MR*. pWSC, VI, 63. Ehrman, *Grand Strategy*, V, 352–53. *R&C*.]

Before Churchill's plea for canceling ANVIL could arrive in Washington, the President sent a telegram strongly endorsing the arguments of the U.S. Joint Chiefs of Staff. (The additions to the draft were made in Roosevelt's handwriting.)

R–573

Washington [via U.S. Navy]
June 28, 1944, 12:05 P.M.

Personal and Top Secret, from the President for the Former
Naval Person.
  Your 714.
  I have examined the problem of assistance for OVERLORD by operations in the Mediterranean which our Chiefs of Staff have been discussing. On balance I find I must completely concur in the stand of the U.S. Chiefs of Staff. General Wilson's proposal for continued use of practically all the Mediterranean resources to advance into northern Italy and from there to the northeast is not acceptable to me, and I really believe we should consolidate our operations and not scatter them.
  It seems to me that nothing can be worse at this time than a dead-lock in the Combined Staffs as to future course of action. You and I must prevent this and I think we should support the views of the Supreme Allied Commander. He is definitely for ANVIL and wants action in the field by August 30th preferably earlier.
  It is vital that we decide at once to go ahead with our long agreed policy to make OVERLORD the decisive action. ANVIL, mounted at the earliest possible date, is the only operation which will give OVERLORD the material and immediate support from Wilson's forces. Roosevelt [GCM]

[MR. *R&C*.]

Since General Sir Stewart Graham Menzies was "C"—the head of M.I.6, the British military's Secret Intelligence Service—the "very important information" he sent to Roosevelt was most likely an intelligence report, probably one received in London on June 27 indicating that Hitler expected the Allies to mount a major offensive in Italy in order to follow up their successes. The report, which could not be located in the archives, was most probably based on an ULTRA intercept. It claimed that the Germans had decided to defend the northern Apennines since a breakthrough there "would have 'incalculable military and political consequences.' " (Ehrman, *Grand Strategy*, V, 353, apparently quotes the intelligence report, though without a citation.)

The abbreviation OKW (par. 4 and after) stands for Oberkommando der Wehrmacht—the German Army High Command. Cette (par. 14 and after) is an Anglicized form of Sète, a city on the Gulf of Lions in southern France. General Alexander's plan and General Wilson's support for Alexander's proposals (par. 19) are summarized in Ehrman, *Grand Strategy*, V, 347–49. Smuts' cable to Churchill (par. 19) is reprinted in *WSC*, VI, 61–62.

The Maquis (par. 16) was one of the five main French Resistance organizations. It was made up of young men who had fled into the mountains of the Haute-Savoie to escape German labor drafts.

C–718

London
June 28, 1944, 2045 Z / TOR 0135 Z, June 29

Prime Minister to President Roosevelt. Strictly Private, Personal and Top Secret.

1. Following is memorandum referred to in paragraph two of my number 717. Please also take into consideration the very important information which General Menzies is sending you separately on my instructions.

2. Memorandum begins:— Operations in the European Theatres. Note by the Prime Minister and Minister of Defence.

Part I.

1. I have thought it right to put down a few points which seem to me dominant.

2. At the present stage of the war in Europe, our overall strategic concept should be the engagement of the enemy on the largest scale with the greatest violence and continuity. In this way only shall we bring about an early collapse. Here is the prime test.

3. For this purpose sufficient ports must be acquired to allow the direct and speedy deployment in Europe of the thirty or more American divisions which are in the United States.

4. In choosing points of landing or attack, regard must be paid, first to their tactical relation with the main enterprise and battle proceeding under General Eisenhower in Western France; and, secondly, to the strain produced upon the Central Power of Germany, the OKW. The optimum is to combine both.

5. Political considerations, such as the revolt of populations against the enemy or the submission and coming over of his satellites, are a valid and important factor.

6. It is better to have two ventures than three, and there are certainly not enough LSTS, etc, available for more than two major ventures.

7. The various choices now open should be examined in the light of the above requirements.

Part II.

8. The supreme priority must naturally be accorded to the support of OVERLORD, for it is certain that the number of divisions now assigned to that enterprise up to the end of August, namely, forty plus, are not sufficient to establish mastery over the enemy resources available in Western France (apart from a psychological collapse which should not be reckoned upon). It was understood that United States divisions would directly reinforce OVERLORD after August at the rate of five per month. The number of divisions which can be provided to reinforce OVERLORD in this period should be limited only by shipping possibilities and port accommodation on the western shores of France. The fundamental problem for SHAEF is the reception of the maximum of divisions from any quarter, together with the necessary tail.

9. For this purpose one ought not to consider only the ports envisaged. There are many small ports besides, as port-En-Bassin, Courseulles and Ouistreham, with an aggregate capacity of four thousand tons per diem, have already been found, even on the very closely-studied beaches of the actual OVERLORD assault. The use of landing craft enormously increases the discharge from these small ports. For this reason it would seem a mistake to move large quantities of landing craft from the supreme operation across the channel to any diversion elsewhere which was not in tactical relation to the battle. The question is how to give General Eisenhower the maximum support directly in the shortest time and without causing needless havoc elsewhere.

10. The whole facilities for reception of troops and vehicles along the French Atlantic Coast should be re-examined in the light of newly-won experience. Moreover, the gaining of new ports to the north and south of our present OVERLORD objectives is greatly facilitated

by the use of shore-based airfields or fuelling grounds now soon to be available in France. The taking of Havre and St Nazaire is a necessity in far closer relation to the battle than any ports in the Mediterranean. In short, it is the main interest of OVERLORD to receive the great volume of troops who are waiting in the United States and can, if they can take them and if they can come into action sooner, be drawn from the Mediterranean. It would be a great pity to sweep aside all possibilities of broadening the intake direct from the United States or by stages through the United Kingdom into the western coasts of France.

11. Not only should the quantity of the intake be expanded to the utmost limit, but also the quality should be related to the fighting prospects of the next few months. Attached to this paper will be found, in a note (annex) prepared for me, the arrivals in the United Kingdom during May and the estimate of arrivals for June, July and August. From this it will be seen that 553,356 American soldiers have arrived or are to arrive in these four months, but they only constitute seven divisions. The field troops of seven divisions amount to about 20,000 men a division, and with other fighting accessories, such as tank brigades and independent brigades, etc, to (say) 25,000. Total 175,000. Deducting this from 553,356 leaves 378,356. The question arises whether it might not be possible by severe adjustments, within the limits of existing shipping arrangements, to give a higher priority to at least four or five more fighting divisions at the expense of some 378,356 servicing troops of many details comprised in this immense figure. The battle in France in this period may turn upon the more speedy arrival of these additional fighting units. This would still leave nearly a quarter of a million for the tail. Here also it must be observed that the casualties in France have happily been much less than those provided in the scale of build up, and we should be justified on the results of May and June alone in sending in two additional formed divisions instead of fifty thousand replacements.

12. There are three French divisions which could be withdrawn from North Africa and a further four French divisions which might be withdrawn from Italy if ports and shipping and tail could be found for them. General Eisenhower in his number SCAF 53, para 7 B, plainly foresees this possibility as his second choice.

13. Thus there are possibilities of a considerable increase on the schedule of arrivals in the OVERLORD area in the next three months. Let us be sure that we are right in discarding these possibilities before we turn to more sombre alternatives, for it is certain that in no other way can so great or so timely a reinforcement be given to OVER-LORD.

Part III.

14. We must consider the application of the axioms set forth in Part I to the Mediterranean in relation to the remarks in Part II about reinforcement of OVERLORD from the west. If there were any way of capturing Bordeaux within the present fighting season by a thrust from the Gulf of Lions, and thus opening Bordeaux and other smaller ports near it to the advance across the ocean of the main United States Army, this would clearly take priority over any purely Mediterranean enterprise which could be launched. Let us therefore examine in this setting the variants of ANVIL which have for so many months held our thoughts. Two projects have been put forward, to wit, a landing of, say, ten divisions with a three-division lift and a seven-division follow-up at Cette or at Marseilles. Cette has the great advantage of being only 225 miles from Bordeaux and is without any serious mountain obstructions. It is, I understand, admitted by all sides that there is no possibility of any landing on the 1st August and the earliest possibility is the 15th August, and that even this is doubtful. If we attack Cette between the 15th and 30th August, we are told it would be conceivable to land up to ten divisions by the end of September or the middle of October. There would then be the 225-mile march to accomplish in the face of such opposition as might be offered. If there were any opposition worthy of the name, it would be very surprising if a rate of more than 5 miles a day could be maintained by a substantial force. Thus we could not expect to take Bordeaux from the back before the beginning or middle of December. Thereafter there would be the need to put the port in order, and therefore the Cette operation, even if the naval objection to the landing-places were overcome, would not influence the war in 1944 except in so far as German troops now on the Riviera or despatched from OKW were kept out of the OVERLORD theatre. On this plan there could not be any large oversea intake from the United States. This heavy-footed method of approach to Bordeaux is not to be compared with the results to be obtained by a descent upon Bordeaux either from Bayonne or from neighbouring small landing points. This might by a Coup-De-Main give a port and bridgehead into which French troops from Africa and the Mediterranean could enter France, and another great port be opened directly on the Atlantic. Anyhow, in view of the naval objections, Cette has been ruled out.

15. We are therefore left with the Toulon-Marseilles operation. The more I have thought about this, the more bleak and sterile it appears. It adds another 130 miles to the march upon Bordeaux,

making a total of 355 miles in all. This march would present a flank to any German forces to the northward. The landing itself cannot be begun till the 30th August, and then only if the LSTS, etc, can be spared from OVERLORD by the 10th July. All that can be said against Cette as a means of access to Bordeaux is reinforced in the case of Marseilles by these facts. Indeed the march to Bordeaux from Marseilles could not begin in ten division strength till a month after the 30th August, and could not be accomplished for probably three months after that. For these reasons I cannot feel convinced that the attack on Bordeaux from the Gulf of Lions is a practical possibility.

16. But the successful capture of Toulon and Marseilles by the 30th August and the landing of ten divisions by the 30th September would also have as a possible objective a march up the Rhone valley with Lyons, 160 miles to the north, as its first objective. Here we should have, if successful, the advantage of putting in all the French available and such American divisions as were withdrawn from Italy, from Africa or diverted from the United States at the cost of OVERLORD. We should also be in close contact with the Maquis, who have developed a moderate guerilla in the mountains. We should have a first-class port through which to pour American troops into this part of France if and as desired. It is as easy to talk of an advance up the Rhone valley as it is of a march from Italy to Vienna. But very great hazards, difficulties and delays may menace all such projects. Once we are committed to the landing at Marseilles, all the enemy troops along the Riviera, at present seven or eight divisions, can be brought to oppose us. It will always be possible for OKW to move any forces they have in Italy through the tunnels under the Alps or till winter comes along the great motoring roads which have been made over them, and intercept our northward advance at any point they chose. The country is most formidable. Without the enemy withdrawing a single division from the OVERLORD battle, we could be confronted with superior forces at every step we advance up the Rhone valley. The evacuation by the enemy of Piedmont would not entail more than his guarding the Corniche roads along the Riviera and the mountain passes which, with the winter coming on, would not be difficult. He can always blow up the tunnels at his discretion. If we blow them up by air action, he can always, except in the depth of winter, escape over the top or along the Riviera coast.

17. It seems to me very difficult to prove that either the Cette or the Marseilles operation would have any tactical relation to the battle we have to fight now and throughout this summer and autumn for OVERLORD. The distance, as the crow flies, from Marseilles to Cherbourg is 600 miles, and from Marseilles to Paris 400 miles. It would

seem clear that, even with great success, neither of these operations would directly influence the present battle in 1944.

18. Moreover, before we embark upon either of these two forms of ANVIL in the hopes of helping OVERLORD, it would be well to count the cost that must be paid for either of them.

Part IV.

19. General Wilson's number B 12995, General Alexander's private and personal number T 1322/4 to me, and Field-Marshal Smuts's private and personal to me, put before us the project of an attack eastward across the Adriatic or/and around its shores, and General Wilson conceives it possible that, on this plan, he and General Alexander could have possession of Trieste by the end of September. This movement is of course equally unrelated tactically to OVERLORD as are the variants of ANVIL.

20. Whether we should ruin all hopes of a major victory in Italy and all its fronts and condemn ourselves to a passive role in that theatre, after having broken up the fine Allied army which is advancing so rapidly through that peninsula, for the sake of ANVIL with all its limitations, is indeed a grave question for His Majesty's Government and the President, with the Combined Chiefs of Staff, to decide. For my own part, while eager to do everything in human power which will give effective and timely help to OVERLORD, I should greatly regret to see General Alexander's army deprived of much of its offensive power in northern Italy for the sake of a march up the Rhone valley, which the Combined Chiefs of Staff have themselves described as unprofitable, in addition to our prime operation of OVERLORD.

21. To sum up—

(A) Let us reinforce OVERLORD directly, to the utmost limit of landings from the west.

(B) Let us next do justice to the great opportunities of the Mediterranean Commanders, and confine ourselves at this phase to minor diversions and threats to hold the enemy around the Gulf of Lions.

(C) Let us leave General Eisenhower all his landing craft as long as he needs them to magnify his landing capacity.

(D) Let us make sure of increasing to the maximum extent the port capacity in the OVERLORD battle area.

(E) Let us resolve not to wreck one great campaign for the sake of winning the other. Both can be won.

WSC 10 Downing Street, SW 1, 28th June, 1944

Annex U S Army, including AAF arrivals in U.K., May to August 1944:

1. Serial
2. Detail
3. Arrivals in U.K. during May 1944
4. U.S. estimate of arrivals in U.K. for
    (a) June
    (b) July
    (c) August

1.	2.	3.	4.	
1	US Army (excluding Air Force)	88,432	(a)	135,775
			(b)	107,639
			(c)	189,541
2	US Army Air Force	16,257	(a)	7,196
			(b)	3,301
			(c)	5,215
3	Total US Army (including AAF)	104,689	(a)	142,971
			(b)	110,940
			(c)	194,756
4	Number of Inf Divs	1	(a)	1
			(b)	0
			(c)	2
5	Number of Armd Divs	0	(a)	1
			(b)	0
			(c)	1
6	Number of A/B Divs	0	(a)	0
			(b)	0
			(c)	1

[MR. *pWSC*, VI, 716–21.]

C–719

London [via U.S. Army]
June 28, 1944, 2240 Z /TOR 0015 Z, June 29

Prime Minister to President Roosevelt. Personal and Top Secret.

1. I have just received your number 573. But you had not then received my number 717. Nor the memorandum referred to in paragraph two thereof, nor the important information which General Menzies is sending

you separately on my instructions, nor the latest reply by the British Chiefs of Staff to the United States Chiefs of Staff.

2. I earnestly hope you will take all these into consideration and then let me know what you think. A meeting will have to be arranged unless agreement can be reached by correspondence. I agree with you that a deadlock on fundamental questions on strategy would be a cruel injury to our soldiers, who are now fighting so vehemently side by side. For this reason a careful and patient discussion is indispensable and not an over-riding decision by either side.

[MR*. p*FRUS, Quebec Conf.*, 1944, pp. 8–9.]

Roosevelt's answer was drafted by the Joint Chiefs of Staff and expressed, in detail, the viewpoint of the American military. (Paragraphs 1 and 15 were added at the suggestion of Admirals Leahy and Brown; the change in paragraph 3 and the final paragraph were added by the President. There is also some evidence indicating that the last sentence of paragraph 10 was inserted by Roosevelt.) Although written by the JCS, the statement in paragraph 9 that the United States "cannot agree" to deploy troops in the Balkans, plus the warning that Stalin would have to approve any such change in plans, were consonant with the President's long-held position that eastern Europe, unlike western Europe, was beyond America's sphere of influence. Field Marshal Albert Kesselring was the German Commander in Chief in the Italian theater.

R–574

Washington [via U.S. Navy]
June 29, 1944, 2:40 P.M.

Personal and Top Secret. From the President for the Former Naval Person.

1. I have given careful personal consideration to your Number 718 and I have had our Joint Staffs give the whole subject further consideration.

2. I agree with you that our over-all strategic concept should be to engage the enemy on the largest scale with the greatest violence and continuity, but I am convinced that it must be based on a main effort together with closely coordinated supporting efforts directed at the heart of Germany.

3. The exploitation of OVERLORD, our victorious advances in Italy, an early assault on Southern France, combined with the Soviet drives to the West—all as envisaged at Teheran—will most surely serve to realize our object,—the unconditional surrender of Germany. In this connection also I am mindful of our agreement with Stalin as to an operation against

the south of France and his frequently expressed views favoring such an operation and classifying all others in the Mediterranean ~~as unimportant~~ of lesser importance to the principal objective of the European campaign.

4. I agree that the political considerations you mention are important factors, but military operations based thereon must be definitely secondary to the primary operations of striking at the heart of Germany.

5. I agree that the OVERLORD build-up must receive continuing attention, but consider this to be definitely Eisenhower's responsibility. The forces we are sending him from the United States are what he has asked for. If he wants divisions ahead of service troops he has but to ask—the divisions will be ready.

6. Until we have exhausted the forces in the United States, or it is proved we cannot get them to Eisenhower when he wants them, I am opposed to the wasteful procedure of transferring forces from the Mediterranean to OVERLORD. If we use shipping and port capacity to shift forces from one combat area—the Mediterranean—to another—OVERLORD, it will certainly detract from the build-up of OVERLORD direct from the United States and the net result is just what we don't want—fewer forces in combat areas.

7. My interest and hopes center on defeating the Germans in front of Eisenhower and driving on into Germany, rather than on limiting this action for the purpose of staging a full major effort in Italy. I am convinced we will have sufficient forces in Italy with ANVIL forces withdrawn, to chase Kesselring north of Pisa-Rimini and maintain heavy pressure against his army at the very least to the extent necessary to contain his present force. I cannot conceive of the Germans paying the price of 10 additional divisions, estimated by General Wilson, in order to keep us out of northern Italy.

8. We can—and Wilson confirms this—immediately withdraw 5 divisions (3 U.S. and 2 French) from Italy for ANVIL. The remaining 21 divisions plus numerous separate brigades will certainly provide Alexander with adequate ground superiority. With our air superiority there is obviously sufficient air in the Mediterranean to furnish support both for operations in Italy and for ANVIL, and to provide over-whelming air support during the critical moments of either operation. We also have virtual mastery of the sea in the Mediterranean.

9. I agree that operations against Bordeaux or Cette with Mediterranean forces are out of the picture. As to Istria, I feel that Alexander and Smuts for several natural and very human reasons are inclined to disregard two vital considerations: the grand strategy firmly believed by us to be necessary to the early conclusion of the war and the time factor as involved in the probable duration of a campaign to debouch from Ljubljana Gap into Slovenia and Hungary. The difficulties in this advance would seem far to exceed those pictured by you in the Rhone Valley,

ignoring the effect of organized resistance groups in France and the proximity to OVERLORD forces. I am informed that for purely logistical reasons it is doubtful if, within a decisive period, it would be possible to put into the fighting beyond the Ljubljana Gap more than six divisions. Meanwhile we will be struggling to deploy in France thirty-five U.S. divisions that are now in continental United States plus an equivalent of corps and army combat troops not to mention the necessary complement of service troops. I cannot agree to the employment of U.S. troops against Istria and into the Balkans, nor can I see the French agreeing to such use of French troops.

10. The beaches, exits, communications and cover in the Toulon area are most suitable. The Rhone corridor has its limitations, but is better than Ljubljana and is certainly far better than the terrain over which we have been fighting in Italy.

11. I am impressed by Eisenhower's statement that ANVIL is of transcendent importance and that he can and will furnish the required additional means to Wilson without undue detriment to OVERLORD, and by Wilson's statement that he can conduct the operation if given an immediate directive.

12. Wilson's plans for ANVIL are well developed and hence the operation can be launched with no delay.

13. Since the agreement was made at Teheran to mount an ANVIL, I cannot accept, without consultation with Stalin, any course of action which abandons this operation. In the event that you and I are unable to agree to issue a directive to General Wilson by 1 July to launch ANVIL at the earliest possible date, we must communicate with Stalin immediately. Furthermore, I feel that if we are to abandon ANVIL we must at once discuss with the French the use of their forces, which might by this decision be kept out of the battle in France, while taking losses in a secondary effort in Italy or the Balkans.

14. I again urge that the directive proposed by the U.S. Chiefs of Staff be issued to General Wilson immediately. It is evident that the drawing out of this discussion if continued will effectively kill the prospects of ANVIL in time to be of major benefit to OVERLORD.

15. At Teheran we agreed upon a definite plan of attack. That plan has gone well so far. Nothing has occurred to require any change. Now that we are fully involved in our major blow, history will never forgive us if we lose precious time and lives in indecision and debate. My dear friend, I beg you let us go ahead with our plan.

16. Finally for purely political considerations over here I would never survive even a slight setback in OVERLORD if it were known that fairly large forces had been diverted to the Balkans. Roosevelt [JCS]

[MR. *WSC*, VI, 721–25.]

In mid-February 1944, a group of military officers led by Colonel Juan Perón seized control of the Argentine government and installed General Edelmiro Farrell as President. The United States insisted, as a precondition to recognition of the new regime, that Axis activities in Argentina be suppressed. Perón, the real power in the new government, refused to meet the American conditions, and his totalitarian policies further antagonized Secretary of State Hull. Although the British government proposed that the Allies reach a working arrangement with the Perón regime, by June the United States had begun to consider withdrawing its Ambassador, Norman Armour. The British Foreign Office argued that such a move would only strengthen Perón's position within Argentina, but the American Ambassador was recalled for "consultations" and the State Department requested that the British do likewise. When the Foreign Office balked, Hull drafted the following cable, which the President approved without any changes. Sir D. Kelly was the British Ambassador in Argentina.

R–575

Washington [via U.S. Navy]
June 30, 1944, 1:10 P.M.

Personal and Top Secret. From the President for the Former Naval Person.

I understand that the Foreign Office is fully informed with regard to the importance which we attach to the proposal that Ambassador Kelly in Buenos Aires be recalled for consultation.

We have announced Armour's recall. Almost all of the other Republics are taking parallel action. However, it is clear beyond any question that the collective effect of this action will be seriously prejudiced if Kelly stays on in Buenos Aires.

In view of the importance of a common stand at this time, I earnestly hope that your decision will be a favorable one. Roosevelt [CH]

[MR. *FRUS*, 1944, VII, 332 (paraphrase).]

The British decided to put off any further arguments about occupation francs.

C–720

London [via U.S. Army]
July 1, 1944, 0900 Z / TOR 0950 Z

Prime Minister to President Roosevelt. Personal and Top Secret.
Reference telegram 572.

I was glad to have your telegram. I see good hopes of reaching a solution on the lines you suggest and entirely agree that we must coordinate closely.

[MR*]

The British Chiefs of Staff shared Churchill's enthusiasm about Allied chances to destroy German forces which had been ordered to make a stand south of the Pisa-Rimini defensive line in Italy, and they opposed the transfer of ten divisions from that theater to be used in ANVIL, an operation which seemed to them unnecessary. But the British Chiefs did not think much of General Alexander's proposal for an attack through Istria toward Vienna (Operation ARMPIT, a codename Churchill surely would have changed had the plan been approved), despite the Prime Minister's strong endorsement. Churchill mistakenly assumed he had the support of his COS, and when Roosevelt insisted that the invasion of southern France proceed (R–574), the Prime Minister drafted an angry reply which included a threat to resign rather than agree to such an "absolutely perverse strategy." He was serious about making an immediate flight to talk to Roosevelt and actually ordered that an aircraft be readied (Bryant, *Triumph in the West*, p. 168).

C-721, draft A, not sent

London
June 30, 1944

Prime Minister to President Roosevelt. Personal and Top Secret.

1. In order that you may know what is going on, I send you this telegram [not printed] just received from General Alexander, which shows that American brigades are actually being pulled out of his battle-front, in order to prepare for ANVIL. I cannot exaggerate the seriousness of this issue. Everything that we have said has been confirmed by our secret reports from the other side. It was understood here, before the Staff separated, that Alexander should have full facilities at least to fight to the Pisa-Rimini line.

2. The whole campaign in Italy is being ruined, and ruined for what? Simply for the amount of damage that 10 divisions, many quite unproved, the French almost entirely black and headed by inexperienced Commanders, can do advancing up the Rhone valley about five months hence.

3. There was only an interval of 48 hours between when your Chiefs of Staff proposed to us a Directive for an attack at ANVIL on August 1. But now, in your telegram No. __ it has become August 30. I really do know where I am or what orders should be given to the troops. If my departure from the scene would ease matters, by tendering my resignation to The King, I would gladly make this contribution, but I fear that the demand of the public to know the reasons would do great injury to the fighting troops.

4. We agreed that you would have the command in OVERLORD, and I am sure none of your officers will say we have not served you well and faithfully, and we are prepared to run every risk and make every exertion to carry forward victory there. Alternatively, we have to have command

in the Mediterranean. But no one ever contemplated that everything that was hopeful in the Mediterranean should be flung on one side, like the rind of an orange, in order that some minor benefice might come to help the theatre of your command.

5. There is nothing I will not do to end this deadlock except become responsible for an absolutely perverse strategy. If you wish, I will come at once across the ocean to Bermuda, or Quebec or, if you like, Washington. The very first weather that can be found, and the very swiftest aeroplane that can be got shall be my chariot. But to agree to the whole great Mediterranean scene, with all its possibilities, being incontinently cast into ruin without any proportionate advantage gained by OVER-LORD, that I cannot stand. I may add that I am supported by the War Cabinet and by the British Chiefs of Staff. Therefore I think I have a right to some consideration from you, my friend, at a time when our joint ventures have dazzled the world with success.

[PREM 3/271/8/531–32]

Field Marshal Sir Alan Brooke, Chief of the Imperial General Staff, summed up the results of a meeting between Churchill and the COS regarding ANVIL: "I thought at first we might have trouble with him; he looked like wanting to fight the President. However, in the end we got him to agree with our outlook, which is: 'All right, if you insist on being damned fools, sooner than fall out with you, which would be fatal, we shall be damned fools with you, and we shall see that we perform the role of damned fools damned well!' " (Bryant, *Triumph in the West*, p. 168). A memo to the Prime Minister from the chiefs of the three military services argued that they should not have to consult Stalin first about a change in ANVIL since that would necessitate disclosing the secret information they had about German intentions in Italy. More important, they concluded that American insistence on ANVIL was motivated by domestic politics, not military factors, and that "further discussion is useless" (Brooke, Portal, and Cunningham to Churchill, June 30, 1944, PREM 3/271/8/527–30). Churchill finally agreed, though the cable which followed made clear his resentment at Roosevelt's refusal to reconsider.

Churchill's recollection of Eisenhower's sentiments failed to mention that they were expressed on November 24, before the latter became SCAF (Supreme Commander Allied Forces), and therefore reflected the General's appraisal of the problems faced in the Italian theater. Nor was it accurate to characterize Eisenhower's attitude toward ANVIL as one of "dislike." As he cabled General Bedell Smith on January 6, 1944: "I agree that OVERLORD must be more broadly based, but I do not agree that a threat of ANVIL will be as effective as the operation itself. . . . Only in event that OVERLORD cannot possibly be broadened without abandonment of ANVIL would I consider making such a recommendation to the Combined Chiefs" (*Eisenhower Papers*, III, 1952). (Eisenhower's discussion on November 24 with Churchill and the Combined Chiefs of Staff is printed in *FRUS, Teheran Conf.*, pp. 360–61.) Eisenhower had not so much changed his mind as become convinced that ANVIL was important enough to warrant even "certain sacrifices to OVERLORD" (Eisenhower to COS, June 26, 1944, SCAF 54, *Eisenhower Papers*, III, 1954–55).

BONIFACE (par. 8) was an earlier codeword for what was properly called ULTRA—intelligence gleaned from the breaking of the German military cipher. This particular piece of intelligence is described in the headnote to C–718. For a fuller explanation of BONIFACE/ULTRA, see the headnote to C–412/2.

C–721

London [via U.S. Army]
July 1, 1944, 1411 Z

Prime Minister to President Roosevelt Personal and Top Secret.
  Your number 574.
  1. We are deeply grieved by your telegram. There are no differences whatever between my War Cabinet colleagues and the British Chiefs of Staff. The splitting up of the campaign in the Mediterranean into two operations neither of which can do anything decisive, is, in my humble and respectful opinion, the first major strategic and political error for which we two have to be responsible.
  2. At Teheran you emphasized to me the possibilities of a move eastward when Italy was conquered and mentioned particularly Istria. No one involved in these discussions has ever thought of moving armies into the Balkans: But Istria and Trieste in Italy are strategic and political positions, which as you saw yourself very clearly might exercise profound and widespread reactions, especially now after the Russian advances.
  3. After Teheran I was made doubtful about ANVIL by General Eisenhower's dislike for it. You will remember his words at Cairo when "General Eisenhower stressed the vital importance of continuing the maximum possible operations in an established theatre since much time was invariably lost when the scene of action was changed, necessitating, as it did, the arduous task of building up a fresh base".
  4. Furthermore, I was impressed by General Montgomery's arguments when at Marrakesh, after he had been nominated to the OVERLORD Command, he explained that it would take 90 days for a force landed at ANVIL to influence the OVERLORD operation. [C–536.]
  5. Both these opinions are in contrast to SCAF 54 [see headnote]. It is no reflexion on these officers that they should now express a different view. But their opinions expressed so decidedly, make me less confident about an ANVIL operation. Moreover in those days the date was to be

early in June. There is no doubt that an advance up the Rhone Valley begun at the end of August could easily be blocked and stemmed by a smaller number of German troops, who could come either through the tunnels from Italy or from Southern Germany. I doubt whether you will find that three American divisions, supported by seven French 80 per cent native divisions from Morocco, Algeria and Tunis, will have any important strategic effect on the tremendous battle which Eisenhower and Montgomery are fighting 500 miles away to the north. It seems more likely to prove a cul-de-sac into which increasing numbers of United States troops will be drawn, and I fear that further demands will be made even upon what is left to us in Italy. It would no doubt make sure of De Gaulle having his talons pretty deeply dug into France.

6. I should not be frank if I did not assure you that I fear a costly stalemate for you unless far more American divisions, at the expense of Eisenhower, are thrust into ANVIL to make it good at all costs by the great power of the United States. Little account is to be taken of Alexander's operations. The last decision given by the British and American Chiefs of Staff here a fortnight ago was: "The destruction of the German armed forces in Italy south of the Pisa-Rimini line must be completed. There should be no withdrawal from the battle of any Allied forces that are necessary for this purpose" (telegram number 3116 dated June 14th from CCS to Generals Wilson and Eisenhower). However, I received from Alexander on June 28th a long distressing telegram in which the following passage occurs:

"The ghost of ANVIL hangs heavily over the battlefront. For example, the Americans have been ordered to send 517 RCT [Regimental Combat Team] and 117 Cav Recce [reconnaissance] Squadrons which are actually in contact with the enemy. They are also required to release now an engineer regiment and other service units required for the conduct of battle. The French do not appear to be putting their hearts into the present operations and reason is undoubtedly because they have their eyes turned in another direction.

The air effort will shortly be curtailed owing to moves of fighting units to Corsica. Eighth Army are not directly concerned with ANVIL, but as long as there is doubt and uncertainty about the future so long will there be a moral weakening. Armies have a very delicate sense and they are beginning to look over their shoulders. You will no doubt remember the Biblical quotation 'For if the trumpet give an uncertain sound, who shall prepare himself to the battle'. If the momentum of my offensive is to be kept to its maximum, I must receive confirmation that Italian campaign is to be backed. If on the other hand it is decided to go all out for ANVIL, then I must know so that I can recast my present plans. In the event of the latter decision I have proposed to General Wilson that I should fly home and table certain proposals aimed at producing best results my emasculated forces will be able to achieve in support of the war effort."

7. I have considered your suggestion that we should lay our respective cases before Stalin. The passage in the very nice telegram I have received from him yesterday (which follows this immediately) seems to suggest that he does not underrate the Italian front. I do not know what he would say if the issue was put to him to decide. On military grounds he might be greatly interested in the eastward movement of Alexander's Army which, without entering the Balkans, would profoundly affect all the forces there and which, in conjunction with any attacks he may make upon Roumania or with Roumania against Hungarian Transylvania, might produce the most far-reaching results. On a long-term political view, he might prefer that the British and Americans should do their share in France in the very hard fighting that is to come, and that east, middle and southern Europe should fall naturally into his control. However it is better to settle the matter for ourselves and between ourselves.

8. What can I do, Mr. President, when your Chiefs of Staff insist on casting aside our Italian offensive campaign, with all its dazzling possibilities, relieving Hitler of all his anxieties in the Po Basin (vide BONIFACE), and when we are to see the integral life of this campaign drained off into the Rhone Valley in the belief that it will in several months carry effective help to Eisenhower so far away in the north?

9. If you still press upon us the directive of your Chiefs of Staff to withdraw so many of your forces from the Italian campaign and leave all our hopes there dashed to the ground, his Majesty's Government, on the advice of their Chiefs of Staff, must enter a solemn protest. I need scarcely say that we shall do our best to make a success of anything that is undertaken. We shall therefore forward your directive to General Wilson as soon as you let us know that there is no hope of reconsideration by your Chiefs of Staff or by yourself. Our Chiefs of Staff are letting yours know the corrections on points of detail which they think necessary in the previous draft.

10. It is with the greatest sorrow that I write to you in this sense. But I am sure that if we could have met, as I so frequently proposed, we should have reached a happy agreement. I send you every personal good wish. However we may differ on the conduct of the war, my personal gratitude to you for your kindness to me and for all you have done for the cause of freedom will never be diminished.

[MR. Ehrman, *Grand Strategy*, V, 575–77. pR&C.]

Although Churchill pointed to Stalin's message as support for the British claim that the Italian theater was more important than an invasion of southern France, Stalin seemed more concerned with general congratulations and encouragement than with choosing between strategic options.

The Soviet leader seemed sure of the strength of British morale in the face of the V-1 attacks, but the War Cabinet was worried, so much so that it considered retaliation with poison gas or bombing raids on non-military targets in Germany.

C–722

London [via U.S. Army]
July 1, 1944, 1526 Z / TOR 1755 Z

Prime Minister to President Roosevelt. Personal and Secret.

Following is text of message from Stalin referred to in Paragraph 7 of my immediately preceding telegram.

> Begins. I have received your message of the 25th June.
>
> In the meantime the Allied forces have liberated Cherbourg, thus crowning their efforts in Normandy with another great victory. I greet the increasing successes of the brave British and American forces who have developed their operations both in northern France and Italy.
>
> If the scale of military operations in northern France is becoming increasingly powerful and dangerous for Hitler, the successful development of the Allies offensive in Italy is also worthy of every attention and applause. We wish you new successes.
>
> Concerning our offensive it can be said that we shall not give the Germans a breathing space but shall continue to widen the front of our offensive operations by increasing the strength of our onslaught against the German armies. You will, of course, agree with me that this is indispensable for our common cause.
>
> As regards to Hitlerite flying bombs, this expedient, it is clear, can have no serious importance either for operations in Normandy or for the population of London whose bravery is known to all.

[MR*. p*Stalin/WSC*, doc. 286.]

The British Foreign Office advised against recalling the British Ambassador from Argentina, arguing that any government there which capitulated to Anglo-American pressure would be overthrown. Moreover, Foreign Secretary Eden believed that Hull was responding to the American presidential election and to criticism of his policy from Undersecretary of State Sumner Welles instead of basing American actions on a realistic appraisal of the situation in

Argentina. There was a certain irony in Churchill's complaint that Britain had been presented with a *fait accompli* following so closely on Roosevelt's similar complaint about the Anglo-Soviet arrangement in the Balkans. Even so, the Prime Minister decided to agree to the American request since Anglo-American cooperation was more important than any other problem which might arise out of that decision.

C–723

London [via U.S. Army]
July 1, 1944, 1340 Z / TOR 1645 Z

Prime Minister to President Roosevelt Personal and Top Secret.
Your number 575.

1. I have discussed matter with Eden and we have decided to act as you wish. Eden has telegraphed to Buenos Aires recalling our Ambassador for consultation.

2. This decision has been taken in response to your appeal for a "common stand". There is a good deal of anxiety in the Foreign Office and the War Cabinet. I do not myself see where this policy is leading to nor what we expect to get out of the Argentines by this method. I only hope it will not adversely affect our vital interests and our war effort.

3. I hope you will not mind my saying, as is my duty, that we ourselves were placed in an invidious position by this American decision, to which we are now asked to conform, being taken without consultation with us. We were faced with a fait accompli.

[MR*]

R–576

Hyde Park, N.Y. [via U.S. Navy]
July 1, 1944, 7:30 P.M.

Personal and Top Secret, from the President for the Former
Naval Person.
Your 722.

I am very much pleased with U.J.'s statement regarding his offensive on the Eastern Front and we all join with him in hoping you will succeed in neutralizing the flying bombs. Roosevelt [WDL]

[MR]

With this cable the first phase of the debate over ANVIL finally ended, although Churchill would again raise the issue before the invasion actually took place. Roosevelt added the underlined paragraphs after Admiral Leahy and the Joint Chiefs of Staff, in Washington, composed the initial draft.

R–577

Hyde Park, N.Y. [via U.S. Navy]
July 1, 1944, 11:00 P.M.

Personal and Top Secret, from the President for the Former Naval Person.

Your 721.

I appreciate deeply your clear exposition of your feelings and views on this decision we are making. My Chiefs of Staff and I have given the deepest consideration to this problem and to the points you have raised. We are still convinced that the right course of action is to launch ANVIL at the earliest possible date.

Perhaps I am more optimistic than you are, but I feel that our commanders in Italy will, with the forces left to them, continue to do great things and attain all the essential objectives there.

I do not believe we should delay further in giving General Wilson a directive. We have had indicated to us the changes which the British Chiefs of Staff think necessary in the directive and they are acceptable to us. Will you ask your Chiefs to despatch it to General Wilson at once.

As a matter of fact I personally cannot see in the short distance to go in Italy to the Pisa-Rimini Line we can destroy even a major part of the German Army. North of that Line if we clear the Po Valley we gain very little in the destruction of Germans as they can retreat even further north.

At Teheran what I was thinking of was a series of raids in force in Istria if the Germans started a general retirement from the Dodecanese and Greece. But it has not happened yet and Tito appears to be in a less strong position than he was then.

On the same line the country in Istria has bad combat terrain in the winter time—worse than southern France.

Therefore I am compelled by the logic of not dispersing our main efforts to a new theater to agree with my Chiefs of Staff and I think we can jointly cut any idea of 90 days to 60 if you and I insist on it.

I honestly believe that God will be with us as he has in OVERLORD and in Italy and in North Africa. I always think of my early geometry "A straight line is the shortest distance between two points." Roosevelt [WDL, JCS]

[MR. *R&C.*]

German submarines based in the Bay of Biscay and in Norway were ordered to the English Channel immediately after the invasion of Normandy, but very few ever reached their destination and only one Allied ship, an LST, was sunk in the beachhead area by a U-boat. Elsewhere in the Atlantic, however, four Allied merchant ships were sunk on June 29 by a submarine which had escaped radar detection because its "Schnorkel" breathing tube allowed it to remain submerged while recharging its batteries. Had the "Schnorkel" appeared earlier in the war it would have caused serious problems, but by July 1944 the Battle of the Atlantic was over.

R–578

Hyde Park, N.Y. [via U.S. Navy]
July 3, 1944, 8:30 P.M.

Personal and Secret, from the President for the Former Naval Person.
I propose the following statement for release on 10 July.

"Proposed anti-submarine statement covering June 1944, to be issued by the Prime Minister and the President.

"Hitler's submarine fleet failed on all counts in June 1944. Not only were the U-boats unable to halt the United Nations' invasion of the continent, but they made little effort to prevent the necessary supplying of our constantly-growing Allied Army in Europe.

"The U-boats apparently concentrated to the west of the invasion during the month, relatively few of them being disposed over the Atlantic. Their sinking of United Nations' merchant vessels reached the lowest figure of the entire war. For every United Nations' merchant vessel sunk by German submarines, several times as many U-boats were sent to the bottom."

Roosevelt [Navy Dept.]

[MR]

In spite of Roosevelt's and Hull's optimism, the Perón regime in Argentina continued in power and stuck to its anti-American program.

R–579

Washington [via U.S. Navy]
July 6, 1944, 9:40 A.M.

Top Secret and Personal. From the President for the Prime Minister.
Your 723 of July 1, 1944 was genuinely welcome. Your favorable decision on the recall of Kelly concurrently with us and others has already

produced significant concrete results. The immediate reaction has been prompt, conciliatory and definitely in the right direction, with complete absence of irritation or threats toward any country. If we continue to stand firm, letting the Farrell regime understand, in a tone not necessarily unfriendly, that it cannot in violation of its pledge of hemispheric unity and solidarity support the Axis in opposition to its sister nations, there is a good chance that this entire matter can soon be cleared up. It is everywhere recognized that the issue at stake in Argentina is the same as that which is involved in the war against the Axis. I am confident, therefore, that there is not any risk in pursuing a firm and forthright policy toward the Farrell regime. Again my heartiest thanks. Roosevelt [CH]

[MR]

The draft message to Churchill submitted by Admiral Leahy incorporated a literal translation of the Stalin-to-Roosevelt message about Polish-Soviet relations. (A more graceful version is printed in *Stalin/FDR*, doc. 206.)

The Roosevelt-Mikolajczyk conversations had not clarified American policy toward Poland. The President, with an eye on the November election, promised the Poles moral support, but refused to jeopardize Soviet-American relations by making specific commitments. Mikolajczyk's frequent requests for an explanation of what Roosevelt meant by moral support suggest that the Polish Prime Minister realized he was being held at arm's length, but he had no choice except to pretend that he had received detailed commitments of American support against Soviet demands. He apparently hoped that expressions of gratitude for American backing would satisfy the hard-liners in his Cabinet and possibly force the British to reconsider their advice that Poland accept the loss of Vilna and Lwow.

R–580

Washington [via U.S. Navy]
July 6, 1944, 4:00 P.M.

Personal and Top Secret. From the President for the Prime Minister.

Referring to my 571 transmitting a message sent by me to U.J. the following quoted reply is received this date:

QUOTE. Thank you for the information regarding your meeting with Mr. Mikolajczyk.

If to bear in mind the establishment of military cooperation between the Red Army and the fighting against Hitlerite invaders forces of the Polish underground movement, then this, undoubtedly, is now an essential matter for the final rout of our common foe.

Great significance, of course, has in this respect the correct solution of the question of Soviet-Polish relations. You are familiar with the point of view of the Soviet Government and its endeavor to see Poland strong, independent and democratic, and the Soviet-Polish relations—good-neighbourly and based upon durable friendship. The Soviet Government sees the most important premises of this in the reorganization of the emigre Polish Government, which would provide the participation in it of Polish statesmen in England, as well as Polish statesmen in the United States and the U.S.S.R., and especially Polish democratic statesmen in Poland itself, and also in the recognition by the Polish Government of the Curson Line as the new border between the U.S.S.R. and Poland.

It is necessary to say, however, that from the statement of Mr. Mikolajczyk in Washington it is not seen, that he makes in this matter any steps forward. That is why it is difficult for me at the present moment to express any opinion in respect to Mr. Mikolajczyk's trip to Moscow.

Your opinion on the question of Soviet-Polish relations and your efforts in this matter are highly valued by all of us. UNQUOTE.

Roosevelt [WDL]

[MR. *R&C.*]

C–724

London [via U.S. Army]
July 7, 1944, 0050 Z / TOR 0305 Z

Prime Minister to President Personal and Top Secret.

Many thanks for your 578 with Draft Anti U-Boat statement for June. The Admiralty have suggested two amendments which I submit for your approval.

(A) In view of the failure of the great efforts made by the U-Boats to interrupt supplies to France, the last part of paragraph 1 after "the continent" be amended to read "but their efforts to prevent the necessary supplying of our constantly growing Allied Army in Europe were made completely ineffective by our counter-measures".

(B) Latest information shows that another ship has been sunk in June and this will bring the total for the month slightly above that for May. Proposed therefore to insert the word "almost" before "the lowest figure" in the second sentence of paragraph 2.

2. I am telegraphing to you separately about a proposed communique on a special point connected with the U-boats' efforts to interrupt supplies to France [C–725].

[MR*]

C–725

London [via U.S. Army]
July 7, 1944, 0103 Z / TOR 0305 Z

Prime Minister to President Roosevelt Personal and Top Secret.
Reference paragraph 2 of my 724.

I see no reason why this attached statement should not be issued without prejudice to our monthly statements. It deals with a special topic and will please the men. Do you mind?

Statement begins.

1. Thousands of Allied ships have been moved across the Channel to Normandy and coastwise to build up the Military forces engaged in the liberation of Europe. No merchant vessel of this vast concourse has been sunk by U-Boat with the possible exception of one ship. In this case doubt exists as to her destruction by U-Boat or Mine.

2. This is despite attempts by a substantial force of U-Boats to pass up-channel from their bases in Norway and France. Such attempts were of course expected and squadrons of coastal command, working in cooperation with the surface forces of the Allied Navies, were ready.

3. From the moment that the U-Boats sailed from their bases they were attacked by aircraft of coastal command. Both aircraft and surface forces followed up sighting reports, hunting and attacking the U-Boats with relentless determination.

4. The enemy were thus frustrated by the brilliant and unceasing work of coastal command and the tireless patrols of the surface forces, and have suffered heavy casualties.

5. Operations continue.

Statement ends.

[MR*]

The Navy Department suggested a small change in Churchill's proposed statement on anti-submarine operations off Normandy so that due credit would be given to U.S. support for the British Coastal Command.

R–581

Washington [via U.S. Navy]
July 7, 1944, 6:45 P.M.

Personal and Secret, from the President to the Prime Minister.
Your 724 and 725.

We think your proposed changes and the additional communique excellent with the single exception that before the word "squadrons" in the second paragraph of the special communique we insert "U. S. and British air" so that the sentence now reads, "Such attempts were of course expected and U. S. and British air squadrons of coastal command, working in cooperation with the surface forces of the Allied Navies, were ready."

Unless we hear to the contrary, we will release statements as amended at scheduled time. Roosevelt [Navy Dept.]

[MR]

DE GAULLE'S VISIT TO WASHINGTON

De Gaulle's long-delayed visit to Washington finally began on July 6. Although the French leader had promised not to raise the question of recognition for the FCNL, the French Committee had become the de facto government of liberated France. Sensing a political victory, de Gaulle was cordial and cooperative during his talks with Roosevelt and other American officials. The President's willingness to extend de facto recognition to the FCNL followed receipt of a memo from Cordell Hull which began, "We should like to suggest to you a fresh approach to the French situation." In spite of caveats about the temporary nature of that recognition and the need for a free choice of government by the French people, it was a major change in American policy (Hull to Roosevelt, n.d., attached to R–582, MR). Ironically, de Gaulle's political gains were somewhat offset by the refusal of the U.S. Army to rearm a number of French divisions or to arm and transport French forces which would be sent to fight in Indo-China. The deployment of those troops was viewed as a political decision which had to await a presidential order.

Roosevelt's cryptic "the visit has gone off very well" was all he ever wrote to Churchill about the talks with de Gaulle, but the Frenchman, both in his memoirs and in discussions with British officials, gave a fuller report. De Gaulle claimed that the President had outlined a postwar structure wherein the United States, working with Britain, China, and the Soviet Union, would set up a "permanent system of intervention" requiring a chain of American military bases located largely in the then British and French colonies of South and Southeast Asia and West Africa. According to the French leader, "Roosevelt thus intended to lure the Soviets into a group that would contain their ambitions and in which America could unite its dependents"—China and Britain being subordinate to American power (de Gaulle, *Unity*, p. 269; Woodward, *British Foreign Policy*, III, 72). Churchill, annoyed by this resurfacing of Roosevelt's decolonization plans, proposed sending a copy of de Gaulle's account to the President since that might force Roosevelt to deny the report. Moreover, it would indicate how de Gaulle interpreted friendliness. Although Eden agreed that he too would like to have the President either confirm or deny the statements attributed to him by de Gaulle, he also feared such a cable might jeopardize the fragile agreement between the FCNL and the United States—an agreement the British had long sought to create.

R–582

Washington [via U.S. Navy]
July 10, 1944, 1:45 P.M.

Personal and Top Secret. From the President for the Prime Minister.

Re your 713, I am prepared to accept Committee as temporary *de facto* authority for civil administration in France provided two things are made clear—first, complete authority to be reserved to Eisenhower to do what he feels necessary to conduct effective military operations, and, second, that French people be given opportunity to make free choice of their own Government. I have asked officials here to take British drafts as a base and modify them to insure these points, and they will shortly be in touch with your people here. Suggest you authorize your political and military officials here to work out details immediately with our officials for final clearance through the Combined Chiefs of Staff. General De Gaulle is leaving behind officials qualified to deal with this matter. I urge that no publicity be given these arrangements until they are finally cleared.

The visit has gone off very well. Roosevelt [CH, War Dept., JCS]

[MR. *FRUS*, 1944, III, 723–24. *R&C*.]

Churchill's and Roosevelt's mutual love of naval affairs continued to offer a chance for personal touches. There is no explanation of the "various items" which Roosevelt thought Churchill might want for his family papers.

R–582/1, letter

Washington
July 10, 1944

Dear Winston:—

I am enclosing a copy of a letter from Captain Powers Symington, U.S.N., Rtd., an old friend of mine during the first World War—also a copy of my letter to him. The signatures, etc., are for you with full freedom to do what you want with them. Keep them in your personal papers or give them to the Admiralty.

I am also sending along various items which relate to some early Churchills. I thought you would like to have them for your family papers.

With my warm regards, As ever yours, Franklin D. Roosevelt

[PSF:WSC]

First Enclosure to R–582/1

Washington
July 7, 1944

My dear Powers:—

It is certainly good to hear from you again—and especially such a nice letter with its enclosures.

I think it is a grand idea that these very interesting documents should be in Britain. I shall send them, at the opportunity, to the Prime Minister as a gift from you via me to the British Prime Minister and the British Navy.

I do hope to see you one of these days soon.

With all good wishes, Very sincerely yours, Franklin D. Roosevelt

[PSF:WSC]

The final two sentences of Symington's letter must have pleased the President more than the naval papers enclosed with it.

Second Enclosure to R–582/1

San Francisco, Calif.
June 30, 1944

Dear Mr. President

It occurs to me that you might be at a loss to find a suitable present to give Mr. Churchill, a gesture of friendship between the two great men of our time. I am enclosing something that I think will interest you and be acceptable to him.

In 1916 I was as you may remember with the Grand Fleet and a short time before the battle of Jutland I got the various Commanders of the Fleet to sign these papers so I could have a souvenir of my pleasant association with that great group of British Seamen. A number of them were killed at Jutland and these documents so became unique. I had thought at one time to give them to the Naval Academy Museum but believe now they should of right be in Britain, perhaps in the Admiralty.

Mr. Churchill was 1st Lord when I went to England and I believe he would appreciate the special significance of these papers to the British Navy.

I don't care if you stay in for five terms. More power to you.

Yours with great respect [signed] P. Symington

[PSF:WSC]

Once Roosevelt agreed to extend de facto recognition to the FCNL, Britain and the United States proceeded rapidly to the logical decision to extend full recognition to the French Committee as the provisional government of France. On July 12, the State Department indicated that it wished to hold discussions with the French about the details in the de facto agreement, and the British happily agreed.

C–726

London [via U.S. Army]
July 13, 1944, 1305 Z

Prime Minister to President Roosevelt. Personal and Top Secret.

Your number 582.

I am glad to hear that the De Gaulle visit went off well and that you agree that the British drafts will do as a basis for agreement with the French Committee.

2. We agree with the procedure you suggest, and we are instructing our people in Washington accordingly.

3. In regard to your two points. I entirely agree that Eisenhower must have all the authority which he wants for his military operations. This was the paramount aim of our officials in the discussions and the necessity was fully recognized by the French. It was not easy to find a form of words which reconciled Eisenhower's supremacy with French susceptibilities but we were satisfied that we had fully safeguarded the position by the agreed wording of articles one to five of the draft main agreement (see my immediately following message). If your people can improve the wording and persuade the French to accept it, we shall, of course, be content. I am sure though that it would be a mistake to delay unduly. Now, after your successful meeting, is the moment to clear the whole business up.

4. Your second point is very important but we did not feel that it was an appropriate provision to insert in an agreement confined to practical administrative and other questions arising out of Allied operations for the liberation of France. Moreover, the French Committee, as you know, have provided in their decree of April 21st for the holding of elections and the appointment of a provisional government by the resultant representative assembly as soon as two-thirds of France, including Paris, have been liberated. I think we can be sure that the very democratically-minded civilian members of the Committee and of the Assembly and the French people inside France will see that these elections are held. We ourselves are satisfied on this point and I hope that you will not press for it to be covered in the actual agreement. Indeed, I do not see how it could be.

5. When the texts have been finally cleared through the Combined

Chiefs of Staff, I take it that you will wish to proceed as in the case of the agreements about other Allied liberated territory, and that you will wish Eisenhower to sign for you on the military level. On our side the Foreign Secretary will sign with a representative of the French Committee. As we, for our part, are already prepared to accept the London texts and it appears from your telegram that there is not much difference between us, I hope that the talks which your people are having with the French in Washington will shortly be concluded and that we can get the various memoranda finally settled within a very few days.

6. I entirely agree that no publicity be given these arrangements until they are finally cleared.

[MR*. R&C.]

General Eisenhower and General Pierre Koenig, who commanded the French Forces of the Interior (organized units of the French Resistance), had reached a working arrangement regarding the authority of the FCNL in liberated France. Their ability to cooperate facilitated the Franco-American talks then taking place in Washington, and the details of a formal agreement were quickly worked out.

C–727

London [via U.S. Army]
July 13, 1944, 1305 Z / TOR 1600 Z

Prime Minister to President Roosevelt Personal and Top Secret.
Following is text referred to in my immediately preceding message. Begins:

1. In areas affected by active military operations the necessity is recognized for the Allied Commander-In-Chief to possess the necessary authority to ensure that all measures are taken which, in his judgment, are essential for the successful conduct of his operations. The necessary arrangements for this purpose are set out in Articles two to six below.

2. (1) Liberated French metropolitan territory will be divided into two zones: A forward zone and an interior zone. (2) The forward zone will consist of the areas affected by active military operations referred to in Article 1; the boundary between the forward zone and the interior zone will be fixed in accordance with the provisions of paragraph subpara 4 below. (3) The interior zone will include all other regions in the liberated territory, whether or not they have previously formed part of the forward zone. In certain cases, having

regard to the exigencies of operations, military zones may be created within the interior zone in accordance with the provisions of Article 5 subpara 2 below. (4) The delegate referred to in Article 3 below will, in agreement with the Allied Commander-In-Chief, effect the delimitation of the zones in accordance with French law. It is understood that this delimitation shall meet the requirements of the Allied Commander-In-Chief, as dictated by military necessity, in regard to the extent of the forward zone.

3. (1) In accordance with Article 1 of the ordonnance made by the French Committee of National Liberation on the 14th March, 1944, a delegate will be appointed for the present theater of operations. Other delegates may be appointed in accordance with the development of operations. (2) The delegate will have at his disposal an administrative organization, a military delegate and liaison officers for administrative duties. The delegate's task will be in particular to centralize and facilitate relations between the Allied military command and the French authorities. (3) When the powers conferred on the delegate by French law are transferred to higher French authorities, it will be for those authorities to execute the obligations of the delegate under this agreement.

4. In the forward zone:— (1) It will be for the delegate to take, in accordance with French law, the necessary measures to give effect to the provisions of Article 1 and, in particular, to issue regulations and to make appointments in the public services. (2) In exceptional cases, where no French authority is in a position to ensure the operation of the administrative services, the Commander-In-Chief may, as a temporary measure and pending the designation of a French authority by the delegate, take such urgent measures as are required by military necessity. (3) The powers under the state of siege will be exercized by the Allied Commander-In-Chief through the French military delegate in accordance with French law.

5. (1) In the interior zone the conduct of the administration of the territory and responsibility therefor, including the powers under the state of siege, will be entirely a matter for the French authorities. Special arrangements will be made between the Allied Commander-In-Chief and the competent French authorities in order that all measures necessary for the conduct of military operations may be taken. (2) Moreover, in accordance with Article 2 subpara 3 and by agreement between the Allied Commander-In-Chief and the delegate, certain portions of the interior zone (known as military zones) may be subjected to a special regime on account of their vital military importance, for example ports, fortified naval areas, aerodromes and troop concentration areas. In the military zones, the Allied Com-

mander-In-Chief may request the French authorities to take all measures resulting from the state of siege which he considers necessary.
The conduct of the territorial administration and the responsibility
therefor will nevertheless be solely a matter for the French authorities.

[MR]

Roosevelt had decided to take a trip to the West Coast and Hawaii—partly
out of curiosity, partly to play the role of Commander in Chief during the
Democratic National Convention scheduled for late July in Chicago, and
partly to settle the argument between General MacArthur and Admiral Nimitz
over strategy in the Pacific. (See headnote to R–564.) The President left
Washington by train on July 13 and, after watching an amphibious-landing
exercize on the beaches near San Diego, embarked on the heavy cruiser USS
Baltimore on July 20 for the voyage to Pearl Harbor. After three days in
Hawaii, Roosevelt sailed on the *Baltimore* to Adak, Alaska, and then shifted
to a destroyer for the rough and uncomfortable trip to Bremerton Naval
Base in the state of Washington. A train from the West Coast brought him
back to the capital on the morning of August 17. The usual arrangements
were made to expedite communications, including the Churchill-Roosevelt
exchanges, but even so their correspondence became briefer and more routine. Only the growing tension between the Soviet Union and the London
Poles received close scrutiny from the two leaders, with Churchill initiating
most of the cables. During the President's travels the Prime Minister tried to
re-institute the old Churchill-Hopkins relationship, since Roosevelt's once-
closest adviser had returned to part-time duty. Churchill sent Hopkins a
strong plea to have the Americans reconsider the decision to invade southern
France (ANVIL), but when Hopkins made it clear that he could no longer
function as the President's unofficial Chief of Staff, the Prime Minister gave
up.

R–583

Washington [via U.S. Navy]
July 13, 1944, 5:15 P.M.

Top Secret and Personal. From the President for the Prime Minister.

The receipt is acknowledged of your 726 and 727. I feel that the small
differences between the British and American drafts of the agreement
can be adjusted by your and my representatives here working with representatives of the French Committee.

It is essential that Eisenhower have all the authority that is necessary
for the conduct of his military operations at the smallest cost in life to
the American and British soldiers.

I am off on my trip and will be gone several weeks but can always be reached. Roosevelt [FDR]

[MR. *R&C.*]

Cordell Hull, who headed an interdepartmental committee on the treatment of war prisoners, had recommended that the President suggest the following compromise in order to facilitate an exchange of prisoners between the Allies and Japan.

R–584

Washington [via U.S. Navy]
July 13, 1944, 6:20 P.M.

Top Secret and Personal. From the President for the Prime Minister.

Both you and we are negotiating to exchange Japanese civilian prisoners held by each of us for British and American civilians held by Japan. The likelihood is that such an exchange may be the only way of saving the lives of hundreds of your and our nationals.

There is a snag on both sides. The Japanese want us to release 300 odd divers and pilots held in Australia; my military people do not agree to their release and as a result your exchange negotiations has bogged down.

In our exchange the snag is that the Japanese Government insists that Japanese officials coming out shall not be searched, while your people insist on search. The immediate case concerns officials coming out of Argentina. In result our negotiations will bog down when we inform the Japanese of this requirement.

It seems to me that the military considerations in either case are now very small. Japanese officials cannot carry any effective quantities even of valuable contraband. On the other hand, our naval affairs in the Pacific are proceeding well, and the Japanese divers and pilots held in Australia cannot be of great help to the Japanese, even in respect to Far Eastern installations, in view of our present sea and air superiority.

My suggestion is that you give directions to your people to waive the search of Japanese officials; I will be prepared to recommend to our people that they let the divers and pilots be exchanged. This at least will give a reasonable chance that both exchanges might go through, saving many hundreds of both Americans and British from slow death. Please cable me your views. I think the technical people are over-emphasizing the importance of considerations quite proper in themselves, but which should be overriden by the higher humanitarian interest. Roosevelt [CH]

[MR]

With American soldiers fighting the Germans in France and a presidential election only four months away, domestic political pressure forced the Roosevelt administration to take a firm stand against neutral trade with Germany. Turkish chromium, Spanish wolfram, and Swedish steel—particularly ball-bearings—were all essential to German military production, and the Normandy invasion made it unlikely that Germany would retaliate against the neutrals. The Foreign Office preferred caution, but Hull felt so strongly about the issue that he recommended "going after the Swedes alone, possibly with Russian help" if the British would not support the American position (memo from Hull to Roosevelt, July 12, 1944, PSF:State Dept., Conf. File). The Secretary of State proposed that the President ask Churchill to intervene personally, and Roosevelt agreed to make that request.

R–584/1

Washington [via U.S. Embassy]
July 13, 1944, 4:00 P.M.

[Roosevelt to Churchill]

Personal for the Ambassador. At the direction of the President please deliver the following message from him to the Prime Minister:

"Swedish exports to the enemy are becoming a very pressing question here. All the circumstances of the war, particularly Soviet successes in the Baltic area, could now be favorably used by us to bring maximum pressure to bear on Sweden to eliminate exports to the enemy. I would appreciate your getting behind the matter personally as Winant is now taking this question up with your people in the Foreign Office."

Hull [CH]

[*FRUS*, 1944, IV, 578–79. PSF:State, Conf. File (draft).]

By the time this cable reached Washington, Roosevelt had already departed.

C–728

London [via U.S. Army]
July 14, 1944, 1517 Z / TOR 1625 Z (Washington)

Prime Minister to President Roosevelt. Personal and Top Secret.

Your number 583.

We agree. Eden and I send you all good wishes for your trip. We wish it was in the other direction.

[MR*]

Austrian Prime Minister John Curtin continued to put national interests ahead of those of the British Empire. Roosevelt instructed his staff to send copies of this and R–584 to General MacArthur.

C–729

London [via U.S. Army]
July 14, 1944, 1524 Z / TOR 1625 Z (Washington)

Prime Minister to President Roosevelt Personal and Top Secret.
   Your number 584.
   We are both of us in full agreement, but the Australians hold the prisoners and have made very strongly the point about the divers and pilots. We have forwarded you[r] telegram to Mr. Curtin with the strongest request that they fall in with your views, which I am sure they will do; then in a few days I hope to be able to report all clear on the British Empire front. Meanwhile we hope you will repeat your telegram so far as is necessary to General MacArthur, telling him you have my agreement.

[MR*]

The British remained concerned that American pressure on Argentina might jeopardize both wartime and postwar agreements for the sale of Argentine beef to Great Britain. Colonel J. J. Llewellin was Minister of Food in Churchill's Cabinet.

C–730

London [via U.S. Army]
July 14, 1944, 1627 Z / TOR 1830 Z (Washington)

Prime Minister to President Roosevelt Personal and Top Secret.
   I ought to send you the immediately following minute I have received from Mr. Llewellin, the British Food Minister. We wish to do everything we can to help you and Mr. Hull with the South American countries; but we think you ought to have the formidable arguments of this minute before you. Please remember that this community of 46,000,000 imported 66,000,000 tons a year before the war and is now managing on less than 25,000,000. The stamina of the workman cannot be maintained on a lesser diet in meat. You would not send your soldiers into battle on the British service meat ration, which is far above what is given to workmen. Your people are eating per head more meat and more poultry than before the war while ours are mostly sharply cut. I believe that if this were put before Mr. Hull he would do all he could to help us to obtain a new

contract and nothing which would jeopardize its chances. I therefore hope that you will do so.

[MR*. *FRUS*, 1944, VII, 333.]

The British argument that the stamina of workingmen could not be maintained without adequate meat was political, not nutritional. As victory came closer, British citizens began to expect some lessening of wartime restrictions, and continuing the drastic rationing of meat could prove a liability at the polls.

C–731

London [via U.S. Army]
July 14, 1944, 1650 Z / TOR 1830 Z (Washington)

Prime Minister to President Roosevelt Personal and Top Secret.
Following is minute referred to in my immediately preceding telegram. Begins:

I am very worried at the position into which we are getting with the Argentine.

I depend upon that country for over 40 per cent of my imported meat. If I fail to get it, the first/second meat ration will have to be reduced by about five D. Even a temporary loss of supplies will reduce the ration.

We are very grateful to the Americans for the meat they are sending us. I do not believe that they can send us such an increase as to make up for the loss of our supplies from the Argentine.

In any event such additional meat would be largely pork and we have too great a proportion of that now. The meat we get from the Argentine is beef and mutton.

My present contract with the Argentine runs out in October. I am anxious to renew it for three to four years, in order to make sure that the people of this country will get the meat they want and need, not only for the rest of the war, but for the period of shortage afterwards.

It is going to be most difficult for me to persuade the Argentines to let me have all their exportable surplus of meat for this period, unless we can surmount the present political difficulties. If we get it it will go the common pool for allocation by the Combined Food Board. If we fail to get it both the Americans and ourselves are running the risk of those liberated countries which have foreign balances competing independently for the meat, running up the prices and thus benefitting only the Argentines.

I think therefore you ought to be warned now of the position which is likely to arise.

The Foreign Secretary has seen this minute and knows that I am sending it to you.

[MR*]

Secretary of the Treasury Morgenthau went to Europe in early August ostensibly to discuss questions of occupation currency in liberated France and occupied Germany, although sheer curiosity was his primary motive. Churchill, knowing of the close personal relationship between Roosevelt and Morgenthau, gave the Secretary a tour of the Map Room and praised the President. More important than his good impression of the Prime Minister was Morgenthau's discovery that both British and American planners seemed willing to leave postwar Germany industrially and economically intact. The Secretary's concern soon led to the "Morgenthau Plan" for Germany.

R–584/2, letter

Washington [?]
July 15, 1944

Dear Winston:

Henry Morgenthau, Jr. will be in England the latter part of this month. He is going over to discuss currency problems and I hope much that you will be able to see him, if only for a short visit.

With my warm regards, Always sincerely,

[PSF:GB:WSC]

Since the invasion of southern France (ANVIL) would take place before the time Churchill proposed for a conference, other matters must have been on his mind. In his memoirs, the Prime Minister claimed that his concerns were "to assure for Britain an honourable share in the final victory" in the Pacific, to avoid over-confidence by planning on a quick German collapse, and "to forestall the Russians in certain areas of Central Europe" (*WSC*, VI, 147–48). In addition, a reading of the PREM 3 materials suggests that the Prime Minister was also deeply concerned about the continuation of lend-lease after the surrender of Germany. The success of Soviet offensives in eastern Europe and the American victories in the Pacific, compared with the failure of the Anglo-American armies to break out from Normandy, may account for the panicky tone of Churchill's plea for a meeting. The Prime Minister had already demonstrated his willingness to make spheres-of-influence arrange-

ments with the Soviets, but he understood that military events could make
that deal irrelevant.

EUREKA had been the codename for the Teheran Conference, hence the
temporary label of EUREKA II for this new meeting.

C–732

London [via U.S. Army]
July 16, 1944, 1514 Z / TOR 1845 Z (Washington)

Prime Minister to President Personal and Top Secret.

When are we going to meet and where? That we must meet soon is
certain. It would be better that U. J. came too. I am entirely in your hands.
I would brave the reporters at Washington or the mosquitos of Alaska!
Surely we ought now to fix a date and then begin negotiating with U. J.
His Majesty's Government would wish to propose "EUREKA II" for the
last ten days of August. For details see my immediately following telegram.
Failing this, Casablanca, Rome or even Teheran present themselves and
many other places too. But we two must meet and if possible three. Please
let me have your ideas on all this.

[MR*. *FRUS, Quebec Conf.*, 1944, p. 10. *R&C*.]

The Duke of Portland's estate at Langwell and the Royal Castle at Balmoral
both lie in northeastern Scotland.

C–733

London [via U.S. Army]
July 16, 1944, 1721 Z / TOR 1845 Z (Washington)

Prime Minister to President Personal and Top Secret.

We suggest that the first attempt should be to arrange a meeting between us three at Invergordon, where each could have his battleship as
headquarters besides a suitable house on land. The King would entertain
us before, after or during the meeting either at Langwell, which he could
borrow from the Duke of Portland, or at Balmoral if a night journey is
acceptable. The weather might well be agreeable in Scotland at that time.
Secrecy, if desired, and security in any case, can be provided. U. J. might
be able to fly or could certainly come by sea in the *Royal Sovereign* which
has now become a part of his fleet. Anyhow please let me know what you
think. Remember you have my standing offer and MacKenzie King's for
Quebec if that is easiest for you.

[MR*. *FRUS, Quebec Conf.*, 1944, pp. 10–11.]

The President had no objection to a meeting of the Allied leaders, though the sense of urgency in Churchill's cable was not present in Roosevelt's reply. Roosevelt's fascination with warships made Churchill's suggestion particularly appealing. The Presidential Special railroad train had left Washington on July 13, and arrived in San Diego on July 19.

R–585

enroute San Diego [via U.S. Navy]
July 17, 1944, 9:00 A.M. (Washington)

Personal and Top Secret, from the President for the Former Naval Person.

Your 732 and 733.

I am half way across the continent and think this is the best opportunity to go through with this trip. This means I will not get back until between the fifteenth and twentieth of August. I ought to be a fortnight in Washington. I wholly agree that we three should meet but it would be a lot easier for me if we could make it the tenth or fifteenth of September. This is just before the Equinox. I am rather keen about the idea of Invergorden or a spot on the west coast of Scotland. I like the idea of the battleship. This would get me back in plenty of time for the election, although that is in the lap of the Gods. I am sending a telegram, as per my next, to Uncle Joe purely as a feeler. If he feels he cannot come you and I should meet anyway. Roosevelt

[MR. PREM 4/75/2. *FRUS, Quebec Conf.*, 1944, p. 11.]

The President's invitation to Stalin brought a reply on July 22 that the military situation would not permit the Soviet Premier to attend such a conference at the time suggested (*Stalin/FDR*, doc. 213).

R–586

enroute San Diego [via U.S. Navy]
July 17, 1944, 10:15 A.M. (Washington)

Personal and Top Secret, from the President for the Former Naval Person.

Following is copy of my wire to Uncle Joe:

"Things are moving so fast and so successfully that I feel there should be a meeting between you and Mr. Churchill and me in the reasonably near future. The Prime Minister is in hearty accord with this thought. I am now on a trip in the far west and must be in

Washington for several weeks on my return. It would, therefore, be best for me to have a meeting between the tenth and fifteenth of September. The most central point for you and me would be the north of Scotland. I could go by ship and you could come either by ship or by plane. Your Army is doing so magnificently that the hop would be much shorter to Scotland than the one taken by Molotov two years ago. I hope you can let me have your thoughts. Secrecy and security can be maintained either aboard ship or on shore."

Roosevelt

[MR. PREM 4/75/2. *FRUS, Yalta Conf.*, p. 3. *Stalin/FDR*, doc. 211.]

Although Churchill's figure of 150 U-boats more than doubled the German submarines available to harass the OVERLORD convoys, the fact was that the Allies had practically neutralized German U-boat strength in the Atlantic.

C–734

London [via U.S. Army]
July 20, 1944, 0910 Z / TOR 1205 Z (Washington)

Prime Minister to President Roosevelt Personal and Top Secret.

I send you a minute to me from the Admiralty, with which I hope you will agree. It really is quite an achievement to have held 150 U boats close at hand and unable to harm our vital convoys. This would not interfere with our monthly statement. If you agree will you please inform your people, and I will do the needful here and with the Canadians. The Admiralty will get all that is put out.

(Minute begins) Admiralty to Prime Minister.

Although the enemy's attempts to interfere with our OVERLORD convoys have failed, it would save us much effort if he could be induced to abandon them altogether, paticularly as we shall shortly have to withdraw escort vessels for the winter Atlantic convoys.

The only way to bring him to abandon them is to make him realize that they have failed and to bring home to him the extent of his losses. If we can succeed in this, we may undermine the morale of his U boat crews altogether.

We should therefore like to put out communiques and stories about the anti U boat operations of OVERLORD, as background for a thorough-going onslaught on U boat morale, without waiting for the usual monthly statements. The stories would of course be strictly censored and not issued without Admiralty permission.

[MR*]

At the request of U.S. naval authorities, Roosevelt opposed any publicity about Allied anti-submarine warfare efforts lest it affect the war in the Pacific, where American submarines had been remarkably effective against Japanese shipping. Churchill's need for favorable propaganda on the home front was less important than the struggle against Japan.

R–587

San Diego [via U.S. Navy]
July 21, 1944, 2:45 A.M. (Washington)

Personal and Top Secret, from the President for the Former Naval Person.

In respect to proposal in your 734 that Admiralty publish communiques and stories regarding anti-submarine activities during OVERLORD, my opinion still is that relaxation of security as to anti-submarine measures will result in improvement of Japanese technique against our submarines which are now on the crest of a wave of success that is having marked influence on the Pacific Campaign. I recall that our surge of superiority over the U-boats was coincident with and possibly connected with adoption of the current policy of silence as to the steps taken to counter them. I am dubious of the effect of newspaper stories on the morale of U-boat crews. I cannot therefore concur in the proposal for publicity in allied press. I suggest instead radio propaganda direct to U-boat personnel stressing names of U-boats known by us to have been sunk as well as total numbers they have lost without any details. Roosevelt [Navy Dept.]

[MR]

Argentina's refusal to break formally with the Axis had become, as far as the British could tell, an obsession with Secretary of State Hull, who condemned "the petty commercial advantages of a long-term bargain with a fascist government" (as quoted in Cadogan, *The Diaries*, p. 650). Roosevelt had drafted a reply to Churchill's cable on the same day it arrived in Washington, but it took Hull a week to add the final two paragraphs and dispatch the message to Churchill.

R–588

enroute Hawaii [via U.S. Navy]
July 22, 1944, 6:50 P.M. (Washington)

Personal and Top Secret from the President for the Former Naval Person.

I would not do anything in the world to cut down the supply of meat of England. Heavens knows that it is already quite short enough. We would do nothing to prevent your getting a new contract.

I hope, however, that you will, in very firm, clear, disgruntled tones of voice let Argentina know beyond a doubt that we are all fed up with her pro-Axis sentiments and practices. She is the only nation of North, Central and South America acting thus. I think it would help if you could instill this into their stubborn heads and, at the same time, get the meat contract.

Argentina knows full well that if, on its own initiative, deliveries of meat to England were to be delayed or stopped at this time, its action would everywhere be considered a betrayal of the United Nations.

I suggest that you examine the full statement of our position on Argentina which was transmitted to Winant for delivery to Eden on Thursday of this week. Roosevelt [FDR, CH]

[MR. *FRUS*, 1944, VII, 333–34. p*FDR LTRS*, p. 1521 (draft of July 14).]

Grasping at straws, the Polish government in London had chosen to interpret Roosevelt's vague promise of "moral support" and the State Department's assumption that the London Poles would return to liberated Poland as firm promises of American support. But the steady advance of Soviet armies made political arguments irrelevant. Apparently convinced that the London Poles would never prove tractable, Stalin took the first step toward establishing and recognizing a rival Polish government by formally making "contact" with a group of pro-Soviet Poles, the Polish Committee of National Liberation, sponsored by the Soviet government. The Prime Minister of the London Polish government, Stanislaw Mikolajczyk, reluctantly agreed to go to Moscow to talk with representatives of the Polish Committee and the Soviet government, although the atmosphere for that meeting was darkened by the Polish Council in London, which publicly condemned the Polish Committee as "usurpers." Tadeusz Romer and Stanislaw Grabski held posts in London as Minister of Foreign Affairs and President of the Polish National Council, respectively.

C–735

London [via U.S. Army]
July 25, 1944, 2235 Z / TOR 0215 Z, July 26 (Washington)

Prime Minister to President Roosevelt. Personal and Top Secret.

1. Please see U.J.'s telegram to me of July 23rd and the answer I have sent off after discussion with Anthony, the text of which immediately follows this.

2. We have pressed Mikolajczyk strongly to go with his Ministers and to make contact with Stalin. It may well be they will receive a friendly welcome, but of course their outburst last night about "Usurpers" etcetera may have worsened the situation. However we still have hope, and aim at fusion of some kind.

3. Meanwhile it is of the utmost importance that we do not desert the

orthodox Polish Government, and Anthony will give answers in the House tomorrow making it clear that our relations remain unchanged. Anything you say to U.J. that will induce him to give Mikolajczyk a good welcome and realise the importance of founding a united Polish Government, will be invaluable. The great hope is fusion of some kind between the Poles relying on Russia and Poles relying on USA and G.B. We are sure that U.J. will be much influenced by your view of these things.

[MR*. R&C.]

C–736

London [via U.S. Army]
July 25, 1944, 2300 Z / TOR 0220 Z, July 26 (Washington)

Prime Minister to President Roosevelt. Personal and Top Secret.

Following are telegrams referred to in paragraph 1 of my immediately preceding telegram.

Premier Stalin to Prime Minister. Dated July 23d.

I have received your message of July 20th. I am writing to you now only on the Polish question.

Events in our front are proceeding at an extremely rapid tempo. Lubin [Lublin], one of the large towns of Poland, was occupied today by our troops, who are continuing to advance.

In these circumstances the question of administration on Polish territory has arisen for us in a practical form. We do not wish to have and shall not set up our administration on the territory of Poland, for we do not wish to interfere in the internal affairs of Poland. The Poles themselves must do this. We therefore considered it necessary to establish contact with the Polish Committee of National Liberation, which was recently set up by the National Council of Poland, which was itself constituted in Warsaw at the end of last year out of representatives of the democratic parties and groups, as you must already have been informed by your Ambassador in Moscow. The Polish Committee of National Liberation intends to undertake the setting up of administration on Polish territory, and this, I hope, will be accomplished. In Poland we have not found any other forces which could have set up a Polish administration. The so-called underground organisations, directed by the Polish Government in London, proved ephemeral and devoid of influence. I cannot consider the Polish Committee as the government of Poland, but it is possible that, in due course, it will serve as a nucleus for the formation of a provisional Polish government out of democratic forces.

As regards Mikolajczyk, I shall of course not refuse to receive him. It would however be better if he were to address himself to the Polish National Committee, whose attitude would be friendly towards Mikolajczyk. (Ends)

Prime Minister to Premier Stalin. Dated July 25th.

Monsieur Mikolajczyk is starting tomorrow night in response to the suggestion in the last paragraph of your message of July 23d. He is bringing with him Monsieur Romer and Monsieur Grabski. His Majesty's Government are making arrangements for his transport to Teheran or Moscow as may be required. He desires a full and friendly conversation with you personally. He commands the full support of all his colleagues in the Polish government which of course we continue to recognise.

2. Our heartfelt wish is that all Poles may be united in clearing the Germans from their country and in establishing that free, strong and independent Poland working in friendship with Russia which you have proclaimed is your aim.

3. I have told the President of the United States of your telegram to me and have sent him also a copy of this. He will no doubt communicate with you.

[MR*. *Stalin/WSC*, docs. 301, 303. p*R&C*.]

C–737

London [via U.S. Army]
July 26, 1944, 2129 Z / TOR 2345 Z (Washington)

Prime Minister to President Roosevelt Personal and Top Secret.

My No. 735. I should like to add:

Begins. I should also be grateful for anything you could do to encourage Mikolajczyk. Perhaps you could send him a telegram to say how glad you are that he is undertaking this journey, that he has your support and that you much hope he may be able to come to an arrangement which will result in the fusion of all Polish forces.

[MR*]

The following document, not released to the public until 1981, demonstrates that Churchill did request that specific intelligence messages, including ULTRA material, be given to Roosevelt. (See also Hinsley, *British Intelligence*, II, 89.) Presumably, the President did the same. Since this message was passed to the President without comment from the Prime Minister, it is not strictly a Churchill-Roosevelt exchange. It is included as an example of the kind of materials which may be found in the intelligence files at the various archives. The deletion (apparently of a file number) was made prior to the declassification of the document.

C–737/1

Washington
27 July 1944

Memorandum for Colonel McCarthy

Subject: Message for the President

1. On 26 July the following was received through British ULTRA channels: "Prime Minister wishes contents of SAR 0059 [deletion] dated 20/7 concerning Chemical Warfare to be shown at his request to President. Please arrange with War Department and report action taken to me."

2. The message referred to is a Japanese Army communication, a copy of which is attached. It was reported in full on page one of the MAGIC—Far East Summary for 20 July 1944. The President's copy of this publication was delivered to the White House on that day.

3. It has now been established that the message involved was dated 15 July; this fact was not known at the time of original publication.

For the Chief, Military Intelligence Service [initialed] Carter W. Clarke   Colonel, General Staff   Special Security Officer, MIS

[MR]

ATTACHMENT TO C–737/1

Date: 15 July 1944
Circuit: Manila-Menado-Salup

"Unless otherwise ordered or instructed, the use of special smoke shells and special shells, including hand thrown type self-exploding bottles, Toyo tubes and Toyo shells*, is to be discontinued. In view of the present state of enemy chemical warfare preparations, every precaution must be taken not to give the enemy cause for a pretext to use gas, thus leading to chemical warfare."

*The significance of the reference to "Toyo" tubes and shells is not known.

[MR]

John Gilbert Winant, the American Ambassador in London, received a lengthy communication from Foreign Secretary Eden which summarized British proposals for concerted Anglo-American-Soviet pressure on Sweden to halt exports to Germany. Winant commented "that there should be no difficulty in working out at a very early date a joint Anglo-American *démarche* supported by the Soviet Government" (*FRUS*, 1944, IV, 590). Various administrative steps taken by the Swedish government, such as refusing insurance to Swedish ships sailing to German-controlled ports, effectively cut trade between the two countries, but the United States continued to insist on a total cessation of strategic trade, particularly sales of ball-bearings to Germany, as well as on a public gesture by the Swedish government. Not until January 1, 1945, was all Swedish trade with Germany cut off. The British concern for postwar relations with Sweden caused the Foreign Office to oppose harsh, coercive measures.

C–738

London [via U.S. Army]
July 27, 1944, 1149 Z / TOR 1315 Z (Washington)

Prime Minister to President Roosevelt Personal and Top Secret.

Your message of July 14 [R–584/1].

I entirely agree on the desirability of cutting off Swedish exports to the enemy. We must, however, avoid jeopardizing:

(A) The substantial economic warfare advantages we have already obtained in Sweden:

(B) Our military requirements, especially in relation to deception plans:

(C) Our sources of intelligence in Sweden:

(D) Our bases in Sweden for underground work in Denmark and Central Europe.

The Foreign Office is communicating with Winant regarding the form and timing of our approach to the Swedish Government.

As soon as this is agreed, it will be necessary to approach the Russian Government and seek their support.

[MR*. *FRUS*, 1944, IV, 587.]

Randolph Churchill survived when, on July 16, 1944, a Dakota transport carrying him and others back to Yugoslavia crashed on landing. The press reported the incident on July 25, so it appears that Roosevelt learned of it from the newspapers.

R–589

Pearl Harbor, Hawaii [via U.S. Navy]
July 27, 1944, 7:00 A.M. (Washington)

Top Secret and Personal. From the President to the Prime Minister.

I am very happy that Randolph has come through all right. Roosevelt [FDR]

[MR]

As Churchill requested, the President asked Stalin to work with Mikolajczyk, though his cable was couched in vague and ambiguous terms.

R–590

Pearl Harbor, Hawaii [via U.S. Navy]
July 27, 1944, 7:00 A.M. (Washington)

Top Secret and Personal. From the President to the Prime Minister.

I am sending you for your information the text of my message to Marshal Stalin.

"I have received your telegram about the Polish situation and I hear from the Prime Minister that Mikolajczyk is leaving to call on you. It goes without saying that I greatly hope you can work this whole matter out with him to the best advantage of our common effort".

Roosevelt

[MR. *FRUS*, 1944, III, 1300. *Stalin/FDR*, doc. 215.]

See R–583 for background on Roosevelt's trip to the West Coast, Hawaii, and Alaska.

R–591

Hawaii [via U.S. Navy]
July 28, 1944, 2:45 A.M. (Washington)

From the President to the Former Naval Person. Top Secret and Personal.

Your number 738 received. My inspection voyage to date has been very interesting and profitable. Roosevelt

[MR]

Roosevelt's "encouragement" to Mikolajczyk was as vague and ambiguous as his message to Stalin. If the Polish leader harbored any hopes that the United States would support a firm stand against Soviet pressure, this must have brought him back to reality.

R–592

enroute Alaska [via U.S. Navy]
July 28, 1944, 7:30 A.M. (Washington)

Personal and Top Secret from the President to the Former Naval Person.
Your 737, I have sent the following to Mikolajczyk:

"I am pleased that you are discussing the Polish problem with the Soviet Government and I hope you can work out the whole matter to the best advantage of the combined Allied effort against our common Nazi enemy."

Roosevelt [WDL]

[MR]

Randolph Churchill's escape from death in the plane crash and fire had been much too close for comfort.

C–739

London [via U.S. Army]
July 28, 1944 / TOR 1155 Z (Washington)

Prime Minister to President Roosevelt. Personal.
Your number 589.
Thank you so much. Ten died and nine survived.

[MR*]

THE WARSAW UPRISING

Perhaps the best characterization of the Polish government came from Soviet Foreign Minister Molotov when he told American Ambassador Harriman that the Poles had consistently been late, "last year and even up to the present. Now they must make up their minds quickly or it will be too late" (*FRUS*, 1944, III, 1312). From the outset of the war the Polish government had taken an all-or-nothing approach to Soviet-Polish problems, and, with Soviet armies approaching Warsaw, "nothing" appeared more likely than "all." Under pressure, Mikolajczyk agreed to go to Moscow and the talks initially seemed to promise some sort of agreement, particularly once the Polish government in London, the Soviet-sponsored Polish Committee (situated in Lublin), and the Soviet leaders all agreed that Mikolajczyk should remain Prime Minister. The Soviets insisted on the Curzon line as their boundary with Poland, but appeared willing to discuss some adjustments. The London Poles agreed to dismiss certain anti-Soviet Ministers, and all sides acknowledged that initial suggestions that the Lublin Poles hold all but four seats in the Polish Cabinet could be scaled down. But any hope of compromise disappeared on August 1 with the start of the Warsaw Uprising.

The idea of a massive national uprising against the Germans (a plan nicknamed the "Big Scheme" and more formally called Operation TEMPEST) had long dominated the thinking of Polish Underground leaders. Claiming that the Soviet Union had refused to cooperate, the Underground offered to coordinate their attack with Anglo-American military activities. In spite of British advice that an uprising in Poland could succeed only with the approval and support of the Soviet Union, the rapid approach of Soviet armies forced Polish leaders to act quickly if they were to play any significant role in liberating their own nation. On August 1, without informing the Soviet armies approaching Warsaw, Underground leader General Bor-Komorowski began the attack. Well planned and executed, it met with initial success, but victory and even survival depended upon aid, primarily an expected Soviet attack against the Germans in Warsaw. But the Russian summer offensive stopped just short of the city. Although Polish leaders claimed they had acted in response to broadcasts on Radio Moscow by the Union of Polish Patriots (pro-Soviet) calling on Poles to rise up against the Germans, that is a half-truth, as are Soviet claims that supply problems and German reinforcements prevented their armies from continuing to push forward. The Soviet army's flank may have been dangerously exposed near Warsaw, but both Poles and Soviets realized that the Uprising was more than a fight against the Germans; it was also a struggle for political power in liberated Poland. The defeat of Germany was only a matter of time; who would replace the Germans was now the issue at hand.

Stalin refused to accept various Anglo-American proposals designed to aid the Poles in Warsaw, proposals recounted in Churchill-Roosevelt exchanges printed below, and Soviet and Polish communist armies did not launch a major attack until after the Germans had completed their grisly work of crushing the Uprising, killing 200,000 and leveling the city in the process. Stalin could not have foreseen that carnage, but to expect him to have intervened in order to rescue forces which were fiercely anti-Soviet was unrealistic. Regardless of later, secret arrangements between Churchill and Stalin, however, the long-term public sympathy for the victims of the Warsaw Uprising was disastrous for Anglo-Soviet relations. In the words of one British historian, "The Polish question, always difficult, now became the conscience of the West, and relations between Britain and Russia suffered a shock from which they never fully recovered" (Ehrman, *Grand Strategy*, V, 376).

The following exchange between Churchill and Stalin, sent to the President for his information, marked the high point of optimism about the chances for compromise between the London Poles and the Soviet Union.

C–740

London [via U.S. Army]
July 29, 1944, 2110 Z / TOR 2315 Z (Washington)

Prime Minister to President Roosevelt. Personal and Top Secret.
This seems to me the best ever received from UJ.

"I have received your messages of the 25th and 27th July one on
the subject of the departure of Mikolajczyk. M. Mikolajczyk and his
party will be given the necessary assistance on arrival in Moscow.

"You know our point of view on the question of Poland who is our
neighbour and relations with whom have an especial importance for
the Soviet Union. We welcome the national committee which has
been created on the territory of Poland from democratic forces and
I think that by the creation of this committee a good start has been
made for the unification of Poles fiendly [friendly] disposed towards
Great Britain, the USSR and the United States and for the sur-
mounting of opposition on the part of those Polish elements who are
not capable of unification with democratic forces.

"I understand the importance of the Polish question for the common cause of the allies and for this very reason I am prepared to
give assistance to all Poles and to mediate in the attainment of an
agreement between them. The Soviet forces have done and are doing
everything possible to hasten the liberation of Poland from the German usurpers and to help the Polish people in the restoration of
their freedom and in the matter of the welfare of their country."

Message of 25th July is contained in my 736 to you. Following is text
of my message to UJ of 27th July.

"1. Mikolajczyk and his colleagues have started. I am sure Mikolajczyk is most anxious to help a general fusion of all Poles on the
lines on which you and I and the President are, I believe, agreed. I
believe that Poles who are friendly to Russia should join with Poles
who are friendly to Great Britain and the United States in order to
establish the strong, free, independent Poland, the good neighbour
of Russia and an important barrier between you and another German
outrage. We will all three take good care there are other barriers
also.

"2. It would be a great pity and even disaster if the western democracies found themselves recognizing one body of Poles and you
recognizing another. It could lead to constant friction and might even
hamper the great business which we have to do the wide world over.
Please therefore receive these few sentences in the spirit in which

they are sent which is one of sincere friendship and our 20 years alliance."

[MR*. *FRUS*, 1944, III, 1300–1301. *Stalin/WSC*, docs. 305, 306. *R&C*.]

See the headnote to R–597 for an explanation of the strategic issues Roosevelt discussed with his High Commands.

R–593

Alaska [via U.S. Navy]
Aug. 3, 1944, 8:25 P.M. (Washington)

Personal and Top Secret. From the President for the Prime Minister.

Your 740 received at sea, indicated that we have reason to hope that the Stalin-Mikolajczyk conversation may bring about a settlement of the Polish controversy that can be accepted by all of us.

My inspection journey to the Pacific has already been fully justified by my conference with the High Commands. Roosevelt

[MR*. *R&C*.]

OCTAGON was the codename for the proposed Churchill-Roosevelt meeting, although neither the British nor the American records have revealed the origin of that designation. The British Fifty-second (Lowland) Division was probably scheduled for a role in the "break-out" strategy which British Field Marshal Montgomery proposed in mid-August. The division eventually took part in the ill-fated airborne assault on Arnhem (Operation MARKET-GARDEN). Field Marshal Erwin Rommel had tactical command over German forces in northwestern France and the Lowlands until he was injured on July 17 when Allied aircraft strafed his car. Roosevelt never replied to the suggestion that Soviet Foreign Minister Molotov be invited to any talks.

C–741

London [via U.S. Army]
Aug. 4, 1944, 0748 Z

Prime Minister to President Roosevelt Personal and Top Secret.

As U.J. cannot come to OCTAGON, would it not be well to invite Molotov?

Many congratulations on the magnificent fighting of your troops and the splendid advances. We have now placed the 52nd British Division at the disposal of General Montgomery, who has already prepared plans for its use. There may easily be a wide-open break and a general retreat of Rommel's Army. The 52nd will give us the equivalent of 20 divisions in Normandy. I wish we had more, but it is better to use what men we have left to fill the ranks.

[MR*. pFRUS, Quebec Conf., 1944, p. 12.]

On July 31, American forces headed by General George Patton's Third Army broke through the German defenses at Avranches, at the western end of the Allied perimeter. Although the port of Brest, on the western tip of Brittany, was not liberated until September 19 (Lorient and St. Nazaire on the south coast of Brittany remained in German hands until the end of the war), by early September Allied forces had driven northeast to the Dutch border and eastward as far as Metz and Nancy on the Moselle River (see map, p. 277). It was too late to divert forces from the buildup for ANVIL (renamed DRAGOON at the end of July) back to the Italian front, but the British still believed that an attack on German-held ports in western France would be the best way to support OVERLORD. With the breakthrough at Avranches, a secondary attack up the Rhone River valley no longer seemed necessary whereas the opening of additional Atlantic ports would speed the flow of men and matériel from the United States to the main battle front. At the same time that Churchill dispatched this cable to Roosevelt, the British Chiefs of Staff sent a similar argument to the American Chiefs of Staff—only eleven days before the invasion of southern France was to begin.

C–742

London [via U.S. Army]
Aug. 4, 1944, 2119 Z / TOR 0010 Z, Aug. 5 (Washington)

Prime Minister to President Roosevelt. Personal and Top Secret.

1. The course of events in Normandy and Brittany and especially the brilliant operations of the United States left wing give good prospects that the whole Brittany Peninsula will be in our hands within a reasonable time. I beg you will consider the possibility of switching DRAGOON into the main and vital theatre where it can immediately play its part at close quarters in the great and victorious battle in which we are now engaged.

2. I cannot pretend to have worked out the details but the opinion here is that they are capable of solution. Instead of having to force a landing against strong enemy defences we might easily find welcoming American troops at some point or other from St. Nazaire north-westward along the Brittany Peninsula. I feel that we are fully entitled to use the extraordinary flexibility of sea and air power to move with the moving scene. The arrival of the ten divisions assigned to DRAGOON with their LST's might be

achieved rapidly, and if this came off it would be decisive for Eisenhower's victorious advance by the shortest route right across France.

3. I most earnestly ask you to instruct your Chiefs of Staff to study this proposal on which our people here are already at work.

[MR*. *WSC*, VI, 66–67.]

The caution exhibited by German U-boats was a function not only of Allied anti-submarine efforts but also of the German loss of submarine bases in western France and the Lowlands, forcing the U-boats to operate out of Norway. With the "milch-cow" supply submarines virtually eliminated, German submarines were forced to use their torpedoes with greater care.

C–743

London [via U.S. Army]
Aug. 5, 1944, 0718 Z / TOR 1159 Z (Washington)

Prime Minister to President Roosevelt Personal and Secret.
    Here is our suggestion for the monthly report on U-boats.
    We are informing Canada in case you have difficulties in communication.

    The number of German U-Boats sunk during the war now exceeds 500. It is therefore understandable that the U-Boats still operating are extremely cautious. Their efforts have been ineffective during July, a month which has been so important for the success of continental operations.
    The number of U-Boats destroyed has been substantially greater than the number of merchant ships sunk. Seventeen U-Boats have been sunk while attempting to interfere with our cross-channel traffic since the first landing of the Army of Liberation.
    The U-Boat fleet is still of impressive size, nevertheless the U-Boat remain the hunted rather than the hunters. They have been attacked from the Arctic to the Indian Ocean, aircraft playing a great part with the surface forces. This pressure will be maintained until all chances of revival of the U-Boat campaign are killed, whatever may be the new devices and methods developed by the enemy.
    The Nazi claims of sinkings continue to be grossly exaggerated. For instance, their claim for June, the latest month for which complete figures are available, was an exaggeration of a 1,000 %.

[MR*]

Convinced that Britain could maintain its world power and influence only within some sort of Anglo-American entente, Churchill continued to try to pin down a date for another major conference. His repeated references to the British role in the Pacific only demonstrated his desire to maintain the closest possible association between Britain and America.

Generals Wilson, Devers, and Alexander held Allied commands in the Mediterranean/Italian theater. Churchill, always preoccupied with the Mediterranean, arrived in Naples via Algiers on August 11 and did not return to England until the end of the month. Although the Prime Minister thoroughly enjoyed visiting military commanders in the field, his trip was dominated by political issues relating to postwar governments in Yugoslavia, Greece, and Italy. Even so, Churchill found time to observe the Allied landings in the south of France.

C-744

London [via U.S. Army]
Aug. 5, 1944, 1006 Z / TOR 1159 Z (Washington)

Prime Minister to President Roosevelt Personal and Top Secret.

Thank you so much for your 593. Things are everywhere approaching a climax, and almost always a climax in our favour.

Please try to give me a firm date for OCTAGON as I have a lot to arrange.

I am sure your journey to the Pacific must have strengthened the already buoyant situation there. One of the most important things we have to settle when we meet is what you want us to do in the Japanese finale and how we can do it, and also, please, what we would like to do ourselves.

Am off to Normandy tomorrow morning, returning evening, and on Wednesday night I leave for 10 days or a fortnight for Wilson, Devers, and Alexander. I shall be in full touch all the time and will communicate as usual, which is saying a lot. Every good wish.

[MR*. *FRUS, Quebec Conf.*, 1944, p. 13.]

The concept of Anglo-American unity may have been more important to Churchill, but Roosevelt had devised the term "United Nations" and was intensely proud of it (*R&H*, p. 453).

C–744/1, letter

London [via British Embassy]
August 5, 1944

My dear Franklin,

Thank you so much for sending me the framed copy of the Declaration by the United Nations of January 1, 1942. I am very glad to have among my possessions this historic document.

Yours ever, [signed] Winston S. Churchill

[PSF:GB:WSC]

R–594

Alaska [via U.S. Navy]
Aug. 8, 1944, 12:30 A.M. (Washington)

Personal and Top Secret from the President for the Former Naval Person.
Your number 743. Monthly report on U-boats is approved. Roosevelt

[MR*]

The President's reluctance to meet Churchill in England or Europe probably followed a cable from Harry Hopkins pointing out that such a trip could be construed "as a political meeting with Russia out in the cold." Hopkins agreed that there were Anglo-American issues to discuss, but thought it best for the Prime Minister to travel to meet the President. Roosevelt characteristically worried about the effect such a conference might have on the election scheduled for November (Hopkins to Roosevelt, July 26, 1944, *FRUS, Quebec Conf.*, 1944, p. 12).

R–595

Alaska [via U.S. Navy]
Aug. 8, 1944, 12:30 A.M. (Washington)

Personal and Top Secret for the Former Naval Person from the President.
Thanks for your number 744. I am still in the Aleutians but will be back in Washington in ten days.

I hope you are right about the climax but I can not feel quite as optimistic in view of the distances involved both in France and on the Russian Front.

Can you give me one week more to consider all the implications of OCTAGON? My present thought is that, for many reasons you will understand, it would be a mistake for me to go to Scotland especially in view of Uncle Joes failure to come. My present inclination is to give greater consideration to Bermuda especially if we can make it a small meeting of Staffs and not a full Staff meeting as it was in Quebec. We could both live on our ships. As you know, domestic problems are unfortunately difficult for three months to come.

I hope you will have a grand trip and wish I could be with you.

Tell Clemmie I am hereby ordering you not to take unnecessary risks. Roosevelt [FDR]

[MR. PREM 4/75/2. *FRUS, Quebec Conf.*, 1944, pp. 13–14.]

Even before Roosevelt replied to Churchill's plea for a cancellation of DRA-GOON (ANVIL), the Prime Minister had cabled Harry Hopkins in hopes of persuading Roosevelt to the British point of view. Hopkins predicted that the President's answer would "be in the negative" (*WSC*, VI, 67–70).

R–596

Alaska [via U.S. Navy]
Aug. 8, 1944, 12:30 A.M. (Washington)

Personal and Top Secret from the President for the Former Naval Person.

Referring to your 742, I have consulted by telegraph with my Chiefs of Staff and am unable to agree that the resources allocated to DRAGOON should be considered available for a move into France via ports on the coast of Brittany.

On the contrary it is my considered opinion that DRAGOON should be launched as planned at the earliest practicable date and I have full confidence that it will be successful and of great assistance to Eisenhower in driving the Huns from France. Roosevelt [WDL]

[MR*. *WSC*, VI, 70–71.]

Unhappy, Churchill acquiesced to DRAGOON.

C–745

London [via U.S. Army]
Aug. 8, 1944, 1507 Z / TOR 1615 Z (Washington)

Prime Minister to President Roosevelt. Personal and Top Secret.

Your number 596:

I pray God that you may be right. We shall, of course, do everything in our power to help you achieve success.

[MR*. *WSC*, VI, 71. *R&C*.]

The "personal convenience" referred to by Churchill is apparently a reference to living arrangements needed to accommodate the President's inability to walk.

C–746

London [via U.S. Army]
Aug. 8, 1944, 1615 Z / TOR 1615 Z (Washington)

Prime Minister to President Roosevelt. Personal and Top Secret.

1. I will certainly come to Bermuda at any time. We could make you very comfortable at Government House. I had preparations made some months ago for your personal convenience in every way. Whatever you wish in these matters will be agreeable to us.

2. By "climax" I did not mean "end".

3. Thank you for your very kind personal thoughts.

[MR*. *FRUS, Quebec Conf.*, 1944, p. 14.]

C–747

London [via U.S. Army]
Aug. 8, 1944, 2046 Z / TOR 2200 Z (Washington)

Prime Minister to President Roosevelt Personal and Top Secret.

In view of your telegram, No. 587, stories regarding anti-submarine activities during OVERLORD were withheld from publication. It is, however, now proposed to release them in the ordinary way on expiry of the one month interval. These combat stories will, of course, as usual, be subject to careful security censorship, intended to avoid release of information likely to be of value to the enemy including especially Japan.

[MR*]

C–748

London [via U.S. Army]
Aug. 8, 1944, 2322 Z / TOR 0115 Z, Aug. 9 (Washington)

Prime Minister to President Roosevelt. Personal and Top Secret.

My telegram number 746.

I am sending you an amended version [C–750] of my reply about OCTAGON on account of later information. Please therefore regard my telegram as cancelled.

[MR. PREM 4/75/2. *FRUS, Quebec Conf.*, 1944, p. 14.]

Churchill may have found Stalin's message on the Polish question "more agreeable" than usual, but it was clear that the Soviets were demanding that the pro-Soviet Polish Committee dominate any postwar government in Warsaw. E. B. Osubka-Morawski and Boleslaw Bierut (Krasnodewski) were leaders of the Polish Committee. (Other identifications are in the headnote to C–735.) The Polish Committee claimed that it drew its authority from the Polish Constitution of 1921 and charged that the London Polish government depended upon the "illegal" 1935 Constitution for its legitimacy.

Stalin sent the same cable to Roosevelt but added that Oscar Lange, Professor of Economics at the University of Chicago, had been appointed a Director of Foreign Affairs for the Polish Committee. Stalin expressed the hope that Lange would be permitted to go to Poland.

C–749

London [via U.S. Army]
Aug. 10, 1944, 0750 Z

Prime Minister to President Roosevelt Personal and Top Secret.

I send you the following telegram from Premier Stalin. The mood is more agreeable than we have sometimes met, and I think that we should persevere.

"Aug. 8, Premier Stalin to Prime Minister.

"I wish to inform you about my meeting with Mikolajczyk, Grabski and Romer. My talk with Mikolajczyk convinced me that he has unsatisfactory information about affairs in Poland. At the same time, I was left with the impression that Mikolajczyk is not opposed to the finding of ways to unite the Poles.

As I did not consider it possible to press any decision on the Poles, I suggested to Mikolajczyk that he and colleagues should meet and themselves discuss their questions with representatives of the Polish Committee of National Liberation and, above all, the question of the speediest possible union of all the democratic forces of Poland on liberated Polish territory. These meetings have taken place. I have been informed about them by both sides. The delegation of the National Committee proposed that the 1921 constitution should be taken as the basis of the activity of the Polish Government, and, in the event of agreement, offered Mikolajczyk's group four portfolios, among them the post of Prime Minister for Mikolajczyk. Mikolajczyk, however, could not bring himself (literally: did not decide) to give his agreement to this. Unfortunately, these meetings have not yet led to the desired results, but they have all the same had a positive significance, inasmuch as they have permitted both Mikolajczyk and also Morawski and Bernt [Bierut], who had only just arrived from Warsaw, to inform each other in a broad way about their points of view and especially of the fact that both the Polish National Committee and Mikolajczyk expressed the wish to work together and to seek the practical possibilities to that end. One may consider this as the first stage in relations between the Polish Committee and Mikolajczyk and his colleagues. We shall hope that the business will go better in future."

[MR*. p*FRUS*, 1944, III, 1307–8 (paraphrase). p*Stalin/FDR*, doc. 218.]

Giving more credence to Foreign Office reports than to the Bermuda Tourist Bureau, Churchill recommended meeting in Quebec, the site of the QUADRANT Conference in 1943. The Prime Minister remained eager to move Allied forces into the Balkans in the event that German resistance in Italy collapsed, and, in the South East Asia theater, hoped for a thrust southward toward Malaya and Singapore. Since the Americans advocated an attack northward toward China, a conference was needed. British proposals for Pacific strategy, including British fleet support for American operations in the central Pacific, were forwarded to the U.S. Joint Chiefs of Staff a week after Churchill sent this cable. (Ehrman, *Grand Strategy*, V, 500–502.)

C–750

London [via U.S. Embassy]
Aug. 10, 1944, 1342 Z

Prime Minister to President Roosevelt Personal and Top Secret.
See my numbers 746 and 748.

1. I have a very bad report on the climatic conditions in Bermuda in the first or second week of September. It is said to be extremely hot and steamy whether ashore or afloat. There is also a persistent southerly wind reported very sticky and unpleasant. I most deeply regret your inability to visit Scotland. The King seemed very much disappointed when I told him. However, I quite see that, with Stalin not coming, you may wish to defer this promised visit. I, therefore, recommend the QUADRANT area. MacKenzie King assured me he would be enchanted. I have no doubt all could be arranged to your comfort and convenience.

2. I agree about reduced staff on the Teheran scale, but I hope that the meeting will not be delayed beyond the early part of September. There are several serious matters in the military sphere which must be adjusted between our staffs. I, too, would greatly welcome a few frank talks with you on matters it is difficult to put on paper. We have to settle the part the British Empire should take in the war against Japan after Germany's unconditional surrender. The situation in Burma causes me much anx-

iety. We have suffered very heavy losses through disease and the prospect of the whole forces of the British Indian Army being tied down indefinitely in the worst part of the country is unattractive. Other tangled questions arise about the position of Alexander's army in Italy including whether it is to be bled white for DRAGOON and thus stripped of all initiative. It is impossible to resolve these thorny matters by correspondence and I am sure that, if we and the staffs were together, good working agreements could be reached.

3. It will be a very great pleasure for me to see you again. I do hope your tour has done you good. Let me know your wishes as soon as possible.

[MR*. *FRUS, Quebec Conf.*, 1944, p. 15. *R&C.*]

On August 18, the President forwarded a copy of this letter to Captain Symington.

C–750/1, letter

London
August 10, 1944

My dear Franklin,

Thank you very much for your letter of July 10 [R–582/1] sending me the most interesting naval signatures and papers relating to some early Churchills, together with the visiting card signed by my Father in 1886 when, as you know, he was Chancellor of the Exchequer.

Much as I should like to keep the naval documents myself, I feel that the Admiralty should have them for their permanent records, and I am accordingly sending them to the First Lord.

I am very glad to have the papers about the early Churchills, which contain a fine signature of Sarah, Duchess of Marlborough. There were two Generals named Charles Churchill. The first was the brother of the first Duke of Marlborough, and was his General of Infantry throughout his great campaigns. The second, to whom these documents mainly relate, was the son of the first, and was for thirty years Member of Parliament for Castle Rising in Norfolk.

Will you please thank Captain Powers Symington very much for his kind thought in sending you these documents for me.

Yours ever, [initialed] W.

[PSF:GB:WSC]

During his visit to Hawaii, Roosevelt presided over a conference between General Douglas MacArthur, Supreme Commander South West Pacific Area, and Admiral Chester Nimitz, Commander in Chief of the Pacific Ocean Area. MacArthur argued for the liberation of the Philippines as the next strategic step in the Pacific, while Nimitz advocated bypassing those islands in favor of an attack on Formosa. Their differences were ones of emphasis, since both agreed that neither Formosa nor the Philippines could be ignored. Those differences were intensified by the kind of interservice and personal rivalries that all too often characterized American military strategy in the Pacific. MacArthur regularly accused the Navy and Nimitz of trying to take over direction of the war against Japan, and Nimitz responded in kind. MacArthur later claimed that the President had promised not to bypass the Philippines, although it is more likely that Roosevelt merely let MacArthur believe that.

When he wrote this telegram, Roosevelt was aboard the destroyer *Cummings*, enroute Bremerton, Washington, from Alaska.

R–597

at sea [via U.S. Navy, Washington]
Aug. 11, 1944, 1:55 A.M. (Washington)

Personal and Top Secret from the President for the Former Naval Person.

Your 750 is received at sea. I also deeply regret my inability to come to Scotland for this meeting.

It appears now that I should be able to arrive in Quebec on the 10th or 11th of September for a meeting of the Combined Staff on the Teheran scale.

My consultations with the military and naval commanders in the Pacific area have been most interesting and valuable. Roosevelt [WDL]

[MR*. *FRUS, Quebec Conf.*, 1944, p. 17.]

W. Averell Harriman, the U.S. Ambassador to the Soviet Union, sent a report to Washington similar to this report from the British Ambassador, Sir Archibald Clark Kerr, concerning the conclusion of the Mikolajczyk-Stalin talks. Both reports noted that Stalin emphasized the need for Poland to develop close relations with the West. Harriman's report also closed with the opinion that the Soviet Union wanted an agreement and that the British and American governments should "bring full pressure on Mikolajczyk and his associates" to work out a merger of all the Polish factions (*FRUS*, 1944, III, 1313–15).

Marshal Konstantin Rokossovsky commanded the Soviet armies south of Warsaw. The aid Stalin promised to the Poles in Warsaw did not materialize until mid-September, and then was much too late with much too little.

C-751

Algiers [via U.S. Army, London]
Aug. 11, 1944, 1050 Z (London)

Prime Minister to President Roosevelt. Personal and Top Secret.

The following telegram received from Ambassador Clark Kerr dated 10 Aug '44 contains our latest news of Polish affairs.

"M. Mikolajczyk left this morning. I did not see him again after his visit to Stalin last night, but he sent me a message to say that the atmosphere at the Kremlin had been much more cordial than last time. Both Stalin and Molotov had shown marked friendliness. Stalin had answered the question I had suggested with a categorical assurance that he had no intention of communising Poland. He had emphasised the need for an alliance between Poland and the USSR but had said that the Poles must have ties with the West also 'alliances with Great Britain, the United States and France'.

"Stalin had agreed to send help to the Poles in Warsaw, and had said that arrangements must at once be made for Marshal Rokossovski to send a Soviet officer to Polish Headquarters here with cyphers and wireless.

"The talk had then turned on Germany. Stalin had said he would do 'everything possible and impossible' to ensure that Germany could never again reap revenge. Mikolajczyk had told Stalin that a German officer captured in Normandy had said that Germany would go communist after the war, and would find in the communist part of the world an outlet for the German capacity for organization. To this, Stalin had replied that communism was 'no more fit for Germany than a saddle for a cow'. This had surprised and pleased the Poles, who had recalled the German origins of the communist theory.

"Mikolajczyk now felt that speed was the first essential.

"It is clear that this talk has put cheerfulness where there had been gloom in the hearts of the Poles."

[MR*. R&C.]

R-598

at sea [via U.S. Navy, Washington]
Aug. 11, 1944, 8:50 P.M. (Washington)

To the Former Naval Person from the President. Top Secret and Personal.

Your 751 received with its pleasing news of the Soviet-Polish conversations. Roosevelt [WDL]

[MR*]

Churchill quickly accepted the date suggested by Roosevelt for the OCTA-GON meeting in Quebec. During his tour of the Mediterranean (see C–744), Churchill's cables to Roosevelt were normally sent "to the President from Colonel Kent" (the Prime Minister's codename) through London, where the usual "Prime Minister to President" heading was inserted.

C–752

Naples [via U.S. Army, London]
Aug. 12, 1944, 0902 Z (London) / TOR 1053 Z (Washington)

Prime Minister to President Roosevelt Personal and Top Secret.
    Your number 597.
    We accept with greatest pleasure. Urgently looking to our meeting. War situation by then may have cleared up many difficulties. I am arranging with Mackenzie King and others.
    How magnificently your troops are fighting and how their logistics have carried them forward.

[MR*]

BRITISH POLICY IN THE BALKANS

British policy in southern Europe was frequently beset by conflicts between long-term postwar and short-term wartime goals. Although ideology colored the decisions of Churchill's government, the basic thrust of British postwar policy in that area was to control the northern Mediterranean littoral. That seemed to dictate cooperation with Franco's Spain, and support for monarchies in Italy, Yugoslavia, and Greece. But first defeating Hitler, as well as fulfilling the growing desire to have British forces liberate the western Balkans and even Austria and Czechoslovakia, required that Partisans in Yugoslavia and Greece receive matériel support from the Allies. Since those Partisans were at the least anti-monarchist and frequently pro-communist, military aid diminished the likelihood that the monarchies could be restored. Furthermore, the Yugoslav and Hellenic monarchies had been both unpopular and pro-German before the war. Thus the British government found itself forced to play the role of mediator, trying to convince the militarily stronger Partisan forces voluntarily to restore some sort of "constitutional" monarchy. What later events showed is that the British failed to appreciate the intensity of nationalism in those two countries. Even though Yugoslavia remained divided by ethnic quarrels between Serbs and non-Serbs, the German occupation had, as in Greece, stimulated a strong sense of national unity. Because only the Partisans effectively opposed the Germans, they captured national support. Moreover, such rising nationalism stimulated anti-British sentiment among leaders who feared swapping one master for another, even if British influence would be economic and political and vastly different from the Nazi occupation. In moves which foreshadowed the "neutralism" of the Cold War, Partisan leaders tried to walk a narrow path between East and West, building military strength while maintaining political independence, at least domestically.

This dilemma was uppermost in Churchill's mind when he met with Partisan leader Marshal Tito and the Prime Minister of the Royal Yugoslav Government, Dr. Ivan Subasić. During two days of talks held at General Wilson's headquarters at Caserta, near Naples, Churchill tried to reconcile the two British policies. He obtained a promise from Tito that Partisan military efforts would be aimed at the Germans, not the anti-Partisan Serbs, and presided over talks between Tito and Subasić which were so friendly that Churchill and Eden feared the two Croats had underestimated the strength of Serbian opposition to Tito.

(Churchill's report of these talks to Stalin was the same as the following cable except for the addition of a reference to the reduction of internal fighting. The word "declaration," apparently omitted by accident from the first sentence of paragraph 3 of the message to Roosevelt, was included in the version sent to Stalin. See *Stalin/WSC*, doc. 320.)

C–753

Caserta, Italy [via U.S. Army, London]
Aug. 14, 1944, 1626 Z (London) / TOR 1915 Z (Washington)

Prime Minister to President Roosevelt Personal and Top Secret.

I have had meetings during the last 2 days with Marshal Tito and the Yugoslav Prime Minister. I told both the Yugoslav leaders that we had no thought but that they should combine their resources so as to weld the Yugoslav People into one instrument in the struggle against the Germans. Our aim was to promote the establishment of a stable and independent Yugoslavia and the creation of a United Yugoslav Government was a step towards this end.

The two leaders reached a satisfactory agreement on a number of practical questions. They agreed that all the Yugoslav Naval Forces will now be united in the struggle under a common flag. This agreement between the Yugoslav Prime Minister and Marshal Tito will enable us with more confidence to increase our supplies of war material to the Yugoslav Forces.

They agreed between themselves to issue simultaneously in a few days time, which I hope will strengthen and intensify the Yugoslav war effort. They are going off together today to Vis to continue their discussions.

I am informing Marshal Stalin of the result of these meetings.

[MR*. *WSC*, VI, 93. *R&C*.]

Comfortable with British predominance in the southern and western Balkans, Roosevelt could maintain his supposed "hands-off" policy in the area.

R–599

enroute Washington [via U.S. Navy, Washington]
Aug. 14, 1944, 10:40 P.M. (Washington)

Personal and Top Secret from the President for the Former Naval Person.
   Your 753. Congratulations on your prospects of success in bringing together the opposing factions in Jugoslavia which should bring to an end the civil war in that country and be of assistance to us in the rapidly approaching defeat of the Nazis. Roosevelt

[MR*. R&C.]

With obvious reluctance, the Navy Department accepted Churchill's proposal that stories about anti-U-boat warfare during OVERLORD be released to the press. The technique which had been so successful combined ULTRA data, radar, and tactics.

R–600

enroute Washington [via U.S. Navy, Washington]
Aug. 15, 1944, 1:45 A.M. (Washington)

Personal and Top Secret from the President for the Former Naval Person.
   Proposals in your 747 are satisfactory, but I hope all concerned with security censorship of U-boat stories will be impressed with the fact that our submarine campaign in the Pacific is far from over, and that we can be done irreparable harm if Japan gains any knowledge of the reasons for successful anti-U-boat technique of British and American forces. Roosevelt [Navy Dept.]

[MR*]

Since he was already in Italy, Churchill seized the opportunity to observe the invasion of southern France (DRAGOON) on August 15. As much as he hoped for success, he was doubly frustrated: first, by the refusal of the commander of his transportation, the destroyer HMS *Kimberley*, to approach any closer than 7,000 yards (3½ miles) from the beach; but more so by the very fact that the landing had even taken place. The Prime Minister's annoyance still showed when he wrote his memoirs eight or nine years later: "I had at least done the civil thing to ANVIL, and indeed I thought it was a good thing

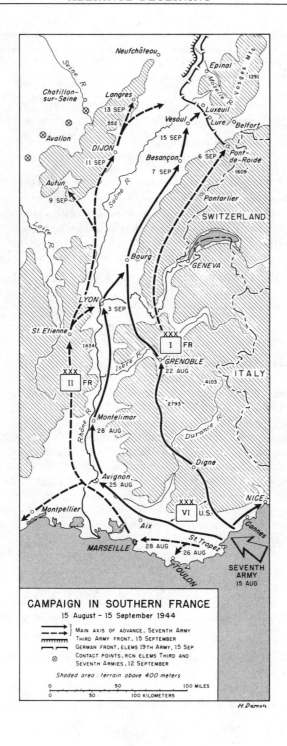

CAMPAIGN IN SOUTHERN FRANCE
15 August – 15 September 1944

Main axis of advance, Seventh Army
Third Army front, 15 September
German front, elems 19th Army, 15 Sep
⊗ Contact points, rcn elems Third and
Seventh Armies, 12 September

Shaded area : terrain above 400 meters

0   50   100 MILES
0   50   100 KILOMETERS

H. Damon

I was near the scene to show the interest I took in it" (*WSC*, VI, 95). Robert Patterson, the Assistant Secretary of War, and Lieutenant General Brehon Somervell, the Commanding General of the U.S. Army Services of Supply, joined Churchill aboard the *Kimberley*.

C–754

Caserta, Italy [via U.S. Army, London]
Aug. 16, 1944, 1621 Z (London) / TOR 2240 Z

Prime Minister to President Roosevelt. Personal and Top Secret.

1. Have just returned from watching the assault from considerable distance. Everything seems to be working like clockwork here and there have been few casualties so far and none that I know of amongst the mass of shipping deployed.

2. All arrangements proceeding for OCTAGON on dates you mention.

3. I had the pleasure of taking Patterson and General Somervell out on my destroyer.

[MR*]

Roosevelt seemed inclined to go along with Churchill's monarchist policies in Greece, but the State Department argued it would be impossible both to support King George II and to prevent a leftist/nationalist revolution. (See Wittner, "American Policy Toward Greece," p. 138.) That may account for the delay in an answer to Churchill's cable (Roosevelt did not answer for over a week; see R–608), although the initial sentence, "Instructions to General Wilson," may have misled the Americans into thinking this was merely a copy of a cable to the Supreme Allied Commander in the Mediterranean. Actually, that phrase belongs at the end of the message, as indicated, and was probably shifted in its location as part of the enciphering process.

All of the sources, including Churchill's memoirs, testify to the Prime Minister's intense concern about the political situation in Greece. Fearful of a communist-led coup in Athens as the Germans withdrew, Churchill wanted to set up contingency plans for a quick British occupation of the Greek capital.

C–755

Italy [via U.S. Army, London]
Aug. 17, 1944, 1820 Z (London)

Prime Minister to President Roosevelt. Personal and Top Secret.

Instructions to General Wilson.

1. We have always marched together in complete agreement about Greek policy, and I refer to you on every important point. The War

Cabinet and Foreign Secretary are much concerned about what will happen in Athens, and indeed in Greece, when the Germans crack or when their divisions try to evacuate the country. If there is a long hiatus after German authorities have gone from city before organized government can be set up, it seems very likely that EAM and the Communist Extremists will attempt to seize the city and crush all other form of Greek expression but their own.

2. You and I have always agreed that the destinies of Greece are in the hands of the Greek people, and they will have the fullest opportunity of deciding between a Monarchy or Republic as soon as tranquility has been restored, but I do not expect you will relish more than I do the prospect either of chaos and street fighting or of a tyrannical Communist government being set up. This could only serve to delay and hamper all the plans which are being made by UNRRA for the distribution of relief to the sorely tried Greek people. I therefore think that we should make preparations through the Allied Staff in the Mediterranean to have in readiness a British force, not exceeding 10000 men, which could be sent by the most expeditious means into the capital when the time is ripe. The force would include parachute troops, for which the help of your air force would be needed. I do not myself expect that anything will happen for a month, and it may be longer but it is always well to be prepared. As far as I can see there will be no insuperable difficulty. I hope, therefore, you will agree that we may make these preparations by the staffs out here in the usual way. If so, the British Chiefs of Staff will submit to the Combined Chiefs of Staff draft [instructions to General Wilson].

[MR*. *WSC*, VI, 111–12. *FRUS*, 1944, V, 132–33. *R&C*.]

C–756

Italy [via U.S. Army, London]
Aug. 17, 1944, 1756 Z (London) / TOR 2100 Z

Prime Minister to President Roosevelt. Personal and Top Secret.

Thank you for your letter dated 15th July [R–584/2]. I had an agreeable conversation with Mr. Morgenthau before I left.

[MR*]

Dr. Ivan Subasić, Prime Minister of the Royal Yugoslav Government, also held the title of Ban of Croatia. British officials believed that Subasić underestimated the intensity of Serbian opposition to Tito.

C–757

Italy [via U.S. Army, London]
Aug. 17, 1944, 1756 Z (London) / TOR 2200 Z

Prime Minister to President Roosevelt Personal and Top Secret.

I am so glad you are cheered by what I told you of my interview with Tito and the BAN [C–753]. They certainly seemed to understand each other very well, but I cannot be sure that BAN gives sufficient expression to Serbians' point of view. How to supply this will be difficult.

Every good wish.

[MR*]

C–758

Italy [via U.S. Army, London]
Aug. 18, 1944, 0850 Z (London) / TOR 1205 Z

Prime Minister to President Roosevelt. Personal and Top Secret.

Your number 600.

I have repeated your telegram to Admiralty who will take every precaution in the matter.

[MR*]

The Soviet decision not to aid directly the Polish Underground in Warsaw seems to have been taken for military reasons, although political considerations pointed to the same conclusion. The Soviet advance during July had been remarkable—over 450 miles in five weeks—but lines of communication and supply were stretched to the breaking point. Moreover, the Soviet offensive and the Warsaw Uprising caused the Germans to dispatch reinforcements (three S.S. panzer divisions) from the Balkan and Italian fronts. A Soviet salient which reached the outskirts of Warsaw early in July was pushed back, and an advance from bridgeheads across the Vistula River, south of Warsaw, failed. In fact, with the exception of some gains in the Carpathians and Lithuania, the entire central and northern sections of the eastern front were stabilized until the Soviet armies resumed the offensive in January 1945. Warsaw did not fall to the Soviets until January 17, three months after the collapse of the Uprising.

Even so, Stalin appeared unwilling even to make *pro forma* gestures of support for the Polish Underground. His instructions for the air-dropping of arms had apparently been ignored or reversed, and by labeling the Uprising an "adventure"—a strong pejorative in the Soviet political lexicon—Stalin indicated that he considered the Underground an enemy of the U.S.S.R. Polish and British aircraft attempted to drop supplies, but with little success.

The Soviets rejected a proposal that British and American aircraft fly from England, drop supplies over Warsaw, and proceed to air bases in Russia, without any explanation beyond a statement that "the Soviet Government did not wish to encourage 'adventuristic actions' which might later be turned against the Soviet Union" (*FRUS*, 1944, III, 1375). Soviet reluctance to permit the presence of any foreign military units within the borders of the U.S.S.R., as evidenced by the negotiations over the use of Siberian air bases by U.S. bombers, only added to Stalin's firmness. The political aspect of the Soviet position is further revealed by Stalin's insistence that Polish Underground forces place themselves under the command of Lieutenant General Zygmunt Berling, leader of a Polish corps sponsored by the Soviet Union. It is quite possible, however, that the Soviets would not have intervened in Warsaw even if the Underground had been led by pro-Soviet communists, although the point is moot since such leaders would have coordinated any uprising with the Soviets.

(The Prime Minister's forwarding instructions were included as part of the message text.)

C-759

Italy [via U.S. Army, London]
Aug. 18, 1944, 1515 Z (London)

Prime Minister to President Roosevelt. Personal and Top Secret.

The Prime Minister has asked that this telegram which he has received from Marshal Stalin should be repeated to the President.

1. After the conversation with M. Mikolajczyk I gave orders that the Command of the Red Army should drop arms intensively in the Warsaw sector. A parachutist liaison officer was also dropped who, according to the report of the Command, did not reach his objective as he was killed by the Germans.

Further, having familiarized myself more closely with the Warsaw affair, I am convinced that the Warsaw action represents a reckless and terrible adventure which is costing the population large sacrifices. This would not have been if the Soviet Command had been informed before the beginning of the Warsaw action and if the Poles had maintained contact with it.

In the situation which has arisen the Soviet Command has come to the conclusion that it must dissociate itself from the Warsaw adventure as it cannot take either direct or indirect responsibility for the Warsaw action.

2. I have received your communication regarding the meeting with Marshal Tito and Prime Minister Subasic. I thank you for the communication.

3. I am very pleased at the successful landing of Allied Forces in the south of France. I wish success from my heart.

[MR*. *Stalin/WSC*, doc. 321. *R&C*.]

Airdrops of supplies for the Polish Underground had proven extremely hazardous with only small success. By mid-August, the aircraft flying out of Italy were ordered to avoid airspace directly over Warsaw, though they continued to drop supplies into the wooded outskirts of the city. By the end of August, the Polish air wing had only three planes left in flying condition, and Allied planes had been withdrawn from the operation, largely because of heavy losses.

(The version of this message printed in Churchill's memoirs appears to be a paraphrase. Since the Prime Minister was then in Italy, it is likely that his original draft was paraphrased before being sent to the President.)

C–760

Italy [via U.S. Army, London]
Aug. 18, 1944, 2220 Z (London) / TOR 0040 Z, Aug. 19

Prime Minister to President Roosevelt Personal and Top Secret.

The refusal of the Soviet to allow the U.S. aircraft to bring succour to the heroic insurgents in Warsaw, added to their own complete neglect to fly in supplies when only a few score of miles away, constitutes an episode of profound and far reaching gravity. If, as is almost certain, the German triumph in Warsaw is followed by a wholesale massacre no measure can be put upon the full consequences that will arise. I am willing to send a personal message to Stalin if you think this wise and if you will yourself send a separate similar message.

2. Better far than two separate messages would be a joint message signed by us both. I have no doubt we could agree on the wording.

3. The situation in Europe is being vastly changed by the glorious and gigantic victories being achieved in France by the U.S. and British forces and it may well be that our armies will gain a victory in Normandy which far exceeds in scale anything that the Russians have done on any particular occasion. I am inclined to think therefore, that they will have some respect for what we say so long as it is plain and simple. It is quite possible Stalin would not resent it but even if he did we are nations serving high causes and must give true counsels towards world peace.

[MR. *WSC*, VI, 135. *R&C*.]

Persuaded that the Warsaw Uprising was doomed, Roosevelt sought only to preserve the image of Allied and Soviet support for the Underground. Nor did he respond to Churchill's suggestion, in the third paragraph of the preceding cable, that military victories in the West would make it possible to take a tougher line with the Soviets.

R–601

Washington [via U.S. Navy]
Aug. 19, 1944, 12:35 P.M.

Personal and Secret, from the President for the Former Naval Person:
Your 760. The following is suggested as a joint message to U.J. which if you approve you may send over both our signatures.

> QUOTE. We are thinking of world opinion if the anti-Nazis in Warsaw are in effect abandoned. We believe that all three of us should do the utmost to save as many of the patriots there as possible. We hope that you will drop immediate supplies and munitions to the patriot Poles in Warsaw, or will agree that our planes should do it very quickly. We hope you will approve. The time element is of extreme importance. UNQUOTE.

Roosevelt [WDL]

[MR*. pWSC, VI, 135–36. pStalin/WSC, doc. 322. R&C.]

The broadcasts referred to in this cable did occur, but subsequent events suggest that the Soviets had expected the Underground to coordinate its revolt with the Soviet offensive. When Underground leader Bor-Komorowski acted alone, the Uprising became a political issue and military considerations became secondary. The Union of Polish Patriots was a Soviet-sponsored organization which evolved into the Polish National Committee and the pro-Soviet Polish government at Lublin.

C–761

Italy [via U.S. Army, London]
Aug. 19, 1944, 1347 Z

Prime Minister to President Roosevelt. Personal and Top Secret.
Further to my 760.
You should see the following telegram which I have just received from Foreign Secretary.

"The Polish Government have reminded me that Soviet broad-casting stations have for a considerable time past repeated appeals to the Polish population to drop all caution and start a general rising against the Germans. As late as July 29th, i.e., three days before the Warsaw rising began, the Moscow radio station broadcast an appeal from the Union of Polish Patriots to the population of Warsaw which, after referring to the fact that the guns of liberation were now within hearing, called upon them as in 1939 to join battle with the Germans, this time for decisive action. 'For Warsaw, which did not yield but fought on, the hour of action has already arrived.' After reference to the German plan to set up defence points which would result in the gradual destruction of the city, the broadcast terminated by re-minding the inhabitants that 'All is lost that is not saved by active affort' and that 'By direct active struggle in the streets, houses, etc., of Warsaw the moment of final liberation will be hastened and the lives of our brethren saved.' "

[MR*. pR&C.]

Andrei Vyshinsky, the First Assistant People's Commissar for Foreign Affairs of the Soviet Union (Deputy Foreign Minister), had made a statement which seemed to object to British and American airdrops of supplies to the Polish Underground in Warsaw. His subsequent statement, quoted below, made it clear that Soviet objections related only to those aircraft continuing on to land at Soviet airbases.

C–762

Italy [via U.S. Army, London]
Aug. 20, 1944, 0808 Z (London) / TOR 1200 Z

Prime Minister to President Roosevelt, Personal and Top Secret.

The message in your Number 601 has been sent on to U.J. over our two signatures. Our thoughts are one.

Following telegram received from our Ambassador in Moscow, dated 17 August:

"United States Ambassador and I are asking urgently for interview with M. Stalin. If his instructions do not arrive in time he will support me on his own responsibility.

"You should, however, know that last night Vyshinski asked the United States Ambassador to call, and, explaining that he wished to avoid the possibility of misunderstanding about what he had said to us the previous afternoon, read out the following statement. Begins:

" 'The Soviet Government cannot, of course, object to English or American aircraft dropping arms in the region of Warsaw since this is American and British affair. But they decidedly object to American or British aircraft, after dropping arms in the region of Warsaw, landing on Soviet territory, since the Soviet Government do not wish to associate themselves either directly or indirectly with the adventure in Warsaw.' " (ends)

[MR*. R&C.]

Intended for the President of Brazil, whose nation had sent a brigade of troops to fight with the United Nations in Italy, Churchill's communicators sent this cable by mistake to President Roosevelt.

C–763

Leghorn, Italy [via U.S. Army]
Aug. 20, 1944, 1636 Z (London) / TOR 1845 Z

Prime Minister to President Roosevelt.

Today I had the honour of inspecting your magnificent troops in the liberated soil of Italy. May I be permitted to express my admiration of the character, quality and bearing of these soldiers. We are most grateful for your help.

[MR]

In addition to inspecting Allied forces during his trip to Leghorn, Churchill held talks with the Commanding General of the Fifth American Army, Mark Clark. Clark agreed with the Prime Minister's arguments against the invasion of southern France, and Churchill's later claim that the Fifth Army "had been stripped and mutilated for the sake of 'ANVIL' " (DRAGOON) reflected Clark's assessment (WSC, VI, 106). During British staff meetings on August 21, Churchill further indicated how strongly he felt about the Italian campaign. In a confidential annex to the minutes of that meeting, the secretary recorded Churchill's position: "A victory would greatly strengthen our hand in the forthcoming discussions with the Americans. . . . He was prepared to go to extreme measures to ensure that the operations of this great Army should not be hamstrung. If the worst came to the worst and the Americans persisted in their desire to withdraw their troops from Italy into France he would be prepared to split the command" (PREM 3/275/1/21). Although Churchill made no such threat during the OCTAGON meetings in Quebec in September, there was no mistaking his support for the Italian campaign.

C–764

Leghorn, Italy [via U.S. Army, London]
Aug. 21, 1944, 0750 Z (London) / TOR 0900 Z

Prime Minister to President Roosevelt, Personal and Top Secret.

Today I spend with your grand Fifth Army and Mark Clark. I also saw the Brazilians, whose bearing was excellent. The spirit of this Army and of the British Eighth Army, standing on its right, is high but of course there is a sense of bewilderment at the repeated and ceaseless withdrawals of important and key elements.

Everything is in train for OCTAGON on the 10th. I am looking forward greatly to meeting you.

[MR*]

Churchill had much more sympathy for the Zionist movement than did most of the British Cabinet, who feared that the creation of a Jewish brigade would be interpreted by Arabs as an endorsement of Zionist goals. The British War Office, tasked with maintaining the peace in Palestine, tried to pigeonhole the proposal, but the Prime Minister refused to let that happen. Nor was Churchill unaware of the effect the creation of such a brigade would have in the United States. As he wrote in a message to one of his Ministers, "Remember the object of this is to give pleasure and an expression to rightful sentiments, and that it certainly will be welcomed widely in the United States" (WSC, VI, 697). The idea of constituting an organized, formal Jewish fighting force had first been broached by Chaim Weizmann, the leader of the World Zionist Organization, shortly after the beginning of the war, but in spite of approval in principle from the British government, domestic and international politics prevented that idea from becoming a reality. Palestinian Jews were enlisted into the British East Kent Regiment where they eventually comprised the "Palestine Regiment." Assigned duty primarily as guards in Palestine, Libya, and Egypt, the leaders of the regiment continued to ask for permission to fight under the Jewish flag. Opposition to sending the Palestine Regiment to the Italian front came from British commanders in the Middle East, who did not want to lose such well-disciplined and effective troops, and from British political figures who feared that such an independent fighting force would only complicate problems in Palestine once the war was over.

C–765

Italy [via U.S. Army, London]
Aug. 23, 1944, 0845 Z (London) / TOR 0945 Z

Prime Minister to President Roosevelt, Personal and Top Secret.

After much pressure from Weizmann I have arranged that the War

Office shall raise a Jewish brigade group in what you would call a regimental combat team. This will give great satisfaction to the Jews when it is published and surely they of all other races have the right to strike at the Germans as a recognisable body. They wish to have their own flag, which is the Star of David on a white background with two light blue bars. I cannot see why this should not be done. Indeed I think that the flying of this flag at the head of a combat unit would be a message to go all over the world. If the usual silly objections are raised I can overcome them, but before going ahead I should like to know whether you have any views upon it.

[MR*. R&C.]

A good deal of the arrangements for the Quebec Conference of September 1944 were made by Churchill and Hopkins in a series of exchanges, most of which are printed in *FRUS, Quebec Conf.*, 1944. As with earlier Churchill-Roosevelt meetings, the President labored unsuccessfully to limit the number of attendees, finally succumbing to a tautological solution whereby each side brought about fifteen "participants" who were then supported by 250 to 300 personnel on each side.

Roosevelt's motives for preferring a small conference appear to have been twofold. First, he wished to avoid the clamor, confusion, and intensive press coverage that went with a full-dress formal meeting. Second, the President wanted to hold candid, personal discussions with the Prime Minister, unencumbered by an army of bureaucrats defending their vested positions with well-rehearsed arguments and reams of statistics. In a very real sense, Roosevelt did not want to be "confused by the facts." Finally, he wanted a small conference which he could control. The last paragraph of this cable was altered by the President to make even more firm his intention of limiting the size of the conference.

Admirals Leahy, Brown, and McIntire, and General Watson, were all on Roosevelt's personal staff.

R–602

Washington [via U.S. Navy]
Aug. 23, 1944, 12:05 P.M.

Personal and Top Secret, from the President for the Former
Naval Person.

Referring to our agreement that the OCTAGON Conference should be on the Teheran scale I find by consultation with my Chiefs of Staff with which I am in agreement that the Teheran scale on the American Staff included the four Chiefs of Staff with their eleven military assistants, a total of fifteen officers.

~~Please let me know that this number is sufficient for your Staff in order that our detailed plans may be completed.~~

I am therefore limiting those officers who will go to Quebec with me to fifteen, not counting Leahy, Watson, Brown and McIntire. Roosevelt [WDL]

[MR*. *FRUS, Quebec Conf.*, 1944, pp. 18–19.]

Roosevelt may have shared some of Churchill's distrust of communism, though uneasiness seems more descriptive of the President's feelings, but he refused to adopt the belligerent policies so often advocated by the Prime Minister. Cooperation, albeit with caution, not confrontation, characterized Roosevelt's goals for Soviet-American relations. A memorandum from Eleanor Roosevelt to the President may offer an insight into his thinking on these matters. Mrs. Roosevelt sent a copy of two paragraphs from a memo written by Churchill on September 15, 1919, in which he summarized Western military efforts during 1919 against the Bolsheviks and then commented:

It is a delusion to suppose that all this year we have been fighting the battles of the anti-Bolshevik Russians. On the contrary, they have been fighting ours; and this truth will become painfully apparent from the moment that they are exterminated and the Bolshevik armies are supreme over the whole vast territories of the Russian Empire (printed in Churchill, *The World Crisis*, IV, 256, 259).

Mrs. Roosevelt's comment was blunt and pointed: "It is not surprising if Mr. Stalin is slow to forget!" (Eleanor Roosevelt to F. D. Roosevelt, Aug. 21, 1944, PSF:GB:WSC).

This brief response to Churchill's pessimistic reports about the Warsaw Uprising fit the pattern of Roosevelt's efforts to temper the Prime Minister's responses to Soviet actions, or inaction.

R–603

Washington [via U.S. Navy]
Aug. 23, 1944, 12:08 P.M.

Personal and Top Secret, from the President for the Former Naval Person.

Your 759, 761 and 762. We must continue to hope for agreement by the Soviet to our desire to assist the Poles in Warsaw. Roosevelt [WDL]

[MR*. *R&C.*]

R–604

Washington [via U.S. Navy]
Aug. 23, 1944, 12:20 P.M.

Personal and Top Secret, from the President for the Former
Naval Person.

Your 763 and 764 noted. I am happy to have your personal observation
that our Fifth and Eighth Armies' spirit is fully up to our expectations.
Roosevelt [WDL]

[MR*]

Among the messages Churchill sent to Harry Hopkins in the course of preparing for the OCTAGON Conference, one raised a number of important
issues and was probably intended for the President and is, therefore, included
here.

"Stage 2" referred to lend-lease assistance to Britain during the period
between Germany's surrender and victory over Japan. Sir John Anderson,
Chancellor of the Exchequer, and Oliver Lyttelton, Minister of Production,
did not atend the Quebec Conference after Hopkins responded that he did
not think the President planned to get into detailed discussions of such questions. Lord Cherwell (Frederick Lindemann) was Churchill's favorite scientist,
although he advised the Prime Minister on any and all issues, and played an
important role in convincing Churchill to accept the Morgenthau Plan for
restructuring Germany.

"T A" stood for TUBE ALLOYS, the joint Anglo-American research project on the military uses of atomic energy (the Manhattan Project). During
talks at Hyde Park immediately following the Quebec Conference, Churchill
and Roosevelt rejected suggestions that atomic energy be subject to international control and further agreed to continue Anglo-American collaboration on the development of military and commercial uses of TUBE ALLOYS
(*FRUS, Quebec Conf.*, 1944, pp. 492–93).

The second paragraph referred to General Alexander's forces in Italy, or
what was "left" of them, and the reference to "unsettlements" was yet another
complaint about denuding the Italian front for the invasion of southern
France.

Churchill's comments about capturing the Brittany ports related to the
longstanding OVERLORD plan to seize those facilities in order to bring in
sufficient men and supplies from the United States for the broad offfensive
against Germany. Because Allied strategists did not expect to have an opportunity to drive quickly to the Rhine, an opportunity presented by the
breakout at Avranches, General Patton's forces were ordered to move westward against the Brittany ports. That was probably just as well, since
OVERLORD logistics were not prepared to sustain the kind of slashing drive
to the Rhine which might have broken German resistance in the West.

Schicklgruber (Schickelgruber) had been the original family name of Alois, Adolf Hitler's father. Born the illegitimate son of Maria Schicklgruber, Alois changed his name to Hitler (a variation of Hüttler or Hiedler, two versions of his supposed father's family name). Schicklgruber sounded ludicrous to the British ear, and the news media frequently referred to Adolf Hitler by that name.

C–765/1

Italy [via U.S. Army, London]
Aug. 23, 1944, 1039 Z

Prime Minister to Mr. Harry Hopkins, Personal, Private, and Top Secret.

For Stage 2 I should require to have with me Chancellor of Exchequer Anderson, Oliver Lyttelton and Lord Cherwell. These complicated discussions could take place side by side with military topics. It might also be well for Anderson and Cherwell to contact your people on T A.

For President's most secret personal information Alexander is going to make a considerable push in the near future, with what he has got left. You know, Harry, that I have here the Army of British Empire, British, Canadian, Australian, South African, and Indian. The airborne army is so representative of whole Empire. They are in grand fettle in spite of unsettlements caused to all ranks by pulling out of key elements, which has gone on for three months, but I hope their action will remind you they cannot possibly be left on side line during later phase of war. I could never consent to this.

I shall now probably come by Boeing [airplane], which gives me four or five days more in London and France, to which I must pay a visit.

Foresee enemy present policy of holding on to all ports to utmost while withdrawing under strong rearguard to Swiss frontier–Dijon–Paris line or farther make it most necessary we shall obtain port facilities and not be jammed up against autumn and winter gales, as is evidently the desire of Schickelgruber.

Looking forward so much to seeing you and our great friend in near future.

[MR]

On August 2, 1944, Churchill had told the House of Commons that the government felt "deep regret and also anxiety" because Argentina had failed to side with the United Nations. He warned that this was "not like some small wars in the past where all could be forgotten and forgiven" and that "nations must be judged by the part they play." Having made that statement, the Prime Minister now argued for a quiet period to permit the Argentine leaders to shift their policies without seeming to submit to pressure from the United States. (Churchill's speech is in *FRUS*, 1944, VII, 337–38.)

Although the President responded favorably (R–607), Secretary of State Hull continued to push for a ban on non-essential meat imports from Argentina to the United States and for continuing the diplomatic pressure aimed at forcing the Colonels, as Churchill called the Argentine leaders, to declare war on the Axis. Annoyed by Hull's intransigence, one British official likened working with him to dealing with Prime Minister William Gladstone in his old age (Woodward, *British Foreign Policy*, IV, 80n). By the time of the Quebec Conference, Hull had convinced the President once again to oppose any long-term Anglo-Argentine meat contract.

C–766

Rome [via U.S. Army, London]
Aug. 23, 1944, 1806 Z (London)

Prime Minister to President Roosevelt. Personal and Top Secret.

I am thankful that you see our point about getting a new Argentine meat contract. We are going ahead accordingly with these difficult negotiations and hope that nothing will happen to hazard them. We have no wish or intention to present the Colonels with anything they can represent as a diplomatic triumph.

2. I hope that you liked my reference to Argentina on August 2nd: from all accounts Argentines do not seem to have liked it. We seem to be agreed as to objectives and I hope that we can also agree as to tactics. We will not send our ambassador back or recognise the Argentine Government until we have discussed with you what we think the situation requires. Our Embassy have now received our views and passed them to your State Department. Now that we have said in public just what we think of the present Argentine Government, I do most earnestly hope that you will ignore the Colonels for a good many weeks, thus giving both of us an opportunity to examine a common policy and the Argentines a chance to mend their ways, which they can never do under the glare of public indictment.

[MR*. *FRUS, Quebec Conf.*, 1944, pp. 163–64.]

Politics aside, there was no question about the dedication and bravery of the Polish Home Army (AK) and the citizens of Warsaw.

C–767

Rome [via U.S. Army, London]
Aug. 23, 1944, 2118 Z (London)

Prime Minister to President Roosevelt. Personal and Top Secret.

The following is an eye witness account of the Warsaw rising. A copy has already been given to the Soviet Ambassador in London.

1. 11th August the Germans are continuing despite all efforts of AK, their ruthless terror methods. In many cases they have burnt whole streets of houses and shot all the men belonging to them and turned the women and children out on to the street where battles are taking place, to find their way to safety. On Krolewska Street many private houses have been bombed out. One house was hit by 4 separate bombs. In one house, where lived old retired professors of Polish Universities, the SS troops forced an entrance and killed many of them. Some succeeded in escaping through the cellars to the other houses. The morale of AK and the civilian population is of the highest standard. The watchword is "Death to the Germans".

2. 11th August.

The German Tank Forces during last night made determined efforts to relieve some of their strong points in the city. This is no light task however, as on the corner of every street are built huge barricades mostly constructed of concrete pavement slabs torn up from the streets especially for this purpose. In most cases the attempts failed, so the tank crews vented their disappointment by setting fire to several houses and shelling others from a distance. In many cases they also set fire to the dead which litter the streets in many places and have begun to smell rather badly. The German Tank Corps have begun to have a great respect for the Polish barricade, for they know that behind each one waits determined troops of AK with petrol bottles. These petrol bottles have caused great destruction to many of their comrades.

3. 13th August.

The German Forces have brutaly murdered wounded and sick people, both men and women who were lying in the hospitals of SS Lazarus on Nmska Str., N. 18, and Karol and Marsa hospitals on Prxejaxd Str., N. 5.

On Aleje Jerozolimskie, when the Germans were bringing supplies by tank to one of their outposts they drove before them 500 women and children to prevent the troops of AK from taking action against them. Many of them were killed and wounded. The same kind of action has been reported from many other parts of the city.

Despite lack of weapons, the Polish forces continue to hold the initiative in the battle for Warsaw. In some places they have broken into German strongholds and captured much needed arms and ammunition. On August 12th, 11,600 rounds of rifle ammunition, 5 machine guns, 8,500 small arms ammunition, 20 pistols, 30 anti tank mines and transport were captured. The German forces are fighting desperately. On Aleje Jeroxolimskie, when AK set fire to a building which the Germans were holding as a fortress 2 German soldiers tried to escape to the Polish lines with a white flag, but an SS Officer saw them and shot them dead. During the night of the 12th/13th August AK received some weapons from Allied aircraft.

4. August 15th.

The dead are buried in backyards and squares. The food situation is continually deteriorating, but as yet there is no starvation. Today there is no water at all in the pipes. It is being drawn from the infrequent wells and house supplies. All quarters of the town are under shell fire and there are many fires. The dropping of supplies has intensified the morale. Everyone wants to fight and will fight but the uncertainty of a speedy conclusion is depressing.

5. August 16th.

Fighting continues to be very bitter in Warsaw. The Germans fight for every inch of ground. It is reported that in some places whole districts have been burnt and the inhabitants either shot or taken to Germany. The inhabitants continue to repeat "When we get weapons we will pay them back".

Fighting for the electric power station began on August 1st at 5.10 P.M. 23 soldiers of the Polish Home Army were stationed in the works before that hour because they were employed in the normal course of things, expecting the outbreak of the rising. The Germans had on the day before raised the strength of the garrison to 150 militarized police stationed in concrete pill boxes and block houses, also in all the works buildings. The signal of action was the explosion of a mine under one of the buildings. After 19 hours of fighting the electric power station was fully in Polish hands. The Polish losses were 17 killed and 27 wounded. The German losses were 20 killed and 22 wounded with 56 taken as Prisoners of War. The detachment which captured the station consisted solely of manual and metal workers of the works. In spite of the fact that the buildings of the station are daily bombarded with 75 MM shells by the Germans, the personnel had succeeded in maintaining the supply of current to the civil population without the slightest interruption.

[MR. *WSC*, VI, 136–38.]

In spite of the poignant tale about the Warsaw Uprising, Roosevelt continued to draw back from applying additional pressure on the Soviets. Stalin's message, dated August 22, made clear his opposition to providing aid to the Underground. He labeled its leaders "power-seeking criminals" and blamed them for exposing the civilian population of Warsaw to the threat of extermination (*Stalin/FDR*, doc. 223).

R–605

Washington [via U.S. Navy]
Aug. 24, 1944, 11:55 A.M.

Personal and Top Secret, from the President for the Former Naval Person.

Thank you for the information in regard to the appalling situation of the Poles in Warsaw and the inhuman behavior of the Nazis described in your 767.

My information points to the practical impossibility of our providing supplies to the Warsaw Poles unless we are permitted to land on and take off from Soviet airfields, and the Soviet authorities are at the present time prohibiting their use for the relief of Warsaw.

I do not see that we can take any additional steps at the present time that promise results.

Stalin's reply of August 23 to our joint message about the Warsaw Poles is far from encouraging to our wishes to assist. Roosevelt [WDL]

[MR*. *WSC*, VI, 139 (paraphrase).]

Churchill's communicators had mistakenly sent a message intended for the President of Brazil to the President of the United States. Since the Prime Minister had been inspecting both Brazilian and U.S. forces, the error caused no embarrassment.

C–768

Siena, Italy [via U.S. Army, London]
Aug. 24, 1944, 2150 Z (London) / TOR 2120 Z

Prime Minister to President Roosevelt Personal and Top Secret.

My 763 was sent to you by mistake. The cipher people had apparently not realized there was any other president in the world.

[MR*]

When Stalin condemned the Polish Underground and ignored the Allied request to use air bases in the Soviet Union, Churchill again tried to persuade Roosevelt to adopt a firm stand. (Stalin's cable is in *Stalin/FDR*, doc. 223.)

The Americans had managed earlier, after lengthy negotiations, to get Soviet approval to land U.S. bombers at three airfields in the Ukraine (Poltava, Mirgorod, and Piryatin) after they had flown raids against targets in eastern Germany and eastern Europe. Operations began at Poltava on June 2, 1944, and a total of seven missions shuttled between western Europe and the Soviet Union. On August 17, 1944, during the Warsaw Uprising, Foreign Minister Molotov told the American Ambassador, Averell Harriman, that the Soviet Air Force planned to reclaim those airfields. No more shuttle-bombing missions were flown, and by the end of October two of the three bases had been closed.

C–769

Siena, Italy [via U.S. Army, London]
Aug. 25, 1944, 1018 Z (London) / TOR 1402 Z

Prime Minister to President Roosevelt. Personal and Top Secret.

Uncle Joe's reply adds nothing to our knowledge and he avoids the definite questions asked. I suggest following reply:

"We are most anxious to send American planes from England. Why should they not land on the refueling ground which has been assigned to us behind the Russian lines without enquiry as to what they have done on the way. This should preserve the principle of your governments dissociation from this particular episode. We feel sure that if wounded British or American planes arrive behind the lines of your armies, they will be succoured with your usual consideration. We do not try to form an opinion about the persons who instigated this rising which was certainly called for repeatedly by radio Moscow. Our sympathies are, however, for the 'almost unarmed people' whose special faith has led them to attack German guns tanks and aircraft. We cannot think that Hitler's cruelties will end with their resistance. On the contrary, it seems probable that that is the time when they will begin with full ferocity. The massacre in Warsaw will undoubtedly be a very great annoyance to us when we all meet at the end of the war. Unless you directly forbid it, therefore, we propose to send the planes."

If he will not give any reply to this I feel we ought to go and see what happens. I cannot conceive that he would maltreat or detain them. Since signing this, I have seen that they are even trying to take away your airfields at Poltava and elsewhere.

[MR*. *WSC*, VI, 139–40 (paraphrase). *R&C*.]

For whatever reason, the President had not answered Churchill's request that the United States support plans to send British forces into Athens to prevent left-wing guerrillas from taking control when the Germans evacuated the city. Roosevelt immediately directed Harry Hopkins and Admiral Leahy to draft a reply.

At the time he drafted this message, Churchill was apparently at the headquarters of the British Eighth Army, near Loreto, Italy.

C-770

Loreto, Italy [via U.S. Army, London]
Aug. 25, 1944, 2111 Z (London)

Prime Minister to President Roosevelt Personal and Top Secret.

Could you very kindly give me an answer to my telegram of August 16th (number 755). We are getting on with the preparations and the crisis may come soon. Should you feel you do not wish to express an opinion on the subject I am quite willing to go ahead on my own.

[MR*. R&C.]

The American Joint Chiefs feared that the "drastic action" Churchill called for might jeopardize American negotiations for the use of air bases in Siberia to fly raids over Japan. (See WSC, VI, 140.)

R-606

Washington [via U.S. Navy]
Aug. 26, 1944, 11:50 A.M.

Personal and Top Secret, for the Former Naval Person from the President.

Your 769. In consideration of Stalin's present attitude in regard to relief of the Polish Underground in Warsaw as expressed in his messages to you and to me, and his definite refusal to permit the use by us of Soviet air fields for that purpose, and in view of current American conversations in regard to the subsequent use of other Soviet bases, I do not consider it advantageous to the long range general war prospect for me to join with you in the proposed message to U.J.

I have no objection to your sending such a message if you consider it advisable to do so. Roosevelt [WDL]

[MR*. WSC, VI, 140 (paraphrase). R&C.]

Even while the President offered no objections to continued British negotiations with Argentina for a long-term meat contract, Secretary of State Hull continued to protest British policy.

R–607

Washington [via U.S. Navy]
Aug. 26, 1944, 11:55 A.M.

Secret and Personal, from the President for the Former Naval Person.

Your 766. We are watching with sympathetic interest your efforts to get Argentina in line with our appetites, and we hope your efforts will be crowned with success. I have no doubt that a satisfactory meat contract will be arranged. After all they must sell their beef and no other diner is in sight. Roosevelt [WDL]

[MR*. *FRUS, Quebec Conf.*, 1944, p. 165.]

No one has yet adequately explained why Roosevelt went against the advice of the State Department at this time and supported British plans to occupy Greece as the Germans withdrew. The President may have been mulling over the question during the ten days which elapsed between Churchill's initial request (C–755) and this reply, but the printed sources give no hint that the White House was engaged in a policy debate. Admiral William Leahy, who helped draft this cable, claimed in his memoirs that his motive was to prevent the United States from becoming involved in European political affairs, and there is no mention of the message in the authorized political biography of the other drafter, Harry Hopkins. (See Leahy, *I Was There*, pp. 284–85; *R&H*, pp. 841ff.) Whatever the reasons, this telegram constituted a major step toward an endorsement of the British policy for liberated Greece.

R–608

Washington [via U.S. Navy]
Aug. 26, 1944, 12:15 P.M.

Top Secret and Personal, from the President for the Former Naval Person.

Your 755 and 770. I have no objection to your making preparations to have in readiness a sufficient British force to preserve order in Greece when the German Forces evacuate that country. There is also no objection to the use by General Wilson of American transport airplanes that are available to him at that time and that can be spared from his other operations. Roosevelt [WDL, HLH]

[MR*. *FRUS*, 1944, V, 133–34. *WSC*, VI, 112.]

The Jewish Brigade proposed by Churchill did become a reality. After training in Egypt it joined the British Eighth Army on the Italian front, taking part in the fighting against German forces in March 1945. It later participated in the occupation of northwestern Europe after the German surrender. The unit was disbanded in the summer of 1946, whereupon most of its members returned to Palestine to join the Israeli Army. Eventually, two members of the Jewish Brigade, M. Makleff and H. Laskov, rose to become Chiefs of Staff of the Israeli Army.

R–609

Washington [via U.S. Navy]
Aug. 28, 1944, 11:50 A.M.

Personal and Secret, from the President for the Former Naval Person.

Your 765. I perceive no objection to your organizing a Jewish Brigade as suggested. Roosevelt [WDL]

[MR*. R&C.]

The upcoming conference at Quebec had increased not only in size but, as the military picture in Europe changed, in importance as well. On the eastern front, Roumania and Bulgaria had surrendered to the Soviet Armies, while in France the Allies had driven eastward to the Marne River, accepting the surrender of German forces in Paris on August 25. Ignoring Hitler's orders to leave the city a "field of ruins," the German commander negotiated a cease-fire inside Paris, though German forces contested the approaches. Even with the Franco-American bickering over administrative and occupation matters, the liberation of Paris was a tremendous psychological victory for the Allies. Surprisingly, the Churchill-Roosevelt exchanges make no mention of the event, possibly because it was the occasion for the triumphant re-entry of General de Gaulle. But all those military victories made a discussion of postwar Anglo-American policies even more imperative.

The time when "Bulgaria proved the lynch pin" was during World War I. Bulgaria had been the first of the Central Powers to capitulate, and within a month and a half the war was over.

C–771

Naples, Italy [?] [via U.S. Army, London]
Aug. 29, 1944 / TOR 0105 Z

Prime Minister to President Roosevelt Personal and Top Secret.

To take part in the conference I shall only bring 14 or 15 persons but I must explain to you that as I and the Chiefs of Staff have to conduct a very great number of import affairs from day to day it will be necessary to have considerable numbers of persons for that purpose. For instance,

My own party and private secretaries 7. Secretariat and Administration 6. Clerical 42. Cipher staff 30. Royal Marine Guard 36. There will also be a small contingent from our element in Washington. These however are only the machinery with which I carry on my work and without which I could not leave the country. You have all your great departments immediately under your hand a few hours away by air.

2. The glorious events in France and in the Balkans have completely altered the whole outlook of the war and with people like the Germans anything might happen. Last time Bulgaria proved the lynch pin which when pulled brought everything crashing down.

3. I must express my admiration to you not only for the valour but for the astonishing mobility and manoeuvering power of the great armies trained in the United States. I am looking forward immensely to seeing you again and trying to clear up with you in the light of our friendship some of the difficulties which beset even the path of dazzling victory. Thank you very much for your telegram about Greece [R–608].

[MR. *FRUS, Quebec Conf.*, 1944, p. 23. *R&C*.]

Allied operations in Italy inevitably suffered from the drain on troops and supplies caused by OVERLORD and DRAGOON. As Churchill had feared, the Italian front became a backwater with a main purpose of merely tying down German forces. Nevertheless, on August 25, General Sir Harold Alexander, commander of Allied armies in Italy, launched a major offensive against the "Gothic" line, a German defense position stretching across the Italian peninsula from Pesaro on the Adriatic to La Spezia on the Ligurian Sea (see map, Vol. II, p. 453). Despite initial successes, a combination of vigorous German defensive action, heavy autumn rains, and depleted Allied forces brought the offensive to a halt at the end of October. By early April 1945, Allied armies still had not broken through, and by the time German defenses collapsed later that month it was too late to realize Churchill's dream of having British troops liberate Austria, Czechoslovakia, and Hungary ahead of the Soviet Union. British forces did liberate Trieste and Istria, but that had little effect in determining the postwar government of Yugoslavia.

Lieutenant General Mark Clark commanded the U.S. Fifth Army until November, when he took command of the Fifteenth Army Group, which included the British Eighth Army.

C–772

Naples, Italy [via U.S. Army, London]
Aug. 29, 1944, 0822 Z (London) / TOR 1210 Z

Prime Minister to President Roosevelt, Personal and Top Secret.
General Alexander received a telegram from SHAEF asking for efforts

to be made to prevent the withdrawal of more [German] divisions from the Italian Front. This of course was the consequence of the great weakening of our Armies in Italy and has taken place entirely since the attack on the Riviera. In all, four divisions have left including a very strong Panzer on route for Chalôns. However, in spite of the weakening process Alexander began about three weeks ago to plan with Clark to turn or pierce the Apennines. For this purpose the British 13 Corps of four divisions has been placed under General Clark's orders and we have been able to supply him with the necessary artillery of which his army had been deprived. This army of eight divisions—four American and four British— is now grouped around Florence in a northerly axis.

By skinning the whole front and holding long stretches with nothing but anti-aircraft gunners converted to a kind of artillery-infantry and supported by a few armoured brigades, Alexander has also been able to concentrate ten British and British controlled divisions representative of the whole British Empire on the Adriatic flank. The leading elements of these attacked before midnight on the 25th and a general barrage opened and an advance began at dawn on the 26th. An advance of about nine miles was made over a large area but the main position, the Gothic Line, has still to be encountered. I had the good fortune to go forward with this advance and was consequently able to form a much clearer impression of the modern battlefield than is possible from the kinds of pinnacles and perches to which I have hitherto been confined.

The plan is that the Eighth Army of ten divisions very heavily weighted in depth will endeavour to pierce the Gothic Line and turn the whole enemy's position entering the Po Valley on the level of Rimini but at the right moment depending on the reactions of the enemy Mark Clark will strike with his eight divisions and the elements of both armies will converge to Bologna. If all goes well I hope that the advance will be much more rapid after that and that the continued heavy fighting will prevent further harm being done to Eisenhower by the withdrawal of divisions from Italy.

I have never forgotten your talks to me at Teheran about Istria [C–717] and I am sure that the arrival of a powerful army in Trieste and Istria in four or five weeks would have an effect far outside purely military values. Tito's people will be awaiting us in Istria. What the condition of Hungary will be then I cannot imagine but we shall at any rate be in a position to take full advantage of any great new situation.

[MR*. WSC, VI, 122–24. FRUS, Quebec Conf., 1944, pp. 221–22.]

R-610

Washington [via U.S. Navy]
Aug. 30, 1944, 12:30 P.M.

Personal and Top Secret, from the President for the Prime Minister.

Your 771. I am pleased that our final arrangements for OCTAGON will keep the number who will participate in the conference to the Teheran level insofar as practicable. Roosevelt [WDL]

[MR. *FRUS, Quebec Conf.*, 1944, p. 24.]

Roosevelt cheerfully acknowledged what Churchill grudgingly admitted: the Italian campaign now served primarily to prevent the Germans from shifting troops out of Italy into France and the Lowlands. Although an advance through the Ljubljana gap was impossible, the President appeared willing to discuss the possibility of an attack on Trieste and Istria, at the head of the Adriatic Sea. Churchill raised the question again during the Quebec Conference, but no firm decisions resulted. Admiral King did tell the British that he could not hold amphibious vessels in the Mediterranean past mid-October 1944 (*FRUS, Quebec Conf.*, 1944, p. 303).

Someone (the handwriting is unidentified) substituted "General Wilson's armies" for "Alexander's Army" in the next-to-last paragraph, probably because the White House wished to emphasize that the chain of command went through the Allied Commander in Chief, Mediterranean, before it reached the Allied commander in Italy (Alexander). That emphasis may have something to do with General Wilson's earlier apparent support for DRAGOON (ANVIL). Whatever the motive, Churchill made a point, in his cable C–774, of stressing Alexander's role in planning the Italian campaign (*WSC*, VI, 124).

Although Admiral Leahy drafted this cable, it is safe to assume that he first consulted the Joint Chiefs of Staff and that it was an expression of U.S. military strategy, not just the President's personal views. Leahy's position later evolved into that of the Chairman of the Joint Chiefs of Staff, but during the war he was only the President's Chief of Staff. General Marshall had suggested that Leahy be appointed to the White House Staff, assuming the Admiral would act as liaison with the Joint Chiefs. As it turned out, to Marshall's chagrin, Leahy frequently acted as *primus inter pares* with the Joint Chiefs.

R-611

Washington [via U.S. Navy]
Aug. 30, 1944, 12:35 P.M.

Personal and Top Secret, from the President for the Prime Minister.

Your 772. I was very glad to receive your account of the way in which General Wilson has concentrated his forces in Italy and has now renewed the offensive. My Chiefs of Staff feel that a vigorous attack, using all the forces available, should force the enemy into the Po Valley. The enemy may then choose to withdraw entirely from northern Italy. Since such action on his part might enable the enemy to release divisions for other fronts, we must do our best to destroy his forces while we have them in our grasp. I am confident that General Wilson has this as his objective.

With an offensive under way and being pressed full strength in Italy, I am sure that General Eisenhower will be satisfied that everything possible is being done in the Mediterranean to assist him by mauling German divisions which might otherwise be moved against his forces in the near future. I understand all available British resources in the Mediterranean are being put into Italy. We are pressing into France all reinforcements and resources we can in order to guarantee that General Eisenhower will be able to maintain the impetus of the joint victories our forces have already won. With the smashing success of our invasion of southern France and the Russians now crumbling the enemy flank in the Balkans, I have great hopes that complete and final victory will not be long delayed.

It is my thought that we should press the German Army in Italy vigorously with every facility we have available and suspend decision on the future use of ~~Alexander's Army~~ General Wilson's armies until the results of his campaign are better known and we have better information as to what the Germans may do.

We can renew our Teheran talk about Trieste and Istria at OCTAGON. Roosevelt [WDL]

[MR*. FRUS, Quebec Conf., 1944, pp. 24, 222–23.]

Churchill arrived back in England after his Italian trip with a fever and his third case of pneumonia during the war. The infection responded to medication (M & B, an antibiotic sulfonamide manufactured by May & Baker), and the Prime Minister was in good health for the Quebec Conference.

C–773

London [via U.S. Army]
Aug. 31, 1944, 0847 Z / TOR 1200 Z

Prime Minister to President Roosevelt Personal and Top Secret.

I had a sudden attack of my former malady with a temperature of between 103 and 104 degrees two hours before my plane reached home. However with vigilance, care and M & B, I am now normal again and have every hope and intention of coming in the *Queen Mary* on the fifth instant, thus reaching OCTAGON on the 10th. The voyage at sea will be better for me than a journey by air.

[MR*. *FRUS, Quebec Conf.*, 1944, p. 26.]

The President added the final paragraph to Leahy's draft about arrangements for OCTAGON. The *Queen Mary* docked at Halifax, Nova Scotia, on September 10.

R–612

Washington [via U.S. Navy]
Aug. 31, 1944, 11:55 A.M.

Personal and Top Secret, from the President for the Prime Minister.

Your 773. I am distressed at the news of your illness. Please guard your health first and above all other considerations.

We can postpone OCTAGON to some later date if it appears advisable to do so.

<u>Where is landing spot? If New York you and I could go to OCTAGON</u>
<u>together on my train.</u> Roosevelt [WDL]

[MR*. *FRUS, Quebec Conf.*, 1944, p. 26.]

Hull continued to press the British to use their negotiations for a meat contract as a lever to force Argentina to join the Allies. A few days after Roosevelt sent this cable, Hull told him that the United States could substantially increase its beef exports to England, making it possible for the British to reduce their imports from Argentina. The Secretary of State made no reference to the long-term implications, however, even though the British had frequently mentioned the matter of postwar trade with Argentina.

R–613

Washington [via U.S. Navy]
Aug. 31, 1944, 7:10 P.M.

Personal and Top Secret, from the President for the Prime Minister.

In connection with the Argentine meat negotiations you have no doubt seen the message to Buenos Aires from the Argentine Ambassador in London in which the Ambassador warned his government that its difficulties were "no longer centered on suspension of relations with the United States" and that Argentina was being placed "in a position of isolation vis-a-vis the Allied and friendly nations." He added that according to a "big meat packer the Allied Nations are now in a position to do without Argentine meat for six months with no trouble at all and for twelve months with some sacrifice." The Ambassador also said that his information tallies with that from the Argentine Commercial Counsellor in Washington and with the view expressed for some time past by the Ambassador himself that the United Nations may make fewer purchases from Argentina.

Since we know that the Colonels are falling all over themselves to get you to buy their meat, I am confident that you will agree that the Ambassador's message was an extremely bad piece of news for them.

All the evidence that has come to my attention reinforces our belief that you are in an excellent position to use the negotiations to support the whole Allied stand in this Hemisphere against this broad Fascist movement. You will certainly have no trouble on the beef and mutton matter in any event. Roosevelt [CH]

[MR*. *FRUS, Quebec Conf.*, 1944, p. 167.]

Alexander was a favorite of Churchill, and the Prime Minister firmly emphasized his role. As it turned out, the offensive in Italy fell far short of Churchill's expectations, whereas the Allied invasion of southern France (DRAGOON) met none of the difficulties Churchill had feared. The Germans opposing DRAGOON concentrated on trying to withdraw in order to avoid being cut off, and by the end of August the Allies had taken Toulon and Marseille. Lyon, 200 miles north of Marseille, was liberated on September 3. DRAGOON forces joined OVERLORD forces on September 12, cutting off almost half the German troops which had occupied southwestern France. (See map, p. 277.)

C–774

London [via U.S. Army]
Aug. 31, 1944, 1532 Z / TOR 1900 Z

Prime Minister to President Roosevelt. Personal and Top Secret.
Your No. 611 SOP.

Now all operations in Italy are conceived and executed by General Alexander in accordance with his general directives from the Supreme Commander. You will see that he is now in contact for twenty miles on the Adriatic flank with the Gothic line, and a severe battle will be fought by the Eighth Army. Also General Clark with the Fifth Army has made an advance from the direction of Florence. I have impressed most strongly upon General Alexander the importance of pressing with his utmost strength to destroy the enemy's armed forces as well as turn his line. It will not be easy for the Germans to effect a general retreat from the Gothic line over the Alps especially if we can arrive in the neighbourhood of Bologna. The western passes and tunnels into France are already blocked by your advance into the Rhone Valley. Only the direct route to Germany is open. We shall do our utmost to engage, harry and destroy the enemy. The decisive battle has yet, however, to be fought.

2. In view of the fact that the enemy on the Italian front has been weakened by four of his best divisions, we no longer ask for further American reinforcements beyond the 92nd Division, which I understand will shortly reach us. On the other hand, I take it for granted that no more will be withdrawn from Italy, i.e., that the four divisions of Clark's army and the elements remaining with them will continue there: and that General Alexander should make his plans on that basis. So much for the present.

3. As to the future: continuous employment against the enemy will have to be found for the Eighth and Fifth Armies once the German armies in Italy have been destroyed or unluckily made their escape. This employment can only take the form of a movement first to Istria and Trieste and ultimately upon Vienna. Should the war come to an end in a few months, as may well be possible, none of these questions will arise. Anyhow, we can talk this over fully at OCTAGON.

4. I congratulate you upon the brilliant success of the landings in Southern France. I earnestly hope the retreating Germans may be nipped at Valence or Lyons and rounded up. Another mob of about 90,000 is apparently streaming back from the south via Poitiers.

[MR. *FRUS, Quebec Conf.*, 1944, pp. 25, 223–24.]

C–775

London [via U.S. Army]
Sept. 1, 1944, 1021 Z / TOR 1205 Z

Prime Minister to President Roosevelt. Personal and Top Secret.

My temperature is normal and I am much better though still eating masses of M & B. The doctors seem quite confident that I can get away on night of fifth. The ship goes to Halifax direct and I will arrive Citadel on the tenth.

I look forward so much to seeing you again and to making good plans with you for the future in these days of glory.

[MR*. *FRUS, Quebec Conf.*, 1944, pp. 27–28.]

Actually, two OSS missions had been sent to work with Mihailović and the Chetniks in Yugoslavia. (See C–638.) One team had the task of evacuating downed Allied fliers who fell into Chetnik-held territory; the other group worked as an intelligence mission at Mihailović's headquarters. The latter group, commanded by a violently anti-Partisan and pro-Chetnik OSS officer, soon became involved in the political struggle between the Chetniks and the Partisans. Ordered to leave Yugoslavia in September, the intelligence mission stayed until November 15, ostensibly because heavy fighting and bad weather prevented U.S. planes from landing (U.S., War Dept., *War Report of the OSS*, II, 131–32; Smith, *OSS*, pp. 150–51).

C–776

London [via U.S. Army]
Sept. 1, 1944, 1046 Z

Prime Minister to President Roosevelt. Personal and Top Secret.

I see that General Donovan has sent an American mission to General Mihailovic. I thought from your telegram, No. 515 in response to my No. 638, that such a step would not be taken. We are endeavouring to give Tito the support and, of course, if the United States back Mihailovic, complete chaos will ensue. I was rather hoping things were going to get a bit smoother in these parts, but if we each back different sides, we lay the scene for a fine civil war. General Donovan is running a strong Mihailovic lobby, just when we have persuaded King Peter to break decisively with him and when many of the Cetniks are being rallied under Tito's National Army of Liberation. The only chance of saving the King is the unity between his Prime Minister, the Ban of Croatia, and Tito. I have been able to arrange for the fusion of the Yugoslav air and naval forces under the title and with the emblem of the Royal Yugoslav Air Force and the Royal Yugoslav Navy.

[MR. *R&C.*]

Clementine (Clemmie) Churchill had as little influence on the Prime Minister's daily routine as did Roosevelt's wife, Eleanor, on the President's.

R–614

Hyde Park, N.Y. [via U.S. Navy]
Sept. 1, 1944, 12:05 P.M. (Washington)

Personal and Top Secret, from the President to the Prime Minister.

So happy your temperature is normal but this is the time to go slow. Remember I am entirely free and can go to OCTAGON literally any time if the doctors suggest a postponement for a week or several weeks. I suggest you make Clemmie the arbiter. The armies keep rolling along and a few weeks of delay on our part will not slow them up. Roosevelt [FDR]

[MR*. *FRUS, Quebec Conf.*, 1944, p. 28.]

After learning that Harry Hopkins felt too ill to attend the Quebec talks, Churchill at first expressed his disappointment to Roosevelt. But the reference was subsequently deleted, possibly because the British knew that Hopkins' prolonged illness had caused the President to look elsewhere for counsel.

C–777

London [via U.S. Army]
Sept. 1, 1944, 1330 Z

Prime Minister to President Roosevelt. Personal and Top Secret.

I hope you will pardon a further transgression of the Teheran scale. I am going to bring Mrs. Churchill with me. I shall be sorry to leave America without seeing Harry.

[PREM 4/75/2/631. pMR. p*FRUS, Quebec Conf.*, 1944, p. 28.]

R–615

Hyde Park, N.Y. [via U.S. Navy]
Sept. 1, 1944, 6:25 P.M. (Washington)

Personal and Top Secret. From the President for the Prime Minister.

Perfectly delighted that Clemmie will be with you. Eleanor will go with me to OCTAGON. Roosevelt

[MR*. *FRUS, Quebec Conf.*, 1944, pp. 28–29.]

C–778

London [via U.S. Army]
Sept. 2, 1944, 1440 Z

Prime Minister to President Roosevelt. Personal and Top Secret.

I am delighted that Eleanor will come.

The doctors are resolute that I can go bar a setback. I cannot reach OCTAGON till noon 11th.

[MR*. *FRUS, Quebec Conf.*, 1944, p. 30.]

American strategy was fixed: a massive, broad advance across northern France and the Lowlands into Germany. Roosevelt softened the tone of Leahy's draft cable restating that strategy, but the President's "open-minded" position, a phrase he added to the draft, did not presage a reversal of American plans.

General Sir Henry Maitland Wilson left his position as Allied commander in the Mediterranean in November and replaced the late Field Marshal Sir John Dill as the British representative on the Combined Chiefs of Staff Committee in Washington. Lieutenant General Alexander Patch commanded the U.S. Seventh Army during the DRAGOON operation.

R–616

Hyde Park, N.Y. [via U.S. Navy]
Sept. 3, 1944, 2:00 P.M. (Washington)

Personal and Top Secret. From the President for the Prime Minister.
Your Number 774.

I share your confidence that the Allied divisions we have in Italy are sufficient to do the task before them and that the battle commanders will press the battle unrelentingly with the objective of shattering the enemy forces. After breaking the German forces on the Gothic Line, we must go on to use our divisions in the way which best aids General Eisenhower's decisive drive into the enemy homeland.

As to the exact employment of our forces in Italy in the future, this is a matter we can discuss at OCTAGON. It seems to me that American forces should be used to the westward but I am completely open-minded on this and, in any event, this depends on the progress of the present battle in Italy and also in France where I strongly feel that we must not stint in any way the forces needed to break quickly through the western defenses of Germany.

The credit for the great Allied success in southern France must go impartially to the combined Allied force, and the perfection of execution of the operation from its beginning to the present belong to General Wilson and his Allied staff and to Patch and his subordinate commanders. With the present chaotic conditions of the Germans in southern France, I hope that a junction of the north and south forces may be obtained at a much earlier date than was first anticipated. Roosevelt [WDL]

[MR*. *FRUS, Quebec Conf.*, 1944, pp. 33, 229.]

On the same day this cable went to Churchill, the President instructed the head of the OSS, General William Donovan, that "in view of British objection, it seems best to withdraw mission to General Mihailovic" (Roosevelt to Donovan, Sept. 3, 1944, MR). From the tone of those instructions, it is unlikely that Roosevelt's failure to act earlier was a "mistake." Correspondence from

Leahy and the Joint Chiefs of Staff to the President on this matter was not sent via the Map Room, probably because it pertained to current intelligence operations. Thus, whatever the discussion, the documents are not in the Map Room files.

R–617

Hyde Park, N.Y. [via U.S. Navy]
Sept. 3, 1944, 5:05 P.M. (Washington)

Personal and Top Secret, from the President for the Prime Minister.
Your No. 776.

The mission of OSS is my mistake. I did not check with my previous action of last April 8th [R–515]. I am directing Donovan to withdraw his mission. Roosevelt [WDL, JCS]

[MR. R&C.]

With remarkable candor, Churchill set forth the political rationale behind British pleas for aid to the Polish Underground. But Stalin, with an equally self-interested appraisal, had no intention of assisting forces which intended to establish an anti-Soviet regime.

C–779

London [via U.S. Army]
Sept. 4, 1944, 2115 Z / TOR 0640 Z, Sept. 5

Prime Minister to President Roosevelt. Personal and Top Secret.

1. The War Cabinet are deeply disturbed at the position in Warsaw and at the far reaching effect on future relations with Russia of Stalin's refusal of airfield facilities.

2. Moreover as you know Mikolajczyk has sent his proposals to the Polish Committee of Liberation for a political settlement. I am afraid that the fall of Warsaw will not only destroy any hope of progress but will fatally undermine the position of Mikolajczyk himself.

3. My immediately following telegram contain the text of a telegram which the War Cabinet in their collective capacity have sent to our Ambassador in Moscow and also of a message which the women of Warsaw have communicated to the Pope and which has been handed by the Vatican to our Minister.

4. The only way of bringing material help quickly to the Poles fighting in Warsaw would be for United States aircraft to drop supplies using Russian airfields for the purpose. Seeing how much is in jeopardy we beg that you will again consider the big stakes involved. Could you not au-

thorize your Air Forces to carry out this operation, landing if necessary
on Russian airfields without their formal consent? In view of our great
successes in the west, I cannot think that the Russians could reject this
fait accompli. They might even welcome it as getting them out of an
awkward situation. We would of course share full responsibility with you
for any action taken by your air force.

[MR*. WSC, VI, 141–42. FRUS, Quebec Conf., 1944, pp. 188–89. R&C.]

On August 29, the United States and Great Britain had issued parallel statements indicating that the Polish Underground forces were part of the armed
forces of the United Nations and should be treated by the Germans in accordance with the "laws and customs of war"; but that futile gesture did
nothing to aid the Warsaw Uprising.

The following cable was apparently sent to the Soviet government via the
British Ambassador in Moscow as an official communication. On September
9, the Soviet Government replied with another denunciation of the "Warsaw
adventure" but agreed to cooperate in aiding the Underground if the British
insisted. After delays caused by bad weather, American bombers dropped
supplies on September 18 and then flew on to Soviet air bases. In addition,
Soviet aircraft made small drops of supplies beginning on September 13.
However, the Soviet government indicated (according to British documents)
that it would not permit another shuttle flight to drop supplies over Warsaw
and then land at Soviet bases (Woodward, British Foreign Policy, III, 221).

The version of this cable printed in Churchill's memoirs includes a final
paragraph which was not sent to Roosevelt. That paragraph is printed below
in brackets and follows the Map Room version of the telegram.

C–780

London [via U.S. Army]
Sept. 4, 1944, 2115 Z / TOR 0040 Z, Sept. 5

Prime Minister to President Roosevelt. Personal and Top Secret.

Following is text of telegram sent to Moscow this evening mentioned
in my immediately preceding telegram:—

"1. The War Cabinet at their meeting today considered the latest
reports of the situation in Warsaw which show that the Poles fighting
against the Germans there are in desperate straits.

2. The War Cabinet wish the Soviet Government to know that
public opinion in this country is deeply moved by the events in Warsaw and by the terrible sufferings of the Poles there. Whatever the
rights and wrongs about the beginnings of the Warsaw rising, the
people of Warsaw themselves cannot be held responsible for the

decision taken. Our people cannot understand why no material help has been sent from outside to the Poles in Warsaw. The fact that such help could not be sent on account of your Government's refusal to allow United States aircraft to land on aerodromes in Russian hands is now becoming publicly known. If on top of all this the Poles in Warsaw should now be overwhelmed by the Germans, as we are told they must be within two or three days, the shock to public opinion here will be incalculable. The War Cabinet themselves find it hard to understand your Government's refusal to take account of the obligations of the British and American Governments to help the Poles in Warsaw. Your Government's action in preventing this help being sent seems to us at variance with the spirit of Allied cooperation to which you and we attach so much importance both for the present and the future."

["Out of regard for Marshal Stalin and for the Soviet peoples, with whom it is our earnest desire to work in future years, the War Cabinet have asked me to make this further appeal to the Soviet Government to give whatever help may be in their power, and above all to provide facilities for United States aircraft to land on your airfields for this purpose."]

[MR*. *FRUS, Quebec Conf.*, 1944, pp. 189–90. *WSC*, VI, 142–43 (with extra par.). *R&C*.]

After reading this appeal, Churchill reportedly suggested cutting off British convoys to Russia, but the Foreign Office convinced him that such a threat would only hurt the Polish cause (Woodward, *British Foreign Policy*, III, 215n).

C–781

London [via U.S. Army]
Sept. 4, 1944, 2115 Z / TOR 0040 Z, Sept. 5

Prime Minister to President Roosevelt. Personal and Top Secret.
Following is text of message from women of Warsaw referred to in my number 779:—

"Most Holy Father, we Polish women in Warsaw are inspired with sentiments of profound patriotism and devotion for our country. For three weeks while defending our fortress we have lacked food and medicine. Warsaw is in ruins. The Germans are killing the wounded in hospitals. They are making women and children march in front of them in order to protect their tanks. There is no exaggeration in reports of children who are fighting and destroying tanks with bottles of petrol. We mothers see our sons dying for freedom and the fatherland. Our husbands, our sons and our brothers are not considered by the enemy to be combatants. Holy Father, no one is helping us. The Russian armies which have been for three weeks at the gates of Warsaw have not advanced a step. The aid coming to us from Great Britain is insufficient. The world is ignorant of our fight. God alone is with us. Holy Father, Vicar of Christ, if you can hear us, bless us Polish women who are fighting for the Church and for freedom."

[MR*. *WSC*, VI, 143.]

The Prime Minister, who was enroute Canada aboard the *Queen Mary*, did not respond to this message, and the monthly anti-submarine warfare statement was released to the American press on September 9.

R–618

Hyde Park, N.Y. [via U.S. Navy]
Sept. 5, 1944, 11:30 A.M. (Washington)

Personal and Secret, from the President for the Prime Minister.
   Following is our suggested text of Anti-U-boat Statement for August:

"Last month, due to the effectiveness of the Allied operations in France, the principal U-boat operating bases in the Bay of Biscay were neutralized. As a consequence the Germans have been forced to operate their underseas craft from Norwegian and Baltic bases, thereby stretching even thinner their difficult lines of operation.
   "The exchange rate between merchant ships sunk and U-boats destroyed continues to be profitable to the United Nations' cause. While U-boat operations continue, they are sporadic and relatively ineffectual."

Roosevelt [Navy Dept.]

[MR*]

The intelligence provided Roosevelt proved incorrect—the Underground did not cease fighting until October 2—but that mattered little, for the President had already decided not to push the Soviets any harder. Leahy's draft of this cable, to which Roosevelt made no changes, had received approval from both the State Department and the Joint Chiefs of Staff.

R–619

Hyde Park, N.Y. [via U.S. Navy]
Sept. 5, 1944, 2:00 P.M. (Washington)

Personal and Secret, from the President for the Prime Minister.

Replying to your 779, 780 and 781, I am informed by my office of Military Intelligence that the fighting Poles have departed from Warsaw and that the Germans are now in full control.

The problem of relief for the Poles in Warsaw has therefore unfortunately been solved by delay and by German action and there now appears to be nothing we can do to assist them.

I have long been deeply distressed by our inability to give adequate assistance to the heroic defenders of Warsaw and I hope that we may together still be able to help Poland be among the victors in this war with the Nazis. Roosevelt [WDL]

[MR*. *FRUS, Quebec Conf.*, 1944, p. 190. *WSC*, VI, 143–44. *R&C*.]

Churchill and his party sailed from the Clyde on September 5 aboard the *Queen Mary* and arrived at Halifax, Nova Scotia, on the tenth.

C–782

Queen Mary [via U.S. Army, London]
Sept. 6, 1944, 0730 Z (London) / TOR 1030 Z

Prime Minister to President Roosevelt Personal and Top Secret.

We are just off. I cannot make Quebec before evening 11th. It might be convenient for you to put off your arrival till 12th as I should wish to have the pleasure of welcoming you and Eleanor at the Citadel but everything will be in readiness anyhow. Every good wish.

[MR*. *FRUS, Quebec Conf.*, 1944, p. 38.]

Churchill so insisted on arriving at Quebec City before the President that, during his voyage, he instructed his staff to make arrangements for air travel from Halifax. Radio silence requirements made that impossible and the Prime Minister calmed down when he discovered his train was scheduled to arrive on the morning of September 11. The President, however, adjusted his travel plans and was waiting in the railroad station when Churchill's train pulled in from Halifax. (The additions indicated below were made in Roosevelt's handwriting.)

R–620

Washington [via U.S. Navy, London]
Sept. 6, 1944, 11:45 A.M.

Personal and Top Secret, from the President for the Former
Naval Person.

Your 782. We will arrive OCTAGON ~~September 12~~ afternoon of September 11th. This time I want to have the privilege and great pleasure of meeting you and Clemmie when you arrive. Roosevelt [WDL]

[MR. *FRUS, Quebec Conf.*, 1944, p. 38.]

Often insensitive to the small personal problems of others, Churchill did worry a good deal about the morale of military personnel. In such instances, this sort of Lincolnesque gesture was typical. (In the PREM 3/472 version of this message, U.S. is substituted for "Uncle Sam.")

C–783

Queen Mary [via U.S. Army, London]
Sept. 7, 1944, 1752 Z (London) / TOR 1900 Z

Prime Minister to President Roosevelt. Personal and Top Secret.

There are a number of Uncle Sam service personnel returning home in this ship for leave, I am told, beginning from their date of embarkation. The sailing of ship was delayed on account of OCTAGON and they may, therefore, lose in some cases as many as seven days leave.

May I indicate through your good offices this will be made up to them? It would be pleasure to me if this could be announced before end of voyage and their anxiety relieved.

[MR*]

Roosevelt instructed the military to comply with his answer to Churchill's request, and General Marshall reported the next day that "the transport commander will amend furlough orders of those personnel affected" (Marshall to Roosevelt, Sept. 8, 1944, MR).

R–621

Washington [via U.S. Navy, London]
Sept. 7, 1944, 5:00 P.M.

Top Secret and Personal. From the President for the Former
Naval Person.

Your 783. Your thoughtfulness greatly appreciated. Necessary adjustments leave will be made in all cases that do not interfere with war effort
which I hope may include all. Roosevelt [WB]

[MR*]

During their meeting in Quebec, Churchill gave Roosevelt an inscribed copy
of *Onwards to Victory: War Speeches by the Right Hon. Winston S. Churchill, C.H.,
M.P., 1943* (London: Cassell and Co., 1944). The inscription is printed below.

C–783/1, inscription

Quebec City
[Sept. 1944]

To F.D.R. from W.S.C.
"A fresh egg from the faithful hen!"
Quebec 1944

[FDRL]

THE SECOND QUEBEC CONFERENCE
(OCTAGON)

As the participants gathered for the OCTAGON Conference, held at the
Citadel in Quebec City, Canada, September 11–16, 1944, optimistic reports
of victory over Germany by Christmas had already begun to circulate. Thus
Churchill and Roosevelt felt a strong sense of urgency to reach a general
political agreement on postwar issues, particularly in Europe, lest the war end
and events decide for them. The President departed from his usual habit of
postponing such issues until a postwar peace conference, although procrastination still remained his instinctive response to acrimony. Only during the
discussions about the Pacific war did military strategy continue to be the
primary issue, and even there the military questions were related to Britain's
postwar role in the Far East.

Whether or not the President went to OCTAGON expecting to discuss
postwar politics in detail is hard to determine. Harry Hopkins had warned

the British that Roosevelt might "be ready to take wider decisions than anyone at present expected," but offered no specific items for the agenda (Halifax to Eden for Churchill, 21 Aug. 1944, CLASP 152, PREM 3/329/1/30–31). The Combined Chiefs of Staff couched its agenda in terms of future military operations, and Roosevelt left Secretary of State Hull and Undersecretary of State Stettinius in Washington, though he promised to send for them if the conference took a political turn. Yet, even when Churchill indicated that there were political decisions to be made (as in C–783/2 and C–783/3), the President did not send for his diplomats, and Roosevelt discouraged Stettinius from attending the political discussions held at Hyde Park after the conclusion of the Quebec Conference. Knowing of Churchill's concern over political matters, the President must have suspected such questions would come up, but with an election only two months away he may have preferred to present a public image of total absorption in military affairs—an image he also hoped would reassure the Soviets that no secret Anglo-American deals were being made. Moreover, the absence of State Department officials meant very little. Roosevelt consulted "striped-pants boys" only when it was convenient, and usually not for major policy advice.

The one potentially significant military decision made at OCTAGON concerning Europe was to keep open the option of an amphibious attack in Istria in the event the Allied campaign in Italy forced a major German retreat. But that never happened. Churchill even managed to get vague approval for a thrust toward Vienna, providing Soviet armies had not already liberated the city, although the British military had no plans for such an operation and considered the move impossible (Pogue, *Organizer of Victory*, p. 437). The Prime Minister's plans for a thrust into eastern Europe, motivated by postwar considerations rather than military strategy, led logically to a discussion of the growing tension between East and West in Greece, Yugoslavia, and Poland. Still, when the Prime Minister suggested a joint message to Stalin expressing grave concern, Roosevelt pulled back (*FRUS, Quebec Conf.*, 1944, p. 490n).

But procrastination on postwar planning for Germany had become impossible. Even though Roosevelt and Churchill assumed that a peace treaty could await the victory, a decision on what to do with the occupying armies could not. The European Advisory Commission, established during the Teheran Conference, had worked out occupation zones satisfactory to all, though the United States and Great Britain both continued to demand occupation rights for the zone in northwestern Germany. But the question of what to do with the Germans quickly overshadowed the dispute over which zone to choose. U.S. Army occupation planners, sharing the assumptions of their British counterparts, had worked up a "handbook of Military Government for Germany" which called for "the gradual rehabilitation of peacetime industry" and a centralized German administration, all designed to get the Army out of the civil government as soon as possible. Those short-term Army goals dovetailed with a State Department plan aimed at replacing "German economic self-sufficiency for war" with "an economy which can be integrated into an interdependent world economy." All this was too much for Treasury

Secretary Morgenthau, who had scathingly labeled such a rehabilitative approach as "a nice WPA job." The President agreed. During the Teheran talks Roosevelt had argued strongly for the complete disarmament of Germany, Stalin had supported him, and Churchill had acquiesced. State Department plans which called for Germany to be reconstituted as a single, self-sufficient economic unit not only went against the dismemberment concept but also implied a gentle treatment of the Germans, an approach which angered the President. Believing that militarism and Nazi ideology had permanently tainted three generations of Germans, Roosevelt (and Morgenthau) proposed returning the Germans to their primeval agrarian origins to start all over again. As the President crudely put it: "We have got to be tough with Germany and I mean the German people, not just the Nazis. You either have to castrate the German people or you have got to treat them in such a manner so they can't just go on reproducing people who want to continue the way they have in the past."

Morgenthau and his staff had drawn up a counter-plan which called for the dismemberment, de-Nazification, and de-industrialization of Germany, and Roosevelt had endorsed the proposal's basic approach. Believing that he had successfully redirected American policy, the President called Morgenthau to the Quebec Conference to present the plan to Churchill. Initially shocked by the notion of destroying Germany's industrial economy, the Prime Minister changed his mind after advisers convinced him that British industry could move into previously German-dominated markets. In his memoirs, Churchill hinted that he agreed to the Morgenthau Plan reluctantly, and only because he needed Morgenthau's support for continuing lend-lease to Britain (stage II) after the surrender of Germany, theoretically to help in the war against Japan but actually to assist in postwar reconstruction. But in fact, after initially rejecting the Morgenthau Plan as "unnatural, unchristian and unnecessary," the Prime Minister accepted it enthusiastically, even to the point of strengthening the language of the joint memorandum in which he and Roosevelt endorsed the conversion of "Germany into a country primarily agricultural and pastoral in its character." (The preceding quotations are taken from documents printed in Kimball, *Swords Or Ploughshares?*, pp. 99, 89, 23, 96, 38, 3. The word "pastoral" was inserted at Churchill's suggestion.)

Although opponents of the Morgenthau Plan, particularly Hull and Stimson, eventually managed to prevent its implementation, at least in the non-Soviet zones, Roosevelt believed that the United States could now accept the southern zone of occupation in Germany without becoming mired down in French and central European politics. Not only would the Morgenthau Plan quickly eliminate Germany's ability to wage war, enabling the Americans to arrange a speedy end to the occupation, but it would also leave Britain with the task of dismantling Germany's industrial center, the Ruhr Basin. Roosevelt agreed to an American occupation of the southern zone but, in a curious expression of his lack of faith in British promises, he insisted on and received the ports of Bremen and Bremerhaven in northwestern Germany as part of the American zone, thus guaranteeing that communications between the United States and southern Germany would not run through France.

The British came to Quebec prepared to argue strenuously for a major role in the naval war against Japan. A year earlier, American military leaders were eager for all the help they could get, but a series of naval victories in the central Pacific had changed their attitude. Planners still counted on the Soviet Army to pin down the Japanese in Manchuria and northern China, but Admiral King and his staff accused the British of trying to gain part credit for a victory which belonged to the U.S. Navy. Nevertheless, when Churchill offered the British fleet, Roosevelt accepted without hesitation, prompting one British wag to recommend that the official minutes note that "at this point Admiral King was carried out" (Pogue, *Organizer of Victory*, p. 453). But the President understood what motivated the offer. As he later told Morgenthau, "All they want is Singapore back." In the long run, little came of the decision. The British fleet played a minor role in the central Pacific campaign, and a few victories against an already beaten foe could not restore Britain's prestige or its Asian empire.

The Quebec decisions considered to be important, particularly by the British, turned out to be inconsequential. British participation in the war against Japan had little effect, Italy never became the jumping-off point for a preemptive occupation of the southern Balkans, and the Morgenthau Plan was stillborn. But nothing proved a bigger disappointment for the British than the failure of the United States to implement stage II lend-lease aid to Britain. Roosevelt had long doubted the British claims of virtual bankruptcy, for like most Americans he accepted the myth of British opulence. But by the time of the OCTAGON meeting, the President had finally become convinced that Britain's fears were justified. One of the appeals of the Morgenthau Plan was that it promised economic benefits to Britain by opening up markets previously dominated by the Germans, but that was not enough. Although the November presidential election made him cautious—twisting the Lion's tail was still a popular electoral practice in the United States—Roosevelt believed that an economically stable England was important for America's postwar security, and he agreed to assist British reconstruction by providing $6 billion in lend-lease aid during the first year of stage II. But, as with so many commitments Roosevelt made, his death intervened and lend-lease came to an abrupt halt in August 1945.

The most significant agreement reached by Roosevelt and Churchill was not made at Quebec but during personal conversations held on September 18 and 19 at the Roosevelt home in Hyde Park, New York. Out of those discussions came an *aide-mémoire* which committed the United States and Great Britain to "full collaboration . . . in developing TUBE ALLOYS for military and commercial purposes" even after the defeat of Japan. Moreover, they agreed that atomic energy (TUBE ALLOYS) should not come under international control and that the project should remain secret. Although Churchill's motives seem clear—he sought to perpetuate an Anglo-American community of interest after the war and to be in a position to brandish the atomic bomb as a threat against the Soviet Union—the President's goals are more difficult to ascertain. Roosevelt had expected the British to play a major role in leading postwar Europe but had expressed grave concern about its economic plight. Atomic energy would help solve that problem. But the politics of the decision are more complicated. The alternatives suggested in the *aide-mémoire* were either international control or secrecy. Yet, given Roosevelt's belief that the American public retained much of its pre-World War II distrust of internationalism, he may have believed that public disclosure of the Manhattan Project (the codename for atomic-bomb research) would jeopardize not only the important talks regarding a postwar peace-keeping organization, then going on at Dumbarton Oaks in Washington, but also his re-election chances. He knew that the Soviets had learned of the TUBE ALLOYS work through espionage; so his decision not to inform them had to be political, not military. But the desire for "utmost secrecy" related to public disclosure, not secret communications with Stalin. Rather than interpret Roosevelt's position either as a subtle signal to the Soviets that he was willing to discuss the international control of atomic energy or as a desire to monopolize the atomic bomb and thus coerce Anglo-American opponents, it seems likely that the President hedged his bet. Churchill was happy, the American electorate was not offended by the sharing of such a great secret with the Communists in the Kremlin, and internationalization of atomic energy could await the formation of the United Nations organization, all without threatening America's postwar security. Roosevelt believed that a strong Britain was needed in order to balance Soviet power on the Continent, but his espousal of a form of balance-of-power politics is not equivalent to starting the Cold War.

A similar mixture of motives characterized the Hyde Park decisions about politics in Italy. Neither Churchill nor Roosevelt wanted to see a communist government in Italy, Churchill because that would expand Soviet influence into the central Mediterranean, Roosevelt because that would displace the pro-American government of Ivanoe Bonomi. In a joint press release, the two Allied leaders announced plans to grant Italy greater self-government, economic relief through UNRRA, and aid for the long-term economic reconstruction of the country. Roosevelt's later concern over the timing of this press release (R–622) suggests that he had his re-election and the Italian-American vote in mind as well.

The Quebec and Hyde Park conferences accomplished as much as any meeting between a senior and a junior partner could be expected to do. Roosevelt went a long way toward establishing the postwar Anglo-American entente so desired by Churchill, but the growth of Soviet power and importance meant that the OCTAGON meetings could not be definitive. Within the limited realm of Anglo-American hegemony, the decisions were final. But greater questions relating to the economic and geopolitical structure of the world had to await a meeting with Stalin.

(As in previous Churchill-Roosevelt conferences, the two leaders signed or initialed a number of policy statements, orders, and memoranda. These have not been treated as Churchill-Roosevelt exchanges, and most of them can be found in the relevant volumes of *FRUS*.)

19. The junior and senior partners: Churchill greets Roosevelt at
Quebec, September 11, 1944

Two days after writing the following letter, Churchill formally proposed
Harold Macmillan, the British Minister Resident in Italy, to be Chairman of
the Allied Control Commission. As the Prime Minister had hoped, Roosevelt
agreed to extend formal diplomatic recognition to the Italian government.
Fiorello La Guardia, Mayor of New York City, had previously asked to be
commissioned a General and assigned civil-government duties in Italy. Roosevelt, ever conscious of La Guardia's popularity among Italian Americans,
had agreed, but Secretary of War Stimson and General Marshall opposed the
appointment as unprofessional, suggesting instead that a colonelcy would be
sufficient. La Guardia refused, but with a presidential election around the
corner Roosevelt was again looking for some kind of job for the Mayor.

Lord Leathers, British Minister of War Transport, and Rear Admiral Emory
Land, War Shipping Administrator, who coordinated the use of American
shipping assets, were later scheduled to discuss shipping matters with Churchill and Roosevelt on the evening of September 13, but that same night Morgenthau proposed his plan for postwar Germany, and that dominated the
talks.

BONIFACE was Churchill's personal codename for secret ULTRA-type
intelligence gleaned from breaking the German military cipher. The docu-

ments Churchill sent to Roosevelt are not in the available files, but the "speedy results" the Prime Minister hoped for in Italy were not forthcoming.

C–783/2, letter

Quebec City, Quebec
September 12, 1944

My dear Friend,

1. Would it be agreeable to you to discuss with me sometime today our Italian policy? I must fill up the Chairmanship of the Allied Control Commission, and I feel the great need of a competent politician and Minister there, like Macmillan, rather than a General. I was distressed and disquieted by the tales I heard of serious food shortages in some parts of Rome and other great towns. Unemployment looms big in Italy. We may also soon have the populous North flowing on to our hands. I was hoping we might together make up an agreeable programme for Italy, which could be announced, comprising resumption of their export trade, interchange of diplomatic representatives a la Russe, and bringing them into the area of U.N.N.R.A. [sic] as co-belligerents if that can be managed. If not, some other scheme of effective relief. You spoke of La Guardia having a Mission. This also I should like to discuss with you.

2. The Staffs are forming their contacts this morning and browsing over the Agenda on general lines. But would it not be well to have a plenary session tomorrow where you and I can put forward the fundamentals of our future war policy. This will enable them to go ahead much more rapidly and easily.

3. A small point. Leathers is longing for Admiral Lands. You said you were keeping him handy; but if he could come up soon, these two would be together working out their complicated affairs, while we are busy with other things, and have results ready for us at each stage.

4. Some of the BONIFACE I sent you this morning appeared to me to be of profound significance. Alexander's battle is a hard one, but now that Clark has crashed into the centre I am hopeful of speedy results.

Yours always, [initialled] W.

[MR. *FRUS, Quebec Conf.*, 1944, p. 42.]

The Combined Chiefs of Staff did not report back to Churchill and Roosevelt until Saturday morning, but the President still managed to leave Quebec by train that same evening. Churchill followed by train on Sunday, meeting Roosevelt in Hyde Park on September 18.

Roosevelt and Churchill continued to oppose formal recognition of the French provisional government, in spite of recommendations from both Eden and Hull to do so. Anthony Eden noted that when he raised the question both the President and the Prime Minister launched a "tirade against De Gaulle" (Eden, *The Reckoning*, p. 553).

C–783/3, letter

Quebec City, Quebec
September 12, 1944

My dear Friend,

Would you let me have your views on the following suggested timetable:

Wednesday, 13th—Plenary Meeting with Chiefs of Staff.
Thursday, 14th, and Friday, 15th—their further discussions.
They should report to us the evening of Friday, 15th, enabling a final Plenary to take place on Saturday, 16th.

It would probably be in conformity with your wishes to return to Hyde Park on Saturday. If agreeable to you I would follow by Air with Clemmie early on Monday, 18th, and stay with you Monday and Tuesday. We could then have anyone necessary to wind up outstanding points. I must depart on Wednesday, 20th.

I have asked Eden to come over if possible tomorrow, so he should be here on Thursday or Friday. There are several important things to discuss with him including recognition of the French Provisional Government, as to which I am by no means convinced. I do not know whether you would require to have Hull or Stettinius for Friday, 15th.

One of the most important things I have to discuss with you is Stage II. Would Thursday, 14th, do for that?—in which case I hope you could have Morgenthau present. This matter is considered of extreme and vital importance by the British Government, for reasons which are only too painfully apparent.

Yours always, [initialed] W.

[MR. PREM 4/75/2. *FRUS, Quebec Conf.*, 1944, p. 43.]

Roosevelt had sent for Morgenthau on September 12, but Hull and Stettinius never received word to come either to Quebec or to Hyde Park.

R–621/1, letter

Quebec City, Quebec
[September 12, 1944?]

Dear Winston,
    Schedule is good.
    Glad Anthony [Eden] is coming. I will get Cordell [Hull] or Stettinius here on Friday [Sept. 15].
    Morgenthau gets here Thursday at noon.
    Yrs. [initialed] FDR

[PREM 4/75/2/811]

Roosevelt, Churchill, and Richard Law, British Minister of State in the Foreign Office, did meet on September 14 at 11 A.M. A joint decision to provide aid to Italy through UNRRA was announced after the Hyde Park conversations.

C–783/4, letter

Quebec City, Quebec
September 14, 1944

My dear Friend,
    I understand that we are meeting at 11.30 about Stage 2. Dick Law arrived here late last night, and I wonder whether I might bring him at 11 o'clock with or without Anthony, to discuss the application of U.N.N.R.A. [sic] to Italy. He tells me that a compromise proposal would get through whereby 50 million dollars of U.N.N.R.A. [sic] would be available for Italy. I consider this should be an essential part of our friendly gesture to Italy.
    If agreeable then, I will turn up at 11.
    Yours always, [initialed] W.

[MR. FRUS, Quebec Conf., 1944, p. 45.]

Churchill sensed that there were differences between British and American goals in Italy, and he moved cautiously. The appointment of Harold Macmillan as head of the Allied Control Commission, a move to which Roosevelt agreed, indicated just how important Churchill considered Italy to be. At the same time, a State Department memo, sent on September 13 to Harry Hopkins, stated that "we do not believe that Italy will contribute to an orderly and peaceful Europe if it is subject to any one of its more powerful neighbors"

(*FRUS, Quebec Conf.*, 1944, p. 413). That could have meant "subject to" either Britain or the Soviet Union, but in September 1944 it appeared that British influence was the greater threat.

Captain Ellery W. Stone, USNR, was Deputy Chief Commissioner on the Allied Control Commission for Italy. Lieutenant General Sir Frank Mason-MacFarlane had been Chief Commissioner but had become ill and returned to England early in June 1944.

C–783/5, letter

Quebec City, Quebec
September 14, 1944

My dear Friend,

The office of Chief Commissioner of the Allied Control Commission, formerly held by General Macfarlane, is vacant. This is a British appointment. In order to have more political knowledge and experience in this post, so full of economic and political issues and so important for the welfare of the Italian people, I propose to appoint Mr. Harold Macmillan. The Supreme Allied Commander is ex-officio President of the Allied Control Commission. He would in practice delegate his functions to Mr. Macmillan.

I propose to leave Mr. Macmillan his present duties as British Resident Minister at A.F.H.Q., and British Political Adviser to the Supreme Allied Commander. This is a simplification and reduction of British Staff.

It is proposed also that the day to day management of the Control Commission, apart from general political guidance (Macmillan), should be in the hands of the Deputy Chief Commissioner of the Commission, the United States representative, Mr. Stone, in whom we have great confidence. He would, if necessary, have a Lieutenant-General under him to assist in the administration and in carrying out effectively the policy. This would widen his scope and power.

I hope that these arrangements will be agreeable to you, as I should not like to make an appointment, even where it falls to me to do so, that does not work into the scheme of our close Anglo-American cooperation.

I should like to discuss with Anthony a suggestion that came up yesterday, namely, that Mayor La Guardia should pay a visit to Italy as your representative, and that while there he should be invited to attend the meetings of the Allied Control Commission. Thus he would have a chance to see that the machinery was working in the manner most beneficial to the Italians. I have a series of other proposals helpful to the Italians, on which I hope we shall be in full agreement. I would run through these with you, perhaps to-morrow, when Anthony will be here.

It is urgent to appoint Macmillan, because the post of Chief Commissioner has been vacant for two months, and I am becoming blameworthy in the matter, especially if any food shortage or needless unemployment should arise.

Yours always, [initialed] W.

[MR. *FRUS, Quebec Conf.*, 1944, pp. 417–18.]

The Combined Chiefs of Staff submitted their final conference report at noon on September 16, and Roosevelt and Churchill approved it with only minor amendments (*FRUS, Quebec Conf.*, 1944, pp. 377–82). After receiving honorary LL.D. degrees from McGill University, the two leaders met with the press. By six that evening, Roosevelt was aboard a train heading back toward Hyde Park, New York.

C–783/6, letter

Quebec City, Quebec
September 16, 1944

My dear Friend,

I do not think the Chiefs of Staff will be ready before noon. At any rate I believe this would be more convenient for them than 10.30. Moreover I have some amendments to suggest to the report which I have not yet completed.

In these circumstances, would it not be better to tell the Press to come at 3.30 P.M. after the Degrees. This would give plenty of time for you to catch your train around 5 o'clock.

Yours always, [initialed] W.

[MR]

Although Roosevelt and Churchill routinely exchanged staff papers during all of their conferences, only this one included a covering memorandum. In this case, the Prime Minister wanted to treat the paper as a formal communication so that the Foreign Office could officially comment. Given the strategic location of the Italian colonies, particularly Somaliland at the mouth of the Red Sea and various islands in the Mediterranean, the British were deeply concerned about their disposition. The differences between the British and American positions were minor and frequently cosmetic. Certainly Hull showed no sensitivity to the nationalism which came to characterize postwar Africa, and seemed primarily concerned with avoiding transfers of territory in violation of the Atlantic Charter lest it raise memories of the secret treaties of World War I. Ironically, the British proposed a unification of Italian and British Somaliland and the Ogaden district of Ethiopia—all into a unified

Somalia, the same goal of Somali nationalists during a war against Ethiopia in the 1970s.

Roosevelt agreed to Churchill's request for copies of the memorandum written by Cordell Hull (first attachment) and the U.S. Joint Chiefs (second attachment) and asked the Prime Minister to respond to the American position.

C–783/7, memo

Quebec City, Quebec
Sept. 16, 1944

Mr. President.

I return the Memorandum you gave me about Italian Colonies.

The Foreign Office would like to treat this as an official communication if you would allow us to keep a copy of it.

It seems that the usual broad and substantial measure of agreement exists between us, but we should like to look into the details more closely. [Initialed] WSC

[MR. *FRUS, Quebec Conf.*, 1944, p. 418.]

First Attachment to C–783/7

Washington
Sept. 11, 1944

Memorandum for the President

Subject: Proposals of British Chiefs of Staff for Disposition of Italian Overseas Territories

I refer to your memorandum of April 28 in regard to certain proposals of the British Chiefs of Staff for the future disposition of Italian overseas territories.

In accordance with your request, I am enclosing a memorandum on the subject which embodies the comments and recommendations of the experts in the Department charged with these matters. While the conclusions drawn are in no sense final, they represent long and careful study.

I may add that the Joint Chiefs of Staff have expressed the view that from the limited viewpoint of our national security, there are no direct objections to the British proposals for the disposition of Italian overseas territories since United States postwar military interests are not directly affected. From the broader view of national and worldwide security, however, the Chiefs of Staff have expressed the opinion that the United States should not support any such British proposals prior to ascertaining Russian views.

In my memorandum of May 6 I mentioned that according to our information the proposals in question had not been considered by the British War Cabinet and in no way represented the policy of the British Government. I have, therefore, not discussed the subject with the British nor has any indication been given that we are aware of these particular proposals of the British Chiefs of Staff. [Initialed] CH

[MR. *FRUS, Quebec Conf.*, 1944, pp. 408–9.]

SECOND ATTACHMENT TO C–783/7

[Washington]
Aug. 3, 1944

Comment on British Proposals for
Disposition of Italian Overseas Territories

1. The preferred solution to the problem of Eritrea is for all of this territory to be assimilated to Ethiopia under an arrangement whereby the Ethiopian Government would assume certain obligations by agreement with the International Organization. Among these obligations would be an undertaking by Ethiopia, in the event of a threat to the security of the Red Sea or Northeast African areas, to open all ports, airfields and means of communication in Eritrea to the forces of the United Nations. Such obligations would also include the employment, in both Eritrea and Ethiopia, of technical personnel for the operation of ports, railways and roads, and of technical experts and advisers in the central and provincial government and administration.

This arrangement would satisfy the claims of Ethiopia for the return of Eritrea and for an outlet to the sea at Massawa, under safeguards for proper administration and with due regard for the security interests of the United Nations. However, if the British should insist, for overriding strategic reasons, on the dismemberment of Eritrea, so that a portion of the territory would be ceded to the Sudan, no objections are perceived strong enough to justify the opposition of this Government, provided that the area ceded lies north and west of Asmara and Massawa.

The *Greater New Somaliland* as proposed by the British would include Italian and British Somaliland and the Ogaden district of Ethiopia. Since the Ogaden is an integral part of the territory of an independent sovereign state and ally, a change in its status should not be considered. On the other hand, economic, administrative and cultural considerations support the view that Italian Somaliland, together with the British and French Somalilands, might advantageously be placed under International Trusteeship and directly administered as a single unit by an authority appointed by and responsible to the International Organization. Such an authority should be composed of experts or of representatives of the interested powers. If it should prove impossible to obtain French acceptance of this plan, it would still appear desirable to place Italian and British Somalilands under International Trusteeship, with special arrangements for a genuinely free port at Djibouti and the possible purchase of the Addis Ababa-Djibouti railway by Ethiopia.

No objection is perceived to the fusion of the northern frontier district of Kenya with a greater Somaliland, as mentioned in the British proposals.

2. *Libya* The preferred disposition of Libya would be to place this entire area (Cyrenaica and Tripolitania) under International Trusteeship to be administered by a commission of experts responsible to the International Organization. This would not preclude the establishment of an autonomous Amirate of the Senussi, whom the British have declared shall never again come under Italian rule. However, if it should prove difficult to obtain British agreement to this over-all solution, a feasible though less desirable arrangement would be to establish Cyrenaica as an autonomous Senussi Amirate under Egyptian (or possibly British) trusteeship, along the lines of the British proposal, and to place Tripolitania under an International Trusteeship to be exercised by Italy.

3. It would be taken for granted that United Nations air and naval requirements would be satisfied in the Benghazi area. Likewise, should Great Britain wish to use the Castel Benito airfield for security purposes, there would be no objection, provided that no exclusive commercial rights or privileges were involved.

4. Limited frontier rectifications in the Fezzan area favoring the French would not appear objectionable, but any outright cession of territory in violation of the Atlantic Charter would be undesirable.

5. No compelling reasons are perceived for the return of the Uweinat oasis or the Sarra triangle to the Sudan, particularly in view of the possible violation of the Atlantic Charter thereby.

6. The Department is in accord with the British suggestion that some United Nations security scheme might provide for bases in Crete—possibly administered by the British—and for similar facilities in the Islands of the Dodecanese, particularly Rhodes. It is agreed that with the exception of Castelrosso, which would be given to Turkey, sovereignty over the Dodecanese should be transferred to Greece.

7. Pantelleria and the *Isole Pelagie* should be retained by Italy but completely demilitarized.

[MR. *FRUS, Quebec Conf.*, 1944, pp. 409–11.]

Churchill's plan for dealing with war criminals would serve two purposes. First, it would avoid the hypocrisy of declaring the losers "war criminals" on grounds of genocide and the execution of civilians—a touchy question for any colonial power. Second, it would limit the number of people who could be punished as major war criminals.

Written as a draft cable to Stalin, Churchill gave this to Roosevelt during the Quebec talks. The President said he would refer it to the State Department for comment, but before he responded the Prime Minister asked that the proposal be withdrawn in light of Stalin's insistence on war-crime trials. (See C–801.)

C–783/8, not sent

Quebec
Sept. 17, 1944

Churchill to Roosevelt
Draft of a Suggested Telegram to be Sent by the President and the Prime Minister to Marshal Stalin.

1. In the Moscow Conference of Foreign Ministers before Teheran, the Prime Minister of Great Britain submitted a draft proposing the local punishment of war criminals in the countries and, if possible, at the scenes where their atrocities had been committed. With some small amendments this document was approved and has been published to the world with general acceptance and approval. This document however did not attempt to deal with the cases of the major war criminals "whose offences have no particular geographical localization". This matter was touched on in conversation at Teheran without any definite conclusion being reached. It has now become important for us to reach agreement about the treatment of these major criminals. Would you consider whether a list could not be prepared of say 50 to 100 persons whose responsibilities for directing or impelling the whole process of crime and atrocity is established by the fact of their holding certain high offices? Such a list would not of course be exhaustive. New names could be added at any time. It is proposed that these persons should be declared, on the authority of the United Nations, to be world outlaws and that upon any of them falling into Allied hands the Allies will "decide how they are to be disposed of and the execution of this decision will be carried out immediately". Or alternatively, "the nearest General Officer will convene a Court for the sole purpose of establishing their identity, and when this has been done will have them shot within one hour without reference to higher authority."

2. It would seem that the method of trial, conviction and judicial sentence is quite inappropriate for notorious ringleaders such as Hitler,

Himmler, Goering, Goebbels and Ribbentrop. Apart from the formidable difficulties of constituting the Court, formulating the charge and assembling the evidence, the question of their fate is a political and not a judicial one. It could not rest with judges however eminent or learned to decide finally a matter like this which is of the widest and most vital public policy. The decision must be "the joint decision of the Governments of the Allies". This in fact was expressed in the Moscow Declaration.

3. There would seem to be advantages in publishing a list of names. At the present time, Hitler and his leading associates know that their fate will be sealed when the German Army and people cease to resist. It therefore costs them nothing to go on giving orders to fight to the last man, die in the last ditch, etc. As long as they can persuade the German people to do this, they continue to live on the fat of the land and have exalted employments. They represent themselves and the German people as sharing the same rights and fate. Once however their names are published and they are isolated, the mass of the German people will infer rightly that there is a difference between these major criminals and themselves. A divergence of interests between the notorious leaders and their dupes will become apparent. This may lead to undermining the authority of the doomed leaders and to setting their own people against them, and thus may help the break up of Germany.

4. We should be very glad to have your views upon this proposal at your earliest convenience. It is of course without prejudice to the great mass of German war criminals who will be handed over for the judgment of the countries where their crimes have been committed.

[*FRUS, Quebec Conf.*, 1944, pp. 489–90.]

ORGANIZING THE UNITED NATIONS

The conference at Dumbarton Oaks in Washington, D.C., dealt with the formation of a postwar peace-keeping organization. The first session, which began on August 21, 1944, brought British, American, and Soviet representatives together. The second phase began on September 29 with the departure of the Soviets and the seating of Chinese delegates. Such shuffling was necessary since the Soviet Union was not at war with Japan and wished to avoid any provocation until Germany was defeated.

Although the Soviet emphasis on postwar political security differed from the American interest in social and economic questions, two very specific disputes soon threatened to disrupt the conference and dash hopes for an international organization. First was the matter of great-power unanimity on the Security Council of the proposed peace-keeping body. The Soviet Union demanded that all the permanent members of the council agree on all action taken by that body. Since the Security Council was to function in a manner similar to a cabinet in a parliamentary system—combining certain legislative and executive functions—such a rule would guarantee that the great powers (Britain, China, the United States, and the Soviet Union, with France added later) could prevent any action against their own interests. The British argued that this could paralyze the organization and that other nations would resent the great powers putting themselves above the law. The United States had originally proposed great-power unanimity, but on September 13, 1944, Roosevelt sent a message to Stalin opposing the veto concept. Although the President frequently used "public opinion" as an excuse for not revealing his true motives, in this case, with an election in the offing, he may have been sincere when he stated that Americans would never accept any plan which permitted parties to a dispute to vote on their own case (*Stalin/FDR*, doc. 226). Stalin continued to insist on unanimity, and there the matter stood when the OCTAGON talks ended.

The second major crisis was even more a question of image and electoral politics. Stalin had instructed his representatives to insist that each of the sixteen Soviet Socialist Republics—each was theoretically permitted to make its own foreign policy—have a seat in the General Assembly of the new international organization. Even though Roosevelt considered that assembly a mere debating society, since the real decisions would be made in the Security Council, he could not permit the Union of Soviet Socialist Republics to have sixteen seats while the United States had only one. The Soviets eventually dropped the issue during the Dumbarton Oaks Conference, but raised it again later. In this case the British maintained a discrete silence since their request for a seat for India was equally questionable.

In spite of such arguments, the conference drew up a comprehensive proposal "for the Establishment of a General International Organization" which became the United Nations organization.

The minutes, both British and American, of the OCTAGON talks do not indicate that Churchill and Roosevelt ever discussed the Dumbarton Oaks Conference in any depth, although the following memorandum indicates that the subject did come up. There is no such message to Stalin as the one referred to by Churchill, but Roosevelt apparently planned to send one, for on September 18 the Prime Minister cabled Eden with the news that the President was asking Stalin to postpone further discussions because of the Soviet attitude on the question of great-power unanimity (Woodward, *British Foreign Policy*, V, 144). Nor did Churchill ever send a message to Stalin about southeastern Europe. Instead, the Prime Minister visited Moscow in October 1944 for talks with the Soviet Premier. (See C–789ff.) (This memorandum was not addressed to Roosevelt, but John Martin, Churchill's private secretary, apparently delivered it to the President; hence it is treated as a Churchill-Roosevelt exchange.)

C–783/9, memo

Quebec City, Quebec
Sept. 19, 1944

[Churchill to Roosevelt]
Mr. Martin.

Will you ask the President whether I could see the text of the communication he is making to Marshal Stalin about the Dumbarton Oaks Conference, and also any communique that is to be issued.

In view of the fact that this important message will be passing between the President and Marshal Stalin, the Prime Minister thinks it might be well to defer the other message about the Greeks, Yugoslavs and Poles, to a later period. W.S.C.

[MR]

Churchill, his wife, Clementine, and his daughter, Mary, left Hyde Park on the evening of September 19 and boarded the *Queen Mary* the next morning, arriving back in Great Britain on September 25.

During the voyage, Mrs. Churchill wrote a thank-you letter to Eleanor Roosevelt which demonstrated that she was as smooth a diplomat as her husband, the Prime Minister. The letter is not properly part of the Churchill-Roosevelt correspondence, but because it expressed the sentiments of the Prime Minister it is included here.

The Roosevelts' only daughter was their first child, Anna, born in 1906.

C–783/10, letter

Queen Mary, at sea
September 22, 1944

My dear Mrs. Roosevelt

I shall always remember my delightful visit to Hyde Park. I enjoyed it all so much, the picnics, sitting near the President, & my two long walks with you through your woods. This was the first time I had met your daughter. She is a wonderful combination of yourself & the President. She charmed Winston & me with her gay & vivacious personality. Please (though the acquaintance is short!) give her my love. My thoughts will be much with you during the next two months. I cannot but believe that your great country will honour itself by yet again returning its great leader—great in Peace & great in War.

Yours affectionately   Clementine H. Churchill

[MR]

During their talks at Hyde Park, Roosevelt and Churchill agreed on a change in policy toward Italy, and a proposed public statement outlining those changes was sent to the British Foreign Office for comments. In hopes of buoying up the shaky Bonomi government, the United States and Britain—without consulting the other members of the Allied Control Commission—promised to give the Italian government increased authority, economic aid, and a form of diplomatic recognition. Foreign Secretary Anthony Eden had no objection to those commitments, but he opposed a paragraph which indicated that the Allies were willing to consider a revision of the long terms of armistice. Not only would that offend the Soviet Union and those British Dominions which were party to the terms but had not been consulted, but it would open the question of the disposition of the Italian fleet and colonies. In addition, Eden requested a delay in announcing any relaxation of Allied control in Italy because of bitter criticism in the British press about the inability of the Bonomi government to maintain law and order. The attacks followed the lynching on September 18 of the former Vice Director of Regina Coeli Prison in Rome during the trial of another official accused of collaborating with the Germans. Both had been implicated in the massacre of the Ardeatine caves, where the Germans had summarily executed fifty Italian prisoners. Eden further suggested the deletion of the phrase quoted by Churchill in C–784 because, as stated in the proposed public statement, it could place Italy in a more privileged trading position than other members of the wartime alliance. (Eden's comments, which were forwarded by the British Embassy to the State Department, and the draft and final version of the Churchill-Roosevelt press release on policy toward Italy are all printed in *FRUS, Quebec Conf.*, 1944, pp. 493–98.)

Eden had failed to persuade Churchill and Roosevelt to extend formal recognition to the French provisional government, largely because of their personal objections to de Gaulle and the FCNL, but the Prime Minister understood that he could not hold out much longer.

C–784

Queen Mary, at sea [via U.S. Army, London]
Sept. 22, 1944, 2215 Z (London) / TOR 0015 Z, Sept. 23

Prime Minister to President Roosevelt. Personal and Top Secret.

About our Italian Manifesto. Anthony has made some valid comments which you no doubt have now seen. The argument against publication of long armistice terms at this stage is I feel conclusive. I do not think the omission of words "On basis of exchange of goods" would detract from the value of concessions.

I hear that a very bad impression has been produced in England by the Rome lynching. It might therefore be wise to delay a week or so before making the announcement. This will also give time for a review of French situation which I am anxious to go into on my return and about which I will presently cable you. Thank you so much for our delightful visit to your home. Every good wish. May we soon meet again.

[MR. *R&C.*]

In spite of Roosevelt's politically motivated eagerness to publish the joint statement on Italy, the War Cabinet objected and Eden informed the State Department that the issue could not be settled until Churchill returned to London on September 26. The statement was released to the press in London and Washington on the evening of September 26 (Eden to Churchill, Sept. 23, 1944, cordite No. 411, PREM 3/472/219).

R–622

Washington [via U.S. Navy]
Sept. 23, 1944, 10:20 A.M.

Personal and Top Secret, for the Prime Minister from the President.

Your 784. I believe that the present draft of Italian manifesto prepared after discussion with Halifax meets all of the changes suggested by Anthony Eden.

It is extremely important to me that our joint statement be released for publication in the Monday morning, 25 September, papers and I have so informed Halifax.

Please give us your consent to its publication Monday. Roosevelt [WDL]

[MR*]

Churchill admired greatly the wisdom and experience of South African Prime Minister Jan Christian Smuts, and this cable, forwarded to Roosevelt for his information, apparently helped convince Churchill not to insist on modifying the Soviet Union's request for great-power unanimity in the proposed world organization. A second cable from Smuts to Churchill which was not forwarded to the President gave a clearer indication of the South African's overall view of postwar political problems. After discussing the expansion of Soviet influence into the Balkans, Smuts continued:

I do not say this in any spirit of hostility to Russia. It is upon close cooperation between the Big Three that our best hope rests for the near future. . . . But the more firmly Russia can establish herself in the saddle now the farther she will ride in the future. . . . From this standpoint the future dispositions as regards Germany assume an importance for us which may be far greater than . . . they apper at present. A new situation will be created for us in Europe and the world by the elimination of Germany through this war. . . . While a World Organization is necessary, it is equally essential that our Commonwealth and Empire should emerge from this ordeal as strong and influential as possible, making us an equal partner in every sense for the other Big Two (Smuts to Churchill, Sept. 26, 1944, *WSC*, VI, 212–13).

Sir Archibald Clark Kerr was the British Ambassador in Moscow, and Sir Alexander Cadogan, the Permanent Undersecretary in the Foreign Office, was the British representative at the Dumbarton Oaks Conference.

C–785

London [via U.S. Army]
Sept. 25, 1944, 1649 Z

Prime Minister to President Roosevelt. Personal and Top Secret.
You will wish to read the following telegram I have received from Smuts. Begins:

"I feel deeply perturbed over deadlock with Russia in world organisation talks. This crisis, in any case, comes at most unfortunate moment before final end of war. I fear we are being rushed at breakneck pace into momentous decisions, and not in this case only. International aviation, tele-communications, etc., all tell the same tale. Here, however, the consequences may be particularly disastrous, I may therefore be pardoned for sending a warning note about this impasse.

"At first, I thought the Russian attitude absurd and their contention one not to be conceded by other great powers, and not unlikely to be turned down by smaller powers also. But second thoughts have tended the other way. I assume that Russian attitude is sincerely stated by Molotov and correctly interpreted by Clark-Kerr and Cadogan as one involving honour and standing of Russia among her allies. She asks whether she is trusted and treated as an equal or is still the outlaw and pariah. A misunderstanding here is more than a mere difference. It touches Russian amour propre and produces an inferiority complex and may poison European relations with far-reaching results. Russia, conscious of her power, may become more grasping than ever. Her making no attempt to find a solution shows her reaction and sense of power. What will be her future relations with Germany and Japan, even France, not to mention lesser countries? If a world organisation is formed with Russia out of it, she will become the power centre of another group and we shall be heading for World War III. If no such organisation is formed by the United Nations, they will stand stultified before history. The dilemma is a very grave one, and the position into which we may be drifting should be avoided at all costs.

"In view of these dangers, the smaller powers should be prepared to make a concession to Russia's amour propre and should not on this matter insist on theoretical equality of status. Such insistence may have most devastating results for smaller powers themselves. Where questions of power and security are concerned, it would be most unwise to raise theoretical issues of sovereign equality, and United Kingdom and United States of America should use their influence in favour of common sense and safety first rather than status for the smaller countries.

"On the merits there is much to be said for unanimity among the great powers, at least for the years immediately following on this war. If in practice the principle proves unworkable, the situation could be reviewed later when mutual confidence has been established and a more workable basis laid down. At the present stage, a clash should be avoided at all costs. If unanimity for the powers is adopted, even including their voting on questions directly concerning their interests, the result would be that the United Kingdom and the United States of America will have to exert all their influence on Russia to be moderate and sensible and not to flout world opinion. And in this they are likely to be largely successful. If Russia proves impossible, the world organization may have to act; but the blame will be here. At worst the principle of unanimity will only have the effect of a veto, of preventing action where it may be wise or even necessary. It will be negative and slow down action. But it will also be impossible for Russia to embark on crises disapproved of by United Kingdom and United States of America.

"Where people are drunk with new-won power, it may not be so bad a thing to have a brake-like unanimity. I do not defend it, I dislike it, but I do not think it at present so bad that the future of world peace and security should be sacrificed on this issue.

"The talks have so far been on an official advisory level although, no doubt, there may have been intervention on a higher level. I think, before definite decisions are reached on the highest level, the whole situation should be most carefully reconsidered in all its far-reaching implications and some modus vivendi, even if only of a temporary character, should be explored among the great powers, which would prevent a catastrophe of the first magnitude. We simply must agree and cannot afford to differ where so much is at stake for the future."

[MR*. *FRUS*, 1944, I, 836–38. *R&C*.]

When he sent this cable, Churchill did not know that Eden had already suggested September 27 for the release of the Italian statement. The film to which the Prime Minister referred was probably *Wilson*, a motion picture which presented both Anglo-American relations and Woodrow Wilson's leadership during World War I in a favorable light.

C–786

London [via U.S. Army]
Sept. 25, 1944, 2005 Z

Prime Minister to President Roosevelt. Personal and Top Secret.
Your 622.

I have not been able to signal you before as we were among U-Boats (German) and condemned to wireless silence. I shall be making my statement to the House on Thursday, September 28th and should like to refer to our Italian statement. Could we not synchronize publication on that date? This would enable me to add some words of condemnation of lynching in Rome which would, I think, reconcile public opinion and put that episode in its proper proportion, which is not large. If, however, the earlier date is important to you, I will, of course, meet your wishes. I do not know at the moment of signalling what has actually been settled.

2. We all saw Wilson's film with great interest and pleasure. It made a strong impression upon American officers and troops, but some comments were made about it being effective Democratic Party propaganda. My feeling is that it can do nothing but good to common cause. Kindest regards to all.

[MR*]

C–787

London [via U.S. Army]
Sept. 25, 1944 / TOR 2358 Z

Prime Minister to President Roosevelt Personal and Top Secret.

I am now safely back. Please cancel paragraph one of my telegram number 786 as I now feel that publication should be on the 27th as originally planned.

All best wishes.

[MR*]

Gently, Churchill continued to prod Roosevelt toward recognition of de Gaulle's FCNL as the provisional government of France.

C–788

London [via U.S. Army]
Sept. 27, 1944, 1057 Z / TOR 1355 Z

Prime Minister to President Roosevelt. Personal and Top Secret.

I find on arrival here a very strong feeling that we ought to go a bit further than we have done towards recognizing the French Provisional Government. Our Italian announcement has gone well but of course people ask "What about the French?" I hope you will not mind my saying tomorrow that we are carefully studying the question from week to week in the light of changing events. I shall not of course commit you in any way.

[MR*]

To the dismay of the British Foreign Office, Roosevelt continued to delay recognition of the French provisional government. The President's excuse, that de Gaulle had not established Zones of the Interior, was only technically correct. De Gaulle had asked Eisenhower to turn over control of a large portion of France, including Paris, as an Interior Zone.

R–623

Washington [via U.S. Navy]
Sept. 28, 1944, 1:20 P.M.

Personal and Top Secret, from the President for the Prime Minister.

Your 788. I am pleased to know that our Italian announcement went well in the U.K. It seems also to have been well received here.

In regard to the "French Provisional Government" I believe it would be wise to delay any action on our part until the German troops are expelled from all of France including Alsace and Lorraine.

I have no information as yet that General de Gaulle has expressed any desire for the setting up of any "Zones of the Interior" which would be the first change from a military to a civilian administration of the government. Roosevelt [WDL]

[MR*. R&C.]

Roosevelt heartily endorsed the suggestion from Smuts that cooperation and compromise were needed to bring the Soviets into the proposed world organization until that body was able to stand on its own. The President added the underlined phrase to Leahy's draft of this message.

R–624

Washington [via U.S. Navy]
Sept. 28, 1944, 1:35 P.M.

Personal and Top Secret, from the President for the Prime Minister.

Your 785. I have read with great interest your telegram from Field Marshal Smuts, and I think we are all in agreement with him as to the necessity of having the U.S.S.R. as a fully accepted and equal member of any association of the great powers formed for the purpose of preventing international war.

It should be possible to accomplish this by adjusting our differences through compromise by all the parties concerned and this ought to tide things over for a few years until the child learns how to toddle. Roosevelt [WDL]

[MR*. *FRUS*, 1944, I, 849–50. *WSC*, VI, 215–16. *R&C*.]

During the Quebec Conference, Roosevelt and Churchill apparently discussed plans for a tripartite conference with Stalin. (Churchill mentions such talks in his memoirs as does the official British history. The American records do not mention such a discussion, though Lord Moran claims that Churchill contacted the President from England after the Quebec Conference. See *WSC*, VI, 215; Woodward, *British Foreign Policy*, III, 148; Moran, *Churchill*, pp. 204–5.) Roosevelt reportedly claimed that he could not attend such a meeting until after the November presidential election. Churchill, after disdainfully commenting that the Red Army would not stand and wait for the results, decided to arrange his own meeting with Stalin. Convinced that the military successes in France had changed the balance of power between the Soviet Union and the western Allies, Churchill vowed to press the advantage and work out an agreement with Stalin about eastern Europe, particularly Poland. On September 27, Churchill cabled Stalin to suggest a meeting between the two in Moscow, with a Big Three meeting to follow after the American presidential election, possibly in The Hague.

The conversation Churchill mentions between Stalin and the American and British Ambassadors in Moscow, Averell Harriman and Archibald Clark Kerr, is probably the one of September 23 reported in Harriman's memoir (*Special Envoy*, 349–53). During those talks Harriman, at Roosevelt's request, proposed a Big Three meeting in November somewhere in the Mediterranean area. Stalin claimed that his doctors forbade him to travel and when Harriman suggested that the warm Mediterranean sun would be beneficial, the Premier said he was specifically forbidden to travel to a different climate.

There is a certain irony in Churchill's citing BONIFACE as proof that the French provisional government represented all of France. BONIFACE was the Prime Minister's personal label for ULTRA material—the message traffic of the German High Command which could be intercepted and deciphered.

Churchill's surmise that the war would extend into 1945 was well founded. The Germans, counting on new weapons and assuming that the British and Soviets would begin to quarrel over the Balkans, had decided to make a determined defense in the west. Churchill correctly read the signs of this decision and his pessimism was probably further stimulated by the failure of a major operation designed to outflank German defenses in the northwest. Operation MARKET-GARDEN called for airborne attacks by Anglo-American forces against four strategically located Dutch towns, the northernmost being Arnhem on the Rhine (Neder Rijn) River. The airborne forces were to hold the towns and, most important, the bridges, until relieved by British armored units pushing north out of Belgium. Had the operation succeeded the Allies could have crossed the Rhine into Germany early in the fall, bypassing the Siegfried line, the main German defense position in the west. With the withdrawal, on September 25, of the First British Airborne Division from the Arnhem area after heavy casualties, operation MARKET-GARDEN was over, and the thrust into Germany had to wait until 1945. Field Marshal Montgomery subsequently argued for a "narrow front" attack in the north, one made possible by stripping Allied forces in the center and south of supplies and troops, but Eisenhower stuck to his "broad front" strategy. Each of the commanding generals of the three main Allied forces—Montgomery (British Twenty-first Army Group) in the north, General Omar Bradley (U.S. Twelfth Army Group) in the center, and General George Patton (U.S. Third Army) in the south—believed his forces capable of breaking through into Germany, though Bradley's proposal called for a joint attack with the U.S. Third Army. But Eisenhower refused to unleash either Montgomery or Patton, and chose instead to work for a slower buildup of logistic support for all three before launching what he hoped would be the final assault.

The speech mentioned by Churchill was the now-famous Hotel Statler address given by Roosevelt on September 23 in Washington, D.C. In that lively talk, which kicked off the President's active campaign for re-election, he combined ridicule, sarcasm, and attacks on Republican fat cats in an effective and rousing call for support.

C–789

London [via U.S. Army]
Sept. 29, 1944, 1726 Z / TOR 1855 Z

Prime Minister to President Roosevelt. Personal and Most Especially Secret.

1. Your number 624. I am repeating this to Field Marshal Smuts who will be much gratified.

2. U.J. was most expansive and friendly in a conversation with Averell and Clark Kerr the other night. He however "grumbled about his own health". He said he was never well except at Moscow and his doctors did not like him flying. Even his visits to the front did him harm and it took him a fortnight to get over Teheran, etc.

3. In these circumstances Anthony and I are seriously considering flying there very soon. The route is shorter now. We have not yet heard from U.J. in reply to our suggestion. Our two great objects would be, first, to clinch his coming in against Japan and, secondly, to try to effect a friendly settlement with Poland. There are other points too about Greece and Yugoslavia which we would also discuss. We should keep you informed of every point. We would of course welcome Averell's assistance, or perhaps you could send Stettinius or Marshall. I feel sure that personal contact is most necessary.

4. Your number 623. You may be sure that we shall not take any action with the French except after full consultation with you. I hope nothing I said yesterday embarrassed you. I see you use the expression "French Provisional Government" in your 623. It seems to me there would not be much harm in this phrase coming into use without any formal instrument being agreed between the Governments. After all they are the French Provisional Government and it is fully admitted even in the BONIFACE series that they represent all France.

5. It seems to me pretty clear that Germany is not going to be conquered this year. Omar Bradley in a telegram I have seen is already talking about an operation across the Rhine in the Middle of November and I see many other signs of the German resistance stiffening.

6. Off the record—I have read your speech with much gusto and delighted to see you in such vigorous form.

Every good wish.

[MR*. p*WSC*, VI, 216. *R&C*.]

Initially the President chose to remain aloof from the forthcoming Churchill-Stalin talks, neither ignoring them (Harriman attended as an observer) nor sanctioning them (Hull and Stettinius were not sent). Roosevelt's only advice seemed to be not to press Stalin on his commitment to fight the Japanese, and Harriman received instructions to assure the Soviet Premier that the United States had not the slightest doubt about the sincerity of that commitment.

R–625

Washington [via U.S. Navy]
Sept. 30, 1944, 11:50 A.M.

Personal and Top Secret, from the President for the Prime Minister.

Your 789. Please let me know after you hear from U.J. the date when you and Anthony will arrive in Moscow.

It is my opinion that Stalin is at the present time sensitive about any doubt as to his intention to help us in the Orient.

At your request I will direct Harriman to give you any assistance that you may desire. It does not appear practicable or advantageous for me to be represented by Stettinius or Marshall.

In regard to the French problem I will give it further consideration when the Huns are out of France or when "Zones of the Interior" are established. Roosevelt [WDL]

[MR*. pWSC, VI, 217.]

Hoping to gain Roosevelt's endorsement and thus present a unified Anglo-American front during his talks with Stalin, Churchill emphasized the areas of agreement between himself and the President, including the decision to accept great-power unanimity (the veto) on the Security Council of the proposed world organization. Major General John R. Deane was Chief of the U.S. Military Mission in Moscow.

C–790

London [via U.S. Army]
Oct. 3, 1944, 2335 Z

Prime Minister to President. Personal and Top Secret.

1. Anthony and I start Saturday [Oct. 7] and hope in two or three days to reach U.J. We should like you to send a message to him saying that you approve of our mission and that Averell will be available to take part in discussions.

2. Will you tell Averell or General Deane what can be said about your far eastern plans and let us know what you have told them, so that we all keep within the limits prescribed. We want to elicit the time it will take after the German downfall for a superior Russian army to be gathered opposite the Japanese on the frontiers of Manchukuo and to hear from them the problems of this campaign, which are peculiar owing to the lines of communication being vulnerable in the later stages.

3. Of course the bulk of our business will be about the Poles, but you

and I think so much alike about this that I do not need any special guidance as to your views.

4. The point of Dumbarton Oaks will certainly come up and I must tell you that we are pretty clear that the only hope is that the three great powers are agreed. It is with regret that I have come to this conclusion contrary to my first thought. Please let me know if you have any wishes about this matter, and also instruct Averell accordingly.

[MR*. *FRUS*, 1944, IV, 1002. p*WSC*, VI, 219. *R&C*.]

Pleased by the prospect of Anglo-Soviet cooperation and essentially indifferent to the details of any settlement in eastern Europe, so long as they did not become issues in the presidential election, Roosevelt wished Churchill "every success" in his talks with Stalin. But this draft was never sent. Charles Bohlen, Chief of the State Department's Division of Eastern European Affairs, contacted Harry Hopkins and expressed concern that no American observer would attend the talks. Both he and Hopkins agreed that the meeting could either degenerate into a serious Anglo-Soviet dispute or lead to a spheres-of-influence division in Europe, both unacceptable alternatives. Moreover, it would appear as if the United States did not care. Hopkins telephoned the President and received permission to hold up the dispatch of the cable.

R–626, draft A, not sent

Washington
Oct. 4, 1944, 11:20 A.M.

Top Secret and Personal from the President for the Prime Minister.

Your 790. I wish you every success in your visit to U.J.

General Deane is in possession of our Far Eastern plans and has probably already told them to the Soviet Staff.

Harriman will be available for advice and consultation.

Regarding Dumbarton I cherish a hope that you will find some means of reaching an agreement between the three great powers. This is not a hope but a "must" for all three of us. Failure now is unthinkable. Roosevelt [WDL]

[MR]

Convinced by Hopkins' arguments, the President accepted a new draft reply. This time he asked that Averell Harriman be allowed to observe during the Churchill-Stalin talks and further requested that the question of voting in the United Nations organization—a matter of very deep concern to American liberals and to the public and Congress as well—be deferred to a proposed Big Three meeting. The thrust of the cable was that the United States would not be bound by any agreements reached by British and Soviet negotiators.

R–626

Washington [via U.S. Navy]
Oct. 4, 1944, 5:35 P.M.

Top Secret and Personal from the President for the Prime Minister.

I can well understand the reasons why you feel that an immediate meeting between yourself and Uncle Joe is necessary before the three of us can get together. The questions which you will discuss there are ones which are, of course, of real interest to the United States, as I know you will agree. I have therefore instructed Harriman to stand by and to participate as my observer, if agreeable to you and Uncle Joe, and I have so informed Stalin. While naturally Averill will not be in a position to commit the United States—I could not permit anyone to commit me in advance— he will be able to keep me fully informed and I have told him to return and report to me as soon as the conference is over.

I am only sorry that I cannot be with you myself but I am prepared for a meeting of the three of us any time after the elections here, for which your meeting with Uncle Joe should be a useful prelude, and I have so informed Uncle Joe.

Like you, I attach the greatest importance to the continued unity of our three countries. I am sorry that I cannot agree with you, however, that the voting question should be raised at this time. That is a matter which the three of us can I am sure work out together and I hope you will postpone discussion of it until our meeting. There is after all no immediate urgency about this question which is so directly related to public opinion in the United States and Great Britain and in all the United Nations.

I am asking our military people in Moscow to make available to you our Joint Chiefs' statement to Stalin.

You carry my best wishes with you and I will eagerly await word of how it goes. Roosevelt [HLH]

[MR*. *FRUS, Yalta Conf.*, pp. 7–8. WSC, VI, 219–20.]

Churchill insisted on holding some private talks with Stalin, and the President, assured that he would be kept informed, made no objection, particularly since there would be no public disclosure of what took place. If Roosevelt had shared all of Bohlen's and Hopkins' misgivings about the nature of an Anglo-Soviet settlement in eastern Europe, it is unlikely that he would have approved of such conversations, but now he found himself in his favorite position—uncommitted and free to swing his weight to one side or the other.

C–791

London [via U.S. Army]
Oct. 5, 1944, 1725 Z

Prime Minister to President Roosevelt. Personal and Top Secret.
Your number 626.
1. Thank you very much for what you say and for your good wishes. I am very glad that Averell should sit in at all principal conferences; but you would not, I am sure, wish this to preclude private tete-a-tetes between me and U. J. or Anthony and Molotov, as it is often under such conditions that the best progress is made. You can rely on me to keep you constantly informed of everything that affects our joint interests apart from the reports which Averell will send.
2. I gather from your last sentence but one that you have sent some general account of your Pacific plans to your people in Moscow which will be imparted to U. J. and which I shall see on arrival. This will be most convenient.
3. Should U. J. raise the question of voting as he very likely will do, I will tell him that there is no hurry about this and that I am sure we can get it settled when we are all three together.

[MR*. *WSC*, VI, 220. *R&C.*]

The lull in U-boat activity was due to the German need to reorganize following the shift from bases in the Bay of Biscay to Norwegian facilities. The "new types of U-boats" were those with Schnorkels (devices which permitted submarines to "breathe" air while submerged just below the surface), and high-speed boats (types XXI and XXIII) which could, for short distances, make seventeen knots while underwater. The British Admiralty was concerned about the low rate of U-boat sinkings during September and for the remainder of 1944, even though German submarines did very little damage.

C–792

Washington [via U.S. Army]
Oct. 6, 1944, 1056 Z / TOR 1200 Z

Prime Minister to President Roosevelt. Personal and Top Secret.
I attach our suggestion for the September U-Boat report. Canada is being informed at the same time.

Begins:

During September there has been a lull in U-Boat activity, which is possibly seasonal. This year, as last, the enemy may hope to renew his offensive in the autumn and may rely on new types of U-Boats to counter our present ascendancy. Shipping losses have been almost as low as in May 1944, the best month of the war. The rate of destruction of U-Boats in proportion to shipping losses remains satisfactory.

The U-Boat war, however, demands unceasing attention. Only the zeal and vigour of the Allied air and surface forces have procured the comparative safety of our shipping and the enemy's scant success.

[MR*]

R–627

Hyde Park, N.Y. [via U.S. Navy]
Oct. 7, 1944, 5:30 P.M.

Personal and Top Secret, from the President for the Prime Minister.
    Your 792. I agree. Roosevelt [WEB]

[MR*]

Roosevelt's cable to Churchill of August 26 (R–607), expressing confidence that the British could work out a satisfactory meat contract with Argentina, had not been sent to Hull. Thus, when the Secretary of State learned that the British had negotiated a long-term contract, he drafted a strong protest for the President to send Churchill. Roosevelt ignored the thrust of his earlier message and sent Hull's draft without change. American policy remained the same—to force the collapse of the Argentine government of Farrell and Perón.

R–628

Hyde Park, N.Y. [via U.S. Navy]
Oct. 10, 1944, 9:00 P.M.

From the President for the Prime Minister, Personal and Top Secret.
    We have been informed by Winant that the Ministry of Food now intends to conclude a four-year contract for the exportable surplus of Argentine meat with prices firm for the first two years. Winant does not state whether the proposal of the Ministry of Food has been approved by the Government.

I feel very strongly that the conclusion of any contract at the present time would seriously prejudice our entire stand and would create the impression in Argentina, throughout the American republics, and in this country that we are not standing together on this important problem. Your people here in Washington have undoubtedly informed you that the position which we have taken toward Argentina has the overwhelming support of our press and of all sectors of our public.

You will recall that your people negotiated for ten long months before you signed up your last contract with Argentina, and that was done before the Colonels took over in Buenos Aires.

For the reasons which I have expressed to you on several occasions, and which I recently expressed publicly, I hope you will continue on a month to month basis for some time to come. I feel that we can break this problem if we present a firm united stand during the weeks immediately ahead. Roosevelt [CH]

[MR*. *FRUS*, 1944, VII, 363.]

Churchill and Eden left England on October 7, arriving in Naples, Italy, during the morning of the eighth. As the Prime Minister reported to Roosevelt, conversations with Generals Wilson and Alexander left the gloomy and accurate impression that firm German resistance, and a shortage of supplies and reinforcements for the Allies, would prevent an Allied victory in that theater during 1944. Neither Alexander in Italy nor Eisenhower in western Europe could spare the forces required to carry out the amphibious attack planned against Rangoon, Burma (Operation DRACULA). Churchill agreed to its cancellation with great reluctance since he had hoped that DRACULA would be the first step toward a major campaign in the South East Asia theater, aimed at re-establishing British control and prestige after the war.

C–793

Moscow [via U.S. Army, London]
Oct. 11, 1944; 2330 Z, Oct. 10 (London) / TOR 0415 Z

Prime Minister to President Roosevelt Personal and Top Secret.

We reached Moscow from London in 36 hours, 23 hours spent in flight and on the whole I feel better for the voyage.

2. On the way we had four hours at Naples with Generals Wilson and Alexander. I was much distressed by their tale. The fighting has been very hard. Our losses since the battle opened are about 30,000 of which at least four fifths have been British or British controlled. The enemy are estimated to have lost 42,000 including 10,000 prisoners in our hands. Our men are tired and there are no fresh divisions to put in. It seems so

much was taken away from our Italian front against Germany as just to deny a complete victory in this theatre. Alexander and also Clark tried their best with what was left to them but as I told you I could not guarantee results. Thus Kesselring may bring us to a standstill in the Appenines until they are wrapped in snow. He could then withdraw five or six divisions to resist Eisenhower on the Rhine. The German fighting here has been of the utmost tenacity and the troops he could withdraw would be high class.

3. Pressure in Dutch salient seems to me to be growing very severe and our advances are slow and costly. In these circumstances we have with much sorrow had to recommend that we should put off DRACULA from March to November and leave British 3rd Division in France as well as sending the 52nd Division, one of our best, about 22,000 strong in fighting troops and the 6th Airborne Division to the Netherlands. Eisenhower is counting on these for the impending operation on the Rhine and of course this was much the quickest way to bring additional troops into France.

4. Could you not deflect 2 or better still 3 American divisions to Italian ports which would enable them to join Mark Clark's Fifth Army and add the necessary strength to Alexander? They would have to be there in 4 or 5 weeks. I consider the fact that we shall be sending Eisenhower these extra 2 divisions gives me a case for your generous consideration.

5. With regard to Istria, Trieste, etc, General Wilson is forwarding his plan to Combined Chiefs of Staff. This plan will be in accordance with over all strategic objective, namely the expulsion from or destruction in Italy of Kesselring's army.

6. I was overjoyed to hear that General Marshall was in France at Eisenhower's Headquarters. To save time I have ventured to send a copy of the relevant portion of this telegram to him through Eisenhower. I hope you will send him to Italy so that the situation can at least be fairly talked over between high commanders involved.

7. I hope and trust all is going well with you.

[MR*. p*WSC*, VI, 223–24.]

THE MOSCOW CONFERENCE
(TOLSTOY)

The 1944 Moscow Conference between Churchill and Stalin began on the evening of October 9 and concluded on the evening of October 17, an unusually long meeting. Those talks, and the ones held between Foreign Ministers Molotov and Eden, were unique. With the exception of the 1941 discussions between Eden and Molotov, which of necessity that early in the war were exploratory and inconclusive, the TOLSTOY conversations (the British codename for the 1944 talks) were the only time undisguised power politics predominated at a major wartime conference. With the United States represented only by Ambassador Averell Harriman, who acted as an observer rather than a participant, Churchill and Stalin spoke as if matters in eastern Europe were theirs and only theirs to decide. That was particularly true during their private, informal conversations when Harriman was not present. Although both Churchill and Stalin reported the gist of their talks to Harriman and the President, the atmosphere of those talks—an atmosphere that can be re-created from the British minutes—was missing from those reports.

A spheres-of-influence arrangement with the Soviets was nothing new for Churchill. On October 1, 1939, when he was First Lord of the Admiralty, he had justified in part the Nazi-Soviet non-aggression pact as a legitimate expression of Soviet interests. Speaking publicly, Churchill labeled Russia "a riddle wrapped in a mystery inside an enigma," but went on to explain that the puzzle might be solved by looking at "Russian national interest." "That the Russian armies should stand on this line (the Soviet-German border in what had been central Poland) was clearly necessary for the safety of Russia against the Nazi menace." Churchill "wished that the Russian armies should be standing on their present line as the friends and Allies of Poland instead of as invaders." Even in the context of Britain's fears in 1939, that is little short of an endorsement of Soviet boundary claims. In the same speech, Churchill spoke of "the community of interests which exists between England, France and Russia—a community of interests to prevent the Nazis' carrying the flames of war into the Balkans and Turkey." At the same time, he noted that any German designs on the Baltic states threatened "the historic life-interests of Russia." Despite Churchill's claim that he merely "put the best construction on their (the Russians') conduct," he had sent a clear message to Stalin—the Baltic states were in the Soviet sphere of influence. Later in 1939 and again during the Eden-Molotov talks in December 1941, the British refused formal recognition of Soviet annexation of those states. But that refusal stemmed primarily from concern over American opposition to territorial agreements, not because Churchill had changed his mind. In fact, he never recanted his de facto acceptance of Soviet control over Lithuania, Latvia, and Estonia. (The quotations are from Churchill, *Speeches*, VI, p. 6161, and *WSC*, I, pp. 448–49. See also Resis, "Spheres of Influence in Soviet Wartime Diplomacy," pp. 422–24, 431–36.)

Churchill's consistent pursuit of a spheres-of-influence settlement in Europe was further demonstrated by his eagerness in 1944 to sanction Soviet predominance in Roumania in exchange for British control in Greece, a proposal opposed by the U.S. State Department but approved by Roosevelt (C–687, R–557, C–700, R–560).

Despite the President's acceptance of a temporary Soviet sphere of influence in Roumania, he had tried to limit Churchill's freedom of action during the Moscow Conference by asking Stalin to consider the talks "as preliminary to a meeting of the three of us," a phrase that puzzled the Soviet Premier since he had assumed that Churchill spoke for the Anglo-American alliance (*Stalin/ FDR*, Nos. 230–31). Nevertheless, once the TOLSTOY talks began, both Churchill and Stalin did not hesitate to make just the kind of agreements that the Americans professed to oppose. Nor was Roosevelt unaware of such moves. Although Harriman was not present at the most sensitive of the TOL- STOY conversations, he managed to find out what was going on. In an early report to the President, the Ambassador accurately reported the spheres-of- influence arrangement for the Balkans that was developing: "Churchill and Eden will try to work out some sort of spheres of influence with the Russians, the British to have a free hand in Greece and the Russians in Rumania and perhaps other countries. The British will attempt to retrieve a position of equal influence in Yugoslavia. They can probably succeed in the former but I am doubtful about the latter objective" (Harriman to Roosevelt, Oct. 10, 1944, *FRUS*, 1944, IV, 1006). Roosevelt's response illustrates the difference between his concerns and those of his advisers in the White House and the State Department. Hopkins and Hull had expressed grave concern over any spheres-of-influence arrangement in eastern Europe, but the President told Harriman that "my active interest at the present time in the Balkan area is that such steps as are practicable should be taken to insure against the Balkans getting us into a future international war," leaving open the question of spheres of influence (Roosevelt to Harriman, Oct. 11, 1944, *FRUS*, IV, 1009).

The key Churchill-Stalin meeting came on October 9, the first day of the talks. Faced with rapidly expanding Soviet political and military influence in southeastern Europe, Churchill's goal was to protect Britain's position in Greece and Yugoslavia. The British Army had landed in Greece on October 4 and would arrive in Athens on the fourteenth, but Churchill remained concerned about Soviet support for the communist-dominated ELAS Parti- sans. Moreover, he may have suspected that Stalin would permit the Bul- garians, who were about to sign an armistice with the Soviet Union, to realize age-old territorial ambitions by expanding into northern Greece (Thrace and Macedonia) and eastern Yugoslavia (Serbia).

What had been the major eastern European problem in Anglo-Soviet af- fairs, Poland, took a back seat to the more pressing issue of maintaining British dominance in the Mediterranean. Stalin and Churchill exchanged crude re- marks about the Poles, agreed that Poles were quarrelsome (Stalin remarked "that where there was one Pole he would begin to quarrel with himself through sheer boredom"), and put off any further discussions until representatives of the Polish government in London could come to Moscow. The impression left by Churchill's comments was that of a statesman willing to give the Soviets their way in Poland in return for their cooperation elsewhere. The Prime Minister labeled the Polish leaders in London "unwise," callously noted that the leader of the Warsaw Underground, General Bor, would no longer trou- ble the Soviets since "the Germans were looking after him," and accepted Stalin's position that the London Poles would have to negotiate with the Polish Committee of National Liberation—a group controlled by the Soviets.

With the Polish question out of the way for the time being, the two leaders concentrated on the Balkans. American Ambassador Harriman was excluded from the meeting, so Churchill and Stalin could speak in words of blatant power politics, although the Prime Minister cautioned that "it was better to express these things in diplomatic terms and not to use the phrase 'dividing into spheres', because the Americans might be shocked." According to a Foreign Office account, which was later amended before being made official, Churchill "produced what he called a 'naughty document' showing a list of Balkan countries and the proportion of interest in them of the Great Powers" (F.O. 800–302/7505, p. 4). Some of the percentages were later modified during extensive talks between Eden and Molotov, but the basic structure remained: the Soviet Union would have 90 percent influence in Roumania and 75 percent in Bulgaria, while Britain would exercize 90 percent influence in Greece. Yugoslavia and Hungary were to be split 50–50, although Eden later granted the Soviets 75 percent influence in Hungary. During the discussion which followed, Stalin agreed with Churchill's insistence that "Britain must be the leading Mediterranean power," an admission the Soviets followed with a request that they gain unrestricted access to the Mediterranean from the Black Sea, necessitating the cancellation of the Montreux Convention, which permitted Turkey to close the straits leading to the Aegean Sea. Ignoring centuries of British policy aimed at denying Russia such access, Churchill quickly agreed, calling the convention "inadmissible" and "obsolete."

All in all, it was not Mr. Churchill's finest hour, although he had little room to maneuver. His arguments during this first meeting had an air of desperation. Immensely aware and proud of Britain's prewar power and influence, the Prime Minister frequently was forced to use the Soviet Union against the United States and vice versa in order to maintain the form if not the substance of the British Empire. In spite of a request from Roosevelt not to discuss the results of the Dumbarton Oaks Conference, Churchill came out in favor of great-power unanimity (the veto) in any postwar international organization, because without it, "supposing China asked Britain to give up Hong Kong, China and Britain would have to leave the room while Russia and the U.S.A. settled the question." Churchill's plea for Stalin to restrain the Italian communists (Stalin said they were not always controllable, but he would try) likewise demonstrated Britain's dependence upon the good will of the other two great powers.

One last political discussion concerned postwar planning for Germany. Here both Stalin and Churchill came out in support of the kind of harsh settlement proposed in the Morgenthau Plan, with Stalin emphasizing the need to eliminate most of Germany's heavy industry. (Unless otherwise noted, the quotations in this summary of the TOLSTOY meeting are taken from the British minutes found in PREM 3/434/7.)

The British minutes of the TOLSTOY talks add substantially to the reports Churchill (sometimes jointly with Stalin) sent to Roosevelt, reports which made up the bulk of Churchill's memoir account of the conference (*WSC*, VI, 226–43). The first of the Prime Minister's summaries failed to mention the crucial "percentage" arrangement for the Balkans which had been proposed the night before. The results of talks between the London Poles (Prime Minister Mikolajczyk, Ambassador Romer, and Polish National Council President Grabski) and the Soviet-sponsored Polish Committee were reported in subsequent cables (C–799ff.).

C–794

Moscow [via U.S. Army, London]
Oct. 11, 1944; 2330 Z, Oct. 10 (London) / TOR 0415 Z

To President Roosevelt from Marshal Stalin and Prime Minister
Churchill. Personal and Top Secret.

In an informal discussion we have taken a preliminary view of the
situation as it affects us and have planned out the course of our agreement,
social and otherwise. We have invited Messrs Mikolajczyk, Romer and
Grabski to come at once for further conversations with us and with the
Polish National Committee. We have agreed not to refer in our discussions
to Dumbarton Oaks issues and that these shall be taken up when we three
can meet together. We have to consider the best way of reaching an agreed
policy about the Balkan countries including Hungary and Turkey. We
have arranged for Mr. Harriman to sit in as an observer at all meetings
where business of importance is to be transacted and for General Deane
to be present whenever military topics are raised. We have arranged for
technical contacts between our high officers and General Deane on military aspects, and for any meetings which may be necessary later in our
presence and that of the two foreign secretaries together with Mr. Harriman. We shall keep you fully informed ourselves about the progress we
make.

2. We take this occasion to send you our heartiest good wishes and to
offer our congratulations on prowess of United States Forces and upon
the conduct of the war in the west by General Eisenhower. Signed Churchill and Stalin

[MR*. *FRUS*, 1944, IV, 1007–8. p*WSC*, VI, 228. *Stalin/FDR*, doc. 232. *R&C*.]

R–629

Washington [via U.S. Navy]
Oct. 11, 1944, 4:45 P.M.

Top Secret and Personal. From the President for Marshal Stalin
and Prime Minister Churchill.

Thank you for your joint message No. 794 of October 10.

It is most pleasing to know that you are reaching a meeting of your
two minds as to international policies in which we are all interested because
of our common, current and future efforts to prevent international wars.
Roosevelt [WDL]

[MR. *WSC*, VI, 231 (paraphrase). *Stalin/FDR*, doc. 233.]

Although this message was referred to the State Department for preparation of a draft reply covering the political aspects of the cable, no draft ever reached the White House, possibly because Churchill's telegram said nothing of substance. Only the repeated Soviet assurances that they would enter the war against Japan were worth reading.

C–795

Moscow [via U.S. Army, London]
Oct. 11, 1944, 1032 Z (London) / TOR 1241 Z

Prime Minister to President Roosevelt. Personal Private and Top Secret.

We have found an extraordinary atmosphere of goodwill here, and we have sent you a joint message. You may be sure we shall handle everything so as not to commit you. The arrangements we have made for Averell are I think satisfactory to him and do not preclude necessary intimate contacts which we must have to do any good. Of all these I shall give you a faithful report.

It is absolutely necessary we should try to get a common mind about the Balkans, so that we may prevent civil war breaking out in several countries when probably you and I would be in sympathy with one side and U.J. with the other. I shall keep you informed of all this, and nothing will be settled except preliminary agreements between Britain and Russia, subject to further discussion and melting-down with you. On this basis I am sure you will not mind our trying to have a full meeting of minds with the Russians.

I have not yet received your account of what part of the Pacific operations we may mention to Stalin and his officers. I should like to have this because otherwise in conversation with him I might go beyond what you wish to be said. Meanwhile I will be very careful. We have not touched upon Dumbarton Oaks except to say it is barred, at your desire. However Stalin at lunch today spoke in praise of the meeting and of the very great measure of agreement that has been arrived at there. Stalin also in his speech at this same luncheon animadverted harshly upon Japan as being an aggressor nation. I have little doubt from our talks that he will declare war upon them as soon as Germany is beaten. But surely Averell and Deane should be in a position not merely to ask him to do certain things, but also tell him, in outline at any rate, the kind of things you are going to do yourself, and we are going to help you to do.

[MR*. *FRUS*, 1944, IV, 1010–11. *WSC*, VI, 228–29. *R&C*.]

Aware that the maintenance of close Anglo-American relations had to prevail, Churchill agreed not to permit the negotiation of a long-term meat-purchasing contract with Argentina.

C–796

Moscow [via U.S. Army, London]
Oct. 13, 1944, 1625 Z (London) / TOR 1720 Z

Prime Minister to President Roosevelt. Personal and Top Secret.

I have given instructions to Food Minister that no long-term contract is to be negotiated and that we are to proceed on a month to month basis next couple of months or so during which time we can discuss matters further.

We are worried for fear that French, Belgian and presently the Dutch will come into the market with plenty of gold. Nevertheless we shall make no arrangement at present time but later on I must address you again on the subject.

[MR*. *FRUS*, 1944, VII, 364.]

C–797

Moscow [via U.S. Army, London]
Oct. 14, 1944, 2235 Z (London) / TOR 0147 Z, Oct. 15

Prime Minister to President Roosevelt Personal and Top Secret.

Reference my number 796 about Argentine meat contract. In order to make my meaning clear perhaps you will kindly amend the first sentence of this telegram to read as follows:

"I have given instructions to the food minister that no long term contract is to be negotiated for the next couple of months or so and that we are to proceed meanwhile on a month to month basis during which time we can discuss the matter further".

[MR*]

At the same time that Churchill was trying to convince the President to move toward recognition of the French provisional government, Secretary of State Hull was warning Roosevelt that "in innumerable ways it will be represented to the French that the British Government is willing, and even eager, to extend recognition but that the United States remains adamant in its opposition." The Secretary concluded that the United States should extend recognition to the provisional government lest the American position in France be undermined (Hull to Roosevelt, Sept. 21, 1944, and Oct. 3, 1944, *FRUS*, 1944,

III, 737–38, 739). Churchill's report that Eisenhower favored recognition was accurate. Alfred Duff Cooper was the British representative to the French provisional government.

C–798

Moscow [via U.S. Army, London]
Oct. 14, 1944, 2235 Z (London) / TOR 0147 Z, Oct. 15

Prime Minister to President Roosevelt Personal and Top Secret.

I have been reflecting about the question of recognition of the French Provisional Government. I think events have now moved to a point where we could take a decision on the matter consistently with your own policy and my latest statement in the House of Commons [Sept. 28, 1944].

In your telegram number 623 you said that you thought that we should wait until France was cleared of the enemy and you implied that in any case De Gaulle must first show himself ready to take over from Eisenhower full responsibility for the administration of part of France as an interior zone. I for my part took the line of Parliament that the reorganization of the consultative assembly on a more representative basis ought to precede recognition.

I understand that Eisenhower is anxious to comply with the request he has already had from the French to constitute a large part of France into an interior zone. Negotiations between Supreme Headquarters and the French are making good progress and it appears that we may expect about three quarters of France to become an interior zone very shortly.

The enlargement of the consultative assembly is also making good progress. Duff Cooper reports that owing to very real difficulties of communications in France, French have found it impracticable to proceed with the original Algiers plan of getting members of an enlarged assembly confirmed in their mandates by elections in liberated departments. They propose instead to add selected delegates from the resistance movement and parliamentary groups I understand it is hoped to settle matter shortly and publish a new decree defining attributions of the reformed assembly and giving it increased powers over the executive. It is thought that the enlarged assembly should be able to meet at the end of this month.

There is no doubt that the French have been cooperating with Supreme Headquarters and that their Provisional Government has the support of the majority of French people. I suggest therefore that we can now safely recognize General De Gaulle's administration as the Provisional Government of France.

One procedure might be to tell the French now that we will recognize as soon as the enlarged assembly has met and has given De Gaulle's administration a vote of confidence.

An alternative procedure would be to recognize as soon as the interior zone has been formally established. I am inclined to think that this alternative is preferable as it would connect recognition with what will be a mark of satisfactory cooperation between the French authorities and A.E.F. in the common cause against Germany.

Please tell me what you think. If you agree that we should settle the matter by one or other of the procedures suggested above, the Foreign Office and State Dept might at once compare their ideas upon the actual terms in which we should give recognition. It is important that we should take the same line although we need not necessarily adopt exactly the same wording. We should have of course also to inform the Soviet Government of what we intend.

Recognition would not of course commit us on the separate question of French membership of the European Advisory Commission or similar bodies.

[MR*. *FRUS*, 1944, III, 739–41. *WSC*, VI, 246–47. pR&C.]

In spite of Churchill's plea for the transfer of two or three U.S. divisions to the Italian theater, the Joint Chiefs of Staff, who drafted this cable, adamantly insisted upon concentrating all available Allied strength on the western front. Once again, the recommendations of the Supreme Allied Commander in the Mediterranean, British General Sir H. Maitland Wilson, provided the ammunition with which to turn Churchill's arguments aside.

R–630

Washington [via U.S. Navy]
Oct. 16, 1944, 12:15 P.M.

Top Secret and Personal. From the President for the Prime Minister.

Replying to your 793. My Chiefs of Staff and I are in complete agreement that we should not divert any of Eisenhower's badly needed divisions to Italy.

I appreciate your report on the Italian campaign where, up to the present, our combined effort has cost us nearly 200,000 battle casualties, 90,000 of them American. General Wilson's report in his MEDCOS 201 seems to show clearly that German actions in North Italy are more dependent on Russian advances than on our operations in Italy. My Chiefs of Staff accept Wilson's estimate that we cannot now expect to destroy Kesselring's army this winter and that the terrain and weather conditions in the Po Valley will prevent any decisive advance this year. They further consider that the Germans are free to transfer five or six divisions from

Italy to the Western Front whenever they consider such action more profitable than using these divisions in containing our forces south of the Po. Provision of additional U.S. divisions will not affect the campaign in Italy this year.

All of us are now faced with an unanticipated shortage of man power and overshadowing all other military problems is the need for quick provision of fresh troops to reinforce Eisenhower in his battle to break into Germany and end the European war. While the divisions in Italy are undoubtedly tiring as the result of fighting in the present battle since 25 August, Eisenhower is now fighting the decisive battle of Germany with divisions which have been in continuous combat since they landed on the Normandy beaches the first part of June. The need for building up additional divisions on the long front from Switzerland to the North Sea is urgent. Even more urgent is the need for fresh troops to enable Eisenhower to give some rest to our front line soldiers who have been the spear point of the battle since the first days in Normandy. On the basis of General Marshall's reports on the present situation we are now taking the very drastic step of sending the infantry regiments of the divisions ahead of the other units in order that General Eisenhower may be able to rotate some of our exhausted front line soldiers.

Diversion of any forces to Italy would withhold from France vitally needed fresh troops while committing such forces to the high attrition of an indecisive winter campaign in northern Italy. I appreciate the hard and difficult task which our armies in Italy have faced and will face, but we cannot withhold from the main effort forces which are needed in the battle of Germany.

From General Marshall's reports on the problem now facing General Eisenhower, I am sure that both of them agree with my conviction that no divisions should be diverted from their destination in France. Roosevelt [WDL, JCS]

[MR*. p*WSC*, VI, 224–25.]

This cable and the one which follows are largely self-explanatory. With the collapse of the Polish Underground in Warsaw, the London Poles had lost their major element of real power. Wishfully counting on American support in their fight against Soviet territorial demands, Mikolajczyk and his associates were shocked to learn that Roosevelt had supposedly agreed, during the Teheran Conference, to the Curzon line as the Soviet-Polish boundary. The American minutes of that part of the meeting (Dec. 1, 1943) do not show the President specifically mentioning the Curzon line, although he did tell Stalin that the eastern border of Poland should be moved farther west than proposed by the Soviets. However, during the Yalta Conference, Roosevelt claimed that he had generally supported the Curzon line proposal during the Teheran talks (*FRUS, Teheran Conf.*, p. 594; *FRUS, Yalta Conf.*, pp. 667, 677). Whatever the President actually said, the London Poles realized that there was little chance that the United States would confront the Soviet Union on the issue of the Soviet-Polish boundary. When Roosevelt finally responded to Polish inquiries about his position, he merely offered a vague promise of support for a "strong, free and independent Polish state," but refused to guarantee any specific frontiers (Roosevelt to Mikolajczyk, Nov. 17, 1944, *FRUS*, 1944, III, 1335). Averell Harriman's report to the President echoed Churchill's summary of the talks between Soviet and Polish officials (Oct. 14, 1944, *FRUS*, 1944, III, 1322–23).

The situation in Yugoslavia troubled Churchill because the leader of the Partisans, Tito, had gone to Moscow for secret conversations with Soviet officials without first telling the British. In spite of assurances from Stalin that Tito was not a Soviet puppet, Churchill feared that Yugoslavia would fall under Soviet domination. The Prime Minister spoke of a 50–50 division of British-Soviet influence in Yugoslavia, but he presumed that would eventually mean an independent, pro-British government in that country.

C–799

Moscow [via U.S. Army, London]
Oct. 18, 1944, 1215 Z (London) / TOR 1511 Z

Prime Minister to President Roosevelt. Personal and Top Secret.

I send you in my immediately following text of document to which Mikolajczyk's delegation agreed together with two amendments on which Stalin insisted. Mikolajczyk said that if he accepted the first of these amendments he would be repudiated by his own people. Stalin's position is that in this case it is not worth while proceeding to the difficult discussions arising out of the second amendment. These could probably have been surmounted had the first been accepted.

2. Both the London and the Lublin Poles will now return home to consult their colleagues on outstanding points and our communique from here will explain that progress has been made and differences narrowed. Meanwhile, only the London Poles and Russians know of this document and every endeavour will be made to prevent it leaking out, though London Poles will have to consult some of their people.

3. You will see I have not gone at all beyond the position adopted by His Majesty's Government in your presence at Tehran, though possibly the regions to be ceded by Germany have been more precisely stated. I have made it clear throughout that you are not committed in any way by what I have said and done. It only amounts to a promise on the part of His Majesty's Government to support the Curzon Line and its compen-

sations at the armistice or peace conference, which alone can give a final and legal validity to all territorial changes. I have already informed Parliament in open session of our support of Curzon Line as a basis for frontier settlement in the cast, and our twenty year treaty with Russia makes it desirable for us to define our position to a degree not called for from the United States at the present time.

4. I should however mention, though no doubt Averell will have reported, that Molotov stated at our opening meeting with the London Poles that you had expressed agreement with the Curzon Line at Teheran. I informed Stalin afterwards that neither I nor Eden could confirm this statement. Stalin thereupon said that he had had a private conversation with you, not at the table, when you had concurred in the policy of the Curzon Line, though you had expressed a hope about Lwow being retained by the Poles. I could not, of course, deal with this assertion. Several times in the course of my long talks with him, he emphasized his earnest desire for your return at the election and of the advantage to Russia and to the world which that would be. Therefore, you may be sure that no indiscretion will occur from the Russian side.

5. Meanwhile, in other directions, considerable advantages have been gained. You have already been informed about the obvious resolve of the Soviet Government to attack Japan on the overthrow of Hitler, of their detailed study of the problem and of their readiness to begin inter-Allied preparations on a large scale. When we are vexed with other matters, we must remember the supreme value of this in shortening the whole struggle.

6. Arrangements made about the Balkans are, I am sure, the best that are possible. Coupled with our successful military action recently we should now be able to save Greece and, I have no doubt that agreement to pursue a fifty-fifty joint policy in Yugoslavia will be the best solution for our difficulties in view of Tito's behaviour and changes in the local situation, resulting from the arrival of Russian and Bulgarian forces under Russian command to help Tito's eastern flank. The Russians are insistent on their ascendency in Roumania and Bulgaria as the Black Sea countries.

7. Although I hear most encouraging accounts from various quarters about United States politics, I feel the suspense probably far more than you do or more than I should if my own affairs were concerned in this zone. My kindest regards and warmest good wishes.

[MR*. *FRUS*, 1944, III, 1325–27. p*FRUS, Teheran Conf.*, pp. 884–85. *R&C*.]

C–800

Moscow [via U.S. Army, London]
Oct. 18, 1944, 1227 Z (London) / TOR 1512 Z

Prime Minister to President Roosevelt. Personal and Top Secret.

This is text referred to in Paragraph One of my immediately preceding telegram. Text begins:

"British and Soviet Governments, upon conclusions of discussions at Moscow in October 1944 between themselves and with Polish Government, have reached the following agreement.

"2. Upon unconditional surrender of Germany, territory of Poland in west will include the Free City of Danzig, the regions of East Prussia, West and South Konigsberg, the administrative district of Oppeln in Silesia and lands desired by Poland to east of line of the Oder. It is further agreed that possession of these territories shall be guaranteed to Poland by Soviet and British Governments. It is understood that Germans in said regions shall be repatriated to Germany and that all Poles in Germany shall at their wish be repatriated to Poland.

"3. In consideration of foregoing agreement, the Polish Government accept Curzon Line as basis for frontier between Poland and USSR.

"4. Separate Soviet-Polish agreements will regulate reciprocal transfer and repatriation of population of both countries and release of persons detained. It is agreed that necessary measures will be taken for the transfer of all persons of both countries desiring to change their allegiance in accordance with their freely expressed wishes.

"5. It is agreed that a Polish Government of National Unity under Prime Minister Mikolajczyk will be set up at once in territory already liberated by Russian arms.

"6. The Soviet Government take this occasion of reaffirming their unchanging policy of supporting establishment within the territorial limits set forth of a sovereign independent Poland, free in every way to manage its own affairs, and their intention to make a treaty of durable friendship and mutual aid with Polish Government, which it is understood will be established on an anti-Fascist and democratic basis.

"7. The treaties and relationships existing between Poland and other countries will be unaffected by this settlement, the parties to which declare again their implacable resolve to wage war against Nazi tyranny until it has surrendered unconditionally." End of text.

Herewith amendments to text:
Paragraph Five should read as follows:

It is agreed that Polish Government of National Unity in accordance with agreement (or understanding) reached between the Polish Government in London and Polish Committee of National Liberation in Lublin will be set up at once in territory already liberated by Russian armies. (Amendment to Para Five ends).

(Further amendment). Note reference to second amendment Stalin said he agreed that M. Mikolajczyk should be Prime Minister. End of amendment.

[MR*. *FRUS*, 1944, III, 1327–28. *R&C*.]

The State Department had recommended that the United States extend recognition to the French provisional government and had drafted an affirmative answer to Churchill's suggestion that Britain and the United States move toward such recognition. Harry Hopkins disagreed, however, and drafted an answer which required additional steps toward parliamentary democracy—and a limiting of de Gaulle's personal authority—before extending recognition. Roosevelt agreed with Hopkins and signed that draft after making only minor changes.

R–631, draft A, not sent

Washington
Oct. 16, 1944

From: The President
To: The Prime Minister

We have been following the French situation very closely and have kept actively under consideration the question of recognition of the French Provisional Government since we have always felt that this recognition should be extended as soon as the situation in France warranted in the light of the policy which we have consistently followed.

I share the opinion expressed in your 798 that the situation in France has developed to a point where the extension of recognition to the Provisional Government of the French Republic is justified and desirable.

I believe that either the occasion of a vote of confidence to the administration by an enlarged Consultative Assembly or the establishment of the Interior Zone would provide a useful peg on which to hang our action. Of the two alternatives, I share your preference for the latter.

I will have the State Department get in touch with the Foreign Office, and they can work out the necessary details together, and notify the Soviet authorities who might wish to take concurrent action.

I fully agree that our decision in this matter need not involve such separate questions as that of French membership in the European Advisory Commission. [CH]

[MR]

Churchill had contacted pneumonia just before the Quebec Conference, although his fever had disappeared by the time the talks began. Then, on October 15, during the TOLSTOY conversations, his temperature again rose above normal, although Lord Moran, his personal physician, attributed that to intestinal problems, not a recurrence of pneumonia. After a day the fever left, but Lord Moran remained concerned that the Prime Minister had "developed a bad habit of running a temperature on these journeys" (Moran, *Churchill*, pp. 216, 232). The changes in this message were presumably made by the President.

R–631

Washington [via U.S. Navy]
Oct. 19, 1944, 7:40 P.M.

Personal and Top Secret from the President for the Prime Minister.

Replying to your 798. I think until the French set up a real zone of interior that we should make no move towards recognizing them as a provisional government. The enlargement of the Consultative Assembly which has already been extended and made more representative is almost as important and I should be inclined to hang ~~additional~~ recognition on the effective completion of both these acts. I would not be satisfied with De Gaulle merely saying that he was going to do it.

I agree with you that there must be no implication, if and when we do recognize a provisional government, that this means a seat on the European Advisory Council, etc. These matters can be taken up later on their merits.

I am anxious to handle this matter, for the present, directly between you and me and would prefer, for the moment, that the modus operandi not become a matter of discussion between the State Department and your Foreign Office.

Let me know your views upon this message.

Harriman's messages indicate that you have had a good and useful conference and I shall be anxiously waiting to get a final summation from you.

~~I do hope your health has not been undermined.~~

<u>I do hope you are free of the temperature and really feeling all right again.</u> Roosevelt [HLH]

[MR* (with draft). *FRUS*, 1944, III, 741. p*WSC*, VI, 247–48. *R&C*.]

The conversations between Polish Prime Minister Mikolajczyk (Mik) and the chairman of the Soviet-sponsored Polish National Council (the Lublin Poles), Boleslaw Bierut (Berut), accomplished little. Stalin refused to confront Churchill on the issue of the makeup of any Polish coalition, but made it clear that he would settle for nothing less than a pro-Soviet government.

Churchill had long favored some sort of Danubian federation, failing to realize that the forces of nationalism which had destroyed the Austro-Hungarian Empire were too intense for such a union to develop and function, at least voluntarily.

Churchill appears to have been genuinely angered by the refusal of Turkish President Ismet Inönü to bring his country into the war against Germany, even though the British Foreign Office strongly opposed any revision of the Montreux Convention. The curious fears among British policy-makers of a renewal of Franco-Soviet ties surfaced in a memo from Churchill to Eden in which the Prime Minister claimed that the British fleet could cope with any joint Franco-Soviet fleet in the Mediterranean (Woodward, *British Foreign Policy*, IV, 202). Roosevelt's suggestion of a Black Sea port as the site for a Big Three meeting was made through Harry Hopkins.

Churchill left Moscow on October 19, after Stalin had uncharacteristically appeared at the airport to bid the Prime Minister farewell. After meetings in Cairo with Admiral Mountbatten, the Supreme Commander in the South East Asia theater, Churchill and his party flew on to England via Naples.

C–801

enroute London [via U.S. Army, London]
Oct. 22, 1944, 1014 Z (London) / TOR 1437 Z

Prime Minister to President Roosevelt Personal and Top Secret.

Many thanks for your number 631.

1. On our last day at Moscow Mik saw Berut who admitted his difficulties. Fifty of his men had been shot in the last month. Many Poles took to the woods rather than join his forces. Approaching winter conditions behind the front could be very hard as the Russian army moved forward using all transport. He insisted however that if Mik were premier he must have 75% of the cabinet. Mik proposed that each of the five Polish parties should be represented, he naming four out of the five of their best men whom he would pick from personalities not obnoxious to Stalin.

2. Later at my request Stalin saw Mik and had one and one-quarter hours very friendly talk. Stalin promised to help him and Mik promised to form and conduct a government thoroughly friendly to the Russians. He explained his plan but Stalin made it clear that the Lublin Poles must have the majority.

3. After the Kremlin dinner we put it bluntly to Stalin that unless Mik had 50/50 plus himself the western world would not be convinced that the transaction was bona fide and would not believe that an independent Polish government had been set up. Stalin at first replied he would be content with 50/50 but rapidly corrected himself to a worse figure. Meanwhile Eden took the same line with Molotov who seemed more comprehending. I do not think the composition of the government will prove an insuperable obstacle if all else is settled. Mik had previously explained to me that there might be one announcement to save the prestige of the Lublin government and a different arrangement among the Poles behind the scenes.

4. Apart from the above Mik is going to urge upon his London colleagues the Curzon line including Lwow for the Russians. I am hopeful that even in the next fortnight we may get a settlement. If so I will cable you the exact form so that you can say whether you want it published or delayed.

5. Major war criminals U. J. took an unexpectedly ultra-respectable line. There must be no executions without trial otherwise the world would say we were afraid to try them. I pointed out the difficulties in International law but he replied if there were no trials there must be no death sentences, but only life-long confinements. In face of this view from this quarter I do not wish to press the memo I gave you [C–783/8] which you said you would have examined by the State Department. Kindly therefore treat it as withdrawn.

6. We also discussed informally the future partition of Germany. U. J. wants Poland Czecho and Hungary to form a realm of independent anti-Nazi pro-Russian states, the first two of which might join together. Contrary to his previously expressed view, he would be glad to see Vienna the capital of a federation of south-German states, including Austria, Bavaria, Wurtemburg and Baden. As you know, the idea of Vienna becoming the capital of a large Danubian federation has always been attractive to me, though I should prefer to add Hungary, to which U. J. is strongly opposed.

7. As to Prussia, U. J. wished the Ruhr and the Saar detached and put out of action and probably under international control and a separate state formed in the Rhineland. He would also like the internationalization of the Kiel canal. I am not opposed to this line of thought. However, you may be sure that we came to no fixed conclusions pending the triple meeting.

8. I was delighted to hear from U. J. that you had suggested a triple meeting towards the end of November at a Black Sea port. I think this a very fine idea, and hope you will let me know about it in due course. I will come anywhere you two desire.

9. U. J. also raised formally the Montreux Convention, wishing for modification for the free passage of Russian warships. We did not contest this in principle. Revision is clearly necessary as Japan is a signatory and Inonu missed his market last December. We left it that detailed proposals should be made from the Russian side. He said they would be moderate.

10. About recognizing the present French administration as the provisional government of France, I will consult the cabinet on my return. Opinion of UK is very strongly for immediate recognition. De Gaulle is no longer sole master, but is better harnessed than ever before. I am sure he will make all the mischief he can, but I still think that when Eisenhower proclaims a large zone of the interior for France it would not be possible to delay this limited form of recognition. Undoubtedly De Gaulle has the majority of the French nation behind him and the French government hold support against potential anarchy in large areas. I will however cable you again from London. I am now in the air above Alamein of blessed memory. Kindest regards.

[MR*. *FRUS*, 1944, IV, 1022–24. p*FRUS, Yalta Conf.*, pp. 10, 159–60, 206, 328, 400. *R&C*.]

Roosevelt presumed that any settlement of the Soviet-Polish dispute would be unpopular with Polish-American voters, hence his request that any announcement be postponed until after the November election.

At the same time that the President indicated he was not quite ready to recognize the French provisional government, Acting Secretary of State Edward Stettinius was informing American representatives in Europe that Roosevelt had decided to extend such recognition (Stettinius to Caffery, Oct. 21, 1944, *FRUS*, 1944, III, 744).

R–632

Hyde Park, N.Y. [via U.S. Navy]
Oct. 22, 1944, 3:45 P.M.

Personal and Top Secret, from the President to the Prime Minister.

Your 795, 796, 797, 799, 800 and 801 received.

I am delighted to learn of your success at Moscow in making progress toward a compromise solution of the Polish problem.

When and if a solution is arrived at, I should like to be consulted as to the advisability from this point of view of delaying its publication for about two weeks. You will understand.

Everything is going well here at the present time.

Your statement of the present attitude of U.J. towards war criminals, the future of Germany, and Montreux convention is most interesting. We should discuss these matters together with our Pacific war effort at the forthcoming three party meeting.

In regard to recognizing a Provisional Government of France, I will communicate with you on this matter as soon as Eisenhower reports having established a zone of the interior which is expected within the next few days.

The selection of a Black Sea port for our next meeting seems to be dependent upon our ability to get through the Dardanelles safely as I wish to proceed by ship. Do you think it is possible to get U.J. to come to Athens or Cyprus. Roosevelt [WDL]

[MR*. pFRUS, *Yalta Conf.*, pp. 10, 207. pWSC, VI, 242. *R&C*.]

The background to this message is discussed in the headnote to C–783/5.

C–802

enroute London? [via U.S. Army, London]
Oct. 22, 1944, 1125 Z (London) / TOR 1437 Z

Prime Minister to President Roosevelt Personal and Top Secret.

We agreed at Quebec that MacMillan should be appointed acting president of the Allied Control Commission in Italy. In order to put this decision into effect I suggest the following announcement should be issued simultaneously in Washington and London by our two Governments:— "As already announced the President of the United States and Prime Minister of Great Britain recently reviewed the situation in Italy and agreed on a general policy to meet the many economic and other difficulties of that country. In order to facilitate the task they have agreed that the Right Honourable Harold MacMillan, M. P., British Resident Minister at AFHQ, Mediterranean, should, in addition to his present post, become responsible head of the Allied Commission. In order to effect this, General Wilson will delegate to Mr. MacMillan his functions as president of the Commission. Captain Stone of the United States Navy at present acting chief commissioner, will be appointed chief commissioner. Mr. MacMillan as acting president will be specially charged with duty of supervising development of new measures together with any change in structure of commission necessary to carry them out."

Please let me know if you approve.

[MR]

To Churchill's surprise, the State Department won its campaign to recognize the French provisional government. The change in this message resulted when the British asked that it not be delivered to the President until a change arrived in Washington. The initial draft was received at 1955 Z, and the correction came in at 0317 Z, October 23. The Map Room staff and Harry Hopkins were just as surprised as Churchill, as the following log-sheet summary demonstrates:

> This message caused considerable confusion in the Map Room. No previous information had been received in the Map Room that the US and UK would make announcement recognizing the Provisional French Govt at 12:00 noon, 23 Oct 44. Mr. Hopkins phoned James Dunn in State Dept. at 231503Z. Informed that Mr. Stettinius had met with President in New York on Saturday evening, 21 Oct 44, and that President had given his approval to recognition of Provisional Govt. The text of the announcement, together with release time, had been sent via State to London and Moscow (log sheet attached to C–803, MR).

C–803

London [via U.S. Army]
Oct. 23, 1944; 1815 Z, Oct. 22 / TOR 1955 Z, Oct. 22 and 0317 Z, Oct. 23

Prime Minister to President Roosevelt. Personal and Top Secret.

In view of your number 631 in reply to my number 798 I was naturally surprised at the very sharp turn taken by the State Department and on arrival here I find the announcement is to be made tomorrow. We shall, of course, take similar and simultaneous action. ~~I am sure the Russians will be very much offended.~~ I think it likely that the Russians will be offended. Molotov in conversation said that he expected they would be made to appear the ones who were obstructing, whereas they would have recognized long ago but had deferred to American and British wishes. I hope therefore it has been possible to bring them in.

[MR*. WSC, VI, 249. R&C.]

Churchill's bewilderment about the recognition of the French provisional government was finally ended with the receipt of R–633, which crossed this cable in transmission.

Roosevelt did cable Stalin with suggestions about places for a Big Three meeting. (See R–635.)

On Saturday, October 21, Roosevelt had made a four-hour, fifty-mile drive through four of New York City's boroughs, riding in an open car during a steady rain. For a man who had suffered an attack of angina pectoris earlier that summer, it was dangerous, but it proved a huge political success, burying until after the election the rumors of the President's ill-health. The "Group Undecipherable" comment is explained below in C–805.

C–804

London [via U.S. Army]
Oct. 23, 1944, 1552 Z / TOR 1815 Z

Prime Minister to President Roosevelt Personal and Top Secret.

1. I am bewildered by the reference in your No 632 to recognizing the provisional government in France. Matters have already moved far beyond the stage mentioned in your third sentence from the end. However I am in full agreement with the result which is to be announced tonight at five thirty GMT.

2. U. J.'s doctors do not like him flying and I suppose there would be the same difficulties in Russian warships coming out of the Black Sea as of American and British warships coming in. One way would be for Turkey to declare war, which I expect she would be very willing to do. But I am not at all sure that the Russians would welcome this at the present juncture in view of what I told you about their wish for revision of the Treaty of Montreux. Alternatively we could ask Turkey to waive the Montreux Treaty for the passage either way of the said ships. This I expect the Russians would like. But I am not so sure about the Turks. From what I saw of the Crimea it seems much shattered and I expect all other Black Sea ports are in a similar state. We should therefore in all probability have to live on board our ships. I am inquiring about Athens from Eden who will be there in a day or two. Personally I should think it a splendid setting and here again we should have our ships handy. Cyprus is of course available where absolute secrecy, silence and security can be guaranteed together with plain comfortable accommodation for all principals. Will you telegraph to U. J. on the subject, or shall I? Or, better still, shall we send a joint message?

3. I was delighted to see the proofs of your robust vigour in New York. Nevertheless I cannot believe that four hours in an open car and pouring rain with a temperature of 40 and clothes wet through conform to those limits of prudence which you would be so ready to prescribe if it were my case. I earnestly hope you are none the worse and should be grateful for reassurance. I cannot think about anything except this Group Undecipherable election.

[MR*. pFRUS, Yalta Conf., pp. 10–11. pR&C.]

Resting in Hyde Park after his grueling visit to New York City, Roosevelt apologized to Churchill for the confusion regarding recognition of the French provisional government. It is not certain, however, whether the President was being totally candid, although it is possible that the State Department misunderstood the instructions given to Stettinius. (See headnote to C–803.) Roosevelt's personal feelings about de Gaulle, if not his official policy, are perhaps revealed in an anecdote told by Curtis Roosevelt, the President's eldest grandson. During a gathering of the family at Christmas in 1944, Roosevelt offered to let young Curtis keep a large, functional model submarine. When Eleanor Roosevelt cautioned that the model had been a present from Charles de Gaulle and that a gift from a foreign head of state should not be given away, the President dismissed her objection with the statement that de Gaulle was not a head of state but just the head of some French committee or another.

R–633

Hyde Park, N.Y. [via U.S. Navy]
Oct. 23, 1944, 1:15 P.M.

Top Secret and Personal. From the President for the Prime Minister.

Replying to your 803, I am informed that Moscow as well as London had timely information as to time of release of announcement regarding Provisional Government of France.

I regret that my absence from Washington resulted in more precipitate action by State Department than was contemplated in my 631 to you.

I hope that the final result will be beneficial. Roosevelt [WDL, WEB]

[MR*. R&C.]

The Map Room staff titled this message "PM's pun on 1944 election. 'Group undecipherable' election." The pun must have been an in-joke between Churchill and Roosevelt, but it is not a mistake, for the same message is repeated in the British records.

C–805

London [via U.S. Army]
October 23, 1944, 2015 Z / TOR 2200 Z

Prime Minister to President Roosevelt. Personal and Top Secret.
Reference Paragraph 3 of my number 804.
For "group undecipherable", read "six groups undecipherable."

[MR*]

General Joseph Stilwell, who commanded American forces in the China-Burma-India theater and was Deputy Supreme Allied Commander of the South East Asia Command, also served as Joint (Allied) Chief of Staff to Generalissimo Chiang Kai-shek. In that capacity he tried to force Chiang to bring the Chinese communists into a military coalition against the Japanese. Nothing could have better epitomized Stilwell's lack of sensitivity to recent Chinese history. The differences, both personal and political, between Chiang and the communist leaders were irreconcilable, and Chiang demanded Stilwell's recall. Roosevelt tried to get Chiang to reconsider, but the Generalissimo remained adamant. Annoyed by Chiang Kai-shek's uncooperativeness, General Marshall insisted that the Americans no longer accept responsibility for the operations of Chinese forces within China. Moreover, the American Command in China was split, thus diminishing its prestige.

R–634

Washington [via U.S. Navy]
Oct. 24, 1944, 11:25 A.M.

Personal and Top Secret, from the President for the Prime Minister.

I will make the following announcement of changes in the American command in China and Burma at noon October 28 Washington time:

QUOTE. General Stilwell has been relieved as Chief of Staff to Generalissimo Chiang Kai-shek, as Deputy to Admiral Mountbatten, Commander of the South East Asia Command, and as U.S. Commander of the China-Burma-India Theater and has been recalled to Washington. The former China-Burma-India Theater will be divided into two theaters under separate commanders. The U. S. Forces in the China Theater will be commanded by Major General A. C. Wedemeyer, who will also hold a staff position under the Generalissimo. General Wedemeyer is now Deputy Chief of Staff to Admiral Mountbatten. The India-Burma Theater will be commanded by Lieutenant General Daniel I. Sultan, now Deputy Commander of the China-Burma-India Theater. UNQUOTE.

Roosevelt

[MR*]

Roosevelt's message to Stalin, quoted below, may have led the Soviet Premier to believe that the United States agreed with the "percentages" division of eastern Europe worked out at the TOLSTOY Conference. (The third from the last sentence of the message to Stalin spoke of Malta and Cyprus vice Malta and Athens. See *Stalin/FDR*, doc. 237.)

R–635

Washington [via U.S. Navy]
Oct. 24, 1944, 11:40 A.M.

Personal and Top Secret, from the President for the Prime Minister.

Your 804. Regarding the Provisional Government mix-up, I hope it has now cleared to a satisfactory conclusion (see my 633).

I have today sent the following to U.J.:

QUOTE: I am delighted to learn from your message dated October 19 and from reports by Ambassador Harriman of the success attained by you and Mr. Churchill in approaching an agreement on a number of questions that are of high interest to all of us in our common desire to secure and maintain a satisfactory and a durable peace. I am sure that the progress made during your conversations in Moscow will facilitate and expedite our work in the next meeting when the three of us should come to a full agreement on our future activities and policies and mutual interests.

We all must investigate the practicability of various places where our meeting in November can be held such as accessibility, living accommodations, security, etc., and I would appreciate suggestions from you.

I have been thinking about the practicability of Malta, or Athens, or Cyprus if my getting into the Black Sea on a ship should be impracticable or too difficult. I prefer traveling and living on a ship.

We know that the living conditions and security in Malta and Athens are satisfactory.

I am looking forward with much pleasure to seeing you again.

Please let me have your suggestions and advice. UNQUOTE.

I would, of course, prefer to have him come to the Mediterranean which would be more convenient for all of us.

My journey to New York was useful and rain does not hurt an old sailor. Thank you for your advice nevertheless. I am in top form for the "group undecipherable" election. Roosevelt [WDL]

[MR*. p*FRUS, Yalta Conf.*, pp. 11–12. *R&C.*]

Roosevelt and the State Department had no objection to the changes Churchill proposed for the Allied Control Commission in Italy.

R–636

Washington [via U.S. Navy]
Oct. 24, 1944, 11:45 A.M.

Top Secret and Personal, from the President for the Prime Minister.

Your 802. The announcement contained in your message is acceptable to me. Its simultaneous announcement at noon Washington time on November 10 will be satisfactory and it will be announced here at that time unless you fail to agree. Please let me know. Roosevelt [State Dept.]

[MR*]

The reconstruction of the Italian government required a number of adjustments. The status of Italian soldiers in Germany was particularly important to the Italians.

C–806

London [via U.S. Army]
Oct. 24, 1944, 1628 Z / TOR 1915 Z

Prime Minister to President Roosevelt. Personal and Top Secret.

There are two minor matters connected with the change of policy towards Italy which were mentioned in our talks but not covered by our public joint declaration at Hyde Park.

1. There is at present a partial ban on intercourse between British and Italian diplomats throughout the world. We propose that this should be raised.

2. We suggest the British and American governments should declare that they consider the six hundred thousand or so Italian soldiers at present interned in Germany, who are not regarded by the German government as prisoners of war, should be entitled to prisoner of war treatment, and that appropriate measures will be taken against those responsible for maltreating Italian prisoners as soon as they fall into our hands.

Please let me know if you concur.

[MR*]

This cable crossed R–636, in which Roosevelt agreed to the personnel changes proposed by Churchill. The Prime Minister feared the collapse of the Italian government unless food supplies were increased and the Italian leaders had the firm support of the Allies.

C–807

London [via U.S. Army]
Oct. 24, 1944, 1710 Z / TOR 1915 Z

Prime Minister to President Roosevelt. Personal and Top Secret.
   Please see my number 802.
   I am anxious to get this settled. When I passed through Naples three days ago, I had long talks with General Wilson, MacMillan and other authorities there. The situation in Italy is not good and might sharply deteriorate. There was a serious riot in Sicily and there has been trouble at Pisa. General Wilson spoke to me with anxiety about the whole position, particularly that the Allied Control Commission had been without a head now for nearly ten weeks. I certainly take my full share of the blame for this, but I should like to get it settled now; otherwise, there may be trouble for all of us.

[MR*. R&C.]

Cables C–807 and R–636 had crossed in transmission. The delay in announcing the changes in the Allied Commission for Italy was because of the presidential election, scheduled for Tuesday, November 7.

R–637

Washington [via U.S. Navy]
Oct. 24, 1944, 8:45 P.M.

Personal and Top Secret, for the Prime Minister from the President.
   Your 806. I am in agreement with your proposed joint statement in regard to Italian soldiers interned in Germany and not regarded by the German Government as prisoners of war.
   I have no objection to your raising ban on intercourse between British and Italian diplomats. State Department informs me that we have had no such difficulty.
   Your 807 seems to be answered by my 636. I am sure you understand my desire to delay the announcement until November 10 but I am willing to advance the date if you desire. Roosevelt [WDL]

[MR*]

Cable R–635 concerned the French provisional government, the presidential campaign, and a message to Stalin about a Big Three conference.

C–808

London [via U.S. Army]
Oct. 25, 1944, 0812 Z / TOR 1200 Z

Prime Minister to President Roosevelt Personal and Top Secret.
  Your 635.
  I like it all.

[MR*]

Roosevelt and Churchill continued personally to coordinate public statements regarding anti-submarine warfare, and American naval leaders continued to worry about security in the Pacific and distrust Britain's commitment to the Pacific war.

C–809

London [via U.S. Army]
Oct. 25, 1944, 1434 Z / TOR 1635 Z

Prime Minister to President Roosevelt. Personal and Top Secret.
  We want to include in a forthcoming publication of statistics of the British war effort yearly figures of merchant shipping losses—British, Allied and neutral—since the outbreak of the war. We are satisfied no security questions are involved, but in view of our agreement of July 1943, about statements on submarine warfare, I ask your assent to this publication.

[MR*]

R–638

Washington [via U.S. Navy]
Oct. 26, 1944, 8:52 P.M.

Personal and Top Secret, from the President for the Prime Minister.
  Your 809. I find no objection to your publication of shipping losses since outbreak of war to and including December, 1943, but because of security involved prefer to not publish losses since January first, 1944. Please inform me in advance date of issue in order that we may arrange for simultaneous release. Roosevelt [WDL]

[MR*]

Churchill agreed to delay the announcement of charges in the Control Commission for Italy until after the presidential election, although he wanted to get started immediately on programs designed to prop up the Italian government.

C–810

London [via U.S. Army]
Oct. 27, 1944, 1450 Z / TOR 1644 Z

Prime Minister to President Roosevelt. Personal and Top Secret.

Acceptable to us is November 10th as the date reference your 636 of the announcement about Italy and I will arrange for publication here to be simultaneous with the announcement in Washington. Meanwhile we are telling them to get on with the job in anticipation of the formal announcement.

[MR*]

General Stilwell had no love for the British and had previously refused British decorations.

C–811

London [via U.S.Army]
Oct. 27, 1944, 1730 Z / TOR 1940 Z

Prime Minister to President Roosevelt Personal and Top Secret.

I agree with the suggested announcement of changes in the American command contained in your number 634. For the sake of clarity I suggest that the last sentence should read: "General Wedemeyer is now Deputy Chief of Staff to Admiral Mountbatten. The United States Forces in the India/Burma theater will be commanded by Lieutenant General Daniel I. Sultan, now Deputy Commander of the China/Burma/India theater."

2. I had intended to submit General Stilwell's name to the King for KCB. Is there any objection to this?

[MR*]

C–812

London [via U.S. Army]
Oct. 27, 1944, 1725 Z / TOR 1940 Z

Prime Minister to President Roosevelt Personal and Top Secret.

Is there any objection to my publishing my immediately following?

[MR]

On October 20, soldiers from the U.S. Sixth Army made a landing on the east coast of Leyte island, in the central Philippines. As part of a major counter-attack, the Japanese Navy engaged American naval vessels which were defending the invasion force. At the end of the six-day naval battle of Leyte Gulf, which ended on October 27, the Japanese fleet had been eliminated as a major fighting force, having lost twenty-four warships, including four carriers, three battleships, and nine cruisers. By that time the beachhead had been secured and the U.S. Army had begun to move inland. Australian cruisers HMS *Australia* and *Shropshire* operated with the U.S. Seventh Fleet in the South West Pacific theater.

C–813

London [via U.S. Army]
Oct. 27, 1944, 1742 Z / TOR 1940 Z

Prime Minister to President Roosevelt.

Pray accept my most sincere congratulations which I tender on behalf of His Majesty's Government on the brilliant and massive victory gained by the sea and air forces of the United States over the Japanese in the recent heavy battles.

We are very glad to know that one of His Majesty's Australian cruiser squadrons had the honour of sharing in this memorable event.

[MR. *WSC*, VI, 186.]

R–639

Washington [via U.S. Navy]
Oct. 27, 1944, 5:30 P.M.

Top Secret and Personal for the Prime Minister from the President.

Your 811. The suggested changes proposed are accepted.

I have no objection to your submitting Stilwell's name for K.C.B. Roosevelt [WDL]

[MR*]

R–640

Washington [via U.S. Navy]
Oct. 27, 1944, 5:30 P.M.

Top Secret and Personal from the President for the Prime Minister.

Your 812. I will be much pleased if you should make public the message contained in your 813. Roosevelt [WDL]

[MR*]

As preoccupied as Roosevelt was with the presidential election, only five days away, the proposed Churchill-Roosevelt-Stalin conference still held his attention. Stalin's message to Roosevelt (*Stalin/FDR*, doc. 238) was brief and simply agreed to a meeting on the Soviet Black Sea coast, nowhere else. Roosevelt's desire to meet somewhere other than the Soviet Union may have been politically inspired, although his health was a very real concern. Piraeus and Salonica are in Greece; Constantinople is in Turkey.

R–641

Washington [via U.S. Navy]
Nov. 2, 1944, 8:25 P.M.

Personal and Top Secret, from the President for the Prime Minister.

Referring to my 635, I have received a reply from U.J. which is not very helpful in the selection of a place for our next meeting. He states that if our meeting on the Soviet Black Sea Coast is acceptable he considers it an extremely desirable plan.

His doctors to whose opinion he must give consideration do not wish him to make any "big trips."

He gave me no information as to location of the meeting, accessibility, living conditions, etc., except to express a hope that it will be possible to provide a safe entrance for my ship into the Black Sea.

He will be glad to see me as soon as I find it possible to make the trip.

I do not wish to go to the Black Sea if it can be avoided, first because the Congress will be in session at that time which makes it imperative that I be at all times within rapid mail communication with Washington by Air Mail, and, second because of sanitary conditions.

Dr. McIntire tells me that health conditions in Black Sea ports such as Odessa are very bad, and we must think of the health of our staff and our ships' crews as well as ourselves.

What do you think of the possibility of our inducing U.J. to meet with us in Piraeus, Salonica, or Constantinople. Any of these would not be a "big trip" for him.

Please give me your advice as to the best date for the meeting from your point of view, together with any information you may have in regard to a suitable place for the meeting, danger from enemy action, living conditions, etc. I will take a ship to wherever we may go.

I fear that Uncle Joe will insist on the Black Sea. I do think it important that we three should meet in the near future.

All advice and assistance that you can contribute to the solution of this problem will be appreciated. Roosevelt [WDL]

[MR*. *FRUS, Yalta Conf.*, pp. 12–13. pR&C.]

Churchill was just as dubious about the Black Sea area as was Roosevelt, and the Prime Minister was piqued at Stalin's refusal to leave the Soviet Union.

C–814

London [via U.S. Army]
Nov. 5, 1944, 0920 Z / TOR 1312 Z

Personal and Top Secret from the Prime Minister to President Roosevelt.

1. Your number 641. I send you in my immediately following the report which I called for from the First Sea Lord. The whole matter has been carefully studied by the Admiralty and, as you will see, every port is reported on separately. Our sailors have pretty good knowledge of these ports. On all this I consider the Black Sea out of the question and the Piraeus very little better.

2. I am somewhat attracted by the suggestion of Jerusalem. Here there are first-class hotels, government houses, etc., and every means can be taken to ensure security. The warships could probably lie at Haifa unless the weather turned very rough, in which case they could go to Port Said or Alexandria.

3. Alexandria would probably be a feasible proposition.

4. U.J., could come by special train, with every form of protection, from Moscow to Jerusalem. I am having the timetables of the journeys studied and will telegraph to you about them.

5. I think we ought to put the proposition to U.J., and throw on him the onus of refusing. After all, we are respectable people too.

6. In the event of his not coming, I earnestly hope you will pay your long-promised and deferred visit to Great Britain and then visit your armies in France. The right thing would be to have the conference between us in Britain. I have trenched so often on your hospitality. We could not doubt get Molotov to deputize for Stalin. He counts for a lot.

7. Perhaps you would send me a draft of the telegram we should send to Stalin, after considering the information I am now sending you.

[MR*. *FRUS, Yalta Conf.*, pp. 13–14.]

The report by the Admiralty emphasized the problems of all the suggested locations for a Big Three conference, but strongly opposed the Black Sea site.

C–815

London [via U.S. Army]
Nov. 5, 1944, 0920 Z / TOR 1650 Z

Prime Minister to President Roosevelt Personal and Top Secret.
The report of the First Sea Lord referred to in my number 814 follows:

I have examined the various alternatives for the forthcoming meeting. The considerations are as follows.

During November and December weather conditions are such that it is most desirable for ships to be berthed in a protected anchorage.

Weather conditions in the Aegean and Black Sea are usually bad in the winter, but good in the southern part of the eastern Mediterranean.

The northern part of the Black Sea and the approaches to the Crimea have been heavily mined. Russian minesweeping is an unknown quantity.

There may well be great difficulty in obtaining Turkish consent to the passage of warships through the Dardanelles, which is contrary to the Montreux Convention. It is possible that the only solution would be for Turkey to become a belligerent. This question is, however, one for the Foreign Office.

A British cruiser could be sent to pick up passengers at any port in the Aegean or eastern Mediterranean, and, with some risk, at any Black Sea port.

My conclusions in general terms are as follows:

(A) Black Sea and Crimean ports should be ruled out on account of the minefields in the Black Sea and at the entrance to the Dardanelles. I would certainly not advise the safety of valuable units being dependent on Russian minesweeping. In addition, there is the almost certain lack of amenities, and bad weather conditions. The Montreux Convention is also relevant.

(B) In the Bosphorus the weather conditions are slightly better, and there are reasonably good anchorages. There is, however, the mining danger and the Montreux difficulty as in subpara (A) above.

(C) Aegean—battleships cannot enter the Piraeus. Phalerum Bay is a possible alternative but an open anchorage, and here again there is some danger from mines. Salonika, though good anchorage, has no amenities and malaria is rife. Mineable waters which have not yet been swept extend a long way from the port.

(D) Cyprus-Famagusta and Limassol are possible. But both are open anchorages. Malaria is prevalent and they are not recommended.

(E) Levant—Beirut and Haifa are open anchorages, but the weather should be moderate. There is reasonably good accommodation ashore. Haifa has rail and first class road communication with Jerusalem.

(F) Egypt—Alexandria is a first class port with a good climate and excellent accommodation ashore. There is some doubt, however, whether the largest battleships can traverse the approaches to the harbour. This is being confirmed. An alternative is Port Said, where battleships can berth within the harbour.

(G) Malta—An excellent harbour and some accommodation ashore.

Conclusions:

I find great difficulty in making any recommendation to suit all the conditions. The Aegean and Black Sea in my opinion are no places to hold conferences in the winter, let alone the mining danger. Of the ports considered above, I would recommend Alexandria first, with Port Said as its alternative if battleships cannot enter, and secondly Haifa, but this presupposes that Marshall Stalin is prepared to make the long journey by train across Turkey or by sea from a Black Sea port. Failing these, Malta of course provides the necessary battleship anchorage and some accommodation.

Detailed notes on the various ports follow:

Black Sea ports—two considerations apply to all Black Sea ports:

(1) The Montreux Convention:

(2) Widespread mining is known to have been carried out, and the extent of sweeping by the Russians is unknown. The whole of the north-west section of the Black Sea (including Sevastopol, Nikolaev, Odessa and Constanza) is believed to be heavily mined. Nikolaev insufficient depth of water. Odessa open anchorage only. Constanza open anchorage only. Novorossisk open anchorage only. Crimea Sevastopol open anchorage only. Climate very cold. It is presumed that amenities in these ports have been largely wrecked.

Bosphorus—two considerations apply:

(1) The Montreux Convention;

(2) The approaches to the Dardanelles are known to have been heavily mined, and exact details are not known. Possible anchorages are:

(A) Off Istanbul. There is a very strong current.

(B) One ship in Buyukdere Bay, and the other in Beikos Bay (on the other side of the Bosphorus, about two and one quarter miles away). There is not room for two ships in either of these bays. Therapia is within easy distance (about one mile) by boat from both these bays. Climate cold.

Phalerum Bay the nearest anchorage to Athens which ships could use (within easy reach by road). The anchorage is an open one, but ships could shift to Salamis Bay (also within easy reach) in the event of Phalerum becoming untenable. The approaches were all heavily mined but considerable sweeping has been done (operation MANNA) and cruisers now come and go freely. Suggest route from Russia would be by rail from Tiflis to Beirut, and thence by sea—or it may be possible to go direct by rail through Roumania and Bulgaria. Climate temperate.

Salonika a good protected anchorage, but involving a long approach through waters which may be heavily mined. Malaria is rife. Route from Russia as for Phalerum Bay.

Cyprus only open anchorages are available—off Famagusta and Limassol. Ships could shift from one to the other in the event of bad weather. These places are connected by an asphalt all-weather road, but are 60 miles apart. Suggested route from Russia would be by rail from Tiflis to Beirut, and thence by sea. Accommodation Ashore is limited to government buildings and a few small hotels. Climate temperate. There is a danger of Malaria.

Beirut open anchorage. Climate temperate with little risk of gales, but fairly heavy rainfall. Some hotels. Direct rail communication with Tiflis.

Haifa open anchorage. Climate temperate with little risk of gales, but fairly heavy rainfall. Rail and first class road communication with Jerusalem direct rail communication with Tiflis.

Alexandria a good protected anchorage with ample berthing space for both battleships. It is possible to reach Alexandria by rail from Tiflis. Hotel accommodation plentiful. Climate good.

[MR*]

Field Marshal Sir John Dill had worked closely with the Joint Chiefs of Staff, particularly General Marshall. When the British officer died, on November 4, Marshall felt the loss very keenly, and arranged for Dill to be buried in Arlington National Cemetery. Field Marshal Sir H. Maitland Wilson took over Dill's job on the Combined Chiefs of Staff Committee, but never managed to establish the same close relationship with his American counterparts.

R–642

Hyde Park, N.Y. [via U.S. Navy]
Nov. 6, 1944, 2:00 P.M.

Top Secret and Personal from the President for the Prime Minister.
I should like to express to you my personal sorrow and regret at the

loss of Field Marshal Sir John Dill, who as Great Britain's senior representative on your Combined Staff Mission in America contributed his high soldierly talents and his wide experience with conspicuous success to the solution of our many common war problems.

America joins with Great Britain in sorrow at the loss of your distinguished soldier whose personal admirers here are legion. Roosevelt [FDR]

[MR*. pWSC, VI, 263.]

German U-boat operations were severely limited by the loss of bases in western France.

R–643

Hyde Park, N.Y. [via U.S. Navy]
Nov. 6, 1944, 7:15 P.M.

Secret and Personal from the President for the Prime Minister.

Following is our suggested text of Anti-U-boat statement for October:

QUOTE. The scope of the German U-boats' activities in October 1944 was materially below that of any other month of the war; in consequence of which the number of United Nations' merchant vessels sunk by German submarines during the month was also the lowest of any month of the entire war.

Although the number of German U-boats destroyed was less than what has come to be considered a good monthly "bag", it represented a one-sided ratio as compared to the number of Allied merchant vessels sent to the bottom by the U-boats.

The Allies continue to supply on schedule their ever-growing Armies in Europe. UNQUOTE.

Roosevelt [Navy Dept.]

[MR*]

On November 7, American voters once again chose Franklin Roosevelt for President, although his popular-vote percentage, 52.8, was the lowest of any of his four presidential elections. Roosevelt had never acknowledged receiving Churchill's congratulatory message after the election of 1940 (C–37x), so the Prime Minister tried again.

C–816

London [via U.S. Army]
Nov. 8, 1944, 1300 Z / TOR 1600 Z

Prime Minister to President Roosevelt Personal and Top Secret.

I always said that a great people could be trusted to stand by the pilot who weathered the storm. It is an indescribable relief to me that our comradeship will continue and will help to bring the world out of misery.

I send you, as you have forgotten it, a copy of the telegram I sent you in 1940, much of which is true today. Signed Winston.

[MR*. R&C.]

C–817

London [via U.S. Army]
Nov. 8, 1944, 1300 Z / TOR 1600 Z

Prime Minister to President Roosevelt Personal and Top Secret.

My immediately preceding telegram. Here is the text of what I sent you on November 6, 1940.

I did not think it right for me as a foreigner to express any opinion upon American Politics while the election was on but now I feel that you will not mind my saying that I prayed for your success and that I am truly thankful for it. This does not mean that I seek or wish for anything more than the full, fair and free play of your mind upon the world issues now at stake in which our two nations have to discharge their respective duties.

We are entering upon a sombre phase of what must evidently be a protracted and broadening war, and I look forward to being able to interchange my thoughts with you in all that confidence and good-will which has grown up between us since I went to the Admiralty at the outbreak.

Things are afoot which will be remembered as long as the English language is spoken in any quarter of the globe, and in expressing the comfort I feel that the people of the United States have once again cast these great burdens upon you.

I must avow my sure faith that the lights by which we steer will bring us all safely to anchor.

[MR*]

C–818

London [via U.S. Navy]
Nov. 8, 1944, 1300 Z / TOR 1600 Z

Prime Minister to President Roosevelt Personal and Top Secret.

Your number 643 anti-U-boat statement for October. Proposed text is admirable but would you accept following rewording of paragraph 2 in order to make it a bit clearer for our paper?

"Although the number of German U-boats destroyed was less than what has come to be considered a good monthly "bag", it compares very favourably with the number of Allied merchant vessels sunk by U-boats."

[MR*]

R–644

Hyde Park, N.Y. [via U.S. Navy]
Nov. 8, 1944, 7:45 P.M.

Personal and Secret, from the President for the Prime Minister.

Your 818. I agree. Roosevelt [FDR]

[MR*]

Roosevelt's cable expressing sorrow at the death of Field Marshal Dill had been sent in a cipher which was used for previous and subsequent messages; hence publication of the message could compromise that cipher. The "one-time pad" was a cipher which was different for each individual message.

C–819

London [via U.S. Army]
Nov. 9, 1944; 2332 Z, Nov. 8 / TOR 1100 Z

Prime Minister to President Roosevelt Personal and Top Secret.

Your 642. This was not sent in a cypher corresponding to our one time pad and consequently cannot be published as it stands. Will you trust me to paraphrase it and publish it, together with a suitable acknowledgement of thanks from me.

[MR*]

R–645

Hyde Park, N.Y. [via U.S. Navy]
Nov. 9, 1944, 11:05 A.M.

From the President to the Prime Minister. Personal and Top Secret.
   Your 819. Publication of paraphrase of my 642 approved. Roosevelt
[WDL]

[MR*]

R–646

Washington [via U.S. Navy]
Nov. 10, 1944, 1615 Z

Personal and Secret, from the President for the Prime Minister.
   Your 816 and 817. Thank you for your friendly message and for your
repetition of the 1940 message which I certainly had not forgotten. We
should now be permitted to continue our work together until this world-
wide agony is ended and a better future insured. F.D.R. [WDL]

[MR*. *R&C.*]

The following cable is apparently the "suitable acknowledgment" Churchill
referred to in C–819.

C–820

London [via U.S. Army]
Nov. 10, 1944, 1450 Z / TOR 1625 Z

Prime Minister to President Roosevelt.
   I was deeply moved by your message on the death of Field Marshal Sir
John Dill.
   The kindness and goodwill with which he was throughout his mission
treated by all the high officers of the United States and the consideration
which you always showed him made his task fruitful in the highest degree.

[MR*]

The U.S. Navy continued to protest, through the President, what it considered dangerous breaches of security regarding submarines.

R–646/1, letter

Washington
November 10, 1944

My dear Winston,

I realize that it is very trying for many people that we should continue to prevent information from leaking out about anti-submarine methods; but our own submarine campaign in the Pacific is playing such an important role that the Barbarian will seize desperately upon any information what will help him in anti-submarine measures. I do hope, therefore, that we may continue to do all that we can to keep anyone from talking too much. I have no doubt that indiscretions are committed in our press but the enclosed has recently appeared under a London dateline.

I will do what I can to keep the lid on here and I know I may count on you for similar measures.

Cordially yours, "F.D.R."

[PSF:WSC]

Enclosure to R–646/1

Inventions Give U-boats New Life, Briton Asserts.

(By Wireless to the New York Times).
London, Nov. 8—Air Vice Marshal A. B. Elwood, a senior staff officer of the Royal Air Force Coastal Command, said today that the Germans were fitting an extendable air intake to their U-Boats so that they could recharge batteries and ventilate the submarines without surfacing. This and "certain other improvements" under development have given the U-Boats a new lease on life, he added.

Between May and August, 1943, he said, the Germans lost U-Boats at the rate of thirty a month. The number in the Atlantic was reduced by almost half.

[PSF:WSC]

In a series of directives issued in late October and early November, presumably aimed at influencing the Italian-American vote in the election, Roosevelt provided dollar backing for the Italian currency and increased economic aid to Italy, including an increase in the bread ration from 200 to 300 grams per person per day. Both British and American representatives on the Allied Control Commission had long advocated such economic support, but authorities in London, particularly Churchill, were reluctant to do anything which would strengthen the Bonomi government at the expense of the eventual restoration of the monarchy. Moreover, the British believed the Bonomi government to be far too dependent upon the United States. The Italian government, as part of its program to regain complete sovereignty, had requested that the Allied Commission for Italy (the word "control" had been dropped from the name of the commission) be composed only of civilians, and the President had instructed the War Department to move in that direction.

Harold Macmillan, not entirely in agreement with Churchill, supported policies designed to win Italian "gratitude for the post-war Europe" (Macmillan, *The Blast of War*, p. 450), and was deeply concerned about communist strength, particularly in northern Italy. During his visit to London, from November 25 through early December, Macmillan tried to arrange British support for the Bonomi government, although he did agree with Churchill's complaint about the lack of merchant shipping to carry the grain to Italy, a shortage caused particularly by the diversion of more American ships to the Pacific.

C–821

Paris [via U.S. Army, London]
Nov. 12, 1944, 1616 Z (London) / TOR 1835 Z

Prime Minister to President Roosevelt Personal and Top Secret.

I have seen your directive of 1st November to the U.S. Secretary of War about the Italian grain ration, and I hope you will not mind my saying that you have jumped a good many fences. It will be difficult to give our ex enemies in Italy more than our Allies in Greece and Yougoslavia, and I hope your people will bear this in mind.

You will understand why I am rather anxious about commitments of this sort, which are bound to tie up so much shipping. I trust that the U.S. War Department will take steps to provide the additional tonnage, which we cannot ourselves provide, to carry the increased supplies.

As regards economic assistance to Italy generally, dealt with in NAF 810, MacMillan is coming here soon and has asked that this question should be kept open until he has taken over as Acting President of the Allied Commission.

I also hope that United States military personnel will not—as was suggested by the War Department—be withdrawn from commission in the meantime.

[MR*]

In mid-September, R.A.F. bombers flying from an airfield near Archangel, in the Soviet Union, inflicted such heavy damage on the German battleship *Tirpitz* that it could no longer threaten Allied convoys from its base at Alten-fiord, Norway. The Germans moved the *Tirpitz* to Tromsö to act as a floating battery against the expected British invasion of Norway. Warned by ULTRA intercepts, British-based Lancaster bombers from the R.A.F. attacked and sank the warship on November 12. Although the *Tirpitz* had fired her heavy guns only once at an enemy, and that against a land target, her presence in Norway from January 1942 until her sinking had created such major problems for British naval strategists that they had launched sixteen separate attacks against the ship.

This message was stamped "Top Secret ULTRA," possibly because reports on the sinking of the *Tirpitz* had been gleaned from intercepts of German military communications and thus were given special handling in order to prevent the Germans from learning that the Allies had broken those ciphers.

The President's mention of the German Treasury is apparently a reference to the economic woes of the Weimar Republic after World War I, a problem which scholars claimed had given Hitler an opportunity to take over.

R–647

Washington [via U.S. Navy]
Nov. 13, 1944, 1703 Z

Personal and Top Secret, from the President to the Prime Minister.

The death of the *Tirpitz* is great news. We must help the Germans by never letting them build anything like it again, thus putting the German Treasury on its feet. Roosevelt [FDR]

[MR*. R&C.]

Many of Roosevelt's advisers distrusted the Soviet leaders and were pessimistic about what would come of another Big Three conference. To travel to the Soviet Union for such talks only made matters worse. Harry Hopkins was one of the few who insisted that the talks were necessary and that Stalin would not leave the Soviet Union. Roosevelt hoped that the Soviet Premier could be persuaded to travel as far as the northern Adriatic, and suggested a delay until after the convening of Congress and the presidential inauguration.

By the end of the presidential campaign, Roosevelt had dropped the pose of being "above politics," and responded vigorously to Republican candidate Thomas Dewey's attacks. The President disliked Dewey and told one aide shortly after Dewey conceded the election, "I still think he is a son of a bitch" (William D. Hassett as quoted in Burns, *Soldier of Freedom*, p. 530).

Churchill visited France during November 10–14. It was a formal visit designed to improve relations between Churchill and de Gaulle, and proved quite successful. During their talks the British Prime Minister agreed that France should have a zone of occupation in postwar Germany.

R–648

Washington [via U.S. Navy]
Nov. 14, 1944, 1622 Z

Top Secret and Personal from the President for the Prime Minister.

The more I think it over the more I get convinced that a meeting of the three of us just now may be a little less valuable than it would be after I am inaugurated on the twentieth of January. The location of a meeting now is very difficult. All my people advise strongly against the Black Sea. I do not think there is a chance that UJ would agree to Jerusalem, Egypt or Malta.

But there is a real chance that by the end of January or early February he could get rail transportation to head of the Adriatic. He might be willing to come to Rome or the Riviera. I would of course stop in England going or returning. I do not think he wants to fly or take a very difficult and long rail journey to Haifa.

Incidentally it would be far easier for me as I am undergoing the throes of the old session and preparing for the new session on January third.

Ever so many thanks for your wire. I finally got angry toward the end of the campaign and replied to the worst type of opposition I have ever met. However it worked well and people are now sitting back trying to catch their breath.

What do you think of postponement? It appeals to me greatly. My best to you on your Parisian trip. Don't turn up in French clothes. Roosevelt [FDR]

[MR*. pFRUS, Yalta Conf., p. 14. R&C.]

Roosevelt had frequently warned that American armed forces would be withdrawn from Europe within six months after the end of the war against Germany, making closer Anglo-French cooperation necessary. Churchill realized that Roosevelt still disliked and distrusted de Gaulle specifically and the French in general, and this cable was an attempt to persuade the President that his fears were unwarranted. Churchill deleted his reference to de Gaulle's "inferiority complex" when this cable was printed in the Prime Minister's war memoirs in 1953. Georges Bidault was the Foreign Minister of the French provisional government.

Anglo-French discussions about Syria, as well as Lebanon, related to efforts by the French to regain their previous influence in those two nations. Following World War I, France had received a mandate from the League of

Nations to administer that portion of the old Ottoman Empire, but by the 1940s Arab nationalism had become a potent force in the area. Churchill was incorrect in assuming that the Levant was an Anglo-French problem. Roosevelt had frequently condemned French colonialism, and the State Department was as opposed to British influence in the Middle East as to renewed French power in the Levant. Fearful that local opposition to the French in Syria and Lebanon would stimulate nationalist uprisings in British-dominated areas of the Middle East, Churchill and Eden tried to persuade de Gaulle to make concessions to the native governments.

The "brute" referred to in the opening paragraph was the German battleship *Tirpitz*. The "meat" referred to in the final sentence apparently meant the Argentine-British negotiations for a meat contract. (See C–826.)

C–822

London [via U.S. Army]
Nov. 16, 1944; 2145 Z, Nov. 15 / TOR 0308 Z

Prime Minister to President Roosevelt. Personal and Top Secret.

1. Your number 647.

Thank you so much. It is a great relief to us to get this brute where we have long wanted her.

2. Your number 648.

I am very sorry that you are inclined to make no further effort to procure a triple meeting in December, and I will send you a separate telegram [C–825] making some further suggestions about this.

3. Thank you for your kind wishes about the Paris–De Gaulle trip. I certainly had a wonderful reception from about half a million French in the Champs Elysees and also from the party opposition centre at the Hotel de Ville. I reestablished friendly private relations with DeGaulle, who is better since he has lost a large part of his inferiority complex.

4. I see statements being put out in the French press and other quarters that all sorts of things were decided by us in Paris. You may be sure that our discussions on important things took place solely on an ad referendum basis to the three great powers, and of course especially to you who have by far the largest forces in France. Eden and I had a two-hours talk with De Gaulle and two or three of his people after luncheon on the 11th. De Gaulle asked a number of questions which made me feel how very little they were informed about anything that had been decided or was taking place. He is of course anxious to obtain full modern equipment for eight more divisions which can only be supplied by you. SHAEF reasonably contends that these will not be ready for the defeat of Germany in the field and that shipping must be devoted to the upkeep of the actual forces that will win the battles of the winter and spring. I reinforced this argument.

5. At the same time I sympathize with the French wish to take over more line, to have the best share they can in the fighting or what is left of it, and there may be plenty, and not to have to go into Germany as a so-called conqueror who has not fought. I remarked that this was a sentimental point which ought never the less to receive consideration. The important thing for France was to have an army prepared for the task which it would actually have to discharge, namely their obligation first to maintain a peaceful and orderly France behind the front of our armies, and secondly to assist in the holding down of parts of Germany later on.

6. On this second point the French pressed very strongly to have a share in the occupation of Germany not merely as sub-participation under British or American command but as a French command. I expressed my sympathy with this, knowing well that there will be a time not many years distant when the American armies will go home and when the British will have great difficulty in maintaining large forces overseas, so contrary to our mode of life and disproportionate to our resources, and I urged them to study the type of army fitted for that purpose, which is totally different in form from the organization by divisions required to break the resistance of a modern war-hardened enemy army. They were impressed by this argument but nevertheless pressed their view.

7. I see a Reuter message, emanating no doubt unofficially from Paris, that it was agreed France should be assigned certain areas, the Ruhr, the Rhineland, etc, for their troops to garrison. There is no truth in this and it is obvious that nothing of this kind can be settled on such a subject except in agreement with you. All I said to De Gaulle on this was that we had made a division of Germany into Russian, British and United States spheres: roughly, the Russians had the east, the British the north and the Americans the south. I further said that, speaking for His Majesty's Government, the less we had of it the better we should be pleased and that we would certainly favour the French taking over as large a part as their capacity allowed, but that all this must be settled at an inter-Allied table. I could of course issue something which would be a disclaimer of any loose statements made by Reuter, but you may not think this necessary in view of the obvious facts. I am telegraphing to U. J. in the same sense. We did not attempt to settle anything finally or make definite agreements.

8. It is evident however that there are a number of questions which press for decision at a level higher than that of the high commands, without which decisions no clear guidance can be given to the high commands. Here is another reason why we should have a triple meeting if U. J. will not come, or a quadruple meeting if he will. In the latter case the French would be in on some subjects and out on others. One must always realize that before five years are out there must be made a French army to take on the main task of holding down Germany. The main

question of discussion between Eden and Bidault was Syria, which was troublesome, lengthy and inconclusive but primarily our worry.

9. I thought I would give you this account at once in case of further tedentious statements being put out in the press.

10. I thought very well of Bidault. He looks like a younger and better looking Reynaud, especially in speech and smiling. He made a very favourable impression on all of us and there is no doubt that he has a strong share in the power. Giraud was at the banquet apparently quite content. What a change in fortunes since Casablanca. Generally I felt in the presence of an organized government, broadly based and of rapidly-growing strength, and I am certain that we should be most unwise to do anything to weaken it in the eyes of France at this difficult, critical time. I had a considerable feeling of stability in spite of communist threats, and that we could safely take them more into our confidence. I hope you will not consider that I am putting on French clothes when I say this. Let me know your thoughts. I will cable you later about the meeting and the meat.

[MR*. pWSC, VI, 251–53. pFRUS, Yalta Conf., pp. 15, 284–86. pR&C.]

General "Jumbo" Wilson had not only worked well with his American counterparts, but Churchill thought he had all too frequently supported American arguments on the Italian campaign. Lieutenant General Joseph T. McNarney was already Deputy Allied Supreme Commander in the Mediterranean, while Lieutenant General Mark Clark had been in command of the U.S. Fifth Army in Italy. (General Marshall's long campaign to get people to spell his name with a double l had succeeded too well.)

C–823

London [via U.S. Army]
Nov. 17, 1944, 1850 Z / TOR 2250 Z

Prime Minister to President Roosevelt Personal and Top Secret.

1. I feel it of great importance to have Field Marshall [sic] Dill's position filled by someone who would have access to you from time to time and would have a status which would enable him to be in very close touch with Marshall. I can find only one officer with these credentials. General Maitland Wilson as Supreme Commander in the Mediterranean has worked very well with all your people and is in full possession of the general outlook upon the war as a whole. I propose, with your agreement, to appoint him to the vacant post as head of the British Military Mission and as my official representative in military matters at Washington. I consider he has all the qualities necessary for this task.

2. I propose to you that General Alexander should become Allied Supreme Commander in the Mediterranean in succession to General Wilson, with General McNarney as his deputy, and that General Mark Clark should command the 15th Group of Armies in Italy. In Alexander we have a man whom you know and respect and who is in the most friendly relations with Clark. The course of our general strategy has since the capture of Rome not been favourable to Alexander's activities. But he has the entire confidence of his troops and of His Majesty's government. As Supreme Allied Commander, General Alexander would exercise full authority and responsibility for the operations in the field.

3. I have been disturbed by the immense staffs which have grown up in the Mediterranean Theatre, one for the armies at the front and the other for the Allied Supreme Commander at Caserta. These commands should be combed and where possible amalgamated and reduced to the minimum necessary.

4. I hope therefore that I may have your agreement to the following:—

(A) General Maitland Wilson to succeed Dill.

(B) General Alexander to be Supreme Allied Commander in the Mediterranean.

(C) General Mark Clark to command the group of armies on the Italian front.

5. I should be grateful to have your concurrence as soon as possible in these appointments which I am sure are in our common and closely linked interests.

[MR*]

Roosevelt did not agree with Churchill's proposals for the restoration of France as a major European power. The first draft of this cable, drawn up by Leahy and printed below, was bluntly anti-French. A revised version, drafted by Admiral Brown at the President's request to make the cable more "personal," was far more gentle in tone.

R–649, draft A, not sent

Washington
Nov. 16, 1944

President to Prime:

Your 822 received.

Regardless of available shipping and availability of material in the U.S., there does not appear to be at the present time any authority for the United States to equip an eight division post-war French Army.

I also sympathize with the French point of view and hope that France will be able to build up a sufficient military force to meet the needs of a post-war period.

I am not prepared not to agree that the provisional French Government should be a fourth member of our next staff meeting. Such a debating society probably would not expedite the essential business of the conference.

In regard to turning over parts of Germany to France after the collapse of Naziism, this will it seems to me require agreement by the Soviet, the U.K., and the U.S.

Participation by the French Provisional Government in discussions leading to such an agreement does not appear to me to be necessary or helpful.

In this connection I will desire and expect to bring the American troops home as quickly after Germany's collapse as is permitted by all the transportation that can be made available. [WDL]

[MR]

R–649

Washington [via U.S. Navy]
Nov. 18, 1944, 1830 Z

Personal and Top Secret from the President for the Prime Minister.

Your 822. I am sending you in a message to follow a copy of a message I have just sent to Uncle Joe on the subject of our next meeting. It does not seem to me that the French Provisional Government should take part in our next conference as such a debating society would confuse our essential issues. The three of us can discuss the questions you raise in regard to turning over parts of Germany to France after the collapse of Naziism and the further problems of helping to build up a strong France.

Regardless of available shipping and availability of material in the United States, I have no authority at present to equip an eight division post war French army. I, of course, sympathize with the French point of view and hope that we may all be able to help her meet post war responsibilities. You know, of course, that after Germany's collapse I must bring American troops home as rapidly as transportation problems will permit. I shall be glad to have your views about the time and place of our next meeting. Roosevelt [WEB]

[MR*. *FRUS, Yalta Conf.*, pp. 16–17, 286. *R&C*.]

In spite of Hopkins' belief that Stalin would not go outside the Soviet Union for a meeting, the President tried to persuade the Soviet leader to come as far as Italy. The final substantive paragraph referred to attempts by the President's personal representative, Major General Patrick Hurley, to get the communist Chinese in the north and Chiang Kai-shek's armies to work together against the Japanese. Hurley was ignorant of China, believed the British wanted to keep China weak, and was disliked by the State Department. Nevertheless, on the recommendation of Secretary of War Stimson, an old friend, Hurley was appointed Ambassador to China late in November 1944.

R–650

Washington [via U.S. Army]
Nov. 18, 1944, 1807 Z

Personal and Top Secret, from the President for the Prime Minister.
I have today sent the following message to Stalin:

QUOTE. All three of us are of one mind—that we should meet very soon, but problems chiefly geographical do not make this easy at this moment. I can, under difficulties, arrange to go somewhere now in order to get back here by Christmas but, quite frankly, it will be far more convenient if I could postpone it until after the Inauguration which is on January twentieth.

My Navy people recommend strongly against the Black Sea. They do not want to risk a capital ship through the Aegean or the Dardenelles, as it would involve a very large escort much needed elsewhere. Churchill has suggested Jerusalem or Alexandria, and there is a possibility of Athens, though this is not yet sure.

Furthermore, I have at this time a great hesitation in leaving here while my old Congress is in its final days, with the probability of its not adjourning finally until December fifteenth. Also, I have to be here, under the Constitution, to send the Annual Message to the new Congress which meets here in early January.

What I am suggesting is that we should all meet about the twenty-eighth or thirtieth of January, and I should hope that by that time you will have rail travel to some port on the Adriatic and that we should meet you there or that you could come across in a few hours on one of our ships to Bari and then motor to Rome, or that you should take the same ship a little further and that we should all meet in a place like Taormina, in eastern Sicily, which should provide a fairly good climate at that time.

Almost any place in the Mediterranean is accessible to me so that I can be within easy air distance of Washington in order to carry out action on Legislation—a subject with which you are familiar. I must be able to get Bills or Resolutions sent from here and returned within ten days.

I hope that your January military operations will not prevent you from coming at that time, and I do not think that we should delay the meeting longer than the end of January or early February.

Of course, if in the meantime the Nazi Army or people should disintegrate quickly, we should have to meet earlier, though I should much prefer the meeting at the end of January.

A further suggestion as to a place would be one on the Riviera but this would be dependent on the withdrawal of German troops from northwestern Italy. I wish you would let me know your thoughts on this.

I hope to talk over many things with you. We understand each other's problems and, as you know, I like to keep these discussions informal, and I have no reason for formal agenda.

My Ambassador in China, General Hurley, is doing his best to iron out the problem between the Generalissimo and the forces in North China. He is making some progress but nothing has been signed yet.

My warmest regards to you. UNQUOTE.

Roosevelt

[MR*. *FRUS, Yalta Conf.*, pp. 15–16. *Stalin/FDR*, doc. 241.]

C–824

London [via U.S. Army]
Nov. 18, 1944, 1559 Z / TOR 1830 Z

Prime Minister to President Roosevelt Personal.
Your 638.

In deference to your view, we have decided to omit from our publication shipping losses which occurred since the 1st January 1944. We propose to publish about noon on 28 November. We are sending over to you by air via the Embassy copies of the figures of shipping losses which will be included in our publication.

[MR*]

The United States continued to insist that Great Britain refrain from negotiating a long-term trade treaty which would add to the prestige of the Farrell/Perón government in Argentina. The original State Department draft of this cable concluded with reference to the ongoing Anglo-American talks about stage II lend-lease (aid following the surrender of Germany up until the defeat of Japan). Britain depended heavily upon such aid, and the inclusion of that sentence would have been a not-so-subtle threat as to the consequences of signing an agreement with Argentina.

R–651

Washington [via U.S. Navy]
Nov. 18, 1944, 2315 Z

Top Secret and Personal from the President for the Prime Minister.

Early in October you were good enough to agree to defer for a while the signature of a meat contract with the Farrell regime in Argentina. Your refusal to sign a contract has helped us tremendously. It has increased the uncertainty which has driven the Colonels to a desperate condition.

We believe that if our tactics can be continued, we have a very good chance of putting an end within a reasonable time to a Fascist regime that otherwise would be a threat to the peace and security of this continent for many years to come.

I have been concerned to hear recent reports that you may shortly take up the matter of the Argentine meat contract with us again.

It is my strong personal conviction that if you sign a meat contract with the Farrell regime the consequences will be disastrous and much more far reaching than we have been able to make some of your people understand. Such action would be propagandized by the Argentine regime to demonstrate a division between us; it would strengthen both their domestic and their international position; and because our own people feel so strongly about the Nazi threat on this continent while their sons are fighting all over the world, such action would have repercussions in the press, in public discussions, and in Congress at a most unfortunate time.

I would not, of course, urge this so strongly if it meant less meat for your people. As you know, you are getting all the meat you can carry from Argentina right now even though you have no contract, and you will recall that this was also the case for ten months prior to the signing of the last contract.

I know that we can continue to count on your help to liquidate this dangerous Nazi threat. ~~I am glad to say that our people tell me the phase two lend-lease discussions are going well.~~ Roosevelt [ES]

[MR*. *FRUS*, 1944, VII, 365.]

Churchill was more interested in talks with Roosevelt than in meeting with Stalin. The Prime Minister's goal was to make the most of the TOLSTOY agreements by securing American support for the British position. Churchill had become increasingly worried about Soviet expansion into eastern and central Europe, but knew that Roosevelt would not be receptive to such an analysis. The "last time" referred to the remilitarization of Germany following World War I.

C–825

London [via U.S. Army]
Nov. 19, 1944, 2220 Z / TOR 0046 Z, Nov. 20

Prime Minister to President Roosevelt, Personal and Top Secret.

1. Naturally I am very sorry to receive your numbers 649 and 650.

2. Your message to U. J. will, of course, make it certain that he will not come anywhere before the end of January. Also you yourself give independently the important reasons which make it difficult for you to come earlier.

3. These reasons, I fear, destroy the hope which we had cherished that you would now pay your long-promised visit to Great Britain, and that we two could meet here in December and ask U. J. to send Molotov, who would be an adequate deputy. It is a great disappointment to me that this prospect should be indefinitely postponed.

4. There is, in my opinion, much doubt whether U. J. would be willing or able to come to an Adriatic port by January 30th, or that he would be willing to come on a non-Russian vessel through this extremely heavily-mined sea. However, if he accepts we shall, of course, be there. I note you do not wish the French to be present. I had thought they might come in towards the end in view of their vital interests in the arrangements made for policing Germany, as well as in all questions affecting the Rhine frontiers.

5. Even if a meeting can be arranged by the end of January, the two and a half intervening months will be a serious hiatus. There are many important matters awaiting settlement, for example. The treatment of Germany and the future world organization, relations with France, the position in the Balkans, as well as the Polish question, which ought not to be left to moulder.

6. Para two of your 649 causes me alarm. If after Germany's collapse you "must bring the American troops home as rapidly as transportation problems will permit" and if the French are to have no equipped post-war army or time to make one, or to give it battle experience, how will it be possible to hold down western Germany beyond the present Russian occupation line? We certainly could not undertake the task without your

aid and that of the French. All would therefore rapidly disintegrate as it did last time. I hope, however, that my fears are groundless. I put my faith in you.

[MR*. *FRUS, Yalta Conf.*, pp. 17, 286–87. *R&C*.]

As explained in his later cable (C–832), Churchill believed the British had every right to negotiate a long-term meat-purchasing contract with Argentina.

C–826

London [via U.S. Army]
Nov. 19, 1944, 2220 Z / TOR 0007 Z, Nov. 20

Prime Minister to President Roosevelt, Personal and Top Secret.

Your 651. I should be very grateful if you would read again the correspondence which has passed between us on this subject. I have had all the telegrams printed in a convenient form and am sending you two copies by air. It is on this basis that I shall venture to put our case before you.

[MR*]

Although the Americans had no objection to General Wilson as the senior British representative on the Combined Chiefs of Staff Committee in Washington, Wilson never achieved the same close working relationship with Marshall as Sir John Dill had enjoyed. General Marshall had originally suggested Major-General Sir Hastings Ismay, Chief of Staff to the Minister of Defence, as Dill's replacement, but that sentence was deleted from the final version of the cable.

R–652

Washington [via U.S. Navy]
Nov. 20, 1944

Personal and Top Secret, from the President for the Prime Minister.

Your Number 823.

General Maitland Wilson is entirely acceptable to us as a successor for Sir John Dill. We would welcome him to Washington. ~~Have you considered General Ismay who would also be very acceptable to us?~~

As to the command arrangements in the Mediterranean resulting from General Wilson's transfer to Washington, I feel that General Alexander is logically General Wilson's successor and his appointment as Supreme

Commander in the Mediterranean Theater is agreeable to the U.S. Chiefs of Staff and to me.

I appreciate the compliment you pay General Clark in suggesting that he take over the Army Group in Italy as General Alexander's successor. I think that is also a logical arrangement. Generals Alexander and Clark have worked together successfully now for some time and I see no reason to change that combination.

General McNarney's status as Deputy to the Supreme Allied Commander should remain the same under the new arrangements. Roosevelt [GCM]

[MR*]

On the seventieth anniversary of Churchill's birth, Roosevelt sent the Prime Minister a printed quotation by Abraham Lincoln, taken from its frame, with the following inscription. Unfortunately, the records do not reveal the actual Lincoln quotation.

R–652/1, inscription

Washington
Nov. 20, 1944

"For Winston on his Birthday—I would go even to Teheran to be with him again."
Franklin D. Roosevelt   Nov. 30, 1944

[PSF:WSC. *FDR LTRS*, p. 1558.]

The Joint Chiefs of Staff, who drafted this cable, were reacting to the advice of U.S. Army civil administrators in liberated Italy, who believed that economic distress lay at the root of the civil disturbances. The insistence that civilian personnel be substituted for military representatives on the Allied Commission reflected the Army's distaste for the civil/political role it was assigned in liberated Italy. The first two paragraphs of the telegram were inserted by Admiral Leahy, probably at the President's suggestion. The tone of those additions indicates that Roosevelt intended to maintain a high level of American influence in Italy after the war. (See the headnote to C–821 for additional background material.)

R-653

London [via U.S. Navy]
Nov. 21, 1944, 1617 Z

Personal and Top Secret, from the President for the Prime Minister.

Your 821. In regard to the Italian grain ration it is true that I have "jumped some fences" and because of the great number of Italians in this country I must continue in the future to follow the same practice. I know you will understand.

I have not been at all satisfied with the administration of the relief problem to date, especially with the distribution of food in Italy.

In September, 1944, General Wilson reported that from a military standpoint the tranquility of the Mediterranean area might be jeopardized if the 300 gram bread ration were not sanctioned.

The provision of relief to the distressed peoples in liberated areas presents very difficult problems of shipping. My own view is that until after German collapse the import of such supplies must be limited to those supplies for which the Combined Chiefs of Staff can obtain shipping in the light of shipping requirements to carry out current and projected operations. In view of these heavy operational shipping demands, I think that, until German collapse, they can provide shipping in operational areas only for those basic essentials necessary to avoid disease and unrest which would interfere with operations or lines of communication and supply. I agree with your suggestions that we should not discriminate in favor of Italy over other liberated areas, although, in view of shipping limitations, it will only be possible to furnish a minimum relief program necessary to prevent prejudice to military operations.

It is my belief that to continue military personnel in the Allied Commission any longer than is absolutely necessary is inconsistent with the principles you and I announced in our joint statement. I therefore feel that whenever a position in the Commission need no longer be filled by an officer, he should be replaced by a civilian as soon as a suitable replacement can be found. I will, of course, be glad to consider any views which you may have on these matters and other problems of economic assistance to Italy, after your consultation with MacMillan. Roosevelt [JCS, WDL]

[MR*]

The acrimony which came to characterize Anglo-American relations at the International Civil Aviation Conference, held in Chicago, Illinois, November 1–December 4, 1944, is explained with blunt candor in Admiral Leahy's memoirs: "An impasse between England and the United States seemed to have been reached because ... England ... was endeavoring to break the more or less monopolistic control of overseas commercial aviation heretofore held by American companies" (Leahy, *I Was There*, p. 280). In a memorandum sent to the President at the close of the meeting, Assistant Secretary of State Adolf A. Berle, Jr., Chairman of the American delegation to the conference, summarized the British proposals: "through the medium of an extremely intricate formula, ... [the British] offered a good arrangement for the United States across the Atlantic Ocean and possibly across the Pacific, [but] in substance it strangled any United States [air]line beyond the Atlantic gateways" (Dec. 7, 1944, *FRUS*, 1944, II, 604–5). It was that British plan which Roosevelt opposed. The message was drafted initially by Harry Hopkins and then revised by the State Department before the President sent it to Churchill. (The paragraph shown as struck out was written by Hopkins.)

R–654

Washington [via U.S. Navy]
Nov. 21, 1944, 2116 Z

Secret and Personal from the President for the Prime Minister.

The aviation conference is at an impasse because of a square issue between our people and yours. We have met you on a number of points, notably an arrangement for regulation of rates and an arrangement by which the number of planes in the air shall be adjusted to the amount of traffic. This is as far as I can go. In addition, your people are now asking limitations on the number of planes between points regardless of the traffic offering. This seems to me a form of strangulation. It has been a cardinal point in American policy throughout that the ultimate judge should be the passenger and the shipper. The limitations now proposed would, I fear, place a dead hand on the use of the great air trade routes. You don't want that any more than I do.

~~I think we have walked out of the seventeenth century conception of air trade to the twentieth century conception of air trade and stand on the threshold and that we ought to go right on through.~~

The issue will be debated tomorrow. I hope you can get into this yourself and give instructions, preferably by telephone, to your people in Chicago so that we can arrange, if possible, to agree. It would be unfortunate indeed if the conference broke down on this issue. Roosevelt [HLH, State Dept.]

[MR*. *FRUS*, 1944, II, 584. *R&C*.]

In a message to the War Department on November 20, General Eisenhower noted that German morale showed "no sign of cracking," and suggested efforts to reduce the Germans' "will to resist" by employing "deception methods in addition to propaganda" (*Eisenhower Papers*, IV, 2312). The General seems to have wanted to deceive the German armed forces into either surrendering or deserting, but all the President could think of was a public statement.

R–655

Hyde Park, N.Y. [via U.S. Navy]
Nov. 22, 1944, 1842 Z

Top Secret and Personal from the President for the Prime Minister.

1. Apparently the Chiefs of SHAEF would like something done by top level to help break down German morale.

2. I can think of nothing except a joint statement from you and me and therefore suggest something along the line of the following:

QUOTE. We have viewed the overall iron discipline of the Wermacht and strangle-hold of the Nazi party over the individuals of the German nation and we have considered the problem of getting the truth to the people of Germany, for they have been flooded with Nazi propaganda that the Allies seek the destruction of the German people and the devastation of Germany.

Once more we wish to make it clear to the German people that this war does not seek to devastate Germany or eliminate the German people.

Once more we want to make it clear to the people of Germany that we seek the elimination of Nazi control and the return of the German people to the civilization of the rest of the world.

We are winning. There is no question of that.

But we want to save lives and to save humanity.

We hope that this slaughter of Germans can be brought to an end but we are going to bring this war to a conclusion which will satisfy civilization and seek to prevent future wars. The answer lies in the hands of the German people. They are being pressed the whole length of their boundaries on the Rhine. They are being pressed by overwhelming numbers and inexhaustable resources in Poland and Czechoslovakia and Hungary. German towns are daily being destroyed and your enemies draw closer in the closing of an inexorable ring. The simple fact remains that the Allies are united in demanding a complete military victory.

The choice lies with the German people and the German army. Do not prolong the days of death and suffering and destruction. Join all the other people in Europe and Africa and America and Asia in this great effort for decency and peace among human beings. UNQUOTE.

Roosevelt [FDR]

[MR*. *FRUS*, 1944, I, 564–65. *R&C.*]

The Americans, who possessed the overwhelming bulk of commercial airplanes, wanted civil airlines to compete for traffic in a free market. The British, hoping to hold onto their share of the market, advocated pooling arrangements whereby commercial carriers would be guaranteed a portion of the business.

Viscount Swinton, who had become British Minister of Civil Aviation on October 9, 1944, had the reputation in the State Department of being anti-American. He headed the British delegation at the Civil Aviation Conference. The so-called Freedoms of the Air, advocated by the United States, consisted of: "(1) Freedom of innocent transit; (2) Freedom of technical stop; (3) Freedom to take traffic from the homeland out to other countries; (4) Freedom to take traffic from other countries back to the homeland—and possibly, to a limited extent, (5) Freedom to pick up and discharge traffic between points en route—" (*FRUS*, 1944, II, 604).

C–827

London [via U.S. Army]
Nov. 22, 1944, 1833 Z / TOR 2340 Z

Prime Minister to President Roosevelt Personal and Top Secret.

We have sat all day on your message No. 654 which only reached me at 2:15 A. M. this morning.

The cabinet after prolonged discussion desire me to send to you the following expression of their views which I endorse. If there is anything in this message on which you would like further explanation I earnestly request that you should send for Lord Swinton.

Message from Cabinet begins:

1. We would like to draw your attention to the course of the negotiations at Chicago which have been marked by a large measure of concessions on both sides.

2. Whereas, in order to reach a common agreement your Delegation has agreed to a method of regulating the share of the various countries on the different routes and of regulating the fares, we have agreed to the throwing open of our airfields all over the world to aircraft to other nationalities and to such planes being able to carry not only through traffic but local traffic between two neighbouring countries on the route.

3. We had very much hoped that the agreement thus arrived at between your Delegation and ours, which was embodied in the form of the draft of November 17, would be a satisfactory document to submit for the approval of the whole body of the conference.

4. We feel that we have gone to the limit of concession in this draft especially with relation to the so-called Escalator Clause which enabled the share of operators to be increased if they in fact carry more traffic between terminals than they are allotted under the frequency arrangements.

5. In our understanding it was only because of the new proposals brought forward by your Delegation on the evening of November 18 after the agreement had been arrived at, that the present difficulties have arisen. These proposals we could not accept, since they demand a share of the local traffic between two neighbouring countries by the aircraft of a third country far beyond that which the granting of the right to take up traffic on through service would warrant.

6. We were prepared to agree to the so-called Fifth Freedom subject to adequate protection of the local operators by a price differential, to which your Delegates agreed in the draft accepted.

7. We are, of course, prepared to stand by what Swinton had already agreed with Berle, but we cannot see our way to accept these new suggestions put forward, which would gravely jeopardize our own position.

8. We suggest, therefore, that if you are unable to confirm the agreement arrived at on November 17 by our Delegations at Chicago, the Conference should finalise the valuable technical agreements which have been arrived at, and that the rest of the matters should be adjourned for a time during which we can consider the matter more fully and see whether there is some solution of the problem at which we can arrive.

9. We share with you the most earnest desire to come to a fair and satisfactory agreement by which both our countries can play their full part in the development of world wide civil aviation as soon as possible.

10. We hope that you will be able to examine this and we feel sure you will agree that it is a wise and workable compromise between two points of view which originally diverged widely.

[MR*. *FRUS*, 1944, II, 585–86.]

The initial State Department draft response to C–827 was never sent, probably on the recommendation of Harry Hopkins. It clearly explained why the

British proposals were unacceptable to the United States, but was more technical than the usual President-to-Prime-Minister message. This draft was mistakenly printed in *FRUS* as having been sent to Churchill.

R–655/1, draft A, not sent

Washington
Nov. 23, 1944

From the President to Prime Minister Churchill.

I appreciate your message of November 23 [C–827]. No point would be served by discussing past history such as the suggestion that an understanding on November 17 was rejected and a new proposal made by our Delegation. Our people believed that they had substantial assent from your Delegation to a draft which their and our experts interpreted one way and which Lord Swinton has interpreted in another; but all of us recognize that these situations do occur and they are not important. It is better to have them out before rather than after an agreement is signed.

The important thing is that the draft of November 17, as interpreted by your people, does not set up the conditions for operable routes which pass through any considerable number of countries, and particularly which go to distant countries, for instance, a route from the United States to South Africa. It would make a round-the-world direct route almost impossible. All these routes, yours as well as ours, depend for their existence on a reasonable amount of pick-up traffic between points. We could not have pioneered South America, or maintained our present routes, nor could you maintain an economic route from London to India by depending merely on the traffic from London to each terminal point. A reasonable amount of intermediate traffic is necessary between the Panama Canal and Lima on the West Coast South American route, or between say, Rome and Cairo on your Indian route, to make it even remotely possible economically. Of course, each of us could subsidize indefinitely one plane a week but this is an occasional visit rather than a trade route. Our experts were also worried by the fact that this limitation (homeland to each intermediate point and exclusion of point-to-point traffic) would make it difficult, if not impossible, for any small nation to have extensive routes because small nations do not have great reservoirs of terminal traffic. You and we could survive by liberal subsidies but we both want to get away from that. The Dutch and possibly the French would find great difficulty in surviving.

We know perfectly well that we ought not to set up a situation in which our operators could wreck the local establishments between nearby countries, or so fill the air on long routes that nobody else could get in and survive. We are quite prepared to discuss limitations of pick-up traffic to

assure that this does not happen. What we do want is sufficient play so
that the establishment and maintenance of the long routes on a reasonably
economic basis is possible. For your information, the Canadians are tac-
kling the situation on that basis. A real difficulty in the situation is that
Lord Swinton feels he is so bound by instructions that he can make no
suggestions.

[MR. *FRUS*, 1944, II, 587–88.]

Harry Hopkins apparently made changes on a copy of a second State Department draft, and the cable was sent through Ambassador Winant so that
he could add his personal plea. Winant had just complained that he was at
a disadvantage because he had not received information about the issues
being discussed at Chicago (*FRUS*, 1944, II, 586). Rather than send a specific
answer to the items raised in Churchill's message (C–827), Roosevelt and his
advisers decided to let the naked threat of a termination of lend-lease end
the discussion.

R–655/1

Hyde Park, N.Y. [via State Dept.]
Nov. 24, 1944, 1658 Z

Personal and Top Secret, from the President for Ambassador Winant.
    Please take the following message personally to Winston and convince
him that he has got to come through. You will understand how important
it is that he does.

> QUOTE. I have read carefully the message in your 827 ~~and am
> replying to it in my next telegram~~. I am afraid you do not yet fully
> appreciate the importance of reaching a satisfactory agreement. Our
> people have gone as far to meet yours as I can let them go. ~~Swinton's
> hands are tied.~~ If the conference should end either in no agreement
> or in an agreement which the American people would regard as
> preventing the development and use of the great air routes the re-
> percussions would seriously affect many other things.
>   We are doing our best to meet your lend-lease needs. We will face
> Congress on that subject in a few weeks and it will not be in a generous
> mood if it and the people feel that the United Kingdom has not
> agreed to a generally beneficial air agreement. They will wonder
> about the chances of our two countries, let alone any others, working
> together to keep the peace if we cannot even get together on an
> aviation agreement. ~~Furthermore I cannot see your people's point
> on the escalator clause. What good is an escalator clause covering~~

only traffic going all the way from New York to Calcutta and not
touching part-way traffic? We have got to get together on this. Can't
you give Swinton sufficient leeway to work it out? F.D.R. UNQUOTE.

I hope you will review the situation once more and see if we cannot
get together. UNQUOTE.

Roosevelt [State Dept., HLH]

[MR*. *FRUS*, 1944, II, 589.]

Churchill and the Cabinet had mulled over the idea of an appeal for a German
surrender, but decided against it. Any Anglo-American statement to the German people which did not retreat from "unconditional surrender" would be
of little value, but any such retreat would anger the Soviet Union. Germany,
not Russia, was the enemy, and it made no sense to the British to antagonize
the latter in order to please the former.

Allied forces on the western front had launched an offensive in November
designed to establish a broad front at the Rhine River before winter arrived.
French armies in the south, operating between Strasbourg and the Franco-
Swiss border, pushed forward over fifty miles, reaching the Rhine in some
places. In the process they had killed or captured 27,000 German soldiers.
The American Seventh Army, with assistance from the French, captured
Strasbourg on November 23, but Allied forces in the north were less successful. Although Canadian and British armies cleared the Scheldt Estuary
west of Rotterdam and Antwerp, they met stiff German resistance as they
approached the Rhine and the industrialized Ruhr. The American Ninth and
First armies, attacking on a front stretching north from Luxembourg to Aachen,
could advance only a few miles, and finally stopped at the Roer River. Only
General Patton's Third Army achieved major gains, capturing Metz and driving to the German defenses (Siegried line) in the western Saar.

C-828

London [via U.S. Navy]
Nov. 24, 1944, 1845 Z / TOR 2120 Z

Personal and Top Secret Prime Minister to President Roosevelt.

Your Number 655. I have consulted the Cabinet and separately the
Chiefs of Staff and we all gravely doubt whether any such statement
should be made. I do not think that the Germans are very much afraid
of the treatment they will get from the British and American armies or
governments. What they are afraid of is a Russian occupation, and a large
proportion of their people being taken off to toil to death in Russia, or
as they say, Siberia. Nothing that we can say will eradicate this deep seated
fear.

2. Moreover, U. J. certainly contemplates demanding two or three million Nazi youth, Gestapo men, etc., doing prolonged reparation work, and it is hard to say that he is wrong. We could not therefore give the Germans any assurances on this subject without consultations with U. J.

3. It seems to me that if I were a German soldier or general, I should regard any such statement at this juncture, when the battle for Cologne is at its height, as a confession of weakness on our part and as proof positive of the advantages of further desperate resistance. The Chiefs of the Staff and Ministry of Information both independently agree with me that this might well be the consequence of any such announcement now. I do not see any alternative to the General Grant attitude "To fight it out on this line, if it takes all summer". We, therefore, are opposed to any reassurance being volunteered by us at this juncture.

4. The brilliant French success in the south, your capture of Metz and the break-through of the Seventh American Army upon Strassbourg now taken are substantial facts which must be added to the intense pressure of the American First and Ninth Armies and our own British efforts towards Venlo. Even if we do not conquer at the strongest point towards Cologne, enough has been already gained to make the battle a notable step towards our goal. Words, I am sure, would play no part now and we can, it seems to me, speak no words of which the Russians, who are still holding on their front double the number of divisions opposite us, are not parties.

5. I, therefore, earnestly hope that we shall fight the battle out till winter comes about the middle of December and throw extra weight into the points of penetration. I am sure it would be hurtful to our prestige and even to our initiative if we seemed to try high-level appeals to the Germans now. All kinds of propaganda can be thrown across the battle-fronts locally as they do to us, and the staffs are working at a plan on which a separate telegram will be sent, which is designed to meet Eisenhower's desire to get at German morale by underground methods. But to make the great governments responsible for anything which would look like appeasement now would worsen our chances, confess our errors and stiffen the enemy resistance. Please, however, do not hesitate to correct me if you think I am wrong. Meanwhile, I remain set where you put me on unconditional surrender.

[MR*. *FRUS*, 1944, I, 565–66. *R&C*.]

Field Marshal Sir Henry Maitland Wilson served as the senior British representative on the Combined Chiefs of Staff Committee in Washington until the end of the war. Lieutenant General Lucian Truscott had been slated for an Army command in France, but Eisenhower and Marshall agreed that, because of Truscott's experience in Italy, he would be the logical choice to replace General Clark as commander of the Fifth Army. Truscott was disappointed, for he realized that Italy was not the main theater of operations, but he followed Eisenhower's wishes and took command in December.

C–829

London [via U.S. Army]
Nov. 26, 1944; 2245 Z, Nov. 25 / TOR 0416 Z

Prime Minister to President Roosevelt Personal and Top Secret.
   Your 652.
   1. General Wilson has gratefully accepted appointment. My immediately following telegram contains the announcements which I suggest should be made in London and Washington simultaneously at 23.30 GMT on Sunday, November 26.
   2. Alexander has, off the record and very privately expressed a keen desire to have Truscott for the Fifth Army. Thus, we should get the Anzio crowd together. I ventured to mention this to Ike when I saw him last week, and he told me that he had been planning to have Truscott as one of his army commanders, but that this would not mature before next May. In the circumstances, he would not stand in his way for this immediate appointment: indeed, he thought it far the best. I await your decision on this point.

[MR*]

C–830

London [via U.S. Army]
Nov. 26, 1944; 2245 Z, Nov. 25 / TOR 0245 Z

Prime Minister to President Roosevelt Personal and Top Secret.
   My immediately preceding telegram.
   1. I suggest the following for the British Press.

   "The Prime Minister and Minister of Defence has appointed General Sir Henry Maitland Wilson, GCB, GBE, DSO, head of the British Joint Staff Mission in Washington, and his personal representative on military matters with the President of the United States in succession to the late Field Marshal Sir John Dill, GCB, CMG, DSO".
   "Consequent on the above, the following appointments, which are the result of agreement between the Prime Minister and the President of the United States, are announced:—
   "General Sir Harold Alexander, GCB, CSI, DSO, MC, to be Supreme Allied Commander, Mediterranean Theatre".

"Lieut. General Mark Clark, United States Army, to be Commander-in-Chief of the Allied Fifteenth Group of Armies in Italy".

"The War Office announce that the King has been graciously pleased to approve the promotion of General Sir Harold Alexander, GCB, CSI, DSO, MC, (late Irish Guards) to be Field Marshal, supernumerary to establishment, with effect from June 4th, 1944, the date of the capture of Rome".

[MR*]

R–656

Washington [via U.S. Navy]
Nov. 26, 1944, 1609 Z

Personal from the President for the Prime Minister.

The announcement proposed in your Number 830 for 23.30 GMT, Sunday, November 26, is approved. Roosevelt [WDL]

[MR*]

Roosevelt accepted Churchill's arguments against making any public statement aimed at undermining German morale.

R–657

Washington [via U.S. Navy]
Nov. 26, 1944, 1614 Z

Top Secret and Personal from the President for the Prime Minister.

Your 828. Your attitude toward the proposed joint statement, my 655, is accepted and I have informed General Eisenhower in regard thereto.

I share your earnest hope that both the British and American Armies can throw extra weight into the effort and succeed in destroying the German West Wall Armies by the end of this year. Roosevelt [WDL]

[MR*]

Roosevelt paraphrased for Churchill all of Stalin's reply to suggestions that the tripartite meeting be held outside of the Soviet Union (*Stalin/FDR*, doc. 243).

Roosevelt doubted that Congress would continue aiding Britain once Germany surrendered or collapsed; equipping French military forces seemed even more unlikely. Nor had the President given up his belief that France would fall into political disarray and civil violence following the war.

R–658

Washington [via U.S. Navy]
Nov. 26, 1944, 1637 Z

Top Secret and Personal from the President for the Prime Minister.

Your 825. Uncle Joe has now replied to my message in regard to the tripartite meeting forwarded to you in my 650.

He expresses regret that my Naval advisors doubt the expediency of meeting on the shore of the Black Sea. He does not object to a meeting at the end of January or the beginning of February, but he has in mind that we shall choose as a meeting place one of the Soviet port cities. He must consider the opinion of his doctors that a long trip would be a danger to him.

He hopes that we will now or soon finally agree upon a meeting place that will be acceptable to all of us.

I have a feeling that we will not succeed in getting U.J. to travel beyond the Black Sea unless the Germans should have surrendered by that time.

In regard to paragraph six of your 825, there should be no difficulty for us in equipping so much of a French occupation force as they may need in a disarmed Germany from the military equipment that we will take from the German Army when it surrenders or is destroyed.

In any event, I have at the present time no authority under which it would be possible for me to equip any post-war foreign army, and the prospect of getting such authority from the Congress is more than doubtful. Roosevelt [WDL]

[MR*. FRUS, Yalta Conf., pp. 18, 287. R&C.]

Frederick Lindemann, Lord Cherwell, held the formal Cabinet post of Paymaster General, but functioned as Churchill's personal adviser on scientific matters. The "particular field" of Major General Leslie R. Groves was the Manhattan Project—the Anglo-American program to develop an atomic bomb. Cherwell had stayed in the United States after the Quebec/Hyde Park meetings and had visited a number of scientific research establishments. TUVE, named for Dr. Merrill A. Tuve of the Carnegie Institute of Technology, was a branch of the Office of Scientific Research and Development. Tuve himself worked in the Terrestrial Magnetism Department of OSRD, where the proximity fuse had been developed. Proximity-fuse shells were effective against the V-1 "flying bombs," but anti-aircraft was useless against the V-2 rockets, which reached speeds of four thousand miles per hour.

C–831

London [via U.S. Army]
Nov. 26, 1944, 1037 Z / TOR 1330 Z

Prime Minister to President Roosevelt Personal and Top Secret.

Cherwell has told me how very kind the U.S. Army and Navy were in showing him their latest developments in many fields and in entertaining him at their various establishments. Perhaps if you thought it well, you would transmit my thanks to them and especially to General Groves who went to so much trouble to show Cherwell the latest developments in his particular field.

Perhaps you might also think fit to express my gratitude to the TUVE establishment at Silver Springs whose work on the proximity fuses has proved so valuable in defending London against the robot bombs.

[MR*. R&C.]

Not only did the British argue that any cut in supplies obtained from Argentina would force a reduction in civilian allocations in Great Britain and hamper efforts to support Allied forces in Europe, but they also feared that the measures demanded by the United States could severely damage Anglo-Argentine economic relations after the war.

The reference in the first paragraph to Roosevelt's telegram 730 of July 23 should have read 588 of July 22. Churchill's message to Stettinius, also mentioned in that paragraph, asked that the Americans not "forget our beef and mutton" (*FRUS*, 1944, VII, 366n).

C–832

London [via U.S. Army]
Nov. 26, 1944, 1905 Z / TOR 2215 Z

Prime Minister to President Roosevelt. Personal and Top Secret.

1. You will by now have received the print I sent you about the Argentine and British meat contracts. May I ask you to read again my telegram of 14th July 1944, with its enclosure of the minute by the Food Minister in which you will see that the contract mentioned was one of three-four years. It was in reply to this telegram that you sent your 730 of July 23d, which began "I would not do anything in the world to cut down the supply of meat in England. Heaven knows that it is quite short enough. We would do nothing to prevent your getting a new contract". See also the last sentence of my reply to Stettinius of August 5th.

2. It is perfectly clear there that we had your full agreement in making

a three-four years contract in July. However on October 11th you sent me a strongish telegram [R–628] to Moscow asking that we would continue on "a month to month basis for some time to come". In order to meet your wishes at a critical time I agreed "that no long term contract is to be negotiated for the next couple of months or so and that we are to proceed meanwhile on a month to month basis during which time we can discuss matters further" [C–796].

3. The "couple of months or so" is now nearly up and of course the Food Minister wishes to make his contract. I have however already received your number 651 in which you express a wish for further prolongation of the month to month basis. From the beginning I have told my colleagues that owing to our financial relationship and the scale on which you are helping us to play our part in the common war effort and for many other kindly and friendly acts I would not allow money to count in the matter. I have absolved the Minister of Food from his duty of making the most thrifty contracts in his power and have said that only if our food supply in beef and mutton is endangered should we have to resist your desires.

4. I have put this matter strongly to the Cabinet and they agreed about the money aspect and also felt the risk of our losing our meat supply might be accepted in the near future. In consequence we shall be prepared to continue on a month to month basis for six months from 1st December 1944. We do this on the understanding, to which I am sure you will agree, that all your influence and weight will be used to keep other buyers out of the Argentine market and make sure they do not get refrigerated cargo space. We hope this will be satisfactory to you. It is always my earnest desire to assist you in any way we can, having regard to all the many things you do for us.

5. Since however I brought this matter before the Cabinet I received the document contained in my immediately following telegram. I was of course very much hurt that this form of pressure should be applied to us, and I hope it will not be thought that the Cabinet was aware of it or influenced by it at the time they agreed to my request. It seems almost to amount to a threat of indirect blockade arising out of a matter on which I have your promise of July 23d. I feel sure that you yourself were not aware that this document was being sent to us and certainly Ambassador Winant knew nothing of its delivery.

I am therefore withholding it from circulation to the Cabinet.

[MR*. *FRUS*, 1944, VII, 365–66.]

Ambassador Winant's letters to Foreign Secretary Eden, mentioned in the first paragraph of the quoted document, were based on instructions sent to the American Embassy by the State Department. In the first, Winant indicated that the United States planned to cease all purchases of Argentine products except those essential to the war effort. In the second letter, the Ambassador informed the British that the United States planned to cut its exports to Argentina to about 10 percent of their 1941 value, and asked the British to take parallel action. Eden finally replied at length to those letters on December 4. (See *FRUS*, 1944, VII, 367–70.) His main point was that trade with Argentina constituted a far higher percentage of Britain's import-export trade than it did for the United States.

William J. Gallman was Counselor of Embassy in the United Kingdom; J.V.T. Perowne was head of the South American Department in the British Foreign Office.

C–833

London [via U.S. Army]
Nov. 26, 1944, 1815 Z / TOR 2247 Z

Prime Minister to President Roosevelt. Personal and Top Secret.

My immediately preceding telegram.

The following is document dated 20th November 1944, mentioned in paragraph 5.

"Dear Perowne:"

"I wish to refer to previous correspondence with the Foreign Office concerning exports to Argentina and the purchase of Argentine products. These questions were dealt with in detail in Mr. Winant's letters of August 14th and September 9th to Mr. Eden. As you know we are still awaiting the Foreign Office's reply to these questions."

"We have now received a telegram from the State Department calling our attention to a specific problem which has arisen, which has a bearing on this general question of Argentine exports and imports. The facts in the case are as follows: an export licence for thirteen tons of synthetic rubber, which is needed in a sealing compound for the Argentine meat pack that is intended for the United Kingdom is at this time under consideration by the State Department. The granting of such a licence is made difficult by a number of factors, among them being our rubber agreement with Brazil. The agencies of the Government of the United States charged with passing on this export licence would therefore hesitate to approve a licence in view of the failure of the Foreign Office to inform us regarding the steps your Government is prepared to take to reduce exports to and imports from the Argentine."

"The State Department tells us moreover that until this information regarding the steps that your Government is prepared to take with reference to Argentine exports and imports is received, it is reluctant to authorize the export of any products from the United States which would be used in connection with Argentine exports to the United Kingdom. There are many cases besides this particular one involving synthetic rubber which are constantly being presented. This case involving synthetic rubber is however particularly troublesome. Should a request for the concurrence of Brazil be laid in this case and a shipment from the United States be made, it might make it very difficult for the authorities of Brazil to continue to resist pressure for meeting the general rubber needs of Argentina."

"We have been asked by the State Department to bring this case to the attention of the Foreign Office stressing at the same time the urgency of getting a definite and clear indication of your Government's position on the general question of exports to Argentina and purchases of Argentine products."

Sincerely, William J. Gallman

[MR*]

Churchill thanked Roosevelt for agreeing to drop the idea of a joint statement aimed at damaging German morale, but his main concerns were the probable delay in the tripartite conference and American reluctance to help re-arm the French.

C–834

London [via U.S. Army]
Nov. 27, 1944, 1002 Z / TOR 1430 Z

Prime Minister to President Roosevelt Personal and Top Secret.

1. Your 657. Thank you very much. Please tell us if there is anything you think we ought to do.

2. Your 658. I agree with your conclusion that U. J. will not travel beyond the Black Sea but I am sure the ports there will be unfit for us until the winter has passed.

3. Your last paragraph. We have not got to this point yet and I agree with you we should collect a good many arms from the Germans. Still, I think when American divisions begin to return home there would be a strong case for their leaving some of their heavy weapons and equipment behind for the French to take over the job.

[MR*. *FRUS, Yalta Conf.*, pp. 19, 287–88. *R&C.*]

Roosevelt had a longstanding interest in Clipperton Island, located 2,000 miles due west of the Panama Canal along the logical trans-Pacific air route. American officials were suspicious that the British hoped to use Clipperton Island as part of an air route from the Southwestern Pacific through the Caribbean to England, bypassing the United States. In 1943, Roosevelt sent the famed Antarctic explorer, Rear Admiral Richard E. Byrd, on an expedition to survey a number of Pacific islands, including Clipperton. News that the British were about to conduct a similar expedition prompted the President to instruct the Navy to install weather and radio facilities on Clipperton Island. The French, who had gained legal control of the island following a long dispute with Mexico, protested, and even the State Department admitted that the United States had no legal grounds for such actions; but Roosevelt paid no attention.

Roosevelt had fished off Clipperton Island during a cruise in 1934 and again in 1938. Air Vice Marshal R. P. Willock was attached to the British Joint Staff Mission in Washington.

R–659

Washington [via U.S. Navy]
Nov. 27, 1944, 1722 Z

Top Secret and Personal from the President for the Prime Minister.

In mid October Air Vice Marshal Willock informed our Navy Department of his intention to survey Clipperton Island in compliance with instructions from British Air Ministry and we understand that a survey party is now at Acapulco, Mexico. Having in mind the Monroe Doctrine, air agreements now under discussion and American public opinion, I suggest that any plan of development of military bases on Clipperton or any other territory in or near American waters be discussed by the Governments concerned rather than by the Armed forces. I request that you cancel any instructions by your people about a further survey of Clipperton until you and I can discuss it. King is sure he can work out a schedule of your planes through Hawaii to meet military requirements. I have personally visited Clipperton twice. Roosevelt [WEB]

[MR*]

R–660

Washington [via U.S. Navy]
Nov. 27, 1944, 1728 Z

Top Secret and Personal from the President for the Prime Minister.

Referring to your 829, Truscott has been ordered to report in Italy December 5 for duty. Roosevelt [WDL]

[MR*]

The message Roosevelt sent to Churchill via Winant (R–655/1) was probably delivered on November 25, hence the Prime Minister's opening reference. Churchill's next cable contained the British response to the American position on postwar civil aviation.

C–835

London [via U.S. Army]
Nov. 27, 1944, 1751 Z / TOR 2007 Z

Prime Minister to President Roosevelt Personal and Top Secret.

We have spent all the weekend and this morning on the issues raised by the air conference and by your message to me of the 25th, and we have arrived at definite conclusions. I hope you will forgive me for not sending them to you till tomorrow as we have to give reasonable prior notice of our United Kingdom decisions to the Dominions and India. We can, of course, act for ourselves apart from them, but such discordance would represent a failure on our part in managing our own commonwealth affairs. I will make sure that our message placing our full position before you is in your hands during the morning of the 28th.

[MR*]

American leaders may have seen their requests for fewer restrictions on civil aviation as morally justified; the British saw them as a thinly disguised American attempt to profit at Britain's expense. The details of the argument tend to obscure the basic point of contention: U.S. commercial aviation, if granted complete access to all areas without discrimination, would dominate postwar civil aviation, driving the British carriers out of routes they had previously had or wanted. Churchill's response, particularly in the last paragraph where he recounted the facts of American military and economic superiority, was a proud but at the same time painful admission that Britain's status as a major power now depended upon American assistance and cooperation. The Prime Minister avoided an angry tone, for that was a luxury the British literally could not afford.

Sir Stafford Cripps, Minister of Air Production, and Lord Beaverbrook, the Lord Privy Seal, led the special British committee advising Churchill concerning the civil-aviation discussions. The "five freedoms" of the air are given in the headnote to C–827.

C–836

London [via U.S. Army]
Nov. 28, 1944, 1115 Z / TOR 1731 Z

Prime Minister to President Roosevelt Personal and Top Secret.

1. Winant has brought me your message about the air in reply to my number 827, and naturally it has caused me much anxiety. I agree with you that this is a grave matter in which not only governments but parliaments and peoples may become deeply agitated, with consequences which cannot fail to be disastrous both to the prosecution of the war and to the prevention of future wars. I feel it my duty, therefore, to place before you in simple terms the issue as it presents itself to me after hearing all the advice of the special committee under Beaverbrook, of which Stafford Cripps is an important member, as well as the unanimous views of the War Cabinet.

2. The foundations of our position at this conference, which is being held at the time and place which you proposed, are:

(A) The British Empire is asked to put invaluable and irreplaceable bases for air transport all over the world at the disposal of such nations as are capable of using them. This means of course primarily and in bulk placing them at the disposal of the United States.

(B) It was agreed between us as a war measure that you should make the transport aircraft and specialize upon them on account of the character of the war, the need to supply China over the Hump, the vast distances of the Pacific Ocean, etc., and that we should concentrate our efforts upon fighting types. In consequence the United States are in an incomparably better position than we are to fill any needs of air transport that may arise after the war is over, and to build up their civil aircraft industry. We would venture most earnestly to suggest that these two points are not receiving adequate consideration.

3. However, in partial recognition of the above two points, Lord Swinton believed that he had reached an agreement with Mr. Berle at Chicago on November 17th about the amount of aircraft capacity that should be put into service by our respective countries (frequencies) on a basis of "embarked traffic". Agreement was also reached about fares to prevent undercutting, unfair subventions, etc.

4. All the above was satisfactory to us and, I think, to the world. On November 18, however, your side of the table put forward an entirely new set of ideas and arguments which, in our judgment, took away with one hand what had been given with the other in consideration of our fundamental position set forth above in paragraphs 2 (A) and (B).

5. For instance, the escalator clause we sought, not only for traffic to and from your country but also for traffic between any two foreign coun-

tries. This meant that the number of services on any route could be increased when an airplane achieved a load equal to 65% of its full capacity. We had already agreed, reluctantly, that this escalator clause should apply to traffic to and from an aircraft's own country. We had also agreed to a so-called fifth freedom which would grant to an aircraft on through services the right to pick up and set down traffic between foreign countries at intermediate stops. It is true that provision was made for a differentiation of fares to safeguard the local traffic. That seemed to me a valuable line to explore.

6. Mr. Berle then asked for a combination of the escalator clause and the fifth freedom which would enable American aircraft to carry most of the traffic between the United Kingdom and the Dominions and India and all foreign countries, as well as between all nations of the Commonwealth. It would, in fact, give to United States airlines the right to everything save cabotage.

7. We must accept the fact that the arrangements about frequencies will very soon be completely different from those agreed upon before the escalator clause was proposed. There is very little doubt that our position relatively to yours is markedly injured thereby. This applies not only to Great Britain but to many other durable powers who are now in a weak condition to design and build suitable transport aircraft and to embark traffic.

8. On top of this escalator clause, which we have conceded for traffic to and from your country, Mr. Berle now demands the right of duplication over any section of any through route and also provision for increasing frequencies so that any airline could carry all the intermediate traffic it could get. This might well mean that aircraft embarking traffic in the United States would not only excel, as they are welcome to do on merits, but dominate and virtually monopolise traffic not only between our country and yours, but between all other foreign countries and British Dominions besides.

9. I have the opinion that both this point of linking the escalator clause and the fifth freedom together, and the claim for duplication on foreign air routes, require further patient study with a view to reaching agreement between our two countries. Thus, we could make sure that Great Britain and the Dominions and many other countries as well are not in fact run out of the air altogether as a result of your flying start with no regard to the fact that we are willing to throw all our bases all over the world into the common pool. I am sure I could not obtain the agreement of the Cabinet or of either House of Parliament to anything which wore that aspect. Nor would I try.

10. It may be that you will say I have not rightly posed the issues. If this be so, I should be most grateful if you would state them in your own

words. It is [Is it] suggested, for instance, that we are going to challenge the right of all nations of innocent passage in Freedom I, or the consequential right of refuelling and repair in Freedom II, except in so far as these are mixed up in the much more refined issues arising out of your doctrines of escalator and duplication? There may well be other simplifications which could be made.

11. Should it not be possible for us to reach an agreement at this stage on Freedoms III, IV and V, when great battles in which our troops are fighting side by side are at their height and when we are preparing for immense new further efforts against Japan. I cannot see that a temporary adjournment to allow of the aforesaid patient discussions would do any serious harm. On the contrary, I believe that it would be as readily understood as was the postponement of final decision at Dumbarton Oaks. There is always the great body of technical matter upon which agreement has been secured. Therefore, unless complete agreement is reached, I plead that there shall be an adjournment. Such adjournment for a short time, if asked for by an intimately-allied power like us, ought not to be denied, nor ought we to be confronted with such very serious contingencies as are set out in your message received on Saturday [R–655/1]. As [An] open dispute carried out by Parliament and Congress, both of which would have to be informed and in our voluble free press on both sides, would do far more harm to the war effort and to our hopes of the future than an adjournment of a few weeks or even months, while both parties persevered behind the scenes for a settlement.

12. It is my earnest hope that you will not bring on this air discussion the prospect of our suffering less generous treatment on Lend-Lease than we had expected from the Quebec discussions. But even if I thought that we were to be so penalized, I would not feel myself able to agree to a decision contrary to the merits, as we see them, on this matter.

13. I should be ready, of course, to accept impartial arbitration on the points outstanding at the Chicago conference, provided that they were discussed in relation to the general framework. We have not yet got our World Court again, but there are friendly states and neutral states from whom competent judges might be found.

14. Let me say also, that I have never advocated competitive "bigness" in any sphere between our two countries in their present state of development. You will have the greatest navy in the world. You will have, I hope, the greatest air force. You will have the greatest trade. You have all the gold. But these things do not oppress my mind with fear because I am sure the American people under your re-acclaimed leadership will not give themselves over to vainglorious ambitions, and that justice and fair-play will be the lights that guide them.

[MR*. *FRUS*, 1944, II, 590–92. p*R&C*.]

Churchill thanked Roosevelt for sending General Truscott to Italy.

C–837

London [via U.S. Army]
Nov. 28, 1944, 1010 Z / TOR 1230 Z

Prime Minister to President Roosevelt. Personal and Top Secret.
 Your number 660. Thank you so much.

[MR*]

Given the tension which had arisen over the Civil Aviation Conference and
the extension of lend-lease, Churchill chose not to press the British plan to
survey Clipperton Island.

C–838

London [via U.S. Army]
Nov. 28, 1944, 1010 Z / TOR 1230 Z

Prime Minister to President Roosevelt. Personal and Top Secret.
 Your 659. I had not heard of this, but of course all action will now be
suspended till you and I have discussed the matter.

[MR*]

Since October 1943, Lieutenant General Adrian Carton de Wiart had represented Prime Minister Churchill and the Supreme Commander for South
East Asia, Admiral Lord Louis Mountbatten, in Chungking, the wartime seat
of the Chinese government. On November 21, de Wiart had reported that
Chiang Kai-shek wanted to transfer two Chinese divisions from India, where
they came under U.S. command, to China, in order to help stop a Japanese
advance which threatened American air bases in China, particularly Kunming
in southern China. Operation CAPITAL, however, a multistage offensive
against the Japanese in central Burma, called for those same Chinese divisions
to be used in Burma.

C–839

London [via U.S. Army]
Nov. 29, 1944, 1945 Z

Prime Minister to President Roosevelt Personal and Top Secret.
 In a telegram received today (SEACOS 265) Admiral Mountbatten

reports that he has received a warning from General Carton De Wiart that Generalissimo Chiang Kai Shek contemplates withdrawing the divisions which he requires in China from the Chinese Army in India, which is now engaged in carrying out its share of operation "CAPITAL".

The Chiefs of Staff endorse what Admiral Mountbatten says about the deplorable effect of these withdrawals on our operations in Burma. I suggest that you and I send the Generalissimo the following message of protest. If you agree with this suggestion, and with the terms of the message to the Generalissimo, pray send it off as a joint message from us both, with such minor alterations or additions as you think fit.

"Message from President and Prime Minister to Generalissimo."

"Admiral Mountbatten reports that he has received a message from General Carton De Wiart saying that you contemplate the withdrawal of two of your best divisions from the north Burma front as soon as Bhamo has fallen."

"The withdrawal of these forces from north Burma will inevitably bring the southward thrust through Bhamo to a standstill thus jeopardising the success of the whole campaign, and the security of the Mogaung Myitkyina air base."

"Your two divisions are now in contact with the enemy. If they are withdrawn from the battle in Burma by land route they will spend these critical months in weary marches over the rough track northwards. If they are withdrawn by air, they will use up aircraft which might otherwise be carrying to China the supplies you badly need. In neither case could their heavy transport and equipment be moved with them."

"We earnestly request you therefore to reconsider any idea of weakening your gallant forces which are cooperating so successfully with ours with the intention of reestablishing firm communications between China and her Allies."

[MR*. R&C.]

Roosevelt approved without change this cable drafted by Assistant Secretary of State Dean Acheson after consultations with Adolf Berle. It represents, then, a clear statement of the State Department's position in favor of a world open to American commerce without any restrictions, and so goes beyond the specific issue of civil aviation. The smaller nations, most of whom had competed with Britain for air traffic, tended to favor a system which would open the British Empire to their airlines. The British, thus assailed from both sides, tried to argue that "equal opportunity" had to take into consideration the relative size and wealth of the competitors; but the Americans would have none of it.

The President had left Washington on the afternoon of November 27 and traveled by train to Warm Springs, Georgia, to rest after the strain of the election campaign. According to his physician, Roosevelt was tired but healthy, although his appetite still suffered, probably because of the digitalis he took for his heart condition.

R–661

Warm Springs, Ga. [via U.S. Navy]
Nov. 30, 1944, 0120 Z

Personal and Top Secret from the President for the Prime Minister.

I have given careful thought to your 836 and to the problems which you cite. You know that I have no desire for any arrangement by which our people would profit from the sacrifices which yours have made in this war. Your confidence in the justice and fair play of the American people is, I am sure, justified. I have equal confidence that your people have the same qualities in the same measure. I know that they want equal opportunity in the air and unquestionably they should have it. I can not believe that they would want aviation, in which you as well as we have a great future, stifled and suffocated because they were for a moment in a less favorable competitive position.

You say that the British Empire is being asked to put bases all over the world at the disposal of other Nations. Of course it is. Would you like to see a world in which all ports were closed to all ships but their own or open to one foreign ship, perhaps two if they carried only passengers and cargo bound all the way from Liverpool to Shanghai? Where would England be if shipping were subjected to such limitations? Where will it be if aviation is? I am unable to believe that you do not want an agreement at this time.

I can not agree that the answer is to hold everyone back. It must be rather to go forward together. I know the handicaps under which your aviation industry has laboured during the war. We have found ways to help you before and I am confident that we can find ways to help you in overcoming this. We are prepared to make transport aircraft freely available to you on the same terms as our own people can get them. Our only stipulation is that aviation must be permitted to develop, subject only to reasonable safeguards, as far and as fast as human ingenuity and enterprise can take it.

We have no desire to monopolize air traffic anywhere. I do not see how increased frequencies on long routes would dominate traffic on short ones, when all lines would have the same right to increase their frequencies on the same basis. Nor do I see how in the long term such an arrangement would favor us over others, despite our head start.

You asked that I give further consideration to the fundamentals of your position and that I state the issues as I see them. I have done both and I am more convinced than ever that the answer is not to hold back but to go forward together.

I feel that the Conference can still reach an agreement vastly helpful both in the air and in wider fields. Swinton and Berle on November 27 publicly stated our respective positions. The smaller States have spoken and, if I may say so, our position seemed to have by far the greater support. If it is not possible to reach complete agreement when our delegations have so closely approached it, the reasons, despite our best will, would be all too clear.

You speak of impartial arbitration within the general framework. The Canadians undoubtedly see both points of view, have laboured tirelessly to bring us together and on November 27 brought out a new formula which might provide a reasonable line of compromise if the small nations would indeed accept so limited a formula. I will give Berle latitude for one more try on the lines of that formula if you will give Swinton the same.

Given, on both sides, that spirit of justice and fair play of which you speak, I know that an agreement can be reached which will be equally beneficial to both our interests and to the world. Roosevelt [DA]

[MR*. *FRUS*, 1944, II, 594–95. *R&C*.]

Roosevelt scrawled the draft of this greeting on the back of an envelope for dispatch on Churchill's seventieth birthday. A year earlier, during the Teheran Conference, the British Prime Minister had celebrated his birthday by hosting a dinner for Roosevelt and Stalin. The return to the more personal "Former Naval Person" heading was not indicated in the President's draft and may have been his idea or that of someone on the Map Room staff.

R–662

Warm Springs, Ga. [via U.S. Navy]
Nov. 30, 1944, 0310 Z

Personal and Secret from the President for the Former Naval Person.

Ever so many happy returns of the day. I shall never forget the party with you and UJ a year ago and we must have more of them that are even better.

Affectionate regards. F.D.R. [FDR]

[MR*]

Lieutenant General Albert C. Wedemeyer had replaced Stilwell as commander of U.S. forces in China and as a Chief of Staff to Chiang Kai-shek.
One of the goals of Operation CAPITAL was to re-open the Burma Road
so that supplies could be sent overland to China, but Wedemeyer and the
U.S. Joint Chiefs agreed that the direct threat posed by the Japanese offensive
in China was more important, at least to the Chinese, than operations in
Burma.

R–663

Warm Springs, Ga. [via U.S. Navy]
Dec. 1, 1944, 0223 Z

Personal and Top Secret from the President for the Prime Minister.

Since the receipt of your message number 839 of November 29th reference Mountbatten's SEACOS 265 a message has been received from
General Wedemeyer outlining the gravity of the situation in China and
stating that he concurs in the decision of the Generalissimo to transfer
the two best trained divisions of Chinese troops from Burma to the Kunming area. You have undoubtedly seen this message which went to Mountbatten and has been furnished to your Mission here in Washington so I
shall not repeat it.

We have General Wedemeyer's views on the ground as to the gravity
of the situation along with his knowledge of the situation and the plans
for operations in Burma. I feel that he is better informed as to the general
situation and requirements than any other individual at this moment.
Furthermore we are faced by the fact that the Generalissimo in a grave
crisis which threatens the existence of China, has decided that he must
recall these two divisions in order to check the Japanese drive on Kunming. It would avail us nothing to open a land line to China if the Japanese
seized the Kunming terminal for air and ground. Under the circumstances I therefore am of the opinion that we are not in a position to
bring pressure on the Generalissimo to alter his decision.

The U.S. Chiefs of Staff propose to send to General Wedemeyer a
message which approves his recommendation in support of the Generalissimo's decision but requests him to endeavor to develop a scheme for
using other units which might make possible the retention in India of
one or even both of the two crack Chinese divisions. The U.S. Chiefs have
explained their intention to the British Chiefs of Staff and have requested
that they concur with this action and inform Mountbatten accordingly.
Roosevelt

[MR*. R&C.]

The conferees at the Chicago Civil Aviation meeting had agreed to establish an international Interim Council, leading to a permanent organization, which would apply precise rules previously agreed to by all members. It was to this group that the Anglo-American dispute was initially referred.

C–840

London [via U.S. Army]
Dec. 1, 1944, 1532 Z / TOR 1740 Z

Prime Minister to President Roosevelt Personal and Top Secret.

1. We consulted together at once on the issues discussed in your 661. We decided to examine the prospect of an agreement based on the Canadian plan as suggested in the seventh paragraph of your 661, coupled with a further exploration of the differentiation of fares for Fifth Freedom Traffic, of which I spoke in paragraph five of my 836 as a valuable line.

2. By the time we had communicated with Swinton, however, the conference had already decided to approve all the technical decisions and to refer unfinished business to the Council of the International Organization.

3. I must confess to you that we have found it difficult at this distance to form a clear judgment of the rapidly changing phases of a negotiation so complex in character and far-reaching in scope. Swinton's return will give me an opportunity to conduct with him a comprehensive survey of the problem such as cannot be achieved in an exchange of telegrams.

4. Having reached an understanding, I would propose to give you an account of the plan which we can lay before the council in order to meet your wishes and, as far as may be possible, fulfil your expectations. You may be sure that your own desire to lay a sound foundation for the future civil air transport system of the world is paralleled by our own.

[MR*. *FRUS*, 1944, II, 597.]

Although Churchill had to agree that the Japanese offensive in China could not be ignored, he hoped to minimize the loss of transport aircraft available to Mountbatten and Operation CAPITAL by getting General Wedemeyer to submit his air requirements for review by the British before they were approved.

The paragraph about establishing a "bomb line" presumably related to attempts to coordinate Allied heavy bombing in eastern Germany and along the Russian front so as to avoid dropping bombs on Soviet forces.

C–841

London [via U.S. Army]
Dec. 2, 1944, 1418 Z / TOR 1650 Z

Prime Minister to President Roosevelt Personal and Top Secret.

1. I agree fully with your number 663. Events have superseded the views expressed two days ago in my number 839. We must, then, review the new situation created in Burma by these misfortunes at a time when operation CAPITAL has opened well. The one request I make at the moment is that, as the two Chinese divisions are to be carried by air, we should be consulted about what air forces are left for the necessary support of Mountbatten's advancing forces. I have the greatest confidence in Wedemeyer but he cannot know the situation in the south at any moment.

2. I also concur with the United States Chiefs of Staff that, our officers in Moscow having received no answer from the Russians, the Russians should be notified that we shall bomb from December 3 up to the bomb line proposed to the Red Staff on November 28.

[MR*]

Roosevelt and Churchill had great difficulty keeping up with the fast-changing situation at the Civil Aviation Conference. This message was sent at the request of Adolf Berle, who thought the British needed some additional prodding.

R–664

Warm Springs, Ga. [via U.S. Navy]
Dec. 2, 1944, 1519 Z

Top Secret and Personal from the President for the Prime Minister.

Thank you for your 840. I am advised that Swinton's motion, which Berle seconded, to refer unfinished business to the Council has now been deferred on a motion from the floor. The Conference apparently still feels, as do I, that agreement should be reached if possible. I would accordingly appreciate your further urgent consideration of the matter. Roosevelt [ES]

[MR*]

Churchill alluded to his hoped-for Anglo-American partnership in the postwar world at every opportunity.

C–842

London [via U.S. Army]
Dec. 3, 1944, 0935 Z / TOR 1244 Z

Prime Minister to President Roosevelt. Personal.

I am deeply grateful to you for your most kind message [R–652/1, R–662] on my birthday, which gave me the greatest pleasure, and also for the framed quotation from Abraham Lincoln with your own charming note upon it. This reached me, by sure hands, when I awoke.

I cannot tell you how much I value your friendship or how much I hope upon it for the future of the world, should we both be spared.

[MR*. R&C.]

The United States would not subject Wedemeyer's requests for air transport to prior British scrutiny, but the Joint Chiefs did instruct him to limit his demands to the minimum. SEAC stood for South East Asia Command.

R–665

Warm Springs, Ga. [via U.S. Navy]
Dec. 4, 1944, 1802 Z

Top Secret and Personal from the President for the Prime Minister.

Your 841. Generals Wedemeyer and Sultan have been directed to transfer two Chinese divisions to China to meet the emergency.

Wedemeyer has been directed to limit his demands for transport aircraft to those not urgently required for supply of SEAC forces engaged with the enemy unless no other means of meeting the emergency can be found.

New subject—Regarding the bomb line in Balkans, Russians have been notified that we shall attack enemy with bombs up to the line proposed to the Soviet Staff on November 28.

[MR*]

The British continued to worry that too many aircraft would be diverted from Burma to China, but Roosevelt chose not to reply. The "new subject" mentioned in the second paragraph was the notification given to the Soviets about the bomb line that the Allies would observe.

C–843

London [via U.S. Army]
Dec. 5, 1944, 1132 Z / TOR 1335 Z

Personal and Top Secret. Prime Minister to President Roosevelt.
Your number 665:

1. We agree, but we are sure you would not wish to leave SEAC forces in a dangerous plight, especially since operation CAPITAL is the one you favoured. It is most unlikely that there will be any difference between Mountbatten and Wedemeyer, but if this should arise we feel it should be settled by the Combined Chiefs of Staff.

2. New subject: We endorse your action.

[MR*]

This routine thank-you and reassurance that the United States did not intend to threaten Britain on the matter of trade with Argentina almost contained a serious faux pas. As drafted in the State Department, the final sentence of the second paragraph read: "This message was intended to be an inquiry on a matter of common interest and, of course, in a sense a threat." Someone crossed out the word *a* (sense) and substituted "no."

For some reason, although copies of this message found in American files are dated December 5, 1944, the PREM 3 version in the British files bears the date 11.12.44 (Dec. 11, 1944).

R–665/1

Warm Springs, Ga. [via State Dept.]
Dec. 5, 1944, 5:00 P.M. / TOR Dec. 11, 1944 (?)

The Right Honorable
Winston Churchill, M.P.
Prime Minister, London.

I am deeply grateful for your message (No. 832 November 26, 1944) informing me of your decision to continue purchases on a month to month basis for a further six months' period. We will do everything in our power to satisfy your understanding with respect to other buyers as well as with respect to refrigerated cargo space to which you refer in paragraph four.

I am sorry about the apparent misunderstanding mentioned in the last paragraph of your message, and concerning which I, of course, had no prior information. I believe, however, that you will discover, as I did on further investigation, that the document quoted in your 833 did not refer to the matter of the meat contract, on which we exchanged messages in

October, but to the general programming of your other imports from and exports to Argentina about which the Department of State submitted inquiries to the Foreign Office in August and September. This message was intended to be an inquiry on a matter of common interest and, of course, in no sense a threat.

I am confident, however, that this matter can readily be adjusted and I want again to thank you for your helpful message. Franklin D. Roosevelt [ES]

[MR*. *FRUS*, 1944, VII, 371.]

The following plan for the proposed United Nations organization, worked out in the State Department, called for a veto for the permanent members of the Security Council (China, the United States, the United Kingdom, and the U.S.S.R.; France was added later) on all matters pertaining to declaring something a threat to the peace or on all actions, such as economic or military sanctions, designed to remove such a threat. The same cable, with only minor changes, was sent to Premier Stalin. The President approved this message on November 22, but dispatch was delayed to coincide with the return to Moscow of Ambassador Harriman, who had been in the United States since late October.

Churchill favored the Soviet view that the veto should apply more broadly, but Eden and the British Foreign Office disagreed, and considerable discussion ensued. By the time the British agreed to Roosevelt's proposals, Stalin had informed the President that the Soviet Union would not accept anything less than great-power unanimity (the veto) on all issues before the Security Council, even minor procedural questions. Stalin's message was sent on December 26, but the British did not learn of it until January 16, 1945 (*Stalin/ FDR*, doc. 253; Woodward, *British Foreign Policy*, V, 173). Churchill finally decided that, although he could accept Roosevelt's proposals, "I cannot undertake . . . to fight a stiff battle with them [the Soviet Union] on the subject" (Woodward, *British Foreign Policy*, V, 174). Since the President was already on his way to Europe for the Yalta Conference, the Prime Minister decided not to reply by cable, but on January 13 Eden sent a cable, originally prepared for Churchill's signature, accepting Roosevelt's proposals (Winant to Roosevelt, Jan. 13, 1945, MR).

R–666

Warm Springs, Ga. [via U.S. Navy]
Dec. 5, 1944, 1647 Z

Personal and Top Secret, from the President to the Prime Minister. Copy to Ambassador Winant for Background Only.

In view of the fact that prospects for an early meeting between you,

Marshal Stalin and myself are unsettled and because of my conviction, with which I am sure you agree, that we must move forward as quickly as possible in the convening of a general conference of the United Nations on the subject of international organization, I am taking this means of placing before you my present views on the important subject of voting procedure in the Security Council. This and other questions will, of course, have to be agreed between us before the general conference will be possible. I am also taking up this matter with Marshal Stalin.

I am certain that the following draft provision should be eminently satisfactory to everybody concerned:

Proposal for Section C of the
Chapter on the Security Council

C. VOTING

1. Each member of the Security Council should have one vote.

2. Decisions of the Security Council on procedural matters should be made by an affirmative vote of seven members.

3. Decisions of the Security Council on all other matters should be made by an affirmative vote of seven members including the concurring votes of the permanent members; provided that, in decisions under Chapter VIII, Section A, and under paragraph 1 of Chapter VIII, Section C, a party to a dispute should abstain from voting.

You will note that the proposal provides for the unanimity of the permanent members in all decisions of the Council which relate to a determination of a threat to the peace or to action for the removal of such a threat or for the suppression of aggression or other breaches of the peace. I am prepared to accept in this respect the view expressed by the Soviet Government in its memorandum on an international security organization presented at the Dumbarton Oaks meeting. This means, of course, that in decisions of this character the permanent members would always have a vote.

At the same time I am sure that the maintenance of the moral prestige of the great powers is an essential element in any successful system of international cooperation. I am certain therefore that those powers should not insist on exercising a veto in such judicial or quasi-judicial procedures as the international organization may employ in promoting voluntary peaceful settlement of disputes. I am certain that willingness of the permanent members to abstain from the exercise of their voting rights on questions of this sort would immensely strengthen their own position as the principal guardians of the future peace and would make the whole plan far more acceptable to all nations.

If you should be inclined to give favorable consideration to some such approach to the problem of voting in the Council, would you be willing

that there be held as soon as possible a meeting of representatives designated by you, by me, and by Marshal Stalin to work out a complete
provision on this question and to discuss the arrangements necessary for
a prompt convening of a general United Nations conference? Roosevelt
[State Dept.]

[MR*. *FRUS, Yalta Conf.*, pp. 58–60. *Stalin/FDR*, doc. 247. *R&C*.]

De Gaulle's visit to Moscow was made without prior consultation with either
the British or the Americans, although Stalin did cable Churchill on November 20 that the French leader would come to the Soviet Union later that
month. On December 2 and 3, Stalin sent identical telegrams to Churchill
and Roosevelt informing them that the French wanted a Franco-Soviet treaty
of mutual aid and Soviet support for adjustments along the Franco-German
border (*Stalin/WSC*, docs. 352, 354, 360, 364; *Stalin/FDR*, docs. 243, 244).

R–667

Warm Springs, Ga. [via U.S. Navy]
Dec. 5, 1944, 2017 Z

Top Secret and Personal from the President to the Prime Minister.

I have received from U.J. messages dated second and third December
regarding his talks with de Gaulle and am informed he sent you identical
messages.

I would like to have your views before I reply to Stalin. Roosevelt [ES]

[MR*. *FRUS, Yalta Conf.*, p. 289 (draft).]

Postwar politics had come to dominate the Churchill-Roosevelt exchanges,
but winning the war remained the task at hand. Much of the disappointment
expressed in this cable, however, related to military campaigns which were,
in part, aimed at specific postwar goals. The war in Italy had become, in
Churchill's thinking, a way to limit the spread of Soviet influence in southeastern and central Europe, while operations in Burma were aimed at restoring British power and prestige in South and Southeast Asia.

The slowing of the Allied advance on the western front is described in the
headnote to C–828, and the diversion of forces away from the Burma campaign is explained in C–839, R–663, and C–841. The American offensive
in the southwestern Pacific had driven the Japanese out of all the islands east
of the Philippines, and MacArthur's invasion of Leyte, in the Philippines, was
obviously succeeding. In Italy, Allied forces had stalled in the mountains well
south of Bologna and La Spezia, and would not attempt another offensive
until mid-April 1945. (See C–793.) German defenses had stiffened in eastern
Europe as their lines of communication and supply had shortened, and Soviet

offensives on the northern and central sections of the front had been halted in East Prussia and along the Vistula River respectively. On the southern portion of the front, Soviet forces had liberated Belgrade and had reached the Tisza River, fifty miles east of Budapest, by October, and on the thirtieth of that month launched a large-scale offensive toward Budapest. Rugged terrain and stubborn German resistance kept Soviet forces out of the city until February 1945, even though it was encircled and isolated shortly after Christmas. See maps, Vol. II, pp. 111, 453, and Vol. III, p. 525.

C–844

London [via U.S. Army]
Dec. 6, 1944, 0130 Z / TOR 1010 Z

Prime Minister to President Roosevelt Personal and Top Secret.

As we are unable to meet, I feel that the time has come for me to place before you the serious and disappointing war situation which faces us at the close of this year. Although many fine tactical victories have been gained on the western front and Metz and Strasbourg are trophies, the fact remains that we have definitely failed to achieve the strategic object which we gave to our armies five weeks ago. We have not yet reached the Rhine in the northern part and most important sector of the front and we shall have to continue the great battle for many weeks before we can hope to reach the Rhine and establish our bridgeheads. After that again, we have to advance through to Germany.

2. In Italy the Germans are still keeping 26 divisions, equivalent to perhaps 16 full strength or more, on our front. They could however at any time retreat through the Brenner and Ljubljana and greatly shorten their line by holding from Lake Garda to (say) Mouth of the Adige. By this they might save half their Italian forces for home defence. Even after that there are the Alps to which they could fall back, thus saving more men. It seems to me that their reason for standing so long in Italy may have been to extricate the twelve divisions in the Balkans, etc, which are now fighting their way back to Hungary and Austria. Apart from the air and partisans and small commando forces, there are no means of preventing this, and my opinion is that the greater part will escape. About half of these might be available for adding to what may be saved from Italy. This would be a powerful reinforcement to the German homeland available, according to events, either in the east or in the west.

3. We have secured weighty advantages from DRAGOON for the battle on the main front, but the reason why the Fifteenth Group of Armies has not been able to inflict a decisive defeat on Kesselring is that, owing to the delay caused by the weakening of our forces for the sake of DRA-GOON, we did not get through the Appenines till the Valley of the Po

had become waterlogged. Thus neither in the mountains nor on the plains have we been able to use our superiority in armour.

4. On account of the obstinacy of the German resistance on all fronts we did not withdraw the five British and British-Indian-Divisions from Europe in order to enable Mountbatten to attack Rangoon in March, and for other reasons also this operation became impracticable. Mountbatten therefore began, as we agreed at Quebec, the general advance to Burma downstream from the north and the west, and this has made satisfactory progress. Now, owing to the advance of the Japanese in China, with its deadly threat to Kunming and perhaps Chungking to the Generalissimo and his regime, two and possibly more Chinese divisions have to be withdrawn for the defence of China. I have little doubt that this was inevitable and right. The consequences however are serious so far as Mountbatten's affairs are concerned, and no decision has yet been taken on how to meet this new misfortune, which at one stroke endangers China and your air terminal as well as the campaign in northern Burma. All my ideas about a really weighty blow across the Adriatic or across the Bay of Bengal have equally been set back.

5. The vast scale operations which you have conducted in the Pacific are at present the only part of the war where we are not in a temporary state of frustration.

6. We have however happily to consider what the Russians will do. We have Stalin's promise for a winter campaign starting I presume in January. On most of his immense front he seems to have been resting and preparing though only about three or four German divisions have come over to face Eisenhower. I am not in a position to measure the latest attacks he has launched to the southwest of Budapest. We may however I think look forward to more assistance from this and other Russian actions than we have had lately, and the German position is so strained that any heavy penetration might bring about a partial if not a total collapse.

7. I have tried to survey the whole scene in its scope and proportion and it is clear that we have to face in varying degrees of probability—

(A) a considerable delay in reaching and still more in forcing the Rhine on the shortest road to Berlin,

(B) a marked degree of frustration in Italy,

(C) the escape home of a large part of the German forces from the Balkan Peninsula,

(D) frustration in Burma,

(E) elimination of China as a combatant.

When we contrast these realities with the rosy expectations of our peoples in spite of our joint efforts to dampen them down the question very definitely arises:—

"What are we going to do about it?"

My anxiety is increased by the destruction of all hopes of an early meeting between the three of us and the indefinite postponement of another meeting of you and me with our Staffs. Our British plans are dependent on yours, our Anglo-American problems at least must be surveyed as a whole, and the telegraph and the telephone more often than not only darken counsel. Therefore I feel that if you are unable to come yourself before February, I am bound to ask you whether you could not send your Chiefs of Staff over here as soon as possible, where they would be close to your main armies and to General Eisenhower and where the whole stormy scene can be calmly and patiently studied with a view to action as closely concerted as that which signalised our campaign of 1944.

[MR*. WSC, VI, 268–70. R&C.]

ANGLO-AMERICAN DISAGREEMENTS

The Anglo-American relationship had contained its share of disagreements from the start of World War II, but as postwar politics came to dominate the Churchill-Roosevelt exchanges, those differences become sharp and even angry. Churchill accused the United States of trying to monopolize the world's commercial aviation (C–836), and in the cable printed below bitterly attacked the State Department for its criticism of British policy in Italy and Greece. According to reports reaching the British government, Count Carlo Sforza had been selected as Italian Ambassador to the United States and was also trying to arrange his own appointment as either Deputy Prime Minister or Minister of Foreign Affairs. Churchill and the Foreign Office believed Sforza was anti-British, untrustworthy, and far too willing to work with the Italian communists, but they had to move cautiously since Sforza was well thought-of in American government circles. Nevertheless, American newspapers picked up information about the British attempts to prevent Sforza from getting an important position in the Bonomi government and claimed that Great Britain had vetoed Sforza. Concerned about the effect such reports could have on American opinion and annoyed that the British had begun their campaign against Sforza without first consulting the United States, the State Department, on December 5, released a statement which seemed directly aimed at British policy—in Italy and elsewhere. The State Department argued that politics in Italy was purely an internal affair for Italians to decide, and denied that the United States had indicated any opposition to Count Sforza. The statement closed with a remark which was interpreted in the press as directed also at British military intervention in Greece: "we expect the Italians to work out their problems of government along democratic lines without influence from outside. This policy would apply to an even more pronounced degree with regard to governments of the United Nations in their liberated territories" (FRUS, 1944, III, 1162). Indeed, the British military intervention in Greece, to which Roosevelt had agreed earlier (R–608), became a major Anglo-American controversy. (See C–849/1 and related documents which follow.)

In Belgium, the British Army had gone on alert during anti-government demonstrations in Brussels late in November. Members of the Belgian Resistance—including socialists, communists, and Flemish nationalists—had refused to turn in their arms to Allied military authorities and were trying to force the newly installed Belgian government, composed of leaders who had run the Belgian government in exile in London, to make major concessions. A general strike failed when workers feared it would interfere with the military effort against Germany, and the Resistance quickly offered its full support in mid-December when the Germans began their offensive in the Ardennes. Although General Eisenhower had ordered British troops in Belgium to act as they did, the Churchill Ministry received some criticism in the newspapers for seeming to interfere in Belgium's internal politics.

The letter of September 23, 1943, from Count Sforza to Assistant Secretary of State Adolf Berle (printed below) contained Sforza's commitment to support the Italian government, then led by Marshal Badoglio, so long as it was helping to drive the Germans out of Italy. Churchill interpreted this as a promise to support Badoglio or any other successor government approved by the Allies; Sforza believed the commitment pertained only to the crisis which had existed immediately after Italy's surrender in 1943.

Edward R. Stettinius, Jr., had become Secretary of State on December 1, 1944, replacing a tired, frustrated, and sick Cordell Hull. Even though Stettinius came from the world of corporate business, he shared the ideals of his predecessor on most issues. In this instance, the British assumed that State Department underlings had taken advantage of the Secretary's inexperience and rammed through the public statement on Italian politics. But that was not the case. Stettinius, along with most of the State Department, was highly critical of British attempts to maintain monarchies at the expense of democratic governments.

The distribution of the captured Italian fleet among the Allies had come up during the Teheran Conference and in Churchill-Roosevelt exchanges beginning with R–422.

C–845

London [via U.S. Army]
Dec. 6, 1944, 0130 Z / TOR 0800 Z

Prime Minister to President Roosevelt. Personal and Top Secret.

1. In view of the State Department's communique in [on] Italy issued yesterday, there will no doubt be a debate in Parliament. I shall be called upon to reply to its strictures by implication upon his Majesty's Government's policy and action not only in Italy but in Greece and possibly in Belgium. This I am quite prepared to do and I hope you will realise that I must have all liberty in this matter.

2. I should be very much obliged to you if you would authorise me to read the terms of Count Sforza's letter to Mr Berle of September 23, 1943. It was on the faith of this letter [printed below] that the British Government withdrew their opposition which they had a right to have considered to the sending of Count Sforza into Italy. When Count Sforza passed through London I went through this letter with him almost line by line, before witnesses who are available, and he made the strongest declaration amounting to a gentleman's word of honour that this represented his position. However no sooner had he got to Italy than he worked busily at the intrigues which destroyed the Badoglio Government. On account of this behavior I have regarded him as a man in whom no trust could be placed. It has never been our policy and we have no power, to veto the appointment of particular Italian ministers to particular positions. But it is certain that were Count Sforza to obtain the Premiership or the Foreign Secretaryship, the relations between the British Government and the Italian Government would suffer very much from our complete want of confidence in him. If you do not feel able to allow me to quote the letter, I shall none the less feel entitled to mention the substances of the undertakings given by Count Sforza to me.

3. I was much astonished at the ascerbity of the State Department's communique to the public, and I shall do my best in my reply to avoid imitating it. I feel however entitled to remind you that on every single occasion in the course of this war I have loyally tried to support any statements to which you were personally committed for instance, in the Darlan affair I made the greatest possible exertions as you may remember to sustain the action of the United States Government and Commander, which was and still is much criticized in quarters ever ready to be critical. Also, in the matter of the division of the Italian Fleet I not only did all in my power to avoid the slightest appearance of difference between us, though the difference was considerable, but His Majesty's Government have actually supplied fourteen out of the fifteen warships lent to the Russians to make up for their one third share of the Italian Fleet to which you had referred. Finally, it was I who proposed to you the bulk of the mitigations which were introduced into our relationship with Italy as the result of our talks at Quebec and Hyde Park.

4. In all these circumstances I was much hurt that a difference about Count Sforza should have been made the occasion for an attempt on the part of the State Department to administer a public rebuke to His Majesty's Government. In the very dangerous situation in which the war is now it will be most unfortunate if we have to reveal in public controversy the natural differences which arise inevitably in the movement of so great an alliance. I do not remember anything that the State Department has ever said about Russia or about any other allied state comparable to this

document with which Mr. Stettinius has inaugurated his assumption of office. I am sure such things have never been said by the State Department about Russia even when very harsh communications have been received and harsher deeds done.

[MR*. R&C.]

Because the letter from Count Sforza to Berle is not readily available in the printed sources, it is reproduced below:

Text of Letter addressed by Count Sforza to Mr. Berle on the 23rd September, 1943

I have further considered the statement of Marshal Badoglio issued on the 16th September last. As I told you, under existing circumstances there can be only one cause, namely, the cause of Italy, and it becomes the duty of all Italians, irrespective of their political differences, to support the struggle to defeat the German armies and to liberate Italian soil. I should appreciate it if the Department would send forward the following message from me to Allied headquarters in Italy for transmission, if they see fit, to Marshal Badoglio:—

"I have read with extreme interest the statement of Marshal Badoglio, issued on the 16th September, 1943, unequivocally stating that he considers the defeat of Germans and their expulsion from Italy to be his primary duty and urging all Italians to join in this struggle.

"In my view it now becomes the paramount duty of all Italians irrespective of party or political differences to support and assist in the struggle to crush German arms and to drive every German soldier from Italian soil.

"So long as Marshal Badoglio is engaged in that task and is acceptable to Allies in devoting Italian military material resources to that struggle, I consider it criminal to do anything to weaken his position or hamper his work in fighting for the liberation of Italy and the Italian people. I am prepared to offer my full support so long as he is thus engaged, all the more because this is the only way to destroy the last criminal remnants of Fascism.

"Matters of internal Italian politics can, and should be, adjourned for the period of the struggle, and activities, military and political, of all Italians who seek freedom and the future of their Fatherland should be devoted to supporting the organised forces which are endeavouring to overthrow the common enemy. I pledge my honour to do this myself, and urge this course on my many friends and associates."

[PREM 3/243/5/188–89]

Churchill approved of the proposed Franco-Soviet pact and went it one better by proposing a tripartite Anglo-Soviet-French agreement. Like the President, the Prime Minister preferred to postpone territorial questions until the post-war peace conference, although he promoted the idea of low-level discussions on the subject. Churchill also continued to push gently for some sort of French participation in the upcoming tripartite conference between himself, Roosevelt, and Stalin. (See C–89 for the Anglo-Soviet pact.)

C–846

London [via U.S. Army]
Dec. 6, 1944, 1008 Z / TOR 1345 Z

Prime Minister to President Roosevelt Personal and Top Secret.
    I have replied as follows to Stalin's enquiry for my advice on the two questions raised with him by De Gaulle:—

    "1. Your telegram about De Gaulle's visit and the two questions he will raise. We have no objection whatever to a Franco Soviet pact of mutual assistance similar to the Anglo Soviet pact. On the contrary, His Majesty's Government consider it desirable and an additional link between us all. Indeed, it also occurs to us that it might be best of all if we were to conclude a tripartite treaty between the three of us which would embody our existing Anglo Soviet treaty with any improvements. In this way the obligations of each one of us would be identical and linked together. Please let me know if this idea appeals to you as I hope it may. We should both of course tell the United States.

    2. The question of changing the eastern frontier of France to the left bank of the Rhine or alternatively of forming a Rhenish-Westphalian province under international control, together with other alternatives ought to await settlement at the peace table. There is, however, no reason why, when the three heads of government meet, we should not come much closer to conclusions about all this than we have done so far. As you have seen, the President does not expect De Gaulle to come to the meeting of the three. I would hope that this could be modified to his coming in later on when decisions, especially affecting France, were under discussion.

    3. Meanwhile, would it not be a good thing to let the European

Advisory Commission sitting in London, of which France is a member, explore the topic for us all without committing in any way the heads of governments?

4. I am keeping the President informed."

2. There seems much to be said for a tripartite Anglo Franco Soviet pact. In that way we can be sure that our mutual obligations to each other are harmonised from the beginning. Public opinion too would think such a joint agreement more satisfactory than an arrangement whereby relations between the French and ourselves were governed by agreements which each of us had entered into separately with Russia.

3. I should welcome your views.

[MR*. *FRUS, Yalta Conf.*, pp. 289–90. *Stalin/WSC*, doc. 365. *R&C.*]

German technological advances were indeed impressive, but they came too late to change the course of the war at sea.

C–847

London [via U.S. Army]
Dec. 6, 1944, 1020 Z / TOR 1345 Z

Prime Minister to President Roosevelt Personal and Top Secret.

I attach our suggestion for the November U-Boat report. Canada is being informed at the same time.

"Shipping losses from U-Boat action have again been very small and the number of U-Boats sunk in proportion has again been satisfactory.

The enemy has by no means abandoned the struggle and has introduced new devices, such as the extensible air intake and exhaust which enable U-Boats to remain submerged for long periods and so penetrate into areas denied to them for the past three years.

Reports that U-Boat construction has been abandoned are probably German inspired and are untrue. On the contrary, improved types of U-Boats may at any time be thrown into the battle and retention of our present command of the sea will undoubtedly call for unremitting vigilance and hard fighting."

[MR*]

Roosevelt posed no objections to a Franco-Soviet agreement, but continued to insist that boundary questions be referred to a postwar peace conference.

R–668

Warm Springs, Ga. [via U.S. Navy]
Dec. 6, 1944, 1829 Z

Top Secret and Personal from the President for the Prime Minister.
I have this date sent the following message to U.J.:

QUOTE. Thank you for your two informative messages of December two and December three.

In regard to a proposed Franco-Soviet pact along the lines of the Anglo-Soviet pact of mutual assistance, this Government would have no objection in principle if you and General De Gaulle considered such a pact in the interests of both your countries and European security in general.

I am in complete agreement with your replies to General De Gaulle with regard to the post-war frontier of France. It appears to me at the present time that no advantage to our common war effort would result from an attempt to settle this question now and that its settlement subsequent to the collapse of Germany is preferable. UNQUOTE.

I will reply to your 846 in a subsequent message. Roosevelt [WDL, State Dept.]

[MR*. pWSC, VI, 258. pStalin/FDR, doc. 245. R&C.]

Churchill and the British government remained unhappy with the direction taken at the International Civil Aviation Conference in Chicago, and insisted that further thought and consultations were needed.

C–848

London [via U.S. Army]
Dec. 6, 1944, 1752 Z / TOR 2022 Z

Prime Minister to President Roosevelt Personal and Top Secret.
Thank you for your telegram Number 664.

Although I have always felt that these discussions were premature and throw too heavy a burden on our minds at a time when so many anxieties of war weigh down upon us, yet I can assure you that I sympathise completely with your desire to take advantage of these pregnant negotiations at Chicago. It is our considered view, however, that further and, in the end, swifter progress will be made if we have an opportunity here to review the position in every one of its aspects and in its general setting in the world economy.

It is our desire, as it is yours, to reconcile the greatest possible freedom of air commerce with a broad justice to all nations, large and small.

It is your desire, as it is ours, that the free play of enterprise should not degenerate into an exploitation of national advantages which would in the end be found generally intolerable.

We are not satisfied, however, that the projects which have succeeded one another in such profusion during the intricate discussions at Chicago represent the final contribution of human ingenuity towards a solution.

Apart from our own views, we have to take account of Parliament and public opinion.

Criticisms of the Chicago proposals are already appearing in quarters of the press which are in no sense reactionary or narrowly nationalistic. These are symptoms which in the interest of ultimate agreement we cannot ignore. They serve to fortify us in our conviction that we should at this stage consult with our people. From such a consultation we shall expect to reach a clearer comprehension of issues which now seem to us extremely confused and to propound fresh constructive approaches.

[MR*. *FRUS*, 1944, II, 598–99. *R&C*.]

Roosevelt tried to calm Churchill by giving him permission to use the Sforza-to-Berle letter and by pointing out that it was the British, in a statement Eden made to the House of Commons on December 1, who started the public battle over the makeup of the Italian government. Stettinius continued in the same vein on December 7, when he commented that the American position on Greece coincided with that proclaimed by Churchill before the House of Commons on December 5: "Whether the Greek people form themselves into a monarchy or republic is for their decision. Whether they form a government of the right or left is for their decision. These are entirely matters for them" (Stettinius "Record," *FRUS, Yalta Conf.*, p. 433).

R–669

Warm Springs, Ga. [via U.S. Navy]
Dec. 6, 1944, 2237 Z

Top Secret and Personal from the President for the Prime Minister.
Your 845.

As you know, the letter to Berle merely transmitted Sforza's message to Badoglio and in no way involved this Government. I see no reason why you should not use the message itself in any way you see fit. I believe the message has already been made public, having been given to the press by Badoglio at the time of its receipt.

I deplore any offense which the press release on Italy may have given you personally or any implication of my lack of understanding of your responsibility before your country. You must recognize, however, the untenable position in which we were put by Mr. Eden's prior statement in the House regarding the British Government's representations to the Italian Government on the position of Sforza in any new government. While military operations continue, Italy is an area of combined Anglo-American responsibility and our silence on this step made it appear that we agreed with the action taken. Actually this move was made without prior consultation with us in any quarter and it is quite contrary to the policy which we have tried to follow in Italy, since the Moscow Conference last year, in accepting democratic solutions in government worked out by the Italian people themselves. In the circumstances we had no other choice than to make our own position clear.

You will remember my feeling on this score expressed to you at the time Bonomi succeeded Badoglio in forming a Government last June [R–562]. Roosevelt [ES]

[MR*. *FRUS, Yalta Conf.*, p. 271. *R&C.*]

Throughout the war, Roosevelt opposed any steps toward restoring France as a great power. French participation in major conferences, the expansion of French borders at Germany's expense, and an Anglo-Franco-Soviet pact all granted France more prestige than the President could accept.

R–670

Warm Springs, Ga. [via U.S. Navy]
Dec. 6, 1944, 2252 Z

Top Secret and Personal from the President for the Prime Minister.
Your 846.

You will have seen from my reply to Stalin on his talks with De Gaulle that our views are identical on the two questions which he raised.

I still adhere to my position that any attempt to include de Gaulle in the meeting of the three of us would merely introduce a complicating and undesirable factor.

In regard to your suggestion to Uncle Joe that the question of France's postwar frontiers be referred to the European Advisory Commission I feel that since the Commission is fully occupied with questions relating to the surrender of Germany, it would be a mistake to attempt to bring up at this stage before it any questions of postwar frontiers. It seems to me preferable to leave this specific topic for further exploration between us.

I fully appreciate the advantages which you see in a possible tripartite Anglo-Franco-Soviet pact. I am somewhat dubious, however, as to the affect of such an arrangement on the question of an international security organization to which, as you know, I attack the very highest importance. I fear that a tripartite pact might be interpreted by public opinion here as a competitor to a future world organization, whereas a bilateral arrangement between France and the Soviet Union similar to the Soviet-British Pact would be more understandable. I realize, however, that this is a subject which is of primary concern to the three countries involved. Roosevelt [State Dept.]

[MR*. *FRUS, Yalta Conf.*, p. 291. p*WSC*, VI, 259. *R&C*.]

On the advice of the Navy and the Office of War Information, Roosevelt accepted the British draft of the November anti-submarine warfare statement.

R–671

Warm Springs, Ga. [via U.S. Navy]
Dec. 6, 1944, 2304 Z

Secret and Personal from the President for the Prime Minister.
Your 847. We agree with your proposed statement. Roosevelt

[MR*]

Harold Macmillan was scheduled to visit Washington for talks about Anglo-American policy toward Italy, but the trip was canceled when Macmillan was sent to Greece. (See C–850.) It is not clear just which of Eden's telegrams Churchill was referring to, although the Foreign Secretary had, on December 5, sent a message to Ambassador Halifax protesting Secretary of State Stettinius' criticism of British attempts to keep Sforza out of the Italian government (Woodward, *British Foreign Policy*, III, 461). Roosevelt's cable 653, however, concerned increases in the Italian grain ration.

C–849

London [via U.S. Army]
Dec. 8, 1944, 1728 Z / TOR 1825 Z

Prime Minister to President Roosevelt. Personal and Top Secret.
Your telegram Nr. 653.
1. Macmillan is leaving almost at once for Washington and will be able

to discuss Italian questions with your people.

2. I have arranged for our views on the general question raised in your telegram to be taken up by the Foreign Office with the State Department. I fully endorse the line taken in the Foreign Secretary's telegram.

[MR*]

Unlike Churchill, the President rarely offered a written, broad overview of wartime strategy. This cable is even more unusual because it provides an insight into the differences in thinking between Roosevelt and General Marshall. Draft A, printed below, had the approval of Marshall and Admiral King. The President rewrote it entirely and sent it back to them for comments. Marshall's suggested changes, which were accepted by Roosevelt, are indicated by the additions and deletions shown in the final version printed below.

R–672/1, draft A, not sent

Washington
Dec. 7, 1944

[Roosevelt to Churchill]
For the President from Admiral Leahy:

The following quoted draft reply to Prime's 844 is forwarded for your consideration. It has Marshall's and King's approval.

"Your 844.

"We are winning on every front of our global battleline except in China. I agree with you that some of our optimism at Quebec concerning speedy victory has not been justified by the subsequent course of events. However, our agreed broad strategy is developing according to plan. You and I are now in the position of Commanders in Chief who have prepared their plans, issued their orders, and committed all of their resources to battle according to those plans and orders. For the time being, it seems to me the prosecution of the war and the outcome of the battles lie with our field commanders, in whom I have every confidence.

"It is true that our progress in Europe, both in the battle of Germany and in the Mediterranean, has been beset by exasperating delays. The winter brings with it further difficulties. However, with the opening of Antwerp and the assured flow of divisions and supplies to General Eisenhower, I feel the situation is now brighter than it has been for some time. In the battle of Germany our ground and air forces are day by day chewing up the enemy's dwindling manpower and resources. General Eisenhower estimates that on the Western Front alone he is inflicting losses in excess of the enemy's capability to form new units. I cannot see clearly just when, but soon a decisive break in our favor will come. If the

German chooses to continue this battle of attrition to the bitter end, there can be no result but complete destruction of the enemy. Our air and ground force efforts in the Mediterranean all help in this whittling down of Germany. I think our people understand the situation as it has developed. I feel hopeful that Eisenhower's increasing strength and a Russian offensive after the freeze will decisively crush German military resistance by spring.

"I share your concern about the situation in Asia but believe it is now too early to attempt to evaluate it. Admiral Mountbatten's operations are ahead of schedule, and I think there is a good chance that he may achieve his objectives in spite of immediate transfer of U.S. and Chinese resources to China. As to the grave Chinese situation, I do not see how more aid can be given to the Generalissimo than is now being provided by making available to Wedemeyer the resources for which he has asked.

My Chiefs of Staff are now devoting all of their abilities and energies in directing their organizations towards carrying out the plans we have made and in supporting our forces throughout the world. Practically all of these forces are, for the time being, committed. I do not feel that my Chiefs should leave their posts at this time since no requirement exists for broad strategic decisions to guide our field commanders in directing the decisive battles. If you, however, have any ideas or plans, even though not completely formulated, we should give thought to them at once. This would make it even more important that my Chiefs should be here during the period of preliminary consideration where their advice is immediately available to me."

[MR]

The President's redrafting not only added a more personal tone to the cable but also reflected Roosevelt's disagreement with Churchill on strategy in Italy and the Balkans. The earthquake and subsequent tidal wave, which caused heavy damage in Japan, took place on December 7—the third anniversary of the Japanese attack on Pearl Harbor.

Roosevelt continued to hope that Stalin would travel outside of the Soviet Union for the tripartite conference. Taormina, in eastern Sicily, was unacceptable to the Soviet Premier, but Stalin expressed willingness to go to Batumi (Batum) in southern Georgia on the Black Sea.

Intervention by British troops in Greece had brought on a Vote of Confidence in the House of Commons—a vote which Churchill's government won by 279 to 30. (See the headnote to C–849/1 for information on the Greek crisis.)

R–672

Warm Springs, Ga. [via U.S. Navy]
Dec. 9, 1944, 1947 Z

Top Secret and Personal from the President for the Prime Minister.

Your 844. I am at Warm Springs in Georgia taking ten days off after the campaign and everything in the personal line is going well.

Perhaps I am not close enough to the picture to feel as disappointed about the war situation as you are and perhaps also because six months ago I was not as optimistic as you were on the time element.

On the European front I always felt that the occupation of Germany up to the left bank of the Rhine would be a very stiff job. Because in the old days I bicycled over most of the Rhine terrain, I have never been as optimistic as to the ease of getting across the Rhine with our joint armies as many of the Commanding Officers have been.

However, our agreed broad strategy is developing according to plan. You and I are now in the position of Commanders-in-Chief who have prepared their plans, issued their orders, and committed our resources to battle according to those plans and orders. For the time being, even if a little behind schedule, it seems to me the prosecution and outcome of the battles lie with our Field Commanders in whom I have every confidence. We must remember that the winter season is bringing great difficulties but our ground and air forces are day by day chewing up the enemy's dwindling manpower and resources, and our supply flow is much improved with the opening of Antwerp.

General Eisenhower estimates that on the Western Front line he is inflicting losses in excess of the enemy's capability to form new units. I still cannot see clearly just when, but soon a decisive break in our favor is bound to come.

As to the Italian Front, Alexander's forces are doing their bit in keeping those German divisions in Italy, and we must remember that ~~they have always had the probable chance of moving their troops north of the Alps whenever they wanted to do so~~ the Germans are really free to withdraw to the line of the Alps if they so decide.

The same thing applies to their troops in the Balkans. I have never believed that we had the power to capture any large German forces in the Balkans without assistance by the Russians.

On the Russian Front we must also give full allowance to the vile weather and the Russians seem to be doing their bit at the present time. This, of course, you know more about than I do.

The Far Eastern situation is, of course, on a somewhat different footing and I am not at all happy about it.

From the long range point of view other than the measures Wedemeyer is now taking we can do very little ~~at this time to keep China together conducting~~ to prepare China to conduct a worthwhile defense, but Japan is suffering losses in men and ships and materials in the Pacific area that are many times greater than ours and they, too, cannot keep this up. Even the Almighty is helping. This magnificent earthquake and tidal wave is a proof.

The time between now and spring when the freeze is over will develop many things. We will know a lot more than we know now.

My Chiefs of Staff are now devoting all of their abilities and energies in directing their organizations toward carrying out the plans we have made and in supporting our forces throughout the world. Practically all of these forces are, for the time being, committed. That is why I do not feel that my Chiefs should leave their posts at this time since no requirement exists for broad strategic decisions to guide our Field Commanders.

I think I can leave after Inauguration Day. I hoped that Uncle Joe could come to Rome or Malta or Taormina or Egypt but if he will not—and insists on the Black Sea—I could do it even at great difficulty on account of Congress. Harriman suggested Batum which has an excellent climate. You and I could fly there from Malta or Athens, sending ahead one of my transport Flagships on which to live. Yalta is also intact, though the roadstead is open and we should probably have to live ashore.

Congratulations on the vote. Roosevelt [FDR, GCM]

[MR*. p*FRUS, Yalta Conf.*, p. 19. p*WSC*, VI, 270–72. *R&C*.]

TROUBLE IN GREECE

As he had done so often in the past, Churchill asked Harry Hopkins to intercede with Roosevelt, this time over the issue of British military intervention in Greece. Churchill feared that Stettinius' public statement of December 5 (see headnote to C–845), which implied a strong criticism of British actions in Greece, reflected the President's feelings, and the Prime Minister hoped that Hopkins could bring about a change.

Basically, the Americans and the British differed over the form of the postwar government in Greece. The subject had come up before (see the third enclosure to C–414/8 and C–648), but the evacuation of German forces from Greece brought matters to a head. Guerrilla resistance to the German occupation had been led primarily by anti-monarchical forces, particularly the Greek Communist Party (KKE). This National Popular Liberation Army (ELAS) and its political organization (EAM) had gained the respect of much of the Greek populace while the royal government of King George II, already tainted by its association with the prewar dictatorship in Greece, had lost much of its support. Churchill and the British government, however, believed that ELAS would be anti-British and therefore opposed attempts by the anti-monarchists to arrange a plebiscite before the royal government could return to Greece. The fratricidal nature of the struggle was intensified by the German use of "Security Battalions" of armed Greeks against the supposedly communist ELAS, who were accused of planning to hand Macedonia over to the Bulgarians. By the time the Germans left, the hatred between those two groups had reached the point that neither could trust the other.

Expecting EAM/ELAS to attempt to seize control, the British rushed forces into Athens so that they could "restore order" and install the royal government of Prime Minister Georgios Papandreou. Then, in a move which almost guaranteed violence, the British brought in two elements of the Royal Greek Army, the Third "Mountain" Brigade and the "Sacred" Battalion, to help maintain control. Since both those forces had been purged of all but loyal monarchists during the Greek mutinies at Alexandria earlier in 1944 (see C–648), their presence only heightened the tensions. Even more inflammatory was the British use, on what was supposed to be a temporary basis, of the old German-organized "Security Battalions" as a sort of National Guard. Little wonder that members of ELAS refuse to turn in their arms. EAM leaders, including most of the communists, had assumed that their struggle to establish republican political institutions would be political, not military, but the introduction of British-supported rightist forces shattered those assumptions. Even though Papandreou was not eager to bring the King back to Greece, ELAS still believed it had to build up the strength of its forces in Athens in order to prevent the re-establishment of a rightist monarchy. Meanwhile the Greek economy, devastated by the war, fell apart completely, further weakening the Papandreou government.

On December 1, 1944, Lieutenant General Ronald Scobie, who commanded British forces in Greece, announced that he had instructions to protect the Papandreou government against any coup d'état, and he ordered ELAS to disband its armed forces by December 10. That prompted EAM Ministers in the Papandreou government to resign and to call for a general strike and mass demonstration for December 3. In such an atmosphere of mutual hatred and distrust, the inevitable "incident" occurred, and by nightfall between ten and twenty-one demonstrators had been killed and over a hundred wounded. Churchill quickly took charge and, without consulting his Cabinet, gave General Scobie orders to maintain the Papandreou government in power, using military force as necessary (WSC, VI, 288–89). For the next two months Greece was torn apart by a brutal civil war.

Churchill came under heavy attack in both the British and American press for what seemed to be unwarranted intervention in the internal affairs of an ally. The debate and Vote of Confidence in the House of Commons, to which the Prime Minister confidently referred in this message to Hopkins, was far more bitter and serious than Churchill let on, and Stettinius' public statement on Italy, issued on December 5, contained an indirect but obvious reference to Greece which had angered the Prime Minister (C–845). After having telephoned Harry Hopkins to complain about an order from Admiral King which prohibited American ships from carrying supplies to the British in Greece, an order which Roosevelt made King rescind, Churchill tried to persuade Hopkins that the United States should support British policy in Greece. Hopkins forwarded the message to Roosevelt in Warm Springs, Georgia.

C–849/1

London [via U.S. Army]
Dec. 10, 1944, 2240 Z

Prime Minister to Mr. Harry Hopkins Personal Private and Secret.

I hope you will tell our friend that the establishment of law and order in and round Athens is essential to all future measures of magnanimity and consolation towards Greece. After this has been established will be the time for talking. My guiding principle is "No peace without victory". It is a great disappointment to me to have been set upon in this way by ELAS when we came loaded with good gifts and anxious only to form a United Greece which could establish its own destiny. But we have been set upon, and we intend to defend ourselves. I consider we have a right to the President's support in the policy we are following. If it can be said in the streets of Athens that the United States are against us, then more British blood will be shed and much more Greek. It grieves me very much to see signs of our drifting apart at the time when unity becomes even more important, as danger recedes and faction arises.

For you personally. Do not be misled by our majority yesterday. I could have had another 80 by sending out a three line whip instead of only two. On Fridays, with the bad communications prevailing here, members long to get away for the weekend. Who would not?

Every good wish!

[HLH:Sherwood Col. *WSC*, VI, 297.]

By the time Macmillan and Alexander arrived in Athens on December 11, British forces were besieged in the city and an airbase nearby.

The crisis generated by the proposed appointment of Count Sforza to a major Italian Cabinet post ended when Prime Minister Bonomi announced a new government which did not include Sforza.

C–850

London [via U.S. Army]
Dec. 10, 1944, 1628 Z / TOR 1825 Z

Prime Minister to President Roosevelt, Personal and Top Secret.

My telegram Number 849 of December 8th.

I am sorry that circumstances which I know you will understand now compel me to send MacMillan accompanying Field Marshal Alexander to Athens and he will, therefore, be unable, to his great regret and mine, to make his visit to Washington for some time. I want to send another minister to Washington in his place and will let you know about this as soon as possible.

Meanwhile, as regards Italy, Halifax will tell you what we have in mind. We are briefing him fully and he will have the assistance of the officers who are already waiting to meet MacMillan in Washington.

Halifax will tell you how much we all regret this change of plan.

[MR*]

When Churchill telephoned Harry Hopkins to protest the order from Admiral King (COMINCH—Commander in Chief U.S. Fleet) to Vice Admiral H. K. Hewitt, commander of the U.S. Eight Fleet in the Mediterranean, forbidding the use of American shipping to supply British forces in Greece, Hopkins persuaded the Prime Minister not to send the following angry cable to the President. Hopkins interceded to get the naval order withdrawn, but Churchill sent the draft to Hopkins anyway. The Prime Minister's arguments were well taken, for Roosevelt had approved the transfer of British forces to Greece for the very purpose of preventing a coup by EAM/ELAS.

C–850/1, letter

London
December 11, 1944

Private
My dear Harry,

I took your advice but you ought to see what the case was on the point raised and the President might be reminded of our very close agreement on so many occasions about the Greek situation. I must frankly confess I never knew E.A.M. would be so powerful. I only wish they had fought one-tenth as well against the Germans. We have got many troops coming in now but I certainly do not want to fight another war against E.L.A.S. If, using this telegram or the facts in it as you think best, you can get any word of approval spoken by the United States in favour of the Allied intervention in Athens by British troops, you may save many British and Greek lives and set free soldiers who are needed elsewhere. Send me a telegram on receipt.

Thanking you for yr Mediation   Yours always   W[inston Churchill]

[HLH:Sherwood Col.]

ENCLOSURE TO C–850/1

London
Dec. 10, 1944

Prime Minister to President Roosevelt Personal and Top Secret
[Sent to Harry Hopkins, not to the President]
1. General Wilson has sent the following telegram. BEGINS:

1. I have just received information from C.-in-C. Med. that Commander Eighth Fleet has received orders from COMINCH that American L.S.T.'s are to cease forthwith conveying troops, stores and supplies to Greece.

2. 2 of these L.S.T.'s are due to sail to Greek ports on 10th and a total of 7 are engaged in carrying out a phased programme.

3. Please inform me if I am to accept these orders as embodying the decisions of the Combined Chiefs of Staff.

4. For your information, a reversal of the decision by which these L.S.T.'s have been made available for general Mediterranean purposes would gravely endanger the security of the forces now in Greece, and delay the introduction of relief vehicles and supplies.

5. A decision on similar lines prohibiting the use of American aircraft for the conveyance of stores and reinforcements to Greece would further complicate a very difficult situation.

6. Pending a decision I have ordered that movement of American L.S.T.'s should cease and that the two now ready to sail should stand fast but should not be unloaded. You will no doubt appreciate the urgency of a decision on this matter. ENDS.

2. I am sure there has been some mistake about the orders issued to Commander Eighth Fleet, that American L.S.T.'s should forthwith cease convoying troops, stores and supplies to Greece. We are in Greece by virtue of your telegram No. 608 of August 26 in reply to my telegram No. 755 of August 17, of which text were as follows: [the texts of C–755 and R–608, printed above, follow].

3. We made the necessary preparations and the whole matter was confirmed at Quebec and the report approved by you and me contains the following words:—
BEGINS:

We have noted that as long as the battle in Italy continues there will be no forces available in the Mediterranean to employ in the Balkans except:—
(a) The small force of two British brigades from Egypt which is being held ready to occupy the Athens area and so pave the way for

commencement of relief and establishment of law and order and the Greek Government.

(b) The small land forces in the Adriatic which are being actively used primarily for commando type operations. ENDS.

4. Following is extract from directive sent to General Wilson by the Combined Chiefs of Staff on 8 September (FAN 409):
BEGINS:

4. You will centralize directly under your H.Q.

(a) All operations for occupation in Greece in event of a German withdrawal or surrender, and to pave the way for establishment of a Greek Government.

(b) Arrangements for provision relief supplies in Greece.

5. In exercising your responsibility for military operations referred to in paragraph 4 (a) above you will act in your purely British capacity. You will appoint a British Commander and you will nominate a British Force to be under his Command for purposes indicated in paragraph 4 (a), supplemented by use of such U.S. transport aircraft as are available to you and can be spared from your other operations.

6. The arrangement for provision relief supplies in Greece referred to in paragraph 4 (b) will be an Allied undertaking and in exercising your responsibility for their execution you will therefore act in your capacity as Allied C.-in-C. ENDS.

5. We have acted accordingly. We have been attacked by forces far stronger than were anticipated, but we have not diverged in the slightest degree from the policy towards Greece agreed upon by you and me, namely, that the Germans should be driven out, that law and order should be maintained in Athens and that food supplies should be delivered. Furthermore that ultimately, as soon as normal tranquility returned, the Greeks should have a free vote as to whether they want a monarchy or a republic, or a Left Government or a Right. The King of Greece of course wanted to go back to fight for his throne. I persuaded him not to do so. I would, if necessary, have prevented him from leaving England.

6. If, now that we are heavily engaged, orders are given by the United States which have the effect of partially cutting our lines of communication and impeding reinforcement and maintenance of our troops, this might produce a disaster of the first magnitude.

7. I cannot believe that you have seen these orders. If such were your intentions, I am sure you would have let me know in good time in what way I had diverged from our agreement.

8. The reference in the last sentence of Mr. Stettinius's Press release has of course been taken all over the world and in Greece as a suggestion that the United States is against the action we have taken in Greece, and

this undoubtedly makes our task more difficult and costly in British and Greek life. If our forces had not been on the spot, the whole of Greece would now be in the hands of a Communist-run E.A.M. Government against the will of what I am assured is the vast majority of its people. Being upon the spot, our troops could hardly stand by as spectators of the massacre which would have ensued, followed by a ruthless terror in the name of a purge. I am sure you would not like us to abandon this thankless task now and withdraw our troops and let things crash.

9. I am cheered by the last line of your No. 672. If this were known publicly it would probably lead to a peaceful settlement in Greece. However I am not asking you this. We could of course have added another 80 to our majority by sending out a three-line instead of a two-line Whip. But we did not think this necessary in view of the great difficulty of people getting away to their homes for the weekend.

10. I will send you a telegram tomorrow or the next day about the rest of your No. 672. W.S.C.

[HLH:Sherwood Col.]

Misled by the rhetoric of American criticisms of British colonialism, EAM leaders and many Greeks on the streets of Athens believed that the United States would prevent the British from imposing a government on Greece. In reality, Roosevelt sent Churchill a message which supported British policy within the limitations supposedly set by American public opinion. The President granted that Great Britain had full responsibility for Greece and asked only that Churchill understand why the United States government could not publicly support him. The deleted phrase had apparently been added to the State Department draft, possibly by Roosevelt, but was subsequently taken out. The suggestions made in this cable were aimed at resolving the crisis, not at displacing British influence in Greece.

R–673

Warm Springs, Ga. [via U.S. Navy]
Dec. 13, 1944, 2217 Z

Personal and Top Secret, from the President for the Former Naval Person.

I have been as deeply concerned as you have yourself in regard to the tragic difficulties you have encountered in Greece. I appreciate to the full the anxious and difficult alternatives with which you have been faced. I regard my role in this matter as that of a loyal friend and ally whose one desire is to be of any help possible in the circumstances. You may be sure that in putting my thoughts before you I am constantly guided by the fact that nothing can in any way shake the unity and association between our two countries in the great tasks to which we have set our hands.

As anxious as I am to be of the greatest help to you in this trying situation, there are limitations imposed in part by the traditional policies of the United States and in part by the mounting adverse reaction of public opinion in this country. No one will understand better than yourself that I, both personally and as head of State, am necessarily responsive to the state of public feeling. It is for these reasons that it has not been ~~and I am afraid will not be~~ possible for this Government to take a stand with you in the present course of events in Greece. Even to attempt to do so would bring only temporary value to you and would in the long run do injury to our basic relationships. I don't need to tell you how much I dislike this state of affairs as between you and me. My one hope is to see it rectified so we can go along in this as in everything, shoulder to shoulder. I know that you, as the one on whom the responsibility rests, desire with all your heart a satisfactory solution of the Greek problem and particularly one that will bring peace to that ravished country. I will be with you wholeheartedly in any solution which takes into consideration the factors I have mentioned above. With this in mind I am giving you at random some thoughts that have come to me in my anxious desire to be of help.

I know that you have sent MacMillan there with broad powers to find such a solution and it may be that he will have been successful before you get this. I of course lack full details and am at a great distance from the scene, but it has seemed to me that a basic reason—or excuse, perhaps— for the EAM attitude has been distrust regarding the intentions of King George. I wonder if MacMillan's efforts might not be greatly facilitated if the King himself would approve the establishment of a regency in Greece and would make a public declaration of his intention not to return unless called for by popular plebiscite. This might be particularly effective if accompanied by an assurance that elections will be held at some fixed date, no matter how far in the future, when the people would have full opportunity to express themselves.

Meanwhile, might it not be possible to secure general agreement on the disarmament and dissolution of all the armed groups now in the country, including the Mountain Brigade and the Sacred Battalion, leaving your troops to preserve law and order alone until the Greek national forces can be reconstituted on a non-partisan basis and adequately equipped.

I shall be turning over in my mind this whole question and hope you will share your thoughts and worries with me. Roosevelt [ES]

[MR*. WSC, VI, 299–301. FRUS, 1944, V, 150–51. R&C.]

Ernest Bevin, Minister of Labour and National Service, and a leader of the British Labour Party, defended the decision of the British Cabinet to intervene in Greece. Speaking before the Trades Unions Congress on December 13, Bevin persuaded the audience that Churchill's performance had earned their support, even though the Labour Party disliked the Prime Minister's suppression of the left in Greece. Meanwhile, British troops enroute to the Middle East were diverted to Athens and began arriving on December 13, just in time to prevent the ELAS forces from taking control of the city. (Attica is the ancient Greek name for the area around and including Athens.) Churchill did not make a speech on Sunday, December 17, and did not make a major statement on Greece before the House of Commons until January 18, 1945 (Churchill, *Speeches*, VII, 7085–95).

Secretary of State Stettinius' statement (see C–845) continued to anger Churchill, not only because it had stimulated severe criticism of British actions in Greece in the London press, but because he knew he could not get the President to contradict the statement publicly.

Archbishop Damaskinos of Athens had managed to maintain a degree of credibility with most of the warring Greek factions. He had been elected to the See of Athens before the war began, but the Metaxas government had refused to permit him to assume his post. Although the Germans had permitted Damaskinos to take office, the Archbishop had retained sufficient independence to avoid any stain of collaboration. The British thought well enough of him to have proposed him as Regent twice before, in December 1943 and in March 1944. The object of the regency was to bypass King George II, whose support for the dictatorial Metaxas regime, coupled with his refusal to accept increased constitutional limitations, made him highly unpopular.

(The final sentence of this cable was sent in a correction dispatched at 1034 Z, Dec. 15.)

C–851

London [via U.S. Army]
Dec. 15, 1944; 2325 Z, Dec. 14 / TOR 0305 Z

Prime Minister to President Roosevelt Personal and Top Secret.
Your number 673.

I will send you a considered answer to your telegram, for the kindly tone of which I thank you, over the weekend. I hope that the British reinforcements now coming steadily into Attica may make a more healthy situation in Athens. You will realize how very serious it would be if we withdrew, as we easily could, and the result was a frightful massacre, and an extreme left wing regime under Communist inspiration installed itself, as it would, in Athens. My cabinet colleagues here of all parties are not prepared to act in a manner so dishonourable to our record and name. Ernest Bevin's speech to the labour Conference won universal respect. Stern fighting lies ahead, and even danger to our troops in the centre of

Athens. The fact that you are supposed to be against us, in accordance with the last sentence of Stettinius' press release, as I feared has added to our difficulties and burdens. I think it probable that I shall broadcast to the world on Sunday night and make manifest the purity and disinterestedness of our motives throughout and also of our resolves.

Meanwhile I send you a letter [C–852] I have received from the King of Greece, to whom we have suggested the policy of making the Archbishop of Athens Regent. The King refuses to allow this. Therefore an act of constitutional violence will be entailed if we finally decide upon this course. I know nothing to the credit of the Archbishop, except that our people on the spot think he might stop a gap or bridge a gully. You will have "the people on the spot."

[MR*. WSC, VI, 301. FRUS, 1944, V, 154–55. R&C.]

The letter from the King of Greece, George II, indicated how strongly he opposed any compromise which would leave the EAM any sort of political role in Greece. The inflexibility of the King and his supporters strengthened the belief of most British officials that a regency was an essential step toward a resolution of the crisis. As Macmillan wrote to Eden on December 21, "Alex.[ander] and I agree that there is no (repeat no) military solution of the Greek problem. It can only be solved by a political agreement" (Macmillan, *The Blast of War*, p. 517). True to his monarchist sentiments, however, Churchill remained reluctant to force a regency on King George.

C–852

London [via U.S. Army]
Dec. 15, 1944 / TOR 0100 Z

Prime Minister to President Roosevelt Person and Top Secret.

Following is text of letter, dated December 14th, mentioned in my immediately preceding telegram. Begins.

My Dear Prime Minister,

I feel I must convey to you the deep sorrow produced in me by yesterday's discussions. After a common effort of so many years, during which I did not spare myself or my people, I never expected that the time would ever come when I should hear what I heard yesterday.

I have pondered with all possible detachment on the arguments you advanced in support of the immediate establishment of a Regency, and I have studied anew Mr MacMillan's views, to which you seemed to subscribe.

What you demand of me really amounts to this: that I should entrust the regency to the Archbishop, with all the consequences implicit in such an action, without my being told what precisely are the obligations the Rebels would undertake against this concession. You have not assured me that the disarming of the Guerillas would necessarily follow or that General Scobie's terms would be accepted, not even do you inform me of the terms of the agreement now being sought with Rebels. What would be the position if, after the announcement of the Regency, the Guerillas were to persist in their refusal to disarm or were to put forward new terms? And what would be my own responsibility if I were now to surrender my authority to a Regent who would be able to take decisions in my name, without my being sure that the large but unarmed majority of my people would not be handed over tomorrow to the tender mercies of an armed minority?

I do not know whose views Mr MacMillan is referring to when he says that the demand for the Archbishop's appointment as Regent constitutes "a general hope and wish of the people". What I can tell you, from my own information and on the strength of 10 years experience at the head of my people, is that such a course of action would be regarded as an abandonment of the struggle, would bring confusion to the front of resistance to the extreme left, would disgust the Royalists and the Conservatives, and would immediately give birth to innumerable intrigues around the person of the Archbishop, who does not by any means enjoy the general confidence of the political world. We have had many similar disappointments in the past over the choice of persons.

Yet you expect me to take such a momentous decision simply on the strength of Mr MacMillan's recommendation, without even my government being consulted—indeed, against the views of my own Prime Minister and many other political leaders. In considering such a grave matter concerning the future of the crown and bound also with a vital political problem on the settlement of which will depend the future of my country, I think it would constitute no excessive caution on my part if I wished to ascertain the views of all the representatives of the political parties, who should first be made cognisant of all the advantages that would accrue to the people from such a sacrifice on the part of their King.

From my attitude so far you have no reason to believe that I have ever thought of my own self when it came to a question of serving my country. You will no doubt have in mind all the declarations by which I specifically and irrevocably undertook to submit myself to the will of my people. I left the government entirely in the hands of

persons known for their anti-dynastic sentiments, without once pressing for the appointment of any minister faithful to the crown. I
agreed not to proceed to Greece without the previous consent of my
government, and I accepted without demur your own counsel not
to raise this issue at a time when the liberation was being joyfully
celebrated throughout Greece. Surely you are in a position to know
whether there was ever in my heart the disposition to insist on anything that concerned my person. I am ready for any sacrifice: but
this sacrifice must be for my people's benefit and at my people's
demand. I have never solicited anyone's help to safeguard my throne,
and you know—you more than anybody else, my dear Prime Minister—how wronged I am by those who think I would wish to rely
on anything other than the will of my people. But is it a "self-defense
policy" that I should wish to retain intact all my rights and duties
towards my people until such time as they can freely express their
will?

What hurt me most of all during these discussions was your remarks
about the sacrifices the British troops are undergoing in Greece today
to impose order. I can assure you that a feeling of horror goes through
me when I think of this unbelievable tragedy. What purpose would
it serve now to examine how this has come about, and how so many
arms are found in the hands of people who, after using them to seize
power, have no compunction now in turning them against Greece's
best friend? What I would like to say to you once again, after mature
reflexion during the night, is that in my desire to help the position
of your government and yourself, to whose assistance Greece owes
so much, I would not ask your troops to remain in Greece one minute
longer than is absolutely necessary for the liberation of the capital
and its environs and for the arming of the population so that it can
defend itself. Beyond this, it is purely a matter for the occupation
authorities, and will depend exclusively on the general policy which
your government intends to follow with regard to countries liberated
by British arms. But until the arming of the government forces is
effected and the safety of the people is ensured, I cannot believe that
there is any man in this country who would be willing to abandon
the Greek government and that part of the population loyal to it to
the mercy of armed bands equipped by the British authorities. Because quite apart from all considerations of fair play in a situation
where British initiative is so deeply committed, quite apart also from
the most elementary sense of humanity towards an unarmed mass
of human being, the government which you recognize today is your
ally: it was formed at your recommendation; and it derives its legal
status from me, who did not grudge you any sacrifice when my

contribution to the allied cause was still of some weight. I did not stop to consider the Greek soldiers would die by the side of your own men in Macedonia and Crete in a military enterprise doomed in advance, nor that Greece would have to suffer the tragedy of occupation. And when, after the German attack, the political leaders faltered and none came forward to assume responsibility, I took that responsibility on my shoulders, acting as my own prime minister for some time.

This country, where you have so hospitably given me shelter and which I have come to love as my own native land, cannot forget these things quickly, and I feel sure that if it were to see my government being abandoned to this fate, a shock would go through it much stronger than that produced by the present anxiety over the fact that British troops are implicated in Greece. More than that: the whole of Europe would soon appreciate that full significance of such a failure.

With most cordial feelings, Yours very sincerely, George II

[MR*]

CONFUSION OF POLICY TOWARD POLAND

Pressed by members of the Polish government in London who adamantly opposed any territorial concessions to the Soviet Union, Stanislaw Mikolajczyk had resigned as Prime Minister. Churchill believed that the new government of Tomasz Arciszewski would be short-lived and that Mikolajczyk would return with increased strength. However, when Churchill made that prediction in a cable to Stalin (*Stalin/WSC*, doc. 362), the Soviet Premier responded with a call for Britain to support the Polish National Committee (Lublin). Stalin doubted that Mikolajczyk could be of any help and accused the London Poles of supporting anti-Soviet terrorists in liberated Poland.

The Soviet concern about guerrilla warfare was very real and justified. Allied intelligence was apparently unaware of the extensive activities of various insurgent groups operating in Soviet-held territory. The largest of these was the Ukrainian Insurgent Army (UPA), estimated in 1944 to comprise about 100,000 men under arms. That army, which had resisted the Germans but saved its major efforts for the fight against the Soviets, operated in regiment-size military formations in the western Ukraine until 1947. (See Hunczak, *UPA—The Ukrainian Insurgent Army*.)

Mikolajczyk's resignation spawned a debate in the House of Commons on British policy regarding Poland, and on December 15 Churchill made an extensive statement in which he praised Mikolajczyk and condemned the inflexible attitude of the new Polish government. Churchill warned that a reconciliation between the Polish government in London and the Lublin

Committee (National Liberation Committee) seemed unlikely unless Mikolajczyk returned as Prime Minister, and he defended the territorial compromises worked out by Mikolajczyk during his trip to Moscow. Roosevelt's cable was prompted by Churchill's complaint that "the attitude of the United States has not been defined with the precision which His Majesty's Government have thought it wise to use" (Churchill, *Speeches*, VII, 700).

With the election behind him, the President, on the advice of the State Department, began to consider publication of a letter he had sent to Mikolajczyk on November 17. In that letter, Roosevelt supported "a strong, free and independent Poland," but added a vague statement supporting whatever Anglo-Soviet-Polish agreements could be worked out on territorial questions, including the idea of compensating Poland with German territory. To Mikolajczyk's distress, that veiled endorsement of the Curzon line was not accompanied by an American guarantee of Poland's new boundaries. The letter was released to the public on December 18, but without any mention of compensation to Poland in the west (*FRUS, Yalta Conf.*, pp. 218–19, 214–15).

R–674

Warm Springs, Ga. [via U.S. Navy]
Dec. 15, 1944, 2347 Z

Personal and Top Secret, from the President for the Former Naval Person.

I have seen the newspaper reports of your statement in the House on the Polish question. In order that we may cooperate fully in this matter I would appreciate receiving the benefit of your ideas as to what steps we can now take in regard to this question. Particularly I would like to have your evaluation of the possibility of Mikolajczyk's coming back into power with sufficient authority to carry out his plans and what action you feel we should take in the event the Lublin Committee should declare itself to be the provisional government of Poland and Stalin should recognize it as such. In view of this possibility I wonder if it would be helpful if I should send a message to Stalin suggesting that he postpone any positive action on the Polish question until the three of us can get together.

You will recall the contents of the letter I sent to Mikolajczyk by Mr. Harriman which he showed to you and which outlines our policy in regard to Poland. I anticipate strong pressure here for the position of this Government to be made clear, and I may therefore have to make public in some form the four points outlining our position contained in my letter to Mikolajczyk referred to above.

Knowing that we have in mind the same basic objectives in regard to Poland I want to be sure to coordinate with you any steps which I may contemplate in this matter. Roosevelt [ES]

[MR*. *FRUS*, 1944, III, 1344–45. *FRUS, Yalta Conf.*, p. 216. *R&C*.]

Churchill hoped to forestall Soviet recognition of the Lublin Committee as the legitimate Polish government and thus strongly endorsed the President's proposed cable to Stalin.

C–853

London [via U.S. Army]
Dec. 16, 1944, 1109 Z / TOR 1720 Z

Prime Minister to President Roosevelt Personal and Top Secret.

I thank you cordially for your telegram Number 674 about Poland. I trust you will carry out your proposal to send a message to Stalin suggesting that he postpone any positive action on the Polish question until the three of us can get together. This suggestion is most valuable and also I feel extremely urgent. Would it be possible for you to do this today, as I apprehend Stalin may make some move recognizing the Lublin Committee as the government of Poland.

We will send you a fuller account of our views on the other questions you raise as soon as possible, probably tomorrow. I can however tell you at once that the War Cabinet feel that the four points mentioned in your letter to Mikolajczyk are very much in line with our ideas, and that the publication of them could do nothing but good. I also hope to send you a statement about Greece in answer to your Number 673.

I do hope you have benefited by your brief rest at Hot Springs after so strenuous and successful a campaign.

[MR*. *FRUS*, 1944, III, 1345n. p*FRUS, Yalta Conf.*, pp. 216–17. *R&C*.]

Churchill's statement to the House of Commons implying American support for Poland's giving territorial concessions to the Soviet Union unleashed a storm of protests in the American press and in Congress. That, combined with the crisis in Greece, prompted Harry Hopkins to warn Churchill that American public opinion was increasingly critical of the President's policy of cooperation and might force Roosevelt to state publicy "our determination to do all that we can to seek a free and secure world" (Hopkins to Churchill, Dec. 16, 1944, MR). However, as Churchill quickly pointed out, Roosevelt had generally encouraged the British, particularly regarding the Polish settlement, and the President's message to Stalin continued in that vein (Churchill to Hopkins, Dec. 17, 1944, *WSC*, VI, 303).

R–675

Warm Springs, Ga. [via U.S. Navy]
Dec. 16, 1944, 0119 Z

Personal and Top Secret, from the President for the Prime Minister.
Your Number 853. I have today sent the following message to U.J.:

In view of the interest raised in this country by Prime Minister Churchill's statement in the House of Commons yesterday and the strong pressure we are under to make known our position in regard to Poland, I believe it may be necessary in the next few days for this government to issue some statement on the subject. This statement, if issued, will outline our attitude somewhat along the following lines:

QUOTE. 1. The United States Government stands unequivocally for a strong, free, independent and democratic Poland.

2. In regard to the question of future frontiers of Poland, the United States, although considering it desirable that territorial questions await the general postwar settlement, recognizes that a settlement before that time is in the interest of the common war effort and therefore would have no objection if the territorial questions involved in the Polish situation, including the proposed compensation from Germany, were settled by mutual agreement between the parties directly concerned.

3. Recognizing that the transfer of minorities in some cases is feasible and would contribute to the general security and tranquility in the areas concerned, the United States Government would have no objection if the Government and the people of Poland desire to transfer nationals and would join in assisting such transfers.

4. In conformity with its announced aim, this Government is prepared to assist, subject to legislative authority, and in so far as may be practicable, in the economic reconstruction of countries devastated by Nazi aggression. This policy applies equally to Poland as to other such devastated countries of the United Nations. UNQUOTE.

The proposed statement, as you will note, will contain nothing, I am sure, that is not known to you as the general attitude of this Government and is I believe in so far as it goes in general accord with the results of your discussion with Prime Minister Churchill in Moscow in the autumn, and for this reason, I am sure, you will welcome it.

I feel it is of the highest importance that until the three of us can get together and thoroughly discuss this troublesome question there be no action on any side which would render our discussions more difficult. I have seen indications that the Lublin Committee may be intending to give itself the status of a provisional government of Poland. I fully appreciate the desirability from your point of view of having a clarification of Polish authority before your armies move further into Poland. I very much hope, however, that because of the great political implications which such a step would entail you would find it possible to refrain from recognizing the Lublin Committee as a government of Poland before we meet, which I hope will be immediately after my inauguration on January 20. Could you not until that date continue to deal with the Committee in its present form. I know that Prime Minister Churchill shares my views on this point.

Roosevelt [ES]

[MR*. p*Stalin/FDR*, doc. 248. *R&C*.]

Although Churchill doubted that Mikolajczyk would return as Prime Minister of Poland, given the alternatives Britain had little choice but to hope that he would.

C–854

London [via U.S. Army]
Dec. 16, 1944, 2301 Z / TOR 1210 Z

Prime Minister to President Roosevelt Personal and Top Secret.

In your telegram Number 674 you asked for my estimate of the possibility of Mikolajczyk returning to power with enough authority to carry out his plans.

When he resigned it looked to us for the time as though efforts by other Poles to form a government might fail and Mikolajczyk be called back soon. Now that Arciszewski's government has established itself, we no longer see any immediate prospect of this. The majority of the Poles here appear to have accepted Arciszewski faute de mieux, and to be in a fatalistic mood of waiting for something to turn up. But with the Poles these moods do not last. In London Mikolajczyk has the support of all his own Peasant party and of important elements of the Socialist and Christian Labour parties. We have indications that the people in Poland are unhappy about Mikolajczyk's absence from the government. I am hopeful therefore that Mikolajczyk's return to power will still be possible in the new year.

You also asked about the Lublin Committee. We do not regard it as in any way representative of Polish opinion and whatever developments there may be in the Soviet Government's attitude we do not, at present, intend to recognise it. We shall maintain our recognition of the London Government, which is the legal government of Poland and the authority to which the large Polish forces fighting under British command owe allegiance. We hope that we can keep in step and consult beforehand on all this.

[MR*. *FRUS*, 1944, III, 1345n. *R&C*.]

By the time Churchill wrote this cable, Britain was committed to a military solution to the Greek crisis. The bloodshed had ended any immediate hope of political compromise, at least until it became clear that the British could not be dislodged. The regency that Churchill proposed would include Archbishop Damaskinos, whom the British did not fully trust, General Nikolaos Plastiras, head of the EDES—an anti-communist, anti-monarchist partisan organization—and Philippos Dragoumis, a Greek politician who was, according to Macmillan, "a much respected friend of the King" (*Blast of War*, p. 511). Both Harold Macmillan, sent to Greece as a trouble-shooter, and Reginald Leeper, the British Ambassador to the Greek government, recommended such a regency. But whatever the solution, it would have to wait the securing of Athens and its port, Piraeus, by British troops.

The Mountain Brigade had fought against the Germans in Italy and, in 1944, had captured the town of Rimini. The Sacred Battalion had taken part in the attack on Tunis in 1943. Both units were commanded by staunch monarchists and provided the major military support to the forces of the right, and ELAS had demanded their disarmament as a prerequisite to the disarming of its forces. Minister of Labour Ernest Bevin's speech is discussed in the headnote to C–851.

C–855

London [via U.S. Army]
Dec. 17, 1944, 0115 Z / TOR 1210 Z

Prime Minister to President Roosevelt Personal and Top Secret Private and Confidential.

About Greece. The present position is that our representatives on the spot, MacMillan and Leeper, have strongly recommended the appointment of the Archbishop as regent. This is obnoxious to the Papandreou Government though they might be persuaded to advocate a regency of three, namely the Archbishop, General Plastiras and Dragoumis. There is suspicion that the Archbishop is ambitious of obtaining chief political power and that, supported by EAM, he will use it ruthlessly against existing ministers. Whether this be true or not I cannot say. The facts are changing from hour to hour. I do not feel at all sure that in setting up a one-man regency we might not be imposing a dictatorship in Greece.

There is also to be considered the fact that the King refuses, I think inflexibly, to appoint a regency, certainly not a one-man regency of the Archbishop, whom he distrusts and fears. According to the Greek constitution the Crown Prince is Regent in the absence of the King. The King also states that all his ministers under Papandreou advise him against such a step and that, as a constitutional monarch, he cannot be responsible for it.

The War Cabinet decided to await for three or four days the course of military operations. Our reinforcements are arriving rapidly and the British General Staff Intelligence says that there are not more than 12,000 ELAS in Athens and the Piraeus. The Greek King's estimate is 15 to 22,000. Anyhow we shall, by the middle of next week, be far superior in numbers. I am not prepared, as at present informed, to give way to unconstitutional violence in such circumstances.

Our immediate task is to secure control of Athens and the Piraeus. According to the latest reports ELAS may agree to depart. This will give us a firm basis from which to negotiate the best settlement possible between the warring Greek factions. It will certainly have to provide for the disarming of the Guerrilla forces. The disarmament of the Greek Mountain Brigade, who took Rimini, and the Sacred Squadron, who fought so well at the side of British and American troops, would seriously weaken our forces, and in any case we could not abandon them to massacre. They may however be removed elsewhere as part of a general settlement.

I am sure you would not wish us to cast down our painful and thankless task at this time. We embarked upon it with your full consent (see my number 755 and your reply). We desire nothing from Greece but to do our duty by the common cause. In the midst of our task of bringing food and relief and maintaining the rudiments of order for a government which has no armed forces, we have become involved in a furious, though not as yet very bloody, struggle. I have felt it much that you were unable to give a word of explanation for our action but I understand your difficulties.

Meanwhile the cabinet is united and the Socialist ministers approve Mr. Bevin's declarations at the labour conference which, on this matter, endorse the official platform by a majority of 2,455,000 to 137,000 votes. I could at any time obtain, I believe, a ten to one majority in the House of Commons. I am sure you will do whatever you can. I will keep you constantly informed.

[MR*. *FRUS*, 1944, V, 159–60. *WSC*, VI, 303–4. *R&C*.]

C–856

London [via U.S. Army]
Dec. 17, 1944, 1025 Z

Prime Minister to President Roosevelt. Personal and Top Secret.

Your number 675. I am most grateful to you for sending this telegram to U.J. It can do nothing but good.

[MR*. R&C.]

On December 21, Eisenhower had complained to the Combined Chiefs of Staff that a number of German divisions were apparently moving from the eastern to the western front, and he asked that the Soviet Union be asked for information about future operations, particularly the offensive promised for December or January. At the same time, Eisenhower indicated his willingness to share with the Soviets information about Allied plans (*Eisenhower Papers*, IV, 2367).

C–857

London [via U.S. Army]
Dec. 23, 1944, 1102 Z / TOR 1320 Z

Prime Minister to President Roosevelt. Personal and Top Secret.

I and my military advisers entirely agree with Eisenhower (see his SCAF–155) that it is essential for us to obtain from the Russians, at the earliest possible moment, some indication of their strategical and tactical intentions. We think it hopeless to try to get this information through our military mission, or indeed to ask the Russians to commit it to writing. The best, if not the only hope of getting what we want, is for you and me to send a joint telegram to U.J. suggesting that he should allow us to send a high ranking officer, nominated by General Eisenhower, to Moscow at once, in order that he may explain our present dispositions and future intentions on the Western front to the Soviet Government and obtain reciprocal information from them.

If you agree with this, I propose that we should send the following telegram to U.J.:—

"General Eisenhower reports that there has been a tendency for German divisions formed or reforming in East Germany to move to the Western front. The arrival of these divisions clearly influences Eisenhower's dispositions and, if this trend continues, it will affect the decisions which he has to make regarding future strategy in the west. General Eisenhower therefore considers it essential that he should have, at the earliest possible moment, some indication of your strategical and tactical intentions."

"We propose, therefore, that we should send a high ranking officer to Moscow to give you the latest information about the Western front and to receive from your high officers all the information that you feel able to give him about Russian dispositions and future intentions." Roosevelt-Churchill

[MR*. R&C.]

Faced with Stalin's intransigence, Roosevelt agreed to meet at the Black Sea resort of Yalta, in the Crimea. As usual, the President hoped to keep the conference as informal as possible; again as usual, the staffs which arrived far exceeded his plans. It took twenty-five aircraft to bring the 700 members of the British and American delegations to Yalta.

R–676

Washington [via U.S. Navy]
Dec. 23, 1944, 1547 Z

Personal and Top Secret, from the President for the Prime Minister.

I am today sending to Harriman the following message in regard to our projected three party meeting with U.J.

Please let me have your opinion as to the possibilities of this plan from your point of view.

> QUOTE. If Stalin cannot manage to meet us in the Mediterranean I am prepared to go to the Crimea and have the meeting at Yalta which appears to be the best place available in the Black Sea having the best accommodations ashore and the most promising flying conditions.
>
> We would arrive by plane from some Mediterranean port and would send in advance a naval vessel to Sevastopol to provide necessary service and living accommodations if it should be necessary for me to live on board ship.
>
> I would plan to leave America very soon after the inauguration on a naval vessel. You will be informed later of a date of arrival that will be satisfactory to Churchill and to me. My party will be numerically equal to that which was present at Teheran, about 35 total.
>
> I still hope the military situation will permit Marshal Stalin to meet us half way. UNQUOTE.

Roosevelt [WDL]

[MR*. FRUS, Yalta Conf., p. 21.]

Stalin quickly acceded to Roosevelt's request to establish a liaison between the military commanders on the eastern and western fronts. (See *Stalin/FDR*, docs. 250, 251.) Roosevelt's comment about the situation in Belgium was a reference to the German attack in the Ardennes Forest (the Battle of the Bulge; see the headnote to C–870).

R–677

Washington [via U.S. Navy]
Dec. 23, 1944, 1723 Z

Top Secret and Personal from the President for the Prime Minister.
Your 857. I have today sent the following message to Stalin:

QUOTE. I wish to direct General Eisenhower to send to Moscow a fully qualified officer of his staff to discuss with you Eisenhower's situation on the Western Front and its relation to the Eastern Front, in order that all of us may have information essential to our coordination of effort. We will maintain complete secrecy.

I hope you will see this officer of Eisenhower's Staff and arrange to exchange with him information that will be of mutual benefit. The situation in Belgium is not bad but it is time to talk of the next phase.

In view of the emergency an early reply to this proposal is requested. UNQUOTE.

Perhaps you can assist in getting a favorable reply. Roosevelt

[MR*. *Stalin/FDR*, doc. 250.]

For the second year in a row, the Churchill family enjoyed a Christmas tree sent by the President. (Eleanor Roosevelt's name was probably misspelled by the person who deciphered or typed the cable.)

C–857/1

London [via U.S. Army]
Dec. 24, 1944, 1955 Z / TOR 2050 Z

Prime Minister to President Roosevelt. Personal.
Clemmie and I send you and Elinor our warmest wishes for a happy Christmas and a triumphant New Year.

[MR]

R–678

Hyde Park, N.Y. [via U.S. Navy]
Dec. 25, 1944, 0005 Z

Secret and Personal, from the President for the Former Naval Person.

Eleanor joins with me in a happy Christmas to you and Clemmie and the children and an old fashioned good luck for all of you in the new year.

Bless you all. Roosevelt

[MR*]

Churchill made a surprise decision to visit Athens himself after reading his messages on Christmas Eve. From the tone of his memoirs, one suspects that the Prime Minister's motive was more curiosity—particularly about the character and manner of Archbishop Damaskinos—than the belief that the trip would solve the crisis. The request to have the U.S. Ambassador to Greece make contact was unnecessary. Ambassador MacVeagh had kept in touch with British Ambassador Reginald Leeper and had supported the suggestion of Leeper and Macmillan that a regency be established. However, Churchill's pledge that Britain sought "nothing from Greece in territory or advantages" stands in stark contrast to the "percentage" agreements he and Stalin had reached in Moscow a few months earlier.

Churchill and Foreign Secretary Anthony Eden left by airplane on Christmas Day and arrived in Athens that evening. This cable was probably drafted before Churchill departed and sent as soon as news of his arrival reached London.

C–858

Athens, Greece [via U.S. Army, London]
Dec. 26, 1944, 0952 Z (London) / TOR 1209 Z

Prime Minister to President Roosevelt Personal, Top Secret, Eyes Only.

Anthony and I are going out to see what we can do to square this Greek entanglement. Basis of action:

The King does not go back until a plebiscite in his favour has been taken. For the rest, we cannot abandon those who have taken up arms in our cause and must if necessary fight it out with them. It must always be understood that we seek nothing from Greece in territory or advantages. We have given much and will give more if it is in our power. I count on you to help us in this time of unusual difficulty. In particular

I should like you to tell your Ambassador in Athens to make contact with us and to help all he can in accordance with the above principles.

[MR*. *FRUS*, 1944, V, 169–70. *WSC*, VI, 314–15.]

Stalin's answer to Roosevelt is in *Stalin/FDR*, doc. 251.

R–679

Hyde Park, N.Y. [via U.S. Navy]
Dec. 26, 1944, 1519 Z

Personal and Top Secret from the President for the Prime Minister.

Referring to my 677, Stalin has agreed to receive an officer of Eisenhower's Staff and discuss the situation with him.

Eisenhower has been informed. Roosevelt

[MR*]

Just what Roosevelt meant by a "satisfactory solution" was not spelled out, but Churchill had no reason to infer that the President's wishes differed from British policy in Greece.

R–680

Hyde Park, N.Y. [via U.S. Navy, Athens]
Dec. 26, 1944, 2317 Z

From President Roosevelt to Ambassador MacVeagh, for Delivery of the Following Message to Prime Minister Churchill.

QUOTE. Replying to your 858, I have asked our Ambassador to call upon you as soon as possible and I am ready to be of all assistance I can in this difficult situation.

I hope that your presence there on the spot will result in achieving an entirely satisfactory solution. UNQUOTE. Roosevelt [State Dept., FDR]

[MR*. *FRUS*, 1944, V, 170. *WSC*, VI, 315.]

Churchill's meetings with Archbishop Damaskinos convinced the Prime Minister that the churchman "was the outstanding figure in the Greek turmoil" (*WSC*, VI, 316). After a conference with representatives of all the Greek political factions, Churchill concluded that the "Communists [three members of ELAS, one of whom was Georgios Siantos, a KKE leader] did not seem as bad as they had been painted" (Moran, *Churchill*, p. 229). In addition to the British and Greek participants, the French and American Ambassadors and Colonel Gregori Popov, head of a Soviet military mission to ELAS/EAM headquarters, also attended the conference. Popov sat with the Allies and apparently endorsed British policy, something both Churchill and Eden noted with satisfaction.

C–859

Athens, Greece [via U.S. Army, London]
Dec. 28, 1944, 1455 Z (London) / TOR 1840 Z

Prime Minister to President Roosevelt. Personal and Top Secret.

Many thanks for your Number 680 which encouraged me amidst many difficulties. Ambassador Macveagh called yesterday and we had a talk. Like everyone else here he is convinced that a Regency under the Archbishop is the only course open at the moment. I have seen the Archbishop several times and he made a very good impression on me by the sense of power and decision which he conveyed as well as by his shrewd political judgments. You will not expect me to speak here on his spiritual qualities for I really have not had sufficient opportunity to measure these.

Greek conference of which you will have had from other sources full account, was unanimous in recommending a Regency. This was strongly supported by EAM however I do not consider Archbishop is at all Left Wing in Communist sense. On the contrary he seems to be an extremely determined man bent on establishing a small strong executive in Greece to prevent the continuance of Civil War.

I am therefore returning with Anthony to England to press upon the King of Greece to appoint the Archbishop Regent. Effect of this, if King agrees, will of course mean that Archbishop will form a government of ten or less of the best will. I gathered that he would make Plastiras Prime Minister and that Papandreou would not be included. Naturally I could not probe too far while all these matters are hypothetical.

On our return we shall advise our colleagues who are already inclined to this course, that we should put the strongest pressure on Greek King to accept advice of his Prime Minister, Monsieur Papandreou, who changes his mind about three times a day but has now promised to send a telegram in his own words but in sense of my immediately following.

If Ambassador Macveagh's report should on these matters correspond with mine I should greatly hope that you would feel yourself able to send a personal telegram to the King of Greece during the next few days supporting the representation we shall make to him, of which we shall keep you informed. My idea is that the Regency should be only for one year or till a Plebiscite can be held under conditions what is called "normal tranquility".

The Archbishop has left this matter entirely in my hands so that I can put the case in most favorable manner to the King. Of course if after these difficulties have been surmounted and Archbishop is Regent you felt able send him a telegram of support, that would make our task easier. Mr. President, we have lost over 1,000 men and though the greater part of Athens is now clear, it is a painful sight to see this city with street fighting raging now here now there and the poor people all pinched and only kept alive in many cases by rations we are carrying, often at loss of life, to them at the various depots. Anything that you can say to strengthen this new lay out as the time comes will be most valuable and may bring about acceptance by ELAS of the terms of truce set forth by General Scobie. For the rest we are reinforcing as is necessary and military conflict will go on. The vast majority of the people long for a settlement that will free them from the Communist terror.

We have to think of an interim arrangement which can be reviewed when our long hoped for meeting takes place. This date should not now be far distant. It will then be possible to correlate our opinions and actions. In the meanwhile we have no choice but to recommend creation of a new and more competent executive government under Regency of Archbishop, and to press on with our heavy and unsought task of clearing Athens from very dangerous, powerful, well organised and well directed elements which are now pressing the area advance. I should value a telegram when I return on Friday morning.

[MR*. *FRUS*, 1944, V, 173–75. *WSC*, VI, 319–21 (edited). *R&C*.]

In printing the preceding cable (C–859) in his memoirs, Churchill deleted the phrasing which indicated that the following advice given by Greek Prime Minister Georgios Papandreou to his King had been written by British officials, not by Papandreou. On the Map Room copy of this message, someone underlined the phrase "as well as outlook for the Royal House. . . ."

C–860

Athens, Greece [via U.S. Army, London]
Dec. 28, 1944, 1725 Z (London) / TOR 1910 Z

Prime Minister to President Roosevelt. Personal and Top Secret.
Reference Paragraph 4 of my immediately preceding telegram, following is message referred to.

"As Prime Minister of Greece it is my duty to report to Your Majesty that at the conference today all present were unanimously in favour of establishing a Regency. All except members of the Popular Party expressed themselves in favour of Regency being created at once. I myself agreed that an immediate Regency was necessary. The members of the Popular Party thought, however, that establishment of a Regency should be deferred until ELAS had accepted General Scobie's terms for a truce. In view of what happened today and in the interests of Greece as well as outlook for the Royal House, I as Prime Minister formally tend to Your Majesty advice that you should appoint a Regency forthwith. It is further my advice that there should be a single Regent and that he should be the Archbishop of Athens."

[MR*]

Stalin's summary of the Soviet interpretation of events in Poland made it clear that he would not heed Roosevelt's request to hold off on any political decisions until the tripartite conference in January. The shift to the right in the London Polish government apparently convinced the Soviets that there was no reason to continue to talk about a coalition of the London and Lublin Poles. The State Department press release on Poland (Stettinius' letter) is printed in *FRUS, Yalta Conf.*, pp. 218–19, and discussed in the headnote to R–674.

R–681

Hyde Park, N.Y. [via U.S. Navy]
Dec. 29, 1944, 2017 Z

Personal and Top Secret, from the President for the Prime Minister.

I have today received the following message from Marshal Stalin, dated 27 December, in reply to the message quoted to you in my 675. I should like your comments before making a reply.

QUOTE. I have received your message on Polish matters on December 20.

As regards Mr. Stettinius' statement of December 18, I would prefer to express myself about this during our personal meeting. In any case the events in Poland have considerably moved ahead than it is reflected in the said statement.

A number of facts which took place during the time after the last visit of Mikolajczyk to Moscow and, in particular the radio-communications with Mikolajczyk's government intercepted by us from arrested in Poland terrorists—underground agents of the Polish emigré government—with all palpability proves that the negotiations of Mr. Mikolajczyk with the Polish National Committee served as a screen for those elements who conducted from behind Mikolajczyk's back criminal terrorist work against Soviet officers and soldiers on the territory of Poland. We cannot reconcile with such a situation when terrorists instigated by Polish emigrants kill in Poland soldiers and officers of the Red Army, lead a criminal fight against Soviet troops which are liberating Poland, and directly aid our enemies, whose allies they in fact are. The substitution of Mikolajczyk by Arzyshevsky and, in general, transpositions of ministers in the Polish emigré government have made the situation even worse and have created a precipice between Poland and the emigré government.

Meanwhile the Polish National Committee has made serious achievements in the strengthing of the Polish state and the apparatus of governmental power on the territory of Poland, in the expansion and strengthening of the Polish army, in carrying into practice of a number of important governmental measures and, in the first place, of the agrarian reform in favor of the peasants. All this has led to consolidation of democratic powers of Poland and to powerful strengthening of authority of the National Committee among the wide masses in Poland and among wide social Polish circles abroad.

It seems to me that now we should be interested in the support of the Polish National Committee and all those who want and are capable to work together with it and that is especially important for the Allies and for the solution of our common task—the speeding of the defeat of Hitlerite Germany. For the Soviet Union, which is bearing the whole burden for the liberation of Poland from German occupationists, the question of relations with Poland under present conditions is the task of daily close and friendly relations with a power which has been established by the Polish people on its own soil and which has already grown strong and has its own army which together with the Red Army is fighting against the Germans.

I have to say frankly that if the Polish Committee of National Liberation will transform itself into a Provisional Polish Government then, in view of the above-said, the Soviet Government will not have any serious ground for postponement of the question of its recognition. It is necessary to bear in mind that in the strengthening of a pro-Allied and democratic Poland the Soviet Union is interested more than any other power not only because the Soviet Union is bearing the main brunt of the battle for liberation of Poland but also because Poland is a border state with the Soviet Union and the problem of Poland is inseparable from the problem of security of the Soviet Union. To this we have to add that the successes of the Red Army in Poland in the fight against the Germans are to a great degree dependent on the presence of peaceful and trustworthy rear in Poland, and the Polish National Committee fully takes into account this circumstance while the emigré government and its underground agents by their terroristic actions are creating a threat of civil war in the rear of the Red Army and counteract the successes of the latter. On the other hand, under the conditions which exist in Poland at the present time there are no reasons for the continuation of the policy of support of the emigré government, which has lost all confidence of the Polish population in the country and besides creates a threat of civil war in the rear of the Red Army, violating thus our common interests of a successful fight against the Germans. I think that it would be natural, just and profitable for our common cause if the governments of the Allied countries as the first step have agreed on an immediate exchange of representatives with the Polish National Committee so that after a certain time it would be recognized as the lawful government of Poland after the transformation of the National Committee into a provisional government of Poland. Otherwise I am afraid that the confidence of the Polish People in the Allied powers may weaken. I think that we cannot allow the Polish people to say that we are sacrificing the interests of Poland in favor of the interests of a handful of Polish emigrants in London. UNQUOTE.

Roosevelt

[MR*. p*Stalin/FDR*, doc. 254. p*WSC*, VI, 332–34.]

The Admiralty report on conditions at Yalta was unenthusiastic, but Churchill's surmise that Stalin would make appropriate arrangements ashore proved correct. Simferopol is located in the south-central Crimea, north of Sevastopol and Yalta. Anthony Eden was Foreign Minister and Lord Leathers was British Minister of War Transport.

C–861

London [via U.S. Army]
Dec. 29, 1944, 1732 Z / TOR 2028 Z

Prime Minister to President Roosevelt. Personal and Top Secret.

Your 676. I send you in my immediately following the Admiralty report on Yalta. If this place is chosen, it would be well to have a few destroyers on which we can live if necessary. There would be no difficulty in flying from the great air base and weather center at Caserta. I, myself, landed in a York at Simferopol. I dare say, however, Stalin will make good arrangements ashore. Our party will be kept to the smallest dimensions. I think we should aim at the end of January. I shall have to bring Anthony and Leathers.

[MR*. *FRUS, Yalta Conf.*, p. 23. *WSC*, VI, 338. *R&C*.]

C–862

London [via U.S. Army]
Dec. 29, 1944, 1738 Z

Prime Minister to President Roosevelt Personal and Top Secret.

Following is report mentioned in my immediately preceding telegram.

HARBOUR: The harbour at Yalta is small and is unsuitable for ships larger than destroyers. Its quays are believed to be intact. Ships of any size can anchor outside the harbour.

ANCHORAGE: The anchorage is exposed to the prevailing northeast wind which blows along the coast. The strongest winds are those from the northeast which blows in violent squalls from the mountains.

BOAT WORK: Under conditions of strong wind, boat work would become very difficult, if not impossible.

WEATHER: On the whole, however, strong wind conditions are not very frequent. The following figures are typical of the weather in January:

Average Temperature Range	30° to 42° F
Number of Gales per month	1–2
Number of Days of Rain per month	8
Amount per month	1 inch
Number of Fine Days per month	10
Number of Bad Days (Rain and Wind) per month	10

ACCOMMODATION FACILITIES ASHORE: There were a number of palaces and large country houses ashore which were converted into sanatoria and could have been used to provide ample accommodation; but we have no information about the conditions in which the Germans left them—it is believed that at least some of them have been destroyed.

ACCOMMODATION AFLOAT: The question of availability of suitable ships is being looked into.

[MR*]

In mid-December, King George of Greece had written Roosevelt to explain that he had no intention of forcing any form of government on the Greek people and would, once the civil war ended, call for a plebiscite and free elections. On December 28, the President sent a cable to the King expressing sorrow over the events which had transpired but firmly endorsing Archbishop Damaskinos as Regent (*FRUS*, V, 163–64, 177). It was that message for which Churchill was grateful. (He had returned to London that day from Athens.)

C–863

London [via U.S. Army]
Dec. 29, 1944, 1855 Z / TOR 2200 Z

Prime Minister to President Roosevelt Personal and Top Secret.

1. Ambassador Winant has sent me a copy of your message to the Greek King. We are all very much obliged to you for acting so promptly. Anthony and I have just returned. The War Cabinet have endorsed all our actions and have authorized us to urge the King of Greece tonight to appoint the Archbishop as Regent. The Archbishop left it to me to discuss the period of the Regency with the King, so that this gives a little latitude.

2. Failing agreement His Majesty's Government will advise the Archbishop to assume the Office of Regent and assure him that we will recognise him and the Government he forms as the government of Greece.

[MR*. *FRUS*, 1944, V, 178. *WSC*, VI, 321.]

The USS *Catoctin*, a naval auxiliary vessel, was assigned the task of providing communications and alternate living quarters for the President during the Yalta talks. Because of unswept mines, the ship could not berth at Yalta and stayed in Sevastopol during the entire conference.

R–682

Washington [via U.S. Navy]
Dec. 30, 1944, 1614 Z

Top Secret and Personal from the President for the Prime Minister.

Your 861 and 862. I am preparing to leave the U.S. as soon as possible after the Inauguration by warship to the Mediterranean and from there by airplane for Yalta, but have not yet so informed Stalin.

I will give you accurate dates as soon as details are worked out.

My thought now is to send a Naval ex-passenger ship to the Black Sea to provide services and living accommodations if necessary. This ship could berth in Sevastopol if necessary because of weather.

Information from Harriman indicates that suitable quarters and staff meeting place can be made available at Yalta where the city was not damaged during the German occupation.

It is my intention to take with me about 35 persons, including Joint Staff, personal staff, Secret Service, servants, etc.

I will give you more detailed information in the near future. Roosevelt [WDL]

[MR*. *FRUS, Yalta Conf.*, pp. 23–24.]

With the concurrence of the State Department, Roosevelt firmly endorsed the establishment of the Greek regency. Archbishop Damaskinos took the oath of office on December 31, 1944.

R–683

Washington [via U.S. Navy]
Dec. 30, 1944, 1622 Z

Personal and Top Secret, from the President to the Prime Minister.

Your 863 received. I am happy to know of your safe arrival and wish you every success in the solution of the Greek problem which seems very promising as a result of your journey. Roosevelt

[MR*. *WSC*, VI, 322. *R&Cn.*]

Bereft of support within Greece and faced with Churchill's new-found admiration for the proposed Regent, King George reluctantly capitulated when Churchill and Eden indicated that the Archbishop would become Regent with or without the King's sanction. The bitter irony for George II was that Britain, while publicly forswearing any desire to impose a specific form of government on the Greeks, had been accused of intervening to save the monarchy but now had forced its virtual dissolution.

C–864

London [via U.S. Army]
Dec. 30, 1944, 1455 Z / TOR 1727 Z

Prime Minister to President Roosevelt. Personal and Top Secret.

1. Anthony and I sat up with the King of Greece till 4:30 this morning at the end of which time His Majesty agreed to the announcement in my immediately following telegram. I have sent this to Ambassador Leeper in Athens in order that the Archbishop may go to work at once. The Greek translation is now being made and I will furnish you with a copy of it at the earliest moment.

This has been a very painful task to me. I had to tell the King that if he did not agree the matter would be settled without him and that we should recognise the new government instead of him. I hope you will be able to give every support and encouragement to the Archbishop and his government.

2. Your Number 681 enclosing Stalin's reply about Poland shows how serious will be the difficulties we shall have to face. I have consulted the Foreign Secretary and the Cabinet about it and their clear view is that

we shall continue to press Stalin not to recognise the Lublin Committee as the government of Poland and tell him plainly that we shall not do so. The matter should be reserved for the coming conference.

[MR*. *FRUS*, 1944, V, 178. p*FRUS, Yalta Conf.*, p. 233n. *R&C*.]

C–865

London [via U.S. Army]
Dec. 30, 1944, 1503 Z / TOR 1840 Z

Prime Minister to President Roosevelt Personal and Top Secret.

My immediately preceding telegram. The following is the text of the announcement referred to in Paragraph One.

"We, George Second, King of the Hellenes, having deeply considered the terrible situation into which our well-loved people have fallen through circumstances alike unprecedented and uncontrollable, and being ourselves resolved not to return to Greece unless summoned by a free and fair expression of the national will, and having full confidence in your loyalty and devotion, do now by this declaration appoint you, Archbishop Damaskinos, to be our Regent during this period of emergency: and we accordingly authorise and require you to take all steps necessary to restore order and tranquillity throughout our Kingdom. We further declare our desire that there should be ascertained by processes of democratic government, the freely-expressed wishes of the Greek people as soon as these storms have passed, and thus abridge the miseries of our beloved country by which our heart is rent."

[MR*. *WSC*, VI, 322.]

ROOSEVELT AND EASTERN EUROPE

Once again the President tried to convince Stalin not to take the irrevocable step of recognizing the Lublin Committee as the provisional government of Poland. Roosevelt's precise goals in this instance are difficult to determine. It is tempting simply to agree with the weight of historical opinion by claiming that Roosevelt was just procrastinating again, hoping that in some inchoate way the problem would solve itself. But the bulk of the evidence in the Churchill-Roosevelt exchanges indicates that the President, although he did not always keep the State Department informed of his views, was far from the disorganized, random thinker that historians have described. Roosevelt's statement to Edward Stettinius, that the Soviet Union "had the power in Eastern Europe," as well as the President's earlier acquiescence to Anglo-

Soviet bargains regarding power-sharing in eastern and southeastern Europe, all suggest that he accepted the fact of Soviet control in the area. Why then would he challenge that power, even as gently as he did in this message about Poland? It may be that Roosevelt viewed such wartime arrangements as temporary, subject to revision at a postwar peace conference. But that argument would mean that he failed to recognize the thrust of Soviet policy, something which is unlikely after the arguments over the makeup of the Polish government and Stalin's refusal to aid the Warsaw Uprising. It is also possible that the President placed Poland outside what he considered the Soviet Union's legitimate sphere of interest and hoped to preserve a significant degree of independence for the Poles. But again, the events of 1943 and 1944 demonstrated Soviet insistence on what they called a "friendly" Poland, and Roosevelt had continually worked to avoid a confrontation with Stalin. Perhaps the real purpose of the President's moves was merely to get the Soviets to make some sort of small concession, even an unimportant one, just to get them used to cooperating with Britain and the United States. In the short run, this would enhance postwar harmony among the great powers. In the long run, however, Roosevelt may have been thinking of what one historian has called " 'open' spheres of influence" wherein a major power would exercise only enough authority to protect its physical security, as opposed to the traditional "sphere of influence" which also included domination of a nation's internal politics and economic affairs. (See Eduard Mark, "Limits of Soviet Hegemony.") This would fit the President's vague but persistent notion of having "four policemen" who would keep order in the world without resorting to the kind of "spheres of influence" approach which had failed in the past.

R–684

Washington [via U.S. Navy]
Dec. 30, 1944, 1957 Z

Top Secret and Personal from the President for the Prime Minister.

Your 864. I have today sent the following to Stalin. You will see that we are in step.

QUOTE. I am disturbed and deeply disappointed over your message of December 27 in regard to Poland in which you tell me that you cannot see your way clear to hold in abeyance the question of recognizing the Lublin Committee as the provisional government of Poland until we have had an opportunity at our meeting to discuss the whole question thoroughly. I would have thought no serious inconvenience would have been caused your Government or your Armies if you could have delayed the purely juridical act of recognition for the short period of a month remaining before we meet.

There was no suggestion in my request that you curtail your practical relations with the Lublin Committee nor any thought that you should deal with or accept the London Government in its present composition. I had urged this delay upon you because I felt you would realize how extremely unfortunate and even serious it would be at this period in the war in its effect on world opinion and enemy morale if your Government should formally recognize one Government of Poland while the majority of the other United Nations including the United States and Great Britain continue to recognize and to maintain diplomatic relations with the Polish Government in London.

I must tell you with a frankness equal to your own that I see no prospect of this Government's following suit and transferring its recognition from the Government in London to the Lublin Committee in its present form. This is in no sense due to any special ties or feelings for the London Government. The fact is that neither the Government nor the people of the United States have as yet seen any evidence either arising from the manner of its creation or from subsequent developments to justify the conclusion that the Lublin Committee as at present constituted represents the people of Poland. I cannot ignore the fact that up to the present only a small fraction of Poland proper west of the Curzon Line has been liberated from German tyranny, and it is therefore an unquestioned truth that the people of Poland have had no opportunity to express themselves in regard to the Lublin Committee.

If at some future date following the liberation of Poland a provisional government of Poland with popular support is established, the attitude of this Government would of course be governed by the decision of the Polish people.

I fully share your view that the departure of Mr. Mikolajczyk from the Government in London has worsened the situation. I have always felt that Mr. Mikolajczyk, who I am convinced is sincerely desirous of settling all points at issue between the Soviet Union and Poland, is the only Polish leader in sight who seems to offer the possibility of a genuine solution of the difficult and dangerous Polish question. I find it most difficult to believe from my personal knowledge of Mr. Mikolajczyk and my conversations with him when he was here in Washington and his subsequent efforts and policies during his visit at Moscow that he had knowledge of any terrorist instructions.

I am sending you this message so that you will know the position of this Government in regard to the recognition at the present time of the Lublin Committee as the provisional government. I am more than ever convinced that when the three of us get together we can reach a solution of the Polish problem, and I therefore still hope that you can hold in abeyance until then the formal recognition of the

Lublin Committee as a government of Poland. I cannot, from a military angle see any great objection to a delay of a month. UNQUOTE.

Roosevelt

[MR*. *FRUS, Yalta Conf.*, pp. 224–25. *Stalin/FDR*, doc. 255. *R&C*.]

Vice Admiral H. K. Hewitt was commander of the U.S. Mediterranean Fleet.

R–685

Washington [via U.S. Navy]
Dec. 31, 1944, 1626 Z

Personal and Top Secret, from the President for the Prime Minister.

Referring to your 861 in regard to taking off by plane from Caserta, my advisors, medical and otherwise, consider it inadvisable to fly in high altitudes over the mountains between Italy and destination.

Admiral Hewitt has recommended going by Naval vessel from here to Malta and flying from Malta to destination, which can be done without reaching any high altitude. The same applies to Alexandria or Suez, but would necessitate my spending more time on the ship.

Is there any reason why I should not transfer from ship to plane at Malta which might involve remaining overnight?

We are working on the details and hope to give you full information in the early future. Roosevelt [WDL]

[MR*. *FRUS, Yalta Conf.*, p. 25.]

Although the concession made by the United States was very small, it satisfied the British. The message of December 11 to which Churchill referred is, presumably, R–665/1 of December 5.

C–866

London [via U.S. Army]
Dec. 31, 1944, 2035 Z / TOR 0030 Z, Jan. 1, 1945

Prime Minister to President Roosevelt. Personal and Top Secret.

I have not till now had an opportunity of telling you with what pleasure I received from Ambassador Winant your message of December 11th about Argentine meat. The very kind terms of this message gave the greatest satisfaction to the Cabinet. It is always our desire to be of assistance to you in your policies to the utmost of our power.

[MR*]

Eisenhower had proposed sending to Moscow his Deputy Supreme Commander, Air Chief Marshal Sir A. Tedder, along with an American intelligence officer, to exchange information with the Soviets regarding future military operations. Ever sensitive about southeastern Europe, Churchill proposed sending the Supreme Allied Commander in the Mediterranean, General Sir Harold Alexander, to discuss matters in that theater. Churchill also may have hoped to raise Alexander's prestige as part of a campaign to have the general appointed to command all ground forces in the European Theater of Operations (ETO).

C–867

London [via U.S. Army]
Dec. 31, 1944, 2045 Z / TOR 0030, Jan. 1, 1945

Prime Minister to President Roosevelt. Personal and Top Secret.

1. In the instructions which the Combined Chiefs of Staff have sent to General Eisenhower for the guidance of the representative whom he is sending to Moscow for an exchange of information with U.J., it is contemplated that the Russians may wish to discuss the coordination of the action of their forces with those under Alexander's command. In that event, Eisenhower's representative is to say that he is not competent to discuss these questions, but that Alexander himself would probably be ready either to go to Moscow himself or to send a representative.

2. This seems to be a roundabout arrangement, and I feel it would be better for Alexander and Tedder to be in Moscow together. Moreover it is desirable that Alexander's meeting with Stalin should precede his agreed and urgently needed conference at Belgrade with Tolbukhin and Tito. I therefore propose we should instruct the Combined Chiefs of Staff to send instructions to Alexander to proceed to Moscow as soon as he can. As soon as I have your approval I will telegraph to Stalin.

[MR*]

When Jason sailed aboard the *Argonaut* in search of the Golden Fleece, he headed for Colchis, an ancient kingdom on the eastern shore of the Black Sea. Since Yalta was on the Black Sea, Churchill found the codename ARGONAUT quite fitting. The Map Room copy of this message contains the notation that in C–771 Churchill had indicated that the British party at Quebec would consist of 121 plus a few people from Washington.

C-868

London [via U.S. Army]
Dec. 31, 1944, 2055 Z / TOR 0030, Jan. 1, 1945

Prime Minister to President Roosevelt. Personal and Top Secret.

Your 682:—

I will certainly meet you at Yalta. We are preparing to send a small signal ship to Sebastopol, also a civil liner for accommodation if later information indicates that this is necessary to supplement quarters on shore. It will be necessary for me to take with me about the same numbers as attended the last Quebec conference. This includes the provision for a round-the-clock signal service, but any excess over those who can be conveniently put up on shore will live aboard. Pending further news from you I am taking January 28th (January 28th) as target date for arrival of ships. I shall fly direct via Caserta in the C-54 which General Arnold gave me and which is a wonder. Have you a name for this operation? If not I suggest "ARGONAUT" which has a local but not deducible association.

[MR*. *FRUS, Yalta Conf.*, p. 24.]

The reference is to R–646/1, printed above.

C-869

London [via U.S. Army]
Dec. 31, 1944, 2100 Z / TOR 0030 Z, Jan. 1, 1945

Personal and Top Secret. Prime Minister to President Roosevelt.

1. I have had careful inquiries made into Air Vice-Marshal Ellwood's statement about U-boats which you mentioned in your letter of November 10. The script was carefully examined and approved both by the Admiralty and the Air Ministry before it was delivered, and they contend that these statements were within the limits of previous official announcements and disclosed no information which had not already appeared in the press and upon the German broadcast. I have drawn the attention of both departments to the fact that future statements about the U-boat war are to be confined to achievements and should not speak about the forecast of the future, and that newspaper or German-broadcast disclosures are not to be taken as widening the scope of official statements, even though we know from other sources that they are true.

2. I hope you will let me know if you see any further cause for complaint.

[MR*]

Just how much dignity the King of Greece could retain during the all-night session described in C–864 is a matter for conjecture. At any rate he was safely out of the way, and the British could now legitimately deal with the Regent, Archbishop Damaskinos. ELAS had written Churchill on December 30 claiming that they had met General Scobie's terms for a cease-fire. Scobie evaded the issue by referring the request to the new Greek government, but he recommended that truce discussions be terminated and that ELAS be given an ultimatum to disarm or be destroyed. Macmillan and Eden rejected that solution.

It is an indication of the primacy of politics at this stage of the war that not until the final paragraph of this message did either Churchill or Roosevelt mention the German offensive on the western front. That attack had begun on December 16 in the Ardennes, a hilly wooded sector in eastern Belgium near the Luxembourg border. Aided by surprise and bad weather, which grounded Allied planes, it had met with remarkable initial success. Hitler and General Hasso von Mantueffel (with Field Marshal Gerd von Rundstedt opposed) had designed the offensive to cut off and destroy Allied forces north of a line through Antwerp-Brussels-Bastogne, held by the U.S. First Army. SHAEF had assumed that the Ardennes was unsuited to mobile warfare, particularly in winter, and the area was defended by greatly thinned-out forces. The German attack fell far short of Antwerp and Brussels, but did penetrate Allied lines to a distance of nearly sixty miles. In a maneuver which General Omar Bradley later described as "one of the most astonishing feats of generalship of our campaign in the West," General George Patton shifted his Third Army from its front in the Saar northward fifty to seventy miles to attack the southern flank of the "bulge" in the Allied line caused by the German attack. Three days after receiving his orders, Patton had his forces engaged, and on December 26 relieved the key town of Bastogne, where American soldiers had held out for ten days after being surrounded. Threatened by Patton's advance on their flank, German units had to fall back from their positions at Celles, only five miles from the Meuse River.

In the long run, Churchill's analysis of the battle's import was correct. For a brief tactical success, a temporary "bulge" in the Allied lines, the Germans paid heavily in men, equipment, and ammunition. Never again could they launch a major counter-attack or even muster sufficient reserves to reinforce their own positions.

C–870

London [via U.S. Army]
Dec. 31, 1944, 2113 Z / TOR 0030 Z, Jan. 1, 1945

Prime Minister to President Roosevelt. Personal and Top Secret.

1. Many thanks for your 683. The Greek King behaved like a gentleman and with the utmost dignity, and I am sure a private message from you would give him comfort. I shall send only a civil acknowledgment to ELAS

for the published message they have sent me, and hand the matter over to the Archbishop. It is clearly his job now.

2. I have read your 684 to Anthony, and he and I are in entire agreement with it. It will be most valuable to see what Stalin's reaction to it is. We shall of course send a supporting message at any moment you tell us it would be useful. The reason for delay is that you do not state in your 684 whether you have told Stalin that you have shown your message to me.

3. It is very satisfactory that we seem to be getting into step on both these tangled questions.

4. The great battle in the west seems to be turning steadily in our favour and I remain of the opinion that Runstedt's [sic] sortie is more likely to shorten than to lengthen the war.

[MR*. pWSC, VI, 323.]

R–686

Washington [via U.S. Navy]
Jan. 1, 1945, 1913 Z

Personal and Top Secret, from the President for the Prime Minister.
Your 865 and 866 received. Thank you very much. Roosevelt

[MR*]

Churchill refrained from sending the full doggerel he had penned, but he did not spare us when he wrote his memoirs:

> No more let us alter or falter or palter.
> From Malta to Yalta, and Yalta to Malta.
>
> (WSC, VI, 338)

C–871

London [via U.S. Army]
Jan. 1, 1945 / TOR 0420 Z, Jan. 2

Prime Minister to President Roosevelt Personal and Top Secret.
We shall be delighted if you will come to Malta. I shall be waiting on the quay. You will also see the inscription of your noble message to Malta of a year ago. Everything can be arranged to your convenience. No more let us falter! From Malta to Yalta! Let nobody alter!

[MR*. FRUS, Yalta Conf., p. 26. WSC, VI, 338.]

American Navy officials continued to worry that press releases about the successes against German U-boats would help the Japanese develop more successful anti-submarine measures to use against the United States.

R–687

Washington [via U.S. Navy]
Jan. 2, 1945, 1641 Z

Personal and Top Secret, from the President for the Prime Minister.

Thank you for your 869. We feel here that our agreement has been very helpful in preventing premature information reaching the Japs. Nevertheless, we are losing more subs all the time and we therefore feel that we must continue to be on guard. We very much appreciate the action you have taken. Roosevelt [WEB]

[MR*]

Roosevelt did not try to top Churchill's doggerel, though he did seem eager to avoid any extended Anglo-American talks at Malta.

R–688

Washington [via U.S. Navy]
Jan. 2, 1945, 1644 Z

Top Secret and Personal from the President for the Prime Minister.

Your 871. We plan to arrive by ship at Malta early forenoon 1 February and hope to proceed at once by plane without faltering. It will be grand to meet you on the quay. Roosevelt [WDL, WEB]

[MR*. FRUS, Yalta Conf., p. 26. WSC, VI, 339.]

Roosevelt understood that Churchill still held hopes of launching some sort of offensive in the southwestern Balkans, and bluntly warned the Prime Minister not to expect American support for such ventures. Not only were the Americans reluctant to have General Alexander go to Moscow to discuss future operations in the Mediterranean theater, but the British Chiefs of Staff also thought it best to work out a joint policy with the United States before discussing it with the Soviets. Accordingly, neither General Alexander nor his Deputy Commander for the Mediterranean theater, Lieutenant General Joseph T. McNarney, went to Moscow.

Air Chief Marshal Tedder did not reach Moscow until after the beginning of the Soviet offensive, an offensive that permitted Eisenhower to make his own plans sure in the knowledge that the Germans would not be able to transfer forces from the eastern to the western front.

R–689

Washington [via U.S. Navy]
Jan. 2, 1945, 2107 Z

Top Secret and Personal from the President for the Prime Minister.

Replying to your 867, you are aware of the difficulty of my getting involved in any operations in the Balkans that are not essential to the early defeat of Nazi Germany.

Assuming that you will make the necessary arrangements with Stalin, I offer no objections to your sending to Moscow a representative of the Mediterranean theatre.

In regard to sending Alexander, is it not possible that having British Officers as the two senior members of the conference might be a less advantageous arrangement?

With this thought in mind, would it not be wise for you to give favorable consideration to sending the American deputy from the Mediterranean?

It is very important to our operations in France and Belgium that Eisenhower's representatives should not be delayed to await the representative from the Mediterranean. Roosevelt [WDL]

[MR*. R&C.]

At the suggestion of Gilbert Grovesnor, President of the National Geographic Society, Roosevelt had sent the Prime Minister six new maps which the society had prepared shortly before Christmas.

C–872

London [via U.S. Army]
Jan. 3, 1945, 1088 Z [sic] / TOR 1210 Z

Prime Minister to President Roosevelt, Personal.

Thank you so much for the 6 new maps which you sent my Map Cabinet, and which were safely delivered today.

[MR*]

General Alexander did attend the Yalta Conference (ARGONAUT).

C-873

London [via U.S. Army]
Jan. 3, 1945, 1410 Z / TOR 1640 Z

Prime Minister to President Roosevelt. Personal and Top Secret.
   Your Number 689:
   Thank you for the consideration you gave to my Number 867. In the circumstances it will be better for Alexander to meet us when we are all together at ARGONAUT. I fully agree that nothing must stop the immediate dispatch of Eisenhower's representatives to Moscow.

[MR*]

Roosevelt's health may have contributed to his decision to postpone his long-talked-about trip to England. Most observers found him tired and gray-looking, although his personal physician did not find any deterioration in the President's condition. Possibly the tense exchanges with Churchill during December also contributed to Roosevelt's desire to wait until spring. (The changes in the message were apparently made by the President.)

R-690

Washington [via U.S. Navy]
Jan. 3, 1945, 1649 Z

Personal and Top Secret, from the President for the Prime Minister.
   Your 868, I have informed Harriman that I will arrive Yalta February first or second by airplane from Malta and that Chiefs of Staff will arrive at same time possibly from Egypt.
   I have also informed Harriman that we are sending a Naval auxiliary non-combatant vessel to Sevastopol to arrive three or four days in advance of my arrival.
   Your suggestion of ARGONAUT is ~~accepted~~ welcomed. You and I are direct descendants.
   In considering itinerary of visit to Black Sea, it has developed much to my regret that because of my extended absence from Washington it is necessary for me to postpone my projected visit to the United Kingdom until a later date.
   I will make every effort to arrange to visit the U.K. in May or June.
Roosevelt [WDL]

[MR*. *FRUS, Yalta Conf.*, p. 339. pWSC, VI, 339.]

Stalin rejected Roosevelt's call to postpone Soviet recognition of the Lublin Committee as the provisional government of Poland, although the President appeared willing to discuss the matter at the Yalta Conference.

R–691

Washington [via U.S. Navy]
Jan. 4, 1945, 1614 Z

Top Secret and Personal from the President for the Prime Minister.

There is quoted herewith following for your information Stalin's reply to my message in regard to the Polish situation, my No. 684. I am not replying to Stalin, but we may discuss the matter at the meeting:

QUOTE. 1 January 1945. I have received your message of December 31.

I am extremely sorry that I did not succeed in convincing you of the correctness of the position of the Soviet Government on the Polish question. Nevertheless, I hope that events will convince you that the Polish National Committee has all the time rendered and is continuing to render the Allies, in particular the Red Army, important assistance in the fight against Hitlerite Germany whereas the emigré Government in London is bringing disorganization into this struggle and thus is aiding the Germans.

Of course, your suggestion to postpone for a month the recognition of the Provisional Government of Poland by the Soviet Union is perfectly understandable to me. But there is one circumstance which makes me powerless to fulfill your wish. The fact is that on December 27 the Presidium of the Supreme Soviet of the USSR to an appropriate request of the Poles has already informed them that it intends to recognize the Provisional Government of Poland as soon as it is formed. This circumstance makes me powerless to fulfill your wish.

Permit me to congratulate you on the New Year and to wish you health and success. UNQUOTE.

I have not told Stalin that my message to him was shown to you. Roosevelt

[MR*. *FRUS*, 1945, V, 110–11. *FRUS, Yalta Conf.*, pp. 225–26. *Stalin/FDR*, doc. 256.]

In spite of the growing effectiveness of Allied anti-submarine warfare in the Atlantic, German U-boats remained active to the end of the war. Submarine construction had a high priority throughout the war, so much so that at the end Germany had 336 U-boats, although not all of them were operational. In spite of heavy losses (781 U-boats and over 39,000 officers and men), discipline and morale in the submarine service remained high, and raids against Allied shipping continued. The growing number of snorkel-equipped submarines increased their ability to avoid detection and contributed to the greater activity mentioned in this proposed statement.

The enemy agents mentioned in the statement had landed near Bar Harbor, Maine, on the night of November 29, from a snorkel-equipped U-boat. The two spies were to gather technical data from open sources—radio, newspapers, magazines, and books—and either radio it back to Germany or mail it in microdot form to German agents in neutral countries. The mission failed when one agent, William Colepaugh, who had been born and raised in the United States, turned himself in to the FBI. A few days later, on December 30, the other agent, Erich Gimpel, was arrested by the FBI. Both men were found guilty of espionage and sentenced to death, although President Harry Truman commuted their punishments. (See Kahn, *Hitler's Spies*, pp. 3–26.)

R–692

Washington [via U.S. Navy]
Jan. 4, 1945, 1756 Z

Secret and Personal from the President for the Prime Minister.

Following is proposed submarine statement for December, 1944:

QUOTE. The German U-boat warfare flared into renewed activity during December 1944. This is but another index that the European war is far from over.

Substantially increased losses in Allied merchant craft have been officially recorded, as a result of the U-boats' spurt last month.

Despite these, the United Nations regularly continue to supply their expanding armies over the world, enabling them to resist the attackers or drive back the foe. The Allies continue to sink the enemy undersea craft in widely-separated parts of the Atlantic.

The announcement of the recent landing of enemy agents from a U-boat on the Maine coast is yet another indication that the menace of Germany's undersea fleet is real and continuing. UNQUOTE.

[MR*]

Churchill continued to worry about the arrangements for the Yalta (Y) talks, possibly because Roosevelt had handled everything directly with Stalin. As ever, before meeting Soviet representatives the Prime Minister wanted to hold conversations with the Americans in order to develop joint Anglo-American positions and to prevent Stalin from exploiting any divisions between Britain and the United States. One of those divisive issues was Churchill's scheme for an offensive from Italy northeast toward Austria and Prague, hence the reference to the future use of Allied armies in Italy. The Prime Minister's concern about a presidential visit to France and not England was probably stimulated by Roosevelt's oft-mentioned desire to visit American forces fighting in France.

The message sent by Charles de Gaulle to Churchill and Roosevelt protested Eisenhower's decision to evacuate Strasbourg in Alsace in order to counter a German offensive in the northern part of that French province. De Gaulle feared that such a retreat and the subsequent German reprisals against the French inhabitants of the city would jeopardize his Provisional government and create political chaos behind Allied lines. Even before the French leader's protest reached Eisenhower, the Supreme Commander had come to a similar conclusion and had modified his plans so as to permit Allied forces to remain in Strasbourg. Back in Washington, Roosevelt had refused to say anything to Eisenhower, claiming somewhat disingenuously that it was strictly a military question. However, one suspects that the collapse of the de Gaulle government would not have troubled the President. Churchill claimed in this cable that his visit to SHAEF Headquarters at Versailles was coincidental with de Gaulle's arrival, but some years later the Prime Minister admitted that he went at the Frenchman's invitation (Pogue, *Supreme Command*, p. 401n).

Field Marshal Sir Bernard Montgomery commanded British and Canadian forces on the northern sector of the western front, then Holland and Belgium. During the Battle of the Ardennes, he took command of most of the American armies in that area.

C–874

France/Belgium [via U.S. Army, London]
Jan. 4, 1945; 1635 Z, Jan. 5 (London) / TOR 1900 Z, Jan. 5

Prime Minister to President Roosevelt. Personal and Top Secret.
Your 690.

In none of your telegrams about ARGONAUT have you mentioned whether U.J. likes this place and agrees to it and what kind of accommodation he can provide. I am looking forward to receiving this. It has occurred to some of us that he might come back and say "Why don't you come on the other four hours and let me entertain you in Moscow?" However, I am preparing for Y and am sending a larger liner which will cover all our troubles.

Would it not be possible for you to spend 2 or 3 nights at Malta and let the staffs have a talk together unostentatiously? Also, Eisenhower and Alexander could both be available there. We think it very important that there should be some conversation on matters which do not affect the Russians, E.G., Japan, and also about future use of the Italian Armies. You have but to say the word and we can arrange everything.

We are very sorry indeed you will not come to our shores on this journey. We should feel it very much and a very dismal impression would be made if you were to visit France before you come to Britain: In fact, it would be regarded as a slight on your closest ally. I gather however that you will only go the [to] the Mediterranean and Black Sea, in which case it is merely a repetition of Teheran.

The CIGS and I have passed two very interesting days at Eisenhower's Headquarters at Versailles. Quite by chance De Gaulle arrived at the same time on the business about which he has sent you and me, as Heads of Governments, a telegram concerning the Southern Sector. We had an informal conference and the matter has been satisfactorily adjusted so far as he is concerned. Eisenhower has been very generous to him.

I am now in Eisenhower's train going to visit Montgomery, the weather having made flying impossible. The whole country is covered with snow. I hope to be back in England Saturday [Jan. 6]. Every good wish.

[MR*. p*WSC*, VI, 339–40. p*FRUS, Yalta Conf.*, p. 28. R&C.]

Fearful that the Americans would go to Yalta without any preparatory talks with the British, Churchill tried to arrange a Malta meeting for the military Chiefs of Staff.

C–875

London [via U.S. Army]
Jan. 6, 1945, 1242 Z

Prime Minister to President Roosevelt Personal and Top Secret.
ARGONAUT. Please see my number 874.

If you do not wish to spend more than one night at Malta, it could surely be arranged that both our Chiefs of Staffs should arrive there say a couple of days before us and have their preliminary discussions. We would then all proceed by air to ARGONAUT, thus in no way impeding the journey of the two non-military ships to Sebastopol. Our combined Chiefs of Staff discussions would of course also proceed at Sebastopol at periods when military advisers were not required for the general meetings. The British Chiefs of Staff are repeating this to the United States Chiefs of Staff and suggesting an agenda.

[MR*. *FRUS, Yalta Conf.*, p. 29.]

Roosevelt did not want to meet with Churchill prior to the Yalta talks, and arranged the conference schedule accordingly. He selected the date for arrival at Yalta, February 2, and transmitted it to Stalin on the same day this cable was sent to Churchill. The changes made in this telegram were written by

Roosevelt and further indicate his desire to avoid any Churchill-Roosevelt talks in Malta. Stalin's failure to communicate directly with Churchill about the conference arrangements was in direct response to a request from Ambassador Harriman (Harriman to Roosevelt, Dec. 27, 1944, *FRUS, Yalta Conf.*, pp. 22–23).

The Map Room staff in the White House apparently assigned the number 692 to this cable by mistake, since that same number had been assigned to the preceding cable of January 4. The error was never formally corrected. The additional designation "/1" has been added by the editor to differentiate the two messages.

R–692/1

Washington [via U.S. Navy]
Jan. 6, 1945, 1607 Z

Personal and Top Secret, from the President for the Prime Minister.

Your 874 and 875. I am informed by Harriman that U.J. will meet us at Yalta February first or second.

Preparations are being made to take care of us and our Staff in undamaged houses in Yalta. I will send my ship to Sevastopol to arrive three or four days in advance of my arrival.

There is a chance that weather might permit of the ship's anchoring off the place of meeting.

With favorable weather at sea I can arrive Malta February ~~first~~ second, and it is necessary to proceed by air the same day ~~or the next day~~ in order to keep ~~my~~ the date with U.J.

That is why I regret that in view of the time available to me for this journey it will not be possible for us to meet your suggestion and have a British-American Staff meeting at Malta before proceeding to ARGONAUT. <u>I do not think that by not having a meeting at Malta any time will be lost at ARGONAUT.</u>

I am envious of your visits to the great battlefront which are denied to me by distance. Roosevelt [WDL]

[MR*. *FRUS, Yalta Conf.*, p. 29. p*WSC*, VI, 340.]

Stalin's decision to recognize the Polish National (Lublin) Committee as the provisional government of Poland upset the British, not because they had not expected it but because Stalin did so abruptly and without giving the Churchill government any way to avoid embarrassment at home. The British, of course, could not withdraw their recognition of the London Polish government, but the tone of the Prime Minister's message to Stalin remained conciliatory.

C–876

London [via U.S. Army]
Jan. 6, 1945, 1632 Z / TOR 1850 Z

Prime Minister to President Roosevelt Personal and Top Secret.
Yours number 691.

Thank you for the information and it is interesting to see that the "Presidium of the Supreme Soviet of the USSR" has now been brought up into the line.

Stalin has communicated to me your message to him, of which you sent me a copy in your number 691. We have not ourselves communicated with him on this subject since you sent us a copy of your original message to him (number 675) but had already made it clear in earlier telegrams, and I in fact mentioned it in parliament, that we continue to recognize the London Poles as the Government of Poland. I have now replied to Stalin as follows:— "Naturally I and my war cabinet colleagues are distressed at the course events are taking. I am quite clear that much the best thing is for us three to meet together and talk all these matters over, not only as isolated problems but in relation to the whole world situation both of the war and the transition to peace. Meanwhile, our attitude as you know it remains unchanged. I look forward very much to this momentous meeting and I am glad that the President of the United States has been willing to make this long journey. We have agreed, subject to your concurrence, that the codename shall be called "ARGONAUT" and I hope you will use that in any messages that may be interchanged by the staffs who will be consulting about the arrangements."

You may rest assured of our entire support.

[MR*. *FRUS, Yalta Conf.*, p. 226. p*Stalin/WSC*, doc. 382. p*R&C*.]

The German offensive in the Ardennes, the "Battle of the Bulge," provided the British with another opportunity to propose the appointment of a British officer as Commander in Chief of all ground forces on the western front, a job Eisenhower had assumed as part of his responsibilities as Supreme Commander once the Allies had broken out from Normandy and begun the wide-front offensive against Germany. When the German attack disrupted communications between General Omar Bradley's headquarters and the U.S. First Army, Eisenhower temporarily gave command of that army to British Field Marshal Montgomery. "Monty," whose victory at El Alamein had turned him into a war hero in Great Britain, had repeatedly criticized Eisenhower's handling of ground forces, and he seized the opportunity to try to take charge. In a press conference, ostensibly called by Montgomery to defend Eisenhower and the reputation of American troops, the Englishman led reporters to believe that he was sharply critical of American commanders and their forces. General Bradley responded with an announcement that the shift of the U.S. First Army to Montgomery's command was strictly temporary, whereupon the British press took up the attack on Bradley and other American Generals. Churchill quickly rose in Parliament to praise American troops and leaders, even though the Prime Minister continued to favor the establishment of the post of ground forces Commander in Chief. His personal candidate was Field Marshal Alexander.

During the Ardennes offensive, the U.S. Seventh Armored Division had delayed the German advance in the vicinity of St. Vith for several days, while the First and Ninth American divisions had held the northern sector of the "bulge" in the area of Malmédy. The city of Bastogne, located about ninety miles southeast of Brussels, near the Belgium-Luxembourg border, occupied a crossroads vital to the German advance. German forces surrounded the city on December 20, but Brigadier General A. C. McAuliffe, who commanded the American defenders, rejected a surrender proposal from the Germans with an emphatic "Nuts!"

C–877

London [via U.S. Army]
Jan. 7, 1945, 2154 Z / TOR 0255 Z

Prime Minister to President Roosevelt. Personal and Top Secret.

1. CIGS and I have passed the last two days with Eisenhower and Montgomery and they both feel the battle very heavy but are confident of success. I hope you understand that, in case any troubles should arise in the press, His Majesty's Government have complete confidence in General Eisenhower and feel acutely any attacks made on him.

2. He and Montgomery are very closely knit and also Bradley and Patton, and it would be disaster which broke up this combination which has, in nineteen forty four, yielded us results beyond the dreams of military avarice. Montgomery said to me today that the break through would have been most serious to the whole front but for the solidarity of the Anglo-American Army.

3. Although I regret our divisions only amount to seventeen and two-thirds, all units are absolutely up to strength and we have seven or eight thousand reinforcements all ready in addition in France awaiting transfer to their units. The measures we have taken to bring another 250,000 into or nearer the front line enable me to say with confidence that at least our present strength will be maintained throughout the impending severe campaign.

4. I am deeply impressed with the need of sustaining the foot who bear two-thirds of the losses but are very often the last to receive reinforce-

ments. More important even than the sending over of large new units is the keeping up of the infantry strength of divisions already engaged. We are therefore preparing a number of infantry brigades, including several from the Marines, of which the Navy has 80,000. These brigades will liberate mobile divisions from quasi-static sectors and, at the same time, do the particular work which is needed in them. Montgomery welcomed this idea most cordially as regards the Twenty First Army Group. I gathered from General Eisenhower that he takes the same view and that he is longing for more infantry drafts, i.e. rifle and bayonet, to maintain the U.S. Divisions at their proper establishment.

5. I most cordially congratulate you on the extraordinary gallantry which your troops have shown in all this battle, particularly at Bastogne and two other places which Montgomery mentioned to me on his own front, the exact location of which I do not carry in my mind, one at the peak of the salient where the First and Ninth American Divisions fought on and won after extremely heavy losses, and the other in connection with the Seventh U.S. Armoured Division, which seems to have performed the highest acts of soldierly devotion. Also many troops of the First Army have fought to the end holding cross-roads in the area of incursion which averted serious perils to the whole armies of the north at heavy personal sacrifice.

6. As I see there have been criticisms in the American papers of our troops having been kept out of the battle, I take this occasion to assure you that they stand absolutely ready at all times to obey General Eisenhower's commands. I believe that the dispositions which he and Marshall Montgomery under him have made are entirely in accordance with strict military requirements, both as regards the employment of troops in counter-attack and their lateral movement, having regard to criss-cross communications. I have not found a trace of discord at the British and American Headquarters but, Mr. President, there is this brute fact: we need more fighting troops to make things move.

7. I have a feeling this is a time for an intense new impulse, both of friendship and exertion, to be drawn from our bosoms and to the last scrap of our resources. Do not hesitate to tell me of anything you think we can do.

[MR*. *WSC*, VI, 277–78. *R&C*.]

Roosevelt was particularly fond of his daughter, Anna, and had had her serve as unofficial First Lady on a number of occasions when Eleanor Roosevelt was absent.

R–693

Washington [via U.S. Navy]
Jan. 7, 1945, 1616 Z

Top Secret and Personal from the President for the Prime Minister.

If you are taking any of your personal family to ARGONAUT, I am thinking of including my daughter Anna in my party. Roosevelt [WDL]

[MR*]

C–878

London [via U.S. Army]
Jan. 7, 1945, 2109 Z / TOR 2340 Z

Prime Minister to President Roosevelt. Personal and Top Secret.

Our joint monthly statement about U-boat losses. Admiralty suggest the word "substantially" is stronger than the facts justify and might give an unfortunate impression. I leave the matter in your hands.

[MR*]

Churchill likewise enjoyed his daughter's company.

C–879

London [via U.S. Army]
Jan. 7, 1945, 2124 Z / TOR 2340 Z

Prime Minister to President Roosevelt. Personal and Top Secret.

Your 693. How splendid. Sarah is coming with me.

[MR*]

Eisenhower had insisted that he needed more ground combat troops and had proposed equipping five French divisions by May 1945. The shortage had become so serious that he even proposed a transfer of Marine Corps units from the Pacific and the use of Negro volunteers on the battle line. Ironically, it was the German Army that finally got de Gaulle the arms he wanted for his forces.

R–694

Washington [via U.S. Navy]
Jan. 8, 1945, 1622 Z

Top Secret and Personal from the President to the Prime Minister.

Your 876 and 877 received. My Staff is now making every effort to reinforce Eisenhower with all additional forces that can be found and transported and also by arming French divisions as quickly as possible. Roosevelt [WDL]

[MR*]

R–695

Washington [via U.S. Navy]
Jan. 8, 1945, 1746 Z

Secret and Personal from the President for the Prime Minister.

Your 878.

Your suggestion is a good one and we shall issue the statement deleting "substantially." Roosevelt [GE]

[MR*]

As the Yalta meeting approached, Churchill mounted an all-out campaign to convince the Americans of the need for prior consultations. In the face of Roosevelt's reluctance to meet at Malta, the Prime Minister proposed a meeting of the Foreign Ministers of the three great powers so that political as well as military matters could be discussed in surroundings more favorable to the Anglo-American allies than Yalta.

C–880

London [via U.S. Army]
Jan. 8, 1945, 1600 Z / TOR 1915 Z

Prime Minister to President Roosevelt Personal and Top Secret.

1. I am still thinking it of high importance that our military men should get together for a few days before we arrive at ARGONAUT. There will no doubt be opportunities for them to confer together at Sebastopol on days when we are engaged in politics and do not require technical advice. All the same, there are a tremendous lot of questions which should be looked at beforehand, and our agenda ought really to be considered.

2. Even further to this I would add that there would be great advantages in a preliminary conference of about a week's duration between the foreign ministers. If these could be gathered at the Pyramids or Alexandria, about which arrangements are very easy, and could join us at ARGONAUT, an immense amount of preliminary work would be done. I do not know whether you are bringing Stettinius with you, or whether you would bring him for such a conference. If so, I should greatly welcome it, and the moment that such a decision has been taken, we would invite Molotov to come to the rendezvous. You will remember what advantages were gained last time by the discussions which took place in Moscow before we met at Teheran. Pray let me know whether this appeals to you at all.

3. What are your ideas of the length of our stay at ARGONAUT? This may well be a fateful conference, coming at a moment when the great allies are so divided and the shadow of the war lengthens out before us. At the present time I think the end of this war may well prove to be more disappointing than was the last.

[MR*. p*WSC*, VI, 341. *FRUS, Yalta Conf.*, p. 31. *R&C*.]

A few hours later, Churchill again proposed a meeting of the Combined Chiefs of Staff and once again raised the possibility of a brief Roosevelt-Churchill session.

C–881

London [via U.S. Army]
Jan. 9, 1945, 0108 Z / TOR 0400 Z

Prime Minister to President. Personal and Top Secret.

1. Please see paragraph one of my Nr. 880. In spite of your Nr. 692, our Staffs consider it of the highest importance that they meet with yours before we go on to ARGONAUT. I understand that your Chiefs of Staff are flying separately from you. Why then can they not reach Malta say on January 30th and meet our people there? We think this very important, and we do not see how the agenda can be covered unless there is this preliminary talk. I beg you to consider this. I shall only arrive in time to welcome you on February 2nd.

2. We cannot tell what the flying will be from Malta onward and you may easily have to wait an extra day in Malta. However if our staffs have covered some of the ground, we can spend this day discussing with them. Uncle Joe may if the weather is bad have to put up with a delay. But he may comfort himself with the reflection that he has made us come to him, which in all the circumstances we are wise to do.

[MR*. *FRUS, Yalta Conf.*, pp. 31–32.]

The President agreed to send his military chiefs to Malta in time for talks with their British counterparts, but he insisted that Secretary of State Stettinius could not be spared, thus effectively limiting those preliminary talks to military affairs.

The difference between Churchill's and Roosevelt's view of the significance of the Yalta Conference with Stalin is illustrated in their estimates of the number of days needed for the talks. The President, who expected to deal with most postwar issues at a major peace conference after the war, proposed that Yalta last no more than six days. Churchill, convinced that the ARGONAUT meeting would have to deal with the postwar settlement, was ready for serious, protracted negotiations. There are indications that Roosevelt had planned to bring Stettinius with the presidential party aboard the USS *Quincy*. Possibly that plan was changed when the President decided to use the excuse that the Secretary could not be spared from Washington as his reason for not sending Stettinius to Malta for lengthy talks with Eden.

R–696

Washington [via U.S. Navy]
Jan. 9, 1945, 2047 Z

Personal and Top Secret, from the President for the Prime Minister.

Your 880 and 881. I have directed Marshall, King and Arnold, with their assistants, to arrive Malta in time for a conference with your staff in forenoon of January 30.

In regard to an advance conference between the foreign ministers and the Secretary of State in view of my absence from Washington during the time required to proceed by sea to Malta, it is impracticable for Stettinius to be out of the country for the same extended period.

He will join me at Malta and be with us in ARGONAUT.

My idea of the length of stay at ARGONAUT is that it should not be more than five or six days.

I am very desirous of keeping our date with U.J. if it can possibly be done. Roosevelt [WDL]

[MR*. *FRUS, Yalta Conf.*, p. 32. p*WSC*, VI, 341.]

Vice Admiral Sir Harold Martin Burrough became the commander of Allied naval forces in the European theater following the death of Admiral Bertram Home Ramsay in an airplane accident on January 2. Burrough had commanded the eastern portion of the naval forces during the invasion of North Africa and had been in command of the naval approaches to Gibraltar and the Mediterranean.

C–882

London [via U.S. Army]
Jan. 9, 1945, 2137 Z / TOR 2340 Z

Prime Minister to President Roosevelt. Personal and Secret.

I propose to appoint Admiral Sir Harold Burrough to succeed Ramsay. Eisenhower has been sounded, and would cordially welcome this appointment: and I feel sure that you will agree.

[MR*]

The Clipperton Islands, which ultimately remained possessions of France, became much less significant as aircraft ranges increased after the war. (See R–659 for background on this issue.)

C–883

London [via U.S. Army]
Jan. 10, 1945, 0945 Z / TOR 1210 Z

Prime Minister to President Roosevelt. Personal and Top Secret.
Your number 659.

1. I have now looked into the matter of the Clipperton Island survey and am relieved to find that the Air Ministry here did not issue any instructions in this matter until our delegation in Washington had received full approval in writing from the Navy Department for this survey to be carried out. The Navy Department, furthermore, provided facilities in the form of gasoline and oil at Bora Bora. The survey was then carried out, and its results communicated to the Navy Department.

2. The question of a further flight to complete the survey was being discussed with the Navy Department and the State Department at the time your telegram was sent. I mention this to correct any impression which may be in your mind that the Air Ministry acted high-handedly.

3. I entirely agree that we should leave the whole matter till we meet.

[MR*]

The United States had already taken steps to ensure a settlement of the Clipperton Island question which would be satisfactory to the Americans. On December 11, 1944, the Navy had established a weather station on the island. (See Adm. Brown to Roosevelt, Dec. 13, 1943, MR 20/MR-OUT-639.)

R-697

Washington [via U.S. Navy]
Jan. 10, 1945, 1629 Z

Top Secret and Personal from the President for the Prime Minister.

Thank you for your 883. I feel sure that we will be able to work out a solution that will be satisfactory to all concerned. Roosevelt [WDL]

[MR*]

R-698

Washington [via U.S. Navy]
Jan. 10, 1945, 1634 Z

Top Secret and Personal from the President for the Prime Minister.

Your 882. I agree fully with your selection of Admiral Burrough to succeed Admiral Ramsay. Roosevelt [WDL]

[MR*]

Churchill worried primarily about coordinating Anglo-American policy on a wide variety of issues relating to the Soviet Union, but concentrated on the postwar peace-keeping organization as the item most likely to bring Stettinius to Malta for pre-Yalta talks.

The "masterly" State of the Union address, too long to be read in its entirety, was sent to Congress on January 6. In spite of Stettinius' pleas for a strong and unequivocal statement on foreign policy, particularly a call for continued American involvement in world affairs, the President stuck to broad generalities, hardly what Churchill hoped for.

C-884

London [via U.S. Army]
Jan. 10, 1945, 1910 Z / TOR 2200 Z

Prime Minister to President Roosevelt, Personal and Top Secret.

Your Number 696.

1. Thank you very much about the Combined Chiefs of Staff's preliminary meeting.

2. Eden has particularly asked me to suggest that Stettinius might come on 48 hours earlier to Malta with the United States Chiefs of Staff so that he (Eden) can run over the agenda with him beforehand, even though Molotov were not invited. I am sure this would be found very useful. I

do not see any other way of realising our hopes about world organisation in five or six days. Even the Almighty took seven. Pray forgive my pertinacity.

3. I have now read very carefully your message to Congress and I hope you will let me say that it is a most masterly document. Every good wish.

[MR*. p*FRUS, Yalta Conf.*, p. 33. *WSC*, VI, 341–42. *R&C*.]

Dill had been a particular favorite of General Marshall, who had arranged for the medal as well as for Dill's interment at Arlington National Cemetery. Although the President intended to send only the second letter, both versions are found in the PREM 3 records and were presumably received by Churchill.

R–698/1, letter

Washington
January 10, 1945

My dear Mr. Prime Minister:

In connection with the recent posthumous award of an American Distinguished Service Medal to Field Marshal Sir John Dill, I am sending you herewith a copy of a Joint Resolution of Congress enacted on December 20 last, appreciating the services of Field Marshal Sir John Dill. The fact that Congress saw fit to take this action, which is without precedent, and that the Chairman of the Foreign Relations Committee of the Senate, the Honorable Tom Connally, introduced the Resolution, is not only formal recognition of the great service rendered by him in promoting unity of action on the part of our respective countries, but is an evidence of a very wholesome state of mind in the midst of the bickerings that are inevitable at this stage of the war.

I think Sir John Dill rendered both our countries a great service and I am delighted to see it written clearly into the record.

Always sincerely, [signed] Franklin D. Roosevelt [GCM]

[MR*]

R–698/2, letter

Washington [via State Dept.]
January 11, 1945

Dear Winston:—

I thought you would like to see this copy of the Resolution by the Congress recognizing the services of Field Marshal Sir John Dill. The other day we had a very charming little ceremony in my office when I presented the Distinguished Service Medal to Lady Dill.

I will see you soon. As ever yours,

[MR*]

The President's D-day prayer, which had been sent to Churchill as a gift, had been delivered on a nationwide radio broadcast from Washington on June 6, 1944. (The speech, which is not printed here, is in FDR Speech File, 1519, FDRL.)

C–885

London [via U.S. Navy]
Jan. 11, 1945, 1030 Z / TOR 1430 Z

Prime Minister to President Roosevelt Personal and Secret.
I have never yet thanked you for the bound copy of your D-Day Prayer.
As for the 3 bow-ties, you will see me wearing them at ARGONAUT.

[MR*]

As a concession to Churchill, the President agreed to send Stettinius ahead to Malta for talks with Eden, though only a day early. In the past, Roosevelt might have preferred Harry Hopkins even if protocol demanded that the Secretary of State conduct talks with the British Foreign Secretary, but Hopkins' protracted illness had prevented him from keeping in close touch with foreign policy. Instead, he went to London to pacify the Prime Minister after the quarrels of December.

R–699

Hyde Park, N.Y. [via U.S. Navy]
Jan. 12, 1945, 1703 Z

Personal and Top Secret, from the President to the Prime Minister.
Your 884. It is regretted that projected business here for the Secretary of State will prevent Stettinius' arrival Malta before January 31.

It is my present intention to send Harry Hopkins to England some days in advance of the Malta date to talk with you and Eden. Roosevelt [WDL]

[MR*. *FRUS, Yalta Conf.*, p. 34.]

Under the terms of the Montreux Convention, warships could not pass through the straits between the Aegean and Black seas without prior permission from the government of Turkey. Churchill's proposal was designed to preserve security surrounding the Yalta meeting, a special problem in the case of Turkey, which had been sympathetic toward the Germans.

C–886

London [via U.S. Army]
Jan. 13, 1945, 1516 Z / TOR 1733 Z

Prime Minister to President Roosevelt, Personal and Top Secret.

1. Shall we not have to warn the Turks of the impending arrival of the two ships? We could indeed argue that they are "merchant vessels" for the purposes of the Montreux Convention, with purely defensive armament and not bound on any exclusively military mission. They could thus in theory arrive unannounced at the Straits; but the Turks could still insist on stopping and examining them, and in fact they would be obliged under Article Three to stop for sanitary inspection, which might lead to anything.

2. Should we not tell President Inonu about them at the latest possible moment, for his own strictly personal information, and ask him to give all the orders necessary to ensure that the ships shall pass through unquestioned except by formality? There would be no need to tell him more than that there was going to be a meeting of the heads of governments some day somewhere in the Black Sea.

[MR*. *FRUS, Yalta Conf.*, pp. 34–35.]

Given the course of the war, the Turks were in no position to interfere, but the President agreed to have the American Ambassador to Turkey, Laurence Steinhardt, make the arrangements required by the Montreux Convention. This cable, drafted by Admiral Leahy, was sent to Churchill over the President's name before Roosevelt, then resting at his home in Hyde Park, gave his approval.

R–700

Hyde Park, N.Y. [via U.S. Navy]
Jan. 13, 1945, 2132 Z

Personal and Top Secret, from the President for the Prime Minister.

Your 886. I have directed the State Department to take such action at an appropriate time through Steinhardt with the Turkish Government

as is necessary to insure passage to the Black Sea without delay or interference of the "Naval auxiliary *Catoctin*, not a combatant vessel" and also
four smaller Naval vessels which are really mine sweepers and which the
Navy wishes to send to the Black Sea.

We will have Steinhardt give the Turks identical information regarding
the passage of American airplanes to be used by my party and for daily
mail trips. Roosevelt [WDL]

[MR*. *FRUS, Yalta Conf.*, p. 35.]

The Combined (Anglo-American) Policy Committee on Atomic Energy had
been established as a result of agreements reached by Churchill and Roosevelt
during the Quebec Conference in 1943. TUBE ALLOYS was the codename
for the atomic energy programs being conducted jointly by Great Britain and
the United States.

C–887

London [via U.S. Army]
Jan. 14, 1945, 1027 Z

Prime Minister to President Roosevelt.
TUBE ALLOYS.
I should like Field Marshal Wilson to succeed Field Marshal Dill on the
Combined Policy Committee and hope that this will be agreeable to you.

[MR*. *R&C*.]

R–701

Hyde Park, N.Y. [via U.S. Navy]
Jan. 14, 1945, 1837 Z

Top Secret and Personal, from the President for the Prime Minister.
Reference your Number 887. Delighted to have Wilson on the Combined Policy Committee. Roosevelt

[MR*]

In October 1944 the Yugoslav Partisan leader, Marshal Tito, met with the
Prime Minister of the Royal Yugoslav Government, Ivan Subasić, to discuss
the formation of a unified government. Since Tito's forces controlled large
segments of Yugoslavia and also had the clear, if unspoken, support of the
Soviet Union, the best Subasić could do was to accept a compromise which

at least left King Peter, then in exile in London, as the nominal head of state. With Soviet armies about to liberate Yugoslavia from the Germans, Subasić paid little attention to British diplomats and concentrated on satisfying Soviet expectations. By December, the British had concluded that the compromise worked out by Tito and Subasić was the best King Peter could hope for, but the King continued to withhold his approval. On January 11, King Peter had issued a statement to the press outlining his objections to the Tito-Subasić agreement, and the British responded by informing both Roosevelt and Stalin that the King had acted without consulting the British government. Fearful that Tito would repudiate the agreement and govern Yugoslavia on his own, Churchill redoubled his efforts to get King Peter to accept the compromise.

C–888

London [via U.S. Army]
Jan. 14, 1945, 1605 Z / TOR 1808 Z

Prime Minister to President Roosevelt, Personal and Top Secret.

1. Halifax is giving the State Department a full account of the recent talks which Eden and I have had with King Peter of Yugoslavia. We have, with the approval of the War Cabinet, been urging him in his own interests to accept the Tito-Subasic agreements which preserve the principle of the monarchy and which are the best we think he can hope for in the circumstances. We told him that he could preserve his own position by making it clear in a suitable declaration that he could not, while outside Yugoslavia, assume actual responsibility for the way in which the agreements were fulfilled and that he accepted them on the clear understanding that they would be loyally carried out in the spirit and the letter.

2. On Thursday, however, King Peter, without consultation with us or with his own prime minister, issued a declaration stating his own views on the Tito-Subasic agreements. You know my views on these matters so well that I do not need to repeat that we should insist, so far as is possible, on full and fair elections deciding the future regime of the Yugoslav people or peoples.

3. We are now examining the situation to see how we can save the agreements and preserve the title of the Royal Yugoslav Government until the people or peoples of those mountainous regions have a chance of going to the poll. We have telegraphed Stalin [*Stalin/WSC*, doc. 387] on the lines which are explained in our telegram to Halifax, which shows our views at length. I should be glad to talk this over with you when we meet.

[MR*. R&C.]

CRICKET was the codename for Malta, and MAGNETO for Yalta.

C–889

London [via U.S. Army]
Jan. 14, 1945, 2150 Z / TOR 0030 Z, Jan. 15

Prime Minister to President, Personal and Top Secret.

1. Anthony is very pleased that Stettinius will come to CRICKET if possible on the 31st instant. He will be there to receive him.

2. I will meet you there on your arrival. I must point out however that thereafter the weather will be our master. I have received from Stalin a notification that he is expecting me at MAGNETO on the 2nd. Ought we not to make it clear that we are governed by weather? My air staff are considering the possible alternatives for the onward flight and I will telegraph their views as soon as possible, but it seems likely that unless you can arrive at CRICKET on the 1st we shall not meet U.J. till the 3rd.

3. I am delighted that you will send Harry over here. There will certainly be plenty to talk over.

[MR*. *FRUS, Yalta Conf.*, p. 35.]

COMPETITION FOR IRANIAN OIL

In the fall of 1944, the Soviet Union had asked the Iranian government to open discussions about oil concessions in the five northern provinces of Iran. This coincided with attempts by American corporations to obtain oil concessions and posed a dilemma for the United States government. To counteract British influence in the Middle East, American officials had repeatedly called for equal commercial opportunity for all nations, but they opposed any expansion of Soviet economic and political influence in Iran, particularly in the northwest, where Russia had long claimed portions which had historically been part of Azerbaijan, a Soviet republic. Seizing the opportunity, Iranian nationalists forbade further discussions about oil concessions until after the war, a solution which pleased the British most of all since it prevented both Soviet and American expansion. The arguments and protests made by the Soviet Union to the British, which Churchill mentioned, are repeated in a communication from the Soviet Ambassador in the United States to the Secretary of State. In each case, the Soviets accused the British and the Americans of being "unsympathetic" toward Soviet desires for oil concessions (*FRUS, Yalta Conf.*, pp. 334–36).

Iranian Prime Minister/Foreign Minister Mohammed Saed resigned on November 9, 1944, in an attempt to get the Soviet Union to drop its demands for negotiating new oil concessions. Saed, who had tried to preserve close relations with the United States, had alienated Iranian nationalists and had come under sharp attack, although British diplomats reported that those attacks were orchestrated by the Soviet Union and its agents in Iran (Woodward, *British Foreign Policy*, IV, 453). Murteza Quli Bayat, who replaced Saed as Iranian Prime Minister, continued to refuse to discuss new oil concessions, and on December 2 the Iranian Majlis (Parliament), led by Mohammed Mossedegh, passed a law forbidding any Prime Minister to discuss oil concessions without permission of the Majlis.

The State Department, at Roosevelt's request, drafted a reply to Churchill's cable. The department agreed that Iranian oil concessions should be discussed at the Yalta meeting, but opposed putting the issue on the formal agenda lest that "accord it undue importance." The President did not read the State Department draft until after the Yalta Conference and then took no action since the matter had already been discussed at that meeting, although the question remained unresolved (*FRUS, Yalta Conf.*, pp. 338–39).

Churchill insisted upon referring to Iran by its ancient name, Persia, in order to avoid confusion with Iraq.

C–890

London [via U.S. Army]
Jan. 15, 1945, 1639 Z / TOR 2155 Z

President Roosevelt from Prime Minister. Personal and Top Secret.

1. One of the questions which I think should be discussed at our meeting with Stalin, or between the Foreign Secretaries, is that of Persia.

2. In the declaration about Persia which we and Stalin signed at Teheran in December 1943, it is stated that "The Governments of the United States of America, the USSR and the United Kingdom are at one with the Government of Iran in their desire for the maintenance of the independence, sovereignty and territorial integrity of Iran."

3. You will have seen reports of the recent attitude of the Russians in Persia. We here feel that the various forms of pressure which they have been exerting constitute a departure from the statement quoted above. They have refused to accept the Persian decision to grant no concessions until after the war: and they have brought about the fall of a Persian Prime Minister who, believing that there could be no free or fair negotiations so long as Russian (or other foreign) troops were in Persia, refused the immediate grant of their oil demands. The new Persian Prime Minister, supported by the Parliament, has maintained his predecessor's attitude on this question. But the Russians have indicated that they do not intend to drop their demands.

4. This may be something of a test case. Persia is a country where we, yourselves and the Russians are all involved: and we have given a joint undertaking to treat the Persians decently. If the Russians are now able not only to save their face by securing the fall of the Persian Prime Minister who opposed them, but also to secure what they want by their use of the

big stick, Persia is not the only place where the bad effect will be felt.

5. Please let me know whether you agree that this should be taken up with the Russians: and if so, whether you feel that it should be handled by ourselves with Stalin (as signatories of the Teheran declaration) or by the Foreign Secretaries. I think it should be our object to induce the Russians to admit that the Persians are within their rights in withholding a concession if they wish to do so. We could agree, if necessary, that the oil question should be further reviewed after the withdrawal of foreign troops from Persia.

6. We do not wish the Russians to be able to represent that they were not warned in time of the strength of our feelings on this matter. If, therefore, you agree generally with my suggestion, I propose that we should separately or jointly let Stalin know now that we think Persia should be discussed at our next meeting (or by the Foreign Secretaries).

7. Before replying to this telegram, I think that you should see Soviet note of December 29 to Foreign Office, which we have communicated to State Department.

[MR*. *FRUS, Yalta Conf.*, pp. 336–37. pR&C.]

R–702

Washington [via U.S. Navy]
Jan. 16, 1945, 1539 Z

For the Prime Minister from the President, Personal and Top Secret.
Receipt is acknowledged of your 889 of January 14. Roosevelt

[MR*]

Roosevelt did not respond to Churchill's cable about Yugoslavia except with this brief acknowledgment. In a cable to the American Ambassador to the Yugoslav government in exile, Secretary of State Stettinius noted that the United States had "not adopted the activist policy which other Governments may have considered useful with regard to the political elements in Yugoslavia ..." (*FRUS*, 1945, V, 1180–81).

R–703

Washington [via U.S. Navy]
Jan. 17, 1945, 1353 Z

Top Secret and Personal, from the President for the Prime Minister.
Receipt of your 888 is acknowledged. Roosevelt [WDL]

[MR*]

Like the President, Churchill did not want his style cramped at Yalta by the presence of British and American reporters. Great-power negotiations over the postwar world required careful news management, not unrestrained publicity and awkward questions.

C–891

London [via U.S. Army]
Jan. 21, 1945, 1640 Z / TOR 1820 Z

Prime Minister to President Roosevelt Personal and Top Secret.

I suggest that the press should be entirely excluded from ARGONAUT, but that each of us should be free to bring not more than three or four uniformed service photographers to take "still" and cinematograph pictures to be released when we think fit. Please let me know if you agree.

There will of course be the usual agreement communique, or communiques.

I am sending a similar telegram to U.J.

[MR*. *FRUS, Yalta Conf.*, p. 38. *R&C*.]

R–704

Washington [via U.S. Navy]
Jan. 22, 1945, 1624 Z

Personal and Top Secret, for the Prime Minister from the President.

I am in full agreement with the suggestion regarding press representatives and photographers made in your 891. Roosevelt [WDL]

[MR*. *FRUS, Yalta Conf.*, p. 38. *R&Cn.*]

C–892

London [via U.S. Army]
Jan. 22, 1945, 2339 Z / TOR 0042 Z, Jan. 23

Prime Minister to President Roosevelt. Personal and Top Secret.
Your 704.
Please tell U.J.

[MR*. *FRUS, Yalta Conf.*, p. 38n.]

R-705

Washington [via U.S. Navy]
Jan. 22, 1945; 0130 Z, Jan. 23

Personal and Top Secret from the President to the Prime Minister.
 Your 892.
 I have sent the following message to Stalin:

 "I have decided not to have any press representatives at ARGO-
NAUT and to permit only a small group of uniformed service photographers from the American Navy to take the pictures that we will
want.
 Prime Minister Churchill agrees."

 Roosevelt [WDL]

[MR*. *FRUS, Yalta Conf.*, p. 39.]

Roosevelt later took Churchill's advice and left Malta (CRICKET) on February
3 at 3:30 A.M. aboard the presidential airplane, the *Sacred Cow*. They arrived
at Saki airfield in the Crimea shortly after noon that same day. The eighty-
mile drive to Yalta (MAGNETO) did prove tiring, but uneventful, and the
President arrived there in the early evening. (The most complete and entertaining description of the President's trip to Malta and Yalta is in Bishop,
FDR's Last Year, pp. 359–406.)
 This message was delivered to the President aboard the heavy cruiser USS
Quincy enroute Malta from Newport News, Virginia. The ship left the United
States on the morning of January 23 and arrived at Valletta, Malta, on February 2. During that time, messages were delivered to Roosevelt by radio and
by aircraft, which dropped cannisters into the sea where they were picked
up by destroyers escorting the *Quincy*.

C-893

London [via U.S. Navy]
Jan. 23, 1945, 2310 Z

Prime Minister to President, Personal and Top Secret.
 1. My people are now discussing with yours in Naples the plans for our
flight from Malta to the Crimea. These should be drawn up in advance
if possible, so that the flight arrangements can be completed and so that
we can give the necessary warning to Marshal Stalin and to President
Inonu of Turkey. It is, of course, understood that they are liable to change
at the last minute if the weather makes this necessary.

2. The route proposed is from Malta, south of the island of Kythera, passing east of Athens and the islands of Skyros, Lemnos and Samothrace, across European Turkey to Midia and then straight over the Black Sea. The flight would be 1,300 miles long and would take about seven hours.

3. The highest point is in the Island of Samothrace, which is just over 5,000 feet high and this would mean, if the visibility is not good, that the aircraft might have to climb to about 7,000 feet for a short time. The rest of the flight could be done quite low down.

4. We could do the flight either entirely by day or by night with a landing in the morning. As the enemy fighters have now left the Aegean, a daylight flight would be quite safe and the navigational and other arrangements for it would be slightly simpler than for a night one. However there is no serious objection to a night flight and indeed I myself did this part of the journey by night when I went to Moscow. A night flight would, moreover, have the great advantage of getting us to the Crimea in the morning with the whole day before us to drive to Yalta.

5. The Russians have asked us to arrive at the Saki airfield as it has the best runways available. This is about ten miles from Eupatoria and would leave us a drive of at least seventy to eighty miles, and possibly more if the roads across the hills south of Simferopol are blocked by snow. I am told that the Russians have not yet had time to repair the roads, which are still very bad and the going upon them is therefore very slow. The drive to Yalta would, therefore, probably take at least four hours and perhaps longer, even in daylight, and I do not think that we could possibly do it in darkness. After a daylight flight the greater part would necessarily be after dark.

6. I have therefore come to the conclusion that we ought to plan to fly by night arriving at Saki in the morning. If you are in agreement I will have the plans drawn up accordingly.

7. If your advisors consider that the risk of rising to 7,000 feet is not acceptable it might be possible to leave CRICKET about 3:00 AM so as to pass Samothrace at dawn and ensure a daylight drive to MAGNETO.

8. From the foregoing it will be seen that unless you can arrive at CRICKET on 1st February we shall not meet U. J. till the 3rd and I suggest that we should give him an amended date if this is necessary.

[MR*]

Field Marshal Alexander attended both the Malta and Yalta (MAGNETO) meetings, but Eisenhower asked to be excused in order to stay abreast of the military situation on the western front. General Marshall, however, met with Eisenhower just prior to the Combined Chiefs of Staff conference in Malta (CRICKET). (See the headnote to C–867 and the discussion of the Malta talks which follows R–707.)

C–894

London [via U.S. Army]
Jan. 24, 1945, 1032 Z / TOR 1212 Z (Washington)

Prime Minister to President Roosevelt Personal and Top Secret.

It would be a great pity if Eisenhower and Alexander only come to CRICKET and if we do not have them with us at MAGNETO. This will really make it impossible for the Heads of Government to enter fully into the military problems. I hope therefore they may be instructed as originally proposed to come to MAGNETO as well as CRICKET and if they have to be absent from either, it should be CRICKET.

The above of course is subject to battle exigencies.

[MR*. *FRUS, Yalta Conf.*, p. 39. R&C.]

On January 24, Lieutenant George Elsey, USNR, of the White House Map Room staff, drafted a routine acknowledgment of Churchill's messages: "White House acknowledges receipt of the Prime Minister's messages 893 and 894. They have been passed to the President who is embarked and will be unable to reply immediately." That same day Harry Hopkin, in London for talks with Churchill, passed on the Prime Minister's prescription for avoiding disease while at Yalta. Hopkins had gone to England on January 21 with the job of pacifying Churchill, who was still fuming over American accusations of British meddling in Italian politics, State Department criticisms of British actions in Greece, and the dispute which had arisen during the Chicago Civil Aviation Conference. Moreover, the President apparently sensed that the Prime Minister was hurt and troubled at Roosevelt's refusal to attend a pre-Yalta conference. Hopkins characterized his visit as "very satisfactory," but that was strictly his own interpretation. Churchill was pleased to see him, but the American avoided the substantive issues which were on the agenda for the Yalta talks. Moreover, the British were annoyed by a *New York Times* story, dispatched by the newspaper's London correspondent, Raymond Daniell, which claimed to give the gist of a message sent to Churchill from Roosevelt. Although the Foreign Office surmised that the story actually came from Harry Hopkins, they still were troubled by warnings that the American public would not support postwar internationalism if they "get the idea that this war which started out as a crusade for freedom winds up as just another struggle between rival Imperialisms." British moves in Greece and Yugoslavia were singled out as particularly offensive to Americans. The Foreign Office decided not to lodge a protest, however, possibly because Daniell was returning to the United States to be assistant editor of the *New York Times*. (See *New York Times*, Jan. 24, 1945; PREM 4/27/10/929–38; FO 371/44559 AN 328.)

General Edwin "Pa" Watson's seasickness, a chronic complaint, may have been intensified by his poor health. According to the heart specialist who accompanied the presidential party, Watson suffered from congestive heart failure and prostate trouble.

C–894/1

London [via U.S. Army]
Jan. 24, 1945

[Churchill to Roosevelt via Hopkins]
Send following to President:

QUOTE   Have had very satisfactory visit London. Leaving for Paris tomorrow. Churchill well. He says that if we had spent ten years on research, we could not have found a worse place in the world than MAGNETO but that he feels that he can survive it by bringing an adequate supply of whiskey. He claims it is good for typhus and deadly on lice which thrive in those parts. Sorry to hear that Watson seasick as usual. Regards to all. Signed Harry. UNQUOTE.

[HLH:Sherwood Col. MR. *FRUS, Yalta Conf.*, pp. 39–40.]

Because South East Asia was a combined (Anglo-American) command, major appointments were officially a matter of concern to both Churchill and Roosevelt, although the air commander's position was a British appointment. Mallory had died in an airplane crash on November 14. Air Marshal Keith Park's war record was impressive, particularly his performance as commander of the R.A.F. in Malta.

C–895

London [via U.S. Army]
Jan. 25, 1945, 0841 Z

Prime Minister to President Roosevelt Personal and Secret.

I am appointing Air Marshal Park as Air Commander in Chief, South East Asia, to fill the vacancy created by Air Chief Marshal Leigh Mallory's death. Park has, as you know, a splendid war record, first in the Battle of Britain, then at Malta, and lately in the Middle East. I am sure you will like my selection.

[MR]

Fortunately for both Roosevelt and Churchill, the drive from ALBATROSS (Saki airfield in the Crimea) to MAGNETO (Yalta) was without serious problems. DISRAELI was the British S.S. *Franconia* (Cunard Lines), moored at Sevastopol with a number of U.S. naval vessels in the event that the conferees decided to move the meetings to shipboard.

C–896

London [via U.S. Army]
Jan. 26, 1945, 0900 Z / TOR 1207 Z (Washington)

Prime Minister to President Roosevelt Personal and Top Secret.

The attached telegram has been received from Group Captain Pickard, The Commanding Officer of the staging post we are setting up at AL-BATROSS airfield.

Begins:—

"Am compelled to advise you of my great concern regarding extreme difficulty in communicating with MAGNETO from ALBA-TROSS by road. Two attempts made by American General Hill resulted in failure to pass mountainous track in blizzard. Personally accompanied General at first attempt and endured most terrifying experience. Am informed under favourable conditions journey takes six hours. Similar difficulty anticipated in road communication AL-BATROSS to DISRAELI." Ends.

We must hope we get better weather when we arrive.

[MR*]

When the Chicago Civil Aviation Conference failed to produce an international agreement, the United States went ahead with bilateral negotiations. A Spanish-American agreement was signed on December 2, 1944, and talks with the Irish Republic (what Churchill called the "Southern Irish") were proceeding, to the distress of the British Prime Minister, who believed Ireland should not only be punished for failing to join the Allied war effort but also be treated as part of the British Commonwealth rather than as a fully independent nation.

C–897

London [via U.S. Army]
Jan. 27, 1945, 2243 Z

Prime Minister to President Roosevelt Personal and Top Secret.

1. I have just heard from Dublin that your people are asking the Government of Southern Ireland to sign a bilateral civil aviation agreement.

Naturally everyone here is astonished that this should have been started without our being told beforehand. We already complained when they were invited to the Chicago conference without a mention to us. We were together at Hyde Park and I thought you felt that my attitude deserved consideration. It was because of their behavior in the war that the Southern Irish were not asked to talk civil aviation with the rest of the British Commonwealth and Empire at Montreal. I cannot feel sure this affair has been brought to your notice and I am certain that you would have wished at least to acquaint us with your intentions beforehand.

2. The War Cabinet have very strong feelings on this episode and we all earnestly hope as good friends that you will consider the matter personally yourself. We went far to meet your requests about the Argentine meat in spite of the grave and growing injury to ourselves and the risk to the general war effort, which is now becoming evident. I am sure we may ask you to postpone these negotiations with the Southern Irish until at least you and I have a chance of talking it over together.

[MR*. R&C.]

As things turned out, the journey from Malta to Yalta proved relatively easy.

R–706

USS *Quincy*, at sea [via U.S. Navy, Washington]
Jan. 28, 1945; 0300 Z, Jan. 29 (Washington)

Personal and Top Secret from the President to the Prime Minister.
Thank you for your 893 and 896.

The approaches to ARGONAUT appear to be much more difficult than at first reported. I will have my advance party make recommendations as to how I shall travel after Malta.

I agree that we must notify U.J. as soon as we can fix our schedule in the light of present information. Roosevelt

[MR*. *FRUS, Yalta Conf.*, p. 40. *WSC*, VI, 342.]

C–898

London [via U.S. Army]
Jan. 29, 1945, 0853 Z

Prime Minister to President Roosevelt, Personal and Top Secret.
Have just received your letter of January 11 [R–698/1, R–698/2] about the resolution of the Congress recognizing the services of Sir John Dill.

I am deeply touched by this impressive recognition of his work for our cause and I have asked the Secretary of State for War that the document which you have forwarded to me shall be framed and preserved in the War Office in the room of the Chief of the Imperial General Staff.

[MR*]

Franklin Roosevelt celebrated his sixty-third birthday on January 30, 1945.

C–899

London [via U.S. Army]
Jan. 29, 1945, 1705 Z / TOR 1900 Z (Washington)

Prime Minister to President Roosevelt. Personal.
   Again we both send you and yours our best wishes for many happy returns of the day.

[MR*]

Roosevelt received Churchill's cables on a number of important and controversial subjects, but the President had no desire to deal with those issues before the Yalta meeting began.

R–707

USS *Quincy*, at sea [via U.S. Navy, Washington]
Jan. 31, 1945, 2232 Z

Top Secret and Personal from the President for the Prime Minister.
   Your 894, 895, 897, 898, and 899 received.
   Many thanks to both of you for your birthday greetings. All are well here. Roosevelt

[MR*]

THE MALTA AND YALTA CONFERENCES
(CRICKET AND ARGONAUT)

Roosevelt and Churchill exchanged no more cables or letters until almost the end of the Yalta Conference. The President's sea voyage aboard the USS *Quincy* ended with his arrival at Malta on the morning of February 2.
   The Malta Conference, which brought Churchill, Eden, Stettinius, and the Combined Chiefs of Staff together, had begun on January 30, but its major

20. The guns of politics: John Gilbert Winant, Roosevelt,
Edward Stettinius, and Harry Hopkins aboard the USS *Quincy*, Alexandria,
Egypt, February 15, 1945

decisions were foreshadowed by the results of talks between Generals Marshall
and Eisenhower, held on January 28 near Marseille, France. Marshall's side-
trip not only served as a public show of confidence in the Supreme Commander—an important gesture given Churchill's continued pressure to have
Field Marshal Alexander appointed Commander in Chief of Allied ground
forces in Europe—but it also gave Marshall, as the American Army Chief of
Staff, an opportunity to review and approve Eisenhower's strategy for a broad
offensive against the Germans on the northern sector of the front. Thus,
when Marshall arrived at Malta, he was ready to deal with the two issues the
British wanted to raise. Probably sensing that Marshall would not agree,
Churchill and the British Chiefs of Staff did not propose any changes in the
command structure of SHAEF, although they did bring the matter up later
in February. At that time, Field Marshal Montgomery insisted that he did
not want any additional command interposed between himself and Eisenhower, and that ended the dispute over command. Marshall answered British
questions about Eisenhower's strategy by explaining that the Supreme Com-

mander would not spread out his forces on a long front but would hold back reserves which could be used to exploit any breakthrough in the north, where the main Allied attacks would take place. The Combined Chiefs also agreed with General Alan Brooke's comment that "there was now no question of operations aimed at the Ljubljana Gap and in any event the advance of the left wing of the Russian army made such an operation no longer necessary." As a result, the military leaders recommended the transfer of a number of Allied divisions from Italy to the western front, although Churchill was not comfortable with such reasoning (*FRUS, Yalta Conf.*, p. 486).

The political discussions preceding the President's arrival at Malta were brief and inconclusive, for without Roosevelt and Stalin no decisions could be taken. Stettinius, Eden, and their subordinates discussed important issues—occupation policy in Germany and Austria, the Soviet presence in Iran, Allied participation in the reorganization of Roumania, Hungary, and Bulgaria, the proposed postwar international organization, and the Polish-German frontier. The most revealing comment came from Eden when he recommended a "fusion" of the Polish governments in London and Lublin (then situated in Warsaw), leading to free elections. At the same time, Eden noted that "there are no good candidates from the Government in London," although the inclusion of men like Mikolajczyk would make it easier for the Allies to recognize a new Polish government (*FRUS, Yalta Conf.*, p. 508). That sort of reasoning, which seemed to be a confused attempt to combine public promises to the London Poles with the secret arrangements made during the Anglo-Soviet talks of October 1944 in Moscow (TOLSTOY), characterized the later discussions about Poland which took place during the Yalta Conference.

To Churchill's obvious disappointment, Roosevelt's arrival in Malta did not herald the beginning of serious Anglo-American political conversations. To the contrary, the President avoided any substantive, lengthy talks in spite of the Prime Minister's best efforts. Churchill did manage to air his disagreement with the Combined Chiefs' recommendations on Italy, arguing instead that "we should occupy as much of Austria as possible as it was undesirable that more of Western Europe than necessary should be occupied by the Russians" (*FRUS, Yalta Conf.*, p. 543). It was the first time Churchill had suggested to the Americans that military forces be positioned so as to limit Soviet expansion, and may be an indication of the kind of pre-Yalta consensus he hoped to achieve. (Churchill had long recognized that the territory occupied by the victorious armies at war's end would affect the "balance of power." See Churchill to Eden, Jan. 8, 1942, *WSC*, III, 696.) But, in spite of the Prime Minister's best efforts, Roosevelt refused to be drawn into any discussion on that or similar questions.

As for the Far East, the Malta talks illustrated the divergence of British and American interests. American planning centered on preparations for an invasion of the Japanese home islands, whereas British leaders were primarily concerned with the liberation of Southeast Asia and the European colonial possessions. With Roosevelt's tacit approval, the Joint Chiefs of Staff warned that American forces would not be available to support operations in Southeast Asia and that all air and transportation support had been earmarked for use in China. The President, somewhat forlornly, admitted that "three generations of education and training would be required before China could become a serious [political] factor," but General Marshall provided a glimpse into American thinking when he noted that the maintenance of British forces in China was not feasible—leaving the United States as the sole sponsor of Chiang Kai-shek's regime (*FRUS, Yalta Conf.*, pp. 544–45).

The President left Malta aboard a specially fitted Air Transport Command aircraft early in the morning of February 3, less than twenty hours after his arrival on the island. The Prime Minister also headed for Saki airfield, in the Crimea, but on a separate plane. The two did not confer privately again until February 6, the third day of the Yalta talks.

Despite the controversy which has surrounded the Yalta meeting (called the Crimea Conference in the documents), most of the decisions merely fleshed out agreements reached at the Teheran Conference, fourteen months earlier. Only discussions regarding the postwar international organization and the settlement in East Asia broke new ground. Moreover, the Yalta decisions must be understood in light of military events in both Europe and the Pacific. By the start of the conference, Soviet forces had reached the Oder River, only forty miles from Berlin. Their massive offensive, which had begun only three weeks earlier from positions south of Warsaw, had swept 250 miles westward, liberating virtually all of prewar Poland in the process—this at a time when Anglo-American forces were still off balance following the German counter-attack in the Ardennes. Not realizing that Soviet armies had reached the limit of their lines of communication and supply (they did not begin their assault on Berlin until mid-April), a number of American diplomats nervously recommended that the President quickly ratify the occupation zones for Germany worked out by the European Advisory Commission lest Stalin claim no agreement existed and permit his armies to occupy portions of western Germany.

In the Pacific, the tempo of Anglo-American military operations seemed also to have slowed. MacArthur's troops were still fighting to clear the Philippines (Manila was not liberated until March), the British were not quite ready to launch an offensive against the Japanese in southeastern Burma (Rangoon was not taken until early May), and the next American move in the central Pacific—the invasion of Iwo Jima—would not occur until February 19. The outcome was not in doubt, either in the Pacific or in Europe, but the military and psychological initiative lay with the Soviet Union, at least as of February 4, 1945, when the Yalta Conference began.

With victory assured (the planning date for the earliest possible surrender of Germany was July 1, 1945, with the defeat of Japan forecast to follow in eighteen months), most of the military discussions at Yalta dealt with relatively minor questions of coordination between Allied and Soviet forces so as to avoid inflicting casualties on each other. Talks were held about occupation procedures in Germany and Austria, but the basic decisions on those questions lay with the political leaders. Soviet participation in the Pacific war received a good deal of attention, and General Marshall indicated his strong desire to see Soviet forces engaged against the Japanese as quickly as possible. But once again, the politicians settled that issue.

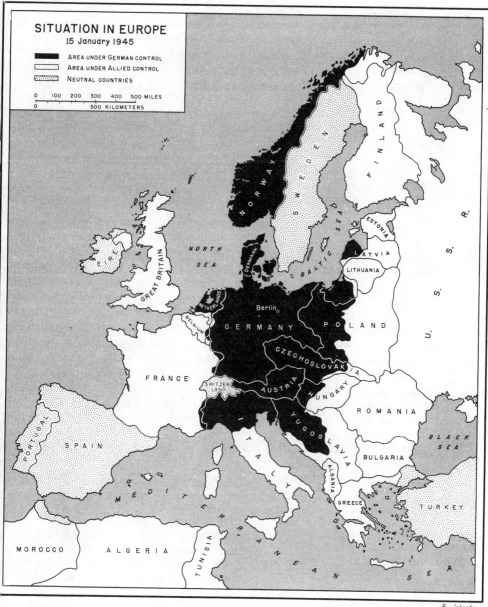

SITUATION IN EUROPE
15 January 1945

▓▓▓ AREA UNDER GERMAN CONTROL
☐ AREA UNDER ALLIED CONTROL
░░░ NEUTRAL COUNTRIES

0   100 200 300 400 500 MILES
0   500 KILOMETERS

R. Johnstone

If frequency of discussion is any gauge, the Polish question dominated the Yalta Conference. The issue was complicated, but it had taken shape long before the three leaders met in the Crimea. By that time, with Soviet military forces firmly in control of Poland, Churchill and Roosevelt were forced to scramble for a compromise acceptable to Stalin and at home. The Prime Minister, already muttering warnings to Eden about a general election in Britain once Germany surrendered, feared both Russian expansion and his own electorate—or at least Parliament—yet he was unwilling to force a confrontation with Stalin over Poland, particularly without full support from the United States. Roosevelt, deeply worried that Americans would reject the activist role in world affairs he favored, did not want controversy over the Polish question to turn domestic and congressional opinion against a postwar international organization or continued great-power cooperation.

The relationship between Poland and the Soviet Union, for that was the basic issue, had been set by the events of World War II and sketched out at the Teheran Conference and the Churchill-Stalin talks in Moscow in October 1944 (TOLSTOY). Given the opportunity to occupy areas which had been claimed by Tsarist and Soviet leaders, Stalin had insisted from the outset of the war that portions of what had been eastern Poland be "returned" to the Soviet Union, with territorial compensation for Poland in eastern Germany (see map, Vol. II, p. 685). Throughout the war, whenever Soviet-Polish relations came up, Stalin made the territorial settlement a prerequisite to agreement on other questions. Churchill and Roosevelt had offered no overall objections to the Soviet demands, although they had both suggested minor modifications to the boundaries proposed by Stalin. The problem was that at no time during the war was the Polish government in London willing to accept such territorial changes. At the same time, the two Allied leaders agreed that Stalin had every right to insist that any postwar Polish government be friendly to the Soviet Union—a requirement which ruled out any restoration of the London Poles to power.

During the Yalta discussions neither Churchill nor Roosevelt challenged those Soviet demands. Rather, they sought to create the impression that any government in postwar Poland would meet the high standards of political freedom set forth in the Atlantic Charter. They hoped the inclusion of a few members of the London Polish regime would legitimize the entire government, whether it was a "new" provisional government or just a broadened version of the Soviet-sponsored Lublin (Warsaw) group. At eight of the nine plenary meetings during the Crimea Conference, Churchill and/or Roosevelt tried to get the Soviets to grant at least cosmetic concessions, but Stalin and Molotov gave very little. All the British and Americans could achieve was a vague promise that "all democratic and anti-Nazi parties" would have a right to take part in "free and unfettered elections" in Poland (*FRUS, Yalta Conf.*, p. 973). A tripartite commission was to discuss the reorganization of the Polish government, but the commission's authority was even less than that of the Allied Control Commission in Italy, which had been used so effectively to deny the Soviets any functional role. Churchill and Roosevelt recognized that implementation of the compromises they had negotiated depended upon

Soviet good will, and the Allied leaders seem to have wishfully believed that Stalin would be lured by the possibility of long-term cooperation instead of immediate gains. They counted on Stalin to understand their requirement for appearances, but both commented to subordinates that the Soviets could implement the agreements as they saw fit, without formally violating them.

The other controversial outcome of the Yalta Conference, the Soviet-American agreement on the Far East, was not a matter of discussion between Churchill and Roosevelt, either at Yalta or in their subsequent correspondence. As early as November 1942, in a conversation with Patrick Hurley, Stalin had alluded to future Soviet cooperation in the Pacific war. By 1945, with any Japanese attack on weakly defended Siberia unlikely, the time had come for a firm quid pro quo. The agreement—which later came in for heavy criticism in the United States—called for Soviet entry into the war against Japan within three months after Germany's surrender. In return, the Soviet Union would regain the southern portion of Sakhalin Island and gain the Kurile Islands from Japan, recognition of the Soviet sphere of influence in Outer Mongolia, and joint Soviet-Chinese operation of the South-Manchurian Railroad, as well as the internationalization of Port Arthur and the leasing of naval facilities in Dairen. Although Chiang Kai-shek was to be consulted, that was a *pro forma* gesture, since the Nationalist Chinese leader was desperate for American and Soviet support against the Chinese communists. Anthony Eden protested that the agreement should not be signed in the absence of Chinese representatives, but Churchill insisted that China was an American concern and that British influence in East Asia would be diminished if he did not sign the protocol. Although the atomic bomb later made Stalin's demands appear excessive, Roosevelt accepted General Marshall's arguments that the entry of the Soviet Union into the war against Japan would shorten the conflict and save many American lives. Moreover, the agreement seemed to guarantee Soviet support for Chiang Kai-shek against the Chinese communists.

What came to be called the United Nations organization received considerable attention at Yalta, although the results were far less controversial than in the case of Poland and East Asia. A lengthy debate sprang up over voting procedures in the Security Council—the body being designed to facilitate great-power cooperation. Negotiators at the Dumbarton Oaks Conference had been unable to resolve the question of great-power unanimity—the veto—on procedural questions, particularly when members were deciding to bring an issue before the council. The Soviets finally accepted a suggestion that seven of eleven votes would be sufficient to refer a matter to the council, but Stalin asked for something in return. His proposal for original membership in the organization for two or three Soviet republics brought objections from Roosevelt on the grounds that the American public would not accept it, but Churchill agreed with Stalin, noting that constituent nations in the British Empire had conducted foreign policy before they became fully independent. The President went along after receiving promises that the United States could also ask for additional votes in the General Assembly of the international organization.

Roosevelt preferred to await the postwar peace conference before taking up the role of Germany in European security, but they did discuss the question of dismemberment. In real or feigned ignorance of shifts in American policy, Stalin assumed that the spirit of the Morgenthau Plan still prevailed, just as Churchill had claimed during their talks in Moscow. The British opposed any commitment to dismemberment and the President compromised by suggesting they merely agree to study the matter. But Stalin and Molotov insisted, and all finally accepted a reference to dismemberment in the surrender terms for Germany, although those terms were to remain secret until the war ended. In spite of what seemed an ideal opportunity, Roosevelt never raised the idea of a security treaty between the United States and the European powers. That kind of guarantee against future German threats had been suggested back in the United States by Senator Arthur Vandenberg, and had been received well in the press and by other opinion makers, and the President had even brought a copy of Vandenberg's speech to the Crimea Conference. Roosevelt may have thought such a treaty would not pass the United States Senate, or he may have feared that it could work against the development of the United Nations as an effective international organization; whatever the reason, the subject never came up at Yalta. (See Gardner, *Architects of Illusion*, pp. 49–50.)

The question of reparations followed the same pattern of postponement, as Roosevelt wanted. To the displeasure of the British, who blamed reparations for the collapse of the peace after World War I, the President supported extensive reparations in principle, agreeing to a $20 billion figure "as a basis for discussion," with 50 percent of that going to the Soviet Union. The one thing which might have lessened Soviet insistence on reparations—a massive loan from the United States—had been proposed by Molotov shortly before the Yalta Conference convened, but Roosevelt had decided previously not to discuss the issue with the Soviets just yet. The President apparently accepted State Department arguments that the loan could be used to gain concessions from the Soviet Union on other issues. (See Blum, *Morgenthau Diaries*, III, 305.)

Other questions, such as giving France an occupation zone in Germany or the establishment of regular meetings between the Foreign Secretaries of the Big Three, caused little argument. American negotiators raised the issue of internationalizing trusteeships—dependencies supervised by larger nations—but when Churchill exploded in protest, the President backed down and agreed to further discussions.

But the essence of Yalta was not in the joint protocols signed by Churchill, Roosevelt, and Stalin. They approached the conference believing that it provided a unique opportunity to create a long-lasting peace, although the President estimated that fifty years without war was the best they could hope for. But each had a different perception of how that peace could best be achieved. The "Declaration on Liberated Europe," part of the final protocols, promised peace, political freedom, and relief to the liberated peoples of Europe, but the three leaders each interpreted those objectives differently. Churchill viewed Europe from the perspective of Soviet expansion and Britain's own economic weakness; Stalin seemed convinced that his nation's security required that

21. Alone at Yalta: Churchill at Livadia Palace, Yalta,
February 8, 1945

22. The Big Two: Roosevelt and Stalin at Yalta,
February 1945

eastern Europe come under Soviet domination; Roosevelt consciously tried to play the role of broker—guarding American interests, placating the Soviets, reassuring the British, converting his own State Department, and maintaining the support of the American Congress and public. The President's attempts to deal with almost all the negotiable problems of the postwar world, from colonialism to buttressing the Chinese government, and to postpone the intractable ones lest they wreck the conference, betray his suspicions that Yalta would be his last chance. Spurred on, perhaps, by his failing health (some medical researchers have even speculated that the President suffered from malignant cancer; *New York Times*, Dec. 2, 1979), Roosevelt seemed intent upon creating great-power harmony then and there, a difficult task even without the suspicion that characterized Anglo-Soviet-American relations. Desperate to satisfy so many constituencies, Roosevelt ended up pleasing none. In Poland, for example, the British saw Soviet expansion as a threat, the Soviets thought they had Anglo-American agreement, the State Department believed that Stalin had lied, and Polish-Americans felt betrayed. Given Roosevelt's penchant for procrastination, there is great irony in suggesting that he could have accomplished more if he had tried to accomplish less.

As was frequently the case in earlier conferences, the correspondence exchanged by Churchill and Roosevelt during the Yalta talks rarely dealt with the major issues of the meeting. The following letter, sent by Roosevelt to Churchill at the Vorontsov Villa, the British quarters in Yalta, concerned provisions of the Lend-Lease Master Agreement between Great Britain and the United States, a topic which had no bearing on the talks with Stalin. Article VII of that agreement called for an end to discriminatory trade practices within the British Empire, that is, equal trading privileges for the United States. The State Department had not succeeded in its efforts to get the British to implement that promise, and Stettinius suspected that "Churchill has obtained the impression that you [Roosevelt] are not very much interested in this subject" (Stettinius to Roosevelt, Feb. 10, 1945, *FRUS, Yalta Conf.*, p. 962). The Secretary of State gave the President a letter to Churchill on the subject, and Roosevelt signed it, apparently without making any changes. The British hoped to separate the question of Article VI from continued discussions over stage II lend-lease, but the Americans steadfastly refused.

R–707/1, letter

Yalta
February 10, 1945

Dear Winston,

I have been hoping to find an opportunity in the course of the present conferences to have a brief word with you on the importance which I attach to a prompt resumption at a high level of conversation between our two Governments on the implementation of Article VII of the Lend-

Lease agreement. As the opportunity for a quiet discussion between us on this matter may still not develop, I do not wish this meeting to close without sending you a brief word on this matter.

Discussion on commercial policies, pursuant to Article VII have been carried on from time to time between our two Governments ever since the Fall of 1943. I think it most important that these talks be re-invigorated and I should like to suggest the prompt naming of full delegations on both sides, to be headed by a Chairman with the rank of Minister. I hope you will find it possible to take the necessary steps to bring this about insofar as your Government is concerned.

Most sincerely yours, [signed] Franklin D. Roosevelt

[PSF:Crimea Conf. *FRUS, Yalta Conf.*, pp. 962–63.]

When Stalin got Churchill's support to seat two or three of the Soviet republics in the world organization's assembly, Roosevelt wrote to both leaders requesting additional seats for the United States. Only then, reasoned the President, would Congress agree to participate in an organization where the British Empire and the Soviet Union had multiple votes. This exchange had apparently been agreed upon in advance.

R–707/2, letter

Yalta
February 10, 1945

Dear Winston:

As I said the other day, I am somewhat concerned over the political difficulties I am apt to encounter in the United States in connection with the ratification by the Senate of the Dumbarton Oaks agreement because of the fact that the United States alone among the three great powers will have only a single vote in the Assembly. I understand from our conversation that you would have no objection if I found it necessary to work out some way of giving the United States additional votes in order to insure parity. I am writing you this letter since I know you understand so well our political situation in the United States and I hope in reply to this letter you can give me your agreement to this suggestion if I find it necessary for our public opinion to make some proposal along those lines at the forthcoming United Nations Conference.

I am enclosing a copy of the letter which I have written to Marshal Stalin on the same subject.

Most sincerely yours, [signed] Franklin D. Roosevelt

[HLH:Sherwood Col. *FRUS, Yalta Conf.*, pp. 966–67.]

ENCLOSURE TO R–707/2, letter

Yalta
February 10, 1945

My dear Marshal Stalin:

I have been thinking, as I must, of possible political difficulties which I might encounter in the United States in connection with the number of votes which the Big Powers will enjoy in the Assembly of the World Organization. We have agreed, and I shall certainly carry out that agreement, to support at the forthcoming United Nations Conference the admission of the Ukrainian and White Russian Republics as members of the Assembly of the World Organization. I am somewhat concerned lest it be pointed out that the United States will have only one vote in the Assembly. It may be necessary for me, therefore, if I am to insure whole hearted acceptance by the Congress and people of the United States of our participation in the World Organization, to ask for additional votes in the Assembly in order to give parity to the United States.

I would like to know, before I face this problem, that you would perceive no objection and would support a proposal along this line if it is necessary for me to make it at the forthcoming conference. I would greatly appreciate your letting me have your views in reply to this letter.

Most sincerely yours, [signed] Franklin D. Roosevelt

[HLH:Sherwood Col. *FRUS, Yalta Conf.*, p. 966.]

Stalin also sent a reply couched in terms similar to those used below by Churchill.

C–899/1, letter

Yalta
February 11, 1945

My dear Franklin,

I have given consideration to your letter of February 10 about the political difficulties which might arise in the United States in connection with the ratification by the Senate of the Dumbarton Oaks Agreement because of the fact that the United States alone among the three Great Powers will have only one vote in the Assembly.

Our position is that we maintained the long-established representation of the British Empire and Commonwealth; that the Soviet Government are represented by its chief member, and the two republics of the Ukraine and White Russia; and that the United States should propose the form in which their undisputed equality with every other Member State should be expressed.

I need hardly assure you that I should do everything possible to assist you in this matter.

Yours very sincerely, [signed] Winston Churchill

[HLH:Sherwood Col. *FRUS, Yalta Conf.*, p. 967.]

Ever since the Italian surrender, American policy had been to push for the speedy reconstruction of the Italian government, particularly when it appeared that anti-monarchist, pro-American political parties would dominate. Unlike the British, who harbored a good deal of resentment toward the Italians and who warned against abandoning the King lest the communists gain power, American officials looked with sympathy upon the requests from the government of Prime Minister Ivanoe Bonomi for a peace treaty and economic aid. This time it was Roosevelt who, in this letter to Churchill, threw up the specter of communism—"those who fish in troubled waters"—in an attempt to gain British support.

The letter was actually drafted by H. Freeman Matthews, Director of the State Department's Office of European Affairs, who was in attendance at the Malta and Yalta Conferences. Sir Alexander Cadogan, the Permanent Undersecretary in the British Foreign Office, was also at the Yalta meeting. Harold Macmillan had been Britain's political representative in Italy until the crisis erupted in Greece in December 1944.

R–707/3, letter

Yalta
February 11, 1945

Dear Winston:

You have expressed some concern with regard to our different viewpoints concerning the policy to be pursued about Italy. I am happy to tell you that Mr. Matthews on behalf of the Department of State went over the ground on this matter with Alec Cadogan yesterday afternoon. As a result of their conversation, Matthews reports that although there are naturally some differences in emphasis in our respective viewpoints, there seems to be no basic reason for any quarrel between us. I find that we are both in accord with the important fact that whatever the Italian attitude and action have been in the past few years, we are faced with a real problem of the future. Italy is and will remain an important factor in Europe whatever we may think of the prospect. It is surely in our joint interest for us to do whatever we properly can to foster her gradual recuperation by developing a return to normal democratic processes, the development of a sense of her own responsibilities and the other steps so necessary in preparing the long hard road of Italy's return to the community of peace-loving democratic states. To this end I believe we are both agreed that we must give her both spiritual and material food. I am impressed with the dangers for us both in Italy's present condition of semi-servitude and of the fact that those who fish in troubled waters will be the only ones to gain from her present condition approaching despair. I know that our soldiers share this view and feel that there is definite inherent danger in the situation to our joint military operations.

I believe that some constructive steps should be taken to move away from the present anomalous situation of onerous and obsolete surrender terms which are no longer pertinent to the situation today. I hope the Foreign Office and the State Department will be able to work out some mutually satisfactory procedure to remedy this situation. As you know, we accepted the Combined Chiefs of Staff's directive to General Alexander along the lines suggested by Mr. MacMillan. Although we felt that the directive was greatly watered down and much of its substance lost, we went along with you in the hope that we may reach some agreement on further steps in the near future.

At any rate, I want you to know that we are determined to pull together with you in Italy as we are in other areas, and that we believe that by full and continuous consultation and goodwill on both sides there is no danger of any serious split between us on this important question.

Most sincerely yours, Franklin D. Roosevelt

[HLH:Sherwood Col. *FRUS, Yalta Conf.*, p. 967. PREM 3/250/3.]

During discussions at Malta and Yalta, the Combined Chiefs of Staff had agreed to shift the two Canadian divisions which remained in Italy and join them with the First Canadian Army, located on the northwest flank on the western front. Canadian Prime Minister Mackenzie King had wished for such a move and expressed his thanks through Churchill.

C–899/2, memo

Yalta
Feb. 11, 1945

Memorandum from Prime Minister

A telegram has been received from Mr Mackenzie King expressing deep satisfaction at the decision to transfer the Canadian Corps from Italy to North Western Europe, thus uniting the whole Canadian army in Europe. He has asked Mr Churchill to express to President Roosevelt the Canadian Government's appreciation of his proposal.

[PSF:Crimea Conf.]

Although the British tried to compartmentalize the various economic discussions taking place with the United States, the single entry in the table of contents to the collection of American documents indicates the attitude of State Department officials: "negotiations relating to the extension of credit to the United Kingdom, the liberalization of world trade, and the settlement of Lend Lease" (*FRUS*, 1945, VI, v). The British were understandably concerned about their postwar economic situation and feared that any massive elimination or reduction of tariffs would jeopardize the reconstruction of British industry. Similarly, the cancellation of the Ottawa agreements, which established preferential trade relationships among the nations of the British Empire, would hamper the redevelopment of the British economy and weaken Britain's hold on her empire. The Americans, conscious that the wartime dislocation of the British economy offered an unparalleled opportunity to force that nation to change its trade policies, demanded such changes as a prerequisite to postwar aid. State Department officials spoke often and forcefully of the need to eliminate the kind of selfish commercial practices which had, in the past, led to tension and war, but they were also conscious of the opportunities for American business which free trade in the British Empire would offer. Their backs to the wall, the British tried to postpone any decision while awaiting further talks.

Harry C. Hawkins, Minister-Counselor for Economic Affairs at the U.S. Embassy in London, was one of many American officials engaged in talks with British representatives, particularly John Maynard Keynes, who advised the British Treasury.

C–899/3, letter

Yalta
February 13, 1945

My dear Franklin,

1. I have to thank you for your letter of February 10 [R–707/1] about Article VII of the Lease-Lend Agreement. I cabled this home to the Cabinet and have now had a full reply from them. It appears that during the past six weeks there has been a regular series of discussions in London between a group of high British officials and three American officials led by Hawkins, who was head of the division in the State Department which deals with Commercial Policy and is now attached to the American Embassy. You may remember that discussions took place in this form at the suggestion of the State Department and were designed to ascertain in-

formally, without of course committing either Government, where both countries now stood as a result of consideration since the talks in Washington rather more than a year ago. Although Commercial Policy was the main subject, the talks covered the whole range of Article VII and seemed to our people to have let light into many obscure corners.

2. Mr. Hawkins went back a week ago to Washington to report and is due to return to London at the beginning of next month to tell us the Washington reaction to the talks. We shall then be able to consider with all practicable speed whether such differences as may be found to remain between the United States and the United Kingdom can be bridged and if so, what should be lines of procedure for consideration of policy by other United Nations.

3. The War Cabinet do not wish to commit themselves at this stage of the war to sending a high-powered delegation to Washington. This must involve bringing other countries into the discussions, notably France, at an early stage and of course the present mood of the Dominions must be ascertained before we go further on general policy.

4. In view of the above, would it not be better to wait till we have both returned home and have been able to review the progress made in the informal discussions? I shall be very glad to talk this over with you when we meet.

[signed] Yours sincerely, Winston S. Churchill

[PSF:Crimea Conf. *FRUS*, 1945, VI, 21.]

Roosevelt's letter about relations with Italy (R–707/3) was the subject of considerable discussion in the British government, and Churchill did not reply until April 8 (C–937/1). Churchill apparently gave this letter to Roosevelt when they met, for the last time, aboard the cruiser USS *Quincy*, anchored in Great Bitter Lake, at the southern end of the Suez Canal. The President had flown there, even before the Yalta communiqués and press releases had been drafted, in order to meet with King Farouk of Egypt, Emperor Haile Selassie of Ethiopia, and King Ibn Saud of Saudi Arabia. The only issue of substance raised during the talks was a request from Roosevelt to Ibn Saud that the Arabs permit more Jews to enter Palestine, a suggestion the King rejected angrily. Saud appeared far more interested in the news about a new wonder-drug, penicillin, than in politics. Not to be outdone, Churchill arranged for talks with Ibn Saud and Farouk after Roosevelt left for the United States aboard the *Quincy*.

C–899/4, letter

Great Bitter Lake, Egypt
February 15, 1945

My dear Franklin,

Thank you for your letter of February 11 about Italy.

Weighty questions are raised in your letter, and I should like to consider them at leisure and send you my considered views after my return to London.

Yours sincerely   Winston S. Churchill [Eden]

[PSF:GB:WSC. PREM 3/250/3.]

Harold Macmillan, the British political adviser to the Supreme Allied Commander in the Mediterranean (SACMED), had just returned to Caserta, Italy, after negotiating a settlement between the warring factions in Greece (the Varkiza agreement). Macmillan urged cooperation with the Americans in Italy because "Italy is a British interest, in the sense that we do not want to see an important Mediterranean power in dissolution or in a state of permanent revolution" (Macmillan, *The Blast of War*, p. 560). Churchill had spoken with Macmillan during a quick trip to Athens, Greece, where the Prime Minister had gone to endorse publicly the Regency of Archbishop Damaskinos and the Ministry of General Nikolaos Plastiras. This cable was probably sent from El Faiyun oasis, south of Cairo, Egypt, where Churchill was meeting with King Ibn Saud. The President was sailing for the United States aboard the USS *Quincy*, with a stop planned at Algiers for February 17. Alexander Kirk was the American political adviser at General Alexander's headquarters (SACMED).

C–900

El Faiyun, Egypt [via U.S. Embassy & Army, London]
Feb. 17, 1945, 1244 Z (London) / TOR 1515 Z (Washington)

Prime Minister to President Roosevelt Personal and Private.

1. Harold Macmillan will gladly come to Algiers anytime February 17th in case you wish to see him. He is very well informed about Italy as head of the Allied Control Commission. You have only to send him a message via Kirk. All good wishes.

[MR*]

Even if Macmillan had had enough time to fly from Caserta, near Naples, to Algiers, Roosevelt was probably too exhausted to hold serious discussions.

R–708

USS *Quincy* [via U.S. Navy, Washington]
Feb. 18, 1945, 2001 Z

Top Secret and Personal from the President for the Prime Minister.
　Thank you for your 900. Sorry received too late to arrange. Roosevelt

[MR*]

Major General Edwin "Pa" Watson, ostensibly a military aide to the President but actually a card-playing, story-telling crony, suffered from a blocked prostate and heart disease. He spent most of the Yalta Conference sick in bed and experienced chest pain after a petty quarrel with an equally ill Harry Hopkins. Watson died aboard the *Quincy* on the morning of February 20.

As Churchill had predicted, the Yalta agreements on Poland received heavy criticism in Parliament. Some members of the Labour Party had grown restive within the constraints of the wartime coalition government, and one of the party's leaders, Arthur Greenwood, who had been Minister without portfolio in the War Cabinet, condemned the Yalta conferees for deciding the fate of Poland without Polish representatives taking part. The Conservative opposition to the agreements came primarily from a group of Tories whose main concern was Bolshevism. These were the same Tories who had favored the appeasement of Germany in the 1930s, once again on the grounds that a strong Germany would limit Bolshevism. Maurice Petherick, a Conservative M.P. for Penryn and Falmouth, introduced an amendment deploring the Yalta agreements on Poland as violations of existing treaties and the Atlantic Charter. The amendment was defeated 396 to 25, but that margin did not hide the "uneasiness" in Parliament. Churchill endorsed a proposal by one M.P. to state publicly that the test of the Crimea protocols would be whether or not the Soviets invited Mikolajczyk and Polish Foreign Minister Tadeusz Romer to talks in Moscow (Nicolson, *The War Years*, pp. 436–37).

Molotov's offer to permit observers into liberated Poland followed British complaints that they were unable to find out what was happening there. The United States and Great Britain quickly accepted the proposal, but the offer was just as quickly withdrawn.

The war on the western front was indeed going well. Allied armies had closed to or near the Rhine by the end of February, and three weeks later launched major attacks across the river.

C–901

London [via U.S. Army]
Feb. 28, 1945, 1240 Z / TOR 1445 Z

Prime Minister to President Roosevelt. Personal and Top Secret.

1. Accept my deep sympathy in your personal loss through the death of General Watson. I know how much this will grieve you.

2. You will probably see the accounts of our three days' debate which began yesterday. Today 21 Conservatives are moving a hostile amendment in favour of Poland, and Greendoow [sic] who speaks for the Labour Party, made a foolish and hostile speech. We shall no doubt defeat the amendment by an overwhelming majority. Nevertheless there is a good deal of uneasiness in both parties that we are letting the Poles down, etc.

3. In these circumstances it is of the utmost importance that as many representative Poles as possible should be invited as soon as possible to the consultations in Moscow and, above all, that Mikolajczyk who is the leading test case should be invited. The London Polish Government is of course trying to prevent any Poles leaving here for Moscow or Poland, and is playing for a breakdown.

4. Clark Kerr telegraphs that Molotov spontaneously offers to allow British and American observers to go into Poland and see what is going on for themselves. I think this is of the highest importance. Nor can I feel that the acceptance of the offer would imply any recognition of the Lublin Government. There are many stories put about of wholesale deportations by the Russians and of liquidations by the Lublin Poles of elements they do not like, and I have no means of verifying or contradicting these assertions.

5. I do hope you have benefited by the voyage and will return refreshed. The battle seems to be going well and I propose to visit the front at the weekend, seeing both Eisenhower and Montgomery. I cannot help feeling there might easily be a good break through in the west. Every good wish to you and all. I hope Harry is recovering.

[MR*. *FRUS*, 1945, V, 131–32. *R&C*.]

Roosevelt returned to Washington on February 28 and attended funeral services for "Pa" Watson at Arlington National Cemetery that same day.

R–709

Washington [via U.S. Navy]
Feb. 28, 1945; 0015 Z, Mar. 1

Personal and Top Secret from the President for the Prime Minister.
    Arrived home safely. Excellent voyage. Thanks for your wire about Pa
Watson. It was a great shock. Otherwise things are quiet. Roosevelt [FDR]

[MR*]

Some of the problems of relief in the liberated nations related to logistics—
but, as this cable and Churchill's immediate answer make clear, there were
political questions as well. The British feared severe food shortages once the
war ended and lend-lease aid diminished or ceased, and they hoped to build
stockpiles to help meet the crisis. The Americans, who continued to refuse
to work out postwar aid agreements with the British, insisted that war supplies
be used only for war-related purposes, including assistance for people in
areas still governed by Allied forces. Although the message below was drafted
in the War Department, it was prepared at the President's direction.

R–710

Washington [via U.S. Navy]
Feb. 28, 1945; 0015 Z, Mar. 1

Top Secret and Personal from the President for the Prime Minister.
    I have been advised that the Supreme Commander, Allied Expedi-
tionary Forces requires an additional 69,000 tons of food during March
to meet civilian supply contingencies arising in the 21st Army Group area
of Belgium and Holland. SCAEF advised the Combined Chiefs of Staff
of these needs in SCAF 215 dated 25 February 1945.
    In order to meet these needs it will be necessary for the supplies to be
shipped from the UK to the 21st Army Group. I understand that the
British Government is now considering whether the 69,000 tons should
be drawn from the stockpile now allocated to SCAEF for use in the B-2
area of Holland (eastern Holland). If so, it appears obvious that the
withdrawal from the B-2 stockpile must be covered by immediate replacement from stocks now in the U.K.
    I hope you will see your way clear to have the U.K. agree to replace
the Dutch B-2 stockpile to the extent required to protect SCAEF against
anticipated Dutch civilian supply needs. Roosevelt [HLS]

[MR*]

C–902

London [via U.S. Army]
Mar. 2, 1945, 0037 Z / TOR 0300 Z

Personal and Top Secret Prime Minister to President Roosevelt.

Reference your telegram Number 710.

1. The total deficiency amounts to 109,000 tons 51,000 tons for March arrival and 58,000 tons for April arrival. We have already made arrangements to meet the 51,000 tons for March arrival by diverting 30,000 tons of wheat in transit to U.K. and 21,000 tons ex SHAEF's general reserve held by us for them in this country. The April deficiency will have to be met from U.K. stocks as there is no time to meet the demand from any other source.

2. We cannot meet certain items at all because we have no stocks available. These details are being arranged with the agencies concerned.

3. I want to impress upon you that we shall require immediate replacement of a large part of these food stuffs, and the provision of ships to carry them.

4. I am sure that the problem will turn out to be bigger than these figures. British Officers are now discussing the matter with SHAEF and will be returning tomorrow. I will send you a further telegram on editing their report.

[MR*. *FRUS*, 1945, II, 1072–73.]

The repatriation of Soviet military personnel liberated from German prisoner-of-war camps by Anglo-American armies, and the return of British and American personnel similarly freed by Soviet forces, should have been easy and quick, but it proved complicated and the cause of bitter recriminations. Embarrassed by the large number of "Soviet" soldiers (frequently men of ethnic minority stock, such as Latvians, Estonians, and Ukrainians) who refused repatriation, Soviet officials began to demand the forcible return of all their personnel. At Yalta, the Big Three leaders had agreed to return "Soviet citizens" to Soviet authorities, but had failed to define that citizenship. At the same time, the Soviets made no attempt to return American prisoners of war found behind their lines, prompting this message from the President. The situation was further complicated by the ongoing dispute over the establishment of a government in liberated Poland. Requests for permission to send Anglo-American teams into Poland to look after ex-prisoners met with Soviet hints that they should work with the Soviet-sponsored Polish provisional government. Stalin responded to Roosevelt's cable by denying that there were any groups of American ex-prisoners located behind Soviet lines (*FRUS*, 1945, V, 1073).

This message was sent to Stalin with instructions to the U.S. Military Mission to send a copy to Churchill via the British Military Mission in Moscow.

R–710/1

Washington [via U.S. Military Mission, Moscow]
Mar. 3, 1945

[Roosevelt to Churchill]

I have reliable information regarding the difficulties which are being encountered in collecting, supplying and evacuating American ex-prisoners of war and American aircraft crews who are stranded east of the Russian lines. It is urgently requested that instructions be issued authorizing ten American aircraft with American crews to operate between Poltava and places in Poland where American ex-prisoners of war and stranded airmen may be located. This authority is requested for the purpose of providing supplementary clothing, medical and food supplies for all American soldiers, to evacuate stranded aircraft crews and liberated prisoners of war, and especially to transfer the injured and sick to the American hospital at Poltava. I regard this request to be of the greatest importance not only for humanitarian reasons but also by reason of the intense interest of the American public in the welfare of our ex-prisoners of war and stranded aircraft crews. Secondly on the general matter of prisoners of war in Germany I feel that we ought to do something quickly. The number of these prisoners of war, Russian, British and U.S., is very large. In view of your disapproval of the plan we submitted what do you suggest in place of it?

[MR. *FRUS*, 1945, V, 1072–73.]

The First Lord's report apparently caused no controversy, for there is no further mention of it in the files.

C–903

London [via U.S. Army]
Mar. 5, 1945, 1208 Z / TOR 1345 Z

Prime Minister to President Roosevelt Personal and Top Secret.

The First Lord of the Admiralty will be making his customary annual statement to Parliament on Wednesday, March 7, in which it will be necessary for him to make a reference in general terms to the history of our submarine warfare in the past year.

This will not conflict in any way with our monthly statement. I have read it myself and it will not touch upon any technical secrets which would be useful to the Japanese.

[MR*]

In spite of what Churchill thought had been promises to the contrary, the United States had signed a civil aviation agreement with the Republic of Ireland. Churchill's anger at the way in which his government had been treated was heightened by his dislike of Irish Prime Minister Eamon de Valera and the fear that the United States would negotiate similar bilateral agreements with other Commonwealth nations.

The printed records of the Malta and Yalta talks do not indicate that Churchill and Roosevelt discussed the matter. Moreover, there is a contradiction in the chronology given in the Prime Minister's cable. Since the Yalta Conference did not begin until February 4, and the Churchill-Roosevelt meeting in Egypt followed, by the time the Irish-American aviation agreement could have been discussed the two governments had already signed the papers. What may have happened, given Roosevelt's style when dealing with small, emotional controversies, is that the President listened to Churchill's angry protests and demands for cancellation of the accord, and, by not disagreeing, gave the Prime Minister the impression that the United States would abrogate the arrangement.

C–904

London [via U.S. Army]
Mar. 6, 1945, 1428 Z / TOR 1650 Z

Prime Minister to President Roosevelt Personal and Top Secret.

1. On January 27 I sent you my telegram 897 about the aviation agreement with the Government of Southern Ireland. You could not at the time reply because of wireless silence. At Yalta, and also later at Alexandria, I understood from you that you did not approve this step and that it had been taken without your agreement. Mr Stettinius also made this clear so far as he was concerned. At the same time as we sent out 897 to you Lord Halifax was instructed to let the State Department have a copy of the telegram at once so that they should hold their hand until you had had an opportunity to comment on it.

2. On January 31 the State Department confirmed that negotiations had been in progress but said that they had not reached readiness for signature. On February 3 however, without further warning, Lord Halifax was informed that the agreement had been signed and shortly afterwards it was published.

3. Our special concern with Eire is obvious on political and geographical grounds, and it is indeed much closer than that of the United States with the Argentine. We and the United States have, moreover, throughout kept in close touch in our general policy towards Eire, e. g., over the recent United States approach to De Valera for the removal of the Axis representatives. For this reason the political effect of the United States action in concluding an agreement with Southern Ireland on an important issue without consulting us seemed to us bound to injure our relations with De Valera politically, and may be embarrassing to the United States also, as it can only encourage him to try to play off one against the other. It has, in fact, been hailed in Southern Ireland as a diplomatic success for them.

4. I trust therefore that you will be able to take the necessary steps to have the agreement annulled. So far no response has been made to our telegrams or representations whether addressed personally to you or handed formally to the State Department.

[MR*. R&C.]

German submarines were numerous but not a military threat, since their bases, manpower, and supplies had all been reduced to the point that the U-boats could operate only sporadically.

R–711

Hyde Park, N.Y. [via U.S. Navy]
Mar. 7, 1945, 1233 Z

Personal and Top Secret from the President for the Prime Minister.
Our suggested text of the February Anti-U-boat Statement follows:

QUOTE. During the month of February a moderate number of Allied merchant vessels fell victim to U-boat activity. However, the anti-submarine forces were successful in destroying more enemy submarines this past month than in January.

Despite satisfactory results now being obtained in the war on undersea raiders our forces must maintain unceasing vigilance because any enemy with a large number of submarines always possesses a potential threat. UNQUOTE.

Roosevelt [Navy Dept.]

[MR*]

A BRITISH REVERSAL ON EASTERN EUROPE

This cable marks a sharp change in British policy toward the Soviet Union's role in eastern Europe. Even though the Prime Minister continued to advocate cooperation with the Soviets and cautioned against any direct confrontation, he now took the position that he and Roosevelt had been "deceived" at Yalta. In spite of an awareness that the Declaration on Liberated Europe, signed at Yalta, was vague and imprecise, Churchill castigated Soviet officials for interpreting it to suit their own purposes. Moreover, the thrust of the Prime Minister's argument was not that he intended to live up to the spirit of his own agreement with Stalin reached during the TOLSTOY talks, but that Britain and the United States need only avoid openly violating those accords. Churchill was well aware of the contradictions inherent in any condemnation of Soviet spheres of influence while Britain struggled to maintain control over Greece, Yugoslavia, and the Middle East. What is unclear is when and why the Prime Minister and his government moved away from the spheres-of-influence settlement outlined in the TOLSTOY talks.

The results of the 1944 Moscow meeting, the spheres of influence, were not challenged during the Yalta Conference, although the Declaration on Liberated Europe did seem contradictory in spirit. But in the absence of specific, firm changes to the Churchill-Stalin arrangements, the declaration was more for public consumption than actual implementation, something Churchill and Roosevelt apparently recognized. Why, then, the change? There is no question that Soviet moves in Roumania, Bulgaria, and Hungary were blunt and brutal. In each of those countries Soviet military power was translated into direct political influence, and regimes presumably faithful to direction from Moscow were soon put into place. But this had not fundamentally changed British or American policy. Appeals from King Michael of Roumania for aid brought only verbal protests from London and Washington that the Soviets had acted without first consulting their allies, and anti-Soviet forces soon realized that they were on their own. Yet, despite the practical if not very pretty agreement with the Soviet Union of November 1944 regarding eastern Europe, Churchill now tried to persuade the President that the time had come to get tough, at least over Poland and, to a lesser degree, Roumania.

But the Prime Minister was playing a tricky game. At the same time he tried to push Roosevelt toward a firmer stand against the Soviets, Churchill chastised his own Foreign Secretary for allowing the Foreign Office and diplomats in Roumania to criticize Soviet actions in that country. "We really have no justification for intervening in this extraordinarily vigorous manner for our late Roumanian enemies," he wrote to Eden on March 5, "thus compromising our position in Poland and jarring Russian acquiescence in our long fight in Athens." A week later, on March 13, Churchill again warned Eden to keep in mind "that we, for considerations well known to you, accepted in a special degree the predominance of Russia in this theatre [Roumania]" (quoted in Carlton, *Eden*, pp. 254, 255). British interests in Greece were clearly too important to risk by confronting the Soviets over an area occupied by the Red Army, but if the Americans could be persuaded to make the challenge

Britain could still appear faithful to the TOLSTOY accords. Churchill had learned well the art of statecraft from his mentor, Lloyd George.

Churchill had come to believe that Stalin was not as eager to cooperate with the West as they had previously hoped. That was particularly true in Poland, a nation that the Soviets had never viewed as a trusted wartime ally. Already predisposed to distrust the "Bolsheviks," Churchill settled on a tougher policy when Stalin moved to consolidate Soviet authority without any pretense of elections or other face-saving gestures for the West. The Prime Minister continued his tactic of subtly placing Great Britain in the position of "broker" by candidly admitting to Roosevelt that any British protest about Poland would "lead to comparisons between the aims of his action and those of ours"—a reference to the Anglo-Soviet arrangement in eastern Europe that left Britain a free hand in Greece. Perhaps Churchill was sincere in arguing that British troops in Athens had protected democracy whereas Soviet political and military power had repressed freedom in Poland, but there is no doubt that he understood that Stalin would not see the distinction. Thus the Prime Minister hoped to get the United States to take the lead over Poland as well, not only because Britain alone would be ineffective, but because it left him free to maneuver, just as he had done at the TOLSTOY talks.

But British electoral politics also played a role in the decision to draw the line over Poland. Even though Churchill assumed that victory against Germany would bring a wave of gratitude from voters, with a general election in the offing, he was searching for a coalition which would return him to office. The political "peace of the castle" in Britain would end with Germany's surrender, and Labour Party chances for a win at the polls appeared good. The Conservatives would provide the bulk of Churchill's support, but they were very sensitive to "Bolshevik" expansion and to the plight of the London Poles. Even Roosevelt and Hopkins detected Churchill's concern about domestic politics from some of the Prime Minister's remarks during the Yalta talks (*FRUS, Yalta Conf.*, p. 729). With the Greek situation well in hand by early March, the Prime Minister may have decided that it was an opportune time to make a gesture toward "saving" the Poles, though it is hard to determine what he thought such opposition could accomplish outside of mending some political fences at home. (See also C–901.)

The State Department and Foreign Office reactions to Soviet moves in eastern Europe leave no doubt that British and American officials were angry and embarrassed that not even the pretense of great-power consultation or "democratic" processes had been preserved. It is likely, however, that many of those officials, not having been at Yalta, failed or refused to understand the cosmetic nature of the Declaration on Liberated Europe. But Churchill did understand and still chose to move toward confrontation with the Soviet Union over eastern Europe—not over some perceived threat to western Europe. A key to figuring out British policy may be found in instructions sent to Ambassador Halifax in Washington. After the United States had rejected a Foreign Office proposal for a strong protest against the Soviet insistence on recognizing the Warsaw (Lublin) government while excluding representatives of the London Poles, Eden instructed Halifax "to point out the danger that, if we did not now intervene to get fair treatment for the anti-Lublin Poles, . . . we and the Americans would then be accused—rightly—of having subscribed at the Crimea Conference to a formula which we knew to be unworkable" (Foreign Office to Halifax, Mar. 5, 1945, as paraphrased in Woodward, *British Foreign Policy*, III, 496). Churchill's repetition of those fears in paragraph 5 of this cable suggests that his public image, not Soviet expansion, was the real problem. Whatever the reason, this message was a call for Anglo-American unity against the Soviet Union.

The congratulations at the end of the telegram were for Roosevelt's March 1 speech to a joint session of Congress. Billed as a report on the Yalta Conference, the President's main message was a plea for the international organization which would be the subject of the forthcoming talks in San Francisco.

C–905

London [via U.S. Army]
Mar. 8, 1945, 1415 Z / TOR 1820 Z

Prime Minister to President Roosevelt. Personal and Top Secret.

1. I feel sure that you will be as distressed as I am by recent events in Roumania. The Russians have succeeded in establishing the rule of a Communist minority by force and misrepresentation. We have been hampered in our protests against these developments by the fact that, in order to have the freedom to save Greece, Eden and I at Moscow in October recognised that Russia should have a largely preponderant voice in Roumania and Bulgaria while we took the lead in Greece. Stalin adhered very strictly to this understanding during the thirty days fighting against the Communists and ELAS in the city of Athens, in spite of the fact that all this was most disagreeable to him and those around him.

Peace has now been restored in Greece and, though many difficulties lie before us, I hope that we shall be able to bring about in the next few months free, unfettered elections, preferably under British, American and Russian supervision, and that thereafter a constitution and government will be erected on the indisputable will of the Greek people, which remains our supreme ultimate objective in all cases, and with which I know you are in sympathy.

2. Stalin is now pursuing the opposite course in the two Black Sea Balkan countries, and one which is absolutely contrary to all democratic ideas. Since the October Anglo-Russian conversations in Moscow Stalin has subscribed on paper to the principles of Yalta which are certainly being trampled down in Roumania. Nevertheless I am most anxious not to press this view to such an extent that Stalin will say "I did not interfere with your action in Greece, why do you not give me the same latitude in Roumania?"

This again would lead to comparisons between the aims of his action and those of ours. On this neither side would convince the other. Having regard to my personal relations with Stalin, I am sure it would be a mistake for me at this stage to embark on the argument.

3. Again I am very conscious of the fact that we have on our hands the much more important issue of Poland, and I do not therefore want to do anything as regards Roumania which might prejudice our prospects of reaching a Polish settlement. Nevertheless, I feel that he should be informed of our distress at the developments which led to the setting up by force of a government in Roumania of a Communist minority, since this conflicts with the conclusions of the declaration on liberated Europe upon which we were agreed at the Crimea conference.

More especially I am afraid that the advent of this Communist Government may lead to an indiscriminate purge of Anti-Communist Roumanians, who will be accused of Fascism much on the lines of what has been happening in Bulgaria. This is as good as foretold in the Moscow broadcast of yesterday, the text of which I have telegraphed to our Embassy.

I would suggest, therefore, that Stalin should be asked to see to it that the new government does not immediately start a purge of all political elements which are in opposition to their views on the ground that they have been encouraged to do so by the Yalta declaration.

We will, of course, give you every support, and if you will show me the text of any message you feel inclined to send Stalin, I will also send one to him supporting it. There is, of course, complete agreement between our representatives on the spot and yours.

4. The news from Moscow about Poland is also most disappointing. I must let you know that the government majorities here bear no relation to the strong under current of opinion among all parties and classes and in our own hearts against a Soviet domination of Poland.

Labour men are as keen as conservatives, and Socialists as keen as Catholics. I have based myself in Parliament on the assumption that the words of the Yalta declaration will be carried out in the letter and the spirit. Once it is seen that we have been deceived and that the well-known communist technique is being applied behind closed doors in Poland, either directly by the Russians or through their Lublin puppets, a very grave situation in British public opinion will be reached.

How would the matter go in the United States? I cannot think that you personally or they would be indifferent. Thus just at the time when everything military is going so well in Europe and when the Japanese policy is also satisfactorily arranged, there would come an open rift between us and Russia not at all confined, in this country at any rate, to government opinion, but running deep down through the masses of the people.

5. After a fairly promising start Molotov is now refusing to accept any interpretation of the Crimea proposals except his own extremely rigid and narrow one. He is attempting to bar practically all our candidates for the consultations, is taking the line that he must base himself on the views of Berut [Bierut] and his gang and has withdrawn his offer that we should send observers to Poland.

In other words, he clearly wants to make a farce of consultations with the "Non-Lublin" Poles—which means that the new government in Poland would be merely the present one dressed up to look more respectable to the ignorant and also wants to prevent us from seeing the liquidations and deportations that are going on and all the rest of the game of setting up a totalitarian regime before elections are held and even before a new government is set up. As to the upshot of all this, if we do not get things right now, it will soon be seen by the world that you and I by putting our signatures to the Crimea settlement have under-written a fraudulent prospectus.

6. I am in any case pledged to Parliament to tell them if the business of setting up a new Polish government etc, cannot be carried out in the spirit of the Yalta declaration. I am sure the only way to stop Molotov's tactics is to send a personal message to Stalin and in that message I must make clear what are the essential things we must have in this business if I am to avoid telling Parliament that we have failed.

I think you will agree with me that far more than the case of Poland is involved. I feel that this is the test case between us and the Russians of the meaning which is to be attached to such terms as Democracy, Sovereignty, Independence, Representative Government and free and unfettered elections.

I therefore propose to send to Stalin a message on the lines set out below. It is as you will see based on the ideas in Eden's telegram to Halifax number 2078 which has been communicated to State Department. I hope you will be ready to send Stalin a similar message containing the same minimum requirements. I shall not send my message till I hear from you. Message begins.

7. "I am sorry to say that the discussions in the Moscow commission on Poland show that M. Molotov has quite a different view from us as to how the Crimea decision on Poland should be put into effect. As you know, nobody here believes that the present Warsaw administration is really representative and criticism of the decision in Parliament to the line that the discussion in Moscow would not result in a really representative government being set up and that, if this was so, all hope of free elections disappeared: All parties were also exercised about the reports that deportations, liquidations and other oppressive measures were being put into practice on a wide scale by

the Warsaw administration against those likely to disagree with them.

Feeling confident of your cooperation in this matter, Eden and I pledged ourselves to Parliament that we would inform them if the fears of our critics were fulfilled. I am bound to tell you that I should have to make a statement of our failure to Parliament if the commission in Moscow were not in the end able to agree on the following basis:

(A) M. Molotov appears to be contending that the terms of the Crimea Communique established for the present Warsaw administration an absolute right of prior consultation on all points. In the English text the passage of the communique in question, of which was in American draft, cannot bear this interpretation. M. Molotov's contention therefore cannot be accepted.

(B) All Poles nominated by any of the three governments shall be accepted for the consultations unless ruled out by unanimous decision of the commission, and every effort made to produce them before the commission at the earliest possible moment: The commission should ensure to the Poles invited facilities for communicating with other Poles whom they wish to consult whether in Poland or outside and the right to suggest to the commission the names of other Poles who should be invited to its proceedings. All Poles appearing before the commission would naturally enjoy complete freedom of movement and of communication among themselves while in Moscow and would be at liberty to depart whither they chose upon the conclusion of the consultations. M. Molotov has raised objections to inviting M. Mikolajczyk but his presence would certainly be vital.

(C) The Poles invited for consultations should discuss among themselves with a view to reaching agreement upon the composition of a government truly representative of the various sections of Polish opinion present before the commission. The discussions should also cover the question of the exercise of the presidential functions. The commission should preside over these discussions in an impartial arbitral capacity.

(D) Pending the conclusion of the commissions discussions the Soviet Government should use its utmost influence to prevent the "Warsaw" administration from taking any further legal or administrative action of a fundamental character affecting social, constitutional, economic, or political conditions in Poland.

(E) The Soviet Government should make arrangements to enable British and American observers to visit Poland and report upon condition there in accordance with the offer spontaneously made by M. Molotov at an earlier stage in the commission's discussions.

8. We must not let Poland become a source of disagreement and

misunderstanding between our two peoples. For this reason I am sure you will understand how important it is for us to reach an early settlement on the basis of the Yalta decision, and it is because I am confident that you will do your utmost to bring this about that I am now telegraphing you". Ends.

9. I should be grateful to know your views. Pray let this telegram be between you and me.

10. Many congratulations on your statement to Congress. Every good wish.

[MR*. *FRUS*, 1945, V, 505–6, 147–50. *R&C*.]

C–906

London [via U.S. Army]
Mar. 8, 1945, 1700 Z / TOR 1820 Z

Prime Minister to President Roosevelt. Personal and Top Secret.
Your number 711. Text of February anti U boat statement. I agree.

[MR*]

Joseph Grew, Acting Secretary of State in the absence of Stettinius (who was in Mexico City trying to get Latin American support for the United Nations), had instructed Ambassador Harriman to protest Soviet policy in Poland. The United States instructed Harriman to argue that the tripartite Moscow Commission, established at the Yalta meeting, was intended to facilitate the creation of a "new provisional government" in Poland, but that Soviet insistence on treating the Warsaw (Lublin) regime as the legitimate Polish government had frustrated the spirit of the Yalta accords. Churchill had no quarrel with that portion of Harriman's instructions, but he was concerned about the suggestion that "the Commission request the rival political groups to adopt a political truce in Poland" (Grew to Harriman, Mar. 8, 1945, *FRUS*, 1945, V, 150–52). Churchill's reference to political problems within his Cabinet (par. 4) lends further support to the idea that domestic political pressure forced a change in his policy toward Soviet-Polish relations.

C–907

London [via U.S. Army]
Mar. 10, 1945, 0115 Z / TOR 0358 Z

Prime Minister to President Roosevelt. Personal and Top Secret.
1. I have now read the instructions to Mr. Harriman which were shown to our Ambassador today. I need not say how cordially I agree with all

the first part of these instructions, but I am distressed at the conclusion which I fear may lead us into great difficulties.

I do not know what the answer of the London-Polish Government would be to a request for a political truce. They continue to assert, with a wealth of detail, that their friends in Poland are being arrested, deported and liquidated on a large scale. At the best they would make conditions of an impossible character.

2. As to the Lublin Poles, they may well answer that their government can alone ensure "The maximum amount of political tranquility inside", that they already represent the great mass of the "Democratic Forces in Poland" and that they cannot join hands with emigre traitors to Poland or fascist collaborationists and landlords, and so on according to the usual technique.

3. Meanwhile we shall not be allowed inside the country or have any means of informing ourselves upon the position. It suits the Soviet very well to have a long period of delay so that the process of liquidation of elements unfavourable to them or their puppets may run its full course.

This would be furthered by our opening out now into proposals of a very undefined character for a political truce between these Polish parties, (whose hatreds would eat into live steel) in the spirit and intent of the Crimea decision and might well imply the abandonment of all clearcut requests such as those suggested in my last telegram to you. Therefore I should find it very difficult to join in this project of a political truce.

4. I have already mentioned to you that the feeling here is very strong. Four ministers have abstained from the divisions and two have already resigned.

I beg therefore that you will give full consideration to my previous telegram number 905 and will suspend the delivery of the latest Harriman instructions till I have received your reply and can reply to it.

[MR*. *FRUS*, 1945, V, 153–54. p*WSC*, VI, 423–24. *R&C*.]

Eisenhower and Marshall were willing to have Alexander replace Tedder as Deputy Supreme Commander in Europe, but were adamantly opposed to Churchill's plan to have Alexander take command of all ground forces in the theater. When Field Marshal Montgomery came out against the proposal, possibly because he could not have the command himself, the Prime Minister dropped it.

C-908

London [via U.S. Army]
Mar. 10, 1945, 1645 Z / TOR 1842 Z

Prime Minister to President Roosevelt Personal and Top Secret.
Repeated to General Marshall.

About my proposal, to which you and General Marshall agreed at Malta, for appointing Field Marshal Alexander as deputy to Eisenhower in place of Air Chief Marshal Tedder. I have had long talks with Eisenhower, who was in every way ready to accept the change and "make it work" on account of his high regard for Alexander. Nevertheless I consider the situation has been changed by the progress of the war, and I therefore withdraw my proposal while thanking you and General Marshall for your ready acceptance of it.

[MR*]

The following cable, based on statements issued by the London Polish government, is largely self-explanatory, although a few identifications may help in understanding it. Whatever the details, Churchill was obviously trying to persuade Roosevelt to take a tough stance.

The Home Army was the Polish Underground force which professed loyalty to the London Polish government. General Zygmunt Berling commanded the Soviet-sponsored Kosciuszko Division. The NKVD was the intelligence arm of the Soviet Army. Marshal I. S. Koniev commanded the Soviet military sector which included Cracow Province. General M. Rola Zymierski commanded the Polish People's Army and became Minister of Defense in the Lublin Polish government in 1944. Stanislaw Radkiewicz was Minister of Public Security in the Lublin government. Tomasz Arciszewski was Prime Minister of the London Polish government. After the British made diplomatic inquiries, Arciszewski's wife was released on the condition that she report daily to the police.

C-909

London [via U.S. Army]
Mar. 10, 1945, 2200 Z

Prime Minister to President Roosevelt. Personal and Top Secret.

Following is summary of "information received from Poland" transmitted to me by Polish Prime Minister here. It will show you how situation is viewed by Poles in this country, and seems to me to be stated with restraint.

Of course we cannot guarantee any of this information, which comes from the Polish Governments Agents in Poland who are not likely to minimise these things nor do we know what opportunities they have of checking their information, as they must be living underground. All this emphasises the need for sending our observers into the country.

(Summary begins) Summary of the more important information sent from Poland in the period 17th January to 1st March.

17 January 45. Kielce Province: The Lublin Committee has assumed civil authority. Arrests of members of the Home Army and the underground administration have begun. Enforced registration of all males in the age groups (question) 19–59.

22 January 45. Cracow Province: On 18th January, groups of the Home Army were fighting the Germans in the western suburbs. Public utility buildings were preserved, thanks to the action of Home Army units. The population greets the Red Army and units of Berling's Army now marching in coldly. The command of Berling's Army is strictly controlled by the NKVD. According to a statement made by one of Berling's officers about 70 percent of the soldiers are in favour of the Government in London.

24 January 45. Cracow Province: Two orders of Marshal Koniev have been posted up on the walls: One regarding right of mobilization, which empowers the Lublin Committee or the Red Army, when so authorized by the committee, to effect mobilization, and a second regarding the surrender of weapons and radio sets, and the registration of typewriters, printing presses and duplicators. Registration of males in the age groups (question) 16–65.

The NKVD has been functioning in Cracow since 21st January. At present they are reading denunciations and observing. Delegates from Lublin speak against the London Government at meetings, and make sharp attacks on the Home Army. The same is evident in the Lublin press, which is already being issued in Cracow and in the soldiers papers.

24 January 45. Miechow District: A number of members of the Home Army have been shot in Miechow and Slomniki. Radziwill was arrested in Balice, and 40 landowners and farmers in Miechow district for belonging to the Home Army or approving it. The Polish Workers party is undertaking the work of denunciation.

27 January 45. Piotrkow District: On the river Pilica in Opoczno District, strong units of the Home Army took part in fighting the Germans. They captured weapons, and destroyed and captured cars. After completing their tasks, these units of the Home Army had to disperse. The Soviet authorities only managed to catch one of the company leaders, and he succeeded in escaping.

The population is treating the new authorities with great reserve. Soviet paratroops are hunting for leaders of the Home Army. Two have already been shot. Soviet officers have announced that the Home Army is to be exterminated as Fascist. Orders have been issued for the surrender of arms, radio sets, typewriters and duplicators.

30 January 45. Piotrkow, Miechow, Czestochowa Districts: In Miechow District, 16 officers of the Home Army have been arrested: In Piotrkow, a number of agents of the underground movement. The food and fuel situation is desperate. The withdrawal of Cracow zloties has produced a complete lack of currency.

Soviet and Lublin agitation against Great Britain is noted. At Czestochowa during the manifestation on 25 January, a banner was carried with the slogan "Down With England".

1 February 45. Cracow Province: The Soviet military authorities take no account of the Lublin Committee and act independently. The Lublin Committee slavishly comply with all their demands. A visa from the Soviet Ambassador and the permission of the peoples commissariat of foreign affairs is necessary in order to travel to Lwow.

The Soviet armies rely on the food stocks of the Polish population for their food supplies. The shops are shut, and there is no bread, water, gas or electricity.

As President of Cracow, an agent of the Committee with the pseudonym of Michalski has been sent from Lublin. So-called Socialists, members of the Peasant Party and Democrats, unknown to anyone have appeared on the town and province councils.

In towns, judges and advocates are the first to be arrested, in the country landowners.

6 February 45. Lodz Province: The situation is similar to that prevailing in other parts: Chaos in administration and the villages have to give up their last remaining food supplies. The NKVD has already begun arresting former members of the Home Army. In Lodz, two officers have been arrested. Zymierski's Army is coldly received by the population.

7 February 45. Warsaw Province: Meetings at which demands for the transformation of the Lublin Committee into a temporary government were adopted here have been organized in villages and small towns by the Soviet Military Commandants on a pattern laid down in advance.

People were compelled by force to attend. Members of the NKVD were mingled with the audience in uniform and in civilian clothes, and they took careful note of the audiences behaviour. Members of the Polish Workers Party, also mixed with the audience, cheered and clapped at the appropriate moments, so as to give an appearance of unanimity and enthusiasm.

9 February 45. Warsaw Province: Dearth everywhere in this area. Shoes cost 2500 zloties, a suit 50,000 zloties, butter 500 zloties a pound. Private people are not allowed to use the postal services. It is not allowed to travel even in your own district without a permit.

Steps are being taken to effect the complete extermination of the Home Army.

14 February 45. Warsaw Province: Public security is under the direction Radkiewicz who is dependent on the NKVD and not on the Lublin Committee. The militia in the villages is similarly situated. The Polish Workers Party is controlled by the NKVD and used for political investigations. The population is required to give personal data on every possible occasion.

16 February 45. Warsaw Province: The Sovietisation of Poland is proceeding apace. Agrarian reform is being carried out in great haste in the territories taken by the Soviet Armies. The land allotted is usually much less than four hectares and may not be built on.

The nationalization of industry and trade is being prepared by the annulling of the stocks of ready cash which may only be changed for Lublin zloties by individuals in person. The Lublin Committee is granting short term credits and in case of non payment the businesses are taken over by the committee.

A totalitarian organization of society is gradually being introduced and is based on enforced one party organizations. Such an organization for the villages is the Peasants' Mutual Aid Association and for workers the appropriate trade union. The Supreme Councils of the trade unions and Mutual Aid are dominated by the Polish Workers Party.

The cooperative movement is in the hands of the one party central cooperative "Spolem". Cinemas and films are in the hands of a cooperative for the exploitation of films taken over by the Lublin Committee from the Germans. The publication and sale of papers, journals and books is concentrated in the hands of one institution, organized to have the appearance of a readers cooperative.

20 February 45. Random District: The NKVD is taking systematic steps to discover the whole organization of the Home Army and to arrest its members. In Kielce Province, about 20 percent of the former members of the Home Army have been arrested. In Sandomierz, more Poles have been arrested during the few months of Soviet occupation than during the whole five years of German occupation.

The local and state authorities are constantly changing, as they cannot cope with the situation: In Kielce, the Wojewoda [governor] is the fourth and the Mayor the sixth in succession. The attitude of the population to the new authorities is indifferent or hostile. Even the enthusiasts change their views in a short time.

Members of the Home Army are grieved that, after so many years of fighting and difficulties, they still have to hide like criminals.

22 February 45. Lwow Province: In January, mass arrests took place, in which 60 percent of those arrested were Poles, among them 21 university professors, priests and all classes of society. The prisons are full to overflowing. In August, 1944, and January, 1945, two trainloads of arrested persons, each containing about 2,000 people, were sent to forced labour camps in Russia.

In connection with these arrests the possession of an old envelope bearing a postage stamp with Hitler's image, or of an old German newspaper is considered sufficient proof of collaboration with the Germans. From 5th February Poles in important positions (professors, doctors and so on) have been forced to sign a memorandum condemning the Polish Government in London and Home Army and praising the Lublin Committee.

22 February 45. Bialystok-Lomza Province: Between 8th and 15th November, 1944, 143 cattle trucks packed full of arrested Poles left Bialystok and Grodno in an easterly director towards Russia.

Up to first January 1945 the total number of Poles arrested and deported to Russia was about 5,000 in Grodno and about 10,000 in Bialystok.

Levies for Berling's Army, carried out by means of manhunts, continue. Up to first February, there were arrested 6 District Chiefs of Staff, 5 inspectors, 3 local commandants, about 1,000 officers 400 non-commissioned officers and some hundreds of soldiers of the Home Army together with their families. The people are unwaveringly behind the Government in London.

East of the Curzon Line, the NKVD are organizing hunts for Poles, and are deporting them to forced labour in Russia. Sometimes they are forcibly expelled on the Lublin side. The Byelorussian population expresses sympathy for the Polish Government in London and wishes these territories to be Polish.

The situation is similar in Vilno and Novogrodek Provinces.

24 February 45. Radom Province: A former inspector has been arrested. The NKVD demanded that he should reveal the whole organization of the Home Army and underground administration.

25 February 45. Lublin Province: In Lubartow, there is a camp for officers of the Home Army and for those officers of Zymierski's Army who have been convicted of belonging to the Home Army or of other "political" crimes. This camp is under the control of the NKVD and contains about 6,000 officers and soldiers. Every few days groups are deported to Russia to an unknown destination.

During the first days of February, the Vice-Wojewoda of Kielce and some officials of the government delegation were arrested.

There is great anxiety at the Crimea decisions. The hostile attitude towards the Lublin Committee is increasing. Nevertheless belief in another more favourable solution of Polish affairs has not been shaken.

26 February 45. Warsaw Province: The wife of Premier Arciszewski was arrested on 20th February. She was working in the Polish Red Cross. Further arrests of members of the Polish Red Cross are taking place. Please inform the British. Allied intervention necessary.

1 March 45. Bialystok Province: The population in Bialystok strongly supports the Legal Polish Government in London. Byelorussians also support the Polish Government in London and wish to be Polish citizens. The minority question simply does not exist in these areas, as there is complete agreement. The population faithfully believes that a better solution of Polish affairs will be found.

They have now become hardened, changed from what they were before the war, they are suffering, but they are fighting on and show no weakness.

In the province of Bialystok, the NKVD are carrying out arrests of former soldiers of the Home Army and of loyal-minded Poles without pause.

In February 1945, 125 cattle trucks from Grodno Province and 242 from Bialystok Province, containing arrested Poles, were sent off to Russia.

The NKVD are keeping those arrested in cellars, air raid shelters and in every possible place. Those arrested sit in darkness, without any bedding or warm clothes. In the course of interrogations, the NKVD beat prisoners, torture them morally, keep them in the cold without clothes. They accuse those arrested of espionage on behalf of the British and of the Polish Government in London, and of collaboration with the Germans. There is a high rate of mortality among the prisoners.

Leaders of the Home Army are carried off into the heart of Russia or perish without any trace.

The NKVD often "work" in the uniforms of Polish officers. Spies and collaborators with the Gestapo were at first arrested by the NKVD— later, however, they were set free and the NKVD employed them as their own spies.

In towns and bigger villages, special posts have been set up to help in the hunt for former soldiers of the Home Army.

1 March 45. Lodz Province: During the last days of February, the NKVD arrested 23 officers of the Home Army, who formerly worked on the District Staff.

The attitude of the population towards the Lublin authorities is unfavourable. Most people in Poland consider the present state of affairs as Soviet occupation.

Note: The dates given are approximately those of the despatch of messages from Poland. (Ends)

[MR*]

Harry Hopkins' poor health and subsequent loss of favor with the President left a gap in the White House staff which was eventually filled by two men— Admiral William Leahy, the President's Chief of Staff, and James F. Byrnes, who had left the Supreme Court to become Director of the Office of Economic Stabilization in 1942. Although Leahy handled most of the wartime foreign and military questions, as postwar economic issues arose Byrnes' influence grew. This response to Churchill's message about food stockpiles in Europe was originally drafted by the War Department and then sent by Roosevelt to Byrnes for additional comments. Byrnes added only the word "here" (under-lined) to emphasize that discussions would be held only in the United States, but his accompanying memo to the President reveals suspicion of British motives. Warning that forecasts for American food production were pessi-mistic, Byrnes argued that "our own people are of the view that the British food stockpile is larger now than warranted by existing war conditions" (Byrnes to Roosevelt, Mar. 8, 1945, MR). The implication was clear: food supplies for peacetime use were not part of the wartime aid program.

R–712

Washington [via U.S. Navy]
Mar. 10, 1945, 2246 Z

Top Secret and Personal from the President for the Prime Minister.
   Reference your Number 902 of 2 March 1945.
   1. I am gratified to learn that you are making arrangements to meet the March and April deficiencies for the 21st Army Group from U.K. stocks.
   2. I share your concern that the problem will prove to be larger than the figures involved in this emergency. I am also very much concerned about the problem of the replacement of your foodstuffs as well as pro-vision of the necessary ships. It seems to me now imperative that discus-sions be resumed <u>here</u> in the immediate future as to these questions and as to the availability of foodstuffs from sources in U.K. and elsewhere in addition to United States.
   3. Eisenhower's estimates of future requirements for Northwest Europe are of such large proportions that they present most difficult problems of shipping availability and inland transport in the United States. Of the 772,000 tons allocated for subsistence procurement responsibility for Northwest Europe for June and July only 20 tons are allocated to the U.K., the remainder being U.S. responsibility. As the total allocations are

only about one-half of Eisenhower's recent estimates it is obvious that discussions leading to definite conclusions must be instituted now between fully authorized representatives of our respective governments and we are prepared to resume such discussions now.

4. I think that the questions you raise in your Number 902 will have to be considered as part of the overall problem which I am most anxious to have fully explored and determined in the immediate future. I should appreciate word as to when your representatives may be expected. Roosevelt [War Dept.]

[MR*. FRUS, 1945, II, 1076–77.]

Roosevelt was genuinely troubled by the ruthless suppression in Poland of any opposition to the Lublin (Warsaw) regime. Whether he expected the Soviets to permit Western-style free elections or merely assumed that Stalin would go through the motions, either way he was disappointed. The President had little respect for the London Poles and his statement supporting land reform would have been unacceptable to them, but he was unable to understand why the Soviets would not permit Anglo-American observers to enter Poland. Churchill guessed that these messages on Poland were being written in the State Department, not by the President, but there is no indication that Roosevelt did not agree with what was said. The drafts were sent to him and his calendar indicates that he was keeping to his usual busy schedule. Roosevelt had complained of weariness and an inability to get enough sleep, but the careful way in which these cables shied away from any direct confrontation with the Soviet Union suggests that his policy of cooperation still governed the matter (WSC, VI, 426, 429). The President's flat refusal to make an issue out of Roumania indicates that he wanted practical solutions, not arguments.

R–713

Washington [via U.S. Navy]
Mar. 11, 1945, 1630 Z

Top Secret and Personal from the President for the Prime Minister.
Your 907.

I had drafted and released for transmission my reply [R–714] to your 905, March 8, before I had received your 907 of March 10. I did not hold up on my first message as I don't believe that the main issues in that reply are basically affected by the points you raise in your 907.

With reference to your observations on the last part of the instructions to Ambassador Harriman in regard to a political truce in Poland, I can assure you that our objectives are identical, namely, to bring about a cessation on the part of the Lublin Poles of the measures directed against their political opponents in Poland to which you refer and vice versa. The only difference as I see it is one of tactics. You would prefer that the demand in regard to the Lublin Poles be put squarely to the Soviet Government as such whereas we feel that the chances of achieving our common objective would be immeasurably increased if it were done under the guise of a general political truce. You will recall at Yalta that Stalin made quite a point of the "terrorist" activities of the underground forces of the London Government against the Red Army and the Lublin Poles. Whether or not these allegations have any foundation in fact is beside the question since it is definitely the position of the Soviet Government. In view of Stalin's attitude we feel we would be inviting certain refusal if we merely demanded that the Lublin Poles alone be forced to cease their persecutions of political opponents. Furthermore, we must be careful not to give the impression that we are proposing a halt in the land reforms. This would furnish the Lublin Poles with an opportunity to charge that they and they alone defend the interests of the peasants against the land lords. However, in view of your feeling on this point we have made sure that Harriman will not deliver those instructions until Clark Kerr has received his. I would also be very glad to consider any suggestions which you may have in order to strengthen this point bearing in mind the considerations which I have set forth above.

The question of sending in observers is being pressed by Harriman under other instructions. We feel, however, that more would be accomplished by pressing for low level observers at this point who would certainly see as much if not more than some more spectacular body. If you feel strongly that some reference to observers should go into the present instructions to Harriman, I will have no objection. Since we wish to get on as speedily as possible with the business of the Commission in Moscow, I would appreciate your letting me have urgently your views on my two messages so that instructions can be issued to Harriman and Clark Kerr for transmission to Molotov. Roosevelt [State Dept.]

[MR*. *FRUS*, 1945, V, 155–56. *R&C*.]

The instructions to Harriman, mentioned below, are apparently the ones in Grew to Harriman, Mar. 8, 1945, *FRUS*, V, 150–52.

R–714

Washington [via U.S. Navy]
Mar. 11, 1945, 1634 Z

Top Secret and Personal from the President for the Prime Minister.
Your 905.
I have of course had very much in mind the considerations in regard

to Rumania and to the Polish question raised in your 905, March 8, and share your concern over these developments. I am fully determined, as I know you are, not to let the good decisions we reached at the Crimea slip through our hands and will certainly do everything I can to hold Stalin to their honest fulfillment. In regard to the Rumanian situation Averell has taken up and is taking up again the whole question with Molotov invoking the Declaration on Liberated Europe and has proposed tripartite discussions to carry out these responsibilities. It is obvious that the Russians have installed a minority government of their own choosing, but apart from the reasons you mentioned in your message, Rumania is not a good place for a test case. The Russians have been in undisputed control from the beginning and with Rumania lying athwart the Russian lines of communications it is moreover difficult to contest the plea of military necessity and security which they are using to justify their action. We shall certainly do everything we can, however, and of course will count on your support.

As to the Polish negotiations in Moscow I most certainly agree that we must stand firm on the right interpretation of the Crimean decision. You are quite correct in assuming that neither the Government nor the people of this country will support participation in a fraud or a mere whitewash of the Lublin Government and the solution must be as we envisaged it at Yalta. We have recently sent instructions to Harriman, a copy of which has been given to your Embassy here, to address a communication to Molotov making this clear and in general very much along the lines of the Foreign Office's suggestions contained in the telegram to Halifax to which you refer. I understand that Clark Kerr will be instructed along similar lines. In the circumstances I feel that it would be much better to await the result of these steps by our Ambassadors before either you or I intervene personally with Stalin particularly since there is no question of either of our Governments yielding to Molotov's interpretation. I feel that our personal intervention would best be withheld until every other possibility of bringing the Soviet Government into line has been exhausted. I very much hope, therefore, that you will not send any message to Uncle Joe at this juncture—especially as I feel that certain parts of your proposed text might produce a reaction quite contrary to your intent. We must, of course, keep in close touch on this question. Roosevelt [State Dept.]

[MR*. *FRUS*, 1945, V, 157, 509–10. *R&C*.]

Unlike Churchill, the President was unwilling to go beyond the text of the Yalta agreements on Poland. Not only did the State Department and Admiral Leahy, who drafted this cable, look with some suspicion on the "alleged" abuses reported by the London Poles, but their answer emphasized the need to be practical. Once again, Roosevelt and his advisers avoided making an appeal to Stalin lest the Soviet Premier give the wrong answer and thus force a confrontation or a retreat.

R–715

Washington [via U.S. Navy]
Mar. 12, 1945, 2017 Z

Personal and Top Secret, from the President for the Prime Minister.

Your No. 909 points directly to an urgent necessity of our taking every practicable means of accomplishing the corrective measures in Poland that are envisaged in the agreements reached at Yalta.

The Yalta agreements, if they are followed, should correct most of the abuses alleged in your 909.

In my opinion as expressed in my 714, we should leave the first steps to our Ambassadors from which we may hope to obtain good results.

When and if it should become necessary because of failure of the Ambassadors we may have to appeal to Marshal Stalin for relief for the oppressed inhabitants of Poland. Roosevelt [WDL, CB]

[MR*. *FRUS*, 1945, V, 158. *R&C*.]

Leahy, acting for Roosevelt, made no comment on Churchill's willingness to drop the plan to make Alexander the Deputy SCAEF.

R–716

Washington [via U.S. Navy]
Mar. 12, 1945, 2019 Z

Personal and Top Secret, from the President for the Prime Minister.
Receipt is acknowledged of your No. 908. Roosevelt [WDL]

[MR*]

This cable illustrates the sharp differences between the British and American positions on the Polish crisis. Churchill and the Foreign Office wanted to draw the line in Poland, making it a clear-cut "test case" on Soviet willingness to cooperate with the West. Roosevelt and the State Department preferred to avoid any kind of ultimatum in the hope that the Soviets could be persuaded to follow more liberal policies. Although Ambassador Harriman and others had come to the conclusion that Soviet leaders understood only harsh language and tough actions, their superiors in the State Department were not yet ready to give up on cooperation, particularly with the San Francisco Conference to plan the international peace-keeping organization about to begin.

Harry Hopkins had attended the Yalta Conference but was too ill to play his usual role, although he did attend all but one of the plenary sessions. To Roosevelt's obvious annoyance, Hopkins had left the USS *Quincy* and the President at Algiers in order to fly back to the United States. Hopkins went to the Mayo Clinic for intensive care on February 27, and was there when Roosevelt died on April 12.

C–910

London [via U.S. Army]
Mar. 13, 1945, 1932 Z / TOR 0240 Z, Mar. 14

Prime Minister to President Roosevelt. Personal and Top Secret.

1. Your numbers 713, 714 and 715.

I thank you for your full and considerate replies to my various messages on Poland. We can, of course, make no progress at Moscow without your aid, and if we get out of step the doom of Poland is sealed.

A month has passed since Yalta and no progress of any kind has been made. Soon I shall be questioned in Parliament on this point and I shall be forced to tell them the truth. Time is, of course, all on the side of Lublin, who are no doubt at work to establish their authority in such a way as to make it impregnable.

2. I am willing to defer addressing Stalin directly for the time being on this subject. But, in that case, I must beg you to agree that the instructions to our Ambassadors should deal with the points which I have proposed to put to Stalin in (A) to (E) of paragraph 7 of my number 905.

You say that some of these might have the opposite effect to what we intend. I wonder which you have in mind. We might be able to improve the wording. But I am convinced that unless we can induce the Russians to agree to these fundamental points of procedure, all our work at Yalta will be in vain.

3. When the discussions following Yalta began at Moscow, we had a perfectly simple objective, namely, to bring together for consultation representative Poles from inside Poland and elsewhere and to promote the formation of a new re-organized Polish Government sufficiently representative of all Poland for us to recognize it.

A test case of progress in this direction would be the inviting of Mikolajczyk and 2 or 3 of his friends who have resigned from the London Polish Government because they realize that a good understanding must be reached with Russia.

4. I fear that your present instructions to Averell will lead to little if any progress on all this, as the only definite suggestion is that there should be a truce between Polish parties. Here we should enter ground of great disadvantage to us both. The Russians would almost at once claim that the truce was being broken by the Anti-Lublin Poles and that Lublin therefore could not be held to it.

I have little doubt that some of the supporters of the Polish Government in London and more particularly the extreme right wing underground force, the so-called N.S.Z., are giving and would give the Russians and Lublin ground for this contention.

As we are not allowed to enter the country to see what the truth is, we shall be at the mercy of assertions. After a fortnight or so of negotiations about the truce, we shall be farther back than in the days before Yalta when you and I were agreed together that anyhow Mikolajczyk should be invited.

5. At Yalta also we agreed to take the Russian view of the frontier line. Poland has lost her frontier. Is she now to lose her freedom? That is the question which will undoubtedly have to be fought out in Parliament and in public here.

I do not wish to reveal a divergence between the British and the United States Governments, but it would certainly be necessary for me to make it clear that we are in presence of a great failure and an utter breakdown of what was settled at Yalta, but that we British have not the necessary strength to carry the matter further and that the limits of our capacity to act have been reached.

The moment that Molotov sees that he has beaten us away from the whole process of consultations among Poles to form a new government, he will know that we will put up with anything. On the other hand, I believe that combined dogged pressure and persistence along the lines on which we have been working and of my proposed draft message to Stalin, would very likely succeed.

6. We are also in presence of the Soviet memorandum of March 9 about inviting representatives of the Lublin Poles to San Francisco. This would amount to a de facto recognition of Lublin. Are we not both pledged not to recognize the Lublin Government until it has been re-organized in accordance with the declaration and spirit of Yalta, and consequently to continue to recognize the London Polish Government as the only one in existence.

The only possible course if no agreement is reached is to invite neither of the present Governments. This is in fact the line agreed upon between us. On the other hand, this very invitation question is well-suited to bring matters to a head at the Moscow conference and make the Soviets see that they must reach a fair and honourable conclusion in accordance with the decisions of Yalta.

7. I trust Harry is progressing. It is very disappointing that he should have had so serious a setback. When he first arrived in London he was better than I had seen him for years.

Kind regards.

[MR*. *FRUS*, 1945, V, 158–60. p*WSC*, VI, 426. p*R&C*.]

Throughout most of the war, the President had usually made changes—adding a personal touch if nothing else—to drafts of Roosevelt-to-Churchill cables. That was particularly true of State Department drafts, which tended to use pompous, stuffy language as far as Roosevelt was concerned. But this telegram, as with most of those drafted after the Yalta Conference, was sent without changes. According to the British records, Harry Hopkins told Eden and Halifax that few of the President's messages after Yalta had been his own, although that must have been hearsay since Hopkins was at the Mayo Clinic in Minnesota the whole time (Woodward, *British Foreign Policy*, III, 503n). Roosevelt made no change in this message, but he did ask the State Department to brief him on the issue.

Neither the Yalta documents nor Sir Alexander Cadogan's published diaries mention the question of American negotiations with Ireland having been discussed at the Crimea Conference. David Gray was the U.S. Ambassador to the Irish Republic.

R–717

Washington [via U.S. Navy]
Mar. 15, 1945, 1643 Z

Top Secret and Personal from the President for the Prime Minister.

I am surprised at your 904. There must have been some misunderstanding of my position. Furthermore, the circumstances of the agreement with Ireland were fully explained to your people, Cadogan in particular, at Yalta.

During the latter days of the Chicago Conference when it became increasingly doubtful that full agreement on aviation would be reached on a multilateral basis we held preliminary discussions looking toward bilateral agreements, as Berle publicly stated, with a number of countries represented there. Ireland was naturally one of these in view of its obvious geographic importance to American air routes. The agreement followed the standard form drawn up with the assistance of your people at Chicago and in no way prejudices your right to make similar arrangements. In the circumstances we saw no need to do more than advise your people, which we authorized Gray to do, before signature. One hour before the scheduled time of signature a copy of your 897 was brought to the attention of Acting Secretary Grew. He advised me that in view of your message he was postponing signature until February 3 to give me time to comment but that, the negotiations having been satisfactorily concluded, we could not in good faith refuse to sign nor could we risk the damage to Anglo-American relations which would result should it become known that your Government had objected to our concluding this agreement with Ireland. I saw no reason to instruct the State Department not to sign on February 3 and I fully approve of its action. There can of course be no question of annuling the agreement. I am sorry but there it is.

I fully realize your concern on political grounds and your opinion, which I share, of Ireland's role during the war. We instructed Gray to make clear to the Irish that signature of the agreement indicated no change what-so-ever in our attitude toward Ireland any more than our signature of a similar agreement with Spain indicated any change in our attitude toward Franco.

This agreement is however a post war matter. You will recall how earnestly I endeavored to secure your cooperation on the future of aviation during the Chicago Conference. These bilateral aviation agreements were made necessary by the failure of that conference to reach a multilateral agreement permitting the natural development of aviation. While I fully understand your own position, I think it only fair to tell you that aviation circles in this country are becoming increasingly suspicious that certain elements in England intend to try to block the development of international flying in general until the British aviation industry is further developed. Of course any feeling of complacence, even though wholly unwarranted at any time, on the part of the Irish has now been somewhat deflated by their being left out of the San Francisco Conference. Roosevelt [State Dept.]

[MR*. R&C.]

By mid-March, the appearance of unity which had characterized the Yalta discussions of Poland had completely disappeared. The Soviet Union now openly insisted that the Lublin Poles could accept or reject all persons proposed by other Polish groups for positions in the provisional government, meaning that all non-communists could be excluded. The British had come to demand open and free elections which would be held under the supervision of representatives of the tripartite Moscow Commission. The United States, trying to find a middle ground acceptable to Churchill, Stalin, and the American public and Congress, pushed for a "new" Polish government rather than just the continuation of the Lublin Committee under a new name. Both Roosevelt and the State Department seemed intent upon preserving great-power cooperation, and were convinced that the British approach would only bring outright rejection from the Soviet Union.

R–718

Washington [via U.S. Navy]
Mar. 15, 1945, 1647 Z

Personal and Top Secret, from the President for the Prime Minister.

I cannot but be concerned at the views you expressed in the second paragraph of point 5 of your 910. I do not understand what you mean by a divergence between our Governments on the Polish negotiations. From our side there is certainly no evidence of any divergence of policy. We have been merely discussing the most effective tactics and I cannot agree that we are confronted with a breakdown of the Yalta agreement until we have made the effort to overcome the obstacles incurred in the negotiations at Moscow. I also find puzzling your statement in paragraph 4 that the only definite suggestion in our instructions to Averell is for a political truce in Poland. Those instructions, of which you have a copy, not only set forth our understanding of the Yalta agreement but they make the definite point that the Commission itself should agree on the list of Poles to be invited for consultation and that no one of the three groups from which the reorganized Government is to emerge can dictate which individuals from the other two groups ought to be invited to Moscow. I must in all fairness point out that while fully aware that time is working against us Averell has had his instructions since March 9 but has not acted on them at your request in order that other points could be included. Our chief purpose at that time was and remains without giving ground to get the negotiations moving again and tackle first of all the point on which they had come to a standstill. I cannot urge upon you too strongly the vital importance of agreeing without further delay on instructions to our Ambassadors so that the negotiations may resume. The need for new instructions to our Ambassadors arose out of the unwillingness of Molotov to accept our proposal concerning the list of Poles to be invited in the first instance. Since our Ambassadors informed him that the matter was being referred to their Governments, the negotiations are held up pending those instructions. With this in mind I have examined the points which you propose to submit to Stalin in your 905 and have the following comments to make:

We are in agreement on point (a) and this is covered in our instructions to Averell.

I cannot believe that Molotov will accept the proposal contained in point (b) that any Pole can be invited unless all three members of the Commission object and I am opposed to putting forward such a suggestion at this time as it would, in my view, almost certainly leave us in a stalemate which would only redound to the benefit of the Lublin Poles. I also think the demand for freedom of movement and communication would arouse needless discussion at this state in the negotiations.

On point (c) we are agreed that the Poles invited for consultation should discuss the composition of the Government among themselves with the Commission presiding in an impartial arbitral capacity so far as possible. Harriman has already been instructed to this effect but feels, and I agree, that this might be pressed later.

I have covered your point (d) in my previous message and continue to feel that our approach would be better calculated to achieve the desired result. With reference to point (e) you will recall that this had been agreed to by Molotov who took fright when Clark-Kerr revealed that you were thinking of a large special mission. I am willing to include in Averell's instructions on wording you propose in point (e).

Please let me know urgently whether you agree that in the light of the foregoing considerations, our Ambassadors may proceed with their instructions.

I heartily agree that we cannot invite the Lublin Poles to San Francisco and the State Department is coordinating a reply to the Soviet note with your Foreign Office.

Harry is getting along well. There is nothing seriously wrong with him and he is getting a good rest. Roosevelt [ES, CB]

[MR*. *FRUS*, 1945, V, 163–65. p*WSC*, VI, 426–28. p*R&C*.]

Shortly before the Yalta Conference began, Roosevelt asked Samuel I. Rosenman, a speechwriter and longtime aide, to head a mission to northwestern Europe to assess wartime and postwar supply requirements. Judge Rosenman (he had once been on the New York State Supreme Court) had to postpone his study when Roosevelt asked him to sail back to the United States on the USS *Quincy* following the Crimea talks in order to draft the President's report to Congress. Rosenman returned to Europe late in February, and his account of talks with Churchill capture the essence of the debate over food stockpiles:

> During the evening conference . . ., Churchill, prompted now and then by Lord Cherwell, his economist, poured onto me statistics of foodstuffs shipped to England, shipped out of England and consumed in England— all to prove that it would be cruel for the United States to divert a substantial amount of the food in the British Isles to the Continent.
>
> Armed with the statistics I had gathered during my weeks of study, I did my best to cope with his arguments. . . . I was armed also with first-hand knowledge of the tragic suffering of the people in the cities of France, Belgium and Holland (Rosenman, *Working with Roosevelt*, p. 545).

Oliver Lyttelton was Minister of Production and a member of the British War Cabinet. Colonel J. J. Llewellin was British Minister of Food.

C–911

London [via U.S. Army]
Mar. 16, 1945, 1335 Z / TOR 1604 Z

Prime Minister to President Roosevelt Personal and Top Secret.

1. Your 712 reached me when I was troubled not only about future requirements for North West Europe but about future requirements for the approaching crisis in world food supplies as a whole. I am advised that there will be enough wheat. But supplies of meat, sugar, fats, dairy produce, etc., will not go anywhere near meeting demands. I agreed at Yalta to a further investigation of our stock levels and we had been led to expect that you would send some one to London for the preliminary part of such survey. But such stock level enquiry is only a small part of the picture and I agree with you that the overall problem must be fully explored and determined in the immediate future.

2. I would, therefore, propose, if agreeable to you, to send over Lyttelton and Llewellin to join with any representatives you may name in determining what steps can and should be taken to cut consumption down to the level of supplies. This enquiry should embrace all major foods in short supply and should cover the whole field including the civil requirements of SHAEF and other military theatres and of the governments of liberated areas, possible further reductions in U.K. stocks, possible reductions in service demands in all theatres and in civilian consumption levels. I realize the difficulties which face producing countries in reducing their standards of consumption. But we shall not get through 1945 without disaster unless reductions are made.

3. Meanwhile situation in North West Europe is so serious that I must ask you at any rate provisionally pending forthcoming discussions, to arrange for the outstanding balance of Eisenhower's stated requirements to be found by U.S.A. I know you realize how important it is that all agreed requirements should arrive to schedule.

4. It would be very helpful if we were able, jointly or severally, to make a statement soon as to how the Allies intend to deal with this emergency.

[MR*]

The British continued to insist that Soviet moves in Poland be protested vigorously, and the United States Ambassador in Moscow, Averell Harriman, tended to agree.

C–912

London [via U.S. Army]
Mar. 16, 1945, 1820 Z / TOR 2150 Z

Prime Minister to President Roosevelt, Personal and Top Secret.

1. Thank you for your No. 718 of 16 March. I am most relieved that you do not feel that there is any fundamental divergence between us and I agree that our differences are only about tactics.

You know, I am sure, that our great desire is to keep in step with you and we realise how hopeless the position would become for Poland if it were ever seen that we were not in full accord.

2. Just before getting your telegram, I received from Clark Kerr the draft of the communication he thinks we should make to Molotov. This was drawn up after long talks with Averell but, of course, does not commit him.

We are instructing Halifax to show Clark Kerr's proposed communication immediately to Stettinius and if possible to you. I like Clark Kerr's draft and must earnestly beg you to consider whether you cannot accept our proposals in this modified form. I hope that when Stettinius has been through it with Halifax you will see your way to instruct Averell to put in the same, or at least a very similar, communication.

3. Halifax will explain to you in detail our views upon the various points the inclusion of which I still consider essential. I welcome your agreement on point (A).

With regard to point (B), what happens if Molotov vetoes every one of our suggestions? And secondly, what is the use of anyone being invited who has no freedom of movement and communications? We had in fact not understood that Molotov had disputed this latter point when it was raised with him earlier but Mikolajczyk has made it a condition of going to Moscow and I gravely doubt whether we could persuade him to leave unless we had some definite assurance to convey to him.

Equally it is in order to reassure the anti-Lublin Poles whom we want to see invited that I should like to come to an agreement with Molotov in regard to the character of the discussions and the commission's arbitral capacity (my point (C)).

If you feel strongly against mentioning the matter of the presidential function at this stage I will give way although it is a matter of great practical importance which the Poles must not be debarred from discussing.

In regards point (D) I fear I cannot agree that your truce plan would achieve the desired result. How can we guarantee that nothing will be said or done in Poland or by the Polish Government's supporters here, which the Russians could not parade as a breach of the truce?

I fear that the truce plan will lead us into interminable delays and a dead end in which some at least of the blame may well be earned by the London Polish Government. I fear therefore that it is impossible for us to endorse your truce proposal, for we think it actively dangerous.

I beg you once more most earnestly to consider whether you cannot accept the revised version of (D) included in Clark Kerr's draft. This would give us something on which to base the work of our observers (point (E), on which I am very glad to see that we are in agreement).

4. At present all entry into Poland is barred to our representatives. An impenetrable veil has been drawn across the scene. This extends even to the liaison officers, British and American, who were to help in bringing out our rescued prisoners of war. According to our information the American officers as well as the British who had already reached Lublin have been requested to clear out.

There is no doubt in my mind that the Soviets fear very much our seeing what is going on in Poland. It may be that apart from the Poles they are being very rough with the Germans. Whatever the reason, we are not to be allowed to see. This is not a position that could be defended by us.

[MR*. *FRUS*, 1945, V, 170–72. p*WSC*, VI, 428–29. p*R&C*.]

Although Churchill phrased the problem in Southeast Asia as one of military coordination, its real nature was political. The British wanted to ensure that their forces liberated Indo-China, so as to restore French sovereignty and defend the principle of European empires. Mountbatten had offered assistance to the French when fighting had broken out on March 9 between the Japanese and French military forces in Indo-China previously loyal to the Vichy regime. Both de Gaulle and the British had asked for American air support, but Roosevelt initially refused. Not only did he agree with General Albert C. Wedemeyer (General Stilwell's replacement as Chiang Kai-shek's Chief of Staff) that the military effort against Japan should concentrate farther north, along the China coast, but the President, Chiang, and Wedemeyer all opposed the restoration of colonial rule in Indo-China. Lord Mountbatten's oral agreement with Chiang would actually give the British a free hand in Southeast Asia since Chinese forces were needed to support the invasion of Japan.

C–913

London [via U.S. Army]
Mar. 17, 1945, 2105 Z / TOR 2359 Z

Prime Minister to President Roosevelt, Personal and Top Secret.
1. I hear that there are certain difficulties between Mountbatten and

Wedemeyer about activities in Indo-China. As Wedemeyer is now in Washington it seems a good moment to try to clear them up.

2. Under existing decisions of the Combined Chiefs of Staff Indo-China is still within the China Theatre. But Mountbatten has a vital interest in Indo-China as well as in Siam, since it is through them that runs the Japanese land and air reinforcement route to Burma and Malaya: and as you know he has an oral understanding with Chiang Kai Shek that both he and the Generalissimo shall be free to attack Siam and Indo-China and that the boundaries between the two theatres shall be decided when the time comes in accordance with the progress made by their respective forces. The Generalissimo agreed after SEXTANT that this understanding extended to pre-occupational activities.

3. I am told that Wedemeyer feels difficulty in recognizing this oral understanding in the absence of instructions to that effect from his superior authorities.

4. This is a situation from which much harmful friction may spring. Could not you and I clear it up by jointly endorsing the oral understanding which seems a sensible and workable arrangement?

5. I well understand Wedemeyer's interest in Indo-China and it is clear that there ought to be the closest liaison about it between him and Mountbatten. If you agree, we might, when endorsing the understanding, direct that appropriate arrangements be made by the Combined Chiefs of Staff for full and frank exchange of intentions, plans and intelligence between Wedemeyer and Mountbatten as regards Indo-China and indeed as regards all matters of mutual concern.

[MR*. R&C.]

No log sheet exists for this telegram, so the President's reaction is unknown. Admiral Leahy scrawled "Reply not necessary" across the top, and the President did not acknowledge the cable until two weeks later. (See R–731.) Churchill had received reports of Roosevelt's failing health and was worried that their special relationship was deteriorating. Although Churchill's decision not to attend the San Francisco Conference was dictated by a combination of protocol (other heads of government were not attending) and the approaching elections in Great Britain, he also understood that Roosevelt needed rest, not visitors.

The mission to Washington was to discuss postwar food supplies, the same subject Samuel Rosenman was in London to discuss. The San Francisco Conference was to work out the postwar international organization.

During a conversation with Stalin at Yalta, Roosevelt mentioned that he and Churchill frequently referred to the Soviet Premier as "Uncle Joe." In spite of Molotov's assurances that Stalin's annoyance was feigned, Churchill seemed unconvinced.

C–914

London [via U.S. Army]
Mar. 17, 1945, 2255 Z / TOR 0155 Z, Mar. 18

Prime Minister to President Roosevelt, Personal and Private.

1. I hope that the rather numerous telegrams I have to send you on so many of our difficult and intertwined affairs are not becoming a bore to you. Our friendship is the rock on which I build for the future of the world so long as I am one of the builders. I always think of those tremendous days when you devised Lend-Lease, when we met at Argentia, when you decided with my heartfelt agreement to launch the invasion of Africa, and when you comforted me for the loss of Tobruk by giving me the 300 Shermans [tanks] of subsequent Almein fame. I remember the part our personal relations have played in the advance of the world cause now nearing its first military goal.

2. I am sending to Washington and San Francisco most of my ministerial colleagues on one mission or another, and I shall on this occasion stay at home to mind the shop. All the time I shall be looking forward to your long-promised visit. Clemmie is off to Russia next week for a Red Cross tour as far as the Urals to which she has been invited by Uncle Joe (if we may venture to describe him thus), but she will be back in time to welcome you and Eleanor. My thoughts are always with you all.

3. Peace with Germany and Japan on our terms will not bring much rest to you and me (if I am still responsible). As I observed last time, when the war of the giants is over, the wars of the pygmies will begin. There will be a torn, ragged and hungry world to help to its feet: and what will Uncle Joe or his successor say to the way we should both like to do it? It was quite a relief to talk party politics the other day. It was like working in wood after working in steel. The advantage of this telegram is that it has nothing to do with shop except that I had a good talk with Rosenman about our daily bread. All good wishes. Winston

[MR*. *WSC*, VI, 429–30. *R&C*.]

Accepting the recommendations of the State Department, Roosevelt agreed to most of the proposals offered by Churchill and the British Ambassador in Moscow, Archibald Clark Kerr, regarding the Polish crisis. The instructions to Harriman are in *FRUS*, 1945, V, 172–76.

R–719

Washington [via U.S. Navy]
Mar. 18, 1945, 1556 Z

Personal and Top Secret, for the Prime Minister from the President.
  Your No. 912.
  The State Department and your Embassy have prepared instructions
to our Ambassadors in Moscow closely following the draft suggested by
Clark Kerr and have agreed upon a text which I have approved and
which I believe meets both our views. I hope that you will concur. Roosevelt [State Dept.]

[MR*. R&C.]

On his own initiative, although with the approval of the War Cabinet, Churchill proposed a public statement designed to persuade German soldiers to
surrender.

C–915

London [via U.S. Army]
Mar. 18, 1945, 1805 Z / TOR 2248 Z

Prime Minister to President Roosevelt, Personal and Top Secret.
  Will you kindly consider the following kind of proclamation to the
German Army by the three of us or by we two: (Begins)

  German soldiers, who are fighting bravely to defend your native
  land, do you realize what will be the consequences of the war being
  carried on throughout the whole of Germany during the present
  spring and summer? You are told you are defending your homes
  and families and the German people. But though you may delay,
  you cannot stop our overrunning your whole country both from the
  east and west in the next few months. We feel it our duty to give you
  this warning, that if by your tenacity you destroy the means of production in your country and prevent or neglect the spring sowings,
  you will condemn Germany to a winter famine the like of which has
  never been seen in Europe.
    It will be quite impossible for us, with out duties to our own peoples
  and to the liberated countries, to accept any responsibility for feeding
  Germany in the winter of 1945/46. We may do what we can, but the
  available transport, and the available food which we could supply
  would be utterly insufficient to handle or bear so heavy a burden. If

therefore you force us to carry the war on through the homelands of Germany, so that these are devastated by war, you will not protect your wives and families from war suffering, but on the contrary you will condemn a very large proportion of the German people to death by starvation when winter comes. Your leaders at the top will not run short as long as you continue fighting; but the population of Germany will assuredly undergo a frightful reduction by famine unless the crops of this year are sown in time and gathered fully in peace.

The decision is yours, and we can only tell you that if you continue to fight, as we can well understand good soldiers would wish to do, you will not save your nation but doom it to horrors far beyond any you have endured so far and far beyond our power to give you help. Ends.

2. I am inclined to think we should send the above or something like it. On the other hand there is this danger to be weighed. The Germans may react by starving all foreigners, including prisoners of war, in Germany on the ground that if they themselves are to starve next winter they must begin to save up now as much food as they can. I should like very much to know what you think.

[MR*]

The State Department had suggested minor changes in point B of Churchill's suggested protest to Molotov (C–905). One eliminated the ability of any member of the Moscow Commission to veto the makeup of the new provisional government; the other deleted the Anglo-American guarantees that the London Poles would have the freedom to leave Poland after meeting with the Lublin regime's representatives. In each case, the Americans tried to be practical. The veto concept violated the cooperative spirit they were trying to foster, and Anglo-American guarantees were not only unenforceable but seemed a gratuitous insult to the Soviets.

The cryptic postscript is unexplained, but may be another of Churchill's excursions into doggerel.

C–916

London [via U.S. Army]
Mar. 19, 1945, 1532 Z / TOR 1715 Z

Prime Minister to President Roosevelt. Personal and Top Secret.
Your number 719.
I have now read the text proposed. I am delighted we are in full

agreement. We will send an identical message to Clark Kerr forthwith.
P.S.: U.J.: OKAY: U.K.

[MR*]

In his memoirs, Churchill wondered why Roosevelt had not made more use
of Bernard Baruch, a longtime contributor to political coffers and adviser to
Presidents (*WSC*, VI, 430). The answer was simple—Roosevelt generally disagreed with Baruch's proposals, even though he seemed to enjoy the South
Carolinian's company and occasionally stayed at Baruch's plantation, Hobcaw.
Churchill had great respect for Baruch, and Roosevelt sent him to London
in hopes of gaining the Prime Minister's agreement on a wide range of postwar
economic issues. It was a revealing choice on Roosevelt's part, since Baruch
thought the British had exaggerated their economic problems. He had also
criticized the stage II lend-lease agreement as "giving too much and weakening ourselves" (Blum, *Morgenthau Diaries*, III, 323). Apparently, the President intended to drive a hard bargain when it came to postwar economic
issues.

R–720

Washington [via U.S. Navy]
Mar. 19, 1945, 2353 Z

For the Prime Minister from the President, Personal and Top Secret.
I would very much appreciate it if you would see Bernie Baruch as
soon as convenient to you, and also appreciate it if you could wire him
as he counts you one of his oldest friends and would much prefer having
your approval before he goes. Roosevelt [FDR]

[MR*. *WSC*, VI, 430. *R&C*.]

In his memoirs, Churchill gave the last phrase of this cable as "when he will
come" vice "when he will see me" (*WSC*, VI, 430).

C–917

London [via U.S. Army]
Mar. 21, 1945, 0913 Z / TOR 1213 Z

Prime Minister to President Roosevelt. Personal and Top Secret.
I am greatly looking forward to seeing Bernie, who is one of my older
friends. I am telegraphing him to say how glad I am that he is coming.
I should like to know when he will see me.

[MR*. *WSC*, VI, 430. *R&C*.]

Generals Marshall and Eisenhower had long preferred that propaganda aimed at breaking German morale be handled by SHAEF.

R–721

Washington [via U.S. Navy]
Mar. 21, 1945, 1701 Z

Top Secret and Personal from the President for the Prime Minister.

I have given careful consideration to your No. 915, and it is my considered opinion that at the present time it is not appropriate for us to issue a proclamation to the German Army such as that suggested by you.

It seems to me that a correct means of getting this information to the German Army and to the German people is through our established propaganda agencies. Roosevelt [WDL]

[MR*. R&C.]

In a reply written in the State Department, except for paragraph 3, which was drafted by War Department officials, the President carefully avoided the real issue—Britain's need for continued aid after the war ended.

R–722

Washington [via U.S. Navy]
Mar. 21, 1945, 1713 Z

Personal and Top Secret, for the Prime Minister from the President.

1. Replying to your 911, I welcome the proposal to send Lyttelton and Llewellin to Washington to discuss food problems and assume they will arrive with power to act. We have here a group competent to deal with the range of questions you have in mind and prepared to make decisions.

2. Any reductions which might have resulted from the investigations of your stock levels have never been considered by me to involve a reduction in your levels of consumption. However, I agree with you that stock levels are only one aspect of the food situation. We are prepared to investigate the position of all major foods in short supply and to consider military as well as civilian requirements.

3. We are making every effort to provide General Eisenhower with his urgent requirements to the full extent of our capabilities and with due regard to U.S. world-wide commitments, including those of U.K. We cannot, however, assume responsibility to meet all Eisenhower's requirements, even provisionally. I am advised that General Eisenhower's requirements are now under urgent study by the Combined Chiefs of Staff

and I believe that his requirements must be considered as part of the general problem to which I referred to my cable No. 712.

4. I agree with you that, if possible, either joint or separate statements should soon be made on proposed steps for handling the food emergency. Roosevelt [State Dept., War Dept.]

[MR*]

C–918

London [via U.S. Army]
Mar. 21, 1945, 1630 Z / TOR 1740 Z

Prime Minister to President Roosevelt. Personal and Top Secret.

Your telegram number 712 of 11th March and my reply number 911 of 16th March.

Lyttelton and Llewellin will leave here for Washington next Friday morning, 23d March.

[MR*]

This intriguing suggestion, which became a casualty of the rising tension between the West and the Soviet Union, came from Donald Nelson, an executive with Sears Roebuck before the war who viewed the problems in Greece from a businessman's standpoint:

> I think it is safe to say that many of Greece's political difficulties have roots in her present productive weakness, and could be resolved by an upsurge in production. . . . As I see it, many important consequences would flow from success in restoring and increasing the productivity of the Greek people. . . . Small nations everywhere would take renewed hope, while American prestige and influence would be further strengthened (Nelson to Roosevelt, Mar. 20, 1945, MR).

After easing Nelson out of his job as chairman of the War Production Board, a post he had held from 1942 through 1944, Roosevelt sent him to China to discuss postwar economic relations. Although Stimson and Hopkins held Nelson in contempt, Roosevelt took this suggestion seriously. (See Thorne, *Allies of a Kind*, p. 462.)

R–723

Washington [via U.S. Navy]
Mar. 21, 1945, 2222 Z

Top Secret and Personal from the President for the Prime Minister.

What would you think of sending a special mission for developing the productive power of Greece rapidly by concerted, non-political action? Such a mission could consist of people like Lyttelton, [A.I.] Mikoyan, the People's Commissar for Foreign Trade of U.S.S.R. and Donald Nelson, who is back after a very successful similar mission in China. It would not take them long and might have a highly constructive effect on world opinion at this time.

I take it that they could meet in Greece in about a month's time.

I am not taking it up with the Soviet Government until I get your slant. Roosevelt

[MR*. *FRUS*, 1945, VIII, 203–4. *R&C*.]

C–919

London [via U.S. Army]
Mar. 22, 1945, 0918 Z / TOR 1220 Z

Prime Minister to President Roosevelt. Personal and Top Secret.

Your 721, I agree with your view about my suggestion. Pray consider it dead.

[MR*]

The Germans did not systematically execute prisoners of war, but as the end of the war drew near, they did try to exterminate inmates in the concentration camps, particularly Jews.

C–920

London [via U.S. Army]
Mar. 22, 1945, 1020 Z / TOR 1455 Z

Prime Minister to President Roosevelt. Personal and Top Secret.

I have seen your recent exchange of messages with Marshal Stalin on prisoners of war matters. As regards the general question of Allied prisoners in German hands, I entirely agree with you that we ought to arrange matters now so that we are in a position to do something quickly at the right time.

We have long foreseen danger to these prisoners arising either in consequence of chaotic conditions resulting from a German collapse or alternatively out of a deliberate threat by Hitler and his associates to murder some or all of the prisoners. The object of this manoeuvre might be either to avoid unconditional surrender or to save the lives of the more important Nazi gangsters and war criminals, using this threat as a bargaining counter, or to cause dissention among the Allies in the final stages of the war. With this in mind we put to the United States and Soviet Governments last October through our diplomatic representatives at Washington and Moscow a proposal for an Anglo-American-Russian warning to the Germans (for text please see my immediately following telegram), but have so far received no reply.

On the 2d March last, the British Minister in Berne was informed by the Head of the Swiss Political Department that he had received reports from Berlin, which he could not confirm, that the Germans intended to liquidate, i.e. massacre, such prisoners of war as were held in camps in danger of being overrun by the advancing Allied forces rather than try to remove the prisoners or allow them to fall into Allied hands. In addition we have, in recent months, received various indications that the Nazis might in the last resort either murder Allied prisoners in their hands or hold them as hostages.

Various proposals of a practical nature for bringing immediate military aid and protection to prisoners of war camps in Germany have been under consideration by the British and United States military authorities. I believe that the issue at the appropriate moment of a joint warning on the lines we have proposed would be a powerful aid to such practical measures as it may be possible to take. An S/S General is now in charge of prisoners of war matters in the German Ministry of Defence and the S/S and Gestapo are believed to be taking over controls of camps. On such people a warning will have only limited effect, though at the worst it can do no harm. On the other hand it is by no means certain that the S/S have completed taking over from the Regular Army Officers and on the latter the warning might have real effect. We should surely miss no opportunity of exploiting any duality of control.

I would therefore earnestly invite you and Marshall Stalin, to whom I am repeating this message, to give this proposal your personal attention, and I very much hope you will agree to go forward with us in issuing it at the appropriate moment.

[MR*. *FRUS*, 1945, III, 703–4 (paraphrase). *R&C*.]

C–921

London [via U.S. Army]
Mar. 22, 1945, 1104 Z / TOR 1455 Z

Prime Minister to President Roosevelt. Personal and Top Secret.
My immediately preceding telegram.
Following is text of proposed warning:—

"The Governments of the United Kingdom, The United States of America and the Union of Soviet Socialist Republics, on behalf of all the United Nations at war with Germany, hereby issue a solemn warning to all commandants and guards in charge of Allied prisoners of war in Germany and German-occupied territory and to members of the Gestapo and all other persons of whatsoever service or rank in whose charge Allied prisoners of war have been placed, whether in the battle zones, on the lines of communication or in rear areas. They declare that they will hold all such persons, no less than the German High Command and the competent German military, naval and air authorities, individually responsible for the safety and welfare of all Allied prisoners of war in their charge.

"Any person guilty of maltreating or allowing any Allied prisoner of war to be maltreated, whether in the battle zone, on the lines of communication, in a camp, hospital, prison or elsewhere, will be ruthlessly pursued and brought to punishment.

"They give notice that they will regard this responsibility as binding in all circumstances and one which cannot be transferred to any other authorities or individuals whatsoever."

[MR*. pFRUS, 1944, I, 1258.]

The real question was not coordination of military operations, but who would liberate Indo-China and thus dominate that region after the war. (See C–913 and C–943.)

R–724

Washington [via U.S. Navy]
Mar. 22, 1945, 1653 Z

Top Secret and Personal from the President for the Prime Minister.

As you say in your No. 913, Indo-China is still within the China Theater, even though Admiral Mountbatten and the Generalissimo have agreed that at the appropriate time Chinese forces will attack Indo-China and Thailand from the north and Mountbatten is expected to attack from the south, and that the boundaries between the two theaters shall be adjusted at that time. This appears perfectly sound to me. However, there appears to be considerable obscurity as to the intent of the parties concerned as to any agreement dealing with preoccupational activities in Indo-China by Mountbatten. I understand that the Generalissimo has insisted that he should control, through his Chief of Staff, General Wedemeyer, all clandestine activities by other than Chinese forces which may be conducted within the China Theater including Indo-China.

I am told that both Mountbatten and Wedemeyer are now each independently conducting in Indo-China air operations and intelligence activities as well as supporting guerrilla forces. This appears to be a likely source of confusion and wasted effort and might result in placing the two theaters unintentionally in direct conflict. I believe it essential that some definite coordination of the activities in Indo-China of these two commanders be quickly provided. Also the Generalissimo is involved.

It seems to me the best solution at present is for you and me to agree that all Anglo-American-Chinese military operations in Indo-China, regardless of their nature, be coordinated by General Wedemeyer as Chief of Staff to the Generalissimo, who is Supreme Commander of the China Theater, at least until any adjustment of theater boundaries is made in connection with an advance by Mountbatten's forces into Indo-China from the south. This would place on Wedemeyer the normal responsibilities of a theater commander and appears to be readily workable and also consistent since I understand Mountbatten now controls similarly operations from China into Burma. At the same time it would provide coordination between future Chinese and American operations in Indo-China and any operations by Mountbatten which may be necessary.

If you agree to this proposal, I suggest that you direct Mountbatten to coordinate his activities in Indo-China with Wedemeyer; and I will direct Wedemeyer to take any steps necessary to insure coordination of all Allied operations in the China Theater including Indo-China.

Your suggestion for the full, free and frank exchange of plans, intentions and intelligence between Wedemeyer and Mountbatten as regards Indo-China and in all matters of mutual concern is excellent. I think we both should issue instructions to this end. Roosevelt

[MR*. R&C.]

Roosevelt quickly agreed to a joint warning to the Germans concerning their treatment of prisoners of war, but Stalin was much slower to respond. The proclamation was finally distributed in leaflets on April 23, from aircraft flying over German-held territory.

R–725

Washington [via U.S. Navy]
Mar. 22, 1945, 2021 Z

Top Secret and Personal, for the Prime Minister from the President.

Your 920 and 921. If Marshal Stalin agrees, I will go forward with you in our issuing the joint warning contained in your 921. Roosevelt [WDL]

[MR*. FRUS, 1945, III, 704n.]

C–922

London [via U.S. Army]
Mar. 23, 1945, 0932 Z / TOR 1238 Z

Prime Minister to President Roosevelt. Personal and Top Secret.
  Your 725. I thank you.

[MR*]

Churchill took a firm stand on the issue of food supplies and refused to ship the additional stocks requested by Eisenhower, apparently as a signal to those American officials who would be discussing supply matters with Lyttelton and Llewellin.

C–923

London [via U.S. Army]
Mar. 23, 1945; 0001 Z, Mar. 24 / TOR 0250 Z, Mar. 24

Prime Minister to President Roosevelt. Personal and Top Secret.
  1. In reply to your 722 Lyttelton and Llewellin have left for Washington today and have power to discuss the whole supply problem and concert plans with you but the War Cabinet must be consulted before any final decisions are taken.
  2. As regards your paragraph 3. I realize your difficulties in meeting General Eisenhower's urgent requirements in full and in time. But assuming these difficulties cannot be entirely overcome I urge most strongly that General Eisenhower should be informed immediately of the amount which can reasonably be expected to be made available by the due date so that he can plan accordingly. Moreover it is to me most important without waiting for the general review, that every effort should be made to procure and ship whatever supplies are available. I hope you will agree to this being done and I regret that there is nothing more that can be shipped from the U.K. towards meeting these requirements at present. This small island dependent for its life upon imported food must be judged by its sacrifices in rations and not by its contributions.
  3. Your paragraph 4. This is being covered in a separate telegram.

[MR*]

See the headnote to R–720 for background on Baruch's trip to England.

R–726

Washington [via U.S. Navy]
Mar. 24, 1945; 0014 Z, Mar. 25

Top Secret and Personal from the President for the Prime Minister.

If it is all right with you, Bernie [Baruch] can leave here Tuesday or Wednesday, the twenty-seventh or twenty-eighth by air, arriving in London within the next two days. Is this all right? Roosevelt [FDR]

[MR*]

C–924

London [via U.S. Army]
Mar. 25, 1945, 1520 Z / TOR 1800 Z

Prime Minister to President Roosevelt. Personal and Top Secret.

Your 726. Delighted. Am telegraphing to Bernie to say times proposed will be perfectly convenient and to invite him to be guest of the British Government during his visit.

[MR*]

On March 23, Molotov answered Anglo-American protests about Poland (R–719 and preceding cables) by rejecting their interpretation of the Yalta agreements. Insisting that the provisional government in Warsaw had to be consulted first about any reorganization, the Soviet Foreign Minister suggested that requests to send observers into Poland be submitted to that government. Molotov agreed that other Polish leaders should consult with the Warsaw regime about reorganization, but only if they accepted the Soviet interpretation of the Yalta accords, and he specifically excluded Mikolajczyk, one of the more moderate of the London Poles. (Molotov's memorandum is summarized in Woodward, *British Foreign Policy*, III, 506–8, and *FRUS*, 1945, V, 180–82.) Once again, Churchill called for a joint protest to Stalin, a move which would bring on a direct confrontation. Although the British did not expect any change in Soviet policy, the Prime Minister believed that public opinion, in both Britain and the United States, would demand that they take a firm stand.

Churchill's list of other signs of tension was accurate. Soviet Deputy Foreign Minister Andrei Vyshinsky had presided over a forced change of government in Roumania in late February, which he defended on the grounds that democracy in Roumania could not exist under a government dominated by fascists who had collaborated with the Germans. But Anglo-American protests concentrated on the lack of consultation among the three major powers, not on what had actually happened in Bucharest. The work of the European Advisory Commission (EAC), charged with mapping out plans for the treatment of Germany, had been held up by Soviet foot-dragging, although Vyshinsky claimed that the Yalta Conference had caused the delays. The Soviet decision to send Andrei Gromyko, their Ambassador in Washington, to the San Francisco Conference instead of Foreign Minister Molotov brought a quick protest from Roosevelt, who feared that the Soviet Union was downgrading the importance of the postwar international organization. In spite of the President's pleas, Stalin publicly announced that Gromyko would head the Soviet delegation, although Molotov finally did go to San Francisco. (See R–727.) For a discussion of Soviet-American problems over prisoners of war, see the headnote to R–710/1.

Operation CROSSWORD (called SUNRISE by the Americans), a small incident in itself, epitomized the increasing distrust in Anglo-American relations with the Soviet Union. In February 1945, the commander of German SS forces in Italy, Obergruppenführer Karl Wolff, who had direct access to Hitler as well as Heinrich Himmler, approached OSS agents with hints that German forces in Italy might surrender. Allen Dulles, head of an OSS mission to Switzerland, eagerly seized the opportunity and began discussions with Wolff. When it appeared that the talks were worth pursuing, both the United States and Great Britain followed the recommendation of the Supreme Allied Commander in Italy, Field Marshal Alexander, and informed the Soviet Union. Molotov quickly approved and requested that Soviet observers attend all further discussions. The British had no objections, providing Alexander's authority remained unchallenged, but the Americans opposed Soviet participation in the talks scheduled for Bern, Switzerland. Although the formal reason given by the Americans was that the Bern talks were preliminary and conducted only to see if the German offer was legitimate, Dulles and others feared that Wolff and his associates would refuse to negotiate if the Soviets were present. Whether or not he hoped the West could exploit German fears of the Russians, Dulles knew that the Allies had received a number of hints that Germany would be willing to surrender and join an alliance against the Soviet Union. When Harriman informed Molotov that Soviet observers could attend any formal surrender talks, which would be held at Alexander's headquarters, but not the preliminary discussions in Bern, the Soviet Foreign Minister demanded that the talks be adjourned. The Soviets believed that the Bern discussions would be decisive, with later talks serving merely to ratify the previous decisions. When the United States refused, Molotov responded in language which revealed Soviet fears: "in the present case [the talks in Bern] it is not a question of . . . misunderstanding—it is something worse" (*FRUS*, 1945, III, 737). Roosevelt's strong reaction to the Soviet moves, so different from his response to Stalin's actions in eastern Europe, stemmed in part from the fear that a Soviet presence at the Bern talks would scare off the Germans. But it also reflected the belief that Italy was an American sphere of interest—a belief that the British had been made aware of sometime earlier. Although the British tended to accept Soviet arguments, Roosevelt and his advisers continued to insist that Soviet participation be limited to formal surrender talks to be held at Alexander's headquarters. That was where the matter stood when Churchill sent the cable printed below. (The controversy is documented in *FRUS*, 1945, III, 722ff., and *Stalin/FDR*, docs. 281ff.)

The "four points" on Poland made by Molotov and referred to by Churchill in paragraph 4 of the following message all related to how the tripartite Moscow Commission, set up at Yalta to work out the details of the Polish settlement, should operate. The sum and substance of those points was that the commission should accept the Polish provisional government (the Lublin/Warsaw Poles) as the "basis" for a new government, and then should concentrate on determining what other Poles might be asked to join the government, subject to the unanimous consent of all three members of the commission. In short, the Soviets could veto candidates proposed by Britain and the United States. (See Woodward, *British Foreign Policy*, III, 506–8.)

C–925

London [via U.S. Army]
Mar. 27, 1945, 1337 Z / TOR 1820 Z

Prime Minister to President Roosevelt. Personal and Top Secret.

1. I am extremely concerned at the deterioration of the Russian attitude since Yalta.

2. About Poland, you will have seen that Molotov in his reply to the agreed communication made to him by our Ambassadors on the 19th March, and in their discussion on the 23rd March, returned a series of flat negatives on every point he dealt with and ignored others.

He persists in his view that the Yalta Communique merely meant the addition of a few other Poles to the existing administration of Russian puppets and that these puppets would be consulted first. He maintains his right to veto Mikolajczyk and other Poles we may suggest and pretends that he has insufficient information about the names we have put forward long ago.

Nothing is said about our proposal that the commission should preside in an arbitral capacity over discussions among the Poles. Nothing on our point that measures in Poland affecting the future of the Polish State and action against individuals and groups likely to disturb the atmosphere should be avoided.

He ignores his offer about observers and tells us to talk to the Warsaw puppets about this. It is as plain as a pike staff that his tactics are to drag the business out while the Lublin Committee consolidate their power.

3. Clark Kerr's proposal for dealing with this was to try by redrafting to build something on the four point formula included in Molotov's reply. We cannot see that any real progress towards getting an honest Polish settlement can possibly be made in this way.

It would merely mean that we allowed our communication to be side tracked, negotiated on the basis of Molotov's wholly unsatisfactory reply and wasted time finding formulae which do not decide vital points. We therefore instructed Clark Kerr that he should not proceed on this basis, and that we are discussing matters with you.

4. As you know, if we fail altogether to get a satisfactory solution on Poland and are in fact defrauded by Russia, both Eden and I are pledged to report the fact openly to the House of Commons. There I advised critics of the Yalta settlement to trust Stalin. If I have to make a statement of facts to the House, the whole world will draw the deduction that such advice was wrong. All the more so that our failure in Poland will result in a set up there on the new Roumanian model.

In other words, Eastern Europe will be shown to be excluded from the terms of the declaration of liberated Europe and you and we shall be excluded from any jot of influence in that area.

5. Surely we must not be maneouvred into becoming parties to imposing on Poland, and on how much more of Eastern Europe, the Russian version of democracy? (You no doubt saw Vyshinsky's public explanations in Roumania of this doctrine). There seems to be only one possible alternative to confessing our total failure. That alternative is to stand by our interpretation of the Yalta declaration.

But I am convinced it is no use trying to argue this any further with Molotov. In view of this, is it not now the moment for a message from us both on Poland to Stalin? I will send you our rough idea on this in my immediately following. I hope you can agree.

6. I see nothing else likely to produce good results. If we are rebuffed, it will be a very sinister sign, taken with the other Russian actions at variants with the spirit of Yalta; such as Molotov's rude questioning of our word in the case of CROSSWORD, the unsatisfactory proceedings over our liberated German prisoners, the coup de'etat in Roumania, the Russian refusal to allow the declaration on liberated Europe to operate, and the blocking of all progress in the EAC by the Russians.

7. What also do you make of Molotov's withdrawal from San Francisco? It leaves a bad impression on me. Does it mean that the Russians are going to run out or are they trying to blackmail us? As we have both understood them, the Dumbarton Oaks proposals, which will form the basis of discussion at San Francisco, are based on the conception of great power unity.

If no such unit[y] exists on Poland, which is after all a major problem of the post war settlement—to say nothing of the other matters just mentioned—what, it will legitimately be asked, are the prospects of success of the new world organization? And is it not indeed evident that, in the circumstances, we shall be building the whole structure of future world peace on foundations of sand?

8. I believe, therefore, that if the success of San Francisco is not to be gravely imperilled, we must both of us now make the strongest possible appeal to Stalin about Poland and if necessary about any other derogations from the harmony of the Crimea. Only so shall we have any real chance of getting the world organization established on lines which will commend themselves to our respective public opinions.

Indeed, I am not sure that we should not mention to Stalin now the deplorable impression Molotov's absence from San Francisco will cause.

[MR*. *FRUS*, 1945, V, 185–87. p*WSC*, VI, 432–33. *R&C*.]

Churchill may have been willing to accommodate the Soviets in the matter of the surrender talks in Bern, but not on the Polish question. The President supported Churchill, but not in language strong enough to suit the Prime Minister. (See R–729, R–730, C–928.)

C–926

London [via U.S. Army]
Mar. 27, 1945, 1455 Z / TOR 1820 Z

Prime Minister to President Roosevelt. Personal and Top Secret.

1. My immediately preceding telegram.

Could we not both tell him that: We are distressed that the work of the Polish Commission is held up because misunderstandings have arisen about the interpretation of the Yalta decisions. The agreed purpose of those decisions was that a new Government of National Unity was to be established after consultations with representatives of Lublin and other Democratic Poles which both our governments could recognize.

We have not got any reply on the various Polish names we have suggested, pleading lack of information. We have given him plenty of information. There ought not to be a veto by one power on all nominations. We consider that our nominations for the discussions have been made in the spirit of confidence which befits allies; and of course there could be no question of allowing Lublin to bar them. We will accept any nominations he puts forward, being equally confident that the Soviet Government will not suggest Pro-Nazi or Anti-Democratic Poles.

The assembled Poles should then discuss the formation of a new government among themselves. The Commission should preside as arbitrators to see fair play. Monsieur Molotov wants the Lublinites to be consulted first. The [Yalta] Communique does not provide for this. But we have no objection to his seeing them first.

We cannot authorize our representatives to do so since we think it contrary to the spirit of the Communique. Also, to our surprise and regret

Molotov, who suggested at an earlier stage that we might like to send observers, has now withdrawn the offer.

Indeed, he appeared to suggest that it had never been made; and has suggested that we should apply to the present Warsaw Administration. Stalin will understand that the whole point of the Yalta decision was to produce a Polish Government we could recognize and that we obviously cannot therefore deal with the present administration.

We feel sure he will honour the offer to send observers and his influence with his Warsaw friends is so great that he will overcome with ease any reluctance they may show in agreeing.

2. Also, Stalin will surely see that while the three great allies are arranging for the establishment of the new Government of National Unity, those in power in Poland should not prejudice the future. We have asked that the Soviet Government should use their influence with their friends in temporary power there. Stalin will, we feel confident, take steps to this end.

3. Stalin will find all this set out in most reasonable terms in our communication of the 19th March. Will he cast his eye over it and judge whether our suggestions are not all in line with the spirit of the Yalta decision, and should they not all be met by our ally in order that the aim of the Yalta settlement of Poland, viz the setting up of a representative government which Britain and the U.S.A. can recognize, may be carried out without further delay.

[MR*. *FRUS*, 1945, V, 187–88. *WSC*, VI, 434–35. *R&C*.]

Roosevelt feared that the Soviet decision to send Gromyko instead of Molotov to the San Francisco Conference indicated unwillingness to participate fully in the postwar international organization being established.

R–727

Washington [via U.S. Navy]
Mar. 29, 1945, 1532 Z

Personal and Top Secret, from the President for the Prime Minister.

The following interchange of messages between Marshal Stalin and myself is quoted for your information.

QUOTE. President to Marshal Stalin, 24 March 1945.

Ambassador Gromyko has just informed the State Department of the composition of the Soviet delegation to the San Francisco Conference. While we have the highest regard for Ambassador Gromyko's character and capabilities and know that he would ably represent his country, I cannot help being deeply disappointed that Mr. Molotov apparently does not plan to attend. Recalling the friendly and fruitful cooperation at Yalta between Mr. Molotov, Mr. Eden, and Mr. Stettinius, I know the Secretary of State has been looking forward to continuing the joint work in the same spirit at San Francisco for the eventual realization of our mutual goal, the establishment of an effective international organization to insure a secure and peaceful future for the world.

Without the presence of Mr. Molotov the Conference will be deprived of a very great asset. If his pressing and heavy responsibilities in the Soviet Union make it impossible for him to stay for the entire Conference, I very much hope that you will find it possible to let him come at least for the vital opening sessions. Since all sponsoring powers and the majority of other countries attending will be represented by their Ministers of Foreign Affairs, I am afraid that Mr. Molotov's absence will be construed all over the world as a lack of comparable interest on the part of the Soviet Government in the great objectives of this Conference. UNQUOTE.

QUOTE. Marshal Stalin to President, 27 March.

We extremely value and attach great importance to the forthcoming Conference at San Francisco, called to found the international organization of peace and security for peoples but circumstances have developed in such a way that Mr. V. M. Molotov, really, is not able to participate in the Conference. I and Mr. Molotov regret it extremely but the convening, on request of the deputies of the Supreme Soviet, in April, of a sessions [sic] of the Supreme Soviet of the USSR where the presence of Mr. Molotov is absolutely necessary, is excluding the possibility of his participation even in the first meetings of the Conference.

You also know that Ambassador Gromyko has quite successfully accomplished his task in Dumbarton Oaks and we are confident that he will with great success head the Soviet delegation in San Francisco.

As regards various interpretations, you understand, this cannot determine the decisions which are to be made. UNQUOTE.

Roosevelt

[MR*. *FRUS*, 1945, I, 156, 165. *Stalin/FDR*, docs. 280, 282.]

Churchill did not respond to the following request until mid-April, and then he made it clear that the British feared retaliatory German attacks on British cities; so the plan to use drone bombers was dropped. The British never objected on the grounds that they would damage industrial and civilian targets indiscriminately—a charge they had frequently leveled against German V-1 and V-2 attacks.

R–728

Washington [via U.S. Navy]
Mar. 29, 1945, 1548 Z

Top Secret and Personal, for the Prime Minister from the President.

My Chiefs of Staff have undertaken during the past few months a project for the employment of war weary U.S. bombers to be launched against large industrial targets in Germany, each bomber to be loaded with some 20,000 pounds of high explosives and set on course to its target with an appropriate timing device to determine its flight duration.

Your Chiefs of Staff originally concurred in the development and employment of this project but have recently withdrawn their concurrence because, it is understood, of the British Government's apprehension that retaliatory action against London by the Germans might result if pilotless bombers were employed.

My Chiefs of Staff inform me that they consider this weapon to be most valuable in our all-out offensive against Germany. Since the original proposal was made last December, developmental work has progressed to a point where we are now able to direct its flight to the target by remote technical control. In view of the large explosive charge carried by each airplane and the present advanced stage of development in remote control, many lucrative targets in the industrial areas in Germany can be leveled and the German war effort correspondingly weakened.

I am assured that pilotless bombers will be launched only from bases on the Continent which would appear to minimize the chances of retaliatory action against England. I believe that if the enemy were able to take effective measures against the cities of England with this type of weapon he would have done so regardless of any use by us of pilotless aircraft. In addition, combat experience with this weapon on the Continent will make possible the most effective use of this type of weapon in the battle against the highly concentrated areas of the Japanese homeland.

In order that the enemy may feel the full weight of our resources at this propitious hour, it is requested that you ask your Chiefs of Staff to reconsider their withdrawal of concurrence in this project. Roosevelt [JCS]

[MR*. R&C.]

Admiral Leahy and State Department officials, who drafted this cable, continued to emphasize that protests about Soviet actions in Poland should relate strictly to the Yalta agreements and not introduce new issues. Unlike Churchill, the Americans were willing to accept the Soviet claim that the Lublin (Warsaw) Polish government had been given special recognition during the Crimea Conference, but only as *primus inter pares*, without the power to veto the inclusion of other parties in the government.

Next to the phrase "a group of Polish leaders that are truly representative" there is a question mark on the draft of this message. In addition, the words "truly representative" are underlined. The question mark is written with the same quavering penmanship that had come to characterize Roosevelt's handwriting in the weeks following the Yalta Conference. Charles Bohlen added the last sentence to the draft.

R–729

Washington [via U.S. Navy]
Mar. 29, 1945, 1953 Z

Personal and Top Secret, from the President for the Prime Minister.
    Your 925 and 926.

I have likewise been watching with anxiety and concern the development of Soviet attitude since the Crimea Conference. I am acutely aware of the dangers inherent in the present course of events not only for the immediate issues involved and our decisions at the Crimea but also for the San Francisco Conference and future world cooperation. Our peoples and indeed those of the whole world are watching with anxious hope the extent to which the decisions we reached at the Crimea are being honestly carried forward. For our part (and I know for yours) we intend to shirk no responsibility which we have assumed under those decisions. I agree with you that we should not neglect any step calculated to demonstrate to the Soviet Government the vital importance of their doing likewise. It is for this reason and because of the magnitude of the issues involved that I consider it essential to base ourselves squarely on the Crimea decisions themselves and not allow any other considerations, no matter how important, to cloud the issue at this time. I have this particularly in mind with respect to the Polish negotiations.

You will recall that the agreement on Poland at Yalta was a compromise between the Soviet position that the Lublin Government should merely be "enlarged" and our contention that we should start with a clean slate and assist in the formation of an entirely new Polish Government. The wording of the resulting agreement reflects this compromise but if we attempt to evade the fact that we placed, as clearly shown in the agreement, somewhat more emphasis on the Lublin Poles than on the other two groups from which the new Government is to be drawn I feel we will expose ourselves to the charge that we are attempting to go back on the Crimean decision. It by no means follows, however, and on this we must be adamant, that because of this advantage the Lublin group can in any way arrogate to itself the right to determine what Poles from the other two groups are to be brought in for consultation. For the foregoing reasons I feel strongly that we should first of all bring the matter to a head on the question that falls clearly within the Yalta agreement, namely, our right to call for consultation a group of Polish leaders that are truly representative and that it is for the Commission and the Commission alone to decide which Poles are representative. Our Ambassadors in Moscow appear to be in agreement that we should proceed on the basis of their redraft, designed to reconcile our basic instructions with the points put forward by Molotov. They will at the same time make it absolutely clear that we have not receded in the slightest from the other points in our instructions of March 19 and shall revert to them at a later stage.

I do feel the other questions of procedure and the proper time for reopening the other points can be safely left to our Ambassadors. They know exactly what we think and feel on the entire question and I am personally completely confident that under no circumstances will they take any step or agree to anything which would impair the objectives we both seek. For example, I believe that if we can get Soviet agreement to the principle that the Commission and the Commission alone shall determine what Poles shall be invited for consultation and a definite list is drawn up and invitations issued then consultation with the Lublin Poles first might even afford certain advantages. They could be told how we interpret the Yalta decision and thus avoid the danger of having the question of interpretation become a matter of dispute between the Polish groups themselves. I feel subject to your approval that our Ambassadors should proceed along this line to bring our differences with Molotov into sharp focus without waiting for us to concert our messages to Stalin. Averell is ready to go ahead on this basis if we can obtain your concurrence which I earnestly hope you will give.

I agree with you, however, that the time has come to take up directly with Stalin the broader aspects of the Soviet attitude (with particular reference to Poland) and my immediate following telegram will contain the text of the message I propose to send.

I hope you will let me have your reaction as soon as possible. Roosevelt [WDL, State Dept.]

[MR*. *FRUS*, 1945, V, 189–90. *R&C*.]

In this case, as with most of the Roosevelt-to-Churchill messages sent after the Yalta meeting, the Map Room log sheet does not indicate that the President made any alterations to the draft sent to him by Admiral Leahy and the State Department. A few minor changes are noted on a copy of that draft, but they appear to be in Leahy's handwriting. Those amendments are noted below. The changes could have been made at the President's request, although past log sheets noted when Roosevelt had asked for changes.

R–730

Washington [via U.S. Navy]
Mar. 29, 1945, 1959 Z

Top Secret and Personal from the President for the Prime Minister.
Following is my suggested message to Stalin:

QUOTE. I cannot conceal from you the concern with which I view the development of events of mutual interest since our fruitful meeting at Yalta. The decisions we reached there were good ones and have for the most part been welcomed with enthusiasm by the peoples of the world who saw in your ability to find a common basis of understanding the best pledge for a secure and peaceful world after this war. Precisely because of the hopes and expectations that these decisions raised their fulfillment is being followed with the closest attention. We have no right to let them be disappointed. So far there has been a discouraging lack of progress made in the carrying out, which the world expects, of the political decisions which we reached at the Conference particularly those relating to the Polish question. I am frankly puzzled as to why this should be and must tell you that I do not fully understand in many respects the <u>apparent indifferent</u> attitude of your Government. Having understood each other so well at Yalta I am convinced that the three of us can and will clear away any obstacles which have developed since then. I intend, therefore, in this message to lay before you with complete frankness the problem as I see it.

Although I have in mind primarily the difficulties which the Polish negotiations have encountered, I must make a brief mention of our agreement embodied in the declaration on liberated Europe. I frankly cannot understand why the recent developments in Rumania should be regarded as not falling within the terms of that agreement. I hope you will find time personally to examine the correspondence between our Governments on this subject.

However, the part of our agreements at Yalta which has aroused the greatest popular interest and is the most urgent relates to the Polish question. You are aware of course that the Commission which we set up has made no progress. I feel this is due to the interpretation which your Government is placing upon the Crimean decisions. In order that there shall be no misunderstanding I set forth below my interpretation of the points of the agreement which are pertinent to the difficulties encountered by the Commission in Moscow.

In the discussions that have taken place so far your Government appears to take the position that the new Polish Provisional Government of National Unity which we agreed should be formed should be little more than a continuation of the present Warsaw Government. I cannot reconcile this either with our agreement or our discussions. While it is true that the Lublin Government is to be reorganized and its members play a prominent role it is to be done in such a fashion as to bring into being a new Government. This point is clearly brought out in several places in the text of the agreement. I must make it quite plain to you that any such solution which would result in a thinly disguised continuance of the present Warsaw regime would be unacceptable and would cause the people of the United States to regard the Yalta agreement as ~~a fraud~~ having failed. It is equally apparent that for the same reason the Warsaw Government cannot under the agreement claim the right to select or reject what Poles are to be brought to Moscow by the Commission for consultation. Can we not agree that it is up to the Commission to select the Polish leaders to come to Moscow to consult in the first instance and invitations be sent out accordingly. If this could be done I see no great objection to having the Lublin group come first in order that they may be fully acquainted with the agreed interpretation of the Yalta decisions on this point. In order to facilitate the agreement the Commission might first of all select a small but representative group of Polish leaders who could suggest other names for the consideration of the Commission. We have not and would not bar or veto any candidate for consultation which Mr. Molotov might propose being confident that he would not suggest any Poles who would be inimical to the intent of the Crimean decision. I feel that it is not too much to ask that my Ambassador be accorded the same confidence. It is obvious to me that if the right of the Commission to select these Poles is limited or shared with the Warsaw Government the very foundation on which our agreement rests would be destroyed. While the foregoing are the immediate obstacles which in my opinion have prevented the Commission from making any progress in this vital matter there are two other suggestions which were not in the agreement but nevertheless have a very important bearing on the result we all seek. Neither of these suggestions has been as yet accepted by your Government. I refer to (1) that there should be the maximum of political tranquility in Poland and that dissident groups should cease any measures and countermeasures against each other. That we should respectively use our influence to that end seems to me so eminently reasonable. (2) It would also seem entirely natural in view of the responsibilities placed upon them by the agreement that representatives of the American and British members of the Commission should be permitted to visit Poland.

I wish I could convey to you how important it is for the successful development of our program of international collaboration that this Polish question be settled fairly and speedily. If this is not done all of the difficulties and dangers to Allied unity which we had so much in mind in reaching our decision at the Crimea will face us in an even more acute form. You are, I am sure, aware that genuine popular support in the United States is required to carry out any Government policy foreign or domestic. The American people make up their own mind and no Governmental action can change it. I mention this fact because the last sentence of your message about Mr. Molotov's attendance at San Francisco made me wonder whether you give full weight to this factor. UNQUOTE.

Roosevelt [WDL, State Dept.]

[MR*. *WSC*, VI, 743–45. *FDR/Stalin*, doc. 284.]

Bernard Baruch's mission is discussed in the headnote to R–720. The Prime Minister's wife, Clementine, visited the Soviet Union as a representative of the "Aid to Russia" fund, administered by the British Red Cross.

Churchill was far too optimistic about Roosevelt's health. Four days at Hyde Park had not restored the President's energy, and he decided that a complete rest was needed. He stopped in Washington long enough to sign four cables to Churchill and hold some luncheon meetings, and then proceeded by train to Warm Springs, Georgia. This telegram from Churchill was forwarded there.

C–927

London [via U.S. Army]
Mar. 30, 1945, 1851 Z / TOR 2139 Z

Prime Minister to President Roosevelt. Personal and Top Secret.

I am delighted to see from the abundance of messages I have received from you this morning that you are back in Washington and in such vigour. I saw Bernie yesterday and he is coming tonight for the weekend. He seems in great form. As you know, I think he is a very wise man. Winant is coming tomorrow. Clemmie is in flight for Moscow and will be flying about there for at least a month, all of which hangs on my mind. By the way, did you ever receive a telegram from me of a purely private character, No. 914? It required no answer. But I should like to know that you received it. I will now address myself to our joint business.

[MR*. p*WSC*, VI, 431. p*R&C*.]

The American decision to ask Stalin personally to accept the Anglo-American interpretation of the Yalta agreements on Poland was a major step toward a confrontation with the Soviet Union, but the British wanted to go a little further and use stronger language.

C–928

London [via U.S. Army]
Mar. 30, 1945, 1851 Z / TOR 2139 Z

Prime Minister to President Roosevelt. Personal and Top Secret.

1. Thank you for your 729 and 730. I am glad you agree that the time has come for us both to address Stalin directly. We consider the draft in your 730 is a grave and weighty document and, although there are a few points in which it does not give full expression to our own views, we will whole-heartedly accept it and I will also endorse it in my parallel message to Stalin, the text of which I will send you before it goes.

2. Perhaps however before deciding on your final text you would consider the importance of making it clear that we shall not enter into any arrangements with the Lublinites before the arrival of our own Poles. There is no harm in discussing with the Lublinites, but I am sure that Mikolajczyk for instance will stipulate that the field shall be open when he arrives. We should be glad if you would provide for this in your draft.

3. More important still is to get rid of Molotov's veto on our candidates. You indicate this in a most polite manner, but would it not be well to emphasize the point by adding a sentence at the appropriate place to the effect that none of the three of us should veto each other's candidates? Otherwise he will simply veto every one that the Lublin Poles wish him to.

4. Finally, could you not mention in the last paragraph of your draft that it was Molotov himself who originally made the suggestion of observers?

5. I do not ask you to delay the dispatch of your draft on account of these desired additions by us. We leave it in your hands. Meanwhile I agree that our two Ambassadors should give Molotov the redraft of the latter's basic principles, making it clear in doing so that we have not receded in the slightest from the other points in our instructions of March 19th and will revert to them at a later stage.

[MR*. *FRUS*, 1945, V, 190–91. *R&C*.]

Churchill's own message to Stalin was even stronger than the President's and indicated that the British government would not compromise on the Polish question.

C–929

London [via U.S. Army]
Mar. 31, 1945, 1040 Z / TOR 1403 Z

Prime Minister to President Roosevelt. Personal and Top Secret.

Following is text of message I propose to send to Stalin. Please let me know what you think. I will not send it off till I hear from you. Text begins:

Prime Minister to Marshal Stalin. Personal and Top Secret.

1. You will by now I hope have received the message from the President of the United States which he was good enough to show to me before he sent it.

It is now my duty on behalf of His Majesty's Government to assure you that the War Cabinet desire me to express to you our whole-hearted endorsement of this message of the President's, and that we associate ourselves with it in its entirety.

2. There are two or three points which I desire specially to emphasize. First, that we do not consider we have retained in the Moscow discussions the spirit of Yalta nor indeed, at points, the letter. It was never imagined by us that the commission we all three appointed with so much good will would not have been able to carry out their part swiftly and easily in a mood of give and take.

We certainly thought that a Polish Government "new" and "reorganized" would by now have been in existence, recognized by all the United Nations. This would have afforded a proof to the world of our capacity and resolve to work together for its future. It is still not too late to achieve this.

3. However, even before forming such a new and reorganized Polish Government, it was agreed by the commission that representative Poles should be summoned from inside Poland and from Poles abroad, not necessarily to take part in the government but merely for free and frank consultation.

Even this preliminary step cannot be taken because of the claim put forward to veto any invitation, even to the consultation, of which the Soviet or the Lublin Government do not approve. We can never agree to such a veto by any one of us three. This veto reaches its supreme example in the case of Monsieur Mikolajczyk who is regarded throughout the British and American world as the oustanding Polish figure outside Poland.

4. We also have learned with surprise and regret that Monsieur Molotov's spontaneous offer to allow observers or missions to enter Poland has now been withdrawn. We are therefore deprived of all means of checking for ourselves the information, often of a most

painful character, which is sent us almost daily by the Polish Government in London.

We do not understand why a veil of secrecy should thus be drawn over the Polish scene. We offer the fullest facilities to the Soviet Government to send missions or individuals to visit any of the territories in our military occupation.

In several cases this offer has been accepted by the Soviets and visits have taken place to mutual satisfaction. We ask that the principle of reciprocity shall be observed in these matters, which would help to make so good a foundation for our enduring partnership.

5. The President has also shown me messages which have passed between him and you about Monsieur Molotov's inability to be present at the conference at San Francisco. We had hoped the presence there of the three Foreign Ministers might have led to a clearance of many of the difficulties which have descended upon us in a storm since our happy and hopeful union at Yalta. We do not however question in any way the weight of the public reasons which make it necessary for him to remain in Russia.

6. Like the President, I too was struck with the concluding sentence of your message to him. What he says about the American people also applies to the British people and to the nations of the British Commonwealth with the addition that His Majesty's present advisers only hold office at the will of the Universal Suffrage Parliament.

If our efforts to reach an agreement about Poland are to be doomed to failure, I shall be bound to confess the fact to Parliament when they return from the Easter recess. No-one has pleaded the cause of Russia with more fervor and conviction than I have tried to do. I was the first to raise my voice on June 22, 1941.

It is more than a year since I proclaimed to a startled world the justice of the Curzon Line for Russia's western frontier, and this frontier has now been accepted by both the British Parliament and the President of the United States.

It is as a sincere friend of Russia that I make my personal appeal to you and to your colleagues to come to a good understanding about Poland with the western democracies and not to smite down the hands of comradeship in the future guidance of the world which we now extend.

[MR*. *FRUS*, 1945, V, 191–93. p*Stalin*/WSC, doc. 416. R&C.]

There is no log sheet to indicate the drafting history of this cable, but the style and phrasing is not typical of messages to Churchill written by Roosevelt himself. The telegram carefully avoids any discussion of the President's health, which was the question raised in Churchill's number 914.

As this cable noted, the war was going very well, particularly against the Germans in western Europe. General Patton's Third Army had crossed the Rhine at Oppenheim, and by March 28 three Allied armies under Field Marshal Montgomery's command had gone twenty miles east of the Rhine at Wesel. More important, Germany's ability to resist was obviously crumbling. In the Pacific, Iwo Jima fell to the Americans on March 26, providing a base for air operations against the Japanese mainland, and the attack against Okinawa was to begin on April 1.

R–731

Warm Springs, Ga. [via U.S. Navy]
Mar. 31, 1945, 2007 Z

From the President for the Prime Minister, Personal and Top Secret.

Your 927. I did receive your very pleasing message No. 914.

The efforts of Bernie, who is a wise man of wide experience, should be of much assistance to both of us.

We hope that Clemmie's long flying tour in Russia will first be safe and next be productive of good which I am sure it will be.

The war business today seems to be going very well from our point of view and we may now hope for the collapse of Hitlerism at an earlier date than had heretofore been anticipated. Roosevelt

[MR*. *WSC*, VI, 431. *R&C*.]

Drafted by Leahy, this message was approved by Roosevelt, apparently without change. Once again, the United States moved closer to the British position on the new Polish government.

R–732

Warm Springs, Ga. [via U.S. Navy]
Mar. 31, 1945; 0038 Z, Apr. 1

Personal and Top Secret, for the Prime Minister from the President.

Thank you for your 928 of March 30 in regard to my proposed message to Stalin. I am very pleased to find that we are in such substantial agreement. I have carefully considered the helpful suggestions that you have made, and I am making the following three additions to cover the points you raise.

In regard to the point raised in your paragraph 2 I am adding immediately after the words QUOTE Yalta decisions on this point UNQUOTE the following sentence: QUOTE It is of course understood that if the Lublin group comes first no arrangements would be made independently with them before the arrival of the other Polish leaders called for consultation. UNQUOTE.

In your paragraph 3 after the words QUOTE accorded the same confidence UNQUOTE, I am adding the phrase QUOTE and that any candidate for consultation presented by any one of the Commission be accepted by the others in good faith UNQUOTE.

In regard to your point 4 after the words QUOTE permitted to visit Poland UNQUOTE, I would add the following sentence: QUOTE As you will recall Mr. Molotov himself suggested this at an early meeting of the Commission and only subsequently withdrew it UNQUOTE.

I have just received your 929, and as I concur in your proposed message I have sent mine to Stalin with the foregoing additions. Roosevelt [WDL]

[MR*. *FRUS*, 1945, V, 193. R&C.]

C–930

London [via U.S. Army]
Apr. 1, 1945, 1312 Z / TOR 1555 Z

Prime Minister to President Roosevelt. Personal and Top Secret.
Your 732. I am delighted with our being in such perfect step. I have bunged off my 929 to the Bear [Stalin].

[MR*]

Although the British had come to assume that the goal of Eisenhower's offensive was to capture Berlin—an assumption which was strengthened during the Malta Conference when General Marshall stated that the overall plan was to drive into Germany along a broad front in the northwest—the objective was actually to destroy German armed resistance. Rumors of a Nazi withdrawal to a mountain "redoubt" in the south, the presence of a Soviet force of almost one million men along the Oder River near Berlin, favorable terrain in central Germany, and a nagging fear that simultaneous Allied and Soviet attacks on Berlin might lead to incidents between the wartime partners—all prompted Eisenhower to direct General Omar Bradley's Twelfth Army Group to move toward Leipzig, where it could link up with the Soviets and cut Germany in two. The British disliked the decision, for it not only diminished the role to be played by Field Marshal Montgomery's Twenty-First Army Group, but also failed to consider the British desire to control the North Sea/ Baltic Sea coast at war's end. That feeling of annoyance increased when General Eisenhower took the unusual step of sending a message directly to Stalin, outlining the Allied military plan. Possibly motivated by a cable from Stalin to Churchill in which the Soviet leader had complained that he lacked information about Allied military operations, Eisenhower told Stalin that the Allies planned an attack toward Leipzig and wanted to "coordinate our action" and "perfect the liaison between our advancing forces" (*Eisenhower Papers*, IV, 2539–40n, 2551).

Churchill's initial objections were to the military wisdom of a swing toward the south, particularly since Eisenhower did not fully explain his decision to the British Chiefs of Staff (COS), but the political aspects of the failure to move on Berlin soon seemed even more important. In the exchanges which followed, the American Joint Chiefs staunchly defended Eisenhower against what seemed like a renewal of British attacks on the Supreme Commander. Churchill, in turn, took umbrage at what he viewed as less than full credit given to British victories.

C–931

London [via U.S. Army]
Apr. 1, 1945, 1800 Z / TOR 2227 Z

Prime Minister to President Roosevelt. Personal and Top Secret.

1. You will have read the telegrams between the British Chiefs of Staff and their United States colleagues, number COS (W) 723 from us and the U.S. COS reply CCS 805–2. I think there is some misunderstanding on both sides which I am anxious to disperse without more ado.

2. We are very much obliged to the U.S. COS for their Para. 9 which gives time for a reasonable interchange of views between our two Chiefs of Staff Committees.

3. I am however distressed to read in Para. 3 of CCS 805–2 that it should be thought that we wish in the slightest degree to discredit or lower the prestige of General Eisenhower in his increasingly important relations with the Russian Commanders in the field.

All we sought was a little time to consider the far-reaching changes desired by General Eisenhower in the plans that had been concerted by the Combined Chiefs of Staff at Malta and had received your and my joint approval. The British Chiefs of Staff were naturally concerned by a procedure which apparently left the fortunes of the British Army, which though only a third of yours still amounts to over a million men, to be settled without the slightest reference to any British authority. They also did not fully understand from General Eisenhower's 252 what actually was intended. In this we may be excused because [U.S. military attaché] General Deane was similarly puzzled and delayed delivery of General Eisenhower's message to Stalin for 24 hours in order to ask for background. I am in full agreement in this instance with the procedure proposed by your Chiefs of Staff in the last sentence of Para. 3 of 805–2 and I am sorry we did not think of it ourselves.

4. At this point I wish to place on record the complete confidence felt by His Majesty's Government in General Eisenhower, our pleasure that our armies are serving under his command and our admiration of the

great and shining qualities of character and personality which he has proved himself to possess in all the difficulties of handling an allied command. Moreover, I should like to express to you, Mr. President, as I have already done orally in the field to General Eisenhower, my heart-felt congratulations on the glorious victories and advances by all the armies of the United States centre in the recent battles on the Rhine and over it.

5. Having thus, I trust, removed to your satisfaction any misunderstanding of our action that may have given any cause of offence on our part, I should like to say that I thought that the implications of the references to the work of the British and Imperial forces in the northern advance in Para. 4 and in the second sentence of Para. 6 did not quite do justice to our efforts or contributions. Both at Caen in the Normandy battle and lately on the front north of Wesel, we have had the task of forming the hinge to the main American swing. Therefore it could not be expected that in discharging this duty very spectacular results could attend our indispensable action. In the Rhine battle we had to fight onwards alone in the northern hinge for 13 days longer than was arranged on account of the opening of the dams by the Germans which inevitably delayed the coming into action of the Ninth U.S. Army. During this period it was natural that the enemy should transfer as many paratroops and other corps d'elite as possible to confront us, and this conjoined with the state of the ground and the weather made our effort a very hard one. From February 9th, when we began, down to March 30th (the latest date of which I have figures) the 12 or 13 divisions of His Majesty's forces which were engaged suffered a loss of over 20,000 casualties. I do not think any of the American armies to the southward suffered more, and some of them, thank God, suffered very much less. Therefore I feel sure that you will not feel discontented with our efforts and that the actual speed of our advance to date will not be contrasted invidiously with the splendid advances made by the United States Armies in the centre. We even think we may have aided them by our work, and we hope that now we are in the open plains of northern Germany we may be able to move more rapidly.

6. Having dealt with and I trust disposed of these misunderstandings between the truest friends and comrades that ever fought side by side as allies, I venture to put to you a few considerations upon the merits of the changes in our original plans now desired by General Eisenhower. It seems to me the differences are small and as usual not of principle but of emphasis. Obviously, laying aside every impediment and shunning every diversion, the allied armies of the north and centre should now march at the highest speed towards the Elbe. Hitherto the axis has been upon Berlin. General Eisenhower on his estimate of the enemy's resist-

ance, to which I attach the greatest importance, now wishes to shift the axis somewhat to the southward and strike through Leipzig, even perhaps as far south as Dresden. He withdraws the Ninth U. S. Army from the northern group of armies and in consequence stretches its front southwards. I should be sorry if the resistance of the enemy was such as to destroy the weight and momentum of the advance of the British Twenty First Army Group and to leave them in an almost static condition along the Elbe when and if they reach it. I say quite frankly that Berlin remains of high strategic importance. Nothing will exert a psychological effect of despair upon all German forces of resistance equal to that of the fall of Berlin. It will be the supreme signal of defeat to the German people. On the other hand, if left to itself to maintain a seige by the Russians among its ruins and as long as the German flag flies there, it will animate the resistance of all Germans under arms.

7. There is moreover another aspect which it is proper for you and me to consider. The Russian armies will no doubt overrun all Austria and enter Vienna. If they also take Berlin, will not their impression that they have been the overwhelming contributor to our common victory be unduly imprinted in their minds, and may this not lead them into a mood which will raise grave and formidable difficulties in the future? I therefore consider that from a political standpoint we should march as far east into Germany as possible and that should Berlin be in our grasp we should certainly take it. This also appears sound on military grounds.

8. To sum up, the difference that might exist between General Eisenhower's new plans and those we advocated, and which were agreed upon beforehand, would seem to be the following, viz, whether the emphasis should be put on an axis directed on Berlin or on one directed upon Leipzig and Dresden. This is surely a matter upon which a reasonable latitude of discussion should be allowed to our two Chiefs of Staff Committees before any final commitment involving the Russians is entered into.

9. I need hardly say that I am quite willing that this message, which is my own personal message to you and not a Staff communication, should be shown to General Marshall.

[MR*. pWSC, VI, 464–65. pR&C.]

In spite of his admission that the Soviet Union had lived up to its promise not to interfere in Greece, Churchill had no intention of asking the Soviets to come in through the front door. But it was not just the Russian bear which worried the Prime Minister. Roosevelt's proposal indicated that American business was interested in the Greek market, and Churchill's suggestion for a joint Anglo-American committee to dispense financial and economic advice to the Greek government suggests that the British wanted to make sure that the United States did not operate alone.

UNRRA, the United Nations Relief and Rehabilitation Administration, had been established to provide only direct relief to areas destroyed by the war. Roosevelt and the Congress had steadfastly opposed any attempt to make UNRRA a vehicle for postwar reconstruction.

C–932

London [via U.S. Army]
Apr. 3, 1945, 1045 Z / TOR 1350 Z, Apr. 5 [3?]

Prime Minister to President Roosevelt, Personal and Top Secret.

I am attracted by the suggestion in your No. 723 that a high-powered economic mission should visit Greece, but I am rather doubtful whether this is an appropriate moment to bring the Russians in. We cannot expect any help from the Russians in the economic sphere, and to include them in the mission would be a purely political gesture. As such, it might be valuable if we could be sure that the Russian representative would behave correctly and make a public demonstration of his solidarity with our policy, but this assumption seems very doubtful. There is the further disadvantage that at a time when the Russians are firmly excluding both you and us from any say in the affairs of Roumania, it would be rather odd to invite them unsolicited to assume some degree of responsibility in Greek affairs.

2. We have ourselves been giving some thought to the future Allied organisation in Greece. I am, of course, most anxious to reduce the number of British troops in the country at the earliest possible moment, but it is clear that this will not be the end of our responsibility there. In fact the Greek Government must for some time be given advice and guidance in many spheres of the administration if they are to govern the country effectively. Without this help, they will be unable to resume control throughout the country, and the withdrawal of our forces may be seriously delayed.

3. Advice for the Greek Government has hitherto been provided mainly under the authority of General Scobie as general officer commanding British troops in Greece. We hope, however, that the "operational phase" is now over and it therefore seems appropriate that Scobie should be relieved of many of the responsibilities which he has so far borne, and that these should be transferred to our two Embassies where they more properly belong. As you will know, it is proposed that UNRRA should take over relief work from the military on April 1, and this seemed to be a convenient date on which the other changes could be made. The War Cabinet have therefore agreed that on the British side the Embassy will be responsible as from April 1 for ten[d]ering advice to the Greek Gov-

ernment. This advice will be particularly important on economic and financial questions, and I much hope that we can count on the continued collaboration of the United States Embassy in Athens. If you agree, I suggest that a joint Anglo-American committee should be established, comprising the appropriate British and American experts and responsible to our two Embassies. Although members of this committee have not been invited by the Greek Government to advise, I have no doubt that they will in fact exercise great influence over the economic and financial policies of the Greek Government.

4. I feel that this committee should be set in motion before we consider sending a mission on the lines you suggest. A further reason for postponement would be in order to see how the transference of relief from the military authorities to UNRRA works out. Once all this new machinery has begun to work, a high-powered mission on the lines you suggest might do great good by smoothing out difficulties and getting things moving. By that time we might also have resolved the troubles in Roumania and be in a position to invite the Russians to join the mission.

5. We should, of course, welcome the assistance of Donald Nelson at any time, and if it convenient for him to visit Greece now, I would certainly not suggest that he should delay his journey until a full Allied mission can be sent. The problems to be overcome in Greece are so formidable and urgent that his presence there even for a short visit would be of the greatest value.

[MR*. *FRUS*, 1945, VIII, 205–6. *R&C*.]

Eisenhower's instructions to his army group commanders (*Eisenhower Papers*, IV, 2576–77) ordered the Central Group to "launch a thrust with its main axis: Kassel–Leipzig." The Northern Group (British and Canadian) was to guard the northern flank of the Central Group, although it was to be ready to seize a bridgehead across the Elbe and prepare to advance east of that river.

No log sheet is attached to the Map Room copy of this message, but Churchill claimed in his memoirs that General Marshall had handled this issue. Certainly the final sentence is not typical of the informal, personal closings Roosevelt frequently added to his messages.

R–733

Warm Springs, Ga. [via U.S. Navy]
Apr. 4, 1945, 1824 Z

Top Secret and Personal from the President to the Prime Minister.

I have given your personal message No. 931 a very careful reading and have gone over the various papers involved, some of which I had not previously read. Further, I have just received a copy of Eisenhower's directive to his Army Group Commanders, dated April 2.

I personally, as you do, deplore any misunderstanding between us in general, particularly at a time of great victories by our Armies. I think you have misunderstood the presentation of the American Chiefs of Staff regarding the matter of Eisenhower's prestige and especially regarding the achievements of the 21st Army Group. In the first instance they were endeavoring to make a point in their argument by enunciating a military principle well known to us all, and not making any accusation.

Regarding the implications that you find in the references to the 21st Army Group, I know that in general the same explanation can be given; the U.S. Chiefs of Staff were discussing a problem in possibly too technical a manner, without going into details with which we are all familiar as to the character of the military obstacles, the strength and quality of the German opposing forces, etc.

As to the "far-reaching changes desired by General Eisenhower in the plans that had been concerted by the Combined Chiefs of Staff at Malta and had received your and my joint approval," I do not get the point. For example, the strength and all the resources agreed upon for the northern Group of Armies were made available to Montgomery. Following the unexpected Remagen bridgehead and the destruction of the German Armies in the Saar Basin there developed so great a weakness on those fronts that the secondary efforts realized an outstanding success. This fact must have a very important relation to the further conduct of the battle. However, General Eisenhower's directive of April 2, it seems to me, does all and possibly a little more to the north than was anticipated at Malta. Liepzig is not far removed from Berlin which is well within the center of the combined effort. At the same time the British Army is given what seems to me very logical objectives on the northern flank.

As to the Ninth Army, it is a matter of record that Eisenhower previously placed the Ninth Army and a large portion of the First Army under Field Marshal Montgomery during the Ardennes affair; he again placed or continued the Ninth Army under the command of Montgomery for the crossing of the Rhine. In all probability he intends to again place the Ninth Army under Montgomery for the operation to the north once the general advance has broken through the German resistance.

I appreciate your generous expressions of confidence in Eisenhower and I have always been deeply appreciative of the backing you have given him and the fact that you yourself proposed him for this command. I regret that the phrasing of a formal discussion should have so disturbed you but I regret even more that at the moment of a great victory by our combined forces we should become involved in such unfortunate reactions.

It appears reasonable to expect that under Eisenhower's present plans the great German Army will in the very near future be completely broken up into separate resistance groups, while our forces will remain tactically intact and in a position to destroy in detail the separated parts of the Nazi Army.

You have my assurance of every cooperation. Roosevelt [GCM?]

[MR*. R&C.]

Stalin was quite correct in claiming that negotiations had taken place between a German commander and Allen Dulles, and other Allied representatives. In one sense those talks were only exploratory, for Dulles and his superiors feared that General Wolff promised more than he could deliver when he hinted that the commander of German forces in Italy, Field Marshal Albert Kesselring, was willing to discuss surrender terms. On the other hand, Wolff did hope to establish some conditions to any further discussions. Stalin was quite incorrect, however, when he claimed that Kesselring had agreed to cease resistance and permit Anglo-American forces to march eastward, even though that was Churchill's secret hope. In fact, the entire SUNRISE/CROSS-WORD talks proved to be fool's gold. Wolff could never gain support from regular German Army commanders, and Allied negotiators, eager for a settlement in what had become the forgotten theater of the war, grasped too quickly at straws. Roosevelt had told Stalin that the entire controversy stood "in an atmosphere of regrettable apprehension and mistrust," but he never addressed directly the Soviet Premier's main question—why were Soviet representatives excluded from the Bern talks? (*FRUS*, 1945, III, 740–41.) German actions and propaganda had made it evident that they feared the Soviets far more than the British and Americans, and that fear prompted the High Command to concentrate German defenses on the Russian front. That, combined with a longstanding suspicion that the West would negotiate a separate peace with Germany and then turn on the Soviet Union, caused Stalin to exaggerate the importance of the Bern talks. As a result, he sent this extraordinarily blunt cable in which he virtually accused Roosevelt of being a liar—diplomatically phrased as "not fully informed."

R–734

Warm Springs, Ga. [via U.S. Navy]
Apr. 4, 1945, 2058 Z

Top Secret and Personal from the President for the Prime Minister.

The following message from Stalin dated 3 April and my reply thereto are quoted for your information:

QUOTE. Marshal Stalin to President.

I have received your message on the question of negotiations in Bern. You are absolutely right that in connection with the affair regarding negotiations of the Anglo-American Command with the German Command somewhere in Bern or some other place "has developed an atmosphere of fear and distrust deserving regrets."

You insist that there have been no negotiations yet.

It may be assumed that you have not yet been fully informed. As regards my military colleagues, they, on the basis of data which they have on hand, do not have any doubts, that the negotiations have taken place and that they have ended in an agreement with the Germans, on the basis of which the German commander on the Western Front—Marshal Kesselring, has agreed to open the front and permit the Anglo-American troops to advance to the East, and the Anglo-Americans have promised in return to ease for the Germans the peace terms.

I think that my colleagues are close to truth. Otherwise one could not have understood the fact that the Anglo-Americans have refused to admit to Bern representatives of the Soviet Command for participation in the negotiations with the Germans.

I also cannot understand the silence of the British who have allowed you to correspond with me on this unpleasant matter, and they themselves remain silent, although it is known that the initiative in this whole affair with the negotiations in Bern belongs to the British.

I understand that there are certain advantages for the Anglo-American troops as a result of these separate negotiations in Bern or some other place since the Anglo-American troops get the possibility to advance into the heart of Germany almost without resistance on the part of the Germans, but why was it necessary to conceal this from the Russians, and why your Allies—the Russians, were not notified?

As a result of this at the present moment the Germans on the Western front in fact have ceased the war against England and the United States. At the same time the Germans continue the war with Russia, the Ally of England and the United States. It is understandable that such a situation can in no way serve the cause of preservation of the strengthening of trust between our countries.

I have already written to you in my previous message and consider it necessary to repeat it here that I personally and my colleagues would have never made such a risky step, being aware that a momentary advantage, no matter what it would be, is fading before the principle advantage on the preservation and strengthing of trust among the Allies. UNQUOTE.

QUOTE. President to Stalin.

I have received with astonishment your message of April 3 containing an allegation that arrangements which were made between Field Mashals Alexander and Kesselring at Bern, "permitted the Anglo-American troops to advance to the East and the Anglo-Americans promised in return to ease for the Germans the peace terms."

In my previous messages to you in regard to the attempts made in Bern to arrange a conference to discuss a surrender of the German Army in Italy, I have told you that,

(1) No negotiations were held in Bern;
(2) That the meeting had no political implications whatever;
(3) That in any surrender of the enemy army in Italy there could be no violation of our agreed principle of unconditional surrender;
(4) That Soviet officers would be welcomed at any meeting that might be arranged to discuss surrender.

For the advantage of our common war effort against Germany, which today gives excellent promise of an early success in a disintegration of the German armies, I must continue to assume that you have the same high confidence in my truthfulness and reliability that I have always had in yours.

I have also a full appreciation of the effect your gallant army has had in making possible a crossing of the Rhine by the forces under General Eisenhower and the effect that your forces will have hereafter on the eventual collapse of the German resistance to our combined attacks.

I have complete confidence in General Eisenhower and know that he certainly would inform me before entering into any agreement with the Germans. He is instructed to demand and will demand unconditional surrender of enemy troops that may be defeated on his front. Our advances on the Western Front are due to military action. Their speed has been attributable mainly to the terrific impact of our air power resulting in destruction of German communications, and to the fact that Eisenhower was able to cripple the bulk of the German Forces on the Western front while they were still West of the Rhine.

I am certain that there were no negotiations in Bern at any time, and I feel that your information to that effect must have come from German sources which have made persistent efforts to create dissension between us in order to escape in some measure for responsibility for their war crimes. If that was Wolff's purpose in Bern your message proves that he has had some success.

With a confidence in your belief in my personal reliability and in my determination to bring about together with you an unconditional surrender of the Nazis, it is astonishing that a belief seems to have reached the Soviet Government that I have entered into an agreement with the enemy without first obtaining your full agreement.

Finally I would say this, it would be one of the great tragedies of history if at the very moment of the victory, now within our grasp, such distrust, such lack of faith should prejudice the entire undertaking after the collossal losses of life, materiel and treasure involved.

Frankly I cannot avoid a feeling of bitter resentment toward your informers, whoever they are, for such vile misrepresentations of my actions or those of my trusted subordinates. UNQUOTE.

Roosevelt [WDL]

[MR*. *FRUS*, 1945, III, 742–43, 745–46. *WSC*, VI, 446–49. *Stalin/FDR*, docs. 286, 287.]

Churchill still would have liked an all-out thrust toward Berlin, but no one could accept defeat more gracefully than he, when he chose to do so. Roosevelt's Map Room staff translated the Latin quotation as "Lovers' quarrels always go with true love."

C–933

London [via U.S. Army]
Apr. 5, 1945, 2015 Z / TOR 0045 Z, Apr. 6

Prime Minister to President Roosevelt. Personal and Top Secret.
    Your No. 733.
    I still think it was a pity that Eisenhower's telegram was sent to Stalin without anything being said to our Chiefs of Staff or to our deputy, Air Chief Marshal Tedder, to [or] to our Commander-in-Chief, Field Marshal Montgomery. The changes in the main plan have now turned out to be very much less than we at first supposed. My personal relations with General Eisenhower are of the most friendly character. I regard the matter as closed and to prove my sincerity I will use one of my very few Latin quotations, "Amantium irae amoris integratio est".

[MR*. *WSC*, VI, 468.]

There was no mistaking Churchill's anger at Stalin's tone in complaining to Roosevelt about the Bern talks. At the same time, Stalin's message gave the Prime Minister another opportunity to push the President toward a harder line. Churchill's fears that the Soviets would refuse to permit the British and

Americans into their zones in Austria proved unfounded, although the issue was not formally resolved until July.

C–934

London [via U.S. Army]
Apr. 5, 1945, 2030 Z / TOR 0045 Z

Prime Minister to President Roosevelt. Personal and Top Secret.
Your No. 734.

1. I am astounded that Stalin should have addressed to you a message so insulting to the honour of the United States and also of Great Britain. His Majesty's Government cordially associate themselves with your reply and the War Cabinet have instructed me to send to Stalin the message in my immediately following.

2. There is very little doubt in my mind that the Soviet leaders, whoever they may be, are surprised and disconcerted at the rapid advance of the Allied armies in the west and the almost total defeat of the enemy on our front especially as they say they are themselves in no position to deliver a decisive attack before the middle of May. All this makes it the more important that we should join hands with the Russian armies as far to the east as possible and if circumstances allow, enter Berlin.

3. I may remind you that we proposed and thought we had arranged six weeks ago provisional zones of occupation in Austria, but since Yalta the Russians have sent no confirmation of these zones. Now that they are on the eve of taking Vienna and very likely will occupy the whole of Austria, it may well be prudent for us to hold as much as possible in the north.

4. We must always be anxious lest the brutality of the Russian messages does not foreshadow some deep change of policy for which they are preparing. On the whole I incline to think it is no more than their natural expression when vexed or jealous. For that very reason I deem it of the highest importance that a firm and blunt stand should be made at this juncture by our two countries in order that the air may be cleared and they realize that there is a point beyond which we will not tolerate insult. I believe this is the best chance of saving the future. If they are ever convinced that we are afraid of them and can be bullied into submission, then indeed I should despair of our future relations with them and much else.

[MR*. *FRUS*, 1945, III, 746–47. p*WSC*, VI, 449. *R&C*.]

Churchill minced no words in rebutting Soviet accusations of bad faith, but, like Roosevelt, he never addressed the question of why the Soviets were not permitted to attend the Bern discussions.

C–935

London [via U.S. Army]
Apr. 5, 1945, 2125 Z / TOR 0045 Z

Prime Minister to President Roosevelt. Personal and Top Secret.
Following is text of my telegram to Stalin referred to in my immediately preceding telegram:

"Prime Minister to Marshal Stalin. Personal and Top Secret.
1. The President has sent me his correspondence with you about the contacts made in Switzerland between a British and an American officer on Field Marshal Alexander's staff and a German General named Wolff relating to possible surrender of Kesselring's army in northern Italy. I therefore deem it right to send you a precise summary of the action of His Majesty's Government. As soon as we learned of these contacts we immediately informed the Soviet Government on March 12th and we and the United States Government have faithfully reported to you everything that has taken place. The sole and only business mentioned or referred to in any way in Switzerland was to test the credentials of the German emissary and try to arrange a meeting between a nominee of Kesselring's, with Field Marshal Alexander at his headquarters or some convenient point in northern Italy. There were no negotiations in Switzerland even for a military surrender of Kesselring's army. Still less did any political-military plot, as alleged in your telegram to the President, enter into our thoughts, which are not as suggested of so dishonourable a character.
2. Your representatives were immediately invited to the meeting we attempted to arrange in Italy. Had it taken place and had your representatives come, they would have heard every word that passed.
3. We consider that Field Marshal Alexander has full right to accept the surrender of the German army of 25 divisions on his front in Italy and to discuss such matters with German envoys who have the power to settle the terms of capitulation. Nevertheless we took especial care to invite your representatives to this purely military discussion at his headquarters should it take place. In fact however nothing resulted from any contacts in Switzerland. Our officers returned from Switzerland without having succeeded in fixing a rendezvous in Italy for Kesselring's emissaries to come to. Of all this the

Soviet Government have been fully informed step by step by Field Marshal Alexander or by Sir Archibald Clark Kerr, as well as through United States channels. I repeat that no negotiations of any kind were entered into or even touched upon, formally or informally, in Switzerland.

4. There is however a possibility that the whole of this request to parley by German General Wolff was one of those attempts which are made by the enemy with the object of sowing distrust between allies. Field Marshal Alexander made this point in a telegram sent on March 11th in which he remarks, "Please note that two of the leading figures are S.S. and Himmler men which makes me very suspicious". This telegram was repeated to the British Ambassador in Moscow on the 12th of March for communication to the Soviet Government. If to sow distrust between us was the German intention, it has certainly for the moment been successful.

5. Sir Archibald Clark Kerr was instructed by Mr. Eden to explain the whole position to M. Molotov in his letter of March 21st. The reply of March 22nd handed to him from M. Molotov contained the following expression: "In this instance the Soviet Government sees not a misunderstanding but something worse". It also complains that, "In Berne for two weeks behind the backs of the Soviet Union, which is bearing the brunt of the war against Germany, negotiations have been going on between representatives of the German military command on the one hand and representatives of English and American commands on the other". In the interests of Anglo-Russian relations, His Majesty's Government decided not to make any reply to this most wounding and unfounded charge but to ignore it. This is the reason for what you call in your message to the President, "The silence of the British". We thought it better to keep silent than to respond to such a message as was sent by M. Molotov, but you may be sure that we were astonished by it and affronted that M. Molotov should impute such conduct to us. This however in no way affected our instruction to Field Marshal Alexander to keep you fully informed.

6. Neither is it true that the initiative in this matter came as you state to the President wholly from the British. In fact the information given to Field Marshal Alexander that the German General Wolff wished to make a contact in Switzerland was brought to him by an American agency.

7. There is no connection whatever between any contacts at Berne or elsewhere with the total defeat of the German armies on the western front. They have in fact fought with great obstinancy and inflicted upon us and the American armies since the opening of our February offensive up to March 28th upwards of 87,000 casualties.

However being outnumbered on the ground and literally overwhelmed in the air by the vastly superior Anglo-American air forces, which in the month of March alone dropped over 200,000 tons of bombs on Germany, the German armies in the west have been decisively broken. The fact that they were outnumbered on the ground in the west is due to the magnificent attacks and weight of the Soviet armies.

8. With regard to the charges which you have made in your message to the President of April 3rd, which also asperse His Majesty's Government, I associate myself and my colleagues with the last sentence of the President's reply."

[MR*. p*WSC*, VI, 449–51. *Stalin/WSC*, doc. 417.]

C–936

London [via U.S. Army]
Apr. 6, 1945, 1009 Z / TOR 1218 Z

Prime Minister to President Roosevelt. Personal and Top Secret.
My number 935.
In Paragraph eight of message to Stalin for "Charges which you have made" read "Charges which are made".

[MR*]

Roosevelt accepted Churchill's gracious acquiescence to Eisenhower's decision not to drive all-out for Berlin. Nonetheless, the President added an endorsement of the Supreme Allied Commander, probably at the suggestion of General Marshall.

R–735

Warm Springs, Ga. [via U.S. Navy]
Apr. 6, 1945, 1746 Z

Top Secret and Personal from the President for the Prime Minister.
Thank you for your 933. I completely subscribe to your Latin quotation.
Today, on our "Army Day," I have sent to Eisenhower a message of appreciation of his leadership and his great victories. [Roosevelt]

[MR*]

For the first time during the war, Roosevelt seemed to place politics ahead of military cooperation with the Soviet Union. The suggestion that the rapid advance of Anglo-American military forces would allow a "tougher" policy seemed to hint at support for Churchill's desire to confront the Soviets. But so cryptic a message as this does not mean that the President had finally accepted the idea of a postwar Soviet threat and was advocating an early form of military containment. This message merely endorsed the strong British protests over Soviet accusations stemming from the German surrender talks in Bern; it did not refer to the broader issue of eastern Europe and Soviet actions there. Moreover, it came right after Roosevelt had rejected Churchill's plea for a drive on Berlin and earlier proposals for Allied forces to move into Austria and Czechoslovakia. Nor was the language that of the President. The cable was drafted by Admiral Leahy, who supported pleas from Ambassador Harriman in Moscow and others for a change in policy toward the Soviet Union. Harriman believed that the Soviets understood only power, and that the United States should demand a quid pro quo for any aid. Sent to Warm Springs for Roosevelt's approval, the telegram was sent back to Washington without comment in only one hour and twenty-eight minutes, hardly time enough for Roosevelt to have reconsidered and redirected the entire thrust of his wartime and postwar policy toward the Soviet Union. In fact, one wonders if the President gave this message any consideration at all, particularly in view of his poor health.

R–736

Warm Springs, Ga. [via U.S. Navy]
Apr. 6, 1945, 1750 Z

Top Secret and Personal from the President for the Prime Minister.

I am in general agreement with your opinion expressed in 934, and I am pleased with your very clear strong message to Stalin No. 935.

We must not permit anybody to entertain a false impression that we are afraid.

Our Armies will in a very few days be in a position that will permit us to become "tougher" than has heretofore appeared advantageous to the war effort. [WDL]

[MR*. R&C.]

Anglo-American naval authorities had been quite concerned about two new German submarines (called types XXI and XXIII) which were capable of much faster underwater speeds than the older U-boats. A few did become operational before the end of the war, but the Allied bombing campaign damaged or destroyed most of the construction facilities. Danzig, a major port situated at the north end of the old Polish "corridor," had fallen to Soviet forces on March 30, 1945.

C-937

London [via U.S. Army]
Apr. 7, 1945, 0829 Z / TOR 1200 Z

Prime Minister to President Roosevelt. Personal and Top Secret.

There follows for your concurrence the draft of the anti-U-boat warfare statement for March. I am also consulting Mr. Mackenzie King.

"During March the U-boat effort continued to increase but fewer successes were obtained against our shipping than in February. Casualties inflicted on U-boats were again severe and the prolonged and extensive bombing and minelaying policy of the Allies has undoubtedly delayed the introduction of the new type U-boats. In a similar manner the capture of Danzig by the Soviet arms helps to cut off the evil at its source."

[MR*]

Drafted by the State Department and presumably approved without change by the President (there is no log sheet), this cable put the resolution of problems in Poland and eastern Europe ahead of attempts to involve the Soviets in collaborative programs in Greece. Therefore, the United States rejected the British proposal for a bilateral mission. Sir Reginald W. A. Leeper was the British Ambassador in Greece. (See headnote to R-723.)

R-737

Warm Springs, Ga. [via U.S. Navy]
Apr. 8, 1945, 0029 Z

Top Secret and Personal from the President for the Prime Minister.

I recognize the force of the observations on the Russian angle in your 932 and agree that it might be better not to go forward with a tripartite economic mission at the present time. On the other hand I think it would be a mistake to set up a bilateral mission. This would look as though we, for our part, were disregarding the Yalta decision for tripartite action in liberated areas and might easily be interpreted as indicating that we consider the Yalta decisions as no longer valid. Such is certainly not the case, as you know, and I therefore feel that we must be careful not to do anything that would weaken the effectiveness of our efforts to get the Russians to honor those decisions on their side.

Our Ambassador at Athens recently put up to us, at the instance of Mr. Leeper, the suggestion of a joint Anglo-American committee of experts, responsible to our two Embassies, to advise the Greek Government on financial and economic policies. Having the above considerations in mind, we told him we could not approve a formal set-up of this kind, but that the Embassy experts should of course continue to keep in close touch with their British colleagues and the Greek authorities and offer the latter such informal advice and assistance as might be called for. We have agreed with your people to accept the Greek Government's invitations to you and to us to send transportation experts to Greece. This is a very specific situation where a coordinated recommendation is essential, since there will be a joint interest in the supply of any equipment necessary to get transportation going again in Greece. Our people are also doing all they can to help UNRRA to do a good job in Greece.

The Greeks have approached us informally for help and we are anxious to give them what economic support we can. We have suggested that they send a competent supply mission to Washington to present their claims to our supply agencies. While it seems impracticable at the moment to set up an economic mission in Greece on a tripartite or bilateral basis, I think it might be helpful if I send Donald Nelson out anyway, with a few assistants, to make a survey of the needs and possibilities for me. I shall discuss this with him and keep you informed of any developments. Roosevelt [State Dept.]

[MR*. *FRUS*, 1945, VIII, 207–8. *R&C*.]

R–738

Warm Springs, Ga. [via U.S. Navy]
Apr. 8, 1945, 1614 Z

Secret and Personal from the President for the Prime Minister.
　Your 937. We agree. Roosevelt

[MR*]

Concerned about reports of the President's poor health, Churchill had warned the Foreign Office in mid-March "not to overwhelm him [Roosevelt] with telegrams about business which I fear may bore him" (PREM 3/250/3/35). Accordingly, the Prime Minister wrote a letter in response to Roosevelt's suggestion that the armistice terms in effect for Italy be relaxed (R–707/3). Initially, Churchill had proposed mentioning in this letter a number of specific issues, such as conflicting Italian and Yugoslavian claims to Trieste and Venezia Giulia (at the head of the Adriatic Sea) or the final disposition of the Italian fleet, in order to sound out the President's views. Foreign Secretary

Eden objected, preferring to have British and American diplomats discuss such problems, and suggested using Churchill's letter to Roosevelt to remind the Americans to coordinate their Italian policy with that of Great Britain, rather than inform the Foreign Office after the fact (Eden to Churchill, Mar. 26, 1945, PREM 3/250/3/28–29).

Roosevelt died before Halifax could have delivered this letter. Moreover, it is not clear if it was actually sent since the British records contain only Eden's draft. The formality of the heading and text suggests that Churchill would have made at least minor amendments to make the tone more personal. A search of the files at both the Franklin D. Roosevelt Library and the Harry S Truman Library did not turn up the letter, and it is possible that Halifax merely discussed its contents with the State Department.

C–937/1, letter, not sent?

London [via British Embassy]
April 8, 1945

My dear Mr. President,

I have given further thought to your letter of February 11 about Italy [R–707/3].

Let me express my entire agreement with your statement that there is no basic reason for any quarrel between us. It is our wish, quite as much as yours, to see Italy restored to political and moral health and re-admitted to the comity of nations. We want her to obtain the material aid necessary to this end. But in helping Italy we cannot ignore our public opinion and we must keep in step with what we are doing for those Allies who have been with us through everything. I am convinced, however, that if our people in Washington and London and in the field keep in close touch at all levels we shall smooth out any difficulties in the way of our approach to this important problem. We are as determined as you are to pull together; and I am grateful for your assurance on this point, unnecessary though it was.

I know what weight you attach to the modification of the armistice regime. I believe that the new Combined Chiefs of Staff's directive goes some way towards satisfying Italian aspirations and encouraging a sense of responsibility in the Italian Government for the management of their own affairs. However, the Foreign Office are going into the whole question again and will before long be approaching the State Department with a view to considering what further steps can be taken with advantage to all.

Yours very sincerely, Winston S. Churchill [Eden]

[PREM 3/250/3]

The British were genuinely worried about the food shortages in areas of the Netherlands still occupied by German forces, but the Foreign Office had also commented that British efforts to build food stockpiles enabled the Americans to appear to be the only ones concerned about the threat of starvation in Holland. The Swedish relief "scheme" called for supplies to be brought into German-occupied areas through neutral Sweden.

C–938

London [via U.S. Army]
Apr. 9, 1945, 2240 Z / TOR 0110 Z, Apr. 10

Prime Minister to President Roosevelt. Personal and Top Secret.

1. The plight of the civil population of occupied Holland is desperate. Between two and three million people are facing starvation. We believe that large numbers are dying daily, and the situation must deteriorate rapidly now that communications between Germany and Holland are virtually cut. I fear we may soon be in the presence of a tragedy.

2. Eisenhower has plans prepared for bringing relief to the civil population when Western Holland is liberated and we have accumulated the stocks for this purpose in suitable proximity. But if we wait until Holland has been liberated, this help may come too late. There is need for action to bring immediate help, on a far larger scale than is afforded by the Swedish relief scheme.

3. I therefore ask you to join me in giving notice to the German Government, through the Swiss Government as the protecting power, to the following effect.

It is the responsibility of the German Government to sustain the civil population in those parts of Holland which remain in German occupation. As they have failed to discharge that responsibility, we are prepared to send food and medical supplies for distribution to the civil population through the agency of the International Red Cross.

We are ready in [to] increase the limited supplies that are already being sent from Sweden and also to send in further supplies, by sea or direct from areas under military control of the allies, subject to the necessary safe conducts being arranged. We invite the German Government to accord the facilities to enable this to be done.

4. In present circumstances I think that the German Government might well accede to this request. If, however, they should refuse, I propose that we should, at this stage, warn the German Commander in Holland and all the troops under his command that by resisting our attempt to bring relief to the civil population in this area they brand themselves as murderers before the world, and we shall hold them responsible with their lives for the fate which overtakes the people of Holland.

Full publicity would be given to this warning so as to bring it home to all German troops stationed in Holland.

5. We must avert this tragedy if we can. But, if we cannot, we must at least make it clear to the world on whose shoulders the responsibility lies.

6. The terms of the communication to be made to the German Government through the protecting power are being drafted and will be sent to you tomorrow.

In the meantime, I hope that you will feel able to agree in principle.

[MR*. *FRUS*, 1945, V, 19–20. *WSC*, VI, 468–69.]

In a message of April 7, sent to both Roosevelt and Churchill, Stalin had rejected all of Roosevelt's arguments about Poland (see R–730 and R–732) and blamed the entire impasse on the United States and Great Britain. The Soviet Premier continued to insist that the Lublin Poles form the nucleus of any provisional Polish government, and insisted that any regime in Poland had to accept the Yalta decisions on the Curzon line (Soviet-Polish boundary). Most important, any Pole invited to talks on the establishment of the provisional government had to "actually want friendly relations between Poland and the Soviet Union"—in other words, had to be acceptable to Stalin (*Stalin/FDR*, doc. 289; *Stalin/WSC*, doc. 418). On the surface, the following message might seem to be an attempt to coordinate a strong response to Stalin, but Roosevelt's cable was not a call for a tough stand on Poland. Instead, it was drafted by Secretary of State Stettinius to discourage Prime Minister Churchill from making some kind of hasty statement to Parliament that negotiations on the Polish issue had broken down (see the log sheet to R–739, MR).

R–739

Warm Springs, Ga. [via U.S. Navy]
Apr. 10, 1945, 1723 Z

Top Secret and Personal, from the President for the Prime Minister.

I assume Stalin repeated to you his reply to my message on Poland, since he sent me his reply to yours. We shall have to consider most carefully the implications of Stalin's attitude and what is to be our next step. I shall, of course, take no action of any kind, nor make any statement without consulting you, and I know you will do the same. Roosevelt [ES]

[MR*. *FRUS*, 1945, V, 209. *R&C*.]

Roosevelt and the State Department, which presumably drafted this cable, continued to predicate American policy toward liberated Europe on the assumption that postwar cooperation with the Soviet Union would work. CROSSWORD was a codename for the surrender talks in Bern, Switzerland.

R-740

Warm Springs, Ga. [via U.S. Navy]
Apr. 10, 1945, 1731 Z

Personal and Top Secret, for the Prime Minister from the President.
Your No. 938.

I agree in principle with your proposal to give notice to the German Government that it is responsible for the sustenance of the civil population in those parts of Holland that remain in German occupation.

In view of Stalin's recent allegations in regard to CROSSWORD, I believe that before making any arrangement through the Red Cross with any German authority we should inform Stalin. Roosevelt

[MR*. *FRUS*, 1945, V, 20. R&C.]

C-939

London [via U.S. Army]
Apr. 10, 1945, 2355 Z / TOR 0003 Z, Apr. 11

Prime Minister to President Roosevelt. Personal and Top Secret.

In paragraph six of my telegram No. 938 of April 10 about relief for occupied Holland I promised to send you our suggested terms for the communication to be made by both our governments to the German Government through the protecting power. Following is text:

"1. According to reliable information received by His Majesty's/ U. S. Government between two or three million people in those parts of Holland which remain in German occupation are facing starvation and large numbers dying.

2. The situation is such that no improvement can be anticipated. As the German Government are aware, they are directly and wholly responsible for sustaining the civil population in areas under their military occupation.

Since the German Government have failed to discharge their responsibility in this matter, H. M. G./U. S. G. are prepared in addition to the limited supplies which can be sent in Swedish vessels to send food and medical supplies for distribution to the civil population in this area through the agency of the International Red Cross direct by sea and land from areas under the military control of the Allies, subject to the necessary safe conducts being arranged.

H. M. G./the U. S. G. accordingly invite the German Government as a matter of urgency to declare their readiness in principle to accord whatever facilities may be required for this purpose."

[MR*]

Stalin had defended his position regarding the Bern talks (CROSSWORD) in a long message to Roosevelt sent on April 7 (*Stalin/FDR*, doc. 288). He also included a letter from Soviet military authorities reporting that some American intelligence regarding German plans on the eastern front had proven to be incorrect. That enclosure was apparently designed to illustrate the superiority of Soviet intelligence as well as the reliability of the informants who had claimed that the Anglo-American negotiators had made a deal with the Germans in Italy. Stalin did not apologize, but he did deny that he intended to cast doubts upon either Churchill's or Roosevelt's integrity.

C–940

London [via U.S. Army]
Apr. 11, 1945, 0015 Z / TOR 0003 Z

Prime Minister to President Roosevelt. Personal and Top Secret.

Your No. 734 about CROSSWORDS. I send you a private message I have received from Stalin covering the official telegram which he has sent to you with copy to me. I have a feeling that this is about the best we are going to get out of them, and certainly it is as near as they can get to an apology.

However, before considering any answer at all from His Majesty's Government, please tell me how you think the matter should be handled so that we may keep in line together.

[MR*. *FRUS*, 1945, III, 752. p*WSC*, VI, 453. *R&C*.]

C–941

London [via U.S. Army]
Apr. 11, 1945, 0003 Z / TOR 0003 Z

Prime Minister to President Roosevelt. Personal and Top Secret.

Reference my immediately preceding telegram. Following is Marshal Stalin's message dated 7 April.

Your message of 5th April received. In my message of 7th April to the President, which I am sending to you also, I have already replied to all the fundamental points raised in your message regarding the negotiations in Switzerland. On the other questions raised in your message I consider it necessary to make the following remarks.

1. Neither I nor Molotov had any intention of "blackening" anyone. It is not a matter of wanting to "blacken" (anyone) but of our having developed differing points of view as regards the rights and obligations of any ally. You will see from my message to the President that the Russian point of view on this question is the correct one, as

it guarantees each ally's rights and deprives the enemy of any possibility of sowing discord between us.

2. My messages are personal and strictly confidential. This makes
it possible to speak one's mind clearly and frankly. This is the advantage of confidential communications.

If, however, you are going to regard every frank statement of mine
as offensive, it will make this kind of communication very difficult.
I can assure you that I had and have no intention of offending
anyone.

[MR*. *FRUS*, 1945, III, 752–53. *WSC*, VI, 453. *Stalin/FDR*, doc. 419.]

After liberating Roumania, Soviet forces had largely been withdrawn as local,
anti-German political groups took over the government. The Ministry of
General Nicolae Radescu was too conservative to suit either local Roumanian
communists or the Soviet leaders, and when violent clashes took place between
police and communist demonstrators, Stalin seized the opportunity to force
a change. Without calling the tripartite Allied Control Commission into session, the Soviets demanded that King Michael install a new government. Given
two hours in which to comply, the King appointed Petru Groze, leader of
the non-communist Plowmen's Front Party, to head a coalition which was
dominated by Communist Party members who held the Ministries of Interior,
Justice, War, and Communications. Radescu sought sanctuary in the British
Embassy in Bucharest. King Michael remained as a constitutional monarch—
the only monarch of a communist state—until December 1947, when Roumania became a people's republic.

Roosevelt died before he could approve any response to this cable. The
State Department recommended against taking the "lead" in Roumania, but
did ask the new Roumanian government not to deprive political leaders of
their civil rights unless they were "demonstrably Quislings or collaborationists," and preferred to push for the Allied Control Commission to become
more effective (*FRUS*, 1945, V, 530).

C–942

London [via U.S. Army]
Apr. 11, 1945, 0044 Z / TOR 0003 [Z?]

Prime Minister to President Roosevelt. Personal and Top Secret.

Roumania: You will have seen our various telegrams to the British
officers on the Control Commission in Roumania. In Roumanian affairs
we have been following your lead because of what I told you in my No.
905, and we shall continue to do so.

We should be grateful if you would take some of the burden of giving refuge to Roumanian personalities whom you and we have supported, should their lives be in danger.

Radescu is already on our hands. Now there is this question of the King and Queen Mother. We have unhesitatingly said that if they have no other sanctuary they may come to us. But I hope you will take some of this weight off us, as you are taking the lead in Roumania.

[MR*. *FRUS*, 1945, V, 531.]

In an earlier cable (R–724), the President had insisted that Mountbatten clear his activities in Indo-China with Wedemeyer, as if the American were a theater commander. But by mid-March, Roosevelt had responded to British requests and ordered American air forces to assist the French who were fighting against the Japanese in Indo-China, a diversion from Wedemeyer's main concern, that of encouraging the Chinese to attack the Japanese farther north, particularly along the Chinese coast where the Americans hoped to gain a port from which to launch attacks on the Japanese home islands. Although the President had originally hoped to prevent the French from regaining control in Indo-China, that had become impractical. He had initially thought China could supervise the transition for Indo-China from colony to nation, but it had become clear that China would not be capable of acting as the "policeman" for East and Southeast Asia. With Britain pushing for France to be treated as an equal ally and with both Churchill and de Gaulle adamantly opposed to any decolonization program, Roosevelt decided that Indo-China in 1945 was neither the time nor the place to push the issue. He apparently relied on his plan for a United Nations trusteeship system to solve the decolonization question. That plan called for the world organization to appoint trustees— not necessarily the former colonial power—to oversee the creation of independent states out of colonies liberated from Japanese occupation. It was opposed by the American Joint Chiefs of Staff, who feared it would interfere with their plans to establish military bases in many of those colonies and who expected the British and French to agree. Roosevelt died before answering this message.

C–943

London [via U.S. Army]
Apr. 11, 1945, 0745 Z / TOR 1030 Z

Prime Minister to President Roosevelt. Personal and Top Secret.
Your 724.

1. Acting on the instructions of the British Chiefs of Staff, Admiral Mountbatten has discussed the whole question of clandestine operations with General Wedemeyer when the latter was in Kandy recently. You will probably have heard from your Chiefs of Staff that they have come to a

very satisfactory agreement and have settled all difficulties outstanding between them.

2. Nevertheless I still think that we should issue directives to Admiral Mountbatten and General Wedemeyer respectively. I, for my part, will telegraph to Mountbatten as follows. Do you agree?

"Directive from Prime Minister to Admiral Mountbatten in accordance with the agreement which you reached after SEXTANT with the Generalissimo, you may conduct from whatsoever base appears most suitable the minimum pre-occupational activities in Indo-China which local emergency and the advance of your forces require. It is essential, however, that you should keep General Wedemeyer, as Chief of Staff to the Generalissimo, continually informed of all your operations, since forces of China Command will also be operating in the same theatre.

You should foster full, free and frank exchange of plans, intentions and intelligence with General Wedemeyer as regards Indo-China in order to ensure the closest correlation of Allied military interests in that area.

General Wedemeyer is receiving similar instructions from the President that he is likewise to keep you informed of all his activities into Indo-China.

If, as is unlikely, there should be any point of disagreement between you and General Wedemeyer, it should be referred to the Combined Chiefs of Staff."

3. Now that the Japanese have taken over Indo-China and that substantial resistance is being offered by French patriots, it is essential not only that we should support the French by all the means in our power, but also that we should associate them with our operations into their country. It would look very bad in history if we failed to support isolated French forces in their resistance to the Japanese to the best of our ability, or, if we excluded the French from participation in our councils as regards Indo-China.

[MR*]

Churchill's hopes for a breakthrough on the Polish issue were soon dashed, in spite of a statement by Mikolajczyk that he accepted the Yalta agreements on Poland. Stalin continued to insist that the Lublin Poles completely dominate any "new" Polish government.

C–944

London [via U.S. Army]
Apr. 11, 1945, 1830 Z / TOR 2005 Z

Prime Minister to President Roosevelt, Personal and Top Secret.
Your 739.

1. Stalin sent me a copy of his reply to your message on Poland. He also sent me an additional private message, of which the last sentence in Para 1, if seriously intended, would be important. I send this message in my immediately following. Please let these personal introductions to his official messages be guarded absolutely as between you and me.

2. I have to make a statement in the House of Commons next Thursday and of course I should like to know your views about how we should answer Stalin as soon as possible. I have a feeling that they do not want to quarrel with us, and your telegram about CROSSWORD may have seriously and deservedly perturbed them. Our angle of approach and momentum remain exactly what they have been in both the matters under dispute as set forth in our telegrams.

[MR*. *FRUS*, 1945, V, 209. *R&C*.]

C–945

London [via U.S. Army]
Apr. 11, 1945, 2100 Z / TOR 2235 Z

Prime Minister to President Roosevelt. Personal and Top Secret.

The private message referred to in my immediately preceding telegram follows:

> Personal and Secret. Premier J. V. Stalin to The Prime Minister Mr. Winston Churchill.
>
> I have received your message of April 1st on the Polish question. In my message on this subject to The President, which I am also sending to you, I answer all the main questions connected with the work of the Moscow Commission on Poland. As regards the other questions which you raise in your message, I have the following remarks to make:
>
> (1) The British and American Ambassadors who are members of The Moscow Commission are unwilling to take account of The Provisional Polish Government and insist on inviting Polish personalities for consultation, without regard to their attitude to the decisions of the Crimea Conference on Poland and to The Soviet Union. They absolutely insist on summoning to Moscow for consultation, for in-

stance, Mikolajczyk, and this they do in the form of an ultimatum: in this they take no account of the fact that Mikolajczyk has come out openly against the decisions of the Crimea Conference on Poland. However, if you think it necessary, I should be ready to use my influence with The Provisional Polish Government to make them withdraw their objections to inviting Mikolajczyk if the latter would make a public statement accepting the decisions of the Crimea Conference on the Polish question and declaring that he stands for the establishment of friendly relations between Poland and The Soviet Union.

(2) You wonder why the Polish theatre of military operations must be wrapped in mystery. In fact there is no mystery here. You ignore the fact that if British observers or other foreign observers were sent into Poland, the Poles would regard this as an insult to their national dignity, bearing in mind the fact, moreover, that the present attitude of The British Government to The Provisional Polish Government is regarded as unfriendly by the latter. So far as The Soviet Government is concerned, it cannot but take account of the negative attitude of The Provisional Government to the question of sending foreign observers into Poland. Further, you are aware that The Provisional Polish Government puts no obstacles in the way of entrance into Poland by representatives of other states which take up a different attitude towards it, and does not in any way obstruct them; this is the case, for instance, in regard to the representatives of The Czechoslovak Government, The Yugoslav Government and others.

[MR*. *Stalin/WSC*, doc. 418.]

Roosevelt and his advisers chose to treat Stalin's message about the Bern talks as an apology, and the President's response carefully concentrated on the strongest part of the wartime coalition—the common desire to crush Germany.

R–741

Warm Springs, Ga. [via U.S. Navy]
Apr. 11, 1945; 0159 Z, Apr. 12

Top Secret and Personal from the President to the Prime Minister.

Your 940. I am sending the following message to Stalin and quoting it for your information:

QUOTE. President to Marshal Stalin.

Thank you for your frank explanation of the Soviet point of view of the Bern incident which now appears to have faded into the past without having accomplished any useful purpose.

There must not, in any event, be mutual distrust and minor misunderstandings of this character should arise in the future. I feel sure that when our armies make contact in Germany and join in a fully coordinated offensive the Nazi Armies will disintegrate. UNQUOTE.

Roosevelt [WDL]

[MR*. *WSC*, VI, 453. p*FRUS*, 1945, III, 756. p*Stalin/FDR*, doc. 290.]

In one of the very few messages the President drafted personally during his stay in Warm Springs, he characteristically chose to emphasize the optimistic side of Anglo-American relations with the Soviet Union. Roosevelt's advisers may have been concerned primarily with preventing Churchill from making rash public statements, but the President had long ago committed himself to a policy of cooperation after the war. The suggestion that they "minimize" the problems caused by the Soviet Union epitomizes Roosevelt's approach to a host of issues. Partly creative procrastination, based on the belief that many crises solve themselves if left alone, and partly an attempt to direct the thinking of others, on the belief that the way one approaches a problem can be the key to the solution, Franklin Roosevelt's style was an integral part of his substance.

R-742

Warm Springs, Ga. [via U.S. Navy]
Apr. 11, 1945; 0213 Z, Apr. 12

Top Secret and Personal from the President for the Prime Minister.

Your 944. I would minimize the general Soviet problem as much as possible because these problems, in one form or another, seem to arise every day and most of them straighten out as in the case of the Bern meeting.

We must be firm, however, and our course thus far is correct. Roosevelt [FDR]

[MR*. *FRUS*, 1945, V, 210. *WSC*, VI, 454. *R&C*.]

Although there is no log sheet to indicate who drafted this cable, its tone fit Roosevelt's desire to allay Soviet suspicions. The British protested, claiming that they should only keep Stalin informed about ultimatums issued to the German government, not ask his permission, since there would not be direct contact with German authorities and hence no separate peace negotiations.

But events overtook this problem. On April 24, the United States told the Soviets that Eisenhower had been authorized to negotiate a truce in the Netherlands, and that Soviet representatives could attend all discussions with the Germans (*FRUS*, 1945, V, 20–22).

R–743

Warm Springs, Ga. [via U.S. Navy]
Apr. 11, 1945; 0149 Z, Apr. 12

Top Secret and Personal from the President for the Prime Minister.

The proposed message to the German Government quoted in your 939 meets with my approval.

You may send it as a joint message provided it is approved by Stalin.

If at a later date any promise of punishment is proposed, as suggested in your 938, it will require careful consideration in view of probable retaliation against our prisoners in Germany. Roosevelt

[MR*]

Roosevelt's message number 743 ended the Churchill-Roosevelt correspondence. In Warm Springs, Georgia, at 1:15 in the afternoon of April 12, the President complained of "a terrific headache," held his forehead, and then slumped over in his chair. At 3:35 P.M., physicians pronounced Franklin D. Roosevelt dead, following a massive cerebral hemorrhage.

Stalin appeared "deeply distressed" when Ambassador Harriman met with him the next day. The Soviet Premier made a number of inquiries about the circumstances of Roosevelt's death, and later revealed something of himself when he sent a cable to the State Department requesting that an autopsy be performed to determine if the President had been poisoned (*FRUS*, 1945, V, 826–29; Bishop, *FDR's Last Year*, p. 892).

Churchill, in a cable to Eleanor Roosevelt, mourned the loss of "a dear and cherished friendship which was forged in the fire of war," told Harry Hopkins of his "true affection for Franklin," and then, mindful of the future, sent a personal telegram to the new President, Harry S Truman. Churchill expressed his sense of personal loss, but the main thrust of the message was a plea for the creation of an "intimate comradeship"—a phrase reminiscent of his call for a "righteous comradeship" in a speech before a joint session of the United States Congress, shortly after the Pearl Harbor attack (*WSC*, VI, 472).

Churchill to Truman

London
Apr. 13, 1945

Prime Minister to President Truman. Personal.

Pray accept from me the expression of my personal sympathy in the loss which you and the American nation have sustained in the death of our illustrious friend. I hope that I may be privileged to renew with you the intimate comradeship in the great cause we all serve that I enjoyed through these terrible years with him. I offer you my respectful good wishes as you step into the breach in the victorious lines of the United Nations.

[PREM 3/473. *WSC*, VI, 480.]

Harry S Truman came to the presidency with little experience or expertise in international relations. He had been Vice President for only three months, scarcely time to become familiar with foreign relations even if Roosevelt had tried to get him involved. But Roosevelt had had little time for his new Vice President. Between the Yalta Conference, trips to Hyde Park, and his final journey to Warm Springs, Roosevelt was in Washington for less than two months after his fourth inauguration. Truman announced shortly after taking the oath of office that he planned to carry on Roosevelt's foreign policies, but his knowledge of those policies depended heavily on what he was told by the President's aides. On April 13, Secretary of State Edward Stettinius submitted a summary of international problems facing the United States (printed below). Stettinius' views, in both direct and subtle ways, differed from Roosevelt's policies and style, particularly with regard to the Soviet Union and France. That difference in style and content was translated into action by Truman within two weeks after Roosevelt's death. Soviet Foreign Minister Molotov had been sent to the San Francisco Conference after all, as a gesture of good will toward the new American President. Enroute he stopped in Washington for talks with Truman. When the President upbraided the Soviets for their actions, particularly in East Europe, Molotov complained: "I have never been talked to like that in my life." "Carry out your agreements and you won't get talked to like that," Truman answered (Harry S Truman, *Memoirs*, I, 82). Averell Harriman, who had returned to Washington for talks with Truman, was in the room with Molotov and Truman, and later claimed that he was surprised by Truman's vigorous attack. Harriman recognized the shift in attitude, expressing displeasure "that Truman went at it so hard because his behavior gave Molotov an excuse to tell Stalin that the Roosevelt policy was being abandoned. I regretted that Truman gave him the opportunity" (Harriman, *Special Envoy*, pp. 453–54).

State Dept. memo

Washington
Apr. 13, 1945

[Stettinius to Truman]

Special Information for the President

I have been submitting regularly to Mr. Roosevelt a two-page daily report summarizing current secret developments in the field of *foreign affairs*. I shall of course continue this practice but in this my first report to you I felt it would be useful, rather than merely to transmit the developments of the last 24 hours, to present for your information a very brief summary of the background and present status of the principle problems now confronting this Government in its relations with other countries. This summary follows:

UNITED KINGDOM. Mr. Churchill's policy is based fundamentally upon cooperation with the United States. It is based secondarily on maintaining the unity of the three great powers but the British Government has been showing increasing apprehension of Russia and her intentions. Churchill fully shares this Government's interpretation of the Yalta Agreements on Eastern Europe and liberated areas. He is inclined however to press this position with the Russians with what we consider unnecessary rigidity as to detail. The British long for security but are deeply conscious of their decline from a leading position to that of the junior partner of the Big Three and are anxious to buttress their position vis-a-vis United States and Russia both through exerting leadership over the countries of Western Europe and through knitting the Commonwealth more closely together.

FRANCE. The best interests of the United States require that every effort be made by this Government to assist France, morally as well as physically, to regain her strength and her influence.

It is recognized that the French Provisional Government and the French people are at present unduly preoccupied, as a result of the military defeat of 1940 and the subsequent occupation of their country by the enemy, with questions of national prestige. They have consequently from time to time put forward requests which are out of all proportion to their present strength and have in certain cases, notably in connection with Indochina, showed unreasonable suspicions of American aims and motives. It is believed that it is in the interest of the United States to take full account of this psychological factor in the French mind and to treat France in all respects on the basis of her potential power and influence rather than on the basis of her present strength. Positive American contributions toward the rebuilding of France include: present and future rearming of the French Army; support of French participation in the European Advisory Commission, the control and occupation of Germany, the Reparations Commission and other organizations; and the conclusion of a Lend-Lease Agreement. De Gaulle has recently stated his appreciation of the necessity for the closest possible cooperation between France and the United States.

SOVIET UNION. Since the Yalta Conference the Soviet Government has taken a firm and uncompromising position on nearly every major question that has arisen in our relations. The more important of these are the Polish question, the application of the Crimea agreement on liberated areas, the agreement on the exchange of liberated prisoners of war and civilians, and the San Francisco Conference. In the liberated areas under Soviet control, the Soviet Government is proceeding largely on a unilateral basis and does not agree that the developments which have taken place justify application of the Crimea agreement. Permission for our contact teams to go into Poland to assist in the evacuation of liberated prisoners of war has been refused although in general our prisoners have been reasonably well treated by Soviet standards. The Soviet Government appears to desire to proceed with the San Francisco Conference but was unwilling to send their Foreign Minister. They have asked for a large post-war credit and pending a decision on this matter have so far been unwilling to conclude an agreement providing for the orderly liquidation of lend-lease aid. In the politico-military field, similar difficulties have been encountered in collaboration with the Soviet authorities.

POLAND. The present situation relating to Poland is highly unsatisfactory with the Soviet authorities consistently sabotaging Ambassador Harriman's efforts in the Moscow Commission to hasten the implementation of the decisions at the Crimea Conference. Direct appeals to Marshal Stalin have not yet produced any worthwhile results. The Soviet Government likewise seeks to complicate the problem by initiating and supporting claims of the Warsaw Provisional Polish Government to represent and speak for Poland in international matters such as the San Francisco Conference, reparations and territorial questions. Because of its effect on our relations with the Soviet Union and other United Nations and upon public opinion in this country, the question of the future status of Poland and its government remains one of our most complex and urgent problems both in the international and domestic field.

THE BALKAN AREA. The chief problem facing this Government in Rumania, Bulgaria and Hungary concerns the operation of the Allied Control Commissions which were set up for the execution of the respective armistices. The essence is in the relations with the Soviet Government which, as the power in military control and as the predominant element in the ACC's, uses its position for unilateral political interference in the respective countries. This conflicts with the definite responsibilities of this Government under the Yalta Declaration on Liberated Europe. We have invoked this declaration for Rumania (a minority Government imposed by intimidation) and Bulgaria (in anticipation of unfair elections). The Soviet Government rejected the first, but we are renewing the request, and has not yet replied to the second.

There are no immediate problems in Yugoslavia though here too we may be obliged to invoke the Yalta Declaration unless the government shows more moderation toward democratic elements in the country which are not yet represented in the administration.

GERMANY. The policy of the United States toward Germany was outlined in a memorandum approved by President Roosevelt on March 23, 1945. The principal features of that policy are: destruction of National Socialist organizations and influence, punishment of war criminals, disbandment of the German military establishment, military government administered with a view to political decentralization, reparation from existing wealth and future production, prevention of the manufacture of arms and destruction of all specialized facilities for their production, and controls over the German economy to secure these objectives.

Agreements have been reached with the United Kingdom and the Soviet Union on the text of the instrument of unconditional surrender, on control machinery for Germany, and on zones of occupation. France has approved the first two agreements. The War Department is now studying the zone originally allocated to the United States with a view to transferring a portion of it to France in conformity with the Crimea undertaking.

No tripartite or quadripartite agreement on the treatment of Germany during the period of military government has been reached. This Government, however, has submitted the memorandum of March 23 for negotiation in the European Advisory Commission meeting in London. This Government has prepared a program of reparation for presentation to the forthcoming conference in Moscow on that subject.

AUSTRIA. The four principal Allies have declared their intention to liberate Austria from German domination and reestablish it as a free and independent country. The European Advisory Commission is this week actively discussing plans for the zoning of Austria for occupation by forces of these countries, and for an inter-Allied military government of Austria pending the reestablishment of a democratic Austrian state.

ITALY. Although a cobelligerent since October 1943, Italy is still subject to an armistice regime and considerable control by the Allied Commission. Chiefly through our efforts, Italy's status has improved, but less than we desire in view of the British policy of keeping Italy dependent. We have been unable to end the anomaly of Italy's dual status as active cobelligerent and as defeated enemy. Great pressure is being brought to bear by groups in this country to make Italy one of the United Nations—a step essentially in accordance with our policy but not with that of certain other allied governments.

Our gravest problem at present, aside from the country's economic distress, is to forestall Yugoslav occupation of an important part of northeastern Italy, prejudicing by unilateral action a final equitable settlement of this territorial dispute and precipitating serious trouble within Italy. Difficulties may be encountered in maintaining Allied (Anglo-American) military government in this area.

SUPPLIES FOR LIBERATED AREAS. A problem of urgent importance to the U.S. is that of supplies for areas liberated from enemy occupation. The chaos and collapse which may result in these countries from starvation, unemployment and inflation can be averted principally by making available essential civilian supplies. Political stability and the maintenance of democratic governments which can withstand the pressures of extremist groups depend on the restoration of a minimum of economic stability. To do our part we must carefully analyze the needs and reserves of all claimants, military and civilian, domestic and foreign, and insist that they be reduced to absolute essentials. This will involve a reexamination both of U.S. military requirements and supply procedures and of U.S. civilian consumption. Two British Cabinet Members are here to discuss critical food and other supply problems with the U.S. and Canada and have authority to reach decisions. It is essential that we organize ourselves at once to meet this problem. The Department is prepared to play its full role in this matter.

ARGENTINA. After a 13 months' period of non-recognition due to Argentine failure to comply with inter-American undertakings for the defense of the continent, Argentina was readmitted to the inter-American family April 9 by unanimous Pan-American agreement. Unconditional acceptance of the Final Act of the Mexico City Conference, including a declaration of war on the Axis, preceded recognition. An immediate change in our economic policy has placed Argentina back in a position comparable to that of the other American republics. But since this Government is not yet fully satisfied from a world as distinct from a hemispheric view with

Argentine developments and cannot vouch for its continuing cooperation, it will not now advocate Argentina's adherence to the United Nations Declaration nor its presence at San Francisco.

[Harry S Truman papers, President's Secretary File, Harry S Truman Library, Independence, Missouri]

Glossary of Codenames, Acronyms, and Common Abbreviations

According to one source, conservative estimates are that World War II produced over 10,000 codenames in Britain alone (L. Bell et al., *The Second World War: A Guide to Documents in the Public Record Office*, London: HMSO, 1972, p. 178). A few of the Anglo-American codenames, such as OVERLORD, have become part of our vocabulary, but most are long forgotten. This glossary provides a brief working definition of the codenames, acronyms, and abbreviations that appear in the Churchill-Roosevelt correspondence. When a more detailed explanation is found in a document or its headnote, the document number is noted.

ABC	American-British-Canadian Conference (R–36x), Jan. 29–Mar. 29, 1941
ABDA(COM)	American-British-Dutch-Australian Command (C–150x), 1942
ACCOLADE	Plan to occupy the island of Rhodes, canceled Sept. 1943
ACROBAT	Plan to clear Tripoli of Axis forces (C–153x), 1942
A.D.G.B.	Air Defence, Great Britain
Admiral Q	British codename for Roosevelt
AFHQ	Allied Forces Headquarters, Mediterranean (C–449), 1943
AK	Polish Home Army (C–767)
AKA	Attack cargo ship (U.S.)
ALBATROSS	Saki airfield, Crimea, U.S.S.R. (C–896)
American Eagle	General Mark Clark
AMGOT	Allied Military Government of Occupied Territory
ANAKIM	Plan for a major invasion of southern and northern Burma
ANFA	The Casablanca Conference; taken from its location at the Anfa Hotel in the Anfa suburb of Casablanca
ANVIL	Invasion of southern France, later named DRAGOON, 1944
ANZAC	American-New Zealand-Australian Command; also used to describe Australian and New Zealand forces (C–82x)
ARCADIA	First Washington Conference, Dec. 20, 1941–Jan. 14, 1942

ARGONAUT	Second Washington Conference, June 1942; also the Crimea (Yalta) Conference, Jan.–Feb. 1945
ARMPIT	Plan for an attack on Vienna through Istria (C–721 A), 1944
ASDIC	Underwater sound-detection equipment (SONAR)
ASPIDISTRA	Transmitter used for jamming German radio stations (C–162)
ASV	Air to surface-vessel radar
ATC	Air Transport Command
AVALANCHE	Amphibious invasion in Naples/Salerno area of Italy (C–414/2), 1943
AVG	American Volunteer Group (Flying Tigers); American pilots flying for China against Japan (C–160x)
BAD	British Admiralty Delegation (Washington)
BASEBALL	Planned occupation of the Cape Verde Islands (1941)
BATTLEAXE	Operations in Libya aimed at relieving Tobruk (1941)
BAYTOWN	British attack on Calabria in southern Italy (Sept. 1943)
B.E.F.	British Expeditionary Force (France, 1939–40)
B.E.W.	Board of Economic Warfare (U.S.)
"Big Scheme"	See TEMPEST
BOLERO	Buildup of supplies and forces in England for OVERLORD (C–106)
BONIFACE	Early codename for ULTRA; used by Churchill throughout the war (C–412/2)
BONUS	Free French occupation of Madagascar (1942)
BRIDE	Charles de Gaulle (R–275/1)
BRIMSTONE	Capture of Sardinia (1943)
BROADWAY	Airfield in northern Burma (C–626), 1944
BUCCANEER	Planned operation against Japanese forces in Nicobar and Andaman Islands, Burma (1943)
CAIRO 3	Teheran Conference (see EUREKA)
Canaries	German U-boats (C–378)
CANNIBAL	Plan to occupy Akyab, Burma (C–258), 1942–43
CAPITAL	Operation against Japanese in central Burma (C–839), Oct. 1944
C.A.S.	Chief of the Air Staff (British)
CBI	China-Burma-India (theater)
CELESTES	Chiang Kai-shek
CHAMPION	Overall codename for combined BUCCANEER/TARZAN operation (R–418/4)

CICERO	Elyesa Bazna, German agent in the British Embassy in Turkey (R–442)
CIGS	Chief of Imperial General Staff (British)
C in C	Commander in Chief (CINC, C-in-C)
Colonel Kent	Winston Churchill
Colonel Warden	Winston Churchill
Colonel White	Clementine Churchill
COMINCH	Commander in Chief, U.S. Navy
COS	Chiefs of Staff
COSSAC	Chief of Staff to the Supreme Allied Commander, Europe (C–258/1)
CRICKET	Malta Conference (Jan.–Feb. 1945)
CROSSWORD	Discussions in Switzerland about the surrender of German forces in northern Italy (British; see also SUNRISE), 1945
CRUSADER	British Eighth Army operations in Libya and Egypt, 1941–42
CULVERIN	Plan for an attack on Malaya and northern Sumatra (1943)
CYPRUS	Habbiyana, Iraq (C–456)
D.F.	Radio direction-finder (D/F)
DIADEM	Operation to link Allied forces at Anzio with those located on the main front to the south (C–668), 1944
DISRAELI	S.S. *Franconia* (C–896)(British)
DON	Name for a series of telegrams (C–593)
DRACULA	Plan for a combined airborne/amphibious attack on Rangoon (C–793), 1944
DRAGOON	Invasion of southern France in conjunction with the invasion at Normandy (previously ANVIL)
EAC	European Advisory Commission (established Oct. 1943)
EAM	Greek National Liberation Front (C–849/1)
ELAS	Greek National Popular Liberation Army (C–849/1)
ENIGMA	Codename for the enciphering machine used by German and Italian military forces
ETO	European Theater of Operations
EUREKA	Teheran Conference, Nov.–Dec. 1943
EUREKA II	Proposed Churchill-Roosevelt or Churchill-Roosevelt-Stalin meeting during second half of 1944 (C–732)
FCC	Federal Communication Commission (U.S.)

FCNL   French Committee of National Liberation

FRANKLAND   Codename for Churchill during planning for the Casablanca Conference (also Commodore FRANKLAND, C–251), Jan. 1943

FROZEN   Name for a series of Churchill's telegrams (C–537)

GRENADINE   Torpedo-plane protection for convoys to northern Russia (C–274–A)

GYMNAST   Anglo-American invasion and occupation of French North Africa, 1942–43

HANDCUFF   Plan for an attack on the Dodecanese Islands, 1943

HARDIHOOD   Program of aid to Turkey once that nation declared war on Germany (R–471), 1943–44

HERCULES   Plan for an Anglo-Turkish attack on Rhodes (C–521), 1943

H.M.G.   His Majesty's Government (Great Britain)

HORRIFIED   Sicily (after the Allied invasion)

HUSKY   The invasion of Sicily, July 1943

HYDRO   Intelligence derived from decrypts of German naval ciphers (later included as part of ULTRA; see C–103x)

HYPO   (Force) H; British naval squadron located at Gibraltar

ILO   International Labor Organization (Office)

IRONCLAD   Planned attack on Diégo-Suarez in northern Madagascar (C–25), Feb.–May 1942 (previously BONUS)

JAEL   Deception plan against Germany (disinformation), later BODYGUARD

JCS   Joint Chiefs of Staff (U.S.)

JUPITER   Plan for an attack on northern Norway

Kent (Colonel)   Winston Churchill

KINGPIN   General Henri Giraud

KKE   Greek Communist Party (C–849/1)

LCT   Tank landing craft

LIFEBELT   Planned attack on the Azores, June 1943

LIGHTFOOT   British Eighth Army offensive in the western desert (Oct. 1942), C–170

LST   Tank landing ship (ocean-going)

MAB   Munitions Assignment Board (combined Anglo-American)

MAGIC   Intelligence gleaned from U.S. breaking of high-level Japanese codes/ciphers

MAGNET   Replacement of British forces in Northern Ireland with U.S. forces (C–153x), Jan. 1942

MAGNETO	Yalta (site of the Crimea Conference)
Manhatten Project	Atomic-bomb research (U.S.)
MARKET-GARDEN	Operation designed to establish a bridgehead across the Netherlands Rhine by airborne (MARKET) and ground (GARDEN) assault, Sept. 1944
MATTERHORN	Long-range bombing of Japan by B-29s based in China
MAUD	British atomic-bomb research organization (R–62)
MAUDSON	See MAYSON
MAYSON	Anglo-American cooperation on atomic-bomb research (R–62), 1941
M.I.6	Military Intelligence (British)
M.T.	Motor transport
navicerts	cargo certification for neutrals (C–5x)
NEPTUNE	The assault portion of OVERLORD, the Normandy invasion, June 1944
NKVD	Soviet military intelligence organization
OBOE	Oran, Algeria
OCTAGON	Second Quebec Conference, Sept. 1944
OKW	*Oberkommando der Wehrmacht*; German military High Command
ONE-THIRD BOLERO	Informal equivalent of SLEDGEHAMMER (C–106)
OSS	Office of Strategic Services, U.S. clandestine intelligence organization
OVERLORD	Overall plan for the Allied invasion of France, 1944
OWI	Office of War Information (U.S.)
PIGSTICK	Plan for landings on the Mayu Peninsula of the Arakan coast in Burma, 1944 (C–521)
PILGRIM	Plan for the occupation of the Canary Islands, 1941
PLOUGH	Special operation by snow-mobile forces against Roumanian oil fields (C–177), 1942–43
POINTBLANK	Combined bombing campaign against Germany, 1943–44
P.Q.	Anglo-American appeal to the Italian people (C–630), July 1943
PQ	Codename for Roosevelt prior to the First Quebec Conference, 1943
PRICELESS	Operations in the Mediterranean after the invasion of Sicily, 1943
PUGILIST	Allied attack against the Mareth line in Tunisia (C–272–A), 1943
PUMA	Attack/occupation of Grand Canary Island, 1941 (see PILGRIM)

PURPLE	Name for the machine used by the Americans to break high-grade Japanese encryptions (see MAGIC)
QUADRANT	First Quebec Conference, August 1943
R.A.F.	Royal Air Force (British)
RANKIN	Contingency plan for an Anglo-American move to the European continent in the event of a German surrender or collapse of German resistance. RANKIN A: in the event of a sudden weakening of German strength and morale making a pre-OVERLORD invasion possible; RANKIN B: in the event of a German withdrawal from the occupied countries in western Europe; RANKIN C: in the event of a German surrender
RAVENOUS	A small operation planned in northern Burma, possibly as part of ANAKIM, 1943
RIVIERA	Atlantic Conference, Placentia Bay, Newfoundland, Aug. 1941
ROUNDHAMMER	Early name for OVERLORD, coined by combining SLEDGEHAMMER and ROUNDUP (R–275/2)
ROUNDUP	Plan for a major invasion of western Europe from England in 1943 (C–106)
SAC	Supreme Allied Commander (Europe)
SACMED	Supreme Allied Commander, Mediterranean
SACSEA	Supreme Allied Commander, South East Asia
SATURN	Plan to put British forces in Turkey following a Turkish declaration of war on Germany, Dec. 1943
SCAEF	Supreme Commander Allied Expeditionary Force (western Europe)
SCAF	Supreme Commander Allied Forces (see SCAEF)
SEAC	South East Asia Command
SEMI-GYMNAST	See SUPER-GYMNAST (C–106)
SEXTANT	Cairo Conference (C–478), Dec. 1943
SHAEF	Supreme Headquarters, Allied Expeditionary Force (western Europe)
SHINGLE	Amphibious invasion at Anzio, south of Rome, Jan. 1944
SIGINT	Signal (radio) intelligence (C–103x)
SLEDGEHAMMER	Plan for an Anglo-American invasion of western Europe in 1942 (C–70) aimed primarily at relieving pressure on the Russian front
SOAPSUDS	See TIDAL WAVE
SOE	Special Operations Executive (British clandestine-operations organization)

SONAR	Sound navigation ranging, a device used to locate submarines and other underwater objects by sound waves
SUNRISE	American codename for CROSSWORD
SUPERCHARGE I	Attack against German defenses (Gen. Rommel) west of El Alamein, Oct.–Nov. 1942
SUPER-GYMNAST	Early name for a large-scale Anglo-American invasion and/or occupation of French North Africa (C–106), later called TORCH, 1941–42
SUPER-ROUNDUP	Never formally assigned, but used as an early codename for what became OVERLORD (R–149)
SYMBOL	Casablanca Conference, Jan. 1943
TARZAN	Combined British attack in central Burma and Chinese attack in northern Burma (R–418/4)
TEMPEST	Uprising by the Polish Underground against the Germans (nicknamed "the Big Scheme"), 1944 (C–740)
THRUSTER	Planned British occupation of one of the Azores (C–94x), 1941
TIDAL WAVE	U.S. bombing of oilfields in Ploeşti, Roumania, from Libya (C–330), 1943
TIGER	Naval convoy of tanks and aircraft from the U.K. to Malta and thence to British forces in Egypt and North Africa (C–86x), May 1941
TOLSTOY	Churchill-Stalin meeting, Moscow, Oct. 1944
TOPFLITE	The "camouflage" series of propaganda broadcasts, made shortly before OVERLORD, designed to confuse the Germans as to the site of the main Anglo-American attack (C–688)
TORCH	Anglo-American invasion/occupation of French North Africa, Nov. 1942 (previously GYMNAST)
TRIDENT	Third Washington Conference, May 1943
TUBE ALLOYS (TA)	British codename for atomic-bomb research
TUVE	A branch of the U.S. Office of Scientific Research and Development (C–831)
UJ (U.J.)	Uncle Joe (Josef Stalin)
ULTRA	Security label assigned to material taken from German ENIGMA ciphers
UNRRA	United Nations Relief and Rehabilitation Administration (R–308)
UPA	Ukrainian Insurgent Army (R–674)
VELVET	Plan to station Anglo-American aircraft units in the Caucasus, 1942–43

VULCAN   Plan for the final conquest of Tunisia, Apr.–May
                        1943
WELFARE   Codename for a series of Churchill's telegrams (C–
                        414/8, first encl.)

List of Sources Cited

This list provides full location and/or publication data on collections and works actually cited in the headnotes. It comprises only a small fraction of the materials which were used. Accordingly, it is organized in strict alphabetical order without the usual division into primary and secondary materials, memoirs, etc. Manuscript and documentary collections used for source texts are listed in the Bibliographical Note.

Allen, Louis. *Singapore, 1941–42*. Newark: University of Delaware Press, 1977.

Ambrose, Stephen E. *The Supreme Commander: The War Years of General Dwight D. Eisenhower*. Garden City: Doubleday, 1970.

Arnold, H. H. *Global Mission*. New York: Harper and Brothers, 1949.

Bennett, William R. "Secret Telephony as a Historical Example of Spread-Spectrum Communication," *IEEE Transactions on Communications*, COM-31 (January 1983), 98–104.

Beschloss, Michael. *Kennedy and Roosevelt: The Uneasy Alliance*. New York: W. W. Norton, 1980.

Bishop, Jim. *FDR's Last Year: April 1944–April 1945*. New York: Pocket Books, 1975.

Blum, John Morton. *From the Morgenthau Diaries*. Vol. III, *Years of War, 1941–1945*. Boston: Houghton Mifflin, 1967.

Brown, Anthony Cave. *Bodyguard of Lies*. New York: Harper and Row, 1975.

Bruenn, Howard G. "Clinical Notes on the Illness and Death of President Franklin D. Roosevelt." *Annals of Internal Medicine* 72 (1970), 579–91.

Bryant, Arthur. *Triumph in the West*. Garden City: Doubleday, 1959.

———. *The Turn of the Tide, 1940–1945*. London: Collins, 1957.

Bullitt, William C. *For the President, Personal and Secret: Correspondence Between Franklin D. Roosevelt and William C. Bullitt*. Orville C. Bullitt, editor. Boston: Houghton Mifflin, 1972.

Burns, James MacGregor. *Roosevelt: Soldier of Freedom, 1940–1945*. New York: Harcourt Brace Jovanovich, 1970.

Cadogan, Sir Alexander. *The Diaries of Sir Alexander Cadogan*. David Dilks, editor. New York: G. P. Putnam's Sons, 1972.

Calvocoressi, Peter. *Top Secret ULTRA*. New York: Pantheon, 1981.

Carlton, David. *Anthony Eden*. London: Allen Lane, 1981.

Chamberlain, Neville. Papers. Birmingham University Library, Birmingham, England.

Churchill, Winston S. *The Second World War*. 6 vols. Boston: Houghton Mifflin, 1948–53.

———. *Winston S. Churchill: His Complete Speeches, 1897–1963*. Robert Rhodes James, editor. Vols. VI, VII. New York: Chelsea House, 1974.

———. *The World Crisis: The Aftermath*. New York: Charles Scribner's Sons, 1929.

Cowling, Maurice. *The Impact of Hitler*. Chicago: University of Chicago Press, 1977.

Dallek, Robert. *Franklin D. Roosevelt and American Foreign Policy, 1932–1945*. New York: Oxford University Press, 1979.

Davis, Lynn Etheridge. *The Cold War Begins: Soviet-American Conflict over Eastern Europe*. Princeton: Princeton University Press, 1974.

de Gaulle, Charles. *Unity, 1942–1944*. Richard Howard, translator. A volume in *The War Memoirs of Charles de Gaulle*. New York: Simon and Schuster, 1959.

Eden, Anthony. *The Reckoning*. Vol. II of *The Memoirs of Anthony Eden, Earl of Avon*. Boston: Houghton Mifflin, 1955.

Ehrman, Howard. *Grand Strategy*. Vols. V and VI of the *History of the Second World War, United Kingdom Military Series*. London: HMSO, 1956.

Eisenhower, Dwight D. Papers. Dwight D. Eisenhower Library, Abilene, Kansas.

———. *The Papers of Dwight David Eisenhower: The War Years*. Alfred D. Chandler, Stephen E. Ambrose et al., editors. 5 vols. Baltimore: The Johns Hopkins University Press, 1970.

Fagan, M. D., editor. *A History of Engineering and Science in the Bell System: National Service in War and Peace, 1925–1975*. N.p.: Bell Telephone Laboratories, Inc., 1978.

Feingold, Henry L. *The Politics of Rescue*. New Brunswick: Rutgers University Press, 1970.

Funk, Arthur L. *The Politics of TORCH: The Allied Landings and the Algiers Putsch 1942*. Lawrence: University of Kansas Press, 1974.

Gardner, Lloyd C. *Architects of Illusion: Men and Ideas in American Foreign Policy, 1941–1949*. New York: Quadrangle, 1970.

Garland, Albert N., and Smyth, Howard McGaw. *Sicily and the Surrender of Italy*. A volume in *The United States Army in World War II: The Mediterranean Theater of Operations*. Washington: OCMH, 1965.

A Gentleman With a Duster (Harold Begbie). *The Mirrors of Downing Street*. London: Mills & Boon, 1921.

Germany. *Führer Conferences on Matters Dealing with the German Navy*. Translated and mimeographed by the Office of Naval Intelligence. Washington: Department of the Navy, ONI, 1947. (Naval Academy Library, Annapolis, Md.)

Gilbert, Martin. *Winston S. Churchill.* Vols. V, VI, and Companion to Vol. V, Pt. II. Boston: Houghton Mifflin, 1977–83.

Godfroy, Vice Admiral René E. *L'Aventure de la Force X (escadre française de la Mediterranée orientale) à Alexandrie (1940–1943).* Paris: Plon, 1943.

Harriman, W. Averell, and Abel, Ellie. *Special Envoy to Churchill and Stalin, 1941–1946.* New York: Random House, 1975.

Hassett, William D. *Off the Record With F.D.R.* New Brunswick: Rutgers University Press, 1958.

Herring, George C. *Aid to Russia, 1941–1946: Strategy, Diplomacy, and the Origins of the Cold War.* New York: Columbia University Press, 1973.

Hinsley, F. H. et al., *British Intelligence in the Second World War.* Vols. I and II. Volumes in the *History of the Second World War: United Kingdom Civil Series.* New York: Cambridge University Press, 1979–81.

Hopkins, Harry L. Papers. Franklin D. Roosevelt Library, Hyde Park, New York.

Howard, Michael. *Grand Strategy.* Vol. IV of the *History of the Second World War, United Kingdom Military Series.* London: HMSO, 1972.

Hull, Cordell. *The Memoirs of Cordell Hull.* 2 vols. New York: Macmillan, 1948.

Hunczak, Taras. Editor. *UPA—The Ukranian Insurgent Army in the Light of German Documents.* 2 vols. Toronto: Litopys UPA, 1981.

Italy. *Diplomatici Italiani.* Nona serie, vol. I. Rome: La Libreria Della Stato, 1954.

Jones, R. V. *The Wizard War: British Scientific Intelligence, 1939–1945.* New York: Coward, McCann and Geoghegan, 1978.

Kahn, David. *Hitler's Spies: German Military Intelligence in World War II.* New York: Macmillan, 1978.

Kennan, George F. *Memoirs, 1925–1950.* Boston: Little, Brown, 1967.

Kennedy, Ludovic. *Pursuit.* New York: Viking, 1974.

Kimball, Warren F. *"The Most Unsordid Act": Lend-Lease, 1939–1941.* Baltimore: The Johns Hopkins University Press, 1969.

———. *Swords Or Ploughshares? The Morgenthau Plan for Defeated Nazi Germany, 1943–1946.* Philadelphia: Lippincott, 1976.

———, and Bartlett, Bruce. "Roosevelt and Prewar Commitments to Churchill: The Tyler Kent Affair." *Diplomatic History* 5 (Fall 1981), 291–311.

Kirby, S. Woodburn. *The Decisive Battles.* Vol. III of the *History of the Second World War: War Against Japan.* London: HMSO, 1961.

Lash, Joseph P. *Eleanor and Franklin.* New York: W. W. Norton, 1971.

———. *Roosevelt and Churchill, 1939–1941: The Partnership That Saved the West.* New York: W. W. Norton, 1976.

Leahy, William D. *I Was There.* New York: Whittlesey House, 1950.

Leighton, Richard M., and Coakley, Robert W. *Global Logistics and Strategy, 1940–1943*. A volume in *The United States Army in World War II: The War Department*. Washington: GPO, 1955.

Leutze, James. *Bargaining for Supremacy: Anglo-American Naval Collaboration, 1937–1941*. Chapel Hill: University of North Carolina Press, 1977.

Lewin, Ronald. *ULTRA Goes to War*. New York: McGraw-Hill, 1978.

Louis, Wm. Roger. *Imperialism at Bay: The United States and the Decolonization of the British Empire, 1941–1945*. New York: Oxford University Press, 1978.

Lukacs, John. *The Last European War: September, 1939–December, 1941*. Garden City: Anchor Press, 1976.

MacLean, Elizabeth Kimball. "Joseph E. Davies and Soviet-American Relations, 1941–1943." *Diplomatic History* (Winter 1980), 73–93.

Macmillan, Harold. *The Blast of War, 1939–1945*. New York: Harper and Row, 1968.

McNeill, William Hardy. *America, Britain and Russia: Their Co-operation and Conflict, 1941–1946*. New York: Johnson Reprint, 1970 (originally published in 1953).

Mark, Eduard. "Charles E. Bohlen and the Acceptable Limits of Soviet Hegemony in Eastern Europe: A Memorandum of 18 October 1945." *Diplomatic History* 3 (Spring 1979), 201–13.

Matloff, Maurice, and Snell, Edwin M. *Strategic Planning for Coalition Warfare, 1941–1942*. A volume in *The United States Army in World War II: The War Department*. Washington: OCMH, 1953.

———. *Strategic Planning for Coalition Warfare, 1943–1944*. A volume in *The United States Army in World War II: The War Department*. Washington: OCMH, 1953.

Medlicott, W. N. *The Economic Blockade*. Vol. II. A volume in the *History of the Second World War: United Kingdom Civil Series*. London: HMSO, 1959.

Medvedev, Dm. *Silnye Dukhom*. Moscow: Soviet Writer, 1957.

Michel, Henri. *The Second World War*. Douglas Parinee, translator. New York: Praeger, 1975.

Montagu, Ewan. *Beyond Top Secret ULTRA*. New York: Coward, McCann and Geoghegan, 1978.

Moran, Lord (Charles Wilson). *Churchill: Taken from the Diaries of Lord Moran: The Struggle for Survival, 1940–1965*. Boston: Houghton Mifflin, 1966.

Morgenthau, Henry, Jr. Diaries and Papers. Franklin D. Roosevelt Library, Hyde Park, New York.

Morison, Samuel Eliot. *The Battle of the Atlantic*. Vol. I of the *History of United States Naval Operations in World War II*. 15 vols. Boston: Houghton Mifflin, 1947–62.

Morton, H. V. *Atlantic Meeting*. London: Methuen & Co., 1943.

Morton, Louis. *Strategy and Command: The First Two Years*. A volume in *The United States Army in World War II: The War in the Pacific*. Washington: GPO, 1962.

Nicolson, Harold. *The War Years, 1939–1945*. Vol. II of *The Diaries and Letters of Harold Nicolson*. Nigel Nicolson, editor. New York: Atheneum, 1967.

Nixon, Edgar, ed. *Franklin D. Roosevelt and Foreign Affairs*. 3 vols. Cambridge, Mass.: Harvard University Press, 1969.

O'Connor, Raymond G. *Diplomacy for Victory: FDR and Unconditional Surrender*. New York: W. W. Norton, 1971.

Parkinson, Roger. *A Day's March Nearer Home*. London: Hart-Davis, MacGibbon, 1974.

Pawle, Gerald. *The War and Colonel Warden: Based on the Recollections of Commander C. R. Thompson, Personal Assistant to the Prime Minister, 1940–1945*. New York: Alfred A. Knopf, 1963.

Pogue, Forrest C. *George C. Marshall: Ordeal and Hope, 1939–1942*. New York: Viking, 1966.

———. *George C. Marshall: Organizer of Victory, 1943–1945*. New York: Viking, 1973.

———. *The Supreme Command*. A volume in *The United States Army in World War II: The European Theater of Operations*. Washington: OCMH, 1954.

Pollock, Fred E. "Roosevelt, the Ogdensburg Agreement, and the British Fleet: All Done With Mirrors." *Diplomatic History* 5 (Summer 1981), 203–19.

Price, Robert. "Further Notes and Anecdotes on Spread-Spectrum Origins," *IEEE Transactions on Communications*, COM-31 (January 1983), 85–97.

Resis, Albert. "Spheres of Influence in Soviet Wartime Diplomacy." *Journal of Modern History* 53 (September 1981), 417-39.

Reynolds, David. *The Creation of the Anglo-American Alliance, 1937–1941: A Study in Competitive Co-operation*. London: Europa, 1981.

———. "Lord Lothian and Anglo-American Relations, 1939–1940," *Transactions of the American Philosophical Society*, 73, pt. 2 (1983), 1–65.

Robertson, Terence. *The Ship with Two Captains*. New York: E. P. Dutton, 1950.

Roosevelt, Elliott. *As He Saw It*. New York: Duell, Sloan and Pearce, 1946.

Roosevelt, Franklin D. Papers. Franklin D. Roosevelt Library, Hyde Park, New York.

———. *F.D.R.: His Personal Letters, 1928–1945*. Elliott Roosevelt, editor. Vol. II. New York: Duell, Sloan and Pearce, 1950.

———. *The Public Papers and Addresses of Franklin Delano Roosevelt*. Samuel I. Rosenman, editor. 13 vols. New York: Macmillan, 1938–50.

Rosenman, Samuel I. *Working With Roosevelt*. New York: Da Capo, 1972 (originally published in 1952).

Sayers, R. S. *Financial Policy, 1939–1945*. A volume in the *History of the Second World War: United Kingdom Civil Series*. London: HMSO, 1956.

Schellenberg, Walter. *The Labyrinth: The Memoirs of Walter Schellenberg*. Louis Hagen, translator. New York: Harper and Brothers, 1956.

Schrader, Capt. Albert W., USN. Diary. Navy Historical Center, Washington, D.C.

Sherwin, Martin J. *A World Destroyed*. New York: Alfred A. Knopf, 1975.

Sherwood, Robert E. *Roosevelt and Hopkins: An Intimate History*. Rev. ed. New York: Harper and Brothers, 1952.

Smith, R. Harris. *OSS: The Secret History of America's First Central Intelligence Agency*. Berkeley: University of California Press, 1972.

Soames, Mary. *Clementine Churchill*. Boston: Houghton Mifflin, 1979.

Steele, Richard W. *The First Offensive, 1942: Roosevelt, Marshall and the Making of American Strategy*. Bloomington: Indiana University Press, 1973.

Stettinius, Edward R., Jr. *The Diaries of Edward R. Stettinius, Jr., 1943–1946*. Thomas M. Campbell and George C. Herring, editors. New York: New Viewpoints, 1975.

Stevenson, William. *A Man Called Intrepid*. London: Macmillan, 1976.

Stimson, Henry L. Diaries and Papers. Sterling Memorial Library, Yale University, New Haven, Connecticut.

Thorne, Christopher. *Allies of a Kind: The United States, Britain, and the War Against Japan, 1941–1945*. New York: Oxford University Press, 1978.

———. *The Limits of Foreign Policy*. New York: G. P. Putnam's Sons, 1973.

Truman, Harry S. *Memoirs*. Vol. I. Garden City: Doubleday, 1955.

Tuchman, Barbara. *Stilwell and the American Experience in China, 1911–1945*. New York: Macmillan, 1971.

Union of Soviet Socialist Republics, Ministry of Foreign Affairs. *Correspondence between the Chairman of the Council of Ministers of the U.S.S.R. and the Presidents of the U.S.A. and the Prime Ministers of Great Britain during the Great Patriotic War of 1941–1945*. 2 vols. New York: Capricorn Books, 1965 (originally published in 1958).

———. *The Teheran, Yalta and Potsdam Conferences: Documents*. Moscow: Progress Publishers, 1969.

United Kingdom. Prime Minister's Operational and Confidential Files (PREMIER 3 and PREMIER 4). Public Record Office, London, England.

———, Cabinet Office. War Cabinet Files, Public Record Office, London, England.

———, Foreign Office. Foreign Office files, Public Record Office, London, England.

United States. *Foreign Relations of the United States.* Washington: GPO, Printing Office, 1865–.

————, Congress, Joint Committee on the Investigation of the Pearl Harbor Attack. *Hearings.* 39 parts. Washington: GPO, 1946–47.

————, Department of State. Decimal files. National Archives, Washington, D.C.

————, War Department, History Project, Strategic Services Unit. *The Overseas Targets.* Vol. II of the *War Report of the OSS.* New York: Walker, 1976.

Weigley, Russell F. *Eisenhower's Lieutenants.* Bloomington: Indiana University Press, 1981.

Wheeler-Bennett, Sir John. Editor. *Action This Day.* New York: St. Martin's, 1969.

————. *Special Relationships: America in Peace and War.* London: Macmillan, 1975.

Wilson, Theodore A. *The First Summit: Roosevelt and Churchill at Placentia Bay 1941.* Boston: Houghton Mifflin, 1969.

Wittner, Lawrence. "American Policy toward Greece during World War II." *Diplomatic History* 3 (Spring 1979), 129–49.

Woodward, Sir Llewellyn. *British Foreign Policy in the Second World War.* 5 vols. London: HMSO, 1970–76.

Zebel, Sydney H. "Harold Macmillan's Appointment as Minister Resident at Algiers, 1942." *The Journal of the Rutgers University Libraries* 42 (December 1979), 79–103.

Index

ABC-1 talks, **I**: 8, 165, 283
ABDA command, **I**: 312, 325, 330, 336, 353, 363, 365; changes in, **I**: 361; debates over representation, **I**: 339-344, 348-350; relief for, **I**: 307; terminated, **I**: 385-386
Acheson, Dean, **III**: 423
Adler, Elmer E., **I**: 672; **II**: 57-59
Adriatic Sea, **II**: 350, 389; **III**: 212, 454
Advisory Council for Italy, **II**: 643-644, 693; **III**: 53, 97, 176, 178, 190, 199
Aegean campaign, **II**: 121, 555-557
Aegean Islands, **II**: 442, 445, 455, 477, 498; Allied policy, **II**: 504-517, 558; fighting in, **II**: 513; Italians in, **II**: 341
Aegean Sea, **II**: 329, 501, 611; **III**: 351, 378, 508
Africa, **I**: 56; **II**: 73-74, 222; British in, **I**: 184; **II**: 126, 529; ferrying planes across, **I**: 209, 210; Germans in, **I**: 96, 103; Italians in, **II**: 300; supply routes to, **I**: 206, 209
Afrika Korps, Rommel's army, **I**: 152, 165
Agheila, Libya, **I**: 673; **II**: 11
Aid, military: to Britain from United States, **I**: 197; to Britain, **I**: 203
Aid, United States: to Britain, **I**: 45, 48, 56, 60, 72-73, 80, 115, 153-154; Churchill request for, 1941, **I**: 91-92; Roosevelt on, **I**: 42-43, 102
Aid, wartime, **I**: 227
Air Force, Allied, **III**: 164; for Soviet front, **I**: 545-546, 600; in Mediterranean, **II**: 350, 353, 362, 511; **III**: 228; in Middle East, **II**: 499; on D-Day, **III**: 164-165
Air Force, Australian Royal, **II**: 254
Air Force, British (R.A.F.), **I**: 96, 103, 199-200, 202, 254, 272, 316, 449, 537, 580, 598, 607; **II**: 47, 140, 559-560, 746; and aid to Soviets in Caucasus, **II**: 57-60 (*see also* Caucasus); and cross-channel invasion, **I**: 568; **II**: 39, 133; and daylight bombing, **II**: 119; and German submarines, **I**: 434; and lack of planes from U.S., **I**: 487-488; and landing in Soviet Union, **III**: 280-

285; and North African invasion, **I**: 626; and Soviets' southern flank, **I**: 543; and strategic bombing, **I**: 596-598; and V-1 bombing, **III**: 196; attack on Berlin, **III**: 195-196; bomber force, **II**: 218; bombing of France, **III**: 122; Churchill on, **I**: 304; deployment of, **III**: 348; in Blitz, **I**: 74; in Egyptian campaign, **I**: 660; in India, **I**: 411; in Italy, **II**: 565; in Mediterranean, **II**: 529; in North Africa, **I**: 316; **II**: 145; in Pacific theater, **III**: 38; 1943 manpower plans for, **II**: 94; Roosevelt on, **I**: 61, 503; sink *Tirpitz*, **III**: 388; Slessor as commander in Mediterranean, **II**: 732
Air Force, Dutch, **II**: 746
Air Force, French, **II**: 746
Air Force, German, **I**: 333, 350, 436, 469, 503, 596; **II**: 49, 134, 139-140, 266; **III**: 122; Allied policy toward, **I**: 579; and aid to Soviets in Caucasus, **I**: 621-623, 637; and convoys to Soviet Union, **I**: 527-528, 530, 537, 595, 609; **II**: 160-164; and cross-channel invasion, **III**: 164; at Stalingrad, **II**: 52; bombers, types of, **II**: 26-27; Churchill on, **I**: 302, 651; compared to British, **I**: 316; deployment of, **I**: 532, 538; **II**: 247, 267, 509-511; in Ceylon, **I**: 438; in Crete, **I**: 202-203; in Eastern Mediterranean, **II**: 498-499; in Japan, **I**: 305; in Soviet Union, **I**: 598; in Western Europe, 1942, **I**: 568; in Yugoslavia and Greece, 1943, **II**: 410-411; losses, **I**: 42; 1943 production plans for, **II**: 94-95; on Malta, **I**: 467; pilotless planes of, **III**: 161; strength of, **I**: 497; **II**: 152; to Azores, **II**: 330-331; to Turkey, **II**: 196-197
Air Force, Italian, **I**: 318; **II**: 424; and Germans, 1943, **II**: 455; fighting for Allies, **II**: 725; in Yugoslavia, **II**: 411
Air Force, Japanese, **I**: 306; **II**: 154; difficulty in replenishing losses, **I**: 322; losses at Midway, **I**: 507; losses in Ceylon, **I**: 461; losses of, **III**: 193
Air Force, New Zealand, **II**: 36

Air Force, Norwegian, **II**: 746
Air Force, Polish, **II**: 741; **III**: 282
Air Force, Soviet, **I**: 304; **II**: 58-59, 558
Air Force, United States, **I**: 37, 45-46,
    343-344, 382, 455-456, 503; **II**: 46,
    140, 559; **III**: 626; aid to Britain, **I**:
    199-200, 484-488; aid to Soviets in
    Caucasus, **I**: 544, 579-581; **II**: 77-78,
    185 (*see also* Caucasus); aid to Soviets
    in south, **I**: 562; and Azores, **II**: 564;
    and Burma, **II**: 112; and cross-chan-
    nel invasion, **II**: 39, 133; and landing
    in Soviet Union, **III**: 280-285; and
    strategic bombing, **I**: 596-598;
    Churchill on, **I**: 454; **II**: 518; deploy-
    ment of, 1942, **I**: 392-393, 509; Ferry-
    ing Command, **I**: 199-200; in Battle
    of Philippine Sea, **III**: 193; in Britain,
    I: 509, 604; **II**: 218; **III**: 220; in
    China, **II**: 294, 294, 542, 690; **III**: 12;
    in India, **I**: 450; **II**: 294; in Italian
    campaign, **II**: 436, 553, 565; in Medi-
    terranean, **I**: 318; **II**: 529, 628; in
    North Africa, **II**: 145; Roosevelt on
    priorities for, **I**: 390-393; strength of,
    1942, **I**: 315; use of in battles, 1941, **I**:
    222
Air Force, Yugoslav, **III**: 306
Air Ministry, British, **I**: 66
Air power: Allied superiority expected,
    1943, **I**: 499; Allied superiority in
    Egyptian campaign, **I**: 659; Allied su-
    periority in Mediterranean, **III**: 222;
    Allied vs. German strengths, 1942, **I**:
    497; Allied, Stalin on, **II**: 287; and
    second-front negotiations, **I**: 495;
    British in Mediterranean, **I**: 216; Brit-
    ish in North Africa, **I**: 543; British in
    India, **III**: 49-50; British vs. German,
    I: 245; Churchill on, **I**: 303, 562, 651;
    discussed at Atlantic Conference, **I**:
    226; Germans at Stalingrad, **I**: 618-
    619; Germans in Mediterranean, **I**:
    175; in central Mediterranean, 1943,
    II: 12; in cross-channel invasion, **III**:
    186; in European theater, **III**: 611; in
    Italian campaign, **II**: 444; inferiority
    of British in Far East, **I**: 350-351; Jap-
    anese, Stalin on, **I**: 305; Japanese in
    ANZAC area, **I**: 385; Japanese at Sin-
    gapore, **I**: 361; Japanese on Java, **I**:

    364-365, 367-368; key in defeat of
    Rommel, **I**: 210; Mountbatten on, **III**:
    51, 55; Roosevelt on for Pacific, **II**:
    755; Roosevelt on importance of
    1943, **II**: 46; Soviet weakness in, late
    1942, **I**: 672
Air Training Conference, **I**: 457
Air Transport Command, U.S., **III**: 49-
    50, 50-52, 56
Aircraft, Allied:
    against submarines, **II**: 217
    bombers, **I**: 367; B-29, **III**: 193;
    better target-finding techniques, **I**:
    424; importance of, **I**: 210-211
    British needs for 1941, **I**: 105, 107
    ferrying of, **I**: 206-207, 210, 369,
    370
    in Burma and China, **III**: 427-430
    losses over Poland, **III**: 282
    Mountbatten requests, **III**: 50-52,
    56
    Roosevelt on needs for 1943, **II**: 44-
    45
    to Soviet Union, **II**: 57-58, 65, 172-
    174, 190-191
    to Turkey, **II**: 133
Aircraft, Soviet: 1942 production fig-
    ures, **I**: 566; 1943 needs for, **II**: 94-95
Aircraft, United States, **I**: 203; **III**: 297;
    and aid to Soviets, **I**: 629; bombers, **I**:
    297, 453, 566; **II**: 11, 26-27, 594;
    Churchill requests, **I**: 414; deploy-
    ment of, **I**: 596-598; ferrying of, **I**:
    202-203; losses at Midway, **I**: 507;
    production of, **I**: 241, 597-598, 638-
    639; **II**: 46; to Australia, **II**: 254; to
    Britain, **I**: 40, 74, 80, 153, 435, 484-
    488, 509-510, 513, 518, 524, 532, 538,
    598; **II**: 27; to India, **I**: 462, 464; to
    India and Burma, **I**: 449-450; to So-
    viet Union, **I**: 507, 566
Ajeta, Marquis, **II**: 428
Akyab, Burma, **II**: 112; **III**: 19-20
Alam el Halda, battle of, **I**: 585
Alaska, **I**: 392, 609; **II**: 54-55; **III**: 191,
    243, 258
Alaska-Siberian route, **I**: 609, 619
Alba, Duke of, **II**: 101; **III**: 99, 106
Albania, **I**: 67, 144-145, 153, 209; **II**:
    349, 350, 459; Axis brutalities re-
    ported in, **II**: 418-419; guerrilla activ-

ity in, 1943, **II**: 184, 409-410
Aleutian Islands, **I**: 381, 382, 507; **II**:
216; **III**: 266
Alexander I of Russia, **II**: 54
Alexander, Sir Harold, **I**: 189, 424, 461-
462, 635; **II**: 98, 122, 128, 131, 304,
481-482, 562-563, 573, 592, 607, 621-
624, 627-629, 632, 641, 651, 658; **III**:
265, 393, 410, 411, 485, 489-490, 494,
522, 534, 563, 614, 615; and invasion
of southern France, **III**: 214, 219,
222; and liberation of Rome, **III**: 163;
and New Zealand troops, **II**: 207; and
Stilwell, **I**: 422-423; at Malta and Yalta
Conferences, **III**: 491, 516-517;
Churchill view of, **I**: 417, 552, 554-
555; **III**: 498; command changes of,
II: 639; Egyptian campaign, report
on, 1942, **I**: 659-660, 663; in Burma,
I: 417-418; in Greece, **III**: 451, 458;
in Italy, **II**: 307, 632, 435-436; **III**:
110-112, 139, 143, 150, 162-163, 167,
197-198, 225, 228, 289-290, 299-301,
304-305, 347-348, 448, 586, 611; in
North Africa, **I**: 611; **II**: 11-12, 23,
136, 138-139, 140-141; in Sicily, **II**:
188-190; in western Europe, **III**: 552-
553; LIGHTFOOT campaign operations, **I**: 604; on Australian troops in
Egypt, **I**: 645; on Italian campaign, **II**:
728-729
Alexandria, Egypt, **I**: 132-133, 301, 517,
521-522, 525; **II**: 84-85, 147-148, 572-
573, 568, 600; **III**: 378, 381, 395, 450,
502
Algeria, **I**: 54, 56, 176, 669; **II**: 30, 68,
75, 145; **III**: 228; Allied landing in,
1942, **I**: 667; in North African invasion, **II**: 3; post-TORCH situation, **II**:
12; Roosevelt on invasion of, **I**: 533
Algiers, Algeria, **I**: 180, 669; **II**: 66-67,
74, 187, 209, 227, 238, 273, 274, 463,
568, 600, 626, 642; **III**: 537-538; and
North African invasion, **I**: 577-578, 581,
582-583, 585-590, 593, 667; **II**; 9;
Churchill visit to, 1943, **II**: 136, 216-
217, 219
Ali, Rashid, **I**: 178, 185, 188
Allied Coastal Command, **II**: 366
Allied Control Commission, Italy, **II**:
467-469, 487-488, 539-540, 643-644,

679-680, 693, 727; **III**: 30, 189, 323-
324, 333, 371-373, 375, 387, 400-401,
526, 537, 625, 635, 636
Allied Military Government, **II**: 529
Almagia, Carlos, **II**: 486
Alois, Hitler's family name, **III**: 290
Alpes Maritimes, France, **II**: 692
Alsace, France, **III**: 338
Ambrosio, d'Armata Vittorio, **II**: 423
Amenia, New York, **II**: 163-164
American Expeditionary Force (WWI),
I: 615
American Federation of Labor, **I**: 87
American Gifts Committee, **I**: 512, 526
American Red Cross, **I**: 116-118, 125;
II: 86-87, 105
American Regional Council, **II**: 223-224
American Volunteer Group (China), **I**:
332-333, 461-462, 464-465; **II**: 205
Amery, L. S., **III**: 105
Ammunition, Allied, production of, **I**:
615
Ammunition, U.S., production of, **I**:
631-632
Anatolia, Turkey, **I**: 295, 319
Anders, Wladyslaw, **II**: 392; warned Al-
lies on Soviet intentions, **II**: 392, 703-
704
Anderson, F. L., **II**: 517-518
Anderson, K.A.N., **I**: 578; **II**: 145, 517-
518; and Darlan deal, **II**: 28; in North
Africa, **II**: 12
Anderson, Sir John, **I**: 279; **II**: 359-360;
III: 34-35, 289-290
Andrews, Frank, **I**: 422; **II**: 281
Anfa Hotel, Casablanca, **II**: 96
Anglo-American Caribbean Commission,
I: 323
Anglo-American Mission: to Soviet
Union, September l941, **I**: 239
Anglo-American relations: and ABDA
command controversies, **I**: 339-343;
and atomic research cooperation, **II**:
214; and breaking enemy codes, **I**:
215; and civil aviation policy, **III**: 402,
567; and Greek crisis, **III**: 450-452,
455-456; and Imperial preference system, **I**: 356; and invasion of southern
France debate, **III**: 225-229; and Italy, **II**: 539-540; and joint naval units
in Pacific, **II**: 60-61; and joint staff

Anglo-American relations (*cont.*)
meetings, **II**: 70; and Madagascar invasion, **I**: 434; and North African invasion plans, **I**: 576-579, 581-592; and pooling of new ships, **I**: 538-539, 541; and postwar economic arrangements, **II**: 743-744; and postwar issues, **I**: 19; **II**: 146, 744-745, 754-755; and recognition of French committee, **II**: 310; and Second Washington Conference, **I**: 513; and self-determination issue, **II**: 360; and sharing codes, **I**: 370; and St. Pierre-Miquelon affair, **I**: 325-326; and unity of commands, **I**: 293; and wheat agreement, **I**: 251; Argentina, dispute on, **III**: 231, 354; at Cairo Conferences, **II**: 609-610; at Casablanca Conference, **II**: 117, 121; at Teheran Conference, **II**: 610; atomic research, cooperation on, **I**: 514; Britain as junior partner, **I**: 10, 15; British dollar balances and, **III**: 34-36; changes in after Teheran, **II**: 708; China-Burma-India theater and, **II**: 274-277; Churchill chooses over French, **III**: 102, 170; Churchill defends war policies, **II**: 527-530; Churchill fears for in 1944, **II**: 565; Churchill on as "righteous comradeship," **I**: 309; Churchill on cooperation in, **I**: 125; Churchill on Hopkins role in, **II**: 682; Churchill on over India, **I**: 448-449; Churchill on own conference, **II**: 543-544; Churchill's views on, **I**: 6; **II**: 226-227, 333; **III**: 31; cooperation in, **I**: 9; cooperation on anti-sub campaign, **II**: 228; cooperation on supply, **I**: 212-213, 217, 326-329, 506, 539; Darlan deal, dispute on, **II**: 40; de Gaulle challenges supremacy of, **III**: 62; de Gaulle, dispute over, **II**: 254-257; debate military diplomatic negotiations, **III**: 23; differences in war strategy, late 1942, **I**: 670; differences on Poland after Yalta, **III**: 560-565, 567-572; discord minimized by Churchill, **I**: 4-6; early British view, **I**: 7; economic coordination during war, **II**: 750; European strategy disputes, **III**: 197-199; French, dispute over, **II**: 235; **III**: 194, 315-319; Greek policy, dispute on, **III**: 95-99, 436-437; Italy, disputes over, **II**: 187-190, 202, 230, 455; joint strategic planning, **I**: 165; lend-lease aid, dispute over, **I**: 137-143; military cooperation in, **I**: 182-183; naval cooperation, problems with, **I**: 452; postwar politics in, **III**: 3, 436-439; postwar prospects, **III**: 93, 109, 428-429; press leaks, strain over, **II**: 530-532; production disputes, **I**: 638; Roosevelt favors Soviets, **II**: 596; Roosevelt's views on, **I**: 6; **III**: 34; scientific cooperation, **I**: 249; Sicily invasion as joint effort, **II**: 303-308; southern France invasion, dispute on, **III**: 212-223; U.S. as main military contributor, **II**: 609

Anglo-American Shipping Adjustment Board, **I**: 327-328

Anglo-American Supply Mission (1941), **I**: 242-244

Anglo-American Tank Board, **I**: 213

Anglo-American Tank Commission (WWI), **I**: 212

Anglo-Portuguese Alliance, **II**: 240, 243, 252, 262-263, 533, 674-675

Anglo-Soviet-French agreement, **III**: 440-441, 444-445

Angola, **II**: 239

Ankara, Turkey, **II**: 547, 551

Anti-Comintern Pact of 1939, **I**: 74

Anti-submarine campaign, **I**: 29, 75, 164-165, 207, 424, 538-539, 541; **II**: 646-647, 711; **III**: 11-13, 22-23, 112, 115, 163, 251-252, 542-543; and convoys to Soviets, **II**: 536; and improvements in radar, **II**: 26-27; and Normandy invasion, **III**: 268; and ship production in Britain, 1943, **II**: 94; blinded by German code change, **I**: 451-452; Churchill on, **I**: 651; **II**: 267; **III**: 125-126; during Normandy invasion, **III**: 276; effect of long-range aircraft on, **II**: 216-217; impact of sonar, **I**: 27; improvement in, fall 1943, **II**: 571, 574-575; Irish policy toward, **III**: 57-58; issue of publicity on, **II**: 312-313; **III**: 374, 382, 384, 386; monthly statement on, **II**: 230, 298, 310, 313-314, 316, 370, 382-383, 513-

514, 569, 656, 658-659; **III**: 79, 81, 121-122, 165-168, 233, 235-237, 264, 266, 280, 312, 345-346, 396, 441, 445, 500-501, 544, 551, 618-619; renewed German attacks, fall 1943, **II**: 499-501; report on, winter 1944, **II**: 710; Roosevelt on, **I**: 420-422; **II**: 260-261; Stalin on, **II**: 286; successes in, 1943, **II**: 247, 366-367, 387; U.S. aids, 1941, **I**: 153-154

Antigua, **I**: 67-68

Antwerp, Belgium, **III**: 446, 448, 487

Apennines, Italy, **II**: 443-444; **III**: 300, 434

Arabs, **I**: 557; **II**: 209, 599-600; **III**: 286, 390, 536; and Jewish refugees in North Africa, **II**: 315

Archangel, U.S.S.R., **I**: 503-504, 528, 537, 637; **II**: 51, 528, 535

Arciszewski, Mrs. T., **III**: 553, 558

Arciszewski, Tomasz, **III**: 461, 465, 476, 553

Arctic Ocean, **II**: 442

Ardeatine Caves, Italy, **III**: 333

Ardennes, Belgium, battle at, **III**: 437, 470, 487-488, 494-495, 497-498, 524, 608

Argentina, **I**: 29, 247; **II**: 103; **III**: 224, 230-231, 233-234, 244, 246-248, 297, 303-304, 390, 484, 520, 544; Allied policy toward, **II**: 678-679, 681-684; **III**: 68, 346-347, 354, 396-397, 399, 430-431, 613-616, 636-637; and Axis powers, **III**: 252-253; and Britain, **III**: 290-291; Churchill on, **II**: 668

Armed Forces, Allied, **I**: 542; **II**: 166; Churchill on limited number, 1944, **II**: 556; command structure, **III**: 82-84; deployment of, 1942, **I**: 391-393

Armed Forces, United States: Roosevelt on use of, **I**: 230-231, 541, 555

Armour, Norman, **III**: 224

Army, Allied, **III**: 617, 630; casualties in western Europe, 1945, **III**: 615; European theater, deployment of, **III**: 356-357; size of for D-Day, **III**: 164-165; troops needed on western front, **III**: 499-501

Army, Australian, **I**: 31-35, 81, 368; in Middle East, **I**: 644-645, 653

Army, Brazilian, **III**: 285-286, 294

Army, British, **I**: 43, 360; **II**: 47; **III**: 411; and cross-channel invasion, 1943, **II**: 133, 556; and Greece, **III**: 279; and North African invasion, **I**: 582, 588, 593; casualties, **II**: 529, 627; **III**: 179, 604; Churchill and, **III**: 178; Churchill defends in India, **II**: 528; command structure of, **I**: 256-257, 259; **I**: 129; deployment of, 1942, **I**: 379-380, 383, 438, 498; deployment of, 1943, **I**: 650; **II**: 15; Eighth, **III**: 228, 289, 296, 298, 299-300, 304-305; Eighth, at El Alamein, **I**: 657, 660, 663; Eighth, in Italy, **II**: 358, 454, 663; Eighth, in North Africa, **II**: 136, 144, 187, 189-190; First, at Anzio, **II**: 641; First, in North Africa, **II**: 144; French aid to, **III**: 197; in Balkans, **III**: 198; in France, **III**: 262-263; in Greece, **III**: 350, 447, 450-461, 466-467, 474, 606; in India, **II**: 751; in Italy, **II**: 565; in Mediterranean, **I**: 184; in Middle East, **I**: 235-236; **II**: 50; in North Africa, **I**: 543, 603; **II**: 51; in western Europe, **III**: 348, 408-409, 498-499, 603-604, 607-608; Stain on, **III**: 175, 20, 230; strength of, 1943, **I**: 80, 108, 648, 651-654; Twenty-first in Normandy, **III**: 183

Army, British Imperial, **I**: 159, 256, 257, 259; **III**: 290, 604

Army, British Indian, **III**: 271

Army, Bulgarian, **II**: 554, 714; brutalities in Greece reported, **II**: 416-417; in Yugoslavia, **II**: 403, 406, 410; **III**: 359

Army, Canadian, **I**: 542; **II**: 321-322; **III**: 82-83, 408, 534, 607

Army, Chinese, **III**: 54-55, 422-423, 428-429, 435, 572, 582-583; equipping of, Cairo Conference on, **II**: 608; in India, **I**: 653; in Indo-China, **III**: 627; U.S. responsibility for, **III**: 370

Army, Croatian, **II**: 405, 407, 410

Army, Dutch, **II**: 281

Army, French, **I**: 180; **III**: 634; Allied supplies to, **III**: 500-501; and cross-channel invasion, **III**: 170; and southern France invasion, **III**: 86-88; as relief for U.S. forces in France, **II**: 746-747; Churchill on, **III**: 225; control of

Army, French (*cont.*)

in North Africa, **II**: 237, 254-256, 262, 272-273, 440-442; expedition to Corsica, **II**: 464-466; in Aegean Islands, **II**: 442, 445; in France, **III**: 164; in Italian campaign, **III**: 88, 136, 149-150; in Middle East, **II**: 603; in North Africa, **I**: 589; **II**: 12, 51, 145, 217, 257-258, 274, 335, 439; **III**: 228; in North Africa, Churchill on, **I**: 673; in western Europe, **III**: 216, 218, 222-223, 408-409; rearming of, **II**: 338, 340, 746; **III**: 237, 390-391, 393-394, 411-412, 416, 500-501

Army, French Colonial, **I**: 667

Army, German, **I**: 319; **II**: 102; **III**: 411, 412, 500

and cross-channel invasion, **III**: 164-165

and Hitler, **III**: 330

and second front, **II**: 132; **III**: 90

at Stalingrad, **I**: 672; **II**: 62-63, 138

British proclamation to, **III**: 575-576, 578

brutalities reported, **II**: 414-416, 418-419

casualties in western Europe, **I**: 302; **III**: 408

defeats of, summer 1944, **III**: 298-299

deployment of, **I**: 495-499, 622; **II**: 329; **III**: 217-218, 222-223, 228-229, 280

fears Hess, **I**: 189

in Eastern Europe, **II**: 362, 554; **III**: 434-435

in Finland, **III**: 61

in France, **III**: 127-128, 194, 263, 308, 338

in Greece, 1943, **II**: 407-410; **III**: 449

in Italy, **II**: 349-350, 358, 361, 380-381, 423-429, 434, 435-436, 556; **III**: 119-120, 127-128, 135-136, 137, 142-143, 163-164, 232, 299-300, 356, 395, 586; and surrender talks, **III**: 609-612; Churchill on, **II**: 442-446; Roosevelt on, **III**: 302

in southern France, **III**: 304-305

in Soviet Union, **I**: 208, 307, 544, 567; **II**: 39, 166, 336, 386, 545; **III**: 610

in Warsaw Uprising, **III**: 292-293

in western Europe, **I**: 568; **III**: 608-609, 615-616

in Yugoslavia, **II**: 403-407, 410; **III**: 191

movement to western front, **III**: 468-469

Panzer army in North Africa, **I**: 673

Stalin on, **I**: 562; **II**: 153

treatment of prisoners of war, **II**: 393

Army, Greek, **III**: 450, 466-467; mutiny of, **III**: 95-97, 113, 114 (*see also* Greece)

Army, Hungarian, **II**: 416

Army, Indian, **II**: 248; composition of, **I**: 373-379, 388-389

Army, Iranian, **III**: 9

Army, Israeli, **III**: 298

Army, Italian, **II**: 464, 725; and Germans, **II**: 455, 484; Churchill on, **II**: 517; in Aegean Islands, **II**: 442, 445, 455, 497, 509-511; in Allied declaration, **II**: 307-308; in Balkans, **II**: 403-406, 410, 416, 442; in East African campaign, **I**: 159; in Egypt, **I**: 112, 672; in France, **III**: 164; in Germany, treatment of, **II**: 446; **III**: 372-373; in Greece, **II**: 408-410; in Italian surrender, **II**: 349, 361, 364, 423-424, 426, 428-429, 456; in Libya, **I**: 126-127, 216; in Tunisia, **II**: 152; morale of, **II**: 329, 341, 351; **III**: 190; Roosevelt on, **II**: 300-301, 649-650

Army, Japanese, **I**: 441; **III**: 256; in Saipan, **III**: 193-194; on Guadalcanal defense, **II**: 6

Army, New Zealand, **II**: 32, 33, 35-37

Army, Polish, **I**: 653; **II**: 203-205; **III**: 135; and London Poles, **III**: 73; in Italy, **II**: 741; in Soviet Union, **I**: 529, 532, 593-594; **II**: 194, 199, 201; in Warsaw Uprising, **III**: 291-293; Stalin on, **III**: 476

Army, Roumanian, **III**: 179

Army, Soviet, **I**: 14, 622; **II**: 247, 267, 565, 637; **III**: 316, 339, 427, 523, 630

and Japanese, **III**: 342

and Polish Underground, **III**: 209

and Roumanian army, **III**: 179

and Warsaw Uprising, **III**: 259-261

at Stalingrad, **I**: 672

carries burden of fighting, 1942, **I:** 495-500

Churchill on, **I:** 360, 637; **II:** 154, 266; **III:** 90, 349, 616

controls Stalin, **I:** 637

deployment of in Caucasus, **I:** 565

in Austria, **III:** 605

Eastern Europe, **II:** 724; **III:** 153, 298, 302, 433-434, 625

in Germany, **III:** 602, 605

in Manchuria, **III:** 318

in Poland, **II:** 684, 686-688, 701, 708, 717-718, 723, 736-738, 740, 742; **III:** 48, 60-61, 253-254, 272, 312, 363, 465, 492, 526, 545, 553-558, 561, 618; Churchill on, **III:** 72-73; Roosevelt on, **III:** 79

in Yugoslavia, **III:** 359, 510

losses compared to Anglo-Americans, **II:** 288

Roosevelt on, **I:** 545; **II:** 260, 440; **III:** 94, 251, 611

Stalin on, **II:** 132, 170-180, 476, 545; **III:** 114, 200, 234

Stalin on Allied help to, **I:** 567; **II:** 534

Stalin on Polish threat to, **III:** 476

successes of, **II:** 386; **III:** 13, 159, 172-173, 280-281

Army, Spanish, **II:** 725, 739

Army, United States, **I:** 199-200, 343, 368, 574; **III:** 237, 411; and Burma, **II:** 118; and North African invasion, **I:** 582, 587-588, 641; and Pacific command struggles, **I:** 409; and supplies from India to China, **II:** 693; assists Churchill at Marrakesh, **II:** 668; at Battle of the Bulge, **III:** 498, 499; at Cherbourg, **III:** 194-195; at Luzon, **I:** 360; Churchill and Stalin on, **III:** 352; Churchill fears of standing idle, **I:** 308; Churchill on, **II:** 33, 528; **III:** 74, 163, 203, 274, 299, 604; Churchill on British contacts with, **I:** 454; Churchill on use of token forces, **I:** 201; deployment of, Europe, **III:** 214-220, 222-223, 225, 228, 356-357; distaste for political role, **III:** 400; Fifth, **II:** 663; **III:** 149, 285-286, 289, 299-300, 304-305, 348; First in Belgium, **III:** 487; First in Europe, **III:** 408-409, 487; French aid to, **III:** 197; in China, **III:**

54-55; in France, **III:** 164, 378; in Iran, **III:** 7-8; in Italy, **II:** 436, 565; **III:** 305; in New Zealand, **II:** 36; in Northern Ireland, **II:** 186-187; in Pacific, **III:** 193; in postwar Europe, **I:** 230-231; in Saipan, **III:** 193; in western Europe, **III:** 604-605, 608; losses in North Africa and Italy, **II:** 529; military plans, 1942, **I:** 543, 603-604, 610; newspaper for troops, **I:** 619-620, 625; Nimitz on, **III:** 272; Ninth in Europe, **III:** 408-409; plans for postwar Germany, **III:** 316; Poles in, **II:** 198; Seventh, **II:** 358; **III:** 308, 408-409; Sixth, in Philippines, **III:** 376; size of in Mediterranean, **II:** 628; Stalin on, **III:** 175, 200, 230; strength of, 1942, **I:** 315; Third, **II:** 641; **III:** 170, 263, 340, 408, 487, 601; to Britain, **I:** 530, 650; **II:** 38; **III:** 18; troops to Australia, **II:** 24-26

Army, Yugoslav, **III:** 300, 306

Arnhem, assault on, **III:** 262, 340

Arnold-Evill-McCain: Patterson agreement, **II:** 115

Arnold-Portal agreement on aircraft, **I:** 484-488

Arnold-Towers-Slessor agreement, **II:** 26

Arnold, H. H., **I:** 183, 191-192, 196, 338, 435, 504, 598; **II:** 70, 517-518, 540, 622-623; and aircraft to Britain, **I:** 490, 509, 513; **III:** 150; and Casablanca Conference planning, **II:** 55; and daylight bombing, **II:** 185; at Malta Conference, **III:** 503; on air strength for North Africa, **I:** 514; on American Volunteer Group, **I:** 332; on building up air forces, 1942, **I:** 484-488; on priority of German defeat, **I:** 597; on trip to Cairo, **II:** 606-608; rejects planes for Polish exiles, **I:** 488

Artillery, British, **I:** 256

Artillery, Soviet, **I:** 565

Artillery, United States: in Egypt, **I:** 516; to Middle East theater, **I:** 592-593

ASDIC (underwater sound device), **I:** 27-28, 43, 57

Asia, **II:** 222; American vs. British interests in, **II:** 696, 755-756; Roosevelt on

Asia (cont.)
  "Asia for the Asiatics," **I**: 401; U.S. interests in bases in, **III**: 237
Asia, East: Teheran-Cairo talks and postwar shape, **II**: 613
Asia, Southern: Germans in, **I**: 96, 103
Asmara, Eritrea, **I**: 203; **II**: 526, 545, 547
ASPIDISTRA (British radio transmitter), **I**: 626-627
Assam, India, **III**: 12; Japanese threat to, **III**: 51-52
Athens, Greece, **III**: 278, 296, 366, 368, 371, 380, 395, 449, 451, 453, 466-467, 471, 474, 547, 607
Athlone, Earl of, **II**: 422
Atlantic Charter, **I**: 227-228, 309, 490, 569; **II**: 21, 129-130, 599; **III**: 5-6, 10, 325, 328, 526, 538; and colonialism, **I**: 557-560; and self-determination, **II**: 360, 369; and Soviet territorial claims, **I**: 394
Atlantic Conference (RIVIERA, 1941), **I**: clxv, 225, 227-230, 265-266; **III**: 574
Atlantic Islands, in Churchill strategy, **I**: 298
Atlantic Ocean, **I**: 78, 97; **II**: 442; British Navy in, **I**: 300; Churchill on northern route, **I**: 112; problems of shipping in, 1943, **II**: 158-165; strategic importance of, **I**: 46
Atlantic Ocean, North: strategic importance of, **I**: 29, 90-91, 98, 102, 163-164
Atlantic Ocean, South: strategic importance of, **I**: 28-32, 90-91, 98
Atlantic theater: as U.S.-British command, **I**: 397-699, 430
Atlantic, Battle of, **I**: 96, 177, 191, 225, 285, 414; **III**: 112, 233, 492-493; Allied victory in, **II**: 571, 574-575, 710; **III**: 11-13, 22-23, 251; and British, **I**: 161-162; and convoys to Soviet Union, **I**: 530; Azores important in, **II**: 239; British position in, **I**: 216, 218-219, 362; Churchill on, **I**: 56, 171-175, 298; **II**: 173-176; critical stage, **I**: 152; effect of breaking of codes on, **I**: 241; German successes, **I**: 149-150, 407; in early war, **I**: 24, 89, 95, 103; renewed,

fall 1943, **II**: 160-163, 476-477, 500-501; Roosevelt on, **I**: 165-166, 184, 212; scientific instruments help Allies, **II**: 228-229; shortage of destroyers in, **II**: 21; sinking of *Bismarck*, **I**: 196-198; U.S. aid to Britain for, **I**: 106, 236-237; U.S. patrols in, **I**: 185
Atomic bomb, **III**: 527
Atomic research (TUBE ALLOYS), **I**: 514; **II**: 214; **III**: 289-290, 412-413, 509; Anglo-American sharing of, **I**: 249, 279; **II**: 317, 351, 359-360, 420-421; at Second Washington Conference, **I**: 513-514; decisions on at Quebec, 1943, **II**: 431; discussed at Quebec, 1944, **III**: 318-319
Atrocities, **II**: 551, 554; Allied policy regarding, **II**: 519-521, 547
Attlee, Clement, **I**: 244, 247, 252, 569; **II**: 620
Auchinleck, Sir Claude J. E., **I**: 216, 244, 252, 254, 258, 269, 317, 516, 543; 551; **II**: 248, 542, 598-599; in Libya, **I**: 272-273, 469; in North Africa, **I**: 294-295, 493-494, 532, 538; relieved of command, **I**: 353, 554-555
Australia, **I**: 91, 174-175, 182, 206, 247, 276, 299-301, 300, 307, 364-365, 382, 487; **II**: 35, 102, 168, 207, 269, 443, 759; **III**: 39; aid to India for famine, **III**: 117, 155; Allied forces in, 1942, **I**: 321, 393; and ABDA command, **I**: 9, 339-344, 349; and Britain, **I**: 425, 427-429, 457; and defense of homeland, **I**: 364-365, 369, 384-388; 390-390; **II**: 22-26, 31-35; and Japan, **I**: 136, 361, 381, 383, 398-399, 429-432; **III**: 244, 246; and military command, **I**: 312, 330-332, 335-337, 409; issue of U.S. aid to, **I**: 438; Roosevelt asks troops to Burma, **I**: 366-367; Roosevelt on, **I**: 363, 421; ships in Pacific theater, **III**: 374; U.S. troops to, **I**: 389, 432-433 (*see also* Army, Australian)
Australian Labour Party, **II**: 33
Australian War Council, **I**: 330
Australian-New Zealand command (ANZAC), **I**: 174-175, 342-343, 363, 365, 369, 382, 384-388; command structure in, **I**: 431-432

Austria, **II**: 769; **III**: 147, 159, 364, 434, 493, 523, 605, 613, 617; Allied strategy toward, **III**: 198; and Britain, **III**: 274; in American occupation zone, **II**: 746; liberation of, **III**: 299; occupation of, **III**: 524; U.S. policy toward, 1945, **III**: 635

Austro-Hungarian Empire, **II**: 223; **III**: 363

Avranches, France, battle in, **III**: 263, 289

Axis Powers, **I**: 315; **II**: 103; and British, **I**: 184-185; in North Africa, **II**: 68

Azerbaijan, Soviet Union, **III**: 511

Azores, **I**: 86, 171-173, 177, 186; Allies and, **II**: 214, 239-241, 249-250, 251-252, 254, 262-263, 291-293, 295-296, 298-299, 309, 330-331, 494-495, 506-507, 524-525, 532-533; American negotiations on, **II**: 326, 495-497, 515, 564, 566-567, 574, 590-591, 667-668, 674-675, 677; British plans for, **I**: 200-202; **II**: 513; Churchill on, **I**: 180-181; **II**: 324-326; Roosevelt on, **I**: 178; **II**: 367

Back-door-to-war policy, **I**: 136-137

Baden, Germany, **II**: 708; **III**: 364

Badoglio, Pietro, **II**: 347-349, 358, 360, 366, 369, 384, 423-425, 427, 452, 483, 486, 586, 663, 711-712, 759-760, 766; **III**: 176, 182-183, 185, 188-190, 199, 437-439, 443-444; Allied view of, **II**: 679-680, 697, 723, 725; **III**: 41-46, 52; and Allies and Axis, **II**: 378-381; and Italian fleet, **II**: 665, 670, 697-698; **III**: 88; and surrender negotiations with Allies, **II**: 446-447, 455, 457-459, 461-462, 467, 469, 472, 474, 524, 552-553; anti-Bolshevism of, **II**: 654; remains in power, **III**: 52

Baghdad, Iraq, **I**: 178, 185-186; **II**: 74, 526; Allied troops in, 1942, **I**: 320

Bahama Islands, **I**: 52-53, 59-60, 65, 68. *See also* Windsor, Duke of

Baillieu, Sir Clive, **I**: 327, 329

Baku, Soviet Union: oil fields, **I**: 671, 673; **II**: 17

Balearic Islands, **III**: 16

Balkan Federation, **II**: 223; Churchill on, **II**: 222-223; Roosevelt on, **III**: 133

Balkan nations, **I**: 12, 13, 170, 171, 292, 669; **II**: 13, 102, 130, 283, 331, 349, 425-426, 477, 554, 556, 558; **III**: 147, 227, 299, 334, 429; Allied strategy toward, **II**: 246-247, 498-499, 504-505, 548-549, 549-551; **III**: 80, 198, 221-223; and Italian surrender, **II**: 347; and Soviet Union, **II**: 610-611; **III**: 229; Anglo-Soviet agreement on, **III**: 177-183, 185, 200-201, 207-208, 340; as General Wilson's territory, **III**: 15; at Malta Conference, **III**: 523; at Moscow Conference, 1944, **III**: 359; at Quebec Conference, 1943, **II**: 430; at Quebec Conference, 1944, **III**: 453-454; at Third Washington Conference, **II**: 218; British policy toward, **III**: 270, 274-275; fighting in, **III**: 434-435; Germans in, **I**: 134, 175, 196, 204; **II**: 266-267; Hitler strategy in, **III**: 119; in World War I, **II**: 516; Italian Army in, **II**: 329, 424, 455; postwar, Roosevelt on, **II**: 709; **III**: 160; postwar spheres in, **I**: 221; **II**: 508-509; **III**: 153-154, 351; rivalries in, **II**: 389; Roosevelt on, **III**: 198, 302, 448, 489-490; Stalin wants second front in, **I**: 237-238; strategy in, Churchill on, **I**: 302; **II**: 128, 380, 442, 444-445; **III**: 349-353; U.S. policy toward, **III**: 276, 350, 634-635

Balmoral, Scotland, **III**: 249

Baltic Sea, **II**: 161-162, 173, 746, 765; **III**: 312, 602

Baltic States: and Soviet Union, **I**: 228, 394, 470, 505; **II**: 178; **III**: 349; at Moscow F. M. Conference, **II**: 606; at Teheran Conference, **II**: 611

Ban of Croatia, **III**: 280, 306

Bandar Shahpur, Iran, **II**: 586-587

Bangkok, Thailand, **II**: 617

Bar Harbor, Maine, **III**: 493

Barcelona, Spain, **I**: 125

Barents Sea, **II**: 158, 161, 174, 176, 636

Bari Congress, Italy, **II**: 679

Baruch, Bernard, **I**: 23, 212-213; **III**: 74, 577, 585, 597, 601

Bases, military: Roosevelt on in postwar world, **III**: 237

Basic English, **III**: 104-105, 154

Basque nationalists, **I**: 371-372

Basra, Iraq, **I**: 319, 503-504, 519, 528-532, 541; **II**: 547, 563, 564, 568, 570, 576, 578, 584, 585

Bastogne, Belgium, battle at, **III**: 487, 498

Bataan peninsula, battle at, **I**: 408, 608

Bathurst, Gambia, **I**: 206-207, 209; **II**: 117, 123, 156

Batt, William L., **I**: 327, 329

Batumi, Soviet Union, **III**: 447, 449

Bavaria, Germany, **II**: 223, 708; **III**: 364

Bay of Bengal, **II**: 116, 504, 616-617; **III**: 38-40

Bay of Biscay, **II**: 366-367; **III**: 119, 233, 312, 345; anti-submarine campaign in, **II**: 27; German submarines in, **II**: 323

Bayat, Murteza Quli, **III**: 512

Bazna, Elyesa. *See* CICERO

Beasley, J. A., **I**: 429

Beaverbrook, Lord (William A. Aitken), **I**: 229, 284, 290, 327, 329; **II**: 191, 261, 638, 657-658, 691; **III**: 41 at petroleum conférence, **III**: 195-196, 206; Churchill on resignation of, **I**: 363-364; mission to Moscow, 1941, **I**: 242-244; on Stalin, **I**: 566

Begin, Menachim, **II**: 601

Beirut, Lebanon, **II**: 448

Belfast, Northern Ireland, **II**: 187

Belgium, **I**: 116, 123, 129, 147, 155; **II**: 102, 522; **III**: 354; Allied occupation of, **III**: 211; anti-government demonstrations in, **III**: 437; atrocities in, **II**: 520; Churchill on landing in, 1943, **I**: 302; imperialism of, **III**: 6; in British occupation zone, **II**: 745; postwar, **II**: 223, 708, 767; **III**: 569; relief needed in, **II**: 105-106; **III**: 47, 540

Belgrade, Yugoslavia, **III**: 485; bombing of, **I**: 170; Soviet forces in, **III**: 434

Beneš, Eduard; and Polish peace with Soviets, **II**: 650-651

Bengal-Assam Railroad, **II**: 690; U.S. Army management of, **III**: 12

Bengal, India, **I**: 373-379; **III**: 117

Benghazi, Libya, **I**: 253, 267-268, 532, 538, 673; **II**: 20; **III**: 328

Bering Strait, **II**: 420

Berio, Alberto, **II**: 384, 425

Berle, Adolf A., Jr., **I**: 221; **II**: 462, 483, 711-712; **III**: 30-31, 109-110, 402, 405, 419-420, 428, 566; and civil aviation dispute, **III**: 419-420, 423, 425; letter from Sforza, **III**: 437-439

Berlin, **I**: 61; **III**: 147, 524, 581; British bombing of, **III**: 195-196; capture of, Allied plans for, **II**: 431; **III**: 602-606, 608, 612-613, 616, 617

Berling, Zygmunt, **II**: 715, 718; **III**: 281, 553-554

Bermuda, **I**: 59-60, 65, 68, 166; **II**: 72, 293, 344; **III**: 53, 59, 157, 226, 267-268, 270; and lend-lease bases, **I**: 139-142

Bern, Switzerland, surrender talks in, **III**: 586-587, 589, 609-611, 612-616, 617, 622-624, 629-630

Béthouart, Emile, **II**: 68-69, 76

Bevin, Ernest, **III**: 75, 101-102, 104, 457, 466-467

Bialystok, Soviet Union, **II**: 719

Bidault, Georges, **III**: 389, 392

Bierut, Boleslaw, **III**: 269, 363-364, 549

Bizerta, Tunisia, **I**: 79, 270, 296, 578; **II**: 7, 27, 51, 54-56, 122, 152, 207

"Black radio," **II**: 303

Black Sea, **I**: 136, 145, 295, 579, 669, 674; **II**: 14, 331, 558, 665, 671, 765; **III**: 141, 351, 359, 364-366, 368, 377-381, 412, 416, 485, 495, 508-509, 516; Allied aid to Soviets in, **II**: 50; control of, 1942, **I**: 318, 321; passage of supplies through, **II**: 15

Bladon Churchyard, England: burial site of Churchill, **II**: 388

Blamey, Sir Thomas: and ABDA command controversies, **I**: 339, 344

Blenheim Day, England, **II**: 388

Blenheim Palace, England, **II**: 388

Blockade: British of Europe, **I**: 32-35, 86, 91, 92, 107, 117, 124, 146, 148, 154-155, 188, 296, 499; **II**: 105-106; **III**: 47, 85-86

Blum, Leon, **I**: 459

Bogomolov, Alexander Y., **II**: 193-194, 284

Boheman, Erik, **I**: 639, 642

Bohlen, Charles, **III**: 343, 344, 593

Boisson, Pierre, **II**: 56-57, 72, 80, 91,

98, 229, 231, 244, 279-280, 625-626, 635, 641, 691-692
Bolivia, **II**: 682-684
Bolshevism, **I**: 14, 211; **III**: 288, 538
Bomber Command, British, **I**: 438
Bombing:
    Allied, before D-Day, **III**: 164-165
    British of French civilians, **I**: 426-427
    British, of German rocket centers, **II**: 559-560
    drone bomber proposal, **III**: 591-592
    of Axis, Roosevelt on, **II**: 46
    of Belgrade, Yugoslavia, **I**: 170
    of Bulgaria, **II**: 761
    of Cologne, **I**: 501, 504
    of England, by Germany, **I**: 39, 70, 80, 542, 544; with V-1 bombs, **III**: 195-196, 206, 211, 231, 592
    of France, before channel invasion, **III**: 122-124, 127
    of German ships, 1942, **I**: 300
    of German submarine construction sites, **III**: 617
    of Germany, **I**: 57, 302, 315, 362, 435, 459, 477, 485, 520, 545; **II**: 44, 51, 119, 152, 190, 247, 260; **III**: 427, 616; American vs. British plans, **I**: 614; and use of Soviet air bases, **III**: 295; Churchill on levels of, **I**: 306; Stalin on, **I**: 561; Washington Conference proposals, **II**: 218
    of Germany and Italy, **I**: 304, 651
    of Germany, cities of, **I**: 499, 597; **II**: 387
    of Germany, daylight, **II**: 185-186, 517-518
    of Germany, losses in, **II**: 517
    of Germany, strategic, **III**: 195
    of Italy, **I**: 671; **II**: 11
    of Japan, **II**: 594
    of Japanese cities, Churchill on, **I**: 307
    of London, **I**: 121-123; **II**: 739-740, 751, 753-754
    of Rome, Allies threaten, **II**: 234, 373-374
    of Sofia, Bulgaria, **II**: 714-715, 724, 730
    of 10 Downing Street, London, **II**: 751, 753-754
    of Tokyo, **I**: 442
    strategic, difficulties discussed, **I**: 596-598
Bombing devices, **I**: 565
Bombing policy: British, **I**: 223-224, 437-438; Churchill on, **I**: 297
Bombs, V-1, **III**: 230
Bombsights, **I**: 27-28
BONIFACE intelligence, **I**: xxi; **II**: 388-389, 502-503; **III**: 227, 320-321, 340-341
Bonomi, Ivanoe, **III**: 176, 182-183, 185, 188-190, 199, 319, 333, 387, 436, 444, 451, 533
Bora-Bora, Society Islands (France), **III**: 504
Bor-Komorowski, General, **III**: 260, 283, 350
Bordeaux, France, **III**: 164, 198, 217-218, 222
Boundaries, postwar: discussed at Atlantic Conference, 1941, **I**: 227
Boundary disputes: and postwar France, **III**: 440, 442, 444-445; Czechs and Soviets, **II**: 650-651; Finns and Soviets, **II**: 181-182; Poland and Soviet Union, **II**: 138-140, 192-193, 204, 650-651, 684-688, 700-705; **III**: 60-61, 69-71; Soviets and neighbors, **I**: 394, 465-466, 470
Bourne, Brigadier, **I**: 596
Bracken, Brendan, **I**: 619, 625; **II**: 139, 141-142, 191, 422, 530-531, 569
Bradley, Follette, **I**: 609
Bradley, Omar, **III**: 340-341, 487, 497-498, 498, 602; command changes, **II**: 639
Brand, Robert, **III**: 144, 155, 157
Brazil, **I**: 86, 177, 210; **II**: 239-241, 343-344, 346, 367, 540; **III**: 285, 294, 415-416; and Portugal, **II**: 243; Roosevelt visit to, **II**: 123
Brazzaville, French Equatorial Africa, **II**: 98, 104-105
Bremen, Germany, **II**: 517, 708; **III**: 317; bombing of, **I**: 597
Bremerhaven, Germany, **III**: 317
Brereton, L. H., **I**: 335, 343, 411, 450, 554-555; **II**: 622-623; and command changes, **II**: 646-647

Brett, George H., **I**: 252, 254, 313, 335-
336, 343, 384, 388, 408, 432; and
ABDA command controversies, **I**:
340, 342-343
Brewster, Owen, **II**: 527
Brindizi, Italy, **II**: 455
British Commonwealth, **I**: 89, 92, 95; **II**:
64, 200, 225; **III**: 335, 418, 519-520,
532, 543, 600, 633; and civil aviation
policy, **III**: 420; leaders oppose Lloyd
George appointment, **I**: 114; nations
warn Japanese, **I**: 280-281
British Empire, **I**: 119-120; **II**: 200; **III**:
195, 335, 351, 520, 527, 531, 532; and
Atlantic Charter, **II**: 599; and civil
aviation policy, **III**: 419, 423, 424;
and Germans, **I**: 46; and goals in
Burma-India theater, **II**: 274-277; and
Imperial preference system, **I**: 247,
351, 356-358; **III**: 530, 535-536; and
military planning, **I**: 384; and self-determination issue, **II**: 360; and Soviet-
American Conference, **II**: 278; anti-
interventionist view of, **I**: 227; Australia and New Zealand, Churchill on
disloyalty of, **II**: 32-33; Churchill on,
I: 6, 360, 655; **II**: 609; Churchill on
United States and, **I**: 96, 103; Hess on
Hitler's view of, **I**: 188; in Pacific, **I**:
136; support for war effort, **I**: 205,
320; U.S. view of, **I**: 232, 373; **II**:
696; **III**: 88
British Gambia, **II**: 150
British Guiana, **I**: 59-60, 65, 68
British Imperial General Staff, **III**: 82
British Merchant Shipping Mission, **I**:
327
British Raw Materials Mission, **I**: 327
British Supply Council, **I**: 213
British West Indies, **III**: 27, 323
Brooke, Sir Alan, **I**: 256, 513, 551, 564,
570; **II**: 128, 131, 133, 202, 217, 305-
306, 431, 433, 571, 623, 641; **III**: 495,
498, 523; and Churchill, **I**: 510; **III**:
226; at Moscow Conference, 1942, **I**:
560; on Churchill at Marrakesh, **II**:
644-645; on Trans-Persian Railway, **I**:
572; strategy of attrition, **II**: 48
Brown, Sir William, **III**: 168, 187-188
Brown, Wilson, **II**: 447, 567; **III**: 28,
221, 287, 393

Bruce, Edward, **I**: 359
Bruenn, Howard, **III**: 59-60
Brunswick, Germany, **III**: 147
Brussels, Belgium, **III**: 437, 487
Budapest, Hungary, **III**: 435; Soviet
forces in, **III**: 434
Bulgaria, **II**: 14, 131, 350, 558, 618; **III**:
523, 635; and Allies, **II**: 445, 553-554,
714-715, 723-724, 729-730, 760-761,
765; **III**: 22-23, 32; and Germans, **I**:
134, 144-145; **III**: 60; and Greece,
III: 450; and Moscow Conference,
1944, **III**: 351, 359; and Soviet Union,
III: 15, 298, 350-351, 545, 547, 548;
Anglo-Soviet agreement on, **III**: 200,
202; Churchill on, **II**: 498-499;
Churchill on Soviet conduct toward,
III: 69; in World War I, **III**: 298-299
Bullitt, William C., **I**: 44, 276-277, 534
Bundles for Britain campaign, **I**: 511-
512, 525
Burma, **I**: 287, 339, 343, 353, 362, 369,
405, 414, 415, 452; **II**: 504, 537, 542,
617; **III**: 38-40, 270-271, 573, 582-583
    air reinforcements for, **I**: 461-462
    Allied operations in, **II**: 110-113,
616, 689-690; **III**: 12, 19-20, 54-55,
524
    Allied strategy debates, **I**: 405, 450;
II: 274-277, 549-550, 757, 759; **III**:
435
    American Volunteer Group in, **I**:
333
    Andaman Islands operations (BUC-
CANEER), **II**: 608-609, 610, 612-613,
616, 632-633, 636; **III**: 39
    and Chiang Kai-shek, **II**: 110-113,
115-117
    and operations in China, **III**: 426,
427-429, 429-430
    and South East Asia command
structure, **II**: 294-295
    Arakan operations, **II**: 110-118,
632-633; **III**: 51-52
    Chinese troops in, **II**: 616-617; **III**:
58-59, 422-423
    command controversies in, **I**: 359-
360, 416-418, 422-423; **II**: 294-295
    decisions on at Quebec, 1943, **II**:
430
    defense of, **I**: 280-281, 320, 365,

456, 654
  difficulties in, **II**: 317-318
  Japanese in, **I**: 348, 350; **II**: 528,
  756; **III**: 50-52
  planned recapture of (ANAKIM),
  II: 153, 205-206, 609; British com-
  manders oppose, **II**: 202; postponed,
  II: 184, 186; Roosevelt on, **II**: 156,
  179; shipping crisis and, **II**: 166-167,
  213; U.S. disputes on, **II**: 177
  postwar politics and, **III**: 433-435
  Prime Minister arrested, **I**: 312
  Rangoon, operations in, **I**: 417-418;
  III: 347-348
  Roosevelt on, **I**: 363
  supplies to China through, **II**: 751-
  752, 756
  U.S. air forces in, 1942, **I**: 393
  Wingate campaign in, **III**: 43-44, 46
Burma Road, **I**: 73, 265, 320, 343; **II**:
  110, 112, 115-116, 751; **III**: 426 (*see
  also* Ledo Road); Churchill on, **I**: 299,
  321; defense of, 1942, **I**: 417; impor-
  tance of, **I**: 365
Burmese: Roosevelt on, **I**: 312, 457
Burrough, Sir Harold Martin, **III**: 503-
  505
Burrows, General, **III**: 93-94, 113
Bush, Vannevar, **I**: 249; **II**: 214, 317
Byelorussia, **II**: 685
Byrd, Richard E., **III**: 417
Byrnes, James F., **II**: 388; **III**: 559

Cadogan, Sir Alexander, **I**: 69-70, 279,
  406; **II**: 17-18, 21, 127; **III**: 335, 533-
  534, 566; at Moscow Conference,
  1942, **I**: 560, 564, 566, 569; objects to
  Churchill visit to U.S., **I**: 283
Caen, France, **III**: 604
Cairo Conference (SEXTANT, 1943),
  II: 492, 566, 569, 708; and Pacific war
  policy, **II**: 755; arrangements for, **II**:
  562-570, 572-573, 575-579, 583-586,
  588-589, 591-593, 594-598, 600-605;
  Chiang Kai-shek at, **II**: 569-576, 585,
  595-596, 600-601; dollar balances discussed at, **III**: 35; issue of Soviet observers at, **II**: 563-565; major power
  cooperation, **III**: 6; occupation zones
  discussed at, **II**: 746; Pacific strategy
  decided at, **III**: 38; security arrangements, **II**: 601-602, 604-605; significance of, **II**: 613; Smuts and Roosevelt meet, **I**: 492; summarized, **II**:
  608-610, 612-613; war strategy decisions at, **III**: 227
Cairo, Egypt, **II**: 42-43, 234, 523, 526,
  554, 562, 568, 724, 730, 761, 765; **III**:
  15, 202, 363; Churchill invites Inonu
  to, **III**: 49; Churchill visit to, July
  1942, **I**: 551; Greek government exiled in, **III**: 95-96
Çakmak, Fevsi, **II**: 128, 131
Calabria, Italy, **II**: 434-436
Calcutta, India, **II**: 689-690, 693-694;
  III: 12, 39
Camaroon, **I**: 146
Campbell, Sir Ronald, **I**: 544; **II**: 239-
  240, 249, 262-263, 380
Canada, **I**: 58, 60, 123-124, 182, 202,
  206, 247, 601; **II**: 223, 659; **III**: 103-
  105, 264, 345, 425, 441 (*see also* King,
  Mackenzie); and ANZAC defense, **I**:
  386; and British, **I**: 457; and French
  Committee recognition, **II**: 379, 420,
  431; and PLOUGH training, **II**: 47;
  and Quebec Conference, 1943, **II**:
  333, 341-343, 343-346; and St. Pierre-
  Miquelon affair, **I**: 324-326, 347; and
  war effort, **I**: 327; **III**: 82; Churchill
  in, 1941-1942, **I**: 309; Churchill on
  strategy toward, 1942, **I**: 299; Eden
  visit to, **II**: 178; Irish shipping to permitted by Allies, **III**: 76; on command
  structure, **III**: 82-84; Pacific theater
  responsibilities, **I**: 398-399
Canadian Joint Staff Mission, **III**: 83-84,
  103
Canadian-American Joint Defense
  Board, **I**: 58
Canary Islands, **I**: 86, 171-173; British
  plans for, **I**: 234
Canterbury, England, raid on, **I**: 655
Cape of Good Hope, **I**: 300, 307
Cape St. Vincent, **I**: 227
Cape Town, South Africa, **I**: 120-123
Cape Verde Islands, **I**: 150-151, 171-
  173, 186; British plans for, **I**: 200-202
Caribbean, **II**: 78, 245, 323; German
  submarines in, **I**: 456, 490-491, 515,
  524
Carlton Gardens, England, **II**: 215

Carton de Wiart, Adrian, **III**: 422-423

Casablanca Conference (SYMBOL), **II**: 73, 93, 113, 117, 196, 543, 545, 618; arrangements for, **II**: 85-87, 89-90; British staff needs, **II**: 56; Churchill on, **II**: 117; decisions made on bombing, **II**: 517; discussion of VELVET at, **II**: 59; failed to plan shipping needs, **II**: 166-167; main issues of strategy settled at, **II**: 38; planning for, **II**: 96-98; press censorship at, **II**: 103-104; Roosevelt's view of preparations, **II**: 53-55; summarized, **II**: 117-122

Casablanca, Morocco, **I**: 85, 87, 175, 179, 180, 182, 253, 296, 635; **II**: 7, 55-56, 74, 439, 562, 566; **III**: 249; Allied landing in, 1942, **I**: 667; in North African invasion plans, **I**: 577-578, 582-583, 585-590

Casey, Richard G., **I**: 364-365, 407, 408, 427-428; **II**: 333-334, 569-570, 577, 592, 622-623

Caspian Sea, **I**: 543, 562

Castellano, Giuseppe, **II**: 423

Castelrosso, Dodecanese Islands, **III**: 328

Casualties: Allied in Italy, **III**:347, 356; Allied in western Europe, **III**: 216, 615; British in Greece, **III**: 179, 202; British in Italy, **III**: 43; British in western Europe, **III**: 604; British, of V-1 bombing, **III**: 196; German in Greece, 1943, **II**: 407-408; German in Italy, **III**: 347; German in western Europe, **III**: 408; in bombing of France, **III**: 122-123, 127; in East Africa, **I**: 159; in invasion of southern France, **III**: 278; in Yugoslavia, 1943, **II**: 406; New Zealand in Middle East, **II**: 37; in OVERLORD, **III**: 87

Catalan nationalists, **I**: 371-372

Catholic Church, **II**: 172. *See also* Vatican

Catroux, Georges, **I**: 204; **II**: 209-210, 235, 271, 333-335, 603

Caucasus, **I**: 295, 319, 562, 598; **II**: 50 Allied aid to Soviets in, **I**: 574, 579-581, 615- 618, 621-623, 637; **II**: 57-60, 77-78, 185; British Chiefs on, **I**: 622; U.S. military opposes, **I**: 620 Churchill on defense of, **I**: 543

military situation in, **I**: 307, 318-319, 565, 579, 672; **II**: 14-15, 58, 63-64 Roosevelt on holding of, 1942, **I**: 421 Soviet defense plans for, **I**: 565 Stalin on situation in, late 1942, **I**: 672

Cazalet, Thelma, **III**: 77

Censorship, Allied, **III**: 268; and cross-channel invasion, **III**: 92, 101; in North Africa, **II**: 76

Central America, **I**: 92

Central Pacific Command: and MacArthur, **II**: 205-206

Ceylon, **I**: 381-382, 414, 438, 452, 469; **II**: 24, 757; **III**: 39; air reinforcements for, **I**: 461-462; invasion of and U.S. intelligence, **I**: 455; Japanese attack on, **I**: 391, 442-443, 450, 461; Roosevelt on holding of, 1942, **I**: 421

Chad, **I**: 146; **II**: 30

Chamber of Commerce, U.S., **III**: 201

Chamberlain, Neville, **I**: 7, 23-24, 115; on cultivating Roosevelt, **I**: 25; resignation of, **I**: 36

Chandler, Albert, **II**: 527

Chaney, James E., **I**: 411, 413

Channel Islands, **II**: 132

Charlottesville, Virginia, **III**: 137; Roosevelt visit to, 1943, **II**: 259

Chartwell (Churchill country home), **I**: 484

Chemical warfare, **III**: 256

Chennault, Claire, **II**: 205-206, 213, 264, 275, 294, 537

Chequers, **I**: 189, 206, 535, 642; **II**: 540, 640; Churchill at, **II**: 740; meeting with Polish exiles at, **II**: 716

Cherbourg, battle at, **III**: 194, 199, 203, 230

Cherchel, Algeria, **I**: 634

Cherwell, Lord (Frederick Lindemann), **I**: 279; **II**: 716; **III**: 34-35, 289-290, 412-413, 569; and Churchill, **I**: 437

Chetniks (Cetniks), **II**: 182, 403-406, 660; **III**: 306

Chiang Kai-shek, **I**: 9, 309, 350, 353, 360, 362-362, 365, 397, 398; **II**: 205-206, 213, 264, 537; **III**: 572-573; Allied aid to, **I**: 265-267, 411, 462; **III**:

447, 449; and agreement on Soviet Pacific role, **III**: 527; and American Volunteer Group, **I**: 332-333; and bomber bases in China, **II**: 594, 732; and Burma theater, **I**: 359-360, 422-423, 450; **II**: 110, 112-113, 115-117, 616-617; **III**: 58-59, 426, 435; and CBI command structure, **II**: 274-277, 294-295; and China as major power, **II**: 525; and communists in China, **III**: 395-396; and India, **I**: 373, 550, 556, 558, 563; and Indo-China, **III**: 582-583; and Mao Tse-tung, **II**: 609; and Mountbatten, **III**: 627; and Pacific strategy, **III**: 39; and Stilwell, **I**: 405; **III**: 370; and U.S., **III**: 524; and withdrawal of troops, **III**: 422-423; at Cairo Conference, **II**: 562, 569-570, 572-573, 576-578, 585, 588-589, 595-596, 600-601, 608; Halifax on, **I**: 277; limited war role of, **I**: 293; Roosevelt on, **II**: 492, 561

Chicago Sun, **II**: 490

Chicago Tribune, **I**: 283, 619

Chiefs of Staff, British, **I**: 10, 292, 361, 384, 480, 504, 576; **II**: 33, 122, 148, 206, 442, 503, 638; **III**: 76, 110, 408-409, 426, 612; and Azores, **II**: 496; and Cairo Conference, **II**: 595, 598; and Casablanca Conference, **II**: 97; and conferences, **II**: 565; and cross-channel invasion, **II**: 9-10, 430, 670; and drone bomber project, **III**: 592; and East Asia command, **II**: 263, 265; and Eisenhower, **I**: 54; **III**: 603, 605; and Greece, **III**: 279; and Indo-China, **III**: 626; and invasion of Norway, **I**: 605; and invasion of southern France, **II**: 705; **III**: 163, 204, 207, 212-213, 221, 225-229, 232, 263; and Italian campaign, **II**: 34, 212, 581; **III**: 119; and Italian political situation, **II**: 760; and Italian surrender, **II**: 519, 538; and Japanese offensive in India, **III**: 50; and Mediterranean strategy, **I**: 669, 671; **II**: 13; **III**: 489; and Pacific strategy, **III**: 37, 38; and Southeast Asia command structure, **II**: 294, 301-302, 430; and Soviet offensive, 1944, **III**: 94; and strategy in Southeast Asia, **II**: 202, 757, 759; at

London Conference, 1942, **I**: 535; at Malta Conference, **III**: 495-496, 501-503, 522; at Quebec Conference, 1943, **II**: 372; at Quebec Conference, 1944, **III**: 298-299; on airplanes for Mountbatten, **III**: 56; on cross-channel invasion, **I**: 670; on German surrender terms, **II**: 767-768, 772; on Italian colonies, **III**: 326-327; on occupation zones in Germany, **II**: 708-709; on shipping crisis, **II**: 167; on Soviet and German armies, **I**: 622; on unity of commands, **I**: 293; on war strategy, **II**: 182, 657-757; opposes Churchill, **II**: 480; to Yalta, **III**: 491

Chiefs of Staff, United States, **I**: 380, 384, 576, 613; **II**: 122, 371, 440, 498, 503; **III**: 60, 76, 91, 270, 308, 344, 429, 447, 449; and air bases in Soviet Union, **III**: 296; and ANZAC strategy, **I**: 432; and Azores, **II**: 495-497, 543; and bombing of Japan, **II**: 732; and bombing of Rome, **II**: 250, 373; and British strategy in Pacific, **III**: 40; and Churchill, **III**: 64, 163, 194-195, 436; and codenames, **II**: 280; and command structure debates, **I**: 414; **III**: 83; and cross-channel invasion, **I**: 389; **II**: 41, 502, 562, 713; **III**: 120; and drone bomber project, **III**: 592; and Eisenhower's strategy, **II**: 83-85; **III**: 603, 605, 608; and Far East bases, postwar, **III**: 626; and French Committee, **II**: 89; and India, **III**: 50; and invasion of Norway, **I**: 605; and invasion of southern France, **II**: 653; **III**: 207, 212-213, 221, 223, 228-229, 232, 263-264, 267; and Italian campaign, **II**: 581; **III**: 301-302; and Italian surrender terms, **II**: 351-352, 359-360; and Italy, **III**: 190, 356, 400; and landing craft for British, **III**: 88-89; and MacArthur, **I**: 480; **II**: 301; and North African invasion, **I**: 576; and Pacific theater, **I**: 398-399; **II**: 205-206, 318, 755; and Poland, **III**: 312; and post-TORCH strategy, **II**: 18, 46; and Quebec Conference, 1944, **III**: 287; and Roosevelt, **II**: 479-480, 606-608, 708; and ships for Indian famine relief, **III**: 155; and Soviet offensive,

Chiefs of Staff (*cont.*)
  1944, **III**: 94; and supplies to China,
  III: 50; at Cairo Conference, **II**: 595;
  at Casablanca Conference, **II**: 54-55,
  97; at Malta Conference, **III**: 495-496,
  501-503, 505; at Quebec Conference,
  1943, **II**: 430; on German surrender
  terms, **II**: 767-768, 772-773; on Italian colonies, **III**: 326-328; on occupation zones in Germany, **II**: 708-709;
  on planes for Polish exiles, **II**: 114; on
  relief for Europe, **III**: 47; on Sir John
  Dill, **II**: 613; on Southeast Asia policy,
  II: 757; **III**: 523-524
Chile, **II**: 103
China, **I**: 12-13, 73, 361, 382, 398, 453;
  II: 63, 283, 540, 733, 742; **III**: 270,
  351, 419, 530, 579-580 (*see also*
  Chiang Kai-shek); air route to, **II**:
  263-264; and bombing raids on Japan,
  I: 307; **II**: 732, 755-756; and Britain,
  I: 75; and Burma, **I**: 348-350; **II**: 112,
  118; and India, **I**: 546-549; and Indo-
  China, **I**: 225; and Japan, **I**: 274-276,
  305, 438; **III**: 426-427, 429, 435, 626;
  and Pacific Council, **I**: 330, 430; and
  Quebec Conference, 1943, **II**: 344,
  346; and Southeast Asia command, **II**:
  294-295, 301-302, 318-319; and Soviet
  Union, **III**: 318; and Stilwell, **I**: 405;
  and U.N. organization, **III**: 330-331,
  431; and Yalta Conference, **III**: 527;
  Churchill on, **I**: 265-267, 299, 504; **II**:
  617; communists vs. Chiang Kai-shek,
  III: 395-396; currency problems of,
  II: 620-621; importance of, **I**: 277-
  278, 365; included in four-power declaration, **II**: 606; military coordination
  with, **I**: 293, 343, 397-399, 416-418,
  430; role of, differing Allied view, **II**:
  217, 221-222, 274-277, 408; Roosevelt
  and "Four Policemen," **II**: 608; Roosevelt on, **I**: 266-267, 363; **II**: 156, 179,
  525, 561; **III**: 524; Roosevelt on Japanese in, **I**: 278; Roosevelt's view of as
  postwar power, **I**: 293, 502; **II**: 213,
  608, 609; **III**: 237; Stalin excludes
  from Teheran, **II**: 600-601; supplies
  to, **I**: 266-267, 328-329, 353; **II**: 536,
  542, 550, 609, 689-690, 693-694, 730-
  731, 751-752; **III**: 49, 50-52; U.S. air

forces in, **I**: 393; **III**: 12, 422-423;
  U.S. policy towards, **II**: 295; **III**: 524
China theater, **III**: 370; and Indo-
  China, **I**: 450; **III**: 582-583; Chiang
  Kai-shek as commander of, **I**: 309; **II**:
  282; Roosevelt on, **III**: 446-449
China-Burma-India theater: Anglo-
  American differences in, **II**: 274-277,
  757, 759; at Cairo Conference, **II**:
  608-609; command issues in, **I**: 405;
  II: 274, 282-283, 430; **III**: 370; dis-
  cussed at Washington Conference, **II**:
  213
Chios Island, Aegean, **II**: 341
Chromium ore, **III**: 48-49, 55-56;
  traded to Germany, **III**: 245
Chrysler Company, **II**: 103
Churchill, Charles, **III**: 271
Churchill, Clementine, **I**: 422, 439, 508,
  633, 636, 642, 654-656; **II**: 7, 88, 156,
  163, 421, 624, 638, 644, 648, 650,
  657, 690, 727, 740; **III**: 267, 306, 314,
  322, 332, 470-471, 574, 597, 601; and
  London bombing, **II**: 751, 753-754;
  codename for, **I**: 510; 35th wedding
  anniversary at Hyde Park, **II**: 438;
  view of Roosevelt, **I**: 4; visit to Canada
  and U.S., **II**: 345, 348, 355, 387, 388,
  432, 437, 447
Churchill, Jack, **II**: 640
Churchill, Jenny, **II**: 163-164
Churchill, Mary, **II**: 344-345, 348, 355,
  387, 431-432, 447; **III**: 332
Churchill, Pamela, **I**: 4
Churchill, Randolph, **II**: 92, 660-661,
  668; **III**: 167-168, 257-259
Churchill, Sarah, **II**: 620-621, 640, 644,
  650; **III**: 500
Churchill, Sylvester, **II**: 150-151
Churchill, Winston Spencer:
  alias as a painter, **I**: 358-359
  ancestry of, **II**: 38; **III**: 271
  and codenames, **I**: 491-492; **II**: 344-
  345; **III**: 274
  and command appointments, **III**:
  497-498
  and nicknames, **II**: 344
  and Roosevelt-Stalin relationship,
  II: 595
  and Teheran Conference, **II**: 492-
  493, 610

as Foreign Secretary for Eden, **III**: 110, 112

as junior partner, **I**: 15

as regular writer of strategy papers, **II**: 442

as Roosevelt's "lieutenant," **II**: 30

as "world's worst patient," **II**: 156-157

at Marrakesh, **II**: 628

Biblical references by, **I**: 202-203; **II**: 604; **III**: 288

birth and burial, **II**: 388

birthday at Teheran Conference, **II**: 615; **III**: 425

debate over psychological motives of, **II**: 657

defends Ango-American war policies, **II**: 527-530

difference with Foreign Office, **II**: 650

doggerel by, **III**: 488

fears for 1944 and unity, **II**: 565

fears U.S. aid delay, **I**: 8

French language ability joked about, **I**: 630

health of, **I**: 309-310; **II**: 146, 149-150, 603, 620-621; **III**: 139, 302-303, 305-307, 362-363; after Teheran, **II**: 613; Roosevelt on, **II**: 624

holiday in Canada and U.S., 1943, **II**: 431-434, 437

humor of, **I**: 229, 314

knowledge of American government, **II**: 128

Latin quotes of, **III**: 612

literary references of, **II**: 55-56

Moscow Conference as not finest hour, **III**: 351

observes invasion of southern France, **III**: 276, 278

on Beaverbrook, **I**: 364

on "Phoney War," **I**: 36

on "underbelly of the Axis," **II**: 9, 11

on battles as additions to history, **III**: 18

on burdens of war, **III**: 203

on civil vs. military rule, **II**: 357

on colonial world, **II**: 222

on consultation and foreign affairs, **III**: 178-179

on D-Day, **III**: 162-163

on de Gaulle, **III**: 170

on death of Roosevelt, **III**: 631-632

on defeatism, **I**: 170

on democracy, **III**: 140

on end of war, **III**: 502

on English-speaking world, **I**: 119-120

on first visit to America, **II**: 178

on freedom of the seas, **I**: 98, 105

on friendship for Roosevelt, **III**: 429

on grammar, **II**: 712

on Iran vs. Persia, **I**: 235

on location of Yalta Conference, **III**: 518

on mediocre officials, **III**: 180

on memorial for Roosevelt, **I**: 19-20

on military men, **II**: 480

on morale of military personnel, **III**: 314-315

on overconfidence, **III**: 18

on relations with Roosevelt, **I**: 7

on Roosevelt after Pearl Harbor, **I**: 289

on Soviets as Russians, **I**: 5

on tripartite cooperation, **III**: 202

on two years to make a soldier, **I**: 514

on visit to Hyde Park, **II**: 382

on war, **I**: 303, 308

on war of "giants," then "pygmies," **III**: 574

on war strategy, **I**: 602

on war, 1942, **I**: 670

on warfare as eye for eye, **I**: 437

on weight of war, **I**: 439

on world events, December 1941, **I**: 289

on worries that war appears won, **III**: 18

pessimism of, mid-1941, **I**: 177

political position, **I**: 395, 420

postwar views of, **III**: 528, 530

prefers Roosevelt to de Gaulle, **III**: 170

proclamation on atrocities, **II**: 519-521

receives honorary degree from Harvard, **II**: 433-434, 438

Churchill, Winston Spencer (*cont.*)
recovery at Marrakesh, **II**: 638
relations with military leaders, **II**: 479-480
Roosevelt concern for safety of, **I**: 284, 286
Roosevelt on, **II**: 563, 648; as fun-to-be-in-decade-with, **I**: 337; at Atlantic Conference, **I**: 227; on marvels accomplished by, **II**: 138
speeches, **I**: 177, 211; during Dunkirk, **I**: 42; on United States' promises, **I**: 229; to Generals before OVERLORD, **III**: 87
struggle to be Prime Minister, **I**: 36
supposed meetings with Ribbentrop, **II**: 673
35th wedding anniversary at Hyde Park, **II**: 438
threatens to resign, **III**: 225
threats to U.S. versus Stalin's, **I**: 238
trips, **II**: 206-207, 216-217, 219; to America as child, **II**: 163-164; to Cairo, 1944, **III**: 363; to France, 1944, **III**: 388-389; to Greece, 1944, **III**: 471-475; to Hyde Park, 1943, **II**: 387-388; to Niagara Falls, 1943, **II**: 387; to Normandy beaches, **III**: 183, 185-187; to Quebec, 1944, **III**: 305, 307, 313-314; to Washington, 1943, **II**: 447. *See also* various conferences
views on industrialists and bankers, **I**: 23
vote of confidence: Roosevelt on, 1942, **I**: 336-337
writings, **I**: xviii-xix, 4-6, 20, 23; **III**: 315; biography of Lord Marlborough, **II**: 388; memoirs, **II**: 20
Churchill-Roosevelt correspondence, **III**: 243, 515; after Yalta Conference, **III**: 566, 594; and Pacific war, **III**: 193; and Roosevelt trip to Canada, **II**: 374; anti-submarine publicity in, **II**: 230; at conferences, **II**: 122, 214, 613; **III**: 530; changes in security classifications, **III**: 102; channels for messages, **II**: 706; Churchill on, **III**: 597; concerning D-Day, **III**: 165; discord minimized, **I**: 6; extent of, **I**: 3; fishing trips discussed, **II**: 432-434, 437; German submarines as "canaries," **II**:

327-328; Hopkins role in, **I**: 128, 444, 599; humor in, **III**: 130-131, 369; initiated by Roosevelt, **I**: 23-24; Leahy's role, **II**: 66; log sheets, **I**: 18; **II**: 493; **III**: 88, 367; numbering system, **I**: xxii-xxiii, 349, 351; on Egyptians, **III**: 114; on Stalin, **II**: 233; phases of, **I**: 6-19; pitfalls of interpreting messages, **I**: 18; postwar politics dominate at end, **III**: 433, 436-437; reflects relationship, **II**: 708; refugees, little on, **II**: 293; reports from Moscow Conference, 1944, **III**: 351; Roosevelt buoys Churchill's spirits, **I**: 362-363; Roosevelt not disorganized thinker, **III**: 481-482; Stevenson on, **I**: 196; tone changes, **I**: 17
Churchill-Roosevelt relationship: and Churchill visit to Shangri-la, **II**: 297; and de Gaulle, **II**: 257; and telephone use, **I**: xx-xxi, 211, 281; **II**: 356-357; **III**: 10-11; at conferences, **I**: 19; Atlantic Conference, 1941, and, **I**: 227; between Pearl Harbor and Teheran, **I**: 358; birthday greetings, **I**: 335; **II**: 126-127, 690; **III**: 400, 425, 429, 521; changes, **I**: 602; **II**: 596, 610; **III**: 229; character of, **I**: 3-5; Christmas greetings, **II**: 88, 632, 635; **III**: 470-471; Churchill as "lieutenant," **I**: 594, 648, 651; Churchill on, **I**: 364; **II**: 228, 447; **III**: 162, 180, 212, 499, 573-574; Churchill proposes meeting; **I**: 439; **III**: 53; differences on Soviet Union, **I**: 545; differences over convoys to Soviets, **I**: 481; disagreements discussed, **III**: 221; dispute on southern France invasion, **III**: 163; dispute over military theater demands, **III**: 498; dispute over postwar Greece, **II**: 450; exchange military reports, **I**: 418-419; exchanges of items of interest, **II**: 150-151; first meeting recalled, **II**: 355-356; gifts exchanged, **I**: 484, 491; **II**: 92, 540, 640-641, 644, 651; **III**: 120, 138-139, 189, 266, 315, 429, 490, 507; historians' view, **I**: 4-6; Hopkins role in, **I**: 501-502; humor in, **I**: 630; **II**: 647-648; love of naval affairs, **III**: 238; misunderstanding in, **II**: 761-762; on being first to Quebec,

III: 313-314; on Churchill's birthday at Teheran, **II**: 615-616; personal nicknames, **I**: xxi; personal touches, **I**: 135, 358-359, 539-540; **III**: 238-239; phases, **I**: 6-19; photos sent, **II**: 322, 753-754; pre-war conspiracy issue, **III**: 201; pre-war contacts, **I**: 23; Roosevelt and Stalin meeting, **II**: 283; Roosevelt on, **I**: 337; **III**: 34; Roosevelt on Greek crisis and, **III**: 456; sharpest exchanges, **I**: 16; strain over Cairo Conference plans, **II**: 595-596; strains over India, **I**: 445; unilateral actions discussed, **III**: 207-208

Ciano de Cortellazzo, Count Galeazzo, **II**: 379-380

CICERO, **II**: 663, 669

Ciechanowski, Jan, **II**: 715, 719

Citadel, Quebec City, **II**: 323

Citrine, Sir Walter, **I**: 87; **III**: 124-125

Civil Aviation Conference (1944), **I**: 17; **III**: 402, 404-405, 418, 421, 422, 425, 427, 428, 442-443, 517, 519-520, 566-567

Civil aviation policy dispute, **I**: 10, 16-17; **II**: 451-452, 506-507, 749; **III**: 109, 335, 402, 404-407, 418, 543-544, 566-567; Churchill on, **I**: 19; **III**: 419-421, 436; Roosevelt on, **III**: 423-425

Civil War, United States, **I**: 306

Clark, Mark W., **I**: 575, 613-614, 634, 655; **II**: 29, 171, 437, 622-623; **III**: 392, 400, 410, 411; and Anzio assault, **II**: 640-641; and Churchill, **I**: 618; and Darlan, **II**: 8; and Italian campaign, **III**: 142, 167, 285-286, 299-300, 304-305, 321, 348; and North African invasion, **I**: 589-590, 594, 670-671; and TORCH, **II**: 5; Marshall on, **I**: 516

Clemenceau, Georges, **II**: 121

Clipperton Island, **III**: 417, 422, 504-505

Cobbold, Ivan, **III**: 196

Codenames, **II**: 118, 573 (*see also Glossary*, **III**: 639-646); Churchill and, **I**: 26; **II**: 280, 336, 344, 346, 492; **III**: 225, 274, 485, 497; efforts to clarify, 1942, **I**: 518-519, 522-523; for Atlantic islands plan, **I**: 201-202; for atomic research, **I**: 249; for breaking enemy

codes, **I**: 214-215; for Casablanca Conference, **II**: 107-109

Codes, secret: Allied, German problems with, **II**: 366-367; British break German and Italian, **I**: 155; British break U.S., **I**: 9; Churchill warns Roosevelt on, **I**: 370-371; Japanese naval, deciphered by U.S., 1942, **I**: 465, 483

Coding machines, **I**: 214-215

Cold War, **II**: 606; **III**: 275, 319; and U.S. foreign policy, **I**: 14-15

Colepaugh, William, **III**: 493

Cologne, Germany, **III**: 409; bombing of, **I**: 438, 501, 504

Colombo, Ceylon, **II**: 443

Colonialism, **III**: 530; American view of, **I**: 557; **II**: 360, 691, 696, 733; **III**: 237; British, **III**: 6; British, Roosevelt view of, **II**: 156; Churchill vs. Roosevelt on, **I**: 19; **II**: 609; **III**: 626; in Southeast Asia, **III**: 572; Roosevelt ignorance of, **II**: 269; Roosevelt on, **I**: 400-401; **II**: 609; **III**: 3-10, 237

Colonies:

British in Asia, **II**: 755; **III**: 38

French, **I**: 177, 179, 641; **II**: 272, 310-311; and FCNL, **II**: 340; and Syrian invasion, **I**: 204; controlled by Free French, **II**: 335; German threats to, **I**: 184-185; in North Africa, importance of, **I**: 146-147; Roosevelt on postwar status of, **II**: 607. *See also* Indo-China

German: Hitler view of, **I**: 188

Italian, **III**: 325-328; disposition of, **III**: 333

Portuguese, **II**: 280-281

Colville, J. R., **II**: 716

Combined boards, in postwar world, **III**: 93

Combined Chiefs of Staff, **I**: 338, 342, 343, 348-349, 365, 367, 599; **II**: 42, 133, 140, 148, 179, 217, 235, 239, 264, 481, 498, 514, 638; **III**: 55, 147, 194, 203-204, 238, 348, 468, 485; and ANZAC defense, **I**: 386, 389; and Argentina, **II**: 678; and Australian troop withdrawal, **II**: 31, 33-34; and bombing of Rome, **II**: 250-251; and Burma, **I**: 333; and China-Burma theater, **III**: 429-430; and command structure, **II**:

Combined Chiefs of Staff (*cont.*)
614-615; **III**: 103; and coordination
of Pacific operations, **I**: 412-414; and
cross-channel invasion, **II**: 132, 712-
713; and Darlan, **II**: 3, 29; and Far
East, **III**: 627; and France, **III**: 241;
and Greece, **III**: 279, 454; Indo-
China, **III**: 573; and invasion of
southern France, **III**: 82, 212-213,
226; and Italian ships to Soviets, **II**:
625, 654, 664-665, 675; **III**: 17, 25;
and Italian surrender, **II**: 371, 538;
and Italy, **II**: 760; **III**: 190, 523, 534,
620; and Mediterranean command,
II: 617-618; and Mediterranean strategy, **I**: 699; **II**: 13; and negotiations
with Bulgarians, **III**: 23; and North
African invasion, **I**: 554; and pooling
of new ship production, **I**: 538-539;
and production coordination, **I**: 632;
and relief for Italy, **III**: 401; and relief in liberated areas, **III**: 540, 578;
and representation on, **I**: 330-332,
335-337; and Southeast Asia command structure, **II**: 294-295, 301,
430; and Soviet Union, **II**: 65; and
Spain, **II**: 165; and troop deployment,
III: 534; and U.S. air force deployment, 1942, **I**: 509; and U.S. aircraft
to Britain, **I**: 484-488, 487; at Casablanca Conference, **II**: 103; at Malta
Conference, **III**: 502, 505, 521, 523;
at Quebec Conference, 1943, **II**: 343,
344, 346, 372, 429-430; at Quebec
Conference, 1944, **III**: 316, 321, 325;
Churchill and, **I**: 394; **II**: 584-585;
creation and composition of, **I**: 9,
293; message to Stalin on OVER-
LORD, **III**: 93-94; on ABDA, **I**: 368;
on Canada and command structure,
III: 82-83; on occupation zones in
Germany, **II**: 708-709; war strategy,
I: 399, 432; **II**: 10, 20, 41, 433, 705;
III: 38, 199, 603, 608
Combined Food Board, **I**: 506, 508; **II**:
750; **III**: 247
Combined Munitions Assignments
Board, **I**: 632
Combined Policy Committee on Atomic
Energy, **II**: 420-421; **III**: 509
Combined Production and Resources
Board, **I**: 506, 508, 614, 632; **II**: 750

Combined Raw Materials Board, **I**: 327-
329; **II**: 750
Combined Shipping Adjustment Board,
I: 329, 552, 647; **II**: 45, 220-221, 750
Commando operations, **I**: 381; Allied, **I**:
545; operation PLOUGH, **II**: 47;
raids on French coast as costly, **I**: 574-
575
Commandos, United States: California
training, **I**: 383, 439; Roosevelt orders
creation of, **I**: 322
Commonwealth Air Training Plan, **I**:
457
Communism:
in Balkans, **III**: 153
in France, **II**: 465-466
in Germany, Stalin on, **III**: 273
in Greece, **II**: 450; **III**: 278-279,
457, 547
in Italy, **II**: 360, 666; **III**: 153, 176,
319, 351, 387, 436; Anglo-American
attitudes, **II**: 379-380; prospect of,
III: 42, 45-46
in Poland, **III**: 208, 273
in postwar Europe, **II**: 431
in Roumania, **III**: 547
in Yugoslavia, **II**: 548
postwar spread of, Hurley on, **III**: 6
Roosevelt on, **III**: 288
Soviet: Marshall on, **II**: 480; Roosevelt on vs. Nazism, **II**: 172. *See also*
Bolshevism
Yugoslavia as test case for, **III**: 133
Communist Party, Greece, **III**: 95
Communist Party, Italian, **II**: 679
Communists: and youth of Europe, **I**:
94; in Britain, **III**: 124; in China, **III**:
370, 527; in Greece, **III**: 449, 450,
455, 472, 474; in Italy, **III**: 110, 533;
in Roumania, **III**: 625
Conant, James, **II**: 433-434
Conferences, wartime, **II**: 438-439, 400;
and Churchill-Roosevelt relationship,
I: 9-10, 19; Churchill and Roosevelt's
eagerness for, **I**: 227; power politics
in, **III**: 348-349. *See also* specific conferences
Connally, Tom, **II**: 222, 225; **III**: 506
Conservative Party, Britain, **I**: 36, 53;
II: 261; **III**: 538-539, 546, 548
Constantinople, Turkey (Istanbul): as
conference site, **III**: 377

Convoys, **I**: 221, 243, 416
and German raiders, **I**: 149-151
Churchill on, **I**: 189-190, 649
escorts improved for, **I**: 172-173
in Atlantic, **I**: 92, 107, 164, 218-219; **II**: 313, 500-501
in Caribbean and Gulf of Mexico, **I**: 524; **II**: 78
in Pacific, **I**: 307-308
increased security for, early 1944, **II**: 647
of troops, **I**: 249; **III**: 18
routes threatened, **I**: 75, 350
strategy for, **I**: 193-194, 407-408; **II**: 12
to Malta, **I**: 535
to Soviet Union, **I**: 482-483, 490, 503-504, 551, 607; **II**: 59, 116, 198-199, 636, 654; **III**: 18, 166; Admiralty on, **I**: 622; and German aircraft, **I**: 595; and North African invasion, **I**: 584; and Soviet demand for Italian ships, **II**: 698; British naval losses in, **III**: 25; Churchill on, **I**: 618, 623-624, 629; **II**: 533-537; **III**: 311; independent ship scheme, **I**: 623, 629, 637; losses on, **I**: 594; negotiations over, **II**: 172-177, 474-479; northern route dangers, **II**: 15, 20-21, 48-51; problems of, **I**: 437, 439, 468-469, 471-475, 493, 494, 521-522, 527-533, 535, 537-538; resumed, **II**: 442, 470, 474-479; **III**: 37, 159; Roosevelt on, **I**: 596, 600, 617; Stalin on, **I**: 544-546; **II**: 179-181; **III**: 200; suspended, **I**: 602, 612-613, 615; **II**: 157-165; U.S. and British losses, **II**: 528; U.S. military on, **I**: 608-609, 612
U.S. escorts for, **I**: 138, 153-156, 163-166, 196, 218, 222-223, 236
Cooper, Alfred Duff, **II**: 579-580, 622-623, 691-692, 695; **III**: 87-88, 355
Coral Sea, Battle of, **I**: 483
Corfu, Greece, **II**: 349, 361
Corregidor, Battle of, **I**: 408
Corsica, **II**: 184, 349, 364, 442, 445, 455, 464-466
Cotentin Peninsula, **II**: 132
Council for the Defense of all Ireland, **I**: 99, 107
Council of Four (WWI), **II**: 449-450
Cournaire, Pierre, **II**: 279

Courseulles, France, **III**: 215
Couve de Murville, Maurice, **II**: 333-334
Crete, **I**: 155, 176, 182; **II**: 131, 152, 511; **III**: 328, 461; atrocities in, **II**: 520; Axis brutalities reported in, **II**: 417; British campaign in, **I**: 202-203, 292; fall of, **I**: 196; German air bases in, **I**: 317; Germans in, **I**: 190-192
Crimea, **I**: 295; **III**: 368. *See also* Yalta
Crimea, battle in, **III**: 119
Cripps, Sir Stafford, **I**: 402, 550; **III**: 418, 419; mission to India, **I**: 444-449, 501, 550
Croatia, Yugoslavia, **II**: 428; **III**: 115
Croatians, in Yugoslavia, **I**: 222; **II**: 660; **III**: 115
Croce, Benedetto, **II**: 457, 664, 666; **III**: 28-29, 30-31, 33, 43, 110
Cross-channel invasion, **I**: 452, 514, 529, 532, 554, 564-565, 603; **II**: 118, 140, 296, 386, 422, 470, 632-633, 636, 663; **III**: 39, 64, 151-152, 191
air assets for, **I**: 597; **II**: 730-731; **III**: 122-124, 127, 195
Allied view of, **I**: 436-437, 493-495, 614; **II**: 505-506, 562, 608
and codenames, **I**: 491-492; **II**: 212, 283
and de Gaulle, **III**: 135-138
and invasion of southern France, **III**: 82, 115, 119, 126-128, 185-186, 212-223, 225-229, 304
and Italian campaign, **II**: 9-10, 202, 580-581, 705; **III**: 137, 299
and Italian ships to Soviets, **II**: 655, 664, 666, 670-671, 676, 694, 698, 700
and North African invasion, **I**: 601, 603-604
and occupation of France, **III**: 62
and other operations, **II**: 502-505, 508, 549-551
and relief operations, **III**: 84-86
and supply problems to Soviets, **I**: 482-483
British naval commitments to, **II**: 755
British view of, **I**: 449, 458-459, 495, 520-521; **II**: 9-10, 344, 516; **III**: 225
Churchill on, **I**: 250, 302, 304, 436, 458-459, 504, 509, 515, 516, 528-529, 650; **II**: 38, 39, 48, 246, 266, 442,

Cross-channel invasion (*cont.*)
444, 454, 541, 613-615; **III**: 53-54, 87,
91, 162, 163-164
    command of, **I**: 551-552; **II**: 481,
489, 541, 551, 570-571, 623-624
    commando raids show danger of
for 1942, **I**: 574-575
    delay of, **II**: 153, 157-158, 667
    discussed at: Casablanca Confer-
ence, **II**: 117-118, 121; London Conference, **I**: 541-543; Moscow Conference (1942), **I**: 560, 564-566, 568;
Quebec Conference (1943), **II**: 430;
Second Washington Conference, **I**:
513-516; Teheran Conference, **II**:
610-613; Third Washington Conference, **II**: 212
    French participation in, **III**: 87-88,
128-130, 156-157
    German intelligence on, **III**: 11
    German occupation zones and, **II**:
746
    German submarines and, **III**: 251
    landing craft needs, **II**: 148; Pacific
requirements, **III**: 89
    landing zones in, **II**: 608, 708-709
    Marshall on, **II**: 205, 480
    Mediterranean theater and, **II**: 498-
499, 609
    Molotov discusses, **I**: 397, 490-491,
494-500
    monopolizes resources, **III**: 110
    North African invasion and, **I**: 551-
552, 575
    planning of, **I**: 498, 552, 568; **II**:
132-134, 557, 565, 658, 712-713, 756-
757; **III**: 161, 198
    problems of food for and Argen-
tina, **II**: 678-679
    resources to, **II**: 585, 653
    Roosevelt converted to, **I**: 460
    Roosevelt on, **I**: 420, 436, 466, 502-
504, 533, 536, 610; **II**: 45, 260, 498,
501, 766; **III**: 138-139
    Roosevelt on Churchill and, **III**: 60
    security measures for, **III**: 92, 120-
121
    security of and Irish, **III**: 57
    Soviet offensive and, **III**: 90-91, 100
    Soviets oppose postponement, **II**:
558
    Stalin on, **I**: 560; **II**: 38-39, 244,
282, 285-288, 606; **III**: 230
    troops needed for, **II**: 556; **III**: 215
    U.S. view of, **I**: 608; **II**: 38, 555
    versus bombing of Japan, resources
for, **II**: 732
    weather and, **III**: 161
Cross-channel invasion buildup (BO-
LERO), **I**: 564; **II**: 9, 41; and Italian
campaign needs, **II**: 434; and North
African invasion, **I**: 555; and Second
Washington Conference, **I**: 514; and
Soviet supply problems, **I**: 482-483;
British view of, **I**: 458-459, 520-521,
650; **II**: 38-39; decision on com-
mander delayed, **I**: 527; discussed at
London Conference, **I**: 542-543; discussed at Third Washington Conference, **II**: 212; planning debate on, **I**:
552; Roosevelt on, **I**: 610; **II**: 156,
179; shipping crisis and, **II**: 167
Crowley, Leo, **III**: 36, 65
CRUSADER, **I**: 252. *See also* Army, British
Cuistreham, France, **III**: 215
Cunningham, John, **II**: 632, 651, 658
Cunningham, Sir Andrew, **I**: 165, 183,
184, 252, 301, 590-591, 596, 602, 634-
635; **II**: 4, 144, 264, 295, 305, 518-
519, 551, 575; **III**: 211; and Darlan
deal, **II**: 28; and Italian fleet disposition, **III**: 26; and Middle East strategy, **II**: 517; appointed First Sea
Lord, British Navy, **II**: 317-318
Cunningham Agreement on Italian
Navy, **II**: 518-519, 538-539, 552-553,
655
Curtin, John, **I**: 330-332, 365, 369, 409;
II: 37; **III**: 77-78, 142-143 ; and Australian troop withdrawal, **I**: 413, 644-
645; **II**: 22-26, 31-35, 47; and Mac-
Arthur's troop request, **I**: 477-480;
and prisoner of war exchange, **III**:
245; Churchill annoyance with, **II**: 32-
33; fears on invasion of Australia, **I**:
438; on ANZAC situation, **I**: 384-388;
on appointment of Casey, **I**: 427-428;
on U.S. troops to Australia, **I**: 432-
433; visit to Roosevelt, **I**: 492-493,
500-501, 503. *See also* Australia
Curzon, Lord, **II**: 684; **III**: 70

Curzon Line, *see* Poland
Cyprus, **II**: 491, 724, 730; **III**: 366, 381
Cyrenaica, **I**: 252, 255, 294, 317, 381, 671, 673; **II**: 11, 13, 122, 136-137, 145, 316, 511; **III**: 179, 328. *See also* Lybia
Czechoslovakia, **I**: 16, 124, 209, 221; **II**: 769; **III**: 299, 403, 617, 629
   and Britain, **III**: 274
   and Soviet Union, **II**: 650-651
   atrocities in, **II**: 520
   postwar: Churchill on, **II**: 223; Stalin on, **II**: 716; **III**: 364
   provisional government, **I**: 206

D'Aosta, Duke of, **I**: 165
D'Astier de la Vigerie, Emmanuel R., **II**: 691-692; **III**: 170-171
D'Astier, François, **II**: 91
D'Astier, Henri, **II**: 91
Dakar, French West Africa, **I**: 71-74, 79, 85, 87, 98, 175-176, 180, 209, 297, 302, 586; **II**: 68, 335, 618, 726; **III**: 109; American interests in, **II**: 607; as key port, **II**: 56; de Gaulle in, **II**: 235, 237; German threats to, **I**: 200-201; invasion of, **I**: 146; Roosevelt on, **I**: 250; **II**: 229, 279; Vichy and Allies cooperate in, **II**: 4
Daladier, Edouard, **I**: 36, 459
Dalmatian Coast, **II**: 428, 445
Damaskinos, Archbishop, **III**: 457-459, 466-467, 471-475, 478-481, 487-488, 537
Daniell, Raymond, **III**: 517
Danube Federation, **II**: 223; **III**: 363-364
Danube River, **II**: 556, 558; **III**: 212
Danzig, Poland, **II**: 738; **III**: 617-618
Dardanelles, **III**: 366, 368, 371, 379-380; battle of, 1915, **I**: 570; in British plans, 1943, **II**: 14-15
Darlan, Jean, **I**: 44, 46, 154, 185-186, 269, 297, 334, 350, 353-354, 460-461, 669-670; **II**: 40, 67-68, 98, 229, 237; **III**: 527; and Allies, **II**: 84; and *Dunkerque* issue, **I**: 157-158, 162-164; and Eisenhower, **II**: 76; and French fleet, **I**: 464-465, 674; and invasion of North Africa, **I**: 634; anti-British feelings, **I**: 146-147; assassination of, **II**:

88-89, 91; Churchill on, **II**: 7, 17-19, 50-51; controversy over, **II**: 3-9, 27-29; in post-TORCH administration, **II**: 56-57; Roosevelt on, **II**: 21-22; Stalin on, **II**: 51, 80-81; U.S. press statement on appointment, **II**: 8-9
Darlan deal, **II**: 67-68, 214, 269, 366, 480, 587, 679; Churchill on, **II**: 726; **III**: 30-31; Churchill support for Roosevelt on, **III**: 438
Davies, Joseph E., **II**: 233, 244, 245, 259, 261, 284, 345; mission to Moscow, **I**: 12-14; on Stalin and Roosevelt, **II**: 278, 283
Davis, Elmer, **II**: 499
Davis, Norman H., **I**: 116-117
De Gaulle, Charles, **I**: 20, 90; **II**: 139; **III**: 30-31, 110, 634; Allied relations with, **I**: 297-298; **II**: 254-257, 641; **III**: 144-147, 169-175, 361-362; American view of, **II**: 235-237; and Churchill, **II**: 689, 691-693, 695; **III**: 389-391, 494-495; and cross-channel invasion, **III**: 86-88, 128-130, 135-138, 148-152; and Dakar, **I**: 72; and Darlan deal, **II**: 3-4, 7, 21, 29-30; and Eisenhower, **II**: 480-481, 622; **III**: 494-495; and French Army, **II**: 273, 274, 440-442; and FCNL, **II**: 268, 271-274, 333-336; and French currency question, **III**: 180-181; and German invasion, **I**: 44; and Giraud, **I**: 669-670; **II**: 135, 214-215, 227-232, 464-466; and invasion of southern France, **III**: 228; and invasion of Syria, **I**: 204; and Italy, **II**: 539; and Madagascar, **I**: 467; and North African invasion, **I**: 593, 595, 599, 656-657, 659-662; and recognition of FCNL, **III**: 194-197, 333, 338, 355-356, 365; and St. Pierre-Miquelon affair, **I**: 324-326; and Southeast Asia, **III**: 572; and Soviet Union, **III**: 433, 440-442, 444-445; and Stalin, **I**: 561; and supplies for French Army, **III**: 500-501; anti-Vichy speech, **II**: 29-31; arrests ex-Vichy officials, **II**: 625-626, 635, 641, 642; as issue at Quebec Conference, 1943, **II**: 328; British vs. American view of, **II**: 104-105; **I**: 12; Churchill on, **I**: 12, 297-298, 667; **II**: 310, 333,

De Gaulle, Charles (*cont.*)
335, 374-375, 640, 691-693; **III**: 172, 322; D-Day broadcast by, **III**: 156-157; discussed at Casablanca, **II**: 119, 121; Eisenhower on, **II**: 75; Hull and Roosevelt view, **II**: 642-643; in Normandy, **III**: 183, 185-186; in North Africa, **I**: 146; **II**: 56-57, 89-92, 98-99, 147-148, 244, 279-280; Leahy on, **II**: 137-138; Middle East policies of, **II**: 599-600; on British threat to French Empire, **I**: 660; on decolonialization, **III**: 626; Roosevelt and Churchill on, **II**: 626; Roosevelt on, **I**: 669; **II**: 134-135, 142-143, 208-211, 229-230, 254-257, 310, 337-340; **III**: 62, 181, 183, 187, 322, 369, 494; Stalin on, **II**: 289; strength underestimated, **II**: 277; trip to London for channel invasion, **III**: 162; U.S. and, 1942, **I**: 297-298; visit to Washington, 1944, **II**: 107-109; **III**: 84, 88-90, 102, 104, 108-110, 166-167, 167-168, 193-194, 205, 237-238, 240
De Jean, Maurice, **II**: 214-215
De la Chapelle, Fernand Bonnier, **II**: 88
De Rialp, Don Manuel, **II**: 672-673
De Valera, Eamon, **I**: 53-54, 92; **II**: 186-187, 225, 421; **III**: 81, 543-544; Allied negotiations with, **III**: 57-58, 75-76; Churchill on, **I**: 112-113, 282; Churchill on neutrality of, **I**: 112, 113. *See also* Ireland
Deakin, F.W.D., **II**: 660-661
Deane, John R., **III**: 93-94, 113, 342-343, 352-353, 603
Declaration of the United Nations, **I**: 309, 371-372; **III**: 266
Declaration on German Atrocities, **II**: 547
Declaration on Iran (State Dept.), **III**: 3
Declaration on Liberated Europe, **II**: 611; **III**: 528, 530, 545-546, 548, 562, 588
Defense plans #3 and #4, **I**: 218
Delhi, India, **II**: 482
Democratic Party, United States, **II**: 306; **III**: 243, 337; and Ireland, **I**: 45
Denmark, **III**: 257; atrocities in, **II**: 520; German invasion of, **I**: 36, 200; in British occupation zone, **II**: 745; postwar, Churchill on, **II**: 223; proposed

landing in, **I**: 302
Denmark Straits, **II**: 161
Dennys, L. E., **I**: 417
Desert Army, **II**: 118, 136, 144-145
Desert Victory (film), **II**: 155-156
Destroyer-bases arrangement, **I**: 43, 53-54; Churchill on, **I**: 37-43
Devers, Jacob, **II**: 281, 284, 622-623, 639, 642, 651, 653, 656, 658; **III**: 265
Dewey, Thomas, **III**: 388
DIADEM, **III**: 197
Diego Suarez, **I**: 404, 405, 480, 483, 613; Allied attack on, **I**: 466; Japanese threat to, **I**: 350
Dieppe, France, **I**: 574-575
Dill, Lady, **III**: 507
Dill, Sir John, **I**: 144-145, 223, 226, 284, 360, 481, 510, 551; **II**: 110, 303, 420-421, 571, 613; **III**: 53, 308, 381-382, 384-385, 392, 399, 410, 506-507, 509; as Churchill's representative, **I**: 338-339; honored by U.S. Congress, **III**: 520-521
Disarmament, **II**: 129; of Axis, Churchill wants total, **II**: 129. *See also* Morgenthau Plan
Djibouti, French Somaliland, **II**: 92, 335
Dnieper River, Soviet Union, **II**: 386
Dodecanese Islands, **II**: 126, 131, 134, 139, 152, 184, 341, 349, 361, 430, 445, 497-499, 505, 508, 555; **III**: 232; and Allied strategy, **II**: 197, 509-512; fighting in, **II**: 513; occupied by Italy since WWI, **II**: 197; postwar disposition of, **III**: 328
Dönitz, K., **II**: 157-158
Donovan, William J., **I**: 134-135, 189, 348, 350; **II**: 553-554; **III**: 306, 309; and Balkans guerrillas, **II**: 548-549; and commandos in California, **I**: 439; and Greece, **I**: 144-145; appointed Coordinator of Information, **I**: 263-264; in French Africa, **I**: 353; organizes subversion in North Africa, **I**: 426
Doolittle, James, **I**: 465, 507
Dornberger, Walter, **II**: 589
Douglas, Lewis, **II**: 177, 219, 354, 365
Douglas, Sir Sholto, **I**: 541-542; **II**: 196, 263, 622-623; Churchill praises, **II**: 305-306; issue of anti-Americanism of,

II: 274, 646-647, 649
Dragoumis, Philippos, III: 466
Dresden, Germany, III: 605
Drummond, Air Marshal, I: 673; and VELVET plans, II: 57-59
Dulles, Allen, III: 586, 609
Dumbarton Oaks Agreement, III: 531-533, 588
Dumbarton Oaks Conference, III: 319, 330-332, 334-335, 339, 342, 343, 351-353, 421, 432, 527, 531, 591
Dunkirk, evacuation of, I: 42
Dunn, James, III: 367
Düsseldorf, Germany, bombing of, I: 597

Eaker, Ira, II: 185, 517-518, 622-624, 627, 642; and command changes, II: 646-647
Early, Steve, II: 171
East Asia: decisions on at Yalta, III: 524, 527
East Asia theater: command structure outlined, II: 263-265; renamed Southeast Asia theater, II: 282
East Indies, II: 617; III: 40; Churchill on strategy toward, 1942, I: 299; in S.W. Pacific command area, I: 411
East Prussia, III: 143
Ecuador, II: 223-224
Eden, Anthony, I: 8, 12, 69, 120, 152, 177, 238; II: 127, 136, 157-158, 175, 177, 182-183, 186, 380, 384, 433, 440, 518, 551, 554, 606, 608, 668; III: 183, 253, 283, 331, 363, 368, 415, 445-446, 545, 547, 550, 566, 615
    and Argentina, III: 230-231, 247
    and Balkans, III: 153, 185
    and Casablanca Conference, II: 56
    and convoys to Soviets, II: 533, 536
    and de Gaulle, II: 257; III: 171, 390, 392
    and Eastern Europe, III: 546-547, 549-550
    and France, II: 227-228, 231, 235; III: 144, 206, 241
    and FCNL, II: 333, 374-375; III: 128-129, 237, 321-322
    and Greece, III: 279, 487-488
    and Italian political situation, III: 30, 32, 45, 333-334, 337, 443-444

    and Italian ships to Soviets, II: 659
    and Italian surrender, II: 423, 424, 462-463
    and Katyn Forest massacre, II: 397
    and Middle East strategy, II: 517
    and neutral nations, III: 245
    and Poland, II: 199; III: 253-254, 359, 364, 480-481
    and Polish boundary dispute, II: 716-717, 719-723, 735
    and Polish-Soviet relations, II: 193-194, 763-764
    and postwar political plans, II: 54
    and Roosevelt, II: 146-147, 155-157; III: 620; Churchill on, II: 191
    and shipping crisis, II: 167
    and Soviets, 1941, I: 393
    and Spanish, II: 739
    and Stalin, II: 172
    and Sweden, III: 257
    and Teheran Conference, II: 523, 547
    and Tunis Conference, II: 515-516
    and Turkish negotiations, III: 55
    and U.N. organization creation, III: 431
    and unconditional surrender for Germany, II: 645-646, 652
    and Yugoslavia, III: 275, 510
    appointed Foreign Secretary, I: 115
    as candidate for Prime Minister, I: 36
    at Malta Conference, III: 521, 523
    at Moscow Conference, 1944, III: 345, 347-351
    at Moscow Foreign Ministers' Conference, II: 557-558, 562-563, 576-577, 606
    at pre-Yalta Conference, III: 503, 505, 507, 511
    at Quebec Conference, 1943, II: 354, 372, 422
    at Quebec Conference, 1944, III: 323-324
    at Yalta Conference, III: 477, 526-527, 591
    health of, III: 110-111
    objects to Churchill visit to U.S., I: 283
    on Balkans, I: 144-145
    on Bolivian revolution, II: 683-684

Eden, Anthony (*cont.*)
    on bombing of Bulgaria, **II**: 715
    on Churchill-Roosevelt communica-
tion, **I**: 279
    on Darlan deal, **II**: 7
    on German attack on Soviets, **II**:
285
    on Hull in England, **II**: 269-270
    on Madagascar invasion, **I**: 475
    on North Africa, **II**: 83
    on pre-Teheran talks, **II**: 596
    on Soviets and Italian settlement,
II: 370-371
    on supplies to Soviets, **I**: 473-474
    trip to Greece, 1944, **III**: 471, 480
    visit to Moscow, 1941, **I**: 10, 470,
490, 566; **II**: 283
Edward VIII, *see* Windsor, Duke of
Egypt, **I**: 132-133, 152, 165, 244, 254,
298, 300, 315, 561-562, 632; **II**: 13,
14, 34, 145, 168, 448, 491, 544, 561;
III: 286, 380-381, 449, 453, 502; and
Madagascar invasion, **I**: 441; Anglo-
American policy toward, **I**: 16;
Churchill on, **I**: 181-182; German
threats to, 1942, **I**: 319; Germans driven out of, **II**: 136-137; Greek exile
government in, **III**: 179; Harriman in,
I: 208; impact of Syrian invasion on,
I: 204; neutrality of, **I**: 204; political
situation in, **III**: 110-111, 114, 116,
178-179; Roosevelt on, **I**: 421, 533;
III: 536
Egyptian campaign, **I**: 79, 621, 651,
655-660, 663; aircraft requirements
for, **I**: 317; **II**: 94; Allied troops in,
1942, **I**: 302, 320; and North African
invasion, **I**: 641; Australian troops in,
II: 24; battles in, **I**: 112, 202-203, 208,
545, 592, 594-595, 611, 620-621, 623,
625, 628-629, 636; battles in, effect on
Soviet front, **I**: 607-608; British in, **I**:
216, 294, 438, 653; operation BAT-
TLEAXE, **I**: 207, 210; Rommel and,
I: 518, 640; Roosevelt to Churchill on,
I: 669-670; Stalin to Churchill on, **I**:
672
Eisenhower, Dwight David, **I**: 4-5, 535;
II: 26, 123, 171, 207, 248, 264, 281,
304, 447, 517, 551, 557, 601, 632,
759; **III**: 196, 203-204, 308, 352, 435,
472, 485, 494, 539, 578, 611, 616
    and Army newspaper, **I**: 625
    and Balkans, **II**: 554
    and Berlin, **III**: 616
    and bombing of Rome, **II**: 250-251,
303
    and Canadians, **III**: 103-104
    and Casablanca Conference, **II**: 97,
113
    and Churchill, **I**: 618; **II**: 17-19,
216, 452, 454, 516, 645; **III**: 87, 495
    and command changes, **II**: 627-629,
631, 635, 639; **III**: 409-410, 504, 552-
553
    and cross-channel invasion, **I**: 552;
II: 573, 584, 712-713, 731; **III**: 164,
228
    and Darlan deal, **II**: 3-9, 21-22, 28-
30, 40, 68-71
    and de Gaulle, **II**: 255-257, 662;
III: 170-171, 186
    and demonstrations in Belgium, **III**:
437
    and Eastern Mediterranean strat-
egy, **II**: 508-509
    and France, **II**: 235-236; **III**: 148,
151, 156, 238, 243, 338
    and FCNL, **II**: 310-312, 634-635,
642; **III**: 128-130, 135, 137, 365-366
    and French currency question, **III**:
180-181
    and French in North Africa, **II**:
229, 231-232, 257-258, 273-274, 335,
626
    and German morale, **III**: 409
    and invasion of southern France,
III: 212-213, 215-216, 219, 222, 226-
227, 267
    and Italian campaign, **II**: 218, 234-
235, 300, 307, 314, 319, 324, 327,
483, 501-502, 562-563, 581, 583; **III**:
119
    and Italian fleet disposition, **III**: 26
    and Italian invasion, **II**: 12-13, 327-
328
    and Italian postwar government, **II**:
190-199, 504
    and Italian prisoners, **II**: 384
    and Italian surrender, **II**: 348, 351-
352, 353, 354, 357, 358-359, 362-365,
367-369, 371-373, 426, 436-437, 455-

469, 471, 484, 486, 488, 490, 492, 518-519, 523-524, 538, 552
  and Jews to North Africa, **II**: 315
  and Marshall, **I**: 516; **III**: 516-517, 522
  and North African invasion, **I**: 575, 577, 578, 585-586, 590-591, 594, 602, 656-657, 662-663, 669-671, 673; **II**: 5, 7
  and occupation administration, **II**: 251, 270-271, 480-481
  and occupation of France, **III**: 62-64, 240-241
  and occupation zones for Germany, **III**: 147, 161
  and Normandy invasion, **III**: 92, 161-162, 263-264
  and refugee camps in North Africa, **II**: 321
  and reinforcements, **III**: 500-501
  and relief for civilians, **III**: 559-560, 570, 584, 621
  and Sholto Douglas, **II**: 306
  and Sicilan invasion, **II**: 242
  and Southeast Asia commander, **II**: 317
  and Soviet offensive, 1944, **III**: 489-490
  and Soviet Union, **III**: 468-469, 470
  and Stalin: Churchill on, **III**: 612
  and supply priorities, **III**: 300, 302, 356-357
  and Tunis military conference, **II**: 503, 516-517
  and western front, **III**: 446-449, 631
  as Supreme Commander, **II**: 481, 613, 617-618, 621-622, 648-649; **III**: 497
  Churchill on, **II**: 17-19, 85, 227, 529; **III**: 74, 498-499, 352, 603-604
  in North Africa, **I**: 554-556; **II**: 56-57, 75-77, 83-85, 87, 89-90, 92-93, 98-99, 105, 136-138, 141-142, 145, 282; Roosevelt on, **II**: 77; Stalin on, **II**: 80
  on Alexander, **II**: 624
  on bombing of France, **III**: 122
  on cross-channel invasion, **I**: 601; **II**: 505, 653-654
  on FCNL, **III**: 169, 355
  on German morale, **III**: 403

  on liberation of Rome, **II**: 331-332, 379
  on strategy in Europe, **II**: 212, 230, 756-757; **III**: 198-199, 340, 347-348, 522-523, 602-605, 607-609
  on unconditional surrender for Germany, **III**: 133
  promoted, **II**: 143
  role in postwar European arrangements, **II**: 766
  Roosevelt on, **III**: 608
Eisenhower, Milton, **II**: 8
El Alamein, Battle of, **I**: 635, 644, 656-660, 663, 670-671; **II**: 555; **III**: 365, 497, 574
Elbe River, Germany, **III**: 604, 607
Elections, British, **III**: 573
Elections, United States:
  and Italian-American vote, **III**: 386
  of 1940, **I**: 63, 68; Churchill on, **I**: 80-81
  of 1942, **I**: 576-577, 584, 647
  of 1944, **III**: 78, 157, 211, 266, 373-375, 377; and British dollar balances, **III**: 34, 36; and Eastern Europe, **III**: 343; and health of Roosevelt, **III**: 367-368; and Italian political situation, **III**: 40-41; and oil conference, **III**: 169; and Pacific strategy, **III**: 193; and Poland-Soviet relations, **III**: 365; and Polish-Americans, **III**: 79, 208, 234; and tripartite conference, **III**: 339; and U.N. organization, **III**: 331; and U.S. policy toward Argentina, **III**: 230; and U.S. policy toward Ireland, **III**: 57; Churchill and, **II**: 541; **III**: 195-196, 359, 368-369; Congress and Roosevelt, **III**: 106; impact of Quebec decisions on, **III**: 316, 318-320; Roosevelt and ethnic groups, **III**: 33; Roosevelt and neutral nations and, **III**: 245; Roosevelt concern for, **II**: 611; Roosevelt elected, **III**: 382-383; Roosevelt on, **III**: 250, 371; Roosevelt trip to England, proposed, **III**: 145; Roosevelt's Hotel Statler speech, **III**: 340-341; Stalin on, **III**: 359
Elsey, George, **II**: 493, 589; **III**: 517
Elwood, A. B., **III**: 386, 486
Embrick, Stanley D., **I**: 239, 241
Emergency Fleet Corporation, **I**: 88

Empire air training scheme (British), **II**: 25, 36

England, **II**: 72; as possible site for 1943 conference, **II**: 43

English Channel, **III**: 164; gales in, **III**: 198

Eniwetok, Marshall Islands, **III**: 193

Erikson, Erik, **III**: 8

Eritrea, **I**: 159; **III**: 327

Espionage: Axis and Allied agents in Iberia, **I**: 540; German in Spanish territories, **III**: 67; German in U.S., **III**: 493

Espiritu Santo, **II**: 36

Essen, Germany, bombing of, **I**: 438

Estonia, **I**: 371; **II**: 611; **III**: 349, 541; and Soviet Union, **I**: 393

Ethiopia, **I**: 203, 372; **II**: 459; Italians defeated in, **I**: 159; postwar arrangements for, **III**: 325-328; Sforza proposal on, **I**: 160-161

Europe:
blockade of: and food shortages, **II**: 86

British interests in, **III**: 194

Eastern: British policy shift in, 1945, **III**: 545-551; Churchill on struggles in, **I**: 6; discussed at Quebec, 1944, **III**: 316; liberation of, **III**: 588; Moscow Conference agreements on, **III**: 339, 344-345, 349-351, 370; outside U.S. sphere, **III**: 221; postwar, **II**: 221; Roosevelt and, **III**: 481-482, 586, 617; Soviet views of postwar, **II**: 431; **III**: 398, 530; Truman on Soviets in, **III**: 632; U.S. policy toward, **III**: 618

German propaganda in, Churchill on, **II**: 195

Hitler's problems in, 1942, **I**: 298

invasion of: Churchill on for 1943, **I**: 292, 302-304; Marshall on, **I**: 292; Roosevelt on, 1942, **I**: 421; U.S. military view of 1942, **I**: 389

liberated areas: Churchill to Stalin on, **II**: 687-688

postwar: Churchill on, **II**: 129, 130, 223, 745-747; **III**: 162; Churchill, Stalin, and Roosevelt on, **III**: 528, 530; communism in, **II**: 431; decisions on at Teheran Conference, **II**: 611-613;

food for, **III**: 570; policing of, **II**: 223; rehabilitation of, **II**: 750; role of military vs. civil; **II**: 766; Roosevelt on U.S. troops in, **I**: 230-231; **II**: 608; Soviets in, **II**: 178

relief for, **III**: 47

Roosevelt freezes funds in U.S., **I**: 209

Roosevelt on, **II**: 114

Soviet interests in, **III**: 229

Soviet liberation of North, **I**: 16

European Advisory Commission, **II**: 539, 606, 767-768; **III**: 22, 160, 316, 356, 362, 440-441, 444, 524, 586, 588, 634, 635

European Regional Council, **II**: 222-223

European theater (ETO), **III**: 207; Allied successes in, **III**: 164-165, 538-539, 601; and Soviet offensive, **III**: 490, 524; as primary British concern, 1941, **I**: 136; Battle of the Bulge, **III**: 487-488, 497-498; British favor emphasis on, **II**: 102; Churchill on, **II**: 154; **III**: 198-199, 282, 498-499; command changes in, **II**: 613-615, 617, 621-624, 627-632, 634, 642, 646, 648-649, 656; **III**: 497-498; Eastern, German defenses in, **III**: 433-434; issue of priority, **I**: 556; **II**: 731; **III**: 356-357; joint U.S.-British control, 1942, **I**: 397-399; problems of Allied planning in, **II**: 705; Roosevelt on, **III**: 135, 446-449, 611-612; slowing of Allied advance in, **III**: 248, 433-435; Stalin on, **I**: 567; Stalin to decide plans for, **II**: 550; strategy, **I**: 391; **II**: 38, 430; **III**: 197-199, 212-223, 225-229, 408-409, 522-523, 602-605, 607-609; strength of U.S. in, **III**: 198; Supreme Commander, power of, **III**: 194, 198

European theater, southern: Allied attack on as possible, **I**: 606; strategy, 1942, **I**: 623, 628

Evatt, Dr. Herbert, **I**: 411, 413, 427-429, 493, 500-501, 503

Evill, Douglas C. S., **I**: 354-355, 597; and U.S. planes to Britian, **I**: 487-488

Fairbanks, Alaska, **II**: 420-421

Falalaev, General, **II**: 59

Far East: British and American differences on, **III**: 523-524; Churchill on, **I**: 90-91, 98, 105
Far East Council, **I**: 342
Far East theater, **I**: 318; British control, 1942, **I**: 397-399; Churchill on, **I**: 316-323; **III**: 143; issue of supply lines, **I**: 350; Roosevelt on, 1942, **I**: 363
Faroe Islands, **I**: 56
Farouk, King of Egypt, **III**: 110-111, 116, 179, 536
Farrell, Edelmiro, **III**: 224, 234, 346, 396-397
Fascism, **I**: 14; **II**: 320; **III**: 548; in Italy, **II**: 307-308, 380, 427
Fascists: Churchill on, **I**: 109; in Italy, **II**: 697; in North Africa, **II**: 68-69
Fénard, Raymond, **III**: 150-152, 167-168, 172
Fields, W. C., **II**: 189
Fiji, **I**: 363, 385, 387, 432
Finland, **I**: 12, 208; **II**: 283, 558; and Soviet Union, **I**: 36, 238; **II**: 181-182; **III**: 60-61; Churchill on Soviet conduct toward, **III**: 69
Flandin, Pierre-Étienne, **I**: 127; **II**: 625-626, 635, 641, 691-692
Flemish, **I**: 221
Florence, Italy, **III**: 300, 304
Flower Villa, Marrakesh, **II**: 618-619, 628-629, 645, 650; Churchill on, **II**: 638, 640-641, 668, 672
Force H (HYPO), **I**: 404, 406, 416, 419
Ford Motor Company, **II**: 103
Foreign Ministers, Anglo-American: and pre-Yalta meeting, **III**: 501-503, 507, 511. *See also* Moscow Foreign Ministers' Conference
Formosa, **II**: 609; **III**: 38, 193, 272
Forrestal, James V., **I**: 171, 174, 189-190
Four Freedoms, **III**: 6, 10
Four-Power Declaration on General Security, **II**: 606
France, **I**: 129, 317, 574-575, 576, 653; **II**: 39, 102, 218, 331, 643-644; **III**: 47, 164, 299, 335, 349, 354, 536
    Allied relations with, **I**: 270, **II**: 3-9; **III**: 84, 440-441
    Allied search for strong leader: Darlan deal, **II**: 3-9

Allied strategy toward, **I**: 667
and Britain: in World War I, **I**: 89
and Clipperton Island, **III**: 417, 504
and Control Commission for Italy, **II**: 693
and cross-channel invasion, **III**: 164
and Germany, **I**: 23; armistice, **I**: 52; German pressure on, **I**: 347
and Indo-China, **III**: 572, 626-627
and Madagascar invasion, **I**: 475-477
and North Africa, **I**: 555; **II**: 142-143; Allied problems with, **II**: 98-100; Roosevelt on, **II**: 104-105; invasion, **I**: 561, 576, 578, 581-583, 586-587, 589, 599, 604, 611, 641, 671
and occupation zone in Germany, **III**: 528, 635
and Poland: Stalin on, **III**: 273
and Polish-Soviet War, 1920, **II**: 685
and postwar Italy, **II**: 539-540, 544
and Roosevelt, **III**: 150, 168
and seat on Italian commission, **II**: 680
and Soviet Union, **III**: 433
and Stalin, **III**: 229
and treatment as major power, **II**: 525
and tripartite meeting, **III**: 394, 398
and U.N. organization, **III**: 331, 431
atrocities in, **II**: 520
attack on ports of proposed, **III**: 263
bombing of, **I**: 316; **III**: 122-124, 127
Churchill on, **I**: 295, 313; **II**: 662; **III**: 91, 161-163, 198
Churchill visit to, 1944, **III**: 388-389
colonialism of, **III**: 6, 390; and Madagascar, **I**: 475-476. *See also* Colonialism; French Empire; and specific colonies
Communists in: Allied reaction to, **II**: 465-466
Council of French Resistance, **II**: 214-215
currency question in, **III**: 170-171, 174-175, 180-181, 183, 186-187, 196-197, 210-211, 224

France (*cont.*)
De Gaulle on war in, **II**: 30-31
dollar balances of, **III**: 35
fall of, **II**: 168; Roosevelt and Churchill on, **I**: 43-52
Free, **I**: 372; **II**: 229; and Anglo-Americans, **II**: 579-580; and Darlan deal, **II**: 4, 7, 21; and North African invasion, **I**: 590, 593, 634, 656-657, 659, 662; and post-TORCH negotiations, **II**: 56-57; and prisoners in North Africa, **II**: 72; and Syrian invasion, **I**: 191, 204; and U.S., **II**: 178; British divided on, **II**: 231; British financing of, **II**: 271-272; Churchill on for 1942, **I**: 297-298; in North Africa, **I**: 334; Stalin on, **II**: 289; struggle over leadership, **I**: 669-670; **II**: 147-148, 208-211, 214-215. *See also* French National Committee
French Committee on National Liberation (FCNL), **II**: 277, 285, 580, 643; and Allies, **II**: 257-258, 626; **III**: 84, 89-90, 92; and control of occupied France, **III**: 63-64, 169-172, 174-175, 204-206, 240-243; and control over French Army, **II**: 440-442; and cross-channel invasion, **III**: 128-130, 148-152, 156; and currency question, **III**: 180-181, 210-211; and de Gaulle visit to London, **III**: 162; and Italy, **II**: 539-540; and Middle East colonies, **II**: 599-600; and submarines for Soviets, **II**: 671; and talks on Italy, **II**: 439-440; Churchill on, **III**: 91; de Gaulle and Churchill on, **II**: 691-693; demands by Resistance, **II**: 634-635; recognition of, **II**: 273, 310-312, 333-336, 337-340, 374-377, 379, 420-421, 431; **III**: 135-138, 144-147, 187, 194-197, 237-238, 321-322, 333, 338, 340-341, 365-369, 374; requests part of Italian fleet, **III**: 23-24; Roosevelt on, **II**: 254-256, 607; **III**: 109; Stalin on recognition of, **II**: 289; struggle for control of, **II**: 271-272, 440-442, 464-466, 593
French National Committee, **I**: 68, 372; **II**: 209-210, 214-215, 227-232, 235-236, 244; Roosevelt on, **II**: 121

German invasion of, **I**: 36, 39-40
Germans in, **I**: 296, 498, 667; **II**: 3, 147, 152, 166, 246, 266
in American occupation zone, **II**: 746
in Middle East, **II**: 599-600
issue of relief for, **I**: 147
issue over fleet of, **II**: 147-148
Italy declares war on, **I**: 42
liberated, administration of, **II**: 208, 440
military vs. civil authority in, **III**: 204-206
occupation, Allied plans for, **III**: 22, 62-64, 169-175; Roosevelt on, **II**: 210
political situation in: Allied negotiations over, **III**: 194-197
postwar, **III**: 147, 390-394, 569; American view of, **II**: 691, 767; Churchill to Roosevelt on, **II**: 745-747; Roosevelt on, **II**: 607, 745, 766-767; **III**: 160, 317, 411, 444; Roosevelt on as "British baby," **II**: 708-709; problems of united leadership in, **I**: 667-670
propaganda campaign in, **I**: 626-627
provisional government in, **III**: 361-362; Allied dispute on, **III**: 354-356; Eisenhower on, **II**: 481
Resistance movement in, **III**: 87, 135, 214, 218, 223, 355; Allied relations with, **III**: 128-129; intelligence to British, **III**: 206; participation in Normandy invasion, **III**: 170
role between world wars, **I**: 14
southern, invasion of, **I**: 656; **II**: 616, 632-633, 636, 657, 662, 663, 705; **III**: 93-94, 145, 231-232, 248, 434; and Italian campaign, **III**: 114-115, 230, 289-290, 299-302; and Italian ships to Soviets, **II**: 655, 664, 666, 670-671, 676, 694, 700; approved at Quebec, 1943, **II**: 430; Churchill on, **III**: 88, 149, 243, 267, 276, 286; Eisenhower on, **III**: 199; Roosevelt on, **III**: 302, 308; Stalin on, **II**: 610-611; **III**: 282; strategy debated, **I**: 15; **II**: 613, 653-654, 658, 712-713, 730-731, 756-757; **III**: 88, 118-119, 126-128,

163-164, 185, 197-199, 203-204, 207, 211-223, 225-229; successes in, **III**: 304-305

  Truman and, **III**: 632

  unification of, de Gaulle on, **II**: 90-91

  Unites States attitudes toward, **I**: 34; **III**: 308, 633

  Vichy, **I**: 181, 190, 191; **III**: 144; Allied relations with, **I**: 90-98, 146-149, 208, 440-441, 459-461, 576, 578, 656-657, 659-663; and Allied occupation, **III**: 64; and Dakar attack, **I**: 71-73; and *Dunkerque* issue, **I**: 157-159, 164, 169; and French fleet, **I**: 54, 56, 92, 521-522, 524-525; **II**: 147-148; and Germany, **I**: 75-85, 76-79, 196, 287; **II**: 4; and invasion of Diego Suarez, **I**: 404; and invasion of Madagascar, **I**: 480-483, 613; and Japan in Indo-China, **I**: 274; and Latin America, **I**: 154-155; and Middle East, **II**: 599; and North Africa, **I**: 175-176, 269-270, 333-335, 463-465, 667; **II**: 27-28, 56-57, 68; and North African invasion, **I**: 561, 578, 593, 626, 634-635; and relief, **I**: 116-118, 125, 156; and St. Pierre-Miquelon affair, **I**: 324-326, 346-347; armistice with Germany, **I**: 516-517; Churchill on, **I**: 127-128, 132-133, 181-182, 253, 297-298, 433-434, 673-674; **III**: 195; collaboration with Germans, **I**: 184-186, 186-187, 350; Eisenhower on, **III**: 170; Hull and, **I**: 346-347; in Syria, **I**: 204; in Tunisia, **II**: 27-28; Roosevelt on, **I**: 177, 179, 250, 406, 465

  western, proposed invasion of (CALIPH), **III**: 163-164

Franco, Francisco, **I**: 640, 663, 666; **III**: 567; Allied policy toward, **II**: 725-726, 728; and Hitler, **I**: 86; Churchill and Roosevelt on, **II**: 640-641, 644-645. *See also* Spain

Franco-Soviet agreement, **III**: 440

Frankfurter, Felix, **II**: 355

Fraser, Peter, **I**: 330, 332, 425; **II**: 33, 61-62, 207; **III**: 77-78

Freedoms of the Air, **III**: 404

Freeman, Sir Wilfred, **I**: 223

Freemantle, Australia, **I**: 382

Freetown, Sierra Leone, **I**: 73, 204, 209, 219

French Central Africa, **II**: 335

French Empire, **I**: 79; **II**: 272; Allies recognize, **I**: 333-334; and Germany, **I**: 297; and 1941 war, **I**: 295; British as threat to, **I**: 660; de Gaulle as commander of, **II**: 274; in Giraud-de Gaulle dispute, **II**: 135; issue of control of, **II**: 440-442; Roosevelt on postwar, **II**: 178

French Equatorial Africa, **I**: 146; **II**: 56-57

French North Africa, **I**: 253, 255, 269-270, 317, 353; **II**: 34-35; Allied negotiations with Vichy over, **I**: 333-335, 463-465; Allied victory in, **II**: 11-12; and food shipments to, **I**: 433-434; Churchill on, **I**: 295, 296-298; **II**: 50-51, 144-145; exchange rate issue in, **II**: 135; politics in, **I**: 634-635; **II**: 21-22, 27-29, 68-71, 142, 189-190, 227-232, 279-280, 340; Roosevelt on, **I**: 250; Stalin on Allied victory in, **II**: 17; subversion in, **I**: 348

French Riviera, **III**: 389, 396

French West Africa, **I**: 210-211, 297-298, 353; **II**: 335; dispute over control of, **II**: 234-237; exchange rate issue in, **II**: 135; subversion in, **I**: 348

French West Indies, **II**: 147

Fulton, Dr., **I**: 441

G.G.& S. Howland Company, **III**: 98

Gabon, **I**: 146

Galicia (Poland/Soviet Union), **II**: 684

Gallipoli, Turkey, **II**: 516, 657

Gallman, William J., **III**: 415-416

Gambia, **II**: 156

Gambia River, **II**: 123

Gammell, Sir James, **II**: 656

Gandhi, Mohandas, **I**: 373, 375, 447, 558, 563; Churchill view of, **I**: 375

George II, King of Greece, **I**: 16; **II**: 548, 618-619; **III**: 95-97, 101, 179, 278, 449-450, 454, 456-461, 467, 471, 473-475, 478-481, 487; American vs. British view, **II**: 450-451

George VI, King of England, **I**: 53, 77;

George VI, King of England (*cont.*)
II: 42, 353, 419-420, 464, 470; III:
139, 143, 157-159, 249, 270; visit to
North Africa, II: 245
George, David Lloyd, II: 684; III: 546;
as possible Ambassador to the U.S., I:
113-115
Georges, Alphonse, I: 44, 270; II: 235,
258, 271, 333, 335, 593; Allied view
of, II: 227-228, 230-231; dismissal of,
II: 691-692
German High Command, I: 267; II:
645, 770; III: 214-215, 340, 582, 609
German Naval High Command, I: 214;
II: 728
Germany, I: 209, 529-530, 660; II: 37,
49, 65, 222, 225, 226, 286, 293, 528,
562-563, 575; III: 315, 335, 630
advances in Europe, 1940, I: 36
aircraft production in: Allied intelligence on, I: 618
Allied strategy toward, I: 206, 223-
224, 302-303, 513-516, 597, 612; II:
612; III: 63; British Chiefs on, I: 622;
Roosevelt on, III: 221-223
and Azores negotiations, II: 302
and Britain: rumors of peace between, I: 540
and Bulgaria, II: 553-554
and convoys to Soviet Union, I: 609
and feeding of occupied territories,
I: 117-118; II: 86
and invasion of southern France,
III: 304-305
and Ireland, III: 57
and Italian ships to Soviets, II: 654-
656. *See also* Great Britain, Cabinet;
Great Britain, Parliament
and Italians: Roosevelt on, II: 300-
301
and Katyn Forest massacre, II: 193,
388-402
and new weapons, II: 560
and North Africa, I: 273, 576, 641;
II: 27, 266-267
and oil, II: 131
and Poland, II: 737
and Polish-Soviet relations, II: 192-
195, 685-687
and Portugal, II: 243, 296, 298-299,
674
and South Africa, I: 654
and Soviet Union, I: 294-295; III:
572, 586-587; feared, III: 408-409,
609
and Spain, I: 663-666; II: 165-166,
725-728
and Tripartite Alliance, I: 137
and United States: issue of war declaration, I: 106; Roosevelt closes consulates of, I: 209-210
and Warsaw Uprising, III: 260,
292-293, 312
Argentina breaks relations with, II:
678-679, 681-684
assassination plot at Teheran Conference, II: 610
atrocities of, III: 310-311, 333
attacks on, 1942, I: 420
battle in, III: 446, 448
Battle of the Bulge and, III: 487-
488
blockade of, I: 32-35; III: 245, 257
bombing of, I: 302, 306, 315, 362,
459, 477, 485, 504, 597-598; II: 11,
26-27, 44, 46, 51, 119, 132, 152, 190,
218, 247, 266, 267, 589-590; III: 195-
196, 616; Churchill on, I: 296-297,
435; daylight, II: 185-186, 517; destruction described, II: 387; of civilian
targets, I: 438-439; III: 230; Roosevelt to Stalin on, II: 260; Stalin on, I:
561
borders with Poles and Soviets, II:
704
British relations with, III: 538
British strategy toward, I: 565, 614
chrome ore from Turkey, III: 48-
49, 55-56
Churchill on, I: 20, 91, 97, 205,
295, 302, 574; II: 39, 131; III: 340-
341; expected casualties for OVER-
LORD, III: 87
collapse of, Allied plans for, II: 41,
606, 708-709, 745-746
communism in, Stalin on, III: 273
cross-channel invasion and, II: 555;
III: 161, 164-165
defense of homeland, III: 434-435
disarmament of, II: 746; III: 317
dismemberment discussed, III: 364,
366, 528

expected strategy of, 1941, **I**: 129
food shortages in occupied areas,
III: 621-623
  Hess on, **I**: 187-188
  imperialism of, **III**: 6
  in Allied Declaration on Italy, **II**:
307-308
    in Balkans, **I**: 144-145; **III**: 274
    in Belgium, **III**: 470
    in Dodecanese, **II**: 197
    in Finland, **II**: 181-182
    in France, **I**: 56, 76-79, 97, 104,
673-674; **III**: 187
    in Greece, **III**: 202, 279, 450, 457
    in Ireland, **I**: 45
    in Italy, **II**: 184, 380-381, 452, 454-
456, 502; **III**: 214, 347-348
    in southern France, **III**: 163
    in Soviet Union, 1943 strategy, **II**:
179
    in Yugoslavia, **III**: 203
    invasion of Italy, Allied: intelligence
on, **II**: 356
    invasion of Soviet Union: American
intelligence on, **I**: 177
    Italian soldiers in, **III**: 372-373
    Italy declares war on, **II**: 491-492,
502
    Kirk letter on, **I**: 61
    military in: Churchill on power of,
II: 370
    morale in, **I**: 603-604, 610
    occupation of, **III**: 248, 524, 634,
635; American assumptions on, **II**:
606; Roosevelt view, **II**: 607-608;
zones debated, **II**: 708, 745-747; **III**:
147, 150, 159-161, 317, 391, 394, 524
    Poles in exile on, **II**: 201
    postwar, **III**: 334-335, 398; and Al-
lies, **II**: 178; and Quebec Conference,
1944, **III**: 316-317; decisions on at
Teheran Conference, **II**: 611; discussed at Moscow, 1944, **III**: 351; issue of Allied forces in, **II**: 431; Roosevelt view of, **II**: 766; **III**: 317
    prisoners of war, treatment of, **III**:
580-584
    Roosevelt on, **I**: 229, 264, 533; **II**:
172, 617, 652; **III**: 403-404
    Secret Service in, **II**: 522
    Stalin on, **I**: 570; **II**: 151

    submarine construction in, **III**: 492
    surrender of: Roosevelt on terms
for, **II**: 766-767; terms discussed, **II**:
767-773; **III**: 21-22; unconditional
terms debated, **II**: 119, 128-129, 652;
III: 133-135, 142-143, 145, 149
    surrender of, Allied appeal for, **III**:
408
    troop deployment of, 1943, **II**: 152
    U.S. forces for bombing of, 1942, **I**:
393
    U.S. policy toward, 1945, **III**: 635
    use of flak artillery, **I**: 258
    victories, 1941, **I**: 152
    war criminals in, issue of, **III**: 329-
330
    war declared on, **I**: 24
    weakening of, **III**: 601
Ghormley, Robert, **I**: 170-172, 198, 207-
208, 397, 399, 419, 423, 440
Gibraltar, **I**: 86, 91, 176, 203-204, 219,
313, 404, 406-407, 554, 612, 640-641,
673; **II**: 245, 463, 570, 572, 575-576,
578, 592, 725; **III**: 503; British forces
in, **I**: 423, 654; British plans for, **I**:
234; conference at late 1942, **II**: 17;
Germans and, **I**: 298; issue of troops
to, **I**: 416, 418-419; Stalin concern
with, **I**: 561
Gilbert Islands, battle at, **I**: 348; **II**: 755;
III: 193
Gimpel, Erich, **III**: 493
Giraud, Henri, **I**: 477, 479, 673; **II**: 9,
80, 136-137, 141, 145, 231-232, 236-
237, 244, 258, 271, 279-280, 293; **III**:
392; and de Gaulle, **II**: 104-105, 208-
211, 273, 440-442; and Eisenhower,
II: 76; and Free French movement, **I**:
669-670; and French Army in North
Africa, **II**: 274; and French in North
Africa, **I**: 655-657, 661; **II**: 335; and
Jewish refugees, **II**: 315; and North
African invasion, **I**: 593, 595, 634; **II**:
3; and refugee camps in North Africa,
II: 321; Churchill on, **III**: 91; Corsica
expediton of, **II**: 464-466; dismissal
of, **II**: 691-692; eliminated from
French Committee, **II**: 593; in North
Africa, **II**: 68, 88-89, 90-91, 98, 142-
143, 147-148; removal as Military
chief, **III**: 89-90; Roosevelt on, **II**:

Giraud, Henri (*cont.*)
134-135, 337-338, 340, 662; Stalin on,
II: 289
Gladstone, William, III: 291
Godfroy, René E., I: 517, 521-522; II:
84, 147-148, 231-232
Goebbels, Joseph, II: 198-199; III: 330
Goering, Herman, I: 596; III: 330
Gold standard, I: 23
Gousev, F. T., III: 71
Grabski, Stanislaw, III: 253, 255, 268,
351-352
Grand Fascist Council (Italy), II: 380
Grandi, Dino, II: 486-487
Grant, Ulysses S., I: 318, 436
Gray, David, II: 420; III: 57, 75, 566-
567
Gray's Inn, London, II: 355-356, 419
Graziani, Rudolfo, II: 663
Great Britain, I: 258; II: 222, 264, 484;
III: 351, 518
    Admiralty, I: 66, 170, 192, 198,
227, 300, 451, 504-505; II: 107, 110,
638, 712; III: 271, 280; and German
submarine sinkings, III: 345-346; and
oil, II: 78, 115; 1943 production
plans, II: 94; on American destroyers,
I: 127; on convoys to Soviet Union, I:
481, 527-528, 530, 533, 535, 537, 551,
620-622; II: 49; on Italian ships to Soviets, III: 19, 25-26; on Japanese fleet
movement, I: 461; on ships to Soviets,
III: 56; on U.S. subs to Gibraltar, I:
554; statement on submarines, III:
126, 251; wants U.S. bombers to Britain, I: 435
    aid to, II: 44-46; bundles for Brit-
ain campaign, I: 511-512, 525; prior
to lend-lease, I: 507; Roosevelt on
British gratitude, I: 526; United
States, I: 196; II: 32, 743-744
    air attacks on, I: 37, 56, 80, 91, 96,
97, 103
    air defense, I: 41-42, 259-261
    Air Ministry: and Clipperton Is-
lands, III: 504; and ferrying plans, I:
202
    Allied forces in, II: 51, 132
    and aid for Ethiopian civilians, I:
160-161
    and anti-sub campaign announce-

ments, II: 298
    and atomic research, I: 514
    and attack on French fleet, I: 56
    and Azores, II: 564
    and Balkans: aid to guerrillas, II:
548
    and Cairo Declaration, II: 609
    and civil aviation policy, III: 423
    and France, II: 420; III: 204-205;
Leahy on, II: 137-138
    and French Committee of National
Liberation, recogntion of, II: 431
    and French in Middle East, II: 599-
600
    and free trade proposals, II: 748
    and Germany, I: 23; II: 247; occu-
pation zone in, III: 391
    and Greece, III: 449-461
    and Indo-China, I: 225
    and Italian campaign, U.S. state-
ment on, 303-308
    and Jewish Brigade, III: 286-287
    and Poland: Stalin on, III: 273
    and Polish-Soviet boundary dispute,
II: 650-651
    and St. Pierre-Miquelon affair, I:
324-326
    and shipping: few ships for commit-
ments, I: 468
    and Singapore defeat, I: 420
    and Soviets and French: Churchill
on, III: 349
    and U.N. organization creation, III:
431
    and United States, II: 606-607; de-
pendence on, II: 750; III: 351; policy
toward, 1945, III: 633; relations with
Japan, 277
    and unity of command, I: 312
    and Warsaw Uprising, III: 312
    and Yugoslavia, III: 510
    armed forces in, 1943, I: 653
    army strengths of, fall 1941, I: 261-
263
    assembling of troops in, II: 41
    aviation gasoline supplies, I: 632
    Cabinet, I: 47, 88, 95, 177, 223,
227, 230, 235, 244, 289, 327; II: 118,
119, 122, 132, 442; III: 327, 408;
and administration of Sicily, II: 251;
and Argentina, III: 231, 414, 484;

and Azores, **II**: 214, 240; and bombing of Rome, **II**: 373; and bombings, **III**: 230; and civil aviation policy, **III**: 404, 419, 420, 520; and cross-channel invasion, **I**: 458-459; and Darlan deal, **II**: 4, 7; and de Gaulle, **II**: 261-262, 271, 599; **III**: 156; and food supplies, **III**: 584; and France, **II**: 208; **III**: 144, 205; and Frank Knox death, **III**: 118; and French fleet, 1940, **I**: 54; and German surrender, **III**: 142, 145; and Greece, **III**: 279, 450, 457, 467, 479, 606; and Imperial preference system, **I**: 351; and import level standards, **II**: 169-170; and India, **I**: 448-449; and invasion of southern France, **III**: 207, 212, 226, 227; and Italian campaign, **II**: 581; and Italian political situation, **II**: 587, 760; **III**: 43, 45; and Italian surrender terms, **II**: 358-359; and Italy, **III**: 53, 183, 334; and lend-lease, **I**: 63; and lend-lease aid, postwar, **III**: 535-536; and Macmillan to North Africa, **II**: 90; and Middle East policy, **III**: 17; and oil, **II**: 754; **III**: 27, 188; and Pacific strategy, **III**: 38; and Poland, **III**: 309-311, 463, 480-481, 497, 551, 599; and Polish boundary dispute, **II**: 686; and Polish-Soviet relations, **III**: 29-30, 68-69, 72; and pre-invasion bombing of France, **II**: 123; and Rome bombing, **II**: 378; and Stalin, **III**: 613; and trade issues, **I**: 345-346; and Yugoslavia, **III**: 510; Churchill changes, **I**: 363; Churchill limited by, **II**: 261-262; composition of, **I**: 36; on bombing in Italy, **II**: 234; on Eisenhower in North Africa, **II**: 83-84; on holiday for Churchill, **II**: 433; on independence for India, **I**: 402; on Jewish Brigade, **III**: 286; on Montgomery appointment, **II**: 623-624, 627-629, 631; on war strategy, 1942, **I**: 520; power over foreign policy, **II**: 128; proclamation to Germany, **III**: 575; supports atrocities proclamation, **II**: 521

    casualties in Italy, **III**: 43
    Chiefs of Staff, **I**: 165
    Churchill assesses position, 1940, **I**: 87-112

    Churchill defends vs. U.S. criticism, **II**: 527-530
    Churchill on, **II**: 595; **III**: 17
    Churchill on morale of, **I**: 60
    Churchill on strategic role, **II**: 288
    Churchill on threats to, **I**: 182
    cities threatened by Germans, **III**: 591-592
    colonial mentality on India, **I**: 375
    Darlan deal, opposition to, **II**: 18
    Defense Committee, **I**: 361; **III**: 212; on war strategy, 1942, **I**: 520
    defense of, **I**: 296; **II**: 38
    defenses of criticized, **I**: 268
    dollar balances in U.S., **III**: 65-66
    draft figures, 1943, **I**: 653
    elections in, after war, **III**: 526
    embassy in Washington: messages relayed through lost, **I**: 527
    financial crisis in, **I**: 87-88, 93, 94, 100-101, 114; **III**: 34-36; and lend-lease, **I**: 139; Churchill assesses, late l940, **I**: 108; gold transfer scheme, **I**: 120-124

    food consumption in, **III**: 246-247
    Foreign Office, **I**: 78, 181, 313, 342, 351, 360, 433; **II**: 479; **III**: 270, 325-326, 351, 446; and Anglo-American relations on oil, **II**: 733; and Argentina, **II**: 682-683; **III**: 224, 230-231, 415-416, 431; and Atlantic Islands, **I**: 201; and Azores, **II**: 590; and Balkans, **III**: 200-201; and Big Three Conference, **III**: 379; and Bulgaria, **II**: 765; and convoys to Soviet Union, **III**: 311; and de Gaulle, **II**: 231, 257, 271, 639-640; **III**: 62, 135; and FCNL, **II**: 310-311, 333-334, 374-375; **III**: 87, 128, 338; and France, **II**: 235; **III**: 149, 195, 355, 361-362; and Free French, **II**: 593; and French arrest of Vichy leaders, **II**: 634; and French overseas empire, **II**: 310-311; and German attack on Soviets, **II**: 285; and Iranian oil, **III**: 511-513; and Italian surrender, **II**: 538; and Italy, **III**: 189-190, 333, 534, 620; and messages relayed through, **I**: 527; and neutral nations, **III**: 245; and oil conference, **III**: 169, 187; and Pacific strategy, **III**: 38; and Poland, **II**: 200;

Great Britain (*cont.*)
III: 562, 563, 569; and Polish boundary dispute, II: 685; and postwar political plans, II: 54; and refugee question, II: 293; and Ribbentrop and
British, II: 672; and Roosevelt, III:
619; and Roumania, III: 545; and
Sforza, II: 483; and Soviets in Eastern
Europe, III: 546; and Soviets in Poland, II: 700-701, 703; and Spain, II:
725, 739; and Stalin, II: 173-175; and
Sweden, III: 257; and Tito, III: 131;
and Turkey, III: 55-56, 363; and
U.N. organization creation, III: 431;
and U.S. press, III: 517; and Yugoslavia, II: 660; Churchill in control of,
III: 178; Churchill view of, II: 155-
157; Churchill's troubles with, II: 642-
643; on Lloyd George appointment, I:
113; on Salazar, II: 674; on Sforza,
III: 436-439; on Soviet ambassador to
Italy, III: 42; on Soviet Union, I: 394;
Roosevelt on Stalin's hatred of, I: 421
  foreign policy: and electoral politics,
III: 546, 548; powers of Prime Minister, II: 128; U.S. criticisms of, III:
517
  German invasion threat against, I:
39, 50-52, 56-57, 68-71, 73, 74-75, 78-
80, 89, 127, 129, 134, 150, 211, 216,
219, 253-254, 298, 302, 315-316, 319,
499-500, 603, 610; II: 25, 101
  gold recovered from HMS *Edin-
burgh*, 482
  House of Commons, I: 229, 323,
328; II: 156-157, 232-233; III: 628;
and Churchill, II: 136, 141, 143-146;
III: 461-464, 467; and French in
North Africa, II: 273; and Italy, III:
443-444; and lend-lease, I: 63-64,
140-141; and Poland, III: 588; and
Spain, III: 161-162; Stalin on Churchill speech to, III: 70-71; vote of confidence in, I: 336-337; II: 74, 77-78;
III: 447, 449; vote of confidence on
Greece, III: 450-451, 455
  import needs of, I: 650; II: 44-45,
153, 167-171
  in Africa, Churchill on, II: 529
  in postwar world, III: 335-336;
Roosevelt view, I: 502

in U.N. organization, III: 331
issue of food stockpiles in, III: 569-
570
join Allied unity declaration, I: 206
Katyn Forest massacre and Allied
unity, II: 398-399
military preparations in, I: 315-316;
II: 94-96, 218; German intelligence
on, III: 11
military vs. political authority in, II:
479-481
  Ministry of Agriculture, II: 169
  Ministry of Food, II: 169
  Ministry of Information, I: 131,
244; II: 569; III: 409; and *Chicago
Tribune*, I: 625
  Ministry of Production, II: 169
  Ministry of War: and oil problems,
II: 78
monetary policy: American view of,
II: 743-744
  Montgomery as hero in, III: 497
  naval losses of, III: 15-16, 24-25
  occupation zones in Europe of, II:
745
  oil shortages in, II: 79-80, 82-83
  Parliament, I: 59-60, 74; II: 388,
481-482, 513, 603-604; III: 25; and
Allied oil policy, III: 27; and Argentina, III: 290; and British defeats,
1942, I: 438; and British dollar balances, III: 35; and Churchill,
atempted censure of, I: 516-517; and
Churchill at Yalta, III: 526; and
Churchill on Italy, II: 760; and
Churchill on Polish situation, I: 61;
and Churchill to, I: 42; and civil aviation policy, III: 420-421, 443; and
Curzon line, III: 359; and Darlan
deal, II: 67, 70; and declaration on
liberated Europe, III: 548-549; and
France, III: 144-145, 196-197; and
Free French, II: 335; and French in
North Africa, II: 271; and Imperial
preference system, I: 351; and Italian
fleet, III: 26, 32; and Italian political
situation, III: 31, 46; and lend-lease,
II: 528; and oil policy, I: 734; II: 754-
755; and Poland, III: 497, 538-539,
564-565, 600, 622; and Polish-Soviet
relations, II: 741; III: 54, 72; and rec-

ognition of FCNL, **II**: 334; **III**: 355;
and U.S. military in Europe, **III**: 498;
Italian policies criticized, **III**: 437; on
India, **I**: 448-449

peace movement in, **I**: 49
postwar: Churchill on, **I**: 93; **II**:
130; issue of aid to, **III**: 540; Roosevelt on, **II**, 708-709; **III**: 237; 319
postwar economic situation, **III**:
535-536, 578-579
proposed conference site, **II**: 439
public opinion: and bombing of
Rome, **II**: 373; and civil aviation policy, **III**: 443; and U.N. organization,
III: 344; Churchill on morale in, **II**:
621; on British defeats, 1942, **I**: 438;
on cross-channel invasion, **I**: 437; on
Darlan deal, **II**: 4-5, 7; on food for
France, **I**: 117; on Italy, **II**: 443; **III**:
620; on military leadership, **II**: 627;
on North Africa, **II**: 145; on Poland,
III: 73-74, 548, 565, 585, 600; on Polish-Soviet relations, **II**: 741; on possible Churchill resignation, **III**: 225; on
rationing and war successes, **III**: 247;
on recognition of FCNL, **II**: 365; on
revenge for London bombing, **II**:
377-378; on war progress, **III**: 435
reaction to Roosevelt-Stalin meeting,
II: 278
role between world wars, **I**: 14
role in Asia, **II**: 696
Roosevelt on, **I**: 316
Roosevelt on India and, **I**: 446-447
Roosevelt on Iran and, **III**: 3
Roosevelt on production issues in,
1943, **II**: 47
Roosevelt trip to, proposed, **III**:
491, 494
sabotage activities of, **II**: 417
Secret Intelligence Service, **III**: 214
shipping crisis outlined, **II**: 166-171
Special Operations Executive (SOE),
I: 263; **II**: 548
Stalin on, **III**: 610; in World War I,
570
strategic position, 1939-1940, **I**: 96,
499, 565; **II**: 528
U.S. aircraft needed in, **I**: 598
U.S. bomber force in, **II**: 218
U.S. troops to, **II**: 46-47

war production, 1943 plans, **II**: 93-
96
war strategy of, American view, **II**:
479
wheat interests of, **I**: 247, 249, 251
Greece, **I**: 79, 123-124, 156, 177, 205,
206, 653, 669; **II**: 126, 131, 139, 350,
540, 553-554, 714; **III**: 202, 232, 312,
328, 517, 579-580
Allied air attacks on, **II**: 511
Allied policy toward, **I**: 16; **III**: 101,
110-111, 198, 605-607, 618-619; **II**:
152
and Germans, **I**: 134, 144-145, 152-
153, 174, 317; **II**: 329, 428
and Italians, **I**: 66-67; **II**: 341, 440,
445; and Italian fleet, **III**: 23-24
and Soviet Union, **III**: 137
Anglo-American dispute on, **III**:
95-99
Anglo-Soviet agreement on, **III**:
153, 177-183, 200-202, 349-350, 547;
at Moscow Conference (1944), **III**:
341, 351, 359
atrocities in, **II**: 416-417, 520
British and, **I**: 170; **II**: 13; **III**: 137,
153, 274-275, 278-279, 296-297, 299,
545, 546-547; American views on, **III**:
436-439, 517
Churchill assesses, **I**: 165
Churchill on postwar government
in, **III**: 443
Churchill visit to, 1945, **III**: 537
civil war in, **II**: 548
claims Dodecanese Islands, **II**: 197
Communist party in, **III**: 449
forces in Egypt, **III**: 95
government in exile, **III**: 95-96,
135, 137, 179
guerrilla activity in, **II**: 407-409,
548-549
monarchy, **II**: 618-619
mutiny by forces in Egypt, **III**: 114,
178-179
National Liberation Front (EAM),
II: 548; **III**: 95-96, 135, 137, 153,
179, 202, 279, 449-450, 452, 455-456,
458, 466, 472
National Popular Liberation Army
(ELAS), **II**: 548; **III**: 350, 449-452,
457, 466-467, 473-475, 487, 547

Greece (*cont.*)
partisan group in (EDES), **II**: 548; **III**: 466
political crisis in, **I**: 10; **III**: 447, 449-461, 463, 466, 471-475, 478-481
postwar: as Anglo-American issue, **II**: 449; British concerns over, **II**: 497-499; Churchill view, **II**: 222-223
relief for, **II**: 105; **III**: 85
sabotage in, **II**: 413-414
Greek Islands, **II**: 14
Greenland, **I**: 165-166
Greenwood, Arthur, **III**: 538-539
Grew, Joseph, **III**: 551, 567
Griazovetz, Soviet Union: Polish prisoners in, **II**: 391
Gromyko, Andrei, **III**: 586, 590-591
Groves, Leslie R., **III**: 412-413
Grovesnor, Gilbert, **III**: 490
Groze, Petru, **III**: 625
Guadalcanal, Battle of, **I**: 490, 608, 633, 639, 644, 657, 659; **II**: 6, 36, 41, 102, 138, 142, 205
Guadaloupe, **II**: 337-338
Guards Chapel, England, bombing of, **III**: 196
Guariglia, Raffaele, **II**: 379-380
Gubbins, Sir Colin, **II**: 548-549
Gulf Coast (of Mexico): German submarines threaten, **I**: 456
Gulf of Lions, France, **III**: 217-219
Gulf of Mexico, **I**: 490-491, 515, 524; **II**: 78
Gulf of Sidra, **I**: 670-673; **II**: 11
Gusev, Feodor T., **III**: 61

Haakon, King of Norway, **III**: 156
Habbaniya, Iraq, **II**: 523, 576
Haifa, Palestine, **III**: 144, 378, 381
Haining, Sir Robert, **I**: 216-217
Halifax, Lord (Edward Wood), **I**: 8, 26, 36, 53-54, 277-278, 284, 309, 333, 344, 354, 356, 373, 427; **II**: 17, 40, 71, 100-101, 221, 269; **III**: 74, 144, 445, 452, 510, 543, 546, 549, 562, 566, 620; and Anglo-American monetary questions, **II**: 743-744; **III**: 35, 65; and Balkans, **III**: 153-154, 177, 200; and Italian political situation, **III**: 30, 32, 41-42, 334; and Jewish refugees to North Africa, **II**: 316; and lend-lease,

I: 58, 140; and Polish-Soviet relations, **II**: 193-194, 735; and Roosevelt, **I**: 25, 133-134; and Spain, **III**: chosen Ambassador to United States, **I**: 115-116; on Middle East oil, **II**: 599, 733-734
Halifax, Nova Scotia, **II**: 382
Hamburg, Germany, **I**: 597; **II**: 707, 718
Hamilton, Duke of, **I**: 186
Handy, Thomas T., **II**: 683
Hanover, Germany, **III**: 147
Harbors, synthetic (Mulberries), **III**: 185, 195, 203
Harnish, Johann, **II**: 171
Harriman, W. Averell, **I**: clxv, 12, 155-156, 203-204, 216, 225-226, 270, 290, 373, 541-542, 552, 563, 593-595; **II**: 54-55, 171, 190, 207-208, 259, 261, 292, 365, 440, 610, 718; **III**: 209, 259, 449, 462, 479, 491, 634; and air bases in Soviet Union, **III**: 295; and Bulgaria, **II**: 730, 760-761; and Casablanca Conference, **II**: 54-55, 109-110; and Churchill, **II**: 211; **III**: 139; and Italian ships to Soviets, **II**: 676, 678; **III**: 24; and planes to Soviets, **II**: 185; and Poland, **III**: 272, 358, 551-552, 560-562, 568-569, 570-571; and Polish exiles, **I**: 488; and Roosevelt-Stalin meeting, **II**: 278-279, 283; and Soviet Union, **III**: 586, 617; and Soviet-Polish relations, **II**: 707; **III**: 20, 563-565; and Stalin, **I**: 578; **III**: 631; and Trans-Persian Railway, **I**: 572; and U.N. organization, **III**: 431; and Yalta Conference, **III**: 496; appointed Ambassador to the Soviet Union, **II**: 588; at Moscow Conference, 1942, **I**: 553, 555-556, 560-562, 564-567, 570; at Moscow Conference, 1944, **III**: 39, 341-345, 349-350, 352-353, 359, 362, 371; at Moscow Foreign Ministers' Conference, **II**: 563; at Quebec Conference, 1943, **II**: 354; Churchill on, **I**: 439, 562; in Egypt, **I**: 208; in Middle East, **I**: 204, 208, 210; on India, **I**: 402; on Italian ships to Soviets, **II**: 624-625, 655-656; on Roosevelt, **III**: 162; on Soviets, **II**: 173; on Stalin and Mediterranean strategy, **II**: 606-607; on supplies to the Soviet Union, **I**:

472, 474; on supply/production coordination, I: 638; on Truman, III: 632
Harris, Sir Arthur T., I: 209, 354-355, 361, 435, 597; II: 185-186
Harrison, Mrs. Leland, II: 150-151, 163
Hart, Thomas C., I: 313, 335, 336, 339-344, 348, 352
Hartle, Russell P., II: 38, 40
Harvard University, II: 433-434, 438
Harwood, Sir Henry, I: 517
Hasanain, Ahmad Muhammad, III: 110-111
Haute Savoie, France, II: 692
Havre, France, III: 216
Hawaii, I: 93, 392; III: 191, 243, 258, 272
Hawkins, Harry C., III: 535-536
Hayes, Carlton J. H., I: 540, 663; II: 725; III: 66
Hearst newspapers, I: 421
Helfrich, C.E.L., I: 335-336, 339-342, 344, 348-349, 352, 355, 361
Helmuth, Osmar Alberto, II: 681, 683
Herald Tribune, III: 61
Hess, Rudolph, I: 186-188, 636-638; II: 102
Hewitt, H. K., III: 452, 484
Himalaya Mountains, II: 537; III: 49
Himmler, Heinrich, II: 415; III: 586
Hirohito, Emperor of Japan, II: 228
Hitler, Adolf, I: 3, 8, 13, 24, 27, 44, 58, 221, 496; II: 118, 212, 370, 446, 563; III: 137, 183, 187, 274, 358, 388, 586; and Ardennes offensive, III: 487; and British surrender, I: 49; and German submarines, I: 230; and Iberia, I: 640; and Italy, I: 42; II: 300-301; III: 143; and Japan, II: 247; and Mussolini, II: 347, 349, 361, 455; and North Africa, I: 576, 578; II: 207; and Poland, II: 193, 199; and prisoners of war, III: 580; and Soviet offensive; I: 621; II: 267, 288; and Soviet Union, Churchill fears peace between, I: 393-394; and Stalin, I: 207; and the Balkans, I: 134, 152; and troops to France, III: 194; and United States, I: 106, 283; and Vatican, II: 172; and Vichy French, I: 76; as war criminal, III: 330; Churchill on, I: 96, 103, 176, 249, 253, 309, 315, 439, 671, 673; II: 551, 558, 631;

III: 119; denies Western Europe invasion plans, I: 36; Hess on, I: 186-188; Irish-American view of, II: 184; Kirk letter on goals of, I: 62-63; Malta strategy of, I: 467; occupies southern France, I: 667; on V-1 bombs, III: 195; orders to Germans in Soviet Union, I: 360; overthrow conspiracy, II: 521; problems of feeding Europe, I: 298; Roosevelt on, I: 38, 184, 466; II: 114; Schicklgruber as family name, III: 290
Hitlerism, I: 309; III: 601; Churchill on, I: 124
Hoare, Sir Samuel, I: 663, 666; II: 423-429, 725-726, 728, 739; III: 6, 68, 107-108
Hog Island Scheme, I: 92, 99, 107
Hong Kong, III: 16, 351
Hoover, Herbert, I: 116
Hopkins, Harry L., I: clxv, 12, 148, 165, 177, 185, 221, 223, 238, 241, 244, 335, 338, 348, 362, 364-365, 441, 452, 454, 460-461, 488, 543, 581, 597, 599; II: 53-55, 70, 89, 155, 171, 186, 190, 191, 206, 291, 463, 481, 513, 567, 619-621, 627; III: 266, 296, 297, 323, 402, 405, 407, 538, 579, 613; and Casablanca Conference, II: 54-55, 109, 117; and Churchill, I: 128-129, 138, 143, 406, 465, 508, 527, 536, 651; II: 26, 83, 134, 527; III: 243, 267, 289, 546; and Churchill-Roosevelt correspondence, I: 18, 444; and Churchill-Stalin talks, III: 343; and coordinated Allied supplies, I: 327, 329; and cross-channel invasion, I: 436, 502; II: 41; and Darlan deal, II: 5; and Eastern Europe, III: 344, 463; and French committee, II: 337; III: 367; and India, I: 388, 445-447, 501-502; and lend-lease, I: 486; and planes to Soviets, II: 185; and Roosevelt, I: 370; II: 156, 189; III: 569; and Roosevelt-Stalin meeting, II: 283; and second front, I: 11; and short snorter club, II: 296; and Soviet Union, II: 149; and war supply, I: 463, 471-472, 638; as go-between, I: 4, 540; at British Cabinet meetings, I: 450-451; Churchill on, I: 87, 134-135, 542, 648; II:

Hopkins, Harry L. (*cont.*)
148, 682; **III**: 91, 110, 539; Churchill on visit to London, 1943, **II**: 39, 49, 182-183; Churchill to on dollar balances, **III**: 34-35; Churchill to on France, **II**: 662; Churchill to on Greek crisis, **III**: 449, 451-453; Churchill to on Marshall, **II**: 481; Churchill to on son's death, **III**: 37, 39-40, 46-47; diminished role of, **II**: 454; **III**: 161, 163, 559; health of, **I**: 351, 353, 441; **II**: 454, 649-650, 662, 669, 672, 688-689, 691; **III**: 73-74, 168, 307, 564, 566; on American Volunteer Group, **I**: 332-333; on atomic research sharing, **II**: 214, 317, 351; on Battle of Atlantic, **I**: 212; on British needs, **II**: 177; on central supply board, **I**: 463; on Churchill, **II**: 508; on France, **III**: 361; on Moscow Conference, 1944, **III**: 350; on postwar planning, **II**: 156; on Sicilian occupational government, **II**: 238; on Stalin, **I**: 606-607, 612; **III**: 395; on Tunis Conference, **II**: 515-516; on Winant and Harriman, **I**: 541; on Yalta Conference, **III**: 388; son killed, **II**: 725-727, 729; trip to Soviet Union, **I**: 224-226; trips to London, **I**: 437, 440-443, 444, 448, 458, 466, 497, 533-536; **III**: 507, 511, 517-518
Hopkins, Louise Macy, **I**: 543; **III**: 74
Hovde, Frederick L., **I**: 250, 279
Howe, Clarence D., **II**: 420-421
Hull, Cordell, **I**: 8, 66, 71, 114, 165, 177, 231, 250, 278, 524; **II**: 92, 146, 208, 304, 388, 440, 449, 540, 544, 596; **III**: 5, 35-36, 58, 77, 154, 326; absences from conferences, **II**: 578; **III**: 316, 322-323, 341; and Africa, **III**: 325; and Argentina, **II**: 678; **III**: 224, 230-231, 233, 246, 252, 291, 297, 303, 346; and atrocities statement, **II**: 547; and Balkan policy, **III**: 200-201; and Balkans, **III**: 177, 182; and Britain, postwar, **III**: 65, 99-100; and Cairo Conference, **II**: 576, 579; and Casablanca Conference, **II**: 54; and de Gaulle, **II**: 208, 235; and France, **II**: 104, 642; **III**: 62, 162, 204, 354; and French in North Africa, **II**: 256; and Imperial Preference System, **I**: 356; and Iran, **III**: 140; and Ireland, **III**: 76; and Italian morale, **II**: 341; and Italian political situation, **II**: 587, 679-681, 697; and Moscow Conference, 1944, **III**: 350; and Moscow Foreign Ministers' Conference, **II**: 463-464, 485, 545, 563, 575, 583, 606; and neutral nations, **III**: 245; and Poland, **II**: 706; and Poles in Soviet Union, **II**: 193-194; and prisoner exchange with Japan, **III**: 244; and Roosevelt, **II**: 572; and St. Pierre-Miquelon affair, **I**: 324-326, 346-347; and Spain, **III**: 107-108, 114; and unconditional surrender for Germany, **II**: 645; and Vichy government, **I**: 353; and Yugoslavia, **III**: 115; at oil conference, **II**: 734, 745; **III**: 169, 206; health of, **II**: 490; on Asia resources, **I**: 274; on blockade of Europe, **II**: 105; on FCNL, **III**: 86-88, 148-149, 237, 321-322; on freezing foreign funds, **I**: 209; on occupation government in Sicily, **II**: 188; on postwar economic goals, **I**: 344; **II**: 748-749; on postwar Germany, **II**: 178; on Soviet boundary issues, **I**: 394; on Soviets and Italian surrender terms, **II**: 371; on Spain, **III**: 105-106; on spheres of influence, **III**: 153-154; on transfer of Pacific ships, **I**: 174; on Turkey, **II**: 581; on Welles, **II**: 462; opposes Morgenthau Plan, **III**: 317; resigns, **III**: 437; Roosevelt on, **I**: 324; trip to England, **II**: 269-270
Hungary, **I**: 170; **II**: 131, 350; **III**: 222, 229, 299, 300, 403, 434, 634; Allied strategy toward, Churchill on, **II**: 445; and Allies, **III**: 523; and Moscow Conference, 1944, **III**: 351-352; Churchill on, **II**: 498-499; Soviet Union and, **III**: 364, 545
Hurley, Patrick, **III**: 3-4, 140-141, 395-396, 527
Hyde Park, N.Y., **I**: 533, 551; **II**: 136, 155, 156, 163, 211-212, 420-421, 430, 431-432, 454, 513, 559, 571, 628; **II** 520, 597; Churchill visit to, 1942, **I**: 511; Churchill visit to, 1943, **II**: 348, 365, 382, 447; Churchill visit to, 1944,

III: 289, 316, 318, 321-323, 325, 332-333; Churchills' wedding anniversary at, II: 438; photos at, II: 530-532

Iberian bloc, II: 243
Ibn Saud, King of Saudi Arabia, II: 561, 599; III: 536, 537
Iceland, I: 36, 56, 162, 166, 200-201, 203, 221, 236, 399, 425-426, 612-613; II: 15, 43, 49, 54-55, 72, 158, 163, 283; and convoys to Soviet Union, I: 623-624, 629; U.S. forces to, I: 207, 208, 218-219, 253, 302, 316, 391
Ickes, Harold, II: 222, 733; III: 169
Imperial Preference System, I: 345-346, 356-359
Imperialism, II: 599; III: 3, 6-8; British, U.S. views on, I: 181, 221; II: 480; Churchill on, III: 140-141. See also Colonialism
Imphal, India, III: 56; Japanese in, II: 751-752; III: 19-20, 49-50, 52
India, I: 91, 136, 350, 353, 362, 370, 414, 632, 653; II: 168, 430, 542, 733, 759; III: 418, 420
    air reinforcements for, I: 461-462
    Allied troops in, 1942, I: 321
    and ANZAC defense, I: 384
    and Britain, I: 444-449; II: 110
    and Japan, Churchill on, I: 438
    and Southeast Asia command structure, II: 294-295
    and supplies to China, II: 537, 689-690
    and United Nations organization, III: 331
    and war effort, I: 320, 373-379
    bomber bases in, II: 589-599, 594
    British defense of, 1942, I: 391, 438
    British forces in, I: 653; II: 117
    British in, I: 395-396; II: 599; III: 141
    Chiang and, I: 546-549, 556
    Churchill defends British Army in, II: 528
    Churchill on, I: 447, 550, 557
    Churchill on Roosevelt views, I: 445
    Churchill on to Chiang, I: 563
    Congress Party in, I: 373-379, 402, 444, 546-547, 550, 558, 563
    famine in, III: 116-117, 155

    importance of, I: 365, 381
    in Middle East theater, I: 399, 430
    in postwar world, II: 609
    independence for: British view, I: 388; Churchill on, I: 402; Roosevelt on, I: 8, 373, 388, 400-404
        Japanese threat to, I: 449-450, 455-456; II: 756; III: 19-20, 49-50
        role of, differing Allied view, II: 274-277
        Roosevelt on, I: 19, 363, 421, 445-447
        shipping needs of, II: 153, 167
        troops in Iran, I: 653
        U.S. forces in, I: 414
India theater, III: 426; and Pacific strategy, III: 39; command changes in, I: 216-217; need for troops in, I: 383; second priority to Europe, 1942, I: 450
India-Burma theater, III: 370
Indian Front Command, II: 482
Indian Ocean, I: 97; II: 349, 759; and Burma operation, II: 202; and cross-channel invasion plan, I: 458; and U.S. Pacific fleet, I: 418; British fleet in, I: 411-412; II: 52-53, 112, 116; III: 39-40; defense of, I: 89, 95, 300, 381, 383, 390-391, 397, 438-439, 449-450, 452, 454-456, 468-470; II: 443; III: 14; 17-18
Indo-China, I: 180, 350, 481; II: 276, 733, 742; III: 237, 582-583, 633; Allied policy toward, III: 626-627; Allied view of, 1941, I: 229; and Britain, III: 572-573; and Vichy government, I: 433-434; British and, I: 280; Churchill on, 1942, I: 299; defense of, I: 382; Japanese in, I: 70, 90-91, 98, 105, 135, 225; U.S.-Japanese disputes over, 1941, I: 274-275
Inönü, Ismet, II: 126-128, 135, 140-141, 618-619; III: 49, 53, 55-56, 363, 365, 508, 515
Intelligence, Allied: before D-Day, III: 165; breaking of German codes, I: 370; codenames for, II: 388; on German subs, II: 323; on Hitler's war expectations, III: 214; on insurgents in Poland, III: 461; on Italian morale, II: 351; Stalin on, I: 570

Intelligence, British, **I**: 69-70; **III**: 206, 214, 255-256; and "Schwartz Kapelle," **II**: 521; and French Resistance, **III**: 148; and German invasion, Western Europe, **I**: 36; blinded by German code change, **I**: 451-452; breaks State Department codes, **I**: 26, 28; breaks the enemy code, **I**: 214-215; in Northern France, **II**: 559-560; on German aircraft production, **I**: 619; on German invasion of Soviet Union, **I**: 211; on German ship movements, **I**: 527; on Germans at Soviet front, **I**: 499; on Germans in Caucasus, **I**: 637; on Germans in Italy, **III**: 226; on Greece, **III**: 467; on Japanese and Hitler, **II**: 247; on Japanese in Pacific, **I**: 136; on Libya, **I**: 273

Intelligence, French, **I**: 214; and German invasion of Western Europe, **I**: 36

Intelligence, German, **I**: 188; and *Iroquois* incident, **I**: 25; breaks Allied merchant ship codes, **I**: 451; in Argentina, **II**: 678-679, 681-684; in Ireland, **III**: 57-58; in Turkey, **II**: 663, 669; on Churchill-Roosevelt phone calls, **II**: 356-357

Intelligence, Polish, **I**: 214; for Allies, **I**: 488-489

Intelligence, signals, **I**: xxi-xxii, 214-215
    MAGIC, **I**: xxii, 214-215; **II**: 101; **III**: 256; and Japanese actions, **I**: 278; message on Germans in Tunisia, **II**: 4, 7; on British and Ribbentrop, **II**: 676-677; on British-German contacts, **II**: 672-674; on Italian situation, **II**: 64, 66-67; on Italians and Germans, **II**: 378
    ULTRA, **I**: xxii, 155, 267, 371-372; **II**: 388-389; **III**: 227, 255-256, 320, 340; and anti-submarine campaign, **II**: 366; **III**: 276; and Atlantic submarine sinkings, **II**: 228; and North African invasion, **I**: 594; and sinking of *Tirpitz*, **III**: 388; code changed by Germans, 1942, **I**: 451; discussed, **I**: 214-215; on *Scharnhorst*, **II**: 636; on Italians and Germans, **II**: 378

Intelligence, Soviet, **III**: 624; and cooperation with Allies, **I**: 616; on German

aircraft production, **I**: 619, 625

Intelligence, United States, **III**: 624; and German invasion of Soviet Union, **I**: 134; and invasion of Ceylon, **I**: 455; and Japanese naval movements, **I**: 483; and William Donovan, **I**: 348; breaking Japanese codes, 1942, **I**: 465; breaking enemy codes, **I**: 214-215; in Pacific, **III**: 193; in North Africa, **I**: 561; in Yugoslavia, **III**: 80; on decoding messages, **II**: 100; on German invasion of Soviet Union, **I**: 211; on Japanese fleet movements, **I**: 461; on Japanese Pacific strategy, **I**: 507; OSS created, **I**: 263

International Labor Organization, **II**: 749; **III**: 101-102, 104; Stalin on, **III**: 75

International Labour Office Convention, **I**: 244

International law, **III**: 364

International organization, postwar, **I**: 228; **III**: 319, 398, 505-506, 523, 531, 532-533, 564, 573-574; and Soviets, **III**: 586, 588-591; Churchill on, **II**: 130, 448-449; decisions on at Yalta, **III**: 524, 526, 527; discussed at Moscow Foreign Ministers' Conference, **II**: 606; Roosevelt vs. Churchill-Stalin views, **II**: 611-612; Roosevelt on, **II**: 178; **III**: 547; U.S. resolutions on, **II**: 584-585. *See also* United Nations Organization

International Red Cross, **II**: 192-195, 198-199, 701; **III**: 621, 623

International Wheat Meetings, 1941-42, **I**: 247

Invergordon, Scotland, **III**: 249-250

Iran, **I**: 13, 176, 318, 372; **II**: 59, 144, 194, 199; Allied troops in, 1942, **I**: 320; and Soviet defeat, **I**: 307; and Soviet Union, **I**: 255-256; **III**: 523; as supply route to Soviet Union, **I**: 503; **II**: 534; British forces in, **I**: 572, 653; Churchill on prospects in, 1942, **I**: 295; competition in, **III**: 139-141, 511-513; in British plans, 1943, **II**: 14; occupation of, **I**: 235; out of Middle East theater, **I**: 554; strategic importance of, **I**: 421; U.S. and British interests in, **III**: 13-14, 16-17, 26-27;

U.S. policy toward, **III**: 3-10

Iraq (Persia), **I**: 178, 180, 318, 372; **II**: 144; **III**: 512; Allied troops in, 1942, **I**: 320; battles in, **I**: 204; British forces in, 1943, **I**: 653; British interests in, **III**: 141; Churchill on prospects in, 1942, **I**: 295; Germans in, **I**: 185-186; Hess on, **I**: 188; out of Middle East theater, **I**: 554; revolution in, **I**: 175-176; threatened by Germans, **I**: 196; U.S. and British interests in, **III**: 13-14, 16-17, 26-27

Ireland, **I**: 17, 37, 39, 56, 90, 254, 636; **II**: 172, 192. *See also* DeValera

    Allied negotiations with, **III**: 75-76

    and Britain, **III**: 58

    and U.S., **II**: 420-421; **III**: 543-544, 566-567; aviation agreement between, **III**: 519-520

    British ports in, **I**: 97-99, 101, 104, 112

    Churchill on, **I**: 106, 282; **III**: 519-520

    food for, **I**: 113

    neutrality of, **I**: 45, 53-54, 88, 92; **II**: 186-187

    relations with Allies, **III**: 57-58

    shipping embargo on, **III**: 81

Iron ore: British import of from Spain, **III**: 66-67

Iroquois incident, **I**: 25

Isayev, General, **I**: 500

Ismay, Hastings, **I**: 314, 458-459, 513; **II**: 584-585; **III**: 399; and Churchill, **I**: 510; Churchill on, **III**: 170; on Churchill, **I**: 605

Isole Pelagie, **III**: 328

Israel, **II**: 561

Istanbul, Turkey, **II**: 714, 730; as site for talks with Bulgarians, **II**: 724

Istria, **III**: 232, 299-302, 305, 316, 348; attack from, **III**: 212-213, 222-223, 225, 227

Italian campaign, **I**: 604, 670; **II**: 503, 761; **III**: 146, 207, 222, 316, 373, 375, 453

    Allied forces in, **II**: 529

    Allied problems in, **II**: 632-633; **III**: 433-435

    American support for, **II**: 554-555

    and bombing of cities, **II**: 234

    and cross-channel invasion, **II**: 580-581, 712-713

    and invasion of southern France, **III**: 114-115, 126, 128, 230, 285-286, 289-290, 299-302

    and occupational government, **II**: 270-271

    and offensive during channel invasion, **III**: 94

    and political situation, **II**: 725-726

    and resources to China, **II**: 730-731

    and second front, **II**: 245

    announcement of, **II**: 314

    Anzio, battle of, **II**: 632-633, 635-636, 638, 640-641, 648, 656-658, 668, 705, 728-729, 757; **III**: 16, 18, 119-120, 142, 148-149; Churchill on, **III**: 18; decisions on, **II**: 658; effect in Italy, **II**: 705

    as priority in Mediterranean, **II**: 756

    battle lines in, **III**: 299-300, 304-305, 308

    Brazilian troops in, **III**: 285

    Calabria, attack planned on, **II**: 434-436

    Churchill on, **I**: 15, **II**: 202, 303-308, 562-563, 565, 657; **III**: 90, 132, 493-494, 523

    debates over strategy in, **II**: 216, 502-505, 508-509, 511, 514, 516; **III**: 19, 135, 137, 299-301, 304-305

    decisions on at Quebec, 1943, **II**: 430

    difficulties in, **II**: 498

    discussed at Quebec, 1944, **III**: 318-321

    discussed at Washington Conference, **II**: 212, 218

    French army in, **III**: 88, 136, 138, 144-145, 149-150

    German defense against, **II**: 266, 329, 354, 442-445, 516-517

    German strength in, **III**: 434

    in grand strategy, **II**: 10-15

    invasion of mainland, **II**: 327-328, 344

    lack of fresh troops for, **III**: 356-357

    liberation of Rome, **III**: 142, 148-

Italian campaign (*cont.*)
149, 163-164
   Monte Cassino, battle at, **II**: 711-712, 728-729; **III**: 16, 18, 135; Churchill on, **III**: 18; German defense of, **II**: 663
   opposition to Jewish Brigade in, **III**: 286
   planning of invasion for, **II**: 133-134
   postwar politics and, **III**: 433-434
   problems in, **III**: 110-112, 197-199, 347-348, 523
   resources to, **II**: 585
   Roosevelt on, **II**: 300-301, 501, 723; **III**: 139, 167, 308, 447-448
   Salerno, battle of, **II**: 434-436, 436, 452, 455
   Sicily, invasion of, **I**: 623, 628, 670; **II**: 10, 18, 110, 117-118, 129, 134, 151-152, 184, 186, 230, 285, 298, 300, 303, 320, 327, 334, 358; air preparations for, **II**: 234-235; Allied losses in, **II**: 529; and de Gaulle, **II**: 273; and Italian morale, **II**: 351; and shipping problems, **II**: 157-159, 161-167, 173, 175-177, 179; Churchill on success, **II**: 328; delayed, 1943, **II**: 148-149; discussed, **I**: 604; **II**: 212, 218; message to Italians, **II**: 322-324; and civil administration, **II**: 187-190, 237-239, 251, 270-271; prior bombing of Italy, **II**: 250-251; prisoners taken in, **II**: 353, 384; Roosevelt on, **II**: 156, 185-186; Stalin on, **II**: 153; troop projections for, **II**: 182-183
   Stalin on, **II**: 244, 386; **III**: 113, 230
   U.S. Army in, **III**: 203
   U.S. military view of, 1943, **II**: 182
   U.S. policy: Churchill on, **III**: 286
   vs. southern France invasion, **III**: 207, 212-223, 225-229, 232
Italian East Africa, **II**: 529
Italian Somaliland, **I**: 159
Italians, **I**: 41, 160; aiding Allied forces, **II**: 723; and ships to Soviets, **II**: 664-666, 669-671, 675-676; Churchill on, **II**: 760; little aid to war effort, **II**: 442, 445; military efforts vs. Germans, **II**: 483; morale of, **II**: 341

Italy, **I**: 209, 223-224; **II**: 12-13, 25, 37, 39, 101, 168, 218, 487-488, 528, 530, 532, 544, 755; **III**: 274, 395, 517
   Allied aid to, **III**: 387
   Allied air forces in, **I**: 11
   Allied bombing of, **I**: 671; **II**: 11, 46, 123
   Allied policy on, **I**: 206, 669; **III**: 333-334, 337-338, 619-620
   and Albania, **I**: 66, 153
   and Allied war effort, **II**: 555
   and Balkans, **I**: 144-145
   and Britain (in World War I), **I**: 89
   and Britain, 1940-1941, **I**: 565
   and entry into war, **I**: 37
   and Soviet Union, **II**: 507
   and Tripartite Alliance, **I**: 137
   and World War I, **I**: 221
   anti-Fascists in, **III**: 29
   as British responsibility, **II**: 767
   as U.S. sphere of influence, **III**: 586
   atrocities in, **II**: 520
   Badoglio government in: Churchill on, **II**: 725-726
   British Army in, **III**: 271
   British policy to, U.S. criticizes, **III**: 436-439
   British sabotage plans in, **I**: 645
   Churchill on, **I**: 91, 302-303; **II**: 184, 267, 593
   collapse of, 1941, **I**: 295
   communists in, **II**: 379-380, 666; **III**: 42, 45, 351
   currency question in, **II**: 466-467, 470-471, **III**: 386
   German air bases in, **I**: 317
   Germans in, **III**: 226
   in Albania, **I**: 153
   in North Africa, **I**: 171, 294, 561, 578, 641, 660; **II**: 9
   Macmillan on, **III**: 537
   MAGIC intelligence on, **II**: 666-667
   occupation policy, **II**: 187-190, 438-440
   Political-Military Commission, **II**: 539-540
   political situation in, **II**: 347, 455-464, 466-474, 586-587, 591, 679-681, 759-760, 761-762; **III**: 52-53, 176, 178, 180, 182-183, 185, 188-190, 199-200, 387, 437-439, 445, 451-452, 533-

534, 536-538; Allied debate on, **III**: 443-444; American view, **II**: 697; Churchill on, **III**: 30-32, 41-43, 45-46; Roosevelt on, **III**: 33, 40-41, 44, 187; Stalin on, **III**: 200

politics, **II**: 457

postwar rule in, **II**: 481, 504, 539-540, 766; **III**: 28-29, 323-324; Anglo-American dispute over, **II**: 455; Churchill on, **II**: 223; Roosevelt on, **II**: 709; **III**: 160

prisoners of war in, **II**: 352-353

relief for, **III**: 400-401

Roosevelt on relationship with U.S., **II**: 306

Roosevelt trip to, **II**: 584

ships to Soviets, **II**: 654-656, 709; **III**: 14-19, 23-28, 24

surrender of, Stalin on, **II**: 432

surrender of, negotiations on, **II**: 119, 128-129, 214, 347, 348, 365-366, 378-381, 422-429, 431, 436-437, 440, 470-474, 483-488, 490-492, 500-502, 518-519, 523-524, 538-539, 551-553, 556, 766, 769; **III**: 188-190

talks with Germans in, **III**: 614. *See also* Bern, Switzerland

U.S. policy toward, **III**: 400, 636

United Nations policy toward, **II**: 300-301

Iwo Jima, battle of, **III**: 524, 601

Jacob, Edward, **II**: 96-97

Jadwin, C. L.: mission to Bulgaria, **II**: 729, 765; **III**: 15

Jamaica, B.W.I., **I**: 59-60, 65, 68

Japan, **I**: 8, 14, 174, 177, 180-181, 209, 309; **II**: 37, 64, 102, 168, 222, 283, 477; **III**: 330, 335, 364, 447, 494, 543

air war against, **II**: 263-264

Allied decisions on, **II**: 217

Allied warning to, **I**: 231, 279-280

and Britain, **I**: 73-74, 229; **II**: 443; **III**: 318; in World War I, **I**: 89

and Cairo Declaration, **II**: 609

and China, **III**: 395; Roosevelt view, **II**: 608

and Gandhi, **I**: 563

and Hitler, **II**: 247

and Indo-China, **I**: 225

and Ireland, **III**: 57

and second front, **I**: 88

and Soviet Union, **II**: 575, 577; **III**: 318, 359, 524, 527; entry into war with, **II**: 606; **III**: 341-342, 353; non-aggression pact between, **I**: 207

and Tripartite Alliance, **I**: 137

and U.S. fleet, 1942, **I**: 442

and unconditional surrender, **II**: 119, 128-129

and United States: historical overview, **I**: 274-275; tensions with, **I**: 218

anti-submarine campaign of, **III**: 276, 489

Argentina breaks relations with, **II**: 684

at Guadalcanal, **II**: 138

attack Pearl Harbor, **I**: 280-282

bombing of, **II**: 732; **III**: 601

British participation against, **III**: 77

Churchill on, **I**: 38, 135-137, 198, 278-279, 309, 383, 459; **II**: 332

Churchill on strategy toward, **I**: 91, 265-266, 298-302, 304-309, 306-307, 308

discussed at Quebec, 1943, **II**: 430

imperialism of, **III**: 6

in India and Burma, **III**: 50-52

in Indo-China, **III**: 627

invasion of, proposed, **II**: 213; **III**: 572, 626; Churchill on, **I**: 321

losses in Pacific, **III**: 193, 449

Lyttelton remark on, **III**: 201

Pacific successes, **I**: 293, 611

Roosevelt freezes assets of, 1941, **I**: 274

Roosevelt on, **I**: 250, 265-267, 274-276, 390, 533; **III**: 135

steel industry in, **II**: 594

United States strategy toward, **I**: 229; **II**: 112, 696; **III**: 523

war strategy of, **I**: 225, 438-439, 507; **II**: 551; **III**: 38-40

Japanese Naval High Command, **I**: 453

Java, **I**: 321, 351, 353, 363, 364-365, 382; battle of, **I**: 367-368; Japanese threat to, **I**: 361

Jerusalem, **III**: 378, 389, 395

Jewish Brigade, **III**: 286-287, 298

Jews, **I**: 557; **II**: 68, 209; in Germany, **III**: 580; refugees and Anglo-American policy, **II**: 293; refugees to North

Jews (cont.)
  Africa, **II**: 315-316; to Palestine, **III**:
    536
Jibouti, French Somaliland, **II**: 92, 335
Jinnah, Mohammed Ali, **I**: 375
Joan of Arc, de Gaulle as, **II**: 121
Johnson, Herschel, **I**: 70
Johnson, Louis, **I**: 501-502
Joint Tank Commission, **I**: 631
Jones, Jesse, **II**: 290
Jordana, Count Francisco Gómez, **I**:
    664-666; **II**: 102; **III**: 99
Juin, Alphonse, **I**: 270
Jutland, Battle of, **III**: 239

Karlsruhe, Germany, bombing of, **I**: 597
Kasserine Pass, Tunisia, **II**: 151
Katyn Forest, **II**: 395. *See also* Poland
Kelly, Sir D., **III**: 224, 233
Kennan, George, **II**: 506-507, 590-591,
    592; on Azores decision-making, **II**:
    495
Kennedy, Joseph, **I**: 7, 46-48, 50, 53, 57,
    58, 61; and early war, **I**: 26-27; as
    Ambassador to England, **I**: 63; on
    early Churchill-Roosevelt meeting, **II**:
    355; Roosevelt on, **I**: 139
Kennedy, Joseph, Jr., **I**: 139
Kennedy, Rose, **I**: 139
Kent, Tyler G., **I**: 40-41; **III**: 201
Kenya, **III**: 328
Kerr, Sir Archibald Clark, **II**: 203-204,
    595-596, 701, 703, 716, 729, 740, 747,
    752, 763-765; **III**: 272-273, 335, 539,
    561-562, 569, 571-572, 574-575, 577,
    587-588, 615; and Churchill-Stalin
    meeting, 1944, **III**: 339, 341; and in-
    formation leaks, **III**: 54; and Italian
    ships, **III**: 17-18; and Poles, **III**: 21;
    and Polish-Soviet relations, **III**: 30,
    68-71
Kesselring, Albert, **III**: 221-222, 348,
    434, 609-611, 614
Keynes, Lord John Maynard, **III**: 34-35,
    535
Kharlamov, Admiral, **I**: 500
Khartoum, Egypt, **II**: 54-55, 56, 66, 72,
    74, 247, 268, 601-602
Kidd, Philip, **III**: 8
Kiel Canal, **III**: 364
King, Ernest J., **I**: 223, 338, 348, 407,
    414, 418, 452, 467, 481, 491, 514,
    540-541, 555, 590, 597, 616; **II**: 70,
    291, 296, 312, 499, 569, 605; **III**: 112,
    119, 194, 301, 417, 446; and British,
    I: 440; **II**: 39, 49, 479, 677; and Brit-
    ish in Pacific, **II**: 52-53; **III**: 38, 318;
    and Casablanca Conference, **II**: 55,
    117-118; and convoys to Soviets, **I**:
    478-480, 482, 533, 617; and Greek
    crisis, **III**: 450, 452; and invasion of
    Norway, **I**: 608; and invasion of
    southern France, **III**: 197-199; and
    Pacific command coordination, **II**:
    205-206; and shipping production, **II**:
    45; and U.S. ships to Indian Ocean, **I**:
    450; at Malta Conference, **III**: 503;
    commands U.S. Navy, **I**: 397; on
    cross-channel invasion, **I**: 601; on Eu-
    ropean vs. Pacific theaters, **II**: 20,
    712; on naval aid to Britain, **I**: 406;
    on publicity over sub sinkings, **II**:
    228-229; on RAF and bombing policy,
    I: 423; on submarine publicity, **II**:
    327; on U.S. aircraft to Britain, **I**:
    486; opposes convoys to Soviets, late
    1942, **I**: 620; opposes joint com-
    mands, **I**: 454-455; **II**: 60-61; to Eng-
    land before D-Day, **III**: 150; trip to
    London, 1942, **I**: 533-536; visit to
    Normandy, **III**: 186; war strategy of,
    III: 203-204
King, Mackenzie, **I**: 69, 457, 603; **II**:
    290, 321-322, 328, 333, 420, 431, 571,
    582, 710; **III**: 79, 126, 165, 249, 270,
    534-535, 618; and Quebec Confer-
    ence, 1943, **II**: 341-343, 344-346, 371-
    372, 379, 422; on Allied command
    structure, **III**: 83-84, 103-105
Kipling, Mrs. Rudyard, **II**: 541
Kipling, Rudyard, **II**: 541, 561-562
Kirk, Alan, **II**: 85
Kirk, Alexander C., **I**: 61; **II**: 569-570,
    588, 592; **III**: 537
Kirkpartick, Ivone, **I**: 187
Knox, Frank, **I**: 66, 101, 165, 177, 238,
    456; **III**: 3, 118; limits aid to Britain,
    I: 157; on submarine menace, **I**: 452
Koenig, Pierre Joseph, **III**: 123-124,
    127, 135-138, 241
Kohima, India, **III**: 49-50
Komarnicki, M., **II**: 391

Koniev, I. S., **III**: 553-554
Königsberg, in Polish-Soviet dispute, **II**: 686, 704, 721, 737
Konoye, Fumimaro, **I**: 250
Korea, **II**: 609
Kos, Greek island, **II**: 497-499, 509-512, 517
Kosciusko League, **II**: 762
Kot, Stanislaw, **II**: 701
Kuh, Frederick, **II**: 490, 522, 530
Kukiel, Marjan, **II**: 701
Kunming, China, **III**: 422, 435
Kurile Islands, **III**: 527
Kursk, Soviet Union, **I**: 14; **II**: 247; Soviet victory at, 1943, **II**: 386
Kuznetsov, Nikolai, **II**: 610

La Guardia, Fiorello, **III**: 320-321, 324
Labour Party, Britain, **II**: 261; **III**: 124, 457, 538-539, 546, 548
Lake of the Snows, Canada, **II**: 431-433
Lambert, de Bois, **II**: 236
Lampson, Sir Miles (Lord Killearn), **III**: 178-179
Land, Emory S., **I**: 236-237, 327, 329; **II**: 219; **III**: 320-321
Landis, James M., **III**: 3, 8
Lange, Oscar, **II**: 762, 764; **III**: 269
Langwell, Scotland, **III**: 249
Lanza, d'Ajeta, Marchese Blasco; **II**: 379-380
Laskov, H., **III**: 298
Laskowski, Janusz, **II**: 395
Lateran Treaty (Italy and Vatican), **II**: 265
Latin America, **I**: 155; **III**: 101, 200; Roosevelt on German intentions toward, **I**: 264
Latin Bloc, **II**: 243
Latvia, **I**: 371-372; **II**: 611; **III**: 349, 541; and Soviet Union, **I**: 393
Laval, Pierre, **I**: 85, 127, 146, 154, 481; and French fleet, **I**: 521-522; and French fleet negotiations, **I**: 517; in Vichy government, 1942, **I**: 459-461; returns to power, 1942, **I**: 466-467; struggle with Petain, **I**: 76-79
Layton, Sir Walter, **I**: 79, 80
Le Troquer, André, **III**: 169, 171
League of Nations, **I**: 14, 228; **II**: 130, 225, 691; **III**: 7, 75, 389-390

Leahy, William D., **I**: 18, 128, 132-133, 148, 158-159, 162, 186, 287, 347, 354, 461, 467, 480, 561, 599; **II**: 106, 109, 117, 255, 259, 279, 304, 343, 567, 606-608, 677, 724, 773; **III**: 47, 59, 221, 232, 234, 296, 303, 308, 393, 400, 508, 563, 617; and British role in Asia, **II**: 696; and cross-channel invasion security, **III**: 120; and France, **III**: 150; and Italian political situation, **II**: 697; **III**: 28; and Poland, **III**: 562-563, 592, 594; and recognition of FCNL, **II**: 337; and Roosevelt, **III**: 161; and Roosevelt correspondence, role in, **III**: 88; as Chief of Staff to Roosevelt, **II**: 66; **III**: 301, 559; on British troops to Greece, **III**: 297; on Burma operations, **II**: 752; on civil aviation dispute, **III**: 402; on de Gaulle, **I**: 669; **II**: 104, 208; on de Gaulle and Giraud, **II**: 137-138; on occupation zones in Germany, **II**: 709; on Petain, **I**: 184, 270; **III**: 128; on trip to Cairo, **II**: 606-608; on U.S. planes to Azores, **II**: 330; on Vichy, **I**: 333-335, 661; to Quebec Conference, 1944, **III**: 287-288
Leathers, Lord, **I**: 474, 541; **II**: 202, 219, 365, 372, 654; **III**: 159, 320-321; at Quebec Conference, 1943, **II**: 354-355; at Yalta Conference, **III**: 477
Lebanon, **I**: 191; **III**: 135, 137, 179; and France, **II**: 599-600; **III**: 389-390; British and French dispute on, **II**: 333-334; de Gaulle on independence for, **I**: 204; French in, **II**: 691-692
Leclerc, Jacques Philippe, **II**: 209-210; **III**: 86, 88, 170
Ledo, India, **II**: 751-752
Ledo Road, Burma, **II**: 274, 277, 282, 430, 757, 759; **III**: 19-20, 54-55
Leeper, Reginald W. A., **III**: 95, 98, 466, 471, 480, 618-619
Leese, Sir Oliver, **III**: 167
Legentilhomme, Paul, **I**: 660-661
LeHand, Marguerite, **I**: 186, 222
Lehman, Herbert H., **II**: 315-316
Leigh-Mallory, Sir Trafford, **II**: 629, 635
Leipzig, Germany, **III**: 602, 605, 607, 608

Lend-Lease Act, **I**: 63, 102, 119, 145, 232-233, 507; **III**: 530-531, 535-536, 574, 634; and Anglo-American relations, **I**: 137-143; in U.S. Congress, **I**: 129

Lend-Lease Administration, **III**: 8-9

Lend-Lease aid, **I**: 7, 114, 207, 209, 346, 487; **II**: 39, 149, 527; **III**: 322-323, 396, 577, 634; Allies threaten cutoff to China, **III**: 58; American senators on, **II**: 733; and civil aviation dispute, **III**: 421, 422; and Neutrality Act amendments, **I**: 245; and Russian and British imperialism, **III**: 6-9; as aid to British economy, **II**: 743-744; Churchill on, **I**: 39-40; **II**: 528-529; debate over compromises, **I**: 351; issue of British dollar balances, **III**: 34-36; issue of use of, **I**: 118, 232-234; **III**: 65-66, 140-141; Master agreement, **I**: 344, 356-359; negotiations over, **I**: 36-43, 63-68; Pearl Harbor lessens, **I**: 285-286; postwar continuation of, **III**: 248, 289-290, 317-318; Roosevelt and, **I**: 88; Roosevelt threatens cutoff, **I**: 17; **III**: 407; Stalin on, **I**: 618; to Soviet Union, **I**: 239; **II**: 233; transport problems, 1942, **I**: 391

Lend-Lease bill: and British colonies, **I**: 140-143

Lend-Lease Protocol, **I**: 507

Lenin, V., **II**: 396

Leningrad, **I**: 226, 295; **II**: 102; **III**: 175; battle of, **II**: 63; **III**: 60

Leros, Greek island, **II**: 497-499, 509-511, 517, 518, 555, 557

Lethbridge, J. S., **III**: 50-51

Lewis, John L., **II**: 290

Leyte, Philippines, invasion of, **III**: 127

Liberia, **I**: 209; Roosevelt visit to, **II**: 123

"Liberum veto" (Poland), **II**: 715, 722

Libya, **I**: 144, 152, 176, 177, 186, 287, 294, 315, 362, 399; **II**: 30, 145; **III**: 286, 328. *See also* Cyrenaica

Libyan campaign, **I**: 112, 171, 252, 268-274, 296, 436, 453, 485, 493-494, 497; **II**: 136-137; British successes in, **I**: 295; Churchill on, **I**: 165, 300, 504; Roosevelt on, **I**: 277; Stalin on British

victory at, **II**: 17. *See also* North African campaign

Lincoln, Abraham, **III**: 7, 400, 429

Linlithgow, Marquess of, **II**: 248

Lippmann, Walter, **II**: 529; and Darlan deal, **II**: 21

Lisbon, Portugal, **II**: 240, 299, 321, 326, 384; British meetings with Germans in, **II**: 672

Lisbon Report on German rockets, **II**: 521

Lithuania, **I**: 371; **II**: 611, 715; **III**: 349; and Soviet Union, **I**: 393

Little, Sir Charles, **I**: 236-237; and supplies to Soviets, **I**: 472-473

Litvinov, Maxim, **I**: 420-421, 490; **II**: 284-285; **III**: 61

Ljubljana Gap, Yugoslavia, **I**: 16; **III**: 198, 222-223, 301, 523

Llewellin, J. J., **II**: 150, 420-421; **III**: 246, 570, 578-579, 584

Lodge, Henry Cabot, **II**: 527

Lombardy, Italy, **II**: 444

London, **I**: 138; **II**: 439, 490, 696; **III**: 230; bombing of, **I**: 70, 121-123; **II**: 373, 377, 739-740, 751, 753-754; Churchill on, **III**: 196; V-1 bombs;

London Conference (1942), **I**: 533-536, 541-543

Longfellow, Henry Wadsworth, **I**: 131

Lorient, France, **III**: 263

Lorraine, France, **III**: 338

Lothian, Lord (Philip Kerr), **I**: 32, 35, 39-40, 52-54, 57, 83, 88, 91, 101; and Dakar invasion, **I**: 72-73; and lend-lease, **I**: 58, 63, 65, 66-67, 68-69, 71; and relief for France, **I**: 116-117; death of, **I**: 111-113

Low, Francis, **III**: 112, 115

Low Countries, **II**: 39; **III**: 308; German forces in, 1942, **I**: 498; postwar, Churchill on, **II**: 223. *See also* Belgium; Netherlands

Lübeck, Germany, bombing of, **I**: 438

Lublin, Poland, **III**: 254

Lucas, John, **II**: 705

Luce, Henry, **I**: 654-656

Lusitania, sinking of, **I**: 203

Luxembourg, **I**: 206; atrocities in, **II**: 520; German invasion of, **I**: 36; in British occupation zone, **II**: 745; postwar, as British responsibility, **II**: 708

Luzon, Philippine Islands, **I**: 360

Lwów, Poland, **II**: 685, 719-720, 735-737, 741, 763; **III**: 13, 21, 29, 359, 364

Lyon, France, **III**: 218, 304-305

Lyster, A. L. St., **II**: 52-53

Lyttelton, Oliver, **I**: 216-217, 278, 489, 491, 501, 506, 638-639, 651, 655, 671; **II**: 42, 77, 93, 95; **III**: 159, 201-203, 208, 289-290, 570, 578-580, 584; and supply and production problems, **II**: 32, 43, 46-47

Macao, **II**: 249-250, 269, 281

MacArthur, Douglas, **I**: 353; **II**: 248; **III**: 243; and Pacific command struggles, **I**: 339-344, 409; and prisoner of war exchange, **III**: 246; and Roosevelt, **II**: 480; **III**: 272; as possible presidential nominee, 1944, **II**: 205; as Supreme Commander, S.W. Pacific, **I**: 408-409, 415; at Port Moresby, **I**: 657; becomes ANZAC Supreme Commander, **I**: 384; demands own theater, **I**: 9; in Pacific, **III**: 193; in Philippines, **I**: 325, 335; **III**: 524; invasion of Leyte, **III**: 433; popular in Australia and New Zealand, **I**: 425; press on, **II**: 482; reinforcement request debated, **I**: 477-480

Macaskie, Sir Nicholas, **II**: 355-356, 419

McAuliffe, A. C. **III**: 498

McCarthy, Leighton, **II**: 343-346

McCloy, John J., **III**: 87, 109-110

McClure, Robert A. **II**: 76

McCormick-Patterson newspapers, **I**: 421

McCormick, Robert R., **I**: 619-620, 625

McCullagh, George, **II**: 191

MacDonald, Malcolm, **II**: 342, 422

Macedonia, Greece, **III**: 350, 450, 461

MacFarlane Sir Frank Mason, **III**: 324

McGill University, **III**: 325

McIntire, Ross T., **I**: 185; **II**: 561, 567, 644; **III**: 59-60, 287, 491; and health of Roosevelt, **III**: 77

Mack, W.H.B., **II**: 100

Maclean, Fitzroy, **II**: 660-661, 668; **III**: 131-132

Macmillan, Harold, **II**: 71, 75, 215, 622-623; **III**: 445; and Allied Control Commission, Italy, **III**: 320-321, 323-324, 366, 372; and arrests by de Gaulle, **II**: 626; and Bulgarians, **III**: 23, 32; and FCNL, **II**: 274, 379, 639-640; and French, **II**: 209-211, 235-236, 579-580; and French in North Africa, **II**: 256, 257-258, 310, 333, 335, 340; and Italian political situation, **II**: 458-459, 462, 587, 679-980; **III**: 30-32, 180; and Italian surrender, **II**: 538; and Portugal, **II**: 242; and postwar Italy, **II**: 693; in Greece, **III**: 451-452, 456, 458-459, 466, 471, 487; in Italy, **III**: 387, 401, 533, 534, 537-538; in North Africa, **II**: 83-85, 87, 89-90, 92-93, 97, 99, 136-137, 228-231, 237, 239, 268, 270, 272; in Sicily administration, **II**: 251; on Italian campaign, **III**: 373

McNarney, Joseph T., **I**: 449-450; **III**: 87, 168, 392, 400, 489

McNaughton, Alexander, **I**: 601, 606

MacVeagh, Lincoln, **III**: 32, 471-473

Madagascar, **I**: 335, 350, 353, 404; **II**: 316, 335

    British forces in, 1943, **I**: 654

    De Gaulle on, **I**: 466-467

    invasion of, **I**: 405-406, 407, 419, 433-434, 439, 467-470, 475-477, 480-483, 613; **II**: 110; and Vichy reaction, **I**: 426; Roosevelt rejects joint action, **I**: 441-442

Madras, India, **I**: 374

Madrid, Spain, **II**: 321

Maglione, Cardinal, **II**: 428

Magruder, John, **I**: 333

Mainz, Germany, bombing of, **I**: 597

Maisky, Ivan, **I**: 544-545, 570, 603, 621-623, 629, 637; **II**: 51, 139-140, 180, 193, 284

Makins, R. M., **II**: 100

Makleff, M., **III**: 298

Malacca Straits, **I**: 382

Malaya, **I**: 177, 279-280, 286, 287, 318, 427; **II**: 213, 276, 480, 755-756, 757, 759; **III**: 39, 76, 270, 573; Allied forces in, 1942, **I**: 350; British troop losses in, **I**: 654; Churchill on strategy toward, 1942, **I**: 299

Mallory, Leigh, **III**: 518

Malone, Dudley F., **II**: 345
Maloney, Harry P., **I**: 137
Malta, **I**: 144, 175, 203, 296, 304; **II**: 145, 242, 264, 455, 575-576, 578, 592-593, 595-596, 600, 602, 618, 619; **III** 515, 518, 520; battle at, **I**: 439, 467-470, 534-535; bombing of by Germans, **I**: 435-436; British forces in, 1943, **I**: 654; Churchill on defense of, **I**: 301; Germans threaten, **I**: 317, 381; in British planning, 1943, **II**: 13; pre-Yalta meeting at, **III**: 488-489, 494-496, 501-507, 516-517; U.S. aid to British in, **I**: 440
Malta Conference (CRICKET), **III**: 543; and European war strategy, **III**: 602-603, 608; described, **III**: 521-524
Manchukuo, **III**: 342
Manchuria, **I**: 225; **II**: 609
Manganese, **III**: 49
Manhattan Project, **III**: 289, 319, 412
Manila, Philippines, **I**: 322; **III**: 524; Churchill on strategy toward, 1942, **I**: 299
Mao Tse-tung, **II**: 609
Maquis, French Resistance group, **III**: 214, 218
Mariana Islands, battle of, **III**: 193
Marin, Charles (AKA Winston Churchill), **I**: 358-359
Marine Corps, United States, **III**: 193, 500; at Guadalcanal, **II**: 6
Marlborough, Duchess of, **III**: 271
Marlborough, Duke of, **II**: 388; **III**: 109, 271
Marne, WWI victory at, **II**: 738
Marne River, **III**: 298
Marrakesh, **II**: 618; **III**: 227; as conference site, Churchill on, **II**: 55-56; Churchill recuperation at, **II**: 613, 620-621, 624, 628, 634, 644-645, 650-651, 668, 689, 695; Churchill-Roosevelt visit to, 1943, **II**: 113, 123
Marseilles, France, **I**: 118, 125; **III**: 217-218, 304
Marshall, George C., **I**: 223, 241, 335, 454-455, 460-462, 555, 581, 593, 646; **II**: 68, 70, 84, 105, 110, 113, 119, 183, 304, 498, 503, 505, 608, 611, 624, 705; **III**: 168-169, 170, 198, 314, 342, 392, 399, 578, 605, 616

and China, **III**: 370, 524
and Churchill, **II**: 216-217
and command changes, **I**: 309; **II**: 635, 639, 642, 646-647; **III**: 409-410, 552-553
and cross-channel invasion, **I**: 292, 436-437, 448-449, 459, 497, 502, 514, 601; **II**: 48, 430, 442, 489, 635; **III**: 53-54, 82, 93-94; command of, **I**: 523, 551-552; **II**: 420, 481-482, 492, 557, 570-571, 573, 613
and Darlan deal, **II**: 3, 5, 8
and de Gaulle, **II**: 254, 256
and Devers, **II**: 281
and Dill, **I**: 338; **III**: 381, 506
and East Asia command structure, **II**: 263
and Eisenhower, **II**: 143; **III**: 130, 522
and European strategy, 1945, **III**: 602
and FCNL, **II**: 440
and invasion of Norway, **I**: 608
and Italian campaign, **II**: 202, 230, 234, 562
and Leahy, **III**: 301
and MacArthur, **I**: 479
and occupation zones in Germany, **III**: 147
and Pacific command coordination, **II**: 205-206
and PLOUGH, **II**: 47
and Roosevelt, **III**: 446-447
and supplies to China, **II**: 537, 542, 550, 689
and tank production, **II**: 46-47
and troop supply question, **I**: 544
and war films, **II**: 528
and western Europe strategy, **II**: 712-713; **III**: 607
at Casablanca Conference, **II**: 54-55, 117-118
at Malta Conference, **III**: 503
Churchill on, **I**: 516; **II**: 232, 629
in France, **III**: 186, 348
on air war, **I**: 10
on Allied aid to Caucasus, **I**: 607
on Anglo-American talks, **II**: 563
on Australian troop withdrawal, **II**: 33
on Burma, **II**: 213, 616, 752

on China-Burma-India theater, **II**: 274

on Eisenhower and Italian surrender, **II**: 348, 372

on European invasions, **II**: 712-713

on Germans in Spain, **II**: 165

on La Guardia appointment, **III**: 320

on landing craft, **III**: 185-186

on Ledo Road, **II**: 430

on MAGIC information, **I**: 215

on Mediterranean theater operations, **II**: 20, 185

on military planning conference, **II**: 42-43

on North African invasion, **I**: 543, 577

on Pacific theater as American, **II**: 318

on political vs. military strategy, **II**: 479-480

on postwar France, **III**: 160

on postwar relations with Soviets, **II**: 431

on priorities of theaters, **I**: 450, 597

on ROUNDUP, **II**: 39

on Sholto Douglas, **II**: 317

on Sicilian occupational government, **II**: 238

on Solomon Islands battle, **I**: 597

on Soviet and Japan, **III**: 524

on Soviet communism, **II**: 480

on Soviet Pacific role, **III**: 527

on Stilwell, **I**: 405; **II**: 301

on supplies for troops, **I**: 542

on trip to Cairo, **II**: 606-608

on troop buildup to Britain, **II**: 38, 212

on troops for western front, **III**: 357

on U.S. aircraft to Britain, **I**: 485-486

on unity of commands, **I**: 293

opposes British imperial goals, **II**: 479-480, 508

proposed visit to London 1943, **II**: 39, 49

Roosevelt overrules, **I**: 514, 533

seeks to limit British role in Asia, **II**: 696

trips to England, **I**: 11, 437, 440-441, 443, 458, 466, 533-536; **III**: 150-152, 157, 167

Marshall Islands, battle at, **I**: 348; **II**: 725-726, 755; **III**: 193

Martin John, **I**: 281, 290, 510, 525; **III**: 331

Martinique, **I**: 324, 350, 353, 522-525; **II**: 147-148, 337-338; de Gaulle controls, **II**: 231

Marx, Karl, **III**: 31, 33

Massawa, Ethiopia, **I**: 203

Massigli, René, **II**: 214-215, 257-258, 271, 333-335, 679-680; **III**: 123-124, 127, 162, 169, 171

Mast, Charles, **II**: 68, 76

Mateur, Tunisia, **II**: 207-208

Matthews, H. Freeman, **I**: 82-84, 162-163; **II**: 71; **III**: 533-534

Maxwell, Russell, **I**: 554-555, 572

May, Stacy, **II**: 169

Mayer, Ernest de Wael, **II**: 75

Mayo Clinic, United States, **III**: 161, 564

Mayu Peninsula, Burma, **III**: 19-20

Mead, James, **II**: 527

Mecca, **II**: 561-562

Mededia, French Morocco, **I**: 667

Medhurst, Charles, **II**: 309

Mediterranean Commission, **II**: 439

Mediterranean Islands, Germans in, **II**: 266; **III**: 325, 328

Mediterranean Sea, **I**: 56; **II**: 570; **III**: 363, 378, 395, 495, 503; Allied control of, **II**: 101; **III**: 222; British interests in, **II**: 188, 480, 497-499; **III**: 95, 178, 274-275; at Moscow talks, 1944, **III**: 350-351; British Navy in, **II**: 755; shipping in, **I**: 469, 674; **II**: 45, 123

Mediterranean theater, **I**: 91, 98, 182, 298; **II**: 444

air war in, **I**: 317-318

and Balkans, **I**: 144

and cross-channel invasion, **III**: 90

and Germans, **II**: 265

and Italian surrender, **II**: 350, 362

and North African invasion, **I**: 561

British in, **I**: 75, 144-145, 300-301; **II**: 117, 369, 621, 756-757; naval losses of, **III**: 24; Stalin on, **II**: 51, 444; want supreme commander, **II**: 481-482

Churchill on, **I**: 254; **II**: 267, 288,

Mediterranean theater (*cont.*)
477; **III**: 226
command changes in, **I**: 430; **II**:
613-615, 617-618, 621-624, 627-632,
634, 642, 646, 648-649, 652, 656; **III**:
392-393
fighting in, **III**: 18
Germans in, **I**: 175-176, 267, 296,
347
impact of lend-lease on, **I**: 65
importance of Turkey to, **II**: 50
Italy as priority, **II**: 756-757
military-political commission in, **II**:
487-488
Roosevelt on, **II**: 260, 628; **III**: 466-
469
sea war in, **I**: 51
situation 1941, **I**: 184-186, 190-192
strategy in, **I**: 670; **II**: 212, 218,
295-296, 430, 432-435, 555-557; **III**:
109-110, 225-229, 453; American
view, **II**: 20; and Soviets, **II**: 278, 609;
III: 489-490; British view, **I**: 15-16;
II: 9-10, 11-15, 39, 246, 606-607, 657,
730-731; British vs. U.S. views, **II**:
554-555
threat to British supply lines, **I**: 81
vs. cross-channel invasion, **II**: 118,
498
vs. northern Europe campaign, **III**:
197-199
vs. Pacific strategy, **III**: 39
vs. southern France invasion, **III**:
185-186, 203-204, 212-223
Mediterranean theater, Eastern, **I**: 136,
191; **II**: 34; British vs. U.S. views on,
II: 182, 184, 502-517; campaign in,
1940, **I**: 86; Churchill on forces in,
1942, **I**: 316, 532; **II**: 152; discussed
at Teheran Conference, **II**: 611; in
1940-1941, **I**: 86, 144-145, 202; issue
of resources for, **II**: 581, 585; relations with Soviets, **II**: 6; **III**: 350-351;
Roosevelt on, **I**: 179
Mediterranean theater, Western: and invasion of Diego-Suarez, **I**: 404; situation worsens, 1940, **I**: 79
Mena House, Cairo, **II**: 601-602
Mendès-France, Pierre, **III**: 174, 180-
181
Menzies, Robert G., **I**: 155-156

Menzies, Sir Stewart Graham, **III**: 214,
220
Mers-el-Kébir, **I**: 634
Metaxas, Ioannis, **II**: 450, 548; **III**: 457
Metz, Germany, **III**: 408-409, 434
Mexico, **II**: 343-344, 346; **III**: 417
Mexico City Conference, **III**: 636
Michael, King of Roumania, **III**: 545,
625-626
Middle East, **I**: 159, 182, 190, 307; **II**:
102, 491; **III**: 380-381
British in, **I**: 78-79; **III**: 390, 511,
545; American view of, **II**: 480
Churchill on, **I**: 134, 208, 557
crisis in with French and Syrians,
II: 603
ethnic rivalries described, **II**: 541
French in, **II**: 333-334; **III**: 390
French influence in, **III**: 390
Iran, Hurley report on, **III**: 3-10
nationalism in, **II**: 599-600
New Zealand troops in, **II**: 61-62
oil in, **II**: 734, 744-745, 754; **III**:
13, 16-17, 187-188
Middle East theater, **I**: 165-166, 254,
285, 369, 453, 551, 611, 616; **II**: 34,
168; **III**: 518
aircraft in, **I**: 414, 426, 607
and Aegean plans, **II**: 502, 509
and cross-channel invasion, **I**: 458
and Greek mutiny, **III**: 96
and Australian and New Zealand
troops, **I**: 382, 384, 389
British in, **I**: 397-399, 438, 653;
troop losses of, **I**: 654; troops available for, **I**: 543; U.S. aid to, **I**: 237-
238; U.S. view of policy in, **I**: 225
British strategy in, **II**: 11-15
Churchill on, **I**: 181-182, 295, 298,
314
command in: as British, **I**: 430;
changes in, **I**: 216; debated, **I**: 554-
555; structure of, **II**: 263
discussed at Atlantic Conference, **I**:
226
Germans in, **I**: 196-197, 201
Iran and, **I**: 235
military situation, 1941, **I**: 175-176,
184-186, 210
Pacific war, effect on, **I**: 136
Rommel and, **I**: 516, 518-519, 659

Roosevelt on, **I**: 206, 485, 610
shipping needs of, **II**: 167
strategy for, **I**: 177, 302, 316-321,
450, 533; **II**: 11-15, 516
strategy in, German, **I**: 319-321
supply lines in, **I**: 350
use of Polish Corps in, **II**: 47
vs. planes to Soviet Union, **II**: 57-58
Midway Island, battle of, **I**: 465; **III**:
193; as turning point in war, **I**: 507-
508; Churchill on, **I**: 509-510, 513
Mihailović, Draza, **II**: 182, 184, 403-406,
425-426, 548, 554; **III**: 80, 86, 115-
116, 131-133, 190, 306, 308-309; and
Britain, **II**: 660-661; Stalin on, **III**: 70
Mikolajczyk, Stanislaw, **II**: 740-741, 762;
III: 461-463, 465, 475-476, 483, 523,
538-539, 550, 564, 571, 585, 587, 598-
599, 627, 629; and Lublin committee,
III: 363-364; and Polish boundary
dispute, **II**: 701-702, 708; and Roosevelt, **III**: 259; and Stalin, **III**: 208-210,
212, 258-262, 269-270, 272; and War-
saw Uprising, **III**: 281; at Moscow
Conference, 1944, **III**: 351-352, 357-
358, 360-361; Churchill on, **III**: 309;
negotiations with British and Soviets,
II: 716-723, 735-738; visit to Moscow,
III: 253-255, 258; visit to United
States, **II**: 637-638; **III**: 20-21, 69, 79-
80, 234-235
Mikoyan, A. I., **III**: 580
Milan, Italy, **II**: 380; **III**: 485; Allied air
attacks on, **II**: 428
Military, British (*see also* Chiefs of Staff;
Army, British; etc.), **I**: 574; **III**: 316;
and cross-channel invasion, **I**: 513,
515; **II**: 48; and invasion of southern
France, **III**: 163; and Italian campaign, **I**: 15-16; and joint Allied planning, **II**: 66, 70, 72; and U.S. in Iran,
I: 595; at Casablanca Conference, **II**:
117, 121; Churchill on, **I**: 254-255; **II**:
480; on Asia theater versus Middle
East, **I**: 177; on invasion of Madagascar, **I**: 433; on war strategy, **II**: 182;
plans for postwar Germany, **III**: 316;
political power of, **II**: 479-481
Military, Soviet: and joint Allied planning, **II**: 66, 72, 74
Military, United States, **II**: 40

and British, **I**: 268, 284; **II**: 121,
479
and British in Iran, **I**: 595
and Burma operations, **II**: 177
and cross-channel invasion, **I**: 436,
514; **II**: 502, 555; **III**: 101, 127;
Churchill on, **II**: 20
and Dill, **I**: 338
and German occupation zones, **II**:
745
and invasion of Norway, **I**: 608-611
and Italian campaign, **II**: 354; **III**:
301-302
and joint Allied planning, **II**: 66,
70, 72
and North African invasion, **I**: 292,
576-577
and Pacific theater, **I**: 275, 670; **II**:
34; and British role in, **III**: 318
and war strategy, early 1943, **II**: 38
at Casablanca Conference, **II**: 117
Churchill's concern for, **III**: 314-
315
forces to Britain, **II**: 247
in Europe, postwar withdrawal of,
III: 389, 391-392, 394
in SHAEF, **II**: 712
on British wartime needs, **II**: 177
on invasion of southern France, **III**:
221-223
on Italy and Eastern Mediterranean, **II**: 182, 184
on mobility as military strategy, **II**:
165
outnumber British forces overseas,
1943, **II**: 609
political power of, **II**: 479-481
rivalry in Pacific, **III**: 272
Roosevelt on leadership of, **II**: 480
strength of in Europe, **III**: 198
to Cairo Conference, **II**: 583
Military-Political Commission, Italy, **II**:
467-469, 487-488
Millspaugh, Arthur C., **III**: 140-141
Mines, magnetic, development of, **I**: 29
Miquelon (French), **I**: 324, 346
Mission to Moscow, 1943 movie, **II**: 345
Molotov, Vyacheslav, **I**: 544, 560, 562;
II: 181, 195, 273, 286, 440, 467, 479,
503-504, 561, 562, 568, 570, 572, 585,
608; **III**: 251, 262, 398, 573, 576, 615;

Molotov, Vyacheslav (*cont.*)
  and air bases in Soviet Union, **III**:
  295; and Balkans, **III**: 185; and Bulgarians, **II**: 724, 730; and Cairo Conference, **II**: 576, 584, 597-598, 600;
  and convoy dispute, **II**: 535-536; and
  Italy, **II**: 487-488, 490, 507, 539-540;
  and Katyn Forest massacre, **II**: 393;
  and Moscow Foreign Ministers' Conference, **II**: 464, 484-485; and Poland,
  II: 707, 718-719, 763-764; **III**: 69, 71,
  259, 273, 364, 538-539, 561-562, 565,
  568-569, 571, 585-590, 596, 598-600,
  602; and pre-Yalta talks, **III**: 502,
  505; and recognition of French committee, **III**: 367; and Roumania, **III**:
  137; and San Francisco Conference,
  III: 586, 588-591, 597, 632; and second front issue, **I**: 397, 490-491, 494-
  500; and Security Council veto, **III**:
  335; and Truman, **III**: 632; at Moscow Conference, 1942, **I**: 564-568,
  570-571; at Moscow Conference,
  1944, **III**: 345, 348-349, 351; at Yalta
  Conference, **III**: 526, 528, 591;
  Churchill on, **III**: 378; on Aegean
  policy, **II**: 558; on Italian ships to Soviets, **II**: 624-625, 655; on North African invasion, **I**: 561; on Soviet boundary issues, **I**: 465-466, 470; on
  Turkey, **II**: 581; on Yalta agreements,
  III: 549-550; Roosevelt on, **I**: 10-11,
  502-504, 506-507
Monarchy:
    British support for, **III**: 274-275,
    437
    Churchill vs. Roosevelt views on, **II**:
    365-368
      Egyptian, **III**: 110-111
    in Greece, **II**: 548; **III**: 110, 480;
    British support for, **II**: 450, 618-619;
    III: 95-97; debate over, **III**: 450-461
    in Italy, **II**: 451, 711-712; Allied de-
    bate on, **II**: 455, 462, 467, 679-681;
    and Eisenhower, **II**: 480-481; British
    support for, **II**: 587; **III**: 387;
    Churchill on, **II**: 593, 697, 702; **III**:
    41
      in Yugoslavia, **II**: 548; **III**: 510;
    British support of, **II**: 660-661
Monnet, Jean, **II**: 209-210, 271, 333,

    335; **III**: 180-181
Monroe Doctrine, **II**: 529; **III**: 417
Montanari, Franco, **II**: 423-424, 428
Montcalm, General L., at Quebec
  (1759), **II**: 323
Monteiro, Armindo, **II**: 262-263
Montevideo, Uruguay, naval battle at, **I**:
  28-32
Montgomery, Sir Bernard, **II**: 98, 122,
  189-190, 207, 482, 621, 623, 624, 626-
  629, 632, 653; **III**: 539, 552, 612
    and Churchill, **II**: 645
    and cross-channel invasion, **III**:
  183, 185, 228
    and Eisenhower, **III**: 497-498
    at El Alamein, **I**: 657. *See also* North
  African campaign
    commander of assault force, Nor-
  mandy, **III**: 87
    in European theater, **III**: 498-499,
  522, 601, 602, 608; at Ardennes battle, **III**: 494-495; in Normandy, **III**:
  262-263
    in Middle East, **I**: 555
    in North Africa, **II**: 23
    in Tripoli, **II**: 152
    in Tunisia, **II**: 172
    in western desert, **I**: 584-585, 592,
  646
    on invasion of southern France, **II**:
  756-757; **III**: 227
    on security for OVERLORD, **III**:
  92
    Roosevelt wants for CBI command,
  II: 276
    war strategy of, Europe, **III**: 340
Montreux Convention, **III**: 351, 363,
  365-366, 368, 379, 380, 508
Moore-McCormack Lines, **I**: 34-35
Moran, Lord (Sir Charles Wilson), **II**:
  156, 387, 621, 621; **III**: 138-139, 339,
  362
Morgan, Frederick, **II**: 570
Morgenthau, Henry, Jr., **I**: 38, 41, 49,
  88, 101, 119, 123, 124, 138, 153, 165,
  177; **II**: 135, 620, 743; **III**: 35-36; and
  aid-to-Britain program, **I**: 78-79; and
  Britain, postwar, **III**: 99-100; and
  British dollar balances, **III**: 65-66; and
  French currency question, **III**: 174,
  196, 210; on Churchill and India in-

dependence, **I**: 388; visit to Europe, **III**: 248

Morgenthau Plan for Germany, **III**: 248, 289, 317-318, 320, 351, 528

Mormons, **II**: 648

Morocco, **I**: 147, 156, 176, 179, 180, 185, 253, 297, 350, 464-465, 665-666; **II**: 30, 68, 74, 76; **III**: 228; Allied troops in, **I**: 302; and Darlan deal, **II**: 27-28; and North African invasion, **I**: 576-578, 583, 667, 669; **II**: 3, 9; Churchill on prospects in, 1942, **I**: 295; post-TORCH situation, **II**: 12; Roosevelt on, **I**: 533

Moscow, **I**: 226; **II**: 65-66, 72, 102, 463-464 (*see also* Moscow Conference); joint mission to suggested, **II**: 10; visit of Mikolajczyk to, **III**: 253-255

Moscow Commission on Poland, **III**: 551, 561-562, 564-565, 567-569, 576, 587, 589, 594-597, 599, 602, 628, 634

Moscow Conference, 1942, **I**: 560, 561-562, 564-572; **II**: 42-43, 278-279

Moscow Conference (TOLSTOY), 1944, **III**: 331, 362, 398, 516, 547; agreement on Poland, **III**: 523, 526; analysis of, **III**: 348-351; and Eastern Europe, **III**: 370-371; and Italian ships to Soviets, **III**: 17-18; Churchill and Stalin at, **III**: 464; discussion of Germany at, **III**: 528; major power cooperation and, **III**: 6; Roosevelt-Churchill messages on, **III**: 339, 341-345, 347; spheres of influence agreement, **III**: 545-547

Moscow Declaration, **III**: 330

Moscow Foreign Ministers' Conference, **II**: 269, 516, 518, 522-523, 536, 543, 545, 550, 557; **III**: 502; and Aegean policy, **II**: 558; and atrocities statement, **II**: 547; and Italian ships to Soviets, **II**: 624-625, 654-655, 665, 669; and Italy, **II**: 539; and Polish boundary question, **II**: 706-707; and postwar economic issues, **II**: 748-749; Churchill on, **II**: 565, 577; decision on international organization, **II**: 611; Hull report on, **II**: 606; leaks on site of, **II**: 490; planning for, **II**: 448, 463-464, 484-485; Roosevelt on, **II**: 563-564; Stalin on, **II**: 489; Turkey discussed,

II: 581; war criminals discussed at, **III**: 329

Moselle River, Germany, **III**: 263

Moslem League, India, **I**: 375-377, 396, 402

Mossedegh, Mohammed, **III**: 512

Mosul, Iraq, **I**: 178, 180, 185

Mountbatten, Lord Louis, **I**: 250, 491, 494, 500, 504, 520, 603; **II**: 148-149, 202, 248, 481-482, 505, 542, 594; **III**: 185-186, 363, 430; and Burma campaign, **III**: 19-20, 54-55, 435; and Chinese, **III**: 422-423, 426, 427-428; and famine in India, **III**: 116-117; and Indo-China, **III**: 626-627; and Japanese offensive in India, **III**: 50; and North African invasion, **I**: 590; and Pacific strategy, **III**: 37-38; and Roosevelt on landing craft, **I**: 489; and Stilwell-Chiang hostility, **II**: 583-584; and supplies to China, **II**: 690; attacked in U.S. press, **II**: 482; Churchill on, **I**: 437-439; **II**: 433; daring schemes of, **I**: 645; in Southeast Asia, **II**: 755-756, 757, 759; **III**: 572-573, 582-583; on Dutch East Indies operation, **II**: 751; on Japanese threat to India, **III**: 50-52, 56; Roosevelt on, **III**: 447; supreme commander, South East Asia, **II**: 430

Mozambique, **II**: 239

Msus, Libya, **I**: 333

Mundt, Karl, **III**: 65-66

Munitions, **I**: 108; American to Britain, **I**: 154; Anglo-American cooperation on, **I**: 539; Churchill requests from U.S., **I**: 138; U.S. increases production of, **I**: 315

Munitions Assignment Board, **I**: 329, 484, 489, 538

Murmansk, U.S.S.R., **I**: 253, 503-504, 637; **II**: 157, 528; Germans threaten, **I**: 528

Murphy, Robert, **I**: 146; **II**: 215, 579, 622-623; and de Gaulle, **II**: 235; and FCNL, **II**: 310-311, 379, 440; and French in North Africa, **II**: 257-258, 335, 340, 465; in North Africa, **I**: 634; **II**: 3, 71, 74, 83-85, 87, 90, 98, 136-137, 228-229, 231, 237, 239, 244, 268; in Sicily administration, **II**: 251;

Murphy, Robert (*cont.*)
  negotiations with Vichy, I: 655; on
  French, II: 254, 256; on Italian political situation, II: 587, 591
Murphy-Weygand agreement, I: 146
Muselier, Émile, I: 326
Muslims, in North Africa, II: 142-143
Mussolini, Benito, I: 37, 65, 67, 159; II:
  51, 307-308, 331, 381, 446, 459, 553,
  586, 663; and Grandi, II: 486; and
  Spanish, I: 86; Churchill on, I: 96,
  103, 309; fall of, II: 347-350, 352,
  360, 362, 369, 427, 556; German res-
  cue of, 1943, II: 455; joins Hitler, I:
  42, 43; Roosevelt on to Italian people,
  II: 300-301; Stalin on, II: 386
Mutual aid agreement, II: 36. *See also*
  Lend-Lease
Myitkyina, Burma, II: 756

Nahas Pasha, III: 110-111, 179
Nalchik, U.S.S.R., I: 672
Naples, Italy, II: 12-13, 184, 443-444,
  452; III: 347, 363, 515; in Allied mili-
  tary planning, II: 435-436
Napoleon I, II: 54; III: 183
Natal, South Africa, I: 209
National Geographic Society, II: 640
National Maritime Board, Britain, I: 107
Nationalism, II: 222; Arab, III: 390; in
  Africa, III: 325; in Austro-Hungarian
  Empire, III: 363; in Balkans, III: 274
Navicerts, I: 33
Navy, Allied, II: 168; in cross-channel
  invasion, III: 186; in Normandy inva-
  sion, III: 236-237; weakness in Pacific,
  1942, I: 304
Navy, British, I: 40-41, 47-48, 64, 66-69,
  105, 254, 267; II: 46-47, 110, 675,
  755; III: 125, 239; and cross-channel
  invasion, III: 91; and Italian fleet, III:
  26; and sinking of *Scharnhorst*, II: 636-
  637; and Soviet Union, II: 534-537;
  Churchill on, II: 158; III: 363; cooperation with Americans, I: 24; Cunningham as First Sea Lord, II: 317; in
  Atlantic, I: 92; in Indian Ocean, II:
  52-53, 112, 116; in Mediterranean, I:
  155-156, 175, 184, 316; II: 529; in
  1941, I: 89, 95; in Pacific, I: 411-412;
  II: 442-443, 702; III: 38-40, 270, 318;

losses in medical, III: 24; oil needs of,
  II: 754; on cross-channel invasion, I:
  568; plans for, 1943, II: 94; Roosevelt
  on defeat of, I: 58-60; scuttle gold-
  carrying ship, I: 481-482; ships, to Soviets, II: 669-671; Stalin on, I: 544;
  II: 287; treatment of by Soviets, II:
  474, 477-479; U.S. reinforcements
  for, I: 419
Navy, Dutch, in Pacific, I: 412
Navy, French, I: 47-49, 52, 56, 97, 98,
  104, 162-164, 180
  and Allies, III: 86, 88
  and German armistice, I: 54
  and Germans, I: 155, 297
  and Vichy French, I: 75-79, 295,
  354
  Churchill on, I: 92, 285
  de Gaulle control of, III: 108-109
  disposition of fleet, I: 81, 146, 463-
  464, 517, 521-522, 524-525, 674; II:
  3, 7, 84-85, 147-148
  in Dakar, II: 56
  in North Africa, I: 334; II: 28;
  Churchill on, I: 634
  surrender to Germans, I: 44
Navy, German, III: 112; and convoys to
  Soviet Union, I: 527-528, 530, 537,
  609; as threat to Britain, I: 90; in
  Norway, II: 49; Stalin on, II: 476
Navy, Greek, mutiny of, III: 95-97, 113,
  114
Navy, Italian, I: 90, 104, 155-156; II:
  475, 518-519, 556; Allied control of,
  II: 587; and Germans, II: 484; and
  invasion of Sicily, II: 184; and surrender of Italy, II: 349, 361, 364, 524,
  551-553; and the monarchy, II: 697;
  at Taranto, I: 83-85; disposition of,
  II: 500, 538; III: 32-34, 333, 437-438,
  619; French claims on, III: 86-88;
  Hitler on, I: 435, 467; in Mediterranean, I: 317; ships of to Soviet, II:
  624-625, 654-656, 664-666, 669-671,
  694-695, 697-700, 702, 747-748; III:
  14-19, 23-28, 56-57; surrenders to Allies, II: 455; use of by Allies, II: 443-
  444, 725-726; weakness of, I: 295
Navy, Japanese, I: 90, 381
  and Coral Sea battle, I: 483
  at Guadalcanal, II: 6

at Singapore, II: 757, 759; III: 38-40
  defeat at Leyte Gulf, III: 376
  in Indian Ocean, I: 441
  in Pacific, I: 135; III: 17-18; strategy of, I: 412; superiority of, I: 287, 289, 304
    losses in New Guinea, II: 154
    Pacific strategy, I: 465, 507-508
    Roosevelt on, I: 466
    ships of for postwar division, III: 25
Navy, Norwegian, III: 125
Navy, Polish: in United Nations forces, II: 741
Navy, Soviet, I: 295, 566; II: 57; and Italian ships, III: 14-16; ship losses in war, II: 765
Navy, United States, I: 46, 199-200, 202, 239, 364, 365; II: 675; III: 125, 276, 445, 515
  aid to Britain in Atlantic, I: 106
  and anti-submarine campaign, II: 228; III: 12-13, 374, 386, 489; Roosevelt on, I: 421-422
  and Azores, II: 525, 564, 675, 677
  and British, I: 24, 190; Churchill on, I: 454
  and Burma, II: 118
  and convoys, 1943, II: 12
  and cross-channel invasion, I: 542
  and German submarines, I: 26, 229-230, 348
  and Italian fleet, III: 26
  and Japanese, 1942, I: 442
  and MacArthur, I: 477; III: 272
  and North African invasion, I: 582, 591, 641
  and Philippine retreat, I: 335
  anti-submarine campaign of, III: 112
  as escorts for convoys, I: 218
  at Casablanca Conference, II: 117
  at Pearl Harbor, I: 39
  Churchill on, I: 300-302, 308
  command changes in, I: 397
  commitments, 1943, I: 615
  forces in Mediterranean, II: 529
  growing strength of, I: 382
  in ANZAC area, I: 382, 390
  in Atlantic, I: 185, 193-194
  in Pacific, I: 299-300, 381; II: 759;

III: 193; and British Navy, I: 411-412; Churchill view, I: 418, 453; command struggle in, I: 409; communications in, I: 384; Seventh, III: 376; strategy in vs. Indian Ocean, I: 442-443; strength of, I: 332; III: 38-40; superiority in, I: 322; view of British in, II: 702; in 1940, I: 91, 99, 102; in 1941, I: 89, 95; in 1942, I: 490
  in postwar Europe, I: 230
  losses at Guadalcanal, I: 657; II: 6
  on ship deployment, I: 505
  on unity of commands, I: 292
  Poles in, II: 198
  Stalin on, II: 287
  use of in battles, 1941, I: 222
Navy, Yugoslav, III: 275
Nazi-Soviet non-aggression pact (1939), I: 144, 209, 393; III: 349
Nazis, I: 95, 102; II: 102; III: 209; and youth of Europe, I: 94; Churchill on, I: 109; III: 349; organizations, III: 635; Roosevelt on, III: 134; Spanish openly supported, II: 725
Nazism, I: 14; Churchill on, II: 370; Roosevelt on, III: 317
Negroes, in battle, III: 500
Nehring, Walther, II: 98-99
Nehru, Jawarharlal, I: 501-502, 558
Nelson, Donald, I: 506, 638; III: 579-580, 607, 619
Netherlands, I: 90, 123, 147, 155, 206, 276, 280; II: 63, 102; III: 11, 47, 147, 354; Allied occupation of, III: 211; and ABDA command, I: 9, 339-344; and Indo-China, I: 225; and Pacific war, I: 398-399, 413; and unity of command, I: 312; atrocities in, II: 520; British troops to, III: 348; Churchill on strategy toward, I: 299, 302; German invasion of, I: 36, 39; imperialism of, I: 401; III: 6; in British occupation zone, II: 745; operations in, III: 340, 348 (see also Arnhem); postwar, III: 569; postwar, as American sphere, II: 708; relief for, III: 540, 621-623; warning to Japanese, I: 279
Netherlands East Indies, I: 91, 98, 105, 275, 279-280, 299, 339, 364-365, 370; II: 757; and involvement in military

Netherlands East Indies (*cont.*)
decisions, **I**: 330-332, 335-337; and
Pacific Council, **I**: 430; Japanese
threaten, **I**: 135; Roosevelt on British
loss of, **I**: 421
Netherlands West Indies, and oil supplies, **II**: 79-80, 83, 115
Neutral nations, **III**: 107, 114, 245; and
freezing of funds by U.S., **I**: 209;
Churchill on, **II**: 667; in Churchill's
postwar world, **II**: 224-225; U.S. handling of criticized, **III**: 78
Neutrality, issue of, **I**: 32-35
Neutrality Act of 1939, **I**: 32, 92, 198,
199, 236, 237, 264; amendments to, **I**:
245-246, 268-269
Neutrality laws, **I**: 87; Roosevelt on, **I**:
196
New Caledonia, **I**: 363, 385, 387, 432
New Deal: Churchill to Roosevelt on, **I**:
23; Willkie criticism of, **I**: 80
New Delhi, India, **II**: 696-697
New Guinea, **I**: 483, 657-659; **II**: 24,
205; battle in, 1942, **I**: 415-416; **II**:
41, 154; in S.W. Pacific command
area, **I**: 409
New Orleans, **I**: 87
New Republic, **I**: 15
New York City, New York, **I**: 121-122;
III: 367-369, 371
New York State, **II**: 451
New York Times, **I**: 218; **III**: 517
New Zealand, **I**: 91, 174-175, 206, 364-
365, 487, 653; **II**: 102, 443
and ABDA command issue, **I**: 349
and involvement in military deci-
sions, **I**: 330-332, 335-337
and Pacific Council, **I**: 430
defense of, **I**: 384-388, 390-392
Japanese threat to, **I**: 136
Pacific theater responsibilities, **I**:
398-399
relations with Britain, **I**: 425
Roosevelt on, **I**: 363
troops: deployment of, **II**: 22, 32-
37, 47, 207; in Middle East, **I**; 413;
II: 61-62
U.S. troops to, **I**: 382, 389
Newfoundland, **I**: 59-60, 65, 166, 173,
200, 218; and base leases, **I**: 140-141
Niagara Falls, New York, **II**: 387

Nicobar Islands, Indian Ocean, **III**: 39
Nicolson, Harold, **III**: 77
Nikopol, U.S.S.R., **III**: 49
Nimitz, Chester A., **III**: 272; in Pacific,
III: 193, 243; receives Pacific Ocean
Command, **I**: 411
NKVD, **III**: 553-558
Nogués, Auguste, **I**: 225; **II**: 27-28, 91,
229
Noon, Sir Firozkhan, **I**: 376
Norman, Montague, **I**: 540
Normandy, France: Churchill visit to,
III: 183, 185-186; de Gaulle to, **III**:
183, 185-186
Normandy invasion (NEPTUNE), **II**:
663; Allied strength in, **III**: 263; and
neutral nations, **III**: 245; Churchill
on, **III**: 282; German submarine activity in, **III**: 236-237; political significance of, **III**: 173; reasons for success
of, **III**: 165; Roosevelt to Churhcill
on, **III**: 194; scope described, **III**:
164-165; Stalin on, **III**: 182-183, 200
North Africa, **I**: 46, 159, 177, 206, 252,
317, 612; **II**: 66, 78, 101, 600; Allied
negotiations with Vichy over, **I**: 333-
335; Allied troops in, 1942, **I**: 320;
and Allied shipping crisis, **II**: 170;
British strategy in, **I**: 175; Churchill
on, **I**: 292, 296, 297, 302, 673; **II**:
288; command structure in, **II**: 136-
138, 144-145; Darlan deal in, **II**: 366,
697; Darlan in, **II**: 3-9, 40; de Gaulle
and Allies in, **II**: 268; French Army
in, **II**: 439; French bases in, 1940, **I**:
77-79; German strategy in, **II**: 267;
Germans threaten, **I**: 201; government in, postwar, **II**: 766; Harriman
in, **I**: 208; Italian fleet escapes to,
1943, **II**: 455; political situation in, **II**:
75-77, 98-100; problems of occupation
of, **II**: 203, 208; refugee camps in, **II**:
293, 321; relief issues in, **II**: 315-316;
Roosevelt on economic aid to, 1942, **I**:
426-427; Roosevelt on strategy for, **I**:
179; Stalin on, **II**: 140, 286; supply
convoy to (TIGER), **I**: 198; U.S. commitments in, 1943, **II**: 46; Vichy and,
I: 186-187, 346-347
North African campaign, **I**: 170; **II**:
110, 152; Allied successes in, **II**: 59;

and French response to, **I**: 655-657,
659-662; and Petain, **I**: 128, 132-133;
and policy toward Spain, **II**: 725; and
Syrian invasion, **I**: 204; and U.S. election, **II**: 41-42; and U.S. Navy resources, **I**: 615; and Vichy role, **I**:
426; British in, **I**: 112, 126-127, 144-
145, 169; Churchill on, **I**: 294-298; **II**:
38; Churchill to Stalin on, **I**: 531-532,
537-538; delays in, **II**: 151-154; fall of
Tobruk, **I**: 514; German operations,
I: 132, 170-171, 493-494; Leahy on,
II: 138; operation CRUSADER described, **I**: 268-274; operation
LIGHTFOOT, **I**: 298-299, 309; operation PUGILIST, **II**: 172-174; planes
needed in, **II**: 58; planning of, disputes on, **I**: 576-592; Rommel in, **I**:
152, 191; Roosevelt favors, **I**: 469;
Roosevelt to Churchill on, **I**: 669-670;
shipping problems and, **II**: 153; status, mid-1941, **I**: 196; supplies in, **I**:
241, 518-519; vs. cross-channel campaign, **I**: 436
North African invasion, **I**: 317, 319,
333-335, 350, 397, 564-566, 586; **II**:
116, 168, 170; **III**: 503; air forces
needed for, **I**: 596-597; Allied forces
in, **I**: 623, 628; Americans on, **I**: 551-
552; and Second Washington Conference, **I**: 513-515; as aid to Soviets, **I**:
605-606, 611-612; as American operation, **I**: 581, 641, 645-646; **II**: 303;
British support, **I**: 493-494, 520-521;
British role in, **I**: 662-663; Churchill
on, **I**: 529, 535, 570-572, 575-576,
598; **II**: 39; **III**: 574; Churchill on as
end-of-beginning, **I**: 670; Churchill to
Stalin on, **I**: 621-623, 628-629; code-
names for, **I**: 519; commanded by Eisenhower, **I**: 554-556; discussed, **I**:
313-314, 541-543, 608-609; drain on
British Navy, **II**: 52-53; effect on shipping, **II**: 123, 168; German troop
movements after, **II**: 49; Marshall on,
I: 543, **II**: 479-480; oil supplies used
in, **II**: 78-79; operation begins, November 1942, **I**: 667; political aspects
of, **I**: 634-635; postponed, **I**: 379-380,
389, 391, 393; propaganda campaign
in, **I**: 626-627, 640-641, 662-663; ram-

ifications of, **II**: 41; requirements exceed estimates, **II**: 38; Roosevelt on, **I**:
11, 533, 536, 555-556, 610, 612; shipping losses in, **II**: 44; Stalin on, **I**:
561-562, 672-673; vs. other military
operations, **I**: 602-604
North African theater:
Churchill on air assets in, **I**: 317
command changes in, **II**: 639
Eisenhower's administration in, **II**:
83-85, 87, 89
issue of oil to, **II**: 82
post-TORCH, **II**: 46
supply convoy to, **I**: 185
Tripoli, planned assault on, **I**: 317,
319; discussed at London Conference,
I: 541-543
North Atlantic, **I**: 470 (*see also* Atlantic
Ocean); British losses in, **I**: 149-150;
convoy problems in, **I**: 138; German
subs withdraw from, **II**: 728-729
North East Africa, **I**: 300
North Pacific Islands: U.S. air forces in,
1942, **I**: 392
North Sea, **I**: 16; **II**: 746, 765; **III**: 602
North West Africa, command stucture
in, **II**: 263
Northern Ireland, **I**: 99, 106, 107, 206,
253-254; **II**: 186-187; British forces
in, **I**: 651; conscription issue in, **II**:
191-192; U.S. troops to, **I**: 296, 314,
316-317, 348, 380, 382, 389, 397, 399,
425
Norway, **I**: 34-35, 36, 56, 90, 147, 155,
192, 206, 253, 292; **II**: 15, 157, 161-
162, 218, 558, 636; **III**: 47, 211, 233,
236, 388; atrocities in, **II**: 520;
Churchill on, **I**: 624, 629; Churchill
on landing in, 1943, **I**: 302; German
submarines in, **III**: 264, 312, 345;
Germans in, **I**: 471, 498, 595, 609,
620-622; **II**: 49; in British occupation
zone, **II**: 745; invasion of, proposed,
I: 493-494, 513-514, 521-522, 529,
531, 537, 541-543, 564, 571, 601, 602-
604, 605, 608-611; **II**: 430, 480; sabotage of electric plants, **I**: 645; relief
for, **II**: 86-87, 105-106
Nova Scotia, **I**: 166, 173; Churchill visit
to, **II**: 382
Novorossisk, U.S.S.R., **II**: 14

Nuremberg, Germany, bombing of, **I**: 597
Nye, Lt. General, **I**: 500

O'Malley, Sir Owen, **II**: 716; report on Katyn Forest massacre, **II**: 390-400
Observer (London), **III**: 54
Occupied territories: Churchill on administration of, **II**: 479; problems of administration of, **II**: 270
Oder River, as Polish-Soviet border, **II**: 685, 738; **III**: 143, 524
Ogden, C. K., **III**: 104
Oglethorpe, Georgia, **II**: 431-432
Oil, **I**: 179, 180, 182; **II**: 17
    and invasion of Syria, **I**: 204
    Anglo-American discussions on, **II**: 733-734, 744-745, 749, 754-755
    Baku fields, **I**: 318-319, 671, 673
    Caspian fields, **I**: 321
    conference in Washington on, 1944, **II**: 744-745; **III**: 16-17, 169, 187-188, 195-196, 206
        in Black Sea, **I**: 136
        in Dutch East Indies, **I**: 135
        in Iran, **I**: 319, 321, 579; **III**: 139-141, 511-513
        Middle Eastern, **I**: 453; **III**: 13
        problems of Allied supplies, **I**: 449, 491; **II**: 78-80, 82-83, 106-107, 115
        problems for Germany, **I**: 27
        Roumanian fields, **II**: 131; bombed by Allies, **II**: 247, 280; Churchill proposes attack on, **I**: 315; vulnerable from Turkey, **II**: 50
        to Spain, Churchill on, **I**: 313
        U.S. embargo of to Spain, **II**: 725-726, 728, 739, 751; **III**: 106
Okinawa, battle of, **III**: 601
OMAHA beach, D-Day landing area, **III**: 165, 185
Oporto, Portugal, **II**: 299, 326
Oppeln, Poland/Germany, **II**: 738
Oppenheim, Germany, **III**: 601
Oran, Algeria, **I**: 79; **II**: 570, 572, 575-576, 578, 583-585, 592, 596, 598, 608; Allied landing in, 1942, **I**: 667; and North African invasion, **I**: 577-588, 665-666
Orkney Islands, **I**: 27, 34; **II**: 245
Orlemanski, Stanislaw, **II**: 762, 764

Osubka-Morawski, E. B., **III**: 269
Ottoman Empire, **III**: 390
Ottowa, Canada, **I**: 121-122; **II**: 430
Ottawa Agreements, **III**: 535
Outer Mongolia, **III**: 527

Pacific (Defense) Council, **I**: 342, 360-361, 398, 430-431, 478; proposed by Australia, **I**: 330-331
Pacific Ocean, **III**: 419; control of, 1941, **I**: 89, 95
Pacific Regional Council, **II**: 223-224
Pacific theater, **I**: 73, 91, 95, 229, 231, 407; **II**: 20, 30, 35-36, 225, 443, 551; **III**: 190, 193, 248, 345, 366, 601
    air assets needed in, **I**: 597; **II**: 730-731
    and Australian defense, **II**: 22-26, 33
    and European rehabilitation, **II**: 750
    and landing craft, **III**: 82, 88-89
    and Quebec Conference, 1944, **III**: 315, 318
    and submarine warfare, **II**: 288; **III**: 374, 382, 384, 386
    at Casablanca Conference, **II**: 117
    British role in, **II**: 52-53, 60-61, 332, 442-443; **III**: 265, 270, 318
    Churchill on, **I**: 74, 315, 381, 453, 513, 557; **II**: 332; **III**: 195, 435
    command questions in, **I**: 397-399, 409, 411-414, 430; **II**: 248-249, 318-319, 608, 702; **III**: 272
    decisions on at Quebec, 1943, **II**: 430
    destroyer losses in late 1942, **II**: 21
    Japanese in, 1941, **I**: 274-276, 286-289
    lack of U.S. ports and ships in, **I**: 616
    Leyte Gulf battle, **III**: 376
    naval movements in, **III**: 17-18
    oil supplies in, **II**: 82
    Portuguese promise action in, **II**: 507
    relative naval strengths, **I**: 135, 287, 289
    Roosevelt on, **I**: 250, 610; **III**: 447-449
    shipping problems in, **II**: 44, 153
    situation in, early 1945, **III**: 524

Soviet participation in, **III**: 353, 524, 527

strategy in, **II**: 9; Allies discuss, **II**: 757, 759; **III**: 272; American vs. British views, **I**: 608; **III**: 37-40; Churchill on, **I**: 265, 292, 298-301, 304-309; Japanese, **I**: 507-508; Roosevelt on, **I**: 533; **II**: 755-756

U.S. commitments to, **I**: 102, 174, 266, 389, 581, 611: **II**: 38

vs. cross-channel invasion, **II**: 712-713

vs. Mediterranean theater: Churchill on, **I**: 319-323

Pacific War Council, **I**: 364-365, 367, 409, 412-413, 457, 539-540, 576; **II**: 112, 319; and Burma, **II**: 116

Packard Company, **II**: 103

Page, Sir Earle, **I**: 430

Paget, Sir Bernard, **II**: 481-482, 622-623, 629, 631, 634-635; **III**: 113

Pakistan, **I**: 376, 388, 395

Palestine, **I**: 176, 235, 318, 361, 532, 557; **II**: 24; **III**: 286, 298, 536; consequences of Soviet defeat, **I**: 307; German threats to, 1942, **I**: 319; Jewish refugees to, 1943, **II**: 316; New Zealand troops in, **I**: 382

Palestine Regiment, **III**: 286

Palewski, Gaston, **II**: 215, 236, 691

Palliser, A.F.E., **I**: 361; and ABDA command controversies, **I**: 339, 341, 344

Pan American Airways, **II**: 507, 566

Panama Canal, **I**: 93

Panama Conference (1939), **I**: 25

Pantelleria (Italian), **II**: 242; **III**: 328

Papandreou, Georgios, **III**: 110-111, 135, 450, 459, 466-467, 473-474

Paris, France: liberation of, **III**: 298

Paris Peace Conference, World War I, **II**: 457; and Polish-Soviet boundary decisions, **II**: 684

Park, Sir Keith, **II**: 264; **III**: 518

Parsons, Geoffrey, **II**: 235-236

Partisans, in Yugoslavia, **II**: 403-406, 548; **III**: 115-116; Allied support for, **III**: 80

Pas de Calais, **I**: 576; **II**: 51, 560; **III**: 164

Patch, Alexander, **III**: 308

Patterson, Robert, **III**: 278

Patton, George, **II**: 75-76; **III**: 170, 289,

340, 408, 498, 601; and Battle of the Bulge, **III**: 487; in France, **III**: 263; in North African invasion, **I**: 670-671; in Tunisia, **II**: 172; on marching toward Moscow, **II**: 480

Paul, Prince of Yugoslavia, **I**: 152

Paulus, Frederich, **II**: 138, 141

Peace conference, postwar, **III**: 482, 527-528; and Balkans, **III**: 153; and boundary disputes, **III**: 359, 687; and currency issues, **III**: 174; boundary disputes to be settled at, **II**: 687; Churchill on, **II**: 129-130; **III**: 73, 440, 442; Roosevelt on, **II**: 192; **III**: 440, 442, 503

Peace treaties, rumors on, **I**: 540

Pearl Harbor attack, **I**: 8, 292, 293, 305, 332, 348, 453, 615; **III**: 201, 243, 447, 631; Churchill on, **I**: 309; Churchill-Roosevelt response to, **I**: 280-282; commemorated, **II**: 63-64

Peenemunde, Baltic Sea Island, **II**: 559-560, 589-590

Pelagian Islands, **II**: 242

Penicillin, **III**: 536

Perón, Juan Domingo, **II**: 681 **III**: 224, 233, 346, 396

Perowne, J.T.V., **III**: 415

Pershing, John J., **I**: 128

Persian Gulf, **I**: 235, 453, 533; **III**: 4, 141; and supply route to Soviet Union, **I**: 531, 537, 609, 612, 616, 623, 629, 630; Churchill on defense of, **I**: 320-321; in Middle East theater, 1942, **I**: 399

Persian Gulf Service Command, **I**: 595

Persian Railway, **III**: 141

Peru, **II**: 223-224

Pétain, Henri, **I**: 44, 51, 146, 148, 186, 460-461, 667; **II**: 3; **III**: 128; and British, **I**: 158-159; and Darlan deal, **II**: 27; and *Dunkerque* issue, **I**: 162, 164, 167; and French fleet, **I**: 75, 82-85, 464-465; and French in North Africa, **I**: 333-335; and Germans, **I**: 184-185; and Madagascar, **I**: 481; and North Africa, **I**: 270; and North African invasion, **I**: 656-657, 659; Churchill and, **I**: 127-128, 132-133; on German threats, **I**: 287; Roosevelt and, **I**: 250, 353-354; struggle with Laval, **I**: 76-79

Peter II, King of Yugoslavia, **I**: 152; **II**:
  660-661; **III**: 80, 115-116, 131-133,
  306, 510
Petherick, Maurice, **III**: 538
Petroleum Conference (1944), **III**: 195-
  196, 206. *See also* Oil
Petroleum Reserves Corporation (U.S.),
  II: 733
Petrolium policy, postwar, **I**: 17
Peyrouton, Marcel, **II**: 229, 625-626,
  635, 641, 691-692
Philip, André, **II**: 209-210, 215, 271
Philippine Sea, battle of, **III**: 193
Philippines, **I**: 267, 286, 325; **III**: 38,
  376, 524; Allied strategy toward, **III**:
  193; Battle of Bataan, **I**: 608; Church-
  ill on strategy, **I**: 301, 308, 321; in
  S.W. Pacific command area, **I**: 411;
  Japanese in, **III**: 433; MacArthur and,
  I: 408-409; **II**: 480; **III**: 272; U.S. pol-
  icy toward, **I**: 400
Phillips, Sir Frederick, **I**: 101, 120, 123;
  III: 144
Phillips, Sir Tom, **I**: 411
Pierlot, Hubert, **III**: 156
Pierse, Sir Richard, **I**: 335-336, 348-349,
  355, 360-361; **II**: 202, 206; and
  ABDA command controversies, **I**:
  342, 343
Pilots, **I**: 191-192, 199-200; British and
  American, number trained, **I**: 488;
  training of, **I**: 182-183
Piraeus, Greece, **III**: 377, 466
Pisa, Italy, **III**: 373
Pisa-Rimini line, Italy, **III**: 225, 228, 232
Pius XII, Pope, **II**: 319-321, 331, 428;
  and Allied prisoners of war, **II**: 357-
  358; and bombing of Rome, **II**: 250-
  253; and Warsaw uprising, **III**: 309,
  311-312
Placentia Bay, Newfoundland: Atlantic
  Conference at, 1941, **I**: 226-228
Plastiras, Nikolaos, **III**: 466, 473, 537
Ploesti, Roumania, **II**: 197, 280, 420
Plog, William, **II**: 540
PLOUGH operation, **II**: 47
Po River, Italy, **II**: 443-444; **III**: 198
Po Valley, Italy, **II**: 505; **III**: 232, 300,
  302, 356, 434-435
Poison gas warfare, **I**: 437, 439; **III**:
  230, 256; Stalin on, **I**: 439

Poland, **I**: 12, 124, 206, 209; **II**: 283,
  698; **III**: 316, 332, 398, 403, 574-575
  Allied policy toward, 1944, **III**: 460-
  465
  Allies view of Soviet rights in, **III**:
  526
  and Soviet Union, **II**: 650-651, 703-
  704, 735-739, 762-765; **III**: 13-14, 29-
  30, 48, 68-71, 137, 202, 208-210, 234-
  235, 243, 273, 365, 576, 592-602, 622,
  634; Allied concerns over, **III**: 20-21;
  and Moscow Conference, 1944, **III**:
  350, 357-361; and Warsaw Uprising,
  III: 280-285, 294-296; Anglo-American policy toward, **III**: 545-551, 585-
  590; boundary dispute, **I**: 490, 505;
  II: 128-130, 178, 636, 668, 684-688,
  700-705, 706-708, 710, 715-723, 740-
  743; **III**: 60-61, 65, 143, 349; British
  position, **III**: 71-74; history of relations, **II**: 396; negotiations with, **III**:
  253-255, 258-261, 269-270; overview
  of relations, **II**: 192-193; Roosevelt
  on, **II**: 192, 202-205, 685; **III**: 79, 208
  and United States, **III**: 618
  and Yalta Conference, **III**: 526-527,
  530
  atrocities in, **II**: 520
  British view of, **III**: 480-481
  Churchill and Roosevelt on, **III**:
  545
  Churchill on, **II**: 223; **III**: 349, 563-
  565
  Curzon line, **II**: 178, 650, 684-686,
  701, 703-704, 715-716, 718-722, 726,
  735, 737, 740-741, 762-764; **III**: 21,
  30, 143, 235, 260, 364, 462, 483, 600,
  622; accepted at Teheran, **III**: 68, 70,
  72, 357-359; discussed at Moscow,
  1944, **III**: 357-360; discussed at Malta,
  III: 523
  Eastern: Soviet occupation of, **II**:
  192-193
  exiles in London, **III**: 48, 243, 269,
  523, 546-547, 552, 564-565, 571-572,
  576, 585, 586-587, 589, 598, 600; and
  British, **II**: 199, 715-723; and Churchill, **II**: 715-723, 726; **III**: 54, 72-73,
  137, 461, 465; and intelligence for Allies, **I**: 488-489; and Lublin committee, **III**: 253-255, 496-497; and Mos-

cow Foreign Ministers' Conference, **II**: 606; and Polish Americans, **III**: 33; and Soviet Union, **II**: 200-202, 637, 700-701, 703; **III**: 259-260; **III**: 20-21, 29-30, 539; and Soviets on boundaries, **II**: 684-688; at Moscow Conference, 1944, **III**: 350-352, 357-361; document on brutalities in Poland, **III**: 553-559; negotiations with Soviets, **II**: 735-739, 740-743, 762-765; on boundaries, **III**: 526; Roosevelt on, **II**: 706-707; **III**: 483; Stalin on, **II**: 203; **III**: 70-71, 235, 475-477, 492; U.S. Poles and, **III**: 79; view of Soviets vs. Germans, **II**: 192-193, 195, 198-199

German invasion of, **I**: 23

Home Army, persecution of, **III**: 553-558

in British theater of operations, **II**: 114

in Churchill-Stalin talks, 1944, **III**: 339, 341-342

Katyn Forest massacre, **II**: 192-195, 198-199, 388-402, 400, 684, 701, 704; Churchill on, **II**: 397

Lublin committee, **III**: 208, 253-255, 269-270, 283, 309, 523, 553-558, 560-561, 564-565, 567-569, 571-572, 576, 585, 587, 589, 593-594, 596, 598-599, 601, 622, 627-629, 634; and Soviet Union, **III**: 551-552; and Stalin, **III**: 260-261, 363-364; at Moscow Conference, 1944, **III**: 350-352, 358-361; recognition of, **III**: 461-465, 475-476, 481-484, 492, 496-497, 526, 539, 546-547

National Council, **II**: 718; **III**: 254

Peasant Party, **II**: 740

Polish National Assembly, **II**: 715

Polish Workers' Party, **II**: 718

postwar: prisoners of war in, **III**: 541

reprisal threats lessen atrocities, **II**: 521

Roosevelt on, **II**: 706-707; **III**: 481-484, 560-563

Secret Service in, **II**: 522

Soviet-sponsored government in, **II**: 198-199, 203, 688

Stalin on, **III**: 350, 364, 475-477

Teheran Conference discussions on, **II**: 611

U.S. policy toward, 1945, **III**: 634

Underground, **II**: 701, 704, 715, 717, 720-723, 740; **III**: 48; and Soviet army, **III**: 209; and Soviet Union, **II**: 736-737; Churchill on, **III**: 72-73; collapse of in Warsaw, **III**: 357; in Warsaw Uprising, **III**: 260, 280-285, 294-296, 357; issue of Allied aid to, **III**: 309-313; Roosevelt on, **III**: 79; Stalin on, **III**: 234, 254, 475, 561

Warsaw Uprising, **III**: 280-285, 294-296, 291-293; Allied response to, **III**: 309-313; and Stalin, **III**: 272-273; described, **III**: 259-260; Roosevelt and, **III**: 283, 288, 294, 313

Yalta agreements on, **II**: 611; **III**: 538-539

Poland, Eastern, **I**: 505; occupied by Soviets, **II**: 396; Soviet annexation of, **I**: 490

Polish corps, **II**: 47-48

Polish Red Cross Society, **II**: 392

Polish Workers' Party, **III**: 555-556

Political-Military Commission (Italy), **II**: 539-540

Poltava, Ukraine, **III**: 295

Popov, Gregori, **III**: 473

Port Arthur, Manchuria, **III**: 527

Port Moresby, New Guinea, **I**: 385, 415, 657

Port Said, Egypt, **II**: 245; **III**: 378, 381

Port-en-Bassin, France, **III**: 215

Portal, Sir Charles, **I**: 226, 284, 513; **II**: 185-186, 202, 305-306, 433, 571; **III**: 122; and U.S. aircraft to Britain, **I**: 485-488; on air reinforcements, **I**: 461-462

Portland, Duke of, **III**: 249

Portugal, **I**: 46, 178, 209; **II**: 166, 521, 728; **III**: 106; American postwar interests in, **II**: 299; and Ireland, **III**: 58; and Jewish refugees, **II**: 315; and North African invasion, **I**: 640-642, 663, 666, 673; Azores negotiations and, **II**: 214, 239-241, 251-252, 262-263, 295-296, 298, 302, 309, 324-326, 497, 506-507, 515, 524-525, 532-533, 542-543, 564, 574, 590-591; Churchill on neutrality of, **II**: 667; German

Portugal (*cont.*)
    threats to, **I**: 129, 171-174, 181, 196,
    200-202, 427; imperialism of, **III**: 6;
    neutrality of, **I**: 86; **II**: 243; rumors
    in, **I**: 540; U.S. handling of criticized,
    III: 78
Portuguese Empire, **II**: 241, 249-250,
    252, 263, 292 (*see also* Timor; Macao);
    Allied postwar guarantees on, **II**: 506-
    507; Roosevelt on, **II**: 269
Postwar world:
        Allied view of, **II**: 606
        and colonialism, **II**: 609
        and military occupations at war's
    end, **III**: 523
        and self-determination, **II**: 369
        British loss of maritime strength in,
    I: 647
        British-American conflicts over, **I**:
    15
        Churchill on, **I**: 93; **II**: 221-227;
    III: 574; Anglo-American relations in,
    II: 333; **III**: 428-429; international or-
    ganization in, **II**: 448-449; in mem-
    oirs, **I**: 6; security in, **II**: 128-132, 221
        civil aviation as issue in, **II**: 749
        cooperation of major powers, **III**: 6
        discussed at Atlantic Conference,
    1941, **I**: 227-228
        discussed at Quebec Conference,
    1944, **III**: 315-319
        discussed at Quebec Conference,
    1943, **II**: 430-431
        discussed at Teheran Conference,
    II: 611-612
        discussed at Yalta Conference, **III**:
    503
        discussions on, **II**: 202-203, 283
        economic issues, **I**: 227-228, 251,
    344; **II**: 748-750; **III**: 535-536, 559-
    560, 577; Churchill on, **I**: 248
        international organization and, **II**:
    584-585
        issue of Azores bases, **II**: 566
        issue of Soviet communism in, **II**:
    178
        military vs. civil administration and,
    II: 480
        planning for, **II**: 54, 156, 192
        reconstruction, **III**: 65, 606
        Roosevelt on, **I**: 73-74; **III**: 237;

    policing of, **I**: 228, 502; **II**: 221, 528,
    608
        U.S. role in, Hurley on, **III**: 10
Potash: British import of from Spain,
    III: 66-67
Pound, Sir Dudley, **I**: 223, 284, 309,
    414, 416, 418, 440, 466, 491, 540-541;
    II: 59, 60-61, 202, 305; and supplies
    to Soviets, **I**: 472-474, 478-479; on
    convoys to Soviets, **I**: 482-483, 617
Pownall, Sir Henry, **I**: 313; **II**: 481-482
Poynton, A. H., **I**: 648
Prague, Czechoslovakia, **III**: 493
Pravda, Soviet Party paper, **II**: 672, 741;
    story on Ribbentrop and British, **II**:
    677
Press, Allied: American versus British, **I**:
    243; and Big Three conference secu-
    rity, **II**: 526; at Casablanca Confer-
    ence, **II**: 103-104, 107-108; at confer-
    ences, **II**: 448; at Teheran
    Conference, **II**: 545; at Yalta Confer-
    ence, **III**: 514-515; leaks in, **II**: 490-
    492, 522; and Soviet-Polish issues, **III**:
    54, 60-61, 71
Press, British, **II**: 530-532; **III**: 421; and
    Greek crisis, **III**: 457; and leaks on
    Polish-Soviet relations, **III**: 54; and
    submarine disclosures, **II**: 313; **III**:
    386; censors in, **II**: 522; Churchill on,
    I: 420; **III**: 46, 498; in North Africa,
    II: 140-141; on American military in
    Europe, **III**: 498; on Churchill and
    Belgium, **III**: 437; on Churchill and
    Greece, **III**: 450; on civil aviation pol-
    icy, **III**: 443; on Italy, **III**: 333; on
    North Africa, **II**: 145
Press, French: on de Gaulle in London,
    III: 148
Press, Polish (Great Britain), **II**: 194;
    anti-Soviet attacks of, **II**: 199
Press, Spanish, **I**: 665
Press, United States, **III**: 201; and Al-
    lied policies in Italy, **III**: 436; and Ar-
    gentina, **III**: 347; and civil aviation
    policy, **III**: 421; and Darlan deal, **II**:
    21-22; and India theater, **II**: 482; and
    lend-lease bill, **I**: 138; and Poland,
    III: 463; and postwar oil arrange-
    ments, **II**: 733; and Roosevelt, **I**: 619-
    620; and Soviet relations, **II**: 233; and

Spain, **III**: 162; and Vichy government, **I**: 287; and submarine warfare disclosures, **II**: 313; **III**: 386; attacks on Mountbatten, **II**: 482; Churchill on, **III**: 499; in North Africa, **II**: 140-141; Italian ships to Soviets, **III**: 14-15; leaks in, **II**: 530-532; on Churchill and Greece, **III**: 450; on Darlan deal, **II**: 18; on Marshall as invasion commander, **II**: 481-482, 489; on postwar security treaties, **III**: 528; on Randolph Churchill, **III**: 257; on Roosevelt's freezing of funds, **I**: 209; Roosevelt on, **I**: 420-421, 633

Prince of Naples, **II**: 586-587, 591

Pripet Marshes, Poland, **II**: 684

Prisoners of war, **I**: 118; **III**: 576; Africa negotiations over among French, **II**: 56-57; Allied in Germany, **III**: 631; Allied in Poland, **III**: 572; Allied-Japanese exchange, **III**: 244, 246; Allied, and Soviets, **III**: 634; Allied in Italy, **II**: 424; American in Soviet Union, **III**: 542; Anglo-American vs. Soviet, problems of, **III**: 541-542, 586, 588; British in Italy, **II**: 349, 352-353, 357-358, 361, 364; German, and Hess, **I**: 189; German treatment of, **II**: 393; **III**: 580-584; Greek in Italy, **II**: 352-353; in German surrender document, **II**: 771; in Libya campaign, **I**: 126; Italian and Allied, exchange of, **II**: 384; Italians in Germany, **II**: 461; **III**: 372-373; Italians in Italy, **II**: 353; Polish and Katyn Forest massacre, **II**: 390-402; Polish in Soviet Union, **II**: 192-193; Polish, number taken by Soviets, 1939, **II**: 390; Polish of Germans, **III**: 310-311; Soviet-German negotiations on, **II**: 180; Yugoslav in Italy, **II**: 352-353

Privy Council, **I**: 87

Propaganda, **II**: 68
    Allied, **III**: 403, 409, 578
    broadcasts before D-Day, **III**: 156-157
    for North African invasion, **I**: 626-627
    Gaullist against Vichy, **II**: 98
    German, **I**: 351, 409; **II**: 199, 201, 710; and Katyn Forest massacre, **II**: 192-195
    in North Africa, **II**: 76

Propaganda Committee (India), **II**: 696-697, 742-743; discontinued, **II**: 733

Propaganda Committees, proposed, **II**: 449

Proximity-fuse shells, effect of, **III**: 412-413

Prussia, **II**: 223, 607, 611; **III**: 364

Prussia, East, **II**: 178, 721, 737; claimed by Soviets, **II**: 704; in Polish boundary dispute, **II**: 685-686

Przemysl, Poland, **II**: 719

Punjab, India, **I**: 395-396

Purić, Bozidar, **III**: 131-133

Purvis, Arthur, **I**: 38-41, 78-79, 80, 88, 124

Pyramids, Egyptian: Churchill and Roosevelt visit, **II**: 601

Quebec City, **II**: 323, 328, 382, 386, 422, 429; **III**: 157, 226, 249, 267, 270; Roosevelt visit to, 1936, **II**: 353

Quebec Conference (OCTAGON, 1944), **II**: 745; **III**: 362, 421, 446, 453; and Argentina, **III**: 291; and Dumbarton Oaks talks, **III**: 331; and tripartite conference, **III**: 339; British delegation to, **III**: 298-299; Burma operations and, **III**: 435; occupation zones decided at, **III**: 160; on French campaign, **III**: 286; on Italian campaign, **III**: 286, 308; planning for, **III**: 195, 272, 274, 286-290, 301-303, 306-307, 313-314; size of delegations, **III**: 485-486; summary of decisions made at, **III**: 315-319; Churchill on, **III**: 438

Quebec Conference (QUADRANT, 1943), **II**: 290, 328, 358, 370, 766; **III**: 213; and atomic research, **III**: 509; and landing craft deployment, **II**: 582; Basic English discussed at, **III**: 105; British goals at, **II**: 344-345; Churchill on, **II**: 556; codenames for, **II**: 336; decisions on channel invasion, **II**: 571; decisions on war strategy, **II**: 388, 504-505; decisions summarized, **II**: 429-431; effect on Roosevelt's health, **II**: 454; film of, **II**: 548, 573; FCNL discussed at, **II**: 375-377; issue of participation in, **II**: 343-346; Mar-

Quebec Conference, 1943 (*cont.*)
  shall as channel invasion leader, **II**:
  481; negotiations with Canada, **II**:
  341-343; Pacific strategy decided at,
  II: 248; preparations for, **II**: 284,
  353-354, 371-373; Roosevelt on postwar world, **II**: 609; European occupation zones decided at, **II**: 746

Rabat, Morocco, **II**: 75
Rabaul, New Britain (Solomon Islands),
  II: 132
Raczyński, Count, **II**: 392, 397, 716,
  719, 740
Radar, **I**: 249; **II**: 26-27, 323, 366, 636;
  III: 193, 276
Radescu, Nicolae, **III**: 625-626
Radio Moscow, **III**: 260, 284
Radkiewicz, Stanislaw, **III**: 553-554, 556
Raeder, Erich, **I**: 25, 283
Ramgarh, India, **II**: 275, 277
Ramírez, Pedro, **II**: 681
Ramsey, Sir Bertram, **I**: 596, 602; **II**:
  629, 631, 635; **III**: 503-505; and
  North African invasion, **I**: 590-591
Rangoon, Burma, **I**: 333, 405, 417-418;
  II: 110, 213; **III**: 347-348, 435, 524;
  Japanese threat to, **I**: 361, 364-365
Rankin, Jeanette, **I**: 282, 336
RAVENOUS, **II**: 115-116. *See also*
  Burma
Rearmament issue, pre-war, **I**: 87
Recife, Brazil, **II**: 367
Red Cross, British, **III**: 574, 597
Red Sea, **I**: 163, 165-166, 169; **II**: 144;
  III: 327; in Middle East theater, 1942,
  I: 399
Refugees: Allied failure on, **II**: 293;
  camps in North Africa, **II**: 321; Jew-
  ish to North Africa, **II**: 315-316
Reilly, Michael F., **II**: 588
Relief:
      Allied policy on, **II**: 105
      for Europe, **II**: 86-87; **III**: 47; and
  cross-channel invasion, **III**: 84-86
      for France, **I**: 116-118, 124, 147-
  148, 158, 179; children, **I**: 427
      for Italy, **III**: 401
      in liberated nations, as issue, **III**:
  540-541
      postwar, **I**: 248, 251; **III**: 569-570,
  573-574, 578-579, 584, 636

Swedish scheme, **III**: 621-623
  to Greece, **III**: 279
Reparations, postwar, **III**: 528
Reparations Commission, **III**: 634
Republican Party, United States, **I**: 80,
  131; **II**: 743; **III**: 201; and British
  dollar balances, **III**: 65; and Mac-
  Arthur, **II**: 480; and Roosevelt, **II**:
  527
Reston, James, **II**: 530
Reunion, Indian Ocean (France), **I**: 350,
  353
Reynaud, Paul, **I**: 36, 44, 46-49, 51
Rhine Province, Germany, **III**: 147
Rhine River, Germany, **III**: 289, 340-
  341, 348, 408, 434-435, 538, 601, 604,
  608, 611
Rhineland, Germany, **III**: 364, 391
Rhodes, Island of, **II**: 445, 497-499,
  503, 505, 508, 511, 517; Allied attack
  on postponed, **II**: 632-633, 636; in
  British plans, 1943, **II**: 14; invasion of
  planned, **II**: 663; postwar disposition
  of, **III**: 328
Rhone River, France, **III**: 263
Rhone Valley, France, **III**: 218-219,
  222-223, 225, 228, 305
Ribbentrop, Joachim, **II**: 379-380, 672-
  673; **III**: 330
Riefler, Winfield, **III**: 85
Riga line, **II**: 736, 741
Rimini line, in Italian campaign, **III**:
  300, 466-467
Riviera, French, **II**: 267, 349; **III**: 164.
  See also France
Robert, Georges, **II**: 147-148, 231-232
Rochat, Charles A., **I**: 167, 169, 333-334
Rocket warfare, German, **II**: 521, 559-
  560, 589-590; **III**: 412
Rokossovsky, Konstantin, **III**: 272-273
Rome, Italy, **II**: 12, 172, 184, 434, 443-
  444, 464, 492, 498, 502, 503, 505,
  554-555, 563, 759; **III**: 97, 249, 321,
  389, 449; Allied air attacks on, **II**:
  428; Allies occupy, June 1944, **III**: 52;
  as open city, **II**: 377-379, 466, 469;
  battle of, **II**: 436, 514, 556; bombing
  threat of, **II**: 234, 250-253, 303-304,
  373-374, 428; German occupation of,
  1943, **II**: 455; in Allied military planning, **II**: 435-436; liberation of, **II**:
  331-332, 587, 593, 680, 697, 725; **III**:

17, 32, 41-42, 45, 110, 119, 136, 142, 163-164, 167, 176, 197

Rome Committee for National Liberation, **III**: 189

Romer, Tadeusz, **II**: 716, 735-736, 740; **III**: 253, 255, 268, 351-352, 538

Rommel, Erwin, **I**: 165, 170, 191, 196, 210, 252, 269, 292, 317, 333, 353, 362, 381, 435-436, 551, 561, 570, 580; **II**: 32, 98, 122-123, 136, 185, 555; army of, **II**: 54-56; at El Alamein, **I**: 656-660, 663; Churchill on, **I**: 531-532, 537-538, 543; helped by Vichy, **I**: 350; in North Africa, **I**: 152, 267, 493-494, 514, 516, 517, 541, 584-585, 604, 640, 671-672; **II**: 5, 144-145, 152; in Tunisia, **I**: 657; **II**: 138

Roosevelt, Anna, **III**: 332, 499-500

Roosevelt, Curtis, **III**: 369

Roosevelt, Eleanor, **I**: 139, 335, 422, 439, 600; **II**: 117, 155, 171-172, 227, 348, 387, 635; **III**: 288, 306, 332, 369, 470-471, 499, 574, 631; view of Churchill, **I**: 4; visit to Britain, 1942, **I**: 541, 633, 636, 639, 642-643, 654-656; **II**: 7, 42; visit to West Indies, **III**: 27

Roosevelt, Elliott, **I**: 203, 204, 206-207, 600, 642; **II**: 438; and Churchill, **I**: 618

Roosevelt, Franklin Delano, **II**: 660
after Yalta, **III**: 593
and ambassadors, **I**: 7, 24
and foreign policy leadership, **II**: 590
and colonialism, **I**: 373; **II**: 269
as member of short snorter club, **II**: 171
at Shangri-la, **I**: 639
Churchill on chivalry of, **I**: 516
Churchill to on journey to So. Car., **III**: 74
Churchill to on second-hand information, **II**: 596
Churchill to on 1944 election victory, **III**: 382-383, 385
death of, **III**: 620, 625, 631-632
devised term "United Nations," **III**: 265
dislike of flying, **II**: 126
domestic vs. foreign policies of, **II**: 252
enjoys secrecy, **II**: 108
fascination with warships, **III**: 250
favorite position as uncommitted, **III**: 345
Four Policemen concept, **I**: 228; **II**: 608-609, 611; **III**: 201, 482
health, **I**: 18, 134, 185-186, 208; **II**: 42, 133-134, 137, 149-150, 155-156, 454, 559, 561, 563, 567, 641-642; **III**: 74, 115-116, 138-139, 145, 162, 191, 376, 424, 530, 573, 597, 600, 617, 619; and election of 1944, **III**: 367-368; and trip to England, **III**: 491; Churchill on, **II**: 644-645; diagnosis of heart condition, **III**: 59-60; ignorance of, **III**: 77-78; view of own, **III**: 59-60
Hopkins on, **III**: 315-316
humor of, **II**: 54-55, 647-648; **III**: 170
infrequent writer of strategy papers, **II**: 442
love of sea stories, **I**: 35
messages buoy Churchill, **I**: 352
on bureaucrats, **II**: 495
on Churchill, **I**: 148. See also Churchill, Winston S.
on geometry and God, **III**: 232
on Hess, **I**: 187-188
on liberation of Rome, **III**: 167
on martinis, **I**: 525
on naval power, **I**: 46
on need to escape from Washington, **II**: 454
on newspapers as running the war, **II**: 489
on politicians at military conferences, **II**: 515
on recording private discussions, **II**: 449-450
on relationship with Churchill, **I**: 4, 6-7
on self as honorary veterinarian, **II**: 562
on Stalin. See Stalin, Joseph V.
on treaties, **III**: 445
on vacations, **I**: 151, 422
on war situation, 1942, **I**: 470, 544
on war strategy, **III**: 446-449
personal diplomacy of, **II**: 610
postwar views of, **III**: 528, 530
procrastination as response to acrimony, **III**: 315

Roosevelt, Franklin Delano (*cont.*)
quotes church proverbs, **II**: 22
rarely looked at broad strategy, **I**: 177
relations with military leaders, **II**: 479-480
speeches, **III**: 340, 507, 547; "Arsenal of Democracy," 1941, **I**: 118-119, 121; "tyranny, like hell," **I**: 370; denounces lend-lease opponents, **I**: 148; Fireside Chat, **II**: 357-359; in Ottawa, 1943, **II**: 433; on German provocation, **I**: 236-237; on German submarine attack, **I**: 264; Pan American Day, 1941, **I**: 196; State of the Union, 1943, **II**: 114; State of the Union, 1944, **II**: 668; **III**: 505-506
style of, **I**: 492; **III**: 543, 630
trip to England, proposed, **II**: 42-43; **III**: 60, 64, 109-110, 143-146, 163, 378, 574
trips, **II**: 117, 186, 189, 259, 348, 370, 374; **III**: 74, 77-78, 88, 167, 191, 193-194, 195, 243-245, 258, 262, 597, 632; to Atlantic Conference, **I**: 227; to Cairo, **II**: 595-596; to Casablanca, **II**: 123; to Ottawa, **II**: 430; to Quebec Conference, 1944, **III**: 307, 313; to Quebec, 1936, **II**: 353; to Teheran, **II**: 613; to West Coast, **I**: 633; to Yalta, **III**: 484, 496, 503, 515-516, 518-519, 520-521, 524; view of professional diplomats, **II**: 155
view on security, **II**: 434-435
visit to factories and military bases, **I**: 608-612
wish to visit French front, **III**: 494
Roosevelt, James, **I**: 23; **III**: 98
Roosevelt, Rebecca Howland, **III**: 98
Roosevelt, Ruth Goggins, **II**: 438
Roosevelt, Sara, **I**: 236
Roosevelt-Stalin conference: Churchill view of, **II**: 290
Rosenman, Samuel I., **III**: 569, 573-574
Rostov on the Don, **II**: 14
Rostov on the Don, Russia, **II**: 39
Roumania, **I**: 16, 208; **II**: 131, 350, 362; **III**: 229, 634-635
and Allies, **II**: 445; **III**: 523
and Moscow Conference, 1944, **III**: 351, 359
and Soviet Union, **I**: 238; **III**: 69,

179, 545, 547-548, 585-586, 588, 595, 606; territorial disputes, **I**: 490
Anglo-Soviet agreement on, **III**: 153, 177-183, 200, 202, 349-350
Churchill on, **II**: 498-499
Germans in, **I**: 134
oil fields of, **I**: 645; **II**: 50
political situation in, **III**: 625-626
Roosevelt on, **III**: 560-562
Soviet Army occupies, **III**: 298
Rowe, James, Jr., **I**: 186
Royal College of Surgeons, England, **II**: 541
Ruhr Basin, Germany, **III**: 317, 364, 391, 408
Russell, Richard, **II**: 527
Russo-Polish War of 1919-1920, **II**: 396

Saar, Germany, **III**: 364
Sabotage, **II**: 68; in Greece, by Britain, **II**: 408-409
Sadat, Anwar el, **II**: 601
Saed, Mohammed, **III**: 511-512
Safi, Morocco, Allied landing in, 1942, **I**: 667
Saigon, Indo-China, **I**: 90, 98, 105
St. Lucia (G.B.), **I**: 59-60, 65, 68
St. Nazaire, France, **III**: 164, 216, 263
St. Pierre (French), **I**: 324, 346
St. Pierre-Miquelon affair, **I**: 324-326, 335, 346-347
St. Vith, Belgium, **III**: 498
Saipan, Mariana Islands, **III**: 193-194
Sakhalin Island, **III**: 527
Salamaua, New Guinea, **I**: 414
Salazar, Antonio de Oliveira, **I**: 200-201, 640; **II**: 243, 295, 673, 728; **III**: 108; and Allies, **II**: 249, 251-252, 254; and Azores, **II**: 239-241, 262-263, 292, 302, 515, 564, 566; and Azores negotiations, **II**: 298-299, 495-497, 506-507, 532-533, 667-668, 674-675, 677; Churchill on, **II**: 668
Salerno, Italy, **II**: 434-436
Salonica, Greece, **II**: 428; **III**: 377, 381
Salter, Sir Arthur, **I**: 236-237, 327, 329
Samoa, **I**: 392
Samos Island, Aegean Sea, **II**: 341, 518
San Diego, California, **III**: 243
San Francisco, California, **III**: 547
San Francisco Conference (1945), **III**:

433, 531, 564, 565, 567, 569, 573-574, 593, 597, 600, 632, 634, 637; Soviet representation at, **III**: 586, 588-591
Sapru, Sir Tej Bahadur, **I**: 375
Sapru Conference, **I**: 375-376
Saracoglu, Sukru, **II**: 139-141
Sardinia, **I**: 604; **II**: 12-13, 184, 218, 349, 361, 442, 445, 455, 459; Allied strategy toward, **I**: 669; invasion of, proposed, **II**: 10, 118, 327
Saudi Arabia, **I**: 372; Churchill on U.S. interests in, **III**: 17; oil in, competition for, **II**: 744
Savoy, House of (Italy), **II**: 354, 366, 369, 591, 692
Scandinavia, **I**: 34; fall of, **II**: 168; postwar, as American sphere, **II**: 708; postwar, Churchill on, **II**: 223; proposed operations, **I**: 316
Scapa Flow, Orkney Islands, **II**: 15, 245, 247, 259, 268, 278, 284, 385
Schacht, Dr. Hjalmar, **I**: 540
Schicklgruber, Maria, **III**: 290
Schleswig, Germany, **III**: 147
Schnorkel, device for subs, **III**: 345
"Schwartze Kapelle," **II**: 521
Schweinfurt, Germany, **II**: 517
Scobie, Ronald, **III**: 450, 459, 474-475, 487, 606
Scotland, **I**: 317; **II**: 245, 247, 268, 452; **III**: 266, 270, 272
Scotland Yard, **I**: 359
Scrambler telephone, **I**: xx-xxi
Scripps-Howard newspapers, **I**: 421
Sea power: Churchill on, **I**: 302-303, 305-306, 496; importance of, **I**: 89, 96, 103; Japanese, **I**: 361, 385
Second front, **I**: 9, 14, 237-238; **II**: 38-39; **III**: 172-173. *See also* Cross-channel invasion
　and North African invasion, **I**: 579, 641
　and Spain, **III**: 67-68
　and Stalin, **I**: 293, 394, 466, 553; **II**: 48-52, 63, 72, 80-81, 132-135, 138-140, 285-288; **III**: 126-128; Allied problems with, **I**: 544-546; Churchill on, **II**: 56-57, 59, 278; Roosevelt and, **II**: 260; Teheran Conference discussions on, **II**: 610
　and supply problems to Soviets, **I**:

482-483
　at Casablanca Conference, **II**: 118-119
　Churchill on, **I**: 448, 498, 530; **II**: 43
　delayed, **II**: 151-154, 157-159, 233, 244-246
　Stalin on, **II**: 153; **III**: 61
　discussed at Moscow Conference, 1942, **I**: 564-566
　Molotov requests, 1942, **I**: 494-500
　Roosevelt on, **I**: 397
Selassie, Haile, Emperor of Ethiopia, **III**: 536
Selective Service Act, United States, **I**: 218
Self-determination, issue of: British vs. American views on, **II**: 360, 369. *See also* Colonialism
Senegal, **I**: 71
Senussi, **III**: 328
Serbia, Yugoslavia, **III**: 131; and Bulgarians, **III**: 350
Serbians, in Yugoslavia, **I**: 222; **II**: 548, 660; **III**: 115, 203, 274-275, 279; massacre of reported, **II**: 416
Servaes, R. M., **II**: 309
Séte, France, **III**: 214, 217-218, 222
Sevastopol, **III**: 479, 501, 519
Seven Years' War, **II**: 323
Sevice d'Ordre Legionnaire (SOL), **II**: 68-69
Seville, Spain, **I**: 125
Sforza, Count Carlo, **II**: 451, 452, 457-458, 462-463, 467, 469, 470, 473, 472-473, 586, 664, 666, 711-712; **III**: 30-31, 33, 43, 110, 176, 436-439, 445, 451; and Allies, **II**: 679; **III**: 188; letter to Berle, **III**: 437-439, 443-444; proposal on Ethiopia, **I**: 160-161
SHAEF, **III**: 156, 170; commands, debate on, **III**: 522
Shah of Iran, **II**: 753; **III**: 3, 9; and Germans, **I**: 235
Shangri-la, Roosevelt retreat, **I**: 638-639; **II**: 322, 347, 559; Churchill visits to, **II**: 211, 297
Shelley, Norman, **I**: 42
Shemiergembeinski, General, and rocket research, **II**: 589-590
Sherwood, Robert, **I**: 12, 211, 284; **II**: 355, 710-711; on Roosevelt, **II**: 615

Shetland Islands, **I**: 56
Shipbuilding, Allied, **I**: 552, 603; **II**: 220-221
Shipbuilding, British, **III**: 25, 91
Shipbuilding, United States: changes in program, 1942, **I**: 610
Shipping, Allied, **I**: 96, 177
　and North African invasion, **I**: 584, 604
　and troop movements, **I**: 391-392; **II**: 33-34
　as key issue in war, **I**: 350
　as limiting factor in troop movement, **I**: 650
　　Churchill on, **I**: 647-651; **II**: 153, 170, 288
　　coordination, **I**: 327
　　discussed at Washington Conference, **II**: 219-221
　　effect on strategy, **II**: 182; **III**: 215-218
　　embargo on Irish, **III**: 75-76, 81
　　improved by anti-sub success, **II**: 217
　　increases for Allies, 1943, **II**: 383
　　in Pacific, **III**: 155
　　issues over neutrality, **I**: 32-35
　　lack of for convoys, **I**: 594
　　landing craft, shortage of, **II**: 133-134, 139-140, 152-154, 218
　　limitations of, **I**: 610; **II**: 156, 247; **III**: 387
　　problems for Allies, **I**: 379-380, 383-384, 600-601; **II**: 93-96, 534; for relief, **III**: 401; in Pacific, **I**: 307; of oil transport, **II**: 82-83; of resources, **II**: 39
　　　production problems, **II**: 166-171, 443-445
　　　Roosevelt on, **II**: 178-179
　　　through Mediterranean, **I**: 674; **II**: 23
Shipping, British, **II**: 168-170; merchant needs assessed, **I**: 90
Shipping, United States, **I**: 32-35, 99, 105, 212; **II**: 220-221; capacity, 1942, **I**: 392; production goals, 1943, **I**: 638; to British, **I**: 425, 650; **II**: 232; to Soviet Union, **I**: 630
Shipping losses, Allied, **I**: 89, 97, 145, 243, 407, 456, 515, 528; **II**: 44, 95-96, 475, 500-501, 514, 571, 574-575, 658-659; **III**: 11-13, 22-23, 37, 79, 122, 165-166, 233, 235-237; 374, 382, 384, 396, 441, 493, 544; Atlantic, **I**: 406, 416, 451-452; **II**: 27, 158, 160, 165; Caribbean, 1942, **I**: 406; Churchill on, **I**: 190-191, 648-650; figures on, **II**: 313; in North African campaign, **II**: 28; Indian Ocean, 1942, **I**: 454; lessen, **II**: 647; **III**: 163, 312; on supply convoys to Soviets, **I**: 471-475
Shipping losses, British, **I**: 97, 104, 107, 191; **III**: 24; ask U.S. help with, **I**: 149-150; in Greece, **III**: 179
Shipping losses, Japanese, **III**: 252
Ships (Naval), Allied:
　escort vessels, lack of, **I**: 610, 615, 649; **II**: 15, 20, 21
　for invasion of southern France, **III**: 197-199
　landing craft, **II**: 656-657; **III**: 82; and cross-channel invasion, **I**: 495-497; **III**: 164; and invasion of southern France, **III**: 114, 119, 126, 128; and Italian campaign, **II**: 632-633, 635; **III**: 137; as priority, **I**: 610; British and production figures, **III**: 77; deployment of, **II**: 580-581, 636, 651; effect on military operations, **II**: 756; for European operations, **II**: 582-583; **III**: 215, 219; shortage of, **II**: 712; **III**: 387
　　pooling of, **I**: 538-539, 541
　　to Soviets for Italian ships, **II**: 670
Ships (Naval), British, **I**: 151, 192, 198, 382, 461, 505; **II**: 97
　and Japanese, **I**: 454
　at Yalta Conference, **III**: 519
　battleship, **I**: 130, 133
　Churchill assesses strength of, **I**: 97, 104
　deployment of, **I**: 468-469; **II**: 60-61; carriers, **II**: 52-53
　destroyers, **I**: 56-57
　Duke of York, **II**: 636
　Exeter, **I**: 28-32
　Illustrious, **I**: 83, 85
　in Aegean, **II**: 509, 511
　in Dakar, **II**: 68
　in Indian Ocean, **I**: 442-443, 453, 461, 491
　　in North African invasion, **I**: 623, 628

in Pacific, **I**: 264, 305-306
losses of, **I**: 195, 451; destroyers, **I**: 50-51; in Italy, **III**: 43; on convoys, **II**: 528
on convoys to Soviet Union, **I**: 474, 482; **II**: 174-176
Prince of Wales, **I**: 308, 411; sunk, 287
production of, **I**: 649; **II**: 94-96
Queen Mary, **II**: 344, 382; **III**: 312-313, 332
Renown, **II**: 452, 463, 584-585, 600
Repulse, **I**: 308; sunk, **I**: 287
Royal Oak, **I**: 27
sinks *Scharnhorst*, **II**: 636
to Soviets, **II**: 752; **III**: 56, 438; Stalin, **II**: 735, 747-748, 762-763; vice Italian ships, **II**: 664-666, 669-671, 694-695, 697-700; **III**: 17-18
to Turkey, **II**: 196
warships sunk by Japanese, **I**: 454
Ships (Naval), French, **I**: 147, 156
de Gaulle and control of, **III**: 108-109
Dunkerque, **I**: 167, 169; debate over, **I**: 157-159
in North Africa, **II**: 335
Jean Bart and *Richelieu*, **I**: 81-85, 97, 105, 164
SS *Normandie*, **I**: 352
Ships (Naval), German, **I**: 169, 173, 192, 193, 196-198, 208, 382; **II**: 52-53
and British, **I**: 369
and convoys, **II**: 173-176; to Soviet Union, **I**: 595
Bismarck, sinking of, **I**: 196-198
British attack *Tirpitz*, **I**: 477
Gneisenau, **I**: 359-362
Graf Spee, **I**: 28-33
Hipper and *Scheer*, **I**: 26-27
in Atlantic, 1942, **I**: 416
in North Atlantic, **I**: 149-150, 156
in Norway, **II**: 15
Prinz Eugen, **I**: 359
Scharnhorst, **I**: 359-362, 530; **II**: 636-638; **III**: 37
Scheer, **I**: 26-27
threaten convoys to Soviet, **II**: 157-162, 164-165
Tirpitz, **I**: 416, 418, 482, 527, 530; **III**: 37, 388
Ships (Naval), Italian, **I**: 301; **II**: 739;

Churchill on, **I**: 97, 104; **III**: 17-19; French demand for, **III**: 90; surrender to Allies, **II**: 424; to Soviets, **II**: 664-666, 669-671, 675-676, 678, 694-695, 697-700, 731
Ships (Naval), Japanese
battleships, **I**: 299
in Indian Ocean, **I**: 442-443, 460-461
in Pacific, **I**: 305-306
losses of, **III**: 193; at Leyte Gulf, **III**: 376; at Midway, **I**: 507
Ships (Naval), Portuguese, **II**: 240
Ships (Naval), Soviet, **I**: 474
Ships (Naval), United States, **I**: 474, 505; **III**: 117
aid to British, **I**: 440, 461-462
and convoys to Soviet Union, **I**: 528
at Yalta Conference, **III**: 479
attacked by German submarines, **I**: 265-267
battleships, **I**: 299, 407; Churchill on new, **I**: 418, 423
Churchill and, **I**: 301; requests for, **I**: 92, 106-107, 453
deployment of carriers, 1943, **II**: 52-53
deployment of, European operations, **III**: 199
destroyers, **I**: 26, 64-65, 99, 103, 106, 112, 126-127, 130; in Atlantic, **I**: 300; to Britain, 101, 118-119
ferrying planes to Malta, **I**: 467-470
Greer, **I**: 236, 238
in Dakar, **II**: 68
in Greek crisis, **III**: 450, 452-454
in North African invasion, **I**: 634-635
in Pacific, **I**: 305-306, 490-491; **II**: 60-61
Iowa, **II**: 567; to Cairo Conference, **II**: 583-584, 596, 598
Kearny, **I**: 264
landing craft, **I**: 489; **III**: 76-77, 88-89, 91
Langley, **I**: 367, 382
losses of, **I**: 236; at Guadalcanal, **I**: 657; at Midway, **I**: 507; on convoys, **II**: 528
Potomac, Presidential yacht, **II**: 596
production of, **I**: 392, 649; Churchill on, **II**: 170

Ships (Naval), United States (*cont.*)
    Quincy, **III**: 515, 521, 536, 537, 538, 569; to Yalta, **III**: 503, 564
    Robin Moor, **I**: 207, 209, 212
    Roosevelt on needs for, **II**: 44-45, 613
        Task Force 39, **I**: 419
        to Indian Ocean, **I**: 464; **III**: 14, 17
        to Malta, **I**: 436
        to Soviet Union; **II**: 709; for Italian ships, **III**: 14-15, 17-18, 56-57, 695, 697-700, 731
        transport planes to India, **I**: 460-461
    Wasp, **I**: 467-469
Short Snorter Club, **II**: 171-172, 291, 296, 312
Siantos, Georgios, **III**: 472
Siberia, **I**: 307; **III**: 296, 527; Soviet Union fears Japanese attack in, **I**: 293
Sicily, Italy, **I**: 176, 605; **II**: 12-13, 139, 218, 425, 439, 440, 459, 556; **III**: 373, 395; Allied strategy toward, **I**: 669; Churchill on for 1943, **I**: 302; German air bases in, **I**: 317; German forces in, 1942, **I**: 435-436; Roosevelt visit to, **II**: 613
Siegfried Line, Germany, **III**: 340
SIGSALY, **I**: xx-xxi
Sikorski, Wladyslaw, **II**: 203, 390, 392, 396; and Germans and Soviets, **II**: 193-195, 198-199; requests aircraft for Polish exiles, **II**: 114-115
Silesia, **II**: 178, 738
Simferopol, Crimea, **III**: 477
Simović, Dušan, **I**: 152
Sinclair Oil Company, **III**: 3
Singapore, **I**: 38, 73-74, 91, 98, 105, 177, 265, 364-365, 381, 427; **II**: 480, 757; **III**: 74, 270, 318
    as U.S. fleet base; Churchill on, **I**: 308
    British defeat at, **I**: 351, 354-355, 359-362, 420; British losses at, **I**: 654; Churchill on, **I**: 438; Roosevelt on, **I**: 421
    Churchill and recapture of, **III**: 76
    Churchill on, **I**: 93, 98, 301, 321-322
    in Middle East theater, 1942, **I**: 399
    Japanese fleet in, **III**: 14, 17-18, 38-40

sinking of British ships at, 1941, **I**: 287
Sino-Japanese War, **I**: 273
Sittang Bridge, Battle of, **I**: 369
Skelton, Red, **II**: 171
Skorzeny, Otto, **II**: 455
Slessor, Sir John, **II**: 732; and aircraft to Britain, **I**: 509-511; and command changes, **II**: 646, 649
Slim, W. J., **III**: 50
Slovenia, **III**: 222
Smith, Ben, **II**: 743-744
Smith, Leonard B., **I**: 198
Smith, Walter Bedell, **I**: 74, 603; **II**: 17, 38, 87-88, 136, 622-623, 629, 631, 632, 651-653, 656, 658, 713; **III**: Allies discuss, late 1942, **II**: 40; and North African invasion, **I**: 669; and southern France invasion, **II**: 705; at Casablanca Conference, **II**: 97
Smolensk, **II**: 391-396
Smuts, Jan C., **I**: 144, 551, 636; **II**: 102, 239, 252, 254, 263; **III**: 142-143, 219, 222, 340; and Madagascar invasion, **I**: 483; Churchill on, **I**: 654-656; on Darlan deal, **II**: 27; on Italian campaign, **II**: 331; on postwar world, **III**: 334-336, 339; visit to Roosevelt, **I**: 492, 494, 500, 503
Sofia, Bulgaria, bombing of, **II**: 553, 714-715, 724, 730
Solomon Islands, battle of, **I**: 411, 483, 597-598, 657, 659; **II**: 6, 526
Somaliland, **III**: 325-328
Somervell, Brehon B., **II**: 481, 542, 583, 588; **III**: 278
Somerville, Sir James, **I**: 183, 411, 438, 453; **II**: 52-53, 112, 116, 202, 206, 264; in Indian Ocean, **I**: 469
SONAR (underwater sound detection), **I**: 27
Soong, T. V., **II**: 318-319
Sosnowski, Kazimierz, **II**: 701, 762-764
Sousse, Tunisia, **II**: 187
South Africa, **I**: 121-123, 300, 335, 350, 653; **II**: 252
South America, **I**: 28-32, 46, 58, 90-91, 92, 98; **III**: 200, 246
South Carolina: Roosevelt visits, **III**: 74, 77-78, 88
South Pacific: Japanese expansion in, **I**: 225

Southeast Asia, **I**: 177, 369; **II**: 276;
British interests in, **III**: 433, 523-524,
572-573; Japanese threaten, **I**: 274-
276, 287, 364-365; Roosevelt view of,
1941, **I**: 250; U.S. interest in bases in,
III: 237
Southeast Asia command, **III**: 518
Southeast Asia theater, **II**: 420, 742-743;
III: 270; Churchill on, **III**: 347; command structure in, **II**: 248, 282-283,
294-295, 301-302, 318-319; debate
over policy in, **II**: 757, 759; decisions
on at Quebec, 1943, **II**: 430; operations in Burma and China, **III**: 54-55,
50-52; strategy in, **III**: 37-40; strategy
for, 1942, **I**: 321-323
Southwest Pacific theater, **I**: 312-313,
325, 611; **II**: 35-36, 46, 269; American campaign in, **III**: 433-435; and
Burma operations, **II**: 177; Australian
concerns over, **I**: 429-432; **II**: 25;
command structure in, **II**: 263; invasion of Rabaul, **II**: 132; Japanese in,
I: 465, 507; MacArthur and, **I**: 408,
409, 425; need for U.S. troops to,
1942, **II**: 41; problems of command
in, **I**: 330-332, 335-337; Roosevelt on,
I: 390-393, 493; **II**: 156; strategy for,
I: 321-323; **II**: 205-206; U.S. air
forces in, 1942, **I**: 392; Wavell commands, **I**: 309
Soviet Embassy, London, **III**: 54; and
press leaks, **II**: 522
Soviet High Command, **I**: 581; **II**: 65
Soviet Union, **I**: 177, 209, 221, 253, 309,
372, 398, 518-519, 579, 584, 594, 607,
618, 630, 637, 671-673; **II**: 34, 77-78,
126, 168, 378, 563, 643-644; **III**: 7,
257, 351, 485, 494, 574, 597
and morale issues, **II**: 20-21
aid to Caucasus, Allied, **I**: 551, 600,
607-608, 623, 629; Allied vs. Soviet
view, **II**: 57-60, 64-65; Allies stall on,
II: 61-62; Churchill on, **I**: 382, 621;
Marshall on, **I**: 607; promised to Stalin, **I**: 623-624, 628-629; Roosevelt on,
I: 620
aid to, Allied, **I**: 226, 285, 380, 453,
481, 519, 601; **II**: 207; acknowledged,
I: 496; air support, **I**: 172-174, 595-
596; amount of, **II**: 149; Atlantic Conference discussion on, **I**: 227; and

southern route, **I**: 449, 571-574; **III**:
9; **II**: 175-176; British, **I**: 238-244;
British Chiefs on importance of, **I**:
622; Churchill on, **I**: 208, 255-256,
399; **II**: 528; decided on at Washington Conference, **II**: 217-218; effect on
British shipping, **II**: 168; lessened,
1942, **I**: 503; over Trans-Persian Railway, **II**: 59; problems of, **I**: 153, 437,
439, 468-475, 482-483, 494; Roosevelt
fears shortages of, **I**: 472-473; Roosevelt on, **I**: 533, 630; Siberian route, **I**:
609; Stalin on, **I**: 564, 671-672; **II**:
179-180; truck requirements, **I**: 571;
United States, **I**: 238-244, 616, 630;
U.S. military view, **I**: 608-612; via
southern route, **II**: 160
and air bases for Allies, **III**: 280-
285, 294-296, 309-310
and Anglo-American unity toward,
II: 555
and atomic research information,
III: 318-319
and Balkans, **I**: 144-145; **II**: 549;
III: 198, 635; Roosevelt on, **III**: 448
and bomb line in Germany, **III**:
427-430
and Britain, **III**: 260, 545, 633; Aegean policy of, **II**: 558; after Warsaw
Uprising, **III**: 260; on Greece, **III**:
179; over convoys, **II**: 474-479
and Bulgaria, **II**: 553-554, 714, 723-
724, 729
and Churchill-Roosevelt relations, **I**:
9-16, 545
and convoys, **II**: 533-537
and Davies mission, **II**: 233
and Eastern Europe, **III**: 398
and France: and FCNL, **II**: 273,
289-290, 335; recognition of FCNL,
III: 136, 138, 367
and Germany, **I**: 436; **II**: 247, 267,
283; **III**: 408-409; aircraft in, **II**: 152;
best troops transferred to, **II**: 166;
Churchill fears peace between, **II**:
284, 290; invasion by, **I**: 134, 175,
206, 209, 211, 267-268, 394, 439, 497,
564; **II**: 285; invasion by, Churchill on
1942, **I**: 319, **II**: 119; invasion by,
Roosevelt on, **I**: 211; occupation zone
in, **III**: 391; surrender of, **III**: 630-
631; threats of in Middle East, **I**: 381

Soviet Union (*cont.*)
    and Greece, **I**: 16; **III**: 473, 605-
607; Churchill view of, **III**: 95
    and Iran, **I**: 235; **III**: 511-513; Roo-
sevelt on, **III**: 3
    and Italian colonies in Africa, **III**:
326
    and Italian political situation, **III**:
42, 45-46
    and Italian surrender, **II**: 350-351,
362, 370, 459, 461, 467-469, 470, 473-
474, 487-488, 490, 507
    and Italy, **II**: 381, 457, 544; Control
Commission, **II**: 693; postwar, **II**:
503-504, 539-540
    and Japan, **I**: 293; **II**: 492, 600;
Churchill on war with, **I**: 307; Roosevelt on war with, **I**: 250
    and North African invasion, **I**: 577
    and Pacific War, **III**: 353; at Yalta,
III: 527
    and Poland, **III**: 475-477, 551-552,
560-563, 563-565, 567-569, 570-572,
627-629; and Katyn Forest massacre,
II: 388-402; and Warsaw Uprising,
III: 260, 280-285, 294-296, 309-313;
Anglo-American relations on, **III**:
592-597, 598-602; Eastern Poland,
dispute on, **I**: 490; **II**: 611; N.K.V.D.
in, **II**: 392; negotiations with Britain,
III: 68-74; Roosevelt on, **III**: 481-484
    and Quebec decisions, 1944, **III**:
316-319
    and Ribbentrop and British, **II**:
672, 677
    and Teheran Conference: courted
by Roosevelt, **II**: 610
    and Tito, **III**: 80
    and tripartite conference, **II**: 579;
III: 266
    and Truman, **III**: 632
    and Turkey, **II**: 131-132, 140-141,
581
    and U.N. organization creation, **III**:
330-331, 339, 431-433, 531, 532-533
    and Washington Conference, **II**:
212, 217-218
    and wheat agreement, **I**: 248, 252
    and Yalta Conference, **III**: 516
    and Yugoslavia, **II**: 661; **III**: 115,
191, 509-510
    Anglo-American policy toward, **II**:

743; **III**: 505, 545-551, 586-591; postwar, discussed at Quebec, 1943, **II**:
431
    at Moscow Conference, 1944, **III**:
348-351
    at Moscow Foreign Ministers' Con-
ference, **II**: 490, 606
    at Yalta Conference, **III**: 524-530
    boundary issues, **I**: 10, 13, 14-15,
393-394, 505. *See also* Poland
    Churchill on, **I**: 12-13, 20, 294-295,
504, 557; **II**: 222-224, 246; **III**: 30,
136-137, 162-163; air force, **I**: 245; as
enigma, **III**: 349; as not consulted on,
II: 268; atrocities in, **II**: 520; bark-
and-bite of, **III**: 69; cooperation with,
II: 200; expansion of, **III**: 523; handling of, **III**: 13; rhetoric vs. action of,
II: 48; southern front of, **I**: 320-321;
strategy toward, 1943, **I**: 302; support
for, **III**: 600; U.S. comments on, **III**:
438; war efforts of, **II**: 142, 148; **III**:
435; warships to, **II**: 675-676; planned
offensive, **III**: 90-91
    Comintern: suppression of, **II**: 389
    convoys to: problems with, **I**: 527-
533, 535, 537-538; sunk by *Scharnhorst*, **II**: 636
    coordination with on materials, **I**:
328-329
    cross-channel invasion as aid to, **I**:
437
    dollar balances of, **III**: 35
    European expansion of: not consid-
ered an issue, late 1942, **I**: 674
    exempt from diplomatic censorship,
III: 92
    ferrying planes to, **II**: 185-186
    fighting in, **II**: 62-63, 179
    foreign policy of, **I**: 636; **II**: 284,
389-390
    guerrillas in territory liberated by,
III: 61
    Hitler and: Hess on, **I**: 188
    Hopkins visit to, 1941, **I**: 225-226
    Hull and Harriman on, **II**: 563
    in British war plans, 1943, **II**: 14-15
    in central Mediterranean, **III**: 319
    in Eastern Europe, **III**: 248
    in postwar world, **III**: 334-335; Al-
lied view of, **II**: 156; Churchill on, **II**:
129, 221; cooperation with Allies, **III**:

622; Eden view of, **II**: 178; Roosevelt's view, **I**: 502; **III**: 237, 319

Italian ships requested by, **II**: 624-625, 654-656, 669-671, 676, 678, 694-695, 697-700, 709, 711, 731; **III**: 14-19, 23-28; Roosevelt on, **III**: 14-15

Italian troops withdraw from, 1943, **II**: 428

not included in strategic planning, **II**: 266

occupation zones in Europe of, **II**: 746

offensive of, 1944, **II**: 662; **III**: 159, 166, 173, 175, 207, 221, 230, 468-469, 489-490; effect on Italian campaign, **III**: 356; Roosevelt on, **III**: 447-448

Presidium of Supreme Soviet, **III**: 492, 497

public opinion in: on Poland, **II**: 195; on second front issue, **I**: 567

Roosevelt and, **I**: 472; **III**: 560-563, 617, 630-631

Roosevelt on, **I**: 11-16, 18-19, 508; **II**: 202-205, 284; China and, **II**: 608; convergence issue, **I**: 593; Italians in, **II**: 300; morale of, **I**: 502-504; 507; obligations to, **I**: 644; over misunderstandings, **I**: 674-675; planes to, **II**: 44-46; psychological support for, **I**: 292; relations with, **II**: 551, 596; **III**: 288; sacrifices of, **I**: 441

second front issue, **I**: 237-238, 293; **II**: 38-39, 118

separatist movement in, **I**: 371

Stalin on little Allied consulting with, **II**: 287-288

treatment of British seamen, **II**: 477-479

U.S. policy toward, 1945, **III**: 634

view of U.S. free trade proposals, **II**: 748

1942 aircraft production figures, **I**: 566

Soviet-British treaties, **II**: 129-130

Soviet-Polish war, **II**: 715

Spaatz, Carl, **I**: 597-598; **II**: 628-632; **III**: 195-196

Spain, **I**: 116-118, 147, 175, 176, 178, 190, 191, 209, 317; **II**: 171

Allied policy toward, **II**: 725-726, 728, 752

Allied relations with, **I**: 208; **II**:

739-740

and Azores negotiations, **II**: 298, 302

and Britain, **III**: 274-275

and Germany, **I**: 297, 334, 663-666; **III**: 99, 105-108

and Ireland, **III**: 58

and Jewish refugees, **II**: 315

and North African invasion, **I**: 561, 576, 577, 578, 586, 599, 604, 640-642, 663-666, 671, 673; **II**: 12, 20

and Portugal, **II**: 251

and refugee camps in North Africa, **II**: 321

and United States, **III**: 78, 567

Churchill on, **I**: 298, 313; **III**: 67, 161-163

collaboration with Germans, **I**: 165-166, 234

German threat to, **I**: 171-174, 181-182, 184-185, 186, 196, 200-202, 427; **II**: 295

in North Africa, **II**: 76

issue of entry into war, **I**: 86

Italian-Allied talks in, **II**: 432

Jewish refugees in, **II**: 293

mutiny on Italian ships in, **III**: 24

neutrality of, **I**: 255

postwar, Churchill on, **II**: 223

rumors in, **I**: 540

separatist groups in, **I**: 371-372

wolfram trade with Germany, **III**: 66-68, 114-115; Allied response, **II**: 751; **III**: 245; Allied response to, **III**: 78, 80-81

Spalding, General, **I**: 572

Spanish American War, **II**: 480

Spanish Morocco, **I**: 665-666; **II**: 68; after TORCH, **II**: 41

Spears, Sir E. L., **II**: 333-334

Spellman, Francis Cardinal, **II**: 171-172

Spheres of influence, **I**: 14; **III**: 248-249, 482; and Iran, **III**: 141; Anglo-Soviet agreement on, **III**: 200-201; Balkan case, **III**: 177-180, 182, 185; downplayed in Churchill's memoirs, **I**: 6; East Asia and Pacific as U.S.-Sino's, Roosevelt view, **II**: 609; in the Balkans, **III**: 153-154; Italy as American, **III**: 586; negotiated at Moscow, 1944, **III**: 349-351

Stalin, Joseph V., **I**: 36, 437, 518-519,

Stalin, Joseph V. (*cont.*)
529, 624; **II**: 15, 39, 102, 109, 129,
136-137, 216, 233, 265, 386, 434, 454,
562, 660; **III**: 49, 115, 146, 163, 167,
207, 212, 231, 259, 332, 391, 425,
468, 472, 477, 479, 503, 514, 634
  aid to: Churchill on, **I**: 468, 543;
Roosevelt on, **I**: 629-630
  aircraft to, **II**: 190-191
  Allied visit to on strategy, **III**: 489-
490
  and Allied aid to Caucasus, **I**: 580,
596; **II**: 57-60, 65, 77-78
  and Allied units behind Soviet lines,
II: 57
  and Allied use of air bases, **III**: 294-
296
  and Atlantic Conference, **I**: 227
  and atomic energy research, **III**:
319
  and Balkans, **III**: 198, 547-548
  and Baltic States, **III**: 349
  and Bern talks, **III**: 610-616
  and Casablanca Conference, **II**: 55-
56, 85
  and Chiang Kai-shek, **II**: 492
  and Churchill, **I**: 551; **III**: 288;
American view, **II**: 606; percentage
agreement with, **I**: 16; **III**: 471
  and convoys, **I**: 528, 535-538, 601-
603; **II**: 157-165, 179-181, 475-476;
Allied message to, **II**: 172-177;
Churchill on, **I**: 595, 602-604; **II**: 533-
537; on termination of, **I**: 544-546;
Roosevelt and, **I**: 473, 482-483
  and Bulgarian negotiations, **III**: 23
  and cross-channel invasion, **II**: 562,
653-654, 662; **III**: 93-94, 110, 113-114
  and Davies mission, **II**: 233
  and de Gaulle, **III**: 444-445
  and Eastern Europe, **III**: 545-551
  and Eisenhower, **III**: 602, 603
  and France, **III**: 433; Churchill on,
III: 440-441; postwar administration,
III: 22; recognition of FCNL, **II**: 277
  and Germany: postwar, **III**: 528;
reparations from, **III**: 409; unpre-
pared for attack by, **I**: 207
  and Greece, **III**: 487
  and international organization, **II**:
611-612; **III**: 431-433, 531, 586, 588-
591; Security Council, **III**: 331
  and invasion of southern France,
III: 226, 229; Roosevelt on delay of,
III: 82
  and Iran, **III**: 3-4, 512-513
  and Italian ships to Soviet Union,
II: 655-656, 659, 664-666, 669-671,
675-676, 678, 694-695, 697-700, 702,
709, 711, 714, 731, 747-748, 752; **III**:
16, 25, 27, 32
  and Italian surrender, **II**: 473-474,
483, 484, 497
  and Italy, **III**: 42, 45, 185, 190
  and Military-Political Commission,
II: 487-488
  and Moscow Conference, 1944, **III**:
339, 341-345, 348-351
  and Moscow Ministers' Conference,
II: 484-485
  and North African invasion, **I**: 578-
579
  and offensive, 1944, **III**: 100, 172-
173, 200; Churchill on, **III**: 90-91
  and Poland, **II**: 740-743, 762-765;
III: 13-14, 33, 48, 208, 253-255, 350,
363-364, 461-465, 492, 560-563, 564-
565, 585, 588-590, 594-602, 622, 627-
629; Allied messages to on, **II**: 193-
202; American policy toward, **II**: 706-
708; and Katyn Forest massacre, **II**:
396-397; and Mikolajczyk, **III**: 253-
255, 258-262, 269-270, 272; and Soviet Army in, **III**: 48; and Warsaw
Uprising, **III**: 260, 280-285, 294-296,
309-311, 482; at Moscow Conference,
1944, **III**: 358-361; boundary dispute
with, **II**: 651, 685-688, 701-704, 715-
717, 720-723, 726; **III**: 526; Churchill
on, **II**: 735-739; **III**: 17, 60-61, 71-74;
message to, **III**: 29-30; message to
Churchill, **III**: 68-71; recognizes Lublin committee, **III**: 496-497; Roosevelt
on, **II**: 202, 204-206, 208-210, 481-
484, 735; **III**: 79; threatens new Polish government, **III**: 20-21
  and postwar issues, **I**: 228; **II**: 178,
748-750; **III**: 528, 530
  and prisoners of war in Germany,
III: 580-581, 583
  and Roosevelt, **I**: 11-12, 504, 613;
II: 119, 244-245, 345, 586, 588-589;
at Teheran Conference, **II**: 610;
changed tone of messages from, **II**:

18; Churchill fears exclusion by, **II**: 277-278; on death of, **III**: 631

and second front, **I**: 495, 553; **II**: 80-81, 132, 138-140, 153; **III**: 126-128; Allied concerns over delay, **II**: 48, 151-154; Allied reassure on, **II**: 118-119; and joint meetings, **II**: 70; Churchill reply to, **II**: 288-289; delays in, **II**: 285-288; negotiations on, 465-466, 470

and Teheran Conference, **II**: 523, 525-526, 544, 547, 572, 598, 600-601

and territorial claims, **I**: 393, 505

and tripartite conference, **II**: 43, 62, 66-67, 323, 330, 332, 336-337, 384-386, 420-421, 432, 438-440, 448, 491, 549-551, 555, 557, 561, 566, 568, 570, 576, 579, 584, 585, 594-595; **III**: 249-251, 262, 267, 339, 341, 388-389, 394-396, 398, 411-412, 416, 447, 449; Roosevelt on, **II**: 53-55

and Truman, **III**: 632

and Turkey, **II**: 140-141

and unconditional surrender, **II**: 645-646; **III**: 133, 142-143

and Yalta Conference, **III**: 367-368, 371, 377-381, 469, 493, 494, 495-496, 510, 515, 516, 520, 526-528, 530; Anglo-American views, **III**: 526-527; Churchill on, **III**: 502

and Yugoslavia, **III**: 510

at Moscow Conference, 1942, **I**: 564-569

at Moscow Foreign Ministers' Conference, **II**: 606

behavior discussed, **I**: 564

Churchill and Roosevelt discuss, **II**: 328

Churchill and Roosevelt name for, **I**: 553

Churchill on, **I**: 6, 294-295, 643; **II**: 246-247; **III**: 260-261, 547-550, 573-574, 612-613; apology of, **III**: 624; approaches to, **II**: 81; as growling bear, **II**: 694; negotiations with, **I**: 563; personal relationship with, **I**: 571-572; *Pravda* story and, **II**: 677; Soviet customs and, **I**: 562; tone of messages of, **II**: 433; pledges to, **I**: 255; supply mission, 1941, **I**: 243

Eisenhower representative to meet with, **III**: 485

fears Allied talks with Germans, **III**: 609-612

fears British-German peace treaty, **I**: 636-637

friendly messages from, late 1942, **I**: 671-673

Halifax on, **II**: 733

health of, **III**: 339-341

negotiating behavior of, **I**: 566

not included in strategic planning, **II**: 266

on Allied successes, **III**: 230

on bombing of Sofia, **II**: 554

on communications among Allies, **III**: 625

on Finland, **II**: 181-182

on International Labor Organization, **III**: 75

on Italy and Normandy invasion, **III**: 182-183

on Japan, **I**: 307; **II**: 575, 577

on lack of support from Allies, **I**: 564, 618-619

on military situation, **I**: 237; **II**: 17

on poison gas usage, **I**: 439

on Poles as not shedding blood, **II**: 764

on Poles in Soviet Union, **I**: 593-594

on role in Italy, **II**: 540

on Roosevelt view of postwar world, **I**: 502

on security leaks to press, **III**: 54

on Soviet role in Pacific, **III**: 527

on U.S. troops to Europe, **I**: 230

on war not won with plans, **I**: 566

on war strategy, 1943, **II**: 244-246

on war-crime trials, **III**: 329

role in alliance, **I**: 293

Roosevelt and, **II**: 259-260; **III**: 482-484, 573

Roosevelt on, **I**: 545-546, 563, 643; **II**: 72-74, 563-564; **III**: 221, 223, 629-630; ability to handle, **I**: 421; proposed meeting with, **II**: 283-284; support for, **I**: 625; treatment of, **II**: 597

Roosevelt to, **II**: 463-464

Stalingrad, Battle of, **I**: 14, 226, 544, 564, 617-619, 636, 671-672; **II**: 14, 17, 51, 52, 63, 102, 138, 141; **III**: 119; Roosevelt on, **I**: 630

Standley, William H., **I**: 616-617, 621; **II**: 180, 233-234

Stark, Harold R., **I**: clxv, 207, 223, 237, 246-247, 338, 348, 399, 411, 413; **II**: 85; **III**: 211; and invasion of southern France, **III**: 197-199; and Mediterranean theater, **III**: 203-204; on convoys to Soviet Union, **I**: 527-528; on ships to Soviet, **III**: 56-57; sent to London, 1942, **I**: 397

Stars and Stripes, **I**: 619

Steel, traded by neutrals, **III**: 245

Steinhardt, Laurence, **III**: 48-49, 508-509

Stettinius, Edward R., Jr., **II**: 743; **III**: 316, 322-323, 341-342, 413, 445, 454, 481-482, 543; Balkans, **III**: 182; and Britain, **III**: 530; and British dollar balances, **III**: 36; and Greece, **III**: 449-450, 457-458; and Italian political situation, **III**: 443; and Latin America, **III**: 551; and occupation zones in Germany, **III**: 147; and Poland, **III**: 622; and recognition of FCNL, **III**: 365, 367, 369; and Truman, **III**: 632; and Yalta and Malta conferences, **III**: 502-503, 505, 507, 511, 521, 523, 591; in London, **III**: 140-141; made Secretary of State, 1944, **III**: 437, 439; on Poland, **III**: 475; on Yugoslavia, **III**: 513; opposes Morgenthau Plan, **III**: 317; trip to London, 1944, **III**: 66, 93, 109-110

Stevenson, Ralph S., **II**: 660

Stilwell, Joseph W., **II**: 117, 205-206, 263, 282, 306, 318, 537; **III**: 117, 426, 572
    and Burma, **II**: 110, 112
    and CBI command structure, **II**: 275-277
    and Chiang, **I**: 405; **II**: 583-584
    and Southeast Asia command, **II**: 294, 301-302; as deputy commander, **II**: 430
    and supplies to China, **II**: 542
    British view of, **II**: 757
    in Burma, **I**: 353, 450; and command situation, **I**: 422-423
    in China, **II**: 751; **III**: 51-52; operations in, **III**: 54
    on Burma operations, **II**: 213
    on Myitkyina, **II**: 756
    recall of, **III**: 370, 375-376

Stimson, Henry L., **I**: 165, 177, 238; **II**: 222, 225-226, 495; **III**: 3, 320, 395, 579; and administration by military, **II**: 480; and China-Burma command disputes, **I**: 405; and Darlan deal, **II**: 8; and Italian campaign, Churchill on, **II**: 202; and Marshall, **II**: 482; on British defenses, **I**: 268; on Chiang Kai-shek, **I**: 417; on Churchill and India, **I**: 447; on cross-channel invasion, **I**: 436, 514; on occupation government in Sicily, **II**: 188; on postwar France, **III**: 160; on U.S. aircraft to Britain, **I**: 485

Stone, Ellery W., **III**: 324, 366

Stowe, Leland, **I**: 456

Straits of Gibraltar, **I**: 86, 179, 576-577, 582-583; **II**: 165-166; threatened by Germans, **I**: 171, 173

Straits of Malacca, **I**: 299

Straits of Sunda, **I**: 299

Strasbourg, France, **III**: 408-409, 434, 494

Strasser, Otto, **I**: 372

Subasić, Ivan, **III**: 115-116, 190, 275, 279, 281, 509

Submarines, Allied: for Soviets, **II**: 671

Submarines, British, **I**: 382, 438; in Pacific, **I**: 305; promised to Soviets, **II**: 702

Submarines, Dutch, **I**: 299, 305, 382, 438

Submarines, German, **I**: 25, 43, 56, 75, 80, 91, 104, 151, 152-153, 164, 170, 172, 174, 193, 212, 219, 221, 227, 238, 554; **II**: 44, 312, 475, 499-501, 514, 605; **III**: 163, 165-166, 235-237, 312, 337, 374, 382, 384, 386, 486, 489, 544; Allies break their codes, **I**: 214-215; American inexperience with, 1942, **I**: 407; and Atlantic shipping losses, **I**: 406; and Azores, **II**: 239; and British ships, **I**: 481; and convoys to Soviet Union, **I**: 527-528, 530, 537; **II**: 157-162; and North African invasion plans, **I**: 577; and U.S. aid to England, **I**: 56; as "canaries," **II**: 327-328, 344; attack U.S. ships, **I**: 265; attack *Greer*, **I**: 236; bombing of bases and construction sites, **I**: 424; British raids on, 1942, **I**: 434-435; British victories over, **I**: 162; changes in tactics, **II**: 647; Churchill on, **I**: 112, 302, 648-649, 671; demoralization of crews of, **III**: 112; diminished activity of, **III**: 11-13, 22-23, 345-346; fleet strength,1940, **I**: 50; Hess on, **I**: 188; improvements in, **III**: 617-618; in Atlantic, **I**: 26, 196, 264, 451-452; in Bay of Biscay, **II**: 366-367; in Caribbean and Gulf, **I**: 515, 524; in Martinique, **I**: 353; in Mediterranean, **I**: 267, 317; in Normandy invasion, **III**: 233; in U.S. waters, **I**: 348, 456; issue of morale on, **II**: 217; issue of publicity on sinkings of, **II**: 327; **III**: 251-252; losses of, **II**: 313-314, 345, 387, 658-659, 728-729; **III**: 79, 121-122, 125-126, 264, 492; number left at end of war, **III**: 492; radar detection of, **II**: 26-27; Roosevelt orders attacks on, **I**: 229-230; shift to Caribbean and Gulf of Mexico, **I**: 490-491; sinking of tankers, **II**: 78; sinkings of, **II**: 28, 228-229, 323-324, 382-383, 571, 574-575, 710; **III**: 37; technological advances in, **II**: 476-477; **III**: 441; 1941 threat of, **I**: 90

Submarines, Italian, **I**: 43, 50, 79; promised to Soviets, **II**: 700

Submarines, Soviet: and Japanese, **I**: 307

Submarines, United States, **I**: 299, 382; in ABDA area, **I**: 390; in Black Sea, **II**: 663; in Pacific, **I**: 305; **III**: 13; propaganda concerning, **II**: 312; losses in Pacific, **III**: 489; Navy's effective weapon in Pacific, **III**: 13; security breaches on, **III**: 386; successes in Pacific, **III**: 252; to Soviet in lieu of Italian ships, **II**: 698-700

Suckley, Margaret, **II**: 438

Sudan, **I**: 203; **III**: 328

Suez Canal, **I**: 91, 159, 163, 298, 302, 519, 541; **II**: 23; **III**: 39, 536; Roosevelt on, **I**: 421

Sugar, Caribbean, **II**: 743

Sultan, Daniel I., **III**: 370, 375, 429

Sumatra, **I**: 321, 351, 353; **II**: 213, 276, 755-756, 757, 759; **III**: 39; Japanese threat to, **I**: 361

Sunda Straits, **I**: 382

Supreme War Council, idea defeated, **I**: 293

Sweden, **I**: 209; **II**: 106, 557, 558; **III**: 106, 108, 621, 623; and Allies, **I**: 639; neutrality of, **III**: 245, 257

Swedish Red Cross, **II**: 86, 105

Swinton, Viscount, **II**: 98; **III**: 404-407, 419, 425, 427, 428

Switzerland, **I**: 129, 209, 225; **II**: 106, 223, 363; **III**: 106, 108, 621

Symington, Powers, **III**: 238-239, 271

Syria, **I**: 179, 185-186, 235; **II**: 102; Anglo-French dispute over, **I**: 210, 660; **II**: 333-334; Allied plans for, 1943, **I**: 671; and Britain, **II**: 14-15; British troops in, **II**: 50; invasion by Britain, **I**: 191, 204; and France, **II**: 599-600; **III**: 389-390; and Madagascar invasion, **I**: 441; Churchill on, **I**: 295; consequences for of Soviet defeat, **I**: 307; German threat to, **I**: 175-176, 196, 319; postwar arrangements in, **I**: 221; Roosevelt on, **I**: 421, 533

Takoradi, Ghana (Gold Coast), **I**: 209, 211

Tananarive, Madagascar, **I**: 613

Tangier, Morocco, **I**: 173, 176; **II**: 384; German consulates in, **II**: 739

Tanks, Allied, **I**: 37, 108: Anglo-American cooperation on, **I**: 212-213, 217, 220; British need for, **I**: 197; Churchill on, **I**: 223-224, 256; **III**: 164; of in North Africa, **I**: 241; production of, **I**: 241-243, 615; Stalin on importance of, **I**: 243; U.S. production of, 1943, **II**: 46-47

Tanks, United States, **I**: 203, 555
and Soviet offensive, 1943, **II**: 179
in Egypt, **I**: 636
in Middle East theater, **I**: 592-593
in North Africa, **I**: 273, 493, 514, 516, 543
production and distribution of, **I**: 631; **II**: 46-47
Sherman: Churchill on, **I**: 646; Omar Bradley on, **I**: 646
to Britain, **II**: 95; **III**: 574
to Soviets, **I**: 569

Tannenberg, battle at, **II**: 738

Taormina, Sicily, **III**: 447, 449

Taranto, Battle of, **I**: 83-85; **II**: 184;
III: 26
Taylor, Myron C, **II**: 315-316
Tedder, Sir Arthur W., **I**: 564, 580; **II**:
295, 306, 621-624, 627-629, 631, 632,
634-635, 651; **III**: 485, 552-553, 612;
advocates strategic bombing, **II**: 234;
at Moscow Conference, 1942, **I**: 560;
in North Africa, **II**: 136, 138-139,
141-142, 145; on bombing of France,
III: 122-123; visit to Moscow, 1944,
III: 489
Teheran, **I**: 235; **II**: 448, 576, 579, 585-
586, 595; **III**: 249
Teheran Conference: Anglo-American
talks before, debate on, **II**: 549-551,
594-598, 600
Teheran Conference (EUREKA, 1943),
I: 6; **II**: 523, 525-526, 544-547, 561,
612, 708; **III**: 53, 502
and cross-channel invasion, **I**: 14;
II: 653, 662, 712; **III**: 90, 94, 110,
113; Soviet offensive and, **III**: 100,
172-173
and Iran, **III**: 140, 512-513
and Italian ships to Soviets, **II**: 624-
625, 654-655, 664-665, 669, 671, 694-
695, 748; **III**: 17-18, 25, 28, 437
and Pacific war policy, **II**: 732, 755
and Poland, **III**: 526; and boundary
dispute of, **II**: 685-686, 706-707; Curzon line accepted at, **III**: 68, 70, 72,
357-359; decisions on, **II**: 735
and postwar economic issues, **II**:
749
and surrender of Germany, **II**: 645;
III: 133, 142-143
codenames for, **II**: 492-494
Istria attack, **III**: 212-213, 227, 232,
300
significance of, **II**: 524, 596, 613
occupation zones for Germany at,
III: 316
planning for, **II**: 493-494, 562-573,
575-579
Roosevelt on, **III**: 221, 223
Roosevelt's personal diplomacy at,
II: 610
war criminals discussed at, **III**: 329
TerPoorten, H., and ABDA command
controversies, **I**: 339, 342, 344

Thailand, **I**: 279-280; **II**: 276; **III**: 573,
582; Churchill on strategy toward, **I**:
299, 382; Japanese in, **I**: 135
Thermopylae, Battle at, **I**: 174-175
Thompson, Charles, **I**: 290, 314, 510,
525
Thompson, Dorothy, **II**: 191
Thomsen, Hans, **I**: 218
Thorez, Maurice, **II**: 465-466
Thorne, Christopher, **I**: 15
Thrace, Greece, **II**: 558; **III**: 350
Tiarks, Henry F., **I**: 540
Tilsit, East Prussia, **II**: 54, 686
Timberlake, Edward J., **II**: 658
Times (of London), **I**: 131; **II**: 63; **III**:
61
Timor (Portugal), **II**: 249-250, 269, 280-
281
Tito (Josip Broz), **II**: 406, 548, 554, 668;
III: 42, 115-116, 190-191, 203, 232,
279-280, 281, 300, 485, 509-510; Al-
lied debate over support for, **III**: 306;
and Churchill, **III**: 131-133, 275; and
Moscow Conference, 1944, **III**: 359;
and Stalin, **III**: 358-359; attack on,
III: 167; British support for, **II**: 182,
660; **III**: 198; Churchill and Roosevelt
on, **II**: 640-641; Churchill on, **II**: 644-
645; efforts against the Germans, **III**:
80
Tobin, Daniel, **I**: 571
Tobin, Jerome F. P., **II**: 164
Tobruk, **I**: 126, 175, 182, 207; **II**: 211;
III: 74, 574; Australian troops at, **II**:
25; battles at, **I**: 168-169, 170-171,
493-494, 514, 516, 532, 538, 673;
British hold, **I**: 351; British losses at,
I: 654
Togliatti, Palmiro, **III**: 110
Tojo, Eiki, **I**: 250
Tokyo, bombing of, **I**: 442, 465-466,
507
Tomlinson, George, **III**: 101-102, 104
Tory Party, British, **I**: 36
Toulon, France, **III**: 223, 304
Towers, John, **I**: 486-488, 490
Trade issues: and Imperial preference
system, **I**: 351; and lend-lease bill, **I**:
137; Britain vs. U.S., **I**: 345-346, 356-
359; United States attitudes toward, **I**:
373

Trades Unions Congress, British, **III**: 457

Trans-Persian Railway, **I**: 532-533, 571-572, 574, 584, 594, 600; **II**: 59, 476

Trans-Siberian Railway, **II**: 175

Transylvania, **II**: 131; **III**: 229

Treaty of Riga, **II**: 685, 703, 720, 722

Treaty of Tilsit, **II**: 54-55

Treaty of Utrecht, **I**: 325-326

Treaty of Versailles, **I**: 14, 61, 221

Trieste, **I**: 83; **III**: 198, 219, 227, 299-302, 305, 348, 619

Trinidad, **I**: 59-60, 65, 68, 142; **II**: 117

Tripartite Alliance, **I**: 74, 137, 152

Tripartite conference proposals, **II**: 565; **III**: 349, 363, 416, 447; Churchill and, **II**: 278, 491; **III**: 436; French participation in, **III**: 440; Roosevelt and, **II**: 260; Stalin and, **III**: 411-412

Tripoli, **I**: 253, 270, 304, 317, 381; **II**: 27, 99, 122; Allies attack, **II**: 12; and Allied invasion, **II**: 9; battle at, **I**: 604; **II**: 118; operation ACROBAT, **I**: 294-295, 314; Rommel in, **II**: 152

Tripolitania, **I**: 673; **II**: 56, 136-137, 144-145, 316; **III**: 328

Truman, Harry S, **III**: 493, 631-632; and Soviet Union, **I**: 19

Truscott, Lucian, **III**: 409-410, 422

Trusteeships, discussed at Yalta, **III**: 528

Tsouderos, Emmanouel, **III**: 95-96, 110

Tuck, S. Pickney, **I**: 480-481

Tunis, Tunisia, **I**: 176, 180, 270, 295, 298, 304, 317, 354; **II**: 4, 11-12, 122, 353, 506, 508-511, 514-516, 568, 584, 592, 618, 626; **III**: 228; Allied losses in, **II**: 529; Allied troops in, 1942, **I**: 320; Allies threaten Germans, 1942, **II**: 7; and North African invasion, **I**: 578; **II**: 9; campaign in, **II**: 54-56, 138, 151, 172, 189, 207; **III**: 466; Churchill at, **II**: 620, 628, 634; conference at, **II**: 518; Roosevelt visit to, **II**: 608, 613

Tunisia, **II**: 20, 30, 68, 98, 118, 139, 145, 147, 384, 511; Allied campaign in, **I**: 673; **II**: 38, 41-42, 51, 76, 118, 133, 136-138, 144-145, 151-153, 157-158, 182-183, 185, 189-190, 207; Allied capture of, **II**: 55-56, 84; and

North African invasion, **I**: 582-583; 185; Germans in, **I**: 657; **II**: 4, 10; Vichy resistance in, **II**: 27-28

Turin, Italy, **II**: 380; **III**: 45

Turkey, **I**: 79, 98, 136, 175, 181, 190, 191, 235-236, 532, 564, 570, 669; **II**: 13-14, 34, 102, 184, 267, 350, 363, 516, 518, 665, 670, 714, 729; **III**: 106, 328, 368

  Allied relations with, **I**: 208, 671, 674; **II**: 14, 49-50, 152, 217, 445, 517, 581, 588, 732; Churchill on, **I**: 301-302

  and Britain, **II**: 126-128, 134, 196-197; **III**: 202; Treaty of Mutual Assistance with, **II**: 140-141

  and chrome, **III**: 55-56

  and Germany, **I**: 579; trade with, **III**: 48-49, 245; Treaty of Friendship with, **II**: 140-141

  and Soviet Union, **II**: 49-50, 127, 131-132; Treaty of Neutrality and Friendship, **II**: 140-141

  and Soviet Union, fear of, **II**: 49-50, 127

  and Yalta Conference planning, **III**: 508-509

  Churchill on role of, **I**: 238, 543; **II**: 498-499

  claims Dodecanese, **II**: 197

  German intelligence activities in, **II**: 663, 669

  German threat to, **I**: 196, 319

  issue of entry into war, **I**: 622; **II**: 128, 130-132, 557-558, 668, 705; British on, **II**: 618; Churchill on, **II**: 612

  Jadwin Mission in, **II**: 765

  military strength of, **I**: 295

  neutrality of: **II**: 10; and Japanese success, **I**: 499; Churchill on, **I**: 255

  Moscow talks, 1944, **III**: 349-353

  plan to put British troops in, **II**: 619, 621

  postwar: Churchill view, **II**: 222-223 Roosevelt on, **I**: 179; **II**: 156 Stalin on, **I**: 566; **II**: 51, 140-141 U.S. aid to, **II**: 527

Tuve, Merrill A., **III**: 412-413

Tweedsmuir, Lord, **II**: 353-354

U Saw, Prime Minister of Burma, **I**: 312

United Nations Relief and Rehabilitation
Administration (UNRRA), **II**: 749-750
Ukraine, **II**: 685; **III**: 532; air bases in,
III: 295; in German plans, 1941, **I**:
129; Insurgent Army in, **III**: 461
Ukranians, **II**: 716, 764; **III**: 541; in Poland, **II**: 701
Umberto, Crown Prince of Italy, **II**:
759; **III**: 31, 33, 52, 110, 176
Unconditional surrender, **II**: 128-129
and German resistance, **II**: 547
discussed at Casablanca, **II**: 119
for Germany, **III**: 133-135, 149,
408-409, 611-612, 635; Roosevelt on,
II: 652; Stalin on, **II**: 645-646
for Italy, **II**: 378, 384, 455, 461,
463, 466-469, 470, 500, 523-524, 552-
553; **III**: 333; debated by Allies, **II**:
347, 358, 363, 370; Eisenhower opposes, **II**: 518-519; Stalin on, **II**: 432;
terms of, **II**: 423, 425-426, 429
for Japan, **II**: 609
in Italy, **II**: 300-301
Stalin on, **II**: 132
Union of Polish Patriots, **III**: 260, 283-
284
United Kingdom Commercial Corporation, **III**: 8-9, 140-141
United Nations (wartime coalition), **I**:
398, 557; **II**: 102, 112, 129-130, 243,
551-553; and de Gaulle, **II**: 272; and
India, **I**: 547-579; and Portugal, **II**:
296; Bulgarians attempt to join, **II**:
729; in Churchill's postwar world, **II**:
224-225; New Zealand view, **II**: 37;
Polish-Soviet dispute and, **II**: 200,
204; Roosevelt on, **I**: 556, 558-559
United Nations Conference on Food
and Agriculture, **II**: 748
United Nations Monetary Conference,
II: 749
United Nations Organization, **III**: 319,
551, 626; at Teheran-Cairo conferences, **II**: 613; debated at Yalta Conference, **III**: 527, 528; proposals on,
III: 75, 431-433; veto debate, **III**:
330-335, 338-339, 342-343, 351; voting question in, **III**: 344-345
United Nations Relief and Rehabilitation
Administration, **II**: 315, 749-750; **III**:
279, 319, 606-607, 619; and aid to It-

aly, **III**: 321, 323
United Press International, **II**: 601
United States, **III**: 351
Africa and, **II**: 529
and Italy: Roosevelt on special relations with, **II**: 306
and Japan: Roosevelt freezes assets
of, **I**: 225; warning to, **I**: 279
and Poland: Churchill urges show
of interest in, **III**: 69; policy on, **II**:
716; Stalin on, **III**: 273
and unity of command in S.W. Pacific, **I**: 312
anti-colonialism in, **I**: 654-656; at
Cairo Conference, **II**: 609
anti-fascism in, **II**: 451
anti-interventionists, **I**: 80, 120, 228;
II: 156; and lend-lease, **I**: 63; and
Roosevelt, **I**: 150, 421
Board of Economic Welfare, **II**:
248, 265, 290
business interests in, **III**: 187; and
British trade, **III**: 535; and Greece,
III: 605; and lend-lease supplies, **I**:
232-234; and postwar Iran, **III**: 10
Cabinet, **I**: 238-239; and Ireland,
II: 421; and Poland, **II**: 198-199
Catholics in: and Roosevelt, **II**: 319-
321, 373
Churchill on, **I**: 176, 182, 235, 292,
649; **II**: 222-223, 227-228, 447-449,
529; as world power, **III**: 421; military security in, **II**: 528-529; Pacific
role of, **I**: 135-137; superiority of, **III**:
418
civil aviation of, **III**: 418-420, 519-
520
Congress, **I**: 211-212; **II**: 114, 296,
454, 526, 563; **III**: 154, 388, 395, 449,
569; aid for Britain, postwar, **III**: 411;
and aid to Britain, **I**: 42, 48-49; and
Big Three conference, **III**: 377; and
British dollar balances, **III**: 36; and
British financial crisis, **I**: 122, 124;
III: 65-66; and civil aviation dispute,
I: 17; and convoying, **I**: 218; **III**: 421;
and destroyer deal, **I**: 38; and European relief program, **III**: 47; and
German war declaration, **I**: 283; and
international organization, **III**: 526,
531; and Japanese war declaration, **I**:

282-283; and lend-lease, **I**: 58, 68, 129, 138, 143; **III**: 407; and Neutrality Act amendments, **I**: 245, 264, 268; and oil agreement, **II**: 733; **III**: 187; and Poland, **III**: 463, 567; and postwar reconstruction, **III**: 606; and Roosevelt, **III**: 160-161, 530; and Roosevelt's foreign policy, **II**: 527-530; and Sir John Dill, **III**: 506, 520-521; and Spain, **III**: 106; and Teheran Conference, **II**: 707; and trade issues, **I**: 345-346; and U.N. organization, **II**: 584-586; **III**: 344; and war mobilization, **I**: 285-286; Churchill on, **II**: 345; Churchill **I**: 292, 306; **III**: 631; Connally Resolution, **II**: 584; Foreign Affairs committee, **III**: 66; Fulbright Resolution, **II**: 584; Hull influence in, **II**: 462; MacArthur's influence in, **I**: 479; Roosevelt aware of opinions in, **I**: 227; Roosevelt on, **II**: 323, 544-546, 568, 578; Roosevelt speech to, **III**: 505-506, 551; Roosevelt to on Yalta, **III**: 547

Constitution, **III**: 5, 10
De Gaulle on, **II**: 210
Department of Agriculture, **I**: 250
ethnic groups and Roosevelt, **III**: 33
Federal Communications Commission, **II**: 248-249, 265
Foreign Economic Administration, **II**: 527
foreign policy: and domestic politics, **II**: 527-530; blames Europeans for world wars, **I**: 14; confusion on Azores, **II**: 590-591; decision-making as lax, **II**: 495-497; powers of President, **II**: 128; Presidents try to control, **I**: 24; Roosevelt and, **II**: 578; **III**: 505; supports British as world power, **III**: 7
Foreign Relief and Rehabilitation Office, **II**: 315-316
House Foreign Affairs Committee: and British dollar balances, **III**: 34
Irish-Americans, **II**: 186; Roosevelt and, **III**: 81
Italian-Americans, **II**: 451, 649; **III**: 646; and election of 1944, **III**: 386; and La Guardia appointment, **III**: 320; and 1944 election, **III**: 319; Roo-

sevelt on, **II**: 306; view of war with Italy, **II**: 188
labor strikes in, 1941, **I**: 276
Lend-Lease Administration, **II**: 315
military vs. political authority in, **II**: 479-481
Navy Department, **III**: 236; and Clipperton Islands, **III**: 504; and lend-lease bill, **I**: 138; and shipments of oil, **II**: 82; on oil supplies, **II**: 106-107; on Pearl Harbor commemoration, **II**: 63
Office of Production Management, **I**: 126, 239, 327
Office of Strategic Services, **I**: 134; **II**: 248-249, 265, 548-549, 729; **III**: 586; and Italian army morale, **II**: 341; created, **I**: 263; mission to Yugoslavia, **III**: 80, 82, 86, 306, 308-309; on Germans in Turkey, **II**: 663
Office of War Information, **I**: 557; **II**: 8, 248-249, 265, 569, 710-711; attack on Italian king, **II**: 354
Polish-Americans, **II**: 192, 198, 611; **III**: 208, 365, 530; Roosevelt attention to, **III**: 33, 79; Stalin on, **II**: 762, 764
political pressure on Roosevelt in, **II**: 42
postwar, **III**: 335-336; Churchill on, **I**: 93; **II**: 130; Roosevelt on, **I**: 502; **II**: 708-709; and less-developed nations, **III**: 4-10
public opinion: and atomic bomb research, **III**: 319; and Clipperton Island, **III**: 417; and Poland, **III**: 597; and U.N. organization, **III**: 344; and war strategy, **III**: 223; Churchill on, **I**: 89; Germany first policy criticized, **I**: 379; on aid to Soviet Union, **I**: 239, 246; on Argentina, **III**: 347; on bombing of Rome, **II**: 252; on British Empire, **I**: 373; on British imperialism, **I**: 205; on British-French-Soviet pact, **III**: 445; on cross-channel invasion, **I**: 437; on Darlan deal, **II**: 5, 8; on escorting convoys, **I**: 218; on France, **III**: 138; on freezing of assets, **I**: 210; on Greek crisis, **III**: 455-456; on Hess, **I**: 186-188; on independence for India, **I**: 402, 445-447; on international organization, **III**: 527; on Ital-

United States (*cont.*)

ian monarchy, **II**: 681; on Italian policies, **III**: 436; on Italian political situation, **III**: 41; on Italy, **III**: 401, 620; on Italy as ally, **II**: 443; on Japan as primary war, **I**: 510; on MacArthur and Philippines, **III**: 193; on Mountbatten, **II**: 489; on neutral trade with enemy, **III**: 106, 108; on Northern Ireland, **II**: 192; on Poland, **II**: 192, 194; **III**: 73-74, 548, 562, 567, 585, 600; on Poland and Greece, **III**: 463; on postwar France, **III**: 160; on postwar internationalism, **III**: 517; on postwar world, **II**: 226; on Roosevelt's foreign policy, **I**: 222-223; **II**: 527-530; on sinking of American ship, **I**: 265; on threat of Vatican bombing, **II**: 303; on U.N. organization, **III**: 526; on U.S. forces to Europe, **I**: 230; on U.S. prisoners of war, **III**: 542; on U.S. support for Britain, **I**: 511-512; on war progress, **III**: 435; optimism on war lowers production, **II**: 327; Roosevelt concern for, **I**: 227, 234, 355; **III**: 526, 530; Willkie on, **I**: 189

Secret Service, **II**: 530, 532, 588

Senate, **III**: 528; and international organization, **III**: 531, 532

shipbuilding program in, **I**: 157, 215

Shipping Administration, **II**: 45

State Department, **I**: 4, 176, 223, 250, 313, 342, 344, 351, 526; **II**: 191, 236, 371, 507, 592, 637-638, 739; **III**: 291, 329, 334, 352, 402, 405, 407, 446, 566, 578; and air agreement with Ireland, **III**: 543-544; and Allied Control Commission, **III**: 371; and American oil interests, **II**: 733-734; and Anglo-American money issues, **II**: 743-744; and Argentina, **III**: 415-416, 430-431; and Atlantic Charter, **I**: 228; and Atlantic Islands plan, **I**: 201; and atrocities proclamation, **II**: 519-521; and Azores, **II**: 495, 506-507, 525, 566-567; and Balkans, **III**: 200-201; and Britain, **III**: 436-438, 517, 530, 535-536; and Bulgaria, **II**: 765; and business protests on lend-lease, **I**: 232; and channel invasion security, **III**:

120; and civil aviation policy, **III**: 423; and Clipperton Island, **III**: 417; 504; and cross-channel invasion, **III**: 101; and Darlan deal, **II**: 8, 726; **III**: 31; and European relief program, **III**: 47; and Foreign Ministers' Conference, **II**: 463; and France, **II**: 579-580; **III**: 356, 361-362; and FCNL, **II**: 337; **III**: 87, 89, 240, 367, 369; and Germany, occupation of, **III**: 316-317; and Germany, postwar, **II**: 178; and Greece, **III**: 278, 297, 349, 455, 480, 618-619; and Imperial preference system, **I**: 356-357; and India, **I**: 546; and Iran, **III**: 5, 8, 10; and Iran, Declaration on, **III**: 3; and Iranian oil, **III**: 511-513; and Ireland, **II**: 421; **III**: 58, 75; and Italian political situation, **II**: 723, 760; **III**: 28-29; and Italian surrender, **II**: 538; and Italy, **II**: 539; **III**: 41, 45, 52-53, 176, 178, 188, 373, 533-534, 620; and Italy, postwar, **III**: 323; and Jews to North Africa, **II**: 316; and lend-lease aid, **I**: 63; and liberated Europe, **III**: 622-623; and Middle East, **III**: 390; and Poland, **III**: 253, 312, 462, 475, 562-563, 563-564, 567-569, 574-575, 592, 594; and postwar economic relations, **II**: 750; and relief for liberated areas, **III**: 636; and relief for Norway, **II**: 105; and reparations, **III**: 528; and Roosevelt, **III**: 530; and Roumania, **III**: 625; and St. Pierre-Miquelon affair, **I**: 326; and Soviet Union, **II**: 119, 233; and Soviets in Eastern Europe, **III**: 546, 549; and Spain, **II**: 751; **III**: 66-67, 78, 105; and Stalin, Roosevelt on, **I**: 421; and the Balkans, **III**: 153-154; and Turkey, **III**: 508; and U.N. organization plan, **III**: 431; and Vichy French, **I**: 426, 440; and war criminals, **III**: 364; and White House, **I**: 521-522; and Yugoslavia, **III**: 191, 510; codes, **I**: 9; Churchill criticizes, **I**: 370-371; excluded from Casablanca Conference, **II**: 53-54, 109; handling of neutrals criticized, **III**: 78; not at Quebec Conference, 1944, **III**: 316; on Atlantic Charter, **I**: 559; on financial aid to China, **II**: 620; on freezing foreign

funds, **I**: 209; on Hess, **I**: 186; on
Hurley, **III**: 395; on Molotov, **I**: 11;
on Pearl Harbor commemoration, **II**:
63; on postwar oil conference, **II**:
744; on propaganda in Asia, **II**: 696;
Roosevelt and, **I**: 276; **III**: 481; Roosevelt on, **II**: 642
    supply program, **II**: 46-47
    tank production in, **I**: 220
    Treasury Department: and Anglo-
American money issues, **II**: 743-744;
and French currency, **III**: 183, 196
    war commitments of, Roosevelt on,
I: 235
    War Department, **I**: 202, 239, 384,
437; **III**: 387, 445, 578, 635; and
command changes, **II**: 656; and Darlan deal, **II**: 40; and Italian surrender
terms, **II**: 368; and lend-lease bill, **I**:
138; and relief, **III**: 559; and relief in
North Africa, **II**: 315; modifies theater arrangements, 1942, **I**: 397; on
Burma command situation, **I**: 422; on
materials and forces to Britain, **II**: 38-
39; on Pearl Harbor commemoration,
II: 63
    war production: defended by Roo-
sevelt 1943, **II**: 114
    war production in, **I**: 211, 238-243
    War Shipping Administration, **I**:
647; **II**: 219, 221
    wheat interests in, **I**: 247, 249, 251
United States Commercial Corporation
(Iran), **III**: 8
United States Maritime Commission, **I**:
327
United States of Europe, **II**: 223
United States Ordnance Board, **I**: 213

Valence, France, **III**: 305
Van Mook, Dr. H. J., **I**: 339-340
Vandenberg, Arthur, **III**: 528
Vargas, Getulio, **II**: 123
Vatican, **II**: 172; and bombing of Rome,
II: 234, 250-253, 265, 269, 303-304,
373-374; and Italian campaign, **II**:
320; and Italian political situation, **II**:
680; and Italian surrender terms, **II**:
363; and prisoner of war exchange,
II: 180
Vegesack, Germany, **II**: 517

Venezia Giulia, **III**: 619
Venice, Italy, **III**: 198
Venizelos, Sophocles, **III**: 95-96
Verdun, Battle at, **I**: 656
Versailles, France: Churchill visit to, **III**:
494-495
Vetterlein, Kurt E., **II**: 356
Victor Emmanuel III, King of Italy, **II**:
347, 349-350, 357-358, 378-379, 452,
459, 470, 471, 473, 486-487, 586-587,
591, 711; **III**: 29, 31, 33, 52, 110, 533
    abdication of, **III**: 176, 178; debate
over, **III**: 41-43, 45-46; Roosevelt supports, **III**: 41
    and declaration of war vs. Germany,
II: 491-492
    and political situation in Italy, **II**:
664, 666-667
    and ships to Soviets, **II**: 698
    and surrender negotiations with Al-
lies, **II**: 455, 458-461, 464, 466, 500-
501
        anti-Bolshevism of, **II**: 654
        British vs. U.S. view of, **II**: 679-681,
697, 723
        issue of abdication of, **II**: 759-760
        Office of War Information attack
on, **II**: 354-355
Victory Production Program (U.S.), **I**:
239-240
Vienna, Austria, **II**: 223; **III**: 198, 305,
316, 364, 605, 613
Viénot, Pierre, **III**: 135, 138, 170-171,
205
Vilna, Poland: disputed city, **II**: 715,
720-721, 735-737, 741, 763; **III**: 13,
21, 29-30, 234
Vis, island in Adriatic, **III**: 167, 190
Vishinsky, A. Y., **II**: 485
Vladivostok, U.S.S.R., **II**: 175
Vlasikavkas, U.S.S.R., **I**: 672
Volhynia, Poland, **II**: 684
Von Arnim, Juergen, **II**: 98-99
Von Coudenhove-Kalergi, Count, **II**:
222
Von Falkenhausen, Alexander Baron,
II: 521
Von Mantueffel, Hasso, **III**: 487
Von Pappen, Fritz, **II**: 663
Von Rundstedt, Gerd, **III**: 487-488
Von Thoma, Wilhelm Ritter, **II**: 555-556

Voroshilov, Marshal, **I**: 580
Vyshinsky, Andrei, **II**: 619, 679-680;
    III: 284, 585-586, 588; and political
    situation, **III**: 30-31

WAFD Party, Egypt, **III**: 110-111
Waley, Sir David, **II**: 743-744
Walker, Frank C., **II**: 388
Wallace, Henry, **I**: 313; **II**: 222, 224-
    225, 227, 290
Walloons (Belgium), **I**: 221
War criminals, **III**: 329-330; Stalin on,
    III: 364, 366
War of Spanish Succession, **II**: 388
War Production Board, **I**: 638
Warm Springs, Georgia, **III**: 424, 448,
    597, 630-631
Warsaw, Poland, **II**: 193, 701, 718; **III**:
    280, 524, 556
Warsaw Uprising. *See* Poland
Washington, D.C., **II**: 696; **III**: 226;
    Churchill visit to, August 1943, **II**:
    431-434, 437-438; oil conference in,
    II: 744-745; **III**: 16-17
Washington Conference (ARCADIA,
    1941-1942), **I**: 292-324, 484; and In-
    dia, **I**: 373; Churchill proposes, **I**:
    283-286; proposed agenda, **I**: 289-290
Washington Conference (ARGONAUT,
    1942), **I**: 495, 513-516
Washington Conference (TRIDENT,
    1943), **II**: 219-221, 233, 296; and sec-
    ond front delay, **III**: 61; Azores dis-
    cussed at, **II**: 239; decisions made at,
    II: 212-215; refugees discussed at, **II**:
    293
Washington Post, **II**: 490
Waterloo, Battle of, **II**: 454
Watkinson, Arnold E., **II**: 384
Watson, Edwin "Pa," **I**: 648; **II**: 134,
    355; **III**: 167, 287, 517-518, 538-540
Watten, France, **II**: 559
Wavell, Sir Archibald P., **I**: 9, 165, 184,
    185, 196, 207, 216, 309, 321, 335-336,
    348-352, 355, 361, 365, 424, 551; **II**:
    112, 117, 202, 206, 248, 353; **III**: 179;
    and ABDA command, **I**: 325, 339-
    344; and British strategy, **I**: 144-145;
    and famine in India, **III**: 116-117; ap-
    pointed to S.W. Pacific command, **I**:
    313; at Moscow Conference, 1942, **I**:
    560, 564, 569; in India, **I**: 395; **II**:

116; in Libya campaign, **I**: 126; on
    Java, **I**: 367-368; on MacArthur as Su-
    preme Commander, **I**: 408
Webb-Johnson, Alfred, **II**: 541
Wedemeyer, A. C., **II**: 757, 759; **III**:
    370, 375, 426, 427-429, 429-430, 447,
    448, 572-573; and Indo-China, **III**:
    626-627; and Pacific strategy, **III**: 37,
    39; in Southeast Asia, **III**: 582-583
Weimar Republic, Germany, **III**: 388
Weizmann, Chaim, **II**: 561; **III**: 286
Welles, Sumner, **I**: 36, 58, 211, 354,
    373, 521-522, 526, 546; **II**: 178, 222,
    226, 440, 462; and Argentina, **III**:
    230; and Polish exiles plane request,
    I: 488; and Vichy negotiations, **I**: 460;
    on Japanese *modus vivendi*, **I**: 277
Wellington, Duke of, **II**: 165, 454; **III**:
    109
Wesel, Germany, **III**: 601, 604
West Africa, **I**: 177, 190, 210; **III**: 237;
    Allies need ports in, **I**: 90, 98, 104;
    British forces in, 1943, **I**: 654;
    Churchill wants troops to, 1942, **I**:
    292; French fleet in, **I**: 93, 105; Roo-
    sevelt to Churchill on, **I**: 669-670
West Indies, **I**: 166; **II**: 528-529; and
    lend-lease bases, **I**: 139-140; British
    colonies in, **I**: 323
Western Hemisphere, **I**: 73; Allies fear
    German bases in, **I**: 426; countries es-
    tablish safety zones, **I**: 25; defense of,
    I: 174
Western Naval Task Force, **I**: 635
Westphalia, Germany, **III**: 147
Weygand, Maxime, **I**: 44, 46, 178, 179,
    186-187, 250, 253, 269-270; on North
    African invasion, **I**: 333-334; removed
    as commander, North Africa, **I**: 287
Weymss, H.C.B., **I**: 338
Wheat Conference, **I**: 263-264; Roose-
    velt on, **I**: 251-252
Wheeler, Burton K., **I**: 218-219
White House Correspondents' Associa-
    tion, **I**: 148
White Russia, **III**: 175, 532
White Russians, **II**: 764
Whitely, J.F.M., **I**: 183, 184; **II**: 435-436
Wilcox, John W., Jr., **I**: 419
Wilhelmina, Queen of Netherlands, **III**:
    156
Willkie, Wendell, **I**: 68, 80, 131, 134,

189-191, 618-619, 654-656; **II**: 108-109

Willock, R. P., **III**: 417

Willson, Russell, **I**: 635

"Wilson," **III**: 337

Wilson, Edwin C., **II**: 579, 691; and FCNL, 639-642

Wilson, Sir Henry Maitland, **II**: 129, 131, 144, 196, 445, 497-498, 553-554, 621, 623-624, 627-629, 631, 632, 642, 651, 656, 658, 700, 723, 727; **III**: 103, 119, 176, 178, 190, 199, 203-204, 228-229, 232, 265, 275, 401, 409-410, 453-454, 509; and Aegean policy, **II**: 518; and aid to Yugoslavia, **III**: 132; and Bulgarian negotiations, **III**: 15, 22-23, 32; and Bulgarians, **III**: 22-23; and Eastern Mediterranean strategy, **II**: 508-514; and French, **III**: 136, 138; and Greece, **III**: 153, 297; and invasion of southern France, **III**: 212-213, 214, 219, 222-223; and Italian campaign, **II**: 728-729; **III**: 167, 301, 347-348, 373; and Italian fleet controversy, **III**: 28; and Italian political situation, **II**: 759-761; **III**: 28-29, 31, 33-34, 41, 356-357; and Middle East strategy, **II**: 517; and war strategy, **III**: 197, 199; command structure and, **III**: 83; moves to Combined Chiefs, **III**: 308; on Combined Chiefs, **III**: 381; replaces Dill, **III**: 392-399; takes over Mediterranean command, **II**: 648-649

Wilson, Woodrow, **I**: 24, 221; **III**: 7, 153, 337; as lesson for Roosevelt, **II**: 462

Wilsonians, and interwar crisis, **I**: 14

Winant, John G., **I**: 139-140, 143, 156, 169, 188, 198, 208, 211, 247, 282, 344, 356, 362, 373, 422, 490-491, 619; **II**: 102, 200, 285, 291, 309, 337, 399, 506, 587, 640, 645, 754; **III**: 53, 172, 253, 346, 418, 419, 479, 484, 597; and Argentina, **III**: 414-415; and civil aviation policy, **III**: 407; and Devers, **II**: 281; and neutral nations, **III**: 245; and oil conference, **III**: 26; and Sweden, **III**: 257; Churchill on, **I**: 439, 505; message on Ireland, **III**: 57; on Churchill, **III**: 139; on North Africa, **II**: 83; on Northern Ireland policy, **II**:

186; on press leaks, **II**: 522; on relief for Europe, **III**: 84-85; on Soviet armies and surrender terms, **II**: 370-371; on Soviet boundary issues, **I**: 394; resented Hopkins role, **II**: 527; with Churchill to Cairo, **II**: 592-593

Windsor, Duchess of, **I**: 489

Windsor, Duke of, **I**: 52-53, 489

Wingate, Orde, **II**: 542, 751; in Burma, **III**: 19-20, 43-44, 46, 55

Winter War (1939-1940), **II**: 181-182

Wolfe, General J., at Quebec, **II**: 323

Wolff, Karl, **III**: 586, 609, 611, 614, 615

Wolfram, trade of, **II**: 298-299; **III**: 245; and Allied policy to Spain, **II**: 751; Spanish trade with Germany, **II**: 725-726, 728, 739; **III**: 66-68, 78, 80-81, 99, 105-108, 114-115

Women's Army Corps, United States, **II**: 431

World War I, **I**: 32-33, 44, 88, 97, 98, 105, 113, 212, 228, 230, 574; **II**: 516; **III**: 7, 388; alliances in, **I**: 89; amount of ammunition used, **I**: 615; and Ottoman Empire, **III**: 389-390; battle mementos to Churchill, **III**: 239; Bulgaria as lynch-pin, **III**: 298-299; Churchill on Russians in, **II**: 738; debt repayment problems, **I**: 101; Europeans, **I**: 345; German naval mutiny in, **III**: 112; German submarine crew morale in, **II**: 729; influence on Allied strategy, **III**: 198; Paris Peace talks and Italians, **II**: 457; Polish boundary decisions in, **II**: 684, 686; reparations in, **III**: 528; Roosevelt on Pétain in, **I**: 656; secret treaties in, **I**: 221; **III**: 325

World Zionist Organization, **II**: 561-562

Wurtenburg, Germany, **II**: 708; **III**: 364

Yalta, **III**: 449

Yalta Conference (ARGONAUT, 1945), **I**: 17; **II**: 611; **III**: 431, 543, 546
    agreement on liberated areas, **III**: 618, 633, 634, 635
    agreements on Poland, **III**: 565, 585, 587-590, 592-593, 595, 598-602, 627, 629; criticized, **III**: 538-539
    and French zone in Germany, **III**: 635
    and Poland, **III**: 492, 523, 562-563, 567-568

Yalta Conference (*cont.*)
    and postwar European arrange-
ments, **II**: 611
    and prisoners of war, **III**: 541
    and spheres of influence, **III**: 545
    Churchill and Roosevelt's views of,
III: 503
      Churchill on, **III**: 502
      decisions at, **III**: 524-530
      impact of military situation on, **III**:
524
      Iranian oil, discussed at, **III**: 512
      military discussions at, **III**: 524
      military representation at, **III**: 517
      negotiations over site, **III**: 364, 367,
374, 377-381
      planning for, **III**: 388-390, 394-396,
398, 411-412, 416, 477-479, 485-486,
491, 493-496, 500-503, 508-509, 511,
518-519
      pre-conference meeting at Malta,
III: 489, 493-496, 501-503, 505, 507
      press at, **III**: 514-515
      Roosevelt as broker at, **III**: 530
      Roosevelt on Curzon line at, **III**:
357-358
      security at, **III**: 508
      Stalin at, **III**: 561
Yamamoto, Admiral, **I**: 507
Yosuke, Matsuoka, **I**: 137
Yugoslavia, **I**: 144-145, 156, 206; **II**:
131, 139, 349, 350, 388-389, 540, 553-
554, 608; **III**: 42, 95, 257-258, 306
    Allied aid to as issue, **III**: 387
    Allied policy toward, **II**: 133-134;
III: 80, 130-133, 198
      and Britain, **II**: 660-661; **III**: 274
      and Italian surrender, **II**: 440
      and Italians, **II**: 428; **III**: 636

    and Moscow Conference, 1944, **III**:
359
    Anglo-Soviet agreement on, **III**:
200-201, 203, 350-351, 358-359
    atrocities in, **II**: 414-416, 520
    British and, **III**: 190-191, 274-275,
545; U.S. views of, **III**: 517
      Churchill on, **III**: 275
      exiled government of, **II**: 405
      fighting in, **II**: 512
      Germans in, **I**: 152-153, 170
      Germans threaten, 1941, **I**: 134
      government in exile, **III**: 203; Stalin
on, **III**: 70
      in Churchill-Stalin talks, 1944, **III**:
341
      liberation of, **III**: 299
      monarchy in, **III**: 133
      OSS mission in, **III**: 80, 82, 86, 306,
308-309
      partisans in, **II**: 182, 184, 402-407,
411-413, 548-549, 644; Allied debated
over support for, **III**: 306; British
support for, **III**: 274-275; relations
with British, **II**: 660-661
      political situation in, **III**: 115-116,
509-510, 513
      postwar: British concerns over, **II**:
497-499
      postwar arrangements in, **I**: 221
      proportion of interest document on,
III: 351
      Roosevelt on, **III**: 276
      sabotage in, 1943, **II**: 411-413

Zionism, Churchill on, **III**: 286
Zog, King of Albania, **I**: 372
Zymierski, M. Rola, **III**: 553, 555

Library of Congress Cataloging in Publication Data

Churchill, Winston, Sir, 1874-1965.
  Churchill & Roosevelt: the complete correspondence.

  Includes bibliographies and index.
  Contents: 1. Alliance emerging, October 1933-
November 1942—2. Alliance forged, November 1942-
February 1944—3. Alliance declining, February
1944-April 1945.
  1. Churchill, Winston, Sir, 1874-1965. 2. Roosevelt,
Franklin D. (Franklin Delano), 1882-1945. 3. World War,
1939-1945—Diplomatic history. 4. Great Britain—Foreign
relations—United States. 5. United States—Foreign
relations—Great Britain. 6. Prime ministers—Great
Britain—Correspondence. 7. Presidents—United States—
Correspondence. I. Roosevelt, Franklin D. (Franklin
Delano), 1882-1945. II. Kimball, Warren F. III. Title.
IV. Title: Churchill and Roosevelt.
DA566.9.C5A4   1984   940.53′22′0922   83-43080
ISBN 0-691-05649-8 (set: alk. paper)
ISBN 0-691-00817-5 (set: pbk.)